European Economic Interaction and Integration
(formerly East–West European Economic Interaction)

Workshop Papers
Series Editor: Philipp Rieger

The Vienna Institute for Comparative Economic Studies organises a series of international workshops concerned with problems of European economic interaction and integration guided by an International Steering Committee consisting of:

The present volume is based on Workshop Session XV held in Vienna, Austria, 1993.

Eastern Europe in Crisis and the Way Out

Edited by

Christopher T. Saunders
Honorary Fellow, Science Policy Research Unit
University of Sussex, UK

MACMILLAN

in association with
THE VIENNA INSTITUTE
FOR COMPARATIVE ECONOMIC STUDIES

Research Director: Prof. Dr Kazimierz Laski
Administrative Director: Dr Ingrid Gazzari

First published 1995 by
MACMILLAN PRESS LTD
Houndmills, Basingstoke, Hampshire RG21 2XS
and London
Companies and representatives
throughout the world

A catalogue record for this book is available from the British Library.

ISBN 0–333–62822–5

10 9 8 7 6 5 4 3 2 1
04 03 02 01 00 99 98 97 96 95

Sponsored by Friedrich Ebert Stiftung, Bonn

Printed and bound in Great Britain by
Antony Rowe Ltd
Chippenham, Wiltshire

TABLE OF CONTENTS

PART III – THE LIBERALISATION OF FOREIGN TRADE

PART IV – PRIVATISATION AND INDUSTRIAL RESTRUCTURING

PART V – SOCIAL PROBLEMS OF TRANSFORMATION

PART VI – COUNTRY COMMENTS

Note: Nomenclature of Country Groups

Political and economic transformation has brought with it new names and new international groupings, some still unfamiliar. The developments covered in this volume overlap changes in constitutions and alignments. To reduce confusion, the following nominal conventions have been adopted wherever appropriate:

- *Eastern Europe,* or "the East", to cover the whole group of countries in transition, including the former USSR. Although geographically inaccurate, the term is familiar and avoids the multiplicity of more novel descriptions (ex-Comecon, ex-socialist/communist, ex-CPEs, Central and East European (CEE). The last is especially ambiguous since easily confused with the French initials of both the European Economic Community and the UN Economic Commission for Europe).
- *The European Community (EC)* generally used here since "EC" applies to most of the period covered until it became the European Union (EU) after the Maastricht Treaty in 1992.
- *The Visegrád* group of four countries more advanced than others in the transition process: the Czech and Slovak Republics, Hungary and Poland; these are also members of the *Central European Free Trade Agreement* (CEFTA). (A partial overlap with the former Austro-Hungarian Empire, minus its base, may be noted.)

ACKNOWLEDGEMENTS

The present volume is based on the proceedings of the Fifteenth *Workshop on East-West European Economic Interaction and Integration* organised by the Vienna Institute for Comparative Economic Studies (WIIW), in collaboration with the Dr. Karl Renner Institute, Vienna and with the support of the Friedrich Ebert Stiftung, Bonn.

It was held in Vienna from 21 to 25 November 1993 under the title "Transformation of the East European Economies, 1989-1993: critical assessments and ways out of the crisis", at a time when most reforming countries found themselves still in the grip of the deep transformational recession.

The arduous task of editing the papers and discussions was again undertaken by Professor C. T. Saunders, ably assisted by Eva Strobl, who was also responsible for organising the Workshop with the assistance of the secretariat of the Vienna Institute. The text was efficiently typeset and prepared for printing by Renate Szumilowski, charts were redrawn by Péter Fóti and Henning Nassler. As always, we are grateful to Mr. T. M. Farmiloe of the Macmillan Press Ltd. for valuable cooperation.

Philipp Rieger
Chairman of the Workshop

EDITOR'S INTRODUCTION

Christopher T. Saunders*)

In 1993 and early 1994 the Eastern European countries were slowly emerging, or seemed about to emerge, from a three to five year decline in output and living standards accompanied by periods of violent inflation. The downturn began in 1989/90 almost simultaneously with the radical political reforms ("velvet revolutions", for the most part) and the initiation by new or reconstructed governments of policies for economic reform aimed at shifting the structure of the economies from Communist central planning and state ownership of the means of production to largely market-led private enterprise.

An indication of the scale of the decline may be seen from the comparative table below; the figures all come from the national official statistics carefully collected and published by the Vienna Institute for Comparative Economic Studies (WIIW).

In most of the countries, the fall in national output (GDP) from 1989 to 1993 was 20-30 per cent; in Croatia over 50 per cent and in Russia almost 40 per cent. Measured declines in real income may have been of similar orders of magnitude. Forecasts for 1994, supported by more recent data for industrial production, suggest some signs of recovery (beginning in 1992 in Poland and 1993 in Slovenia). Registered unemployment rates have of course reached high levels – except in the Czech Republic and Russia which could be attributed to continuing reluctance to reduce overmanning. It is recognised that the disruptions of the time must have hindered the collection of complete data particularly from the massive formation of new privately owned small businesses. The existence of unreported (not necessarily illegal) activities may somewhat modify the picture of dramatic decline (a problem not unknown, too, in Western statistical offices). The indicators display a pattern resembling that of a very severe capitalist slump. But some (e.g. *Kornai* in Ch. 2) insist that the analogy is superficial; the roots of the "transformational recession" in the East lie deep in the social, political and behaviour characteristics formed by the previous

---

*) Science Policy Research Unit, University of Sussex, Brighton, UK.

regimes. Hence Western-type policies for recovery (whether "Keynesian" or "monetarist") are not necessarily applicable.

The varying incidence of the transformational crisis

1. Gross domestic product

	% change from previous year					Index
	1990	**1991**	**1992**	**1993**	**1994** [a]	**1993/1990**
Visegrád group						
Czech Republic	-1.2	-14.2	-6.6	-0.3	+2	78.9
Hungary	-3.5	-11.9	-4.5	-1.5	+2	80.0
Poland	-8.0	-7.6	+2.6	+3.8	+4	86.2
Slovakia	-2.5	-14.5	-7.0	-4.1	0	74.3
Slovenia	-4.7	-9.3	-6.0	+1.0	+3	82.1
Bulgaria	-9.1	-11.7	-7.7	-4.2	-2	71.0
Romania	-5.6	-12.9	-13.5	+1.0	-2	71.8
Croatia	-9.3	-28.7	-23.6	-6.0	-3	46.0
Russia	-2	-12.9	-18.5	-12	-10	60.8

	2. GDP per head $ PPP[b] 1992	*3. Unemployment* %[c] March 1994
Visegrád group		
Czech Republic	7664	3.5
Hungary	5908	12.2
Poland	4148	16.0
Slovakia	5273	14.5
Slovenia	7560	14.8
Bulgaria	2385	16.1
Romania	3058	11.2
Croatia	..	17.6
Russia	5563	1.6

a) Forecast. – b) Purchasing power parities. – c) Registered unemployed as % economically active labour force.

Source: Havlik, P., et al. (1994), "Transition Countries: The Economic Situation in Early 1994 and Outlook Until 1995. More solid recovery in Central and Eastern Europe, continuing decline elsewhere", *WIIW Research Reports,* no. 207, July, Tables 1, 4 and 11.

The present book must be regarded as a progress report; the contributions were mostly written in the second half of 1993; the reader should treat the analyses (and any forecasts) as indications of how things looked at the time of writing to experienced observers (some being influential participants in the process). The following paragraphs take some selected points from their work.[1)]

Part I Stabilisation policies: general assessment (Chh. 1-3)

The results, both positive and negative, of three to five years of transformation in Eastern Europe are examined by *Levcik* (Ch. 1), summarising a fuller study by a team from WIIW[2)]. The authors take a critical view of the "conventional" monetary and fiscal restrictive programmes which have helped to bring down inflation and by liberalisation measures have introduced elements of the market economy – but have also left the economies concerned with heavily reduced output and real incomes, together with much popular disillusion. In the authors' view the time has come, especially in the more advanced Visegrád group, for governments to take steps to stimulate demand and promote steady growth out of the damaging recession of the early 1990s. The overoptimistic view that all problems could be quickly overcome by "shock therapy" and release of market forces should give way to a more gradualist strategy of structural transformation. The argument is taken up by *Kornai* (Ch. 2), pioneer of reformist thinking in the socialist countries. He regards Hungarian experience as an example of incremental and gradual reform with relatively little disruption. He agrees with *Levcik* that demand management must play a primary role in recovery from the "transformational recessions", but sees the solutions in East European circumstances as susceptible to no more than "half-Keynesian" measures of demand management. The collapse in the East is not just a Western-type cyclical recession, but deeply rooted in the disintegration, uncertainties and vacuum left by the disappearance of the coordinating mechanism of central planning, a gap not yet filled by the "hidden hand" of the

---

1) The papers were discussed at the 15th International Workshop on European Economic Interaction and Integration, organised by the WIIW in Vienna in November 1993. The editor gratefully acknowledges summaries of the Workshop sessions made by *Boffito, Bárta, Landesmann* and *Cazes.*

2) Laski, K., et al. (1993), "Transition from the Command to the Market System: what went wrong and what to do now?", *WIIW Working Papers,* no. 1.

market. Apprehensive of renewed inflation, he advocates a "half-turn" rather than a "U-turn" towards a market-led policy; and that requires active government initiatives, economic and social, which can capture public confidence.

Worswick (Ch. 3) turns to a different approach, asking whether Western methods of restoring stability after disruption (e.g. after times of centralised war economies) hold lessons for present stabilisation problems in the East. He insists that "stabilisation" should be taken to cover resumption of economic growth as well as the conquest of inflation which has been the main preoccupation of policy in the Eastern transitions. One example, certainly relevant to Eastern problems, is the cooperative Western effort to restore growth and trade through reduction of trade barriers, combined with the Marshall Plan – the European Recovery Plan. Incidentally, the bilateralism which characterised early postwar trade policies in Western Europe – as it did in the CMEA for much longer – soon gave way to the multilateralism of the GATT and (within its limits) of the European Economic Communities. But after the OPEC actions in the 1970s, the weight of policy was thrown on the control of inflation by attempts to regulate the money supply and restrictive fiscal measures; the cost was stagnation of output and unexpected rises in unemployment. In this respect, over-optimism about the speed and effectiveness of the policy measures characterised Western, as it did many Eastern, policy-makers.

Part II Reform of the financial sector (Chh. 4-6)

In the former system, the function of banks was basically to provide enterprises with funds to fulfil the central plan. The reform administrations had to establish a "universal" commercial banking structure – in effect, a kind of "infant industry" – with, in principle, discretionary powers to finance investment, restructuring and working capital. Lack of reliable channels for personal savings led to a multiplicity of dubious investment funds (not unknown in the West, too); the collapse of the MMM group of shady funds in Russia demonstrated the damaging results of a lack of any adequate regulation.

Describing the evolution of the banking system in Russia, *Boffito* (Ch. 4) points to the proliferation of new commercial banks, mostly privately owned, since reform began, providing extensive statistics. He points, however, to the continuing weaknesses of the new system: lack of trained staffs; inappropriate accounting; weak control of credit and cash flow – in general, managers with little grasp of the concept of banks as profit-seeking enterprises, and with little skill in assessing creditworthiness. One result is a concentration on short-term lending, perhaps natural in inflationary conditions, and reluctance to play their part in the much needed industrial modernisation and restructuring. (For an analysis of credit and monetary policy in the stabilisation process in Russia, see also *Nekipelov* (Ch. 16)). The functions of credit policy in managing stabilisation in a nascent market economy are analysed by *Calvo* and *Kumar* (Ch. 5) from the IMF. They present a model (in algebraic terms) to display their view of the role of credit in determining output and its implications for macroeconomic policy. Their approach suggests that the decline of output in the early 1990s was the result not so much of restrictive credit policies as of decline in the *demand* for credit. An expansionary credit policy would be more likely to create inflation than to increase output. But, as *Hochreiter* points out in a comment, the demand for credit seems itself to be a function of real income which implies a circularity in the credit/output relationship needing further elucidation. On a different aspect of financial reform in the East, *Haiss* (Ch. 6) from Austria displays the variety of Western banking and financial practices, offering to the East a menu for establishing new channels for moving savings into productive investment. He recommends "universal" banks making direct long-term investments (as in Austria, Germany, Switzerland) in preference to share markets based on stock exchanges (as in UK and US).

Part III Liberalisation of international trade (Chh. 7-9)

The breakdown of the CMEA network of intra-trade, based largely on planned, often bilateral, agreements, is obviously one significant reason for the decline of Eastern output although opinions differ about its relative importance; it has been partly offset by increased (diverted?) exports to the West, but that in turn has been more than offset by the attractions to Eastern buyers of the new access to liberalised imports from the West and its depressing impact on domestic markets. Use of the marketing opportunities opened by new relationships with the European Union must depend not only on the bargains negotiated but also on the Eastern countries' gains in international competitiveness through economic reform and restructuring. One feature, in international trade as in other respects, is the divergence between the more "Westernised" Visegrád group of 5 and the others.

In two overall assessments, *Messerlin* (Ch. 7) from Paris and *Smolik* (Ch. 9) of UN/ECE, review the development, especially since 1989, of the course of

East-West trade and of the government and international policies affecting it. On the Western side, there has been significant liberalisation of import quotas and other restrictions, but barriers remain. Although trade with East Europe is still of minor quantitative importance to most Western industrial economies, the European Community has become the major trading partner of each of the Eastern economies. Continuing western restrictions may be partly explained by what *Smolik* calls Western "perceptions" of a threatening flood of imports, as well as by western reluctance (as shown by *Messerlin)* to renounce protection of "sensitive" industries (textiles, steel and of course agriculture), the very industries where the competitive potentialities for the East are strongest. This caution is confirmed by the frequent use against imports from the East of anti-dumping safeguards and by the elaboration of Rules of Origin. On the *Eastern* side, there has been little effort to reconstruct anything like the former CMEA preferential arrangements or specialisation agreements; yet many of the links then established – even if originally owing too much to bureaucratic centralisation – could still offer opportunities in a partly liberalised market system. But, as *Messerlin* suggests, it may well be thought that for both East and West Europe progress should lie in the global network promoted by the GATT rather than in further pursuit of regional trade blocs. *Štouračová* and *Neustadt* (Ch. 8), from Prague, regard liberalising foreign trade as a major instrument for transformation. They report progress in the former Czechoslovakia (CSFR) which has continued since separation (1993) in the Czech Republic. A rather liberal trade policy was introduced early in the reform process with a reduced tariff level (estimated average under 6 per cent), abolition of the State monopoly of foreign trade, but licensing of agricultural imports is continued. Modified free trade agreements with the EC and EFTA have been negotiated; and a Customs Union with Slovakia.

Part IV Privatisation and restructuring (Chh. 10-13)

Four authors discuss various aspects of privatisation. All are much concerned with the failure to foresee that while liberalisation of prices and foreign trade may be achieved – if with much disruption – by shock therapy, the reorganisation and expected efficiency gains of privatisation and market orientation are bound to be a lengthy process impeded by legal, financial and valuation uncertainties, by vested interests and political pressures, and – perhaps most important – by the absence of a sufficient body of managerial expertise with the entrepreneurial talents needed for competitiveness. Moreover the transfer of property rights touches the heart of socialist political philosophy (from Proudhon's drastic "La proprieté c'est le vol").

Thus *Bogomolov* (Ch. 10) raises the intriguing philosophical question of how to identify the ownership of state assets, which he sceptically describes as "nobody's property". The question is relevant to the aims as well as to the machinery of privatisation; the primary objective may be a more efficient economy but, *Bogomolov* insists, social justice should also be involved. Distribution of rights to hold shares by vouchers, even for a small fee, is taken by some critics as making the citizens to buy back "their own property" and leads, in any case, to a rather random redistribution of wealth. He criticises some results of privatisation in Russia: the concentration of privatised assets in the hands of the former Nomenklatura who are unlikely to make the desired change in management methods (it can mean the conversion of state monopolies into private monopolies and the exchange of political power for the "more durable" property rights). The most disputable issue has been the privatisation of *land;* redistribution has been rather reluctantly and tardily put through. A return to the pre-revolutionary peasant system is unlikely, but *Bogomolov* sees a risk of destroying the scale advantages of the big state or collective farms. He concludes that much deeper study is required of the empirical results of privatisation so far; *Bogomolov* has always insisted that the process of transformation must be seen as a long-term strategy.

Hunya (Ch. 11) from the WIIW reviews the progress of privatisation in eight of the Eastern countries. He provides useful data about the proportion and composition of the public and private sectors (although differences between legal and administrative regimes impair comparability). He is chiefly concerned with the "topdown" privatisation of existing state-owned enterprises (SOEs) but also notes that the growth of the private sector is in some countries mainly accounted for by "bottom-up" spontaneous creation of new small enterprises, largely, but not always, in trade, services and construction. It is the general experience that privatisation of the big state monopolies has gone very slowly. The common practice of converting big SOEs into joint-stock companies, retaining their monopolies in practice, is regarded by *Hunya* as no more than preparatory steps to privatisation, rarely doing much to bring about changes in performance or restructuring. Privatisation methods fall into two major classes (with many variants): direct sale, often through a government holding agency (e.g. the

Treuhand in Germany) to private groups of persons who – often difficult to find – have the necessary funds, including management/worker buy-outs; the second class is the issue of vouchers giving the right to buy shares ("mass privatisation"). The first method has the advantage of creating "strong owners" with a long-term interest in developing the assets; the second has the advantage, at least for a time, of promoting wider distribution of wealth.

The various processes of privatisation and restructuring strategies are assessed by *Kennerley* (Ch. 12), of the UN Economic Commission for Europe, which has made extensive studies of the subject over a long period. His main question is whether these strategies have succeeded in increasing economic efficiency. Like other authors, he notes the growth and popularity of small-scale private enterprise, but also the slow progress in transforming the major SOEs. For a long time, governments are likely to retain ownership of much of large-scale industry and must take responsibility for restructuring and infusing capital for modernisation. This is particularly important for improving the infrastructure of transport and communications and for building up the financial and business institutions needed in a market economy. This requires some form of government-coordinated industrial policy – so far almost absent. It is becoming clear that privatisation will not in itself assure the desired transformation. The shortage of domestic funds has led to wide openings for foreign direct investment (FDI) estimated by ECE at close to $ 15 bn in the whole group (1993) – still a small figure in relation to total world capital flows. The new feature is that foreign investors are able to buy ownership stakes in privatised Eastern enterprises (having been restricted in the past mainly to joint ventures). *Kennerley* gives detailed statistics (compiled by ECE) on the recipient and investor companies and industries. He concludes, however, that "experience to date in attracting FDI as a support in the process of privatisation and restructuring has been disappointing".

In some respects (see also *Worswick* in Ch. 3), Western countries have had to face similar problems of reforming state industries. *Aiginger* (Ch. 13) draws some lessons from Austrian experience. The very difficult situation just after World War II, marked by economic collapse and years of Allied occupation, led to rather gradual liberalisation of war controls, but also to formation of the well-known tripartite institutions – the "social partnership" – for a modified supervision of wage and price movements which has been maintained (on the political side, too, an agreed distribution of official posts – the famous "Proporz" – was accepted). In addition, a revolving fund, originating in the counterpart funds from Marshall Aid, together with a special fund for promotion of advanced technology, have continued to be used for investment subsidies to firms selected by rather strict criteria. Since the war, Austria has had a rather large public sector – a heritage of wartime disruption rather than of ideology. These state-owned industries were successful in their early years but, in *Aiginger's* view, have since run into problems. He feels that the economy needs a considered industrial policy to coordinate restructuring, subsidies, taxes, tariffs, regulatory systems etc. This certainly seems relevant to the general issue of the future functions of government in the societies in transition.

Part V Social aspects of transformation policies (Chh. 14 and 15)

The social disruptions and insecurity, unemployment, poverty and inflation which accompanied the reforms were hardly expected and certainly not provided for by government policies. Two accounts, from Polish and Russian authors, help to redress the balance by calling attention to the gap.

From Warsaw, *Supińska* (Ch. 14) sets the social costs of the reform policies against their expected benefits, in the light of Polish experience. While agreeing that not all the disruption can be attributed to the shock therapy of the reform, she shows, from extensive sample surveys, the fall (for many) in living standards, the widening inequalities in income and the surge of recorded unemployment accompanying the sudden liberalisation and fierce inflation – more than offsetting the reappearance of formerly scarce goods in the shops. The initial popular enthusiasm associated with the success of the Solidarity movement has largely given way to disillusion and apathy; one reason being the cuts in social assistance. "Instead of shock therapy, the social services have been offered only a slimming diet." This rigour has led to greatly increased dependence of the poor and sick on *voluntary* welfare services: "charity is expected to fill the gap." In the same vein, *Kollontai* (Ch. 15) from Moscow vigorously criticises the lack of attention to the social aspects of transformation policies. The budgetary crisis, with inflation, has resulted in the dismantling of social provision. It is true that in Russia recorded unemployment remains low; the old Soviet system of full employment by overmanning remains. *Kollontai* stresses the growth of inequality in income and wealth (and, therefore, in power) – impoverishment at one end and, at the other, emergence of a new class of *nouveaux riches.* Statistics suggest a decline in *average* real income (to the extent that it can be measured) of approaching one-third between 1990 and 1993. The well-publicised spread of crime, corruption and organised gangsterism – aspects of "wild capitalism" – contributes to insecurity. *Kollontai* concludes that a complete rebuilding of the social welfare system is required, together with a slower pace in parts of the economic reform (such as privatisation). "At present, few people understand that the real difficulties of economic reform in countries like Russia lie not in the economic but in the social sphere."

Another consequence, less publicised but noted in a comment by *Cazes,* is the demographic effect: the alarming rise in death rates from a variety of medical causes.

Part VI National experiences of transformation (Chh. 16-22)

Authors from seven of the transition countries report on developments, policies and prospects in their own economics: Russia (Ch. 16), Hungary (17) and Poland (18); followed by four countries which have recently achieved separate statehood and face the special problems of the sudden breaking of economic and political links with other parts of large federal states. (It is of course true that limited elements of local autonomy already existed.) Their experience illustrates how greatly both the prosperity and independence of relatively small nations depends on their success in forging international links.

From Moscow, *Nekipelov* (Ch. 16) analyses a particular and controversial element in the Russian reforms – the effectiveness of *monetary policy* in the stabilisation process. Regression analysis of relationships between money supply or ease of credit and rates of inflation leads to some limited evidence of positive correlation (a precise correlation could hardly be expected in the inflationary circumstances of the early 1990s). He points out that any such relationship may run two ways, price inflation affecting the velocity of circulation and *vice versa.* He stresses, however, that a more basic problem, in the transition countries generally, is the inability of institutions to meet the needs of a market economy; he points, for example, to the "whimsicality of motivation and behaviour of liberalised state enterprises".

Török (Ch. 17), from Budapest and Pecs, looks critically at the stages of stabilisation policies in Hungary since the mid-1980s, from restrictive monetary policies to modest expansionary measures. None, in his view, proved successful; hence the title of his chapter: "In quests of lost stabilisation". Policies failed to avert what *Kornai* (Ch. 2, analysing other aspects of Hungarian reform) describes as the "transformational recession". One reason is the unfavourable external environment both in the CMEA and in the West which held back the growth of world demand. A second factor was the collapse of agricultural production, due in part to agricultural protectionism elsewhere but also to neglect of agricultural restructuring in the transformation policies. *Török* adds failure of the tax system to promote investment.

For Poland, *Trzeciakowski* (Ch. 18) from Warsaw gives a comprehensive account of the problems and controversies involved in the Polish transition. Regarding economic reform as "inseparably linked with political and social criteria", he summarises the shifting balance of divergent political interests underlying the formation of economic policy. Poland is generally regarded as a model of the shock therapy treatment which, the author agrees, played its part in short-term stabilisation and may have helped Poland to lead the way in 1993 into a modest recovery of output. But the more serious restructuring of production and institutions is essentially an evolutionary process requiring time and capital. Privatisation and the invisible hand of the market cannot alone assure the restructuring and modernisation of industry and agriculture so much required. Nor can they assure the very necessary consensus in a democratic society. *Trzeciakowski* further stresses the importance of Western assistance in forms acceptable to both donor and recipient – in particular, the wider opening of Western markets to the East.

Kouba (Ch. 19) from Prague, himself much involved in the reform process, reviews developments in Czechoslovakia (CSFR) as a whole, but also gives estimates for the Czech Republic before and after the separation in 1993 (for the Slovak Republic see *Kosír* in the next chapter). Prices and imports were liberalised (not all at once) but the inflationary consequences were moderated, especially by government wage regulation and by partly successful monetary and fiscal measures. Yet output declined, as elsewhere. *Kouba* specifies as reasons the loss of CMEA markets and also the often neglected effect of the running down of the excessive inventories which had characterised central planning. Privatisation, here largely by the issue of vouchers, was quite rapid – as was the speedy formation of many new private enterprises. The author comments that, as elsewhere, privatisation has not generally been accompanied with the much-needed rationalisation; the relatively low unemployment suggests continued overstaffing. Foreign investment (such as the stake by Volkswagen in Skoda) has, however, been important. Policy, in

Kouba's view, should now focus on the "microsphere" – incentives, promotion of good management and the framework of property rights.

The story is taken up by *Kosír* (Ch. 20) from Bratislava. Reform began in Slovakia as a part of the CSFR and continued along similar lines after separation (1 January 1993). But progress has been influenced by the legacy of the former period when Slovakia specialised in armaments and other heavy industry and was thus economically complementary to the Czech lands, and suffered more from falling demand. The next stage, in *Kosír's* view, must be building up new industries and infrastructure for a newly independent economy.

We move now to two more new states emerging from the break-up of the Yugoslav Federation – Slovenia and Croatia.

Mencinger (Ch. 21), from Ljubljana, provides a wealth of data on the economic evolution of Slovenia in the 1990s (separation came in 1991). All the problems of stabilising a small country (population 2 millions) torn away from its main trading connections hit Slovenia and were intensified by the sanctions and conflicts disrupting the rest of the former Federation (fighting in Slovenia itself was mainly limited to the "ten days war" in mid-1991).

A more critical story for Croatia comes from *Vojnić* (Ch. 22), from Zagreb. Since separation (early 1992) the country has had to contend not only, like Slovenia, with loss of trading links but also with direct physical war devastation, the occupation of about a quarter of its territory the massive inflow of refugees and its own military expenditure. The Croatian government was, however, able to introduce a stabilisation programme in 1993 which appears to have brought down the very high inflation rate. A programme of privatisation has also been introduced and is making slow progress; it is complicated by the special form of "social" rather than State property that characterised the former Yugoslavia. *Vojnić* insists on the interdependence between economic transformation and the establishment of an effective political democracy. He also makes it clear that the transition demands an active role by the state but he warns against retreat either to overstressing state functions – described as "neobolshevism" – or to disintegration of state activities – "the Latin American syndrome".

PART I – STABILISATION POLICIES ASSESSED

Chapter 1

ECONOMIC TRANSFORMATION IN THE EAST: A CRITICAL APPRAISAL OF ITS DEVELOPMENT AND SUGGESTIONS FOR A POSSIBLE WAY OUT[1)]

Friedrich Levcik[*)]

The former socialist countries of Eastern Europe have been trying to adopt a system of capitalist market economy with a preponderance of private property. During the transformation process, lasting for more than three years, democratically elected parliaments and governments were installed and various policy steps – of varying intensity – were taken to move towards a market economy.

---

1) This chapter is based on a study, "Transformation from the Command to the Market System: what went wrong and what to do now?", presenting the results of a research project undertaken by The Vienna Institute for Comparative Economic Studies (WIIW) from 1991. The project, under the supervision of Kazimierz Laski, WIIW Research Director, was carried out by the WIIW staff together with WIIW consultants Amit Bhaduri and Friedrich Levcik, as well as several outside experts. References to the fuller treatment in the relevant chapters of the project report (published as *WIIW Working Paper* no. 1, 1993) are given in brackets in the present chapter as "Laski 1993". The authors and titles of auxiliary studies completed within the framework of the project are listed at the end of this chapter.

*) Professor of Economics, Consultant, The Vienna Institute for Comparative Economic Studies, Vienna.

The original euphoric idea that transformation would be over very soon – if only the policies adopted were radical enough – has given way to a general recognition that transformation is a protracted process with uncertain outcome. This may be because the economic results of transformation, besides showing a number of positive features, have so far mostly been disappointing and have had negative social and political consequences.

Empirical results relate largely to the four "Visegrád Group" countries, the Czech and Slovak Republics, Hungary and Poland, but their conclusions may also be applied, at least in part, to other East European countries and to the successor states of the Soviet Union, countries less advanced on the transformation path.

The principal aim is a critical analysis of the generally recommended conventional pattern of transformation policy. Also, an attempt is made to explain why this policy has not yielded the desired results and to suggest modifications that could help to overcome the economic crisis and initiate self-sustained economic growth.

1.1 Background

There can be no doubt that the countries in question are burdened with the legacy of state socialism obstructing all necessary change. This means, *inter alia,* the previous administratively set and distorted prices, largely inefficient state enterprises, an underdeveloped or nearly non-existent private sector, distorted economic structures, poor quality of products, uncompetitive export products, lack of legal institutions, notoriously neglected infrastructure and serious environmental damage. Before the transformation began many of these countries exhibited a considerable monetary overhang, insufficient budgetary discipline and often high external indebtedness. In view of this, governments embarking on transformation spoke of necessary cuts and sacrifices, but they also declared that the inevitable painful adaptation process would be shorter if transformation were radical and fast. After more than three years it is time to review the results.

Positive and negative results of transformation

A number of *positive results* of economic transformation have been observed:

(a) The outward signs of the shortage economy, such as long queues and empty shelves, have disappeared and many previously unavailable goods – mostly western products – are now on sale. New private companies, mostly in trade and services, are being created and are expanding their operations. Privatisation of state enterprises, increasingly also in industry, is taking shape.

(b) Relative prices are approaching international price structures. In some countries inflation rates are falling, although they still reach double digits.

(c) Foreign trade, supported by steeply devalued exchange rates, has largely been liberalised. The earlier, strongly negative current account balances, being closely monitored and supported by IMF credits improving the balance of payments (standby credits), are at least temporarily being brought under control; in some transforming countries there are even current account surpluses, mostly used to increase foreign exchange reserves.

(d) In some countries budgetary discipline has been strengthened.

On the *negative side* fall the results in the "real" economies. During the years of transformation, the countries' economies shrank to an extent that can be compared only with the decline experienced during the deep economic depression of the 1930s. The aggregate gross domestic product (GDP) of the three (now four) Visegrád countries – the Czech Republic, Slovakia, Poland and Hungary – had by 1991 decreased by one-fifth; if Bulgaria and Romania are added, by nearly one-quarter. This process of economic shrinkage slowed down during 1992 and 1993 in the Visegrád four countries. In Russia, the decline was steeper but somewhat less severe in 1993. Industrial production, construction and agriculture were hit most by economic decline. The only improvements came with the rising shares of the previously underdeveloped retail trade and services.

All components of GDP absorption have been declining, especially investment by enterprises. And yet new investments in enterprises would be crucial for stopping decline and bringing about the needed structural changes. Also, consumption and real incomes are still far below their initial levels. Employment is, of course, also on a downward path (even though a part of the newly unemployed workforce is absorbed by the expanding private sector) and the number of unemployed persons is still rising in most countries. However, in general employment is decreasing less than production. Consequently, labour productivity, which had lagged behind that in western market economies before transformation began, continues to decline strongly. Over-staffing in state enterprises inherited from the era of state socialism increased further. (See Laski 1993, A.III)

Some counter-arguments

Official sources in East Europe, but also certain western experts, often draw attention to the fact that the statistics exaggerate actual economic decline because various private, often flourishing, economic activities are not statistically recorded. This may be so, especially since existing tax systems and tax collection procedures still do not meet the requirements of a market economy, and tax evasion is widespread. On the other hand, some previously illegal private activities have been legalised and it is therefore easier to record them statistically. During the first two years of transformation the private sector was still too small to have a significant influence on the general pattern of economic decline. However, by 1992 the private sectors in some countries had grown and statistical recording had improved considerably compared with the two previous years, thus weakening the old argument of the private sector's strong statistical under-representation.

Another frequently heard argument is that the collapse of CMEA trade and the reduced production of unsaleable goods were more responsible for economic decline than shrinking domestic demand. The breakdown of CMEA trade and the substitution of "useless" goods by imported ones certainly had a negative influence on the trade balance and therefore on total demand. However, an analysis of the components influencing GDP revealed that declining investment and, especially, falling consumption, were far more significant.

1.2 The need for, and instruments of, stabilisation

The first stage in the transformation of former command economies into functioning market economies must necessarily be stabilisation. The former centrally planned economies had used their capacities inefficiently (because of low labour productivity, waste of intermediate products and poor product quality) but yet fully and had suffered from shortages. In order to move from a supply-determined shortage economy to a demand-determined market economy total demand must be reduced for a short period because adaptation on the supply side generally takes a longer time. In the Eastern case this process had to be accompanied by a nearly complete liberalisation of prices which before had been set administratively. Consequently, in our attempt to elaborate an alternative transformation policy, we agree with the conventional approach recommended by western institutions, and the West in general, stressing the need for stabilisation.

However, we disagree in many other respects. If actual developments in the major economies in transition are compared with the original assumptions about the magnitude of decline in production and employment, and about the probable duration of the adaptation crisis, it becomes obvious that the difficulties of adaptation were grossly underestimated. In our opinion the reason for such strong divergencies of actual economic development from the expectations of radical reformers and their western advisers lies in the monetarist approach towards stabilisation policy based on the concept of "financial programming". (Laski 1993, A.II)

The quantity theory of money, which is the basis of financial programming, proceeds from the assumption that the velocity of money circulation is roughly constant and that aggregate output is determined exogenously by the demand side. In such conditions, any changes in money supply will lead to corresponding changes in the price level. The control of inflation is therefore by far the most pressing issue to be addressed by conventional stabilisation policy. The usual instruments for fighting inflation are credit restraints, price rationing of credits through high interest rates, restriction of budget expenditures particularly through cuts in subsidies and nearly complete liberalisation of the foreign trade regime, coupled with a substantial devaluation of the domestic currency aiming at a balanced exchange rate. The government tries to maintain, or "anchor", the effectiveness of these instruments of inflation control for a certain period of time through the introduction of wage controls and a limited constancy of the exchange rate. These "nominal anchors" aim at breaking inflationary expectations. Since the liberalisation of prices and foreign trade, combined with a drastically lowered exchange rate, immediately cause strong inflationary pressure, fiscal, monetary and income policy measures must be much more restrictive than would be necessary for immediate stabilisation by itself.

Confusion of aims and means

Our criticism of this conventional concept of stabilisation is directed against the radicality of the measures adopted and against the attempt to solve all problems simultaneously, as well as against confusing transformation targets with the means of reaching them. (This debate is being conducted under the simplifying slogans of "shock therapy" versus "gradualism".) However, what is more important is that the negative effects of a policy of ruthless restriction of real incomes, domestic demand, and consequently of economic growth in general, were grossly underestimated or even ignored. Social unrest and destructive nationalism, leading even to the disintegration of states, must be viewed in the light of the negative social consequences of a certain transformation strategy.

The pivotal role of aggregate demand

This leads to the conclusion that the stabilisation phase can be assessed only in a national accounting framework where total demand plays the central role in determining the level of national output. Only by such an approach can the recommended extent of a restrictive stabilisation programme be weighed against its economic and social consequences. The development of GDP and its components – consumption, investment, public expenditures and the foreign balance of goods and services – are determined by the recommended stabilisation programme. Political decision-makers must decide, on the basis of the macroeconomic implications, what degree of popular sacrifice is compatible with the needed support for the reform path. (Laski 1993, A.IV)

Effective and ineffective inflation control

Attention is justifiably focussed on fighting inflation during stabilisation. We may, however, doubt whether methods appropriate to uncontrolled hyperinflation may be successfully applied in a "normal" inflation occurring concurrently with a drastic reduction of total demand.

Restrictive stabilisation measures eliminating excess demand in the early stages of transformation, if continued during a general economic downturn,will not only deepen the ongoing recession unnecessarily, but also begin to have a negative influence on demand, thus rendering inflation control increasingly difficult. If a cut in public expenditures continues after a drastic fall of production, and if the money supply is kept low through credit restrictions and high interest rates, this can only result in further production slumps. Consequently, investments become unprofitable for private companies, and state enterprises become mutually indebted, increasingly illiquid, or, in some cases, insolvent.

This is compounded by the fact that the prices of most goods – except sources of energy, raw materials and agricultural products – are not determined by demand but by costs and will only stay constant if unit costs also remain so. This is quite likely if capacities were previously under-utilised. If, however, unit costs rise as a consequence of stabilisation policy with capacities still under-utilised, cost-determined prices will also rise, even during deep recession. The costs of intermediate goods per unit of output rise during stabilisation because of steep rises in energy prices, transport charges, rent for office space, and even more because of high variable capital costs caused by high interest rates. Rises in input prices, as well as increases in indirect taxes introduced by governments to lower their budget deficits, heat up inflation further by increasing the cost of intermediate goods. Further devaluations of domestic currencies have a similar effect, as they make imported inputs more expensive. Unit wage costs may also increase during depression if labour productivity decreases more than average real wages. This also happens if nominal wages – while increasing more rapidly than wholesale prices – rise more slowly than consumer prices (this pushes unit labour costs up, even though simultaneously real wages will fall given constant productivity). Under such circumstances what we observe is not inflation caused by excess demand, but cost-induced inflation which cannot be fought with methods appropriate for demand control.

However, conventional stabilisation policy continues to consider inflation caused by excess demand as the main danger. This theoretically incorrect diagnosis of the causes of inflation leads to the continuation of unsuitable inflation control measures. Obviously, in view of the new situation, a loosening of credit restrictions would not only help to overcome recession, but would simultaneously remove some elements of cost-induced inflation. Given free production capacities and surplus of labour in enterprises, an increase in effective demand would lead to an expansion of production rather than price increases. If the workforce and real wages stayed the same, higher effective demand would help to raise labour productivity and lower unit wage costs. Any loosening of demand restrictions would thus, in the circumstances outlined above, not heat up inflation but rather dampen it. (Laski 1993, A.V)

Fiscal policy and budget deficits

During transformation the relationship between reasonable fiscal policy and existing budget deficits is another problem. Stabilisation at first led to some spectacular improvements in the budgets, mainly because of a transient high profitability of state enterprises (due to the revaluation of stocks, high export profits in domestic currency during devaluation and a drastic fall in real wages in the early stages of stabilisation) and consequently to higher government revenues. This situation was soon replaced by a drastic decline in enterprises' profits – caused, *inter alia,* by falling labour productivity and high interest rates – which led to shrinking budget revenues. The expansion of the private sector, often combined with tax exemptions, but also with lenient tax collection and widespread tax evasion, as well as falling employment and decreasing real wages, influenced budget revenues negatively.

This confronted governments with the crucial question: must government expenditures be reduced when a sharp drop in revenues occurs? Conventional stabilisation policy, but also common sense, come up with only one solution: in order to balance the state budget again, expenditures must fall *pari passu* with falling budget revenues. It is obvious that such a policy will lead only to the prolongation or deepening of recession, impairing not only consumption but also profits and savings. Cutting budget expenditures *pari passu* with falling budget revenues makes sense only if effective excess demand – e.g. at the start of transformation – is to be eliminated. During the later phase of transformation depression any further reduction of expenditures is counter-productive and should be replaced by a more flexible fiscal and monetary policy, which would slow down falling aggregate demand and create incentives for private investment. In present circumstances, the real problem about permitting budget deficits, even rising ones, is not the danger of inflation, but the question of what burden may be put on current accounts that are expected to deteriorate at the beginning of the recovery phase. (Laski 1993, A.VI)

Similar arguments apply to monetary policy, which according to the conventional monetarist approach should be rather restrictive (through the application of credit restrictions and positive real interest rates) in order to curb inflation persisting during economic depression. However, if one wants to move from depression to economic recovery and expansion, combined with structural adaptation on the supply side, the continuation of restrictive monetary policy inevitably leading to restrained effective demand will only prolong the depression phase. This will also obstruct the adaptation of the supply side needed for sustained economic growth, since medium and long-term investments in production are too expensive and therefore unattractive at high interest rates. (Laski 1993, A.VII)

1.3 Some measures for effecting institutional and systemic change

Of course, more effective transformation of a centrally planned economy into a decentralised market economy cannot be limited just to the application of a more flexible kind of macroeconomic policy from which rigid patterns of thought have been removed. A series of institutional measures capable of effecting systemic change must be introduced in order to make the macroeconomic framework operative in the first place. We do not attempt to present a comprehensive description and analysis of all such institutional changes. We limit ourselves to discussing a certain number of policy steps towards systemic change that are essential for transformation and closely related to the macroeconomic framework. (Laski 1993, B)

There is general agreement that in order to change over to the market economy the post-communist countries must overcome their tendency for autarky and integrate themselves into the world economy. The market economy furthermore presupposes the existence of economic subjects vested with clear property rights, competing with each other and producing goods and services for a market. The necessity of privatising most state-owned enterprises is therefore not a point of controversy, but there is less agreement regarding the question whether the economy's necessary structural adjustment should be entirely left to the market forces, or whether the state ought to take some responsibility in this respect and conduct a deliberate structural and industrial policy.

Recommendations by the West: unilateral foreign trade liberalisation

Foreign trade liberalisation is generally considered an essential transformation target, allowing the discipline exerted by international prices to act on domestic price structures, to supplement insufficient domestic competition and to give access to western know-how and investments. The conventional approach, adopted in many of the recommendations from the West, is to start transformation by combining the liberalisation of domestic prices with foreign trade liberalisation and at least limited convertibility of the national currency.

Non-tariff, quantitative restrictions are to be completely eliminated, customs duties are to be kept low, export subsidies to be avoided. Moreover, the national currency is to be devalued drastically to reach a balanced exchange rate (corresponding to black market exchange rates) and to ensure current account convertibility. According to conventional "shock therapy", all these measures are to be introduced at the start of transformation, regardless of deficient institutional infrastructures, and unilaterally, without waiting for reciprocity by trade partners.

These recommendations were taken seriously in all transition countries except Hungary. They caused a tremendous price jump which, in turn, had to be fought by draconic fiscal and monetary restrictions. These restrictive measures not only led to avoidable production and employment losses (Laski 1993, A.II and IV), but eventually proved incapable of controlling the ensuing cost inflation in most countries. Moreover, the premature and unilateral liberalisation policy weakened their negotiating positions when they concluded association agreements with the EC.

If only in view of the 1992/1993 recession, when the West was initiating protectionist measures against cheap imports from Eastern Europe, unilateral and comprehensive foreign trade liberalisation may be considered to have been a mistake. It borders on mockery that western protectionist measures against imports from the East are sometimes defended by accusing Eastern wages of being too low (wage dumping), although these low wages are a direct consequence of the West's premature recommendation to introduce convertibility combined with drastically lowered exchange rates. At least some of the countries that have not yet fully elaborated their transformation strategies could infer from this experience that the gradualist strategy adopted by the West European countries after the second world war, and also by Hungary during its reforms aiming at foreign trade liberalisation and convertibility in the 1980s, may actually be more effective. However, other Eastern countries which had introduced import liberalisation, without paying attention to reciprocity, are in fact also beginning to realise that entire economic sectors may be destroyed if there are no introductory periods offering protection, i.e. that specific transitory protective measures may be justified. (Laski 1993, B.VIII)

Conventional privatisation and unconventional summary privatisation procedures

Besides liberalisation, another decisive measure affecting the economic system is privatisation, indispensable for establishing a functioning market economy. Particularly in this context one is often confronted with a confusion of transformation targets and the means of reaching them. Considering their socio-political aims, it is understandable that political leaders in the East wish to privatise all state property as fast as possible by unconventional methods. However, in spite of such efforts, unconventional summary privatisation also takes time, and failure to transform state-owned enterprises into more or less functioning agents of market economy before privatising them causes great – in some cases irreparable – damage to the economy. While the privatisation of existing small and medium-size enterprises, or the founding of new ones, usually does not pose any conceptual problems, too little is done to keep them alive. Tight credit policy in particular puts a heavy burden on such enterprises which often operate on insufficient capital and must struggle for access to new credits.

Privatisation of the large enterprises is difficult because of the lack of domestic capital and foreign companies are not very interested in acquiring enterprises that would first need organisational, financial and technological restructuring; this is why privatisation can proceed only step by step over a number of years. Impatient reformers therefore advocate unconventional summary procedures, whereby state property is distributed by vouchers among nationals free of charge or for an insignificant, nominal sum. The vouchers thus distributed are then exchanged for shares of companies chosen by individuals, or investment funds representing them, by way of several rounds of auctions. The market value of these shares will be determined only at a later stage in the course of transactions on the newly emerging stock exchanges. In the meantime, which may take as much as two years, enterprises selected for this form of privatisation are without supervision and find themselves in a state of "pre-privatisation agony" (a term coined by the inventors of the voucher method). During this interval irreparable damage, or illicit private enrichment by interested parties, may occur. The outcome of this method is still uncertain even in the Czech Republic, where is has been developed furthest. One must assume that a significant number of the new shareholders will try to exchange their shares for cash as fast as possible, so that great pressure will be put on their value in a wave of sales and cause liquidity problems to certain investment funds. It is not clear whether investment funds acting as intermediaries will confine themselves just to administrative functions and the improvement of their portfolios, or whether they will actually exercise ownership rights in joint stock companies whose shares they hold – which would include, where necessary, the formulation and realisation of restructuring and financial rehabilitation programmes. This form of privatisation is superficial and of limited effectiveness regarding improvements in efficiency. It may moreover lead to the destruction of considerable amounts of equity and to illicit enrichment by insiders and thus discredit privatisation in the eyes of the general public.

Conventional privatisation methods will obviously take several years. It follows that large state-owned enterprises will have to be commercialised before privatisation, i.e. they must be removed from direct control by the state as proprietor. They must be transformed into functioning economic agents able to survive in a market-economy environment through the introduction of hard budget constraints, but also through positive motivation of their managements. In many cases there will have to be a phase of rehabilitation and restructuring involving the splitting up and sale or, perhaps, liquidation of non-viable parts of the enterprise, with the state proprietor assisting the process for a strictly limited period and outlining very strict conditions and guidelines. In this case there will be a greater chance that such enterprises can later be directly sold either to private parties at market value, or through placement on the stock exchange. (Laski 1993, B.X)

Can the market solve all problems?

In spite of certain positive results, the transformation process has led the countries concerned into deep economic crisis. Can this crisis be overcome purely by the action of market forces? Official decision-makers and their western advisers answer this question affirmatively without any hesitation. They warn against state interference which is supposed to just conserve outdated structures. The "creative" elimination of indebted enterprises by the market through bankruptcy is considered as part of the necessary recovery process strengthening the economy. Of course, enterprises with no chance of surviving domestic or foreign competition must not be kept alive artificially. But, as outlined above, many existing companies, or parts of them, could be transformed into market-oriented, efficient economic subjects through financial rehabilitation and restructuring programmes. It is interesting to note that the current slight recession of the world economy, which is much milder than that in the East, has led many western governments to elaborate state-supported programmes of structural and industrial policy in order to move out of recession faster. In the developed market economies, both in the past and also at present, the state has intervened actively not only in the case of market failure, but also for the purpose of structural improvement, or to promote activities with good future prospects. Why should this be taboo for the former socialist countries?

Structural and industrial policies are indispensable

Active structural and industrial policy is indeed much more important for Eastern than for western economies, because the Eastern markets, and the reactions of economic agents to market forces, are not yet fully developed. Without active industrial policy they will not be able to tackle the profound structural changes and indispensable modernisation lying ahead. This policy must not, of course, be directed against the unfolding market forces, but must clearly strengthen and support them. New, indirect methods of state intervention need to be elaborated, such as measures giving small and medium-size companies easier access to credit, or regional policies in areas threatened by unemployment, or export promotion for companies with good prospects of achieving high and constant export profits in the future, or infrastructure-related assistance in the fields of research and technology, education or marketing.

Furthermore, governments cannot relinquish their responsibility for the restructuring and financial rehabilitation of major large enterprises with a significant influence on the national or regional economy and decisive for the employment of a great number of people. Structural support for such national flagships of industry should, through cooperation with their managements, staff representatives and with interested foreign partners, aim at the promotion of new activities with good future prospects in various economic branches rather than at the conservation of old production lines. The reconstruction of under-developed and neglected infrastructure in energy, transport and communications, as well as in health and education, should also be targets of active structural and industrial policy.

Such activities must, of course, be financed. Restrictive fiscal and monetary policy leaves no room – or too little – for active industrial policy. However, as said above, existing budget constraints are less the result of excessive public expenditures than of insufficient budget revenues. The economic crisis deepened by prolonged conventional restrictive stabilisation policy is obstructing the execution of an active structural and industrial policy.

1.4 From stabilisation crisis to growth

Transition from stabilisation to growth is politically imperative. Politicians and sociologists observe that people are losing the enthusiasm and willingness for sacrifice which they felt immediately after the breakdown of the communist dictatorship. It is no exaggeration to say that the original social consensus has been shaken by the negative economic and social consequences of the transformation strategy based on the conventional concept of stabilisation. If the economic crisis persists or deepens there is an acute danger that social cohesion will be eroded, that nationalist tensions will mount and that civil wars may break out, threatening peace in all of Europe.

The economy will, of course, not shrink forever – except in the case of civil war or other catastrophes. But may we already count on sustained recovery? One must start by observing that recovery must begin from a level one-fifth lower than before the decline. Many structural, system-oriented adaptations necessary for a functioning market economy are still to take place. Most of these changes will tend to have a negative influence on economic growth. In the course of privatisation it will be unavoidable to liquidate certain enterprises, and all enterprises will have to rationalise, restructure and reduce costs. A significant amount of redundant labour will have to go, and since the developing private sector is expected to absorb only a limited number of the newly unemployed workforce, unemployment will rise and lead to a decrease in domestic demand. This will be compounded by the so far slow recovery from western recession and limit the East's ability to expand exports to the developed market economies. It would therefore be premature to count on sustained and early economic recovery even in the most advanced transition countries.

The role of the West

Of greater significance are middle and long-term expectations, which will have as strong an influence on the economic policies of individual countries in the region as that exerted by western attitudes, recommendations and support. More support would be needed and, particularly, the West should open up its markets more to Eastern products. One cannot escape the impression that the

West, and especially Western Europe, is not aware of the dangers that the unsolved problems of Eastern Europe also pose for them. In our view, a new appraisal of the macroeconomic strategies recommended by the West would be even more important than actual technical and financial assistance, market access or direct investments (whose role should not be cast into doubt), if the conditions for granting the needed assistance are laid down by these strategies.

It is not only necessary but also possible to overcome the transformation crisis if the central role played by effective demand management becomes generally recognised. Two economic policy implications should be stressed: First, economic policy measures with a short-run positive impact are needed. An expansion of total demand brings about the necessary adaptations much faster than an expansion of supply. Second, governments may directly shape fiscal and monetary policy. Of course, budget deficits should not be permitted to serve as instruments for stimulating aggregate demand over long periods. The stimulation of other components of aggregate demand, such as private investments or export surpluses, is certainly of greater and more lasting significance. However, the latter aggregate demand components can be influenced only indirectly and relatively slowly. Budgetary programmes, on the other hand, even allowing higher budget deficits for a limited time, can stimulate the economy and bring socially useful and clearly visible success almost immediately; they may thus have an indirect positive influence on the overall investment climate. (Laski 1993, C.XII) Such an expansion-oriented budgetary policy, complemented by a suitable monetary policy providing easier access to credits at lower interest rates, would not "crowd out" private investments in the current situation of recession and under-utilised capacities; it would, on the contrary, probably "crowd in" more private investments by playing a complementary role. For the same reason demand inflation is not likely under the present circumstances while cost inflation caused by insufficient capacity utilisation is kept under control. (Laski 1993, A.V)

Pressure on the current account due to higher imports could constitute a real obstacle to such an expansion-oriented demand policy in the transition countries. Awareness of this real present stumbling block leads to our conclusions discussed in the context of foreign trade and industrial policy. (Laski 1993, B.VIII and XI) Caution with import liberalisation and selective export promotion, as is normal in western industrialised countries, would be particularly appropriate in the East. Moreover, publicly funded investment programmes should concentrate mainly on projects with a low import share (such as housing programmes). Pressure on the current account could thus be reduced while at the same time the economy would expand. Western support in the form of credits, direct investments and easier market access would greatly strengthen such programmes of economic recovery and expansion. In any case, the conditions imposed for obtaining western financial aid, such as insistence on the reduction of budget deficits even during the current recession phase, ought to be relaxed. In our opinion, the transformation path suggested by us would also have greater chances of success than the conventional stabilisation policies implemented hitherto because it could quickly restore the lost public consensus imperative for the long period of transformation lying ahead.

References

For the research project on which this chapter is based, the following auxiliary studies have been completed; most of them have been published as WIIW Research Reports:

Avramović, D., International Experience with Adjustment Programmes and with Lending for Adjustment.

Bhaduri, A., Conventional Stabilization and the East European Transition.

Fath, J., Industrial Policies for Countries in Transition.

Hunya, G., Speed and Level of Privatization of Big Enterprises in Central and Eastern Europe – General Concepts and Hungarian Practice.

Landesmann, M. A., Industrial Policy and the Transition in East-Central Europe.

Laski, K., Transition from Command to Market Economies in Central and Eastern Europe: First Experiences and Questions.

–, Fiscal Policy and Effective Demand During Transformation.

Levcik, F., The Place of Convertibility in the Transformation Process.

–, The Thorny Path of Transition from Command to Market Economy.

–, Privatization and Restructuring of State Enterprises.

Rosati, D. K., Foreign Trade Liberalization in the Transition to the Market Economy.

Chapter 2

TRANSFORMATIONAL RECESSION:[1) THE EXAMPLE OF HUNGARY

János Kornai[*)

Abstract

All the post-socialist countries of Eastern Europe are in deep recession. This study discusses the common features of these recessions, using the Hungarian economy as an example. The author starts by considering the following general reasons for the phenomenon: 1) the shift from a sellers' to a buyers' market, 2) the transformation of the real structure of the economy, 3) the disturbances in the coordination mechanisms, 4) the macro consequences of the hardening of financial discipline, and 5) the backwardness of the financial system. The components of macrodemand – investment, personal consumption, government consumption, and exports – are then examined one by one. The most important factor here is the dwindling propensity to invest. Finally comes a summary of the conclusions. There are good reasons for placing recovery from the recession at the top of the economic-policy priorities, but without acceleration of inflation or a resumed increase in indebtedness. The study ends by analysing the political and economic-psychological requirements for recovery.

* * *

---

1) The study was made as part of a broad research programme on the subject of the transformation of the Hungarian economy in the period 1986-1992. An initial version of its message for economic policy was conveyed to a broad readership in an article in the Christmas 1992 issue of the newspaper *Magyar Hírlap*. Several of the ideas in the study were put forward at seminars held by the World Bank and the International Monetary Fund in Washington, and at the Political Science Faculty of the Central European University, the Transit Club of the Institute of Economics and Neumann Foundation in Budapest and the Budapest University of Economics. The present text was the author's "Francois Perroux Lecture", delivered in Collège de France, Paris, on 9 June 1993, and published in *Economie Appliquée,* no. 2, 1993, I.S.M.E.A. Paris and Les Presses Universitaires de Grenoble. The contributions to the discussion on those occasions were a great help to me in clarifying my ideas.
I am most grateful to Mária Kovács for her wide-ranging assistance with the research, to Álmos Kovács and György Surányi for their valuable comments, to Brian McLean and Julianna Parti for their excellent translation of the Hungarian text, and to Hungary's National Scientific Research Foundation (OTKA), the European Bank and the AustriaLotto for their financial assistance to the programme.

*) Professor of Economics, Harvard University and Collegium Budapest.

All the East European countries are suffering from a grave economic recession (see *Figure 2.1,* and Tables and Figures at end of chapter). The course of the recessions is remarkably similar, even though the starting-points and specific circumstances differ substantially. The history of the production decline in Poland, the prime example of "shock therapy", is similar to that in Hungary, where the transition has been gradual. Production has fallen sharply in countries which started with high international debts, and also in Romania and Czechoslovakia (or the Czech Republic and Slovakia), which were untroubled by this problem at the beginning of the transition. Production has fallen where there was no reform before the political turning point, and also where there was a process of reform taking place over many years. This strong similarity has prompted me to concentrate in this study on the factors that are common to the histories of this group of countries. Although the discussion throughout this study is about Hungary, I hope that the analytical approaches in it will prove useful when examining other Eastern countries as well.

Since the phenomenon differs substantially from the cases hitherto discussed in the theories of economic fluctuation, there is justification for giving it a separate name. To distinguish it, I have called it *transformational recession*.

The figures for Hungary are shown in *Tables 2.1, 2.2 and 2.3*. These make it clear that the fall in production, which followed a long period of stagnation, is deeper than that in the Great Depression of the early 1930s. Total production has fallen by 19 per cent against 7 per cent then, and industrial production by 36 per cent against 18 per cent. Yet the recession in Hungary so far has been milder than in most other countries in the region.[2)]

It was generally expected that the transition would be accompanied by a range of difficulties, but to my knowledge very few economists predicted this

2) It can be assumed that the share of the informal sector (the "shadow economy") in total production grew in the same period. If this was really so, the fall in the total GDP including both the formal and informal sectors was smaller than the official statistics show.

large-scale decline in production.[3)] A growing number of economists have dealt with the question since then, but the profession has failed to arrive at a consensus about how to explain the phenomenon. Some ascribe it to a single cause (or at least a single main cause) like the collapse of Comecon trade, including the Soviet market. Such simple theories do not seem convincing to me. In my opinion, this is a complex, compound phenomenon that requires a *multi-causal explanation*,[4)] and my research is aimed at contributing to a synthesis of various explanations.

The first Part of the study points out a few *general* factors inducing the recession. The second examines the *special* factors causinig contraction of the main elements of macrodemand (investment, consumption, government spending, and exports). Both Parts discuss causal factors that can be traced back to a common ultimate cause: the post-socialist transformation itself. I am not arguing that no part of any kind is played by factors other than those associated with the process of transformation. A contribution to the decline in the East region has certainly been made, for instance, by the fact that the outside world, including the developed capitalist countries, is going through a recession as well. Apart from the direct economic drawbacks of the tougher export conditions and smaller influx of capital, there is the unfavourable social-psychological effect. It is unfortunate that the former socialist world should have begun to move towards capitalism just when this system was not in its best form. (This factor, however, is not covered in my study, which deals solely with *internal* effects rooted in the transformation itself.)

The third and final Part draws conclusions from the previous causal examination. The emphasis throughout is on positive description and analysis,

---

3) The public in the Eastern countries was not prepared for this eventuality by the new parties and leading politicians, or by the new democratic governments. Nor can any forecast of the serious recession be found in the early theoretical writings to outline the programme for the transition. So it is absent, for instance, from J. Kornai, *The Road to a Free Economy* (1990 (1989)), and from the oft-cited study written by O. Blanchard and other famous Western macroeconomists (1991). Among the very few exceptional early warnings was the writing of Laski (1990).

4) Efforts to provide one are apparent in the articles by Erdős (1992), Commander and Coricelli (1992), Gomulka (1991a, 1991b), and Kolodko (1992). I have taken over several important ideas from them.

but normative proposals also appear, in most cases simply as illustrative examples.

It is worth saying what the study does *not* set out to do. It does not provide a numerical forecast, and it does not put forward a detailed programme of government action. Instead of contributing to the debate on the current situation of the Hungarian economy, I would like to analyse a few major tendencies in the last and next few years, and comment on some strategic problems.

The general factors inducing the recession

Not even in the recessions of a mature capitalist economy does the production of each and every firm and product decline. Even near the trough, successful, expanding enterprises are found at least sporadically. In a transformational recession, this is not exceptional at all; this duality is one of its characteristic features. Contraction and expansion, failure and success, mass exit and mass entry can be observed side by side. To use the phrase of Schumpeter so often quoted these days, "creative destruction" takes place at tempestuous speed. But it is still possible to refer to a recession in the macro sense because the balance of the two processes is negative; for the time being, the pace of the contraction process is greater than the pace of the parallel process of expansion.

This recognition dictates that the examination should not be confined exclusively to the factors that explain the *absolute* decline. The final balance between the expansion and contraction processes with their opposite signs is affected by everything that promotes or impedes either growth or decline.

Each and every trade cycle under capitalism has specific features. Even so, I will attempt a measure of abstraction, by comparing the individual features of the transformational recession with an "ideal type", the typical recession that occurs in a mature capitalist economy.

2.1 From a sellers' market towards a buyers' market

In the normal state of capitalist economy taken here as a basis for comparison, macrolevel monetary equilibrium applies as the long-term trend: macrosupply and macrodemand are in balance at the prevailing level of prices. The usual attendant phenomena are unemployment corresponding to the "natural rate", excess capacities accompanying the imperfect competition that governs the bulk of the market, and a constant process of entries and exits. The balance of power between the producer-cum-seller and the buyer in this kind of economy is tipped in the buyer's favour. There is a buyers' market, in which the sellers compete for the buyers' money, and this is precisely one of capitalism's greatest advantages, because it encourages adaptation to the demand, respect for consumer sovereignty, improvement in quality, and the introduction of new products.[5)]

Compare this with the normal state of classical socialism: a chronic shortage economy, in which macrosupply and macrodemand are out of equilibrium at the prevailing level of prices. The attendant phenomena are a shortage of labour, unsatisfied demand for many products and services, wide-spread queuing, and forced substitution. The expansion of production regularly runs up against bottlenecks and constraints on physical resources.[6)] The balance of power between the producer-cum-seller and the buyer in this kind of economy is tipped towards the seller. This is a sellers' market, in which the buyers compete for the products for sale.

Not even at the peak of the trade cycle in mature capitalism does the state of the market switch over to a general, intensive and chronic shortage economy. The ball remains in the same half-court, i.e. the buyers' market basically continues to prevail, and at most the balance of power shifts slightly in the direction favourable to the seller. At the trough, there is an increase of unemployment and under-utilisation of resources, which further intensifies the competition.

Transformational recession, on the other hand, is combined with a profound and *unique* change. The game moves to the other side of the net, so that the economy changes from a sellers' into a buyers' market – from a supply-constrained economy into a demand-constrained economy. This process is to some extent consciously controlled by economic policy (monetary and fiscal policy, as well as pricing policy), out of a desire to bring the shortage economy to an end. But its course is influenced by several uncontrolled, spontaneous

---

5) On the advantages of a buyers' market, see the articles by Scitovsky (1951) (1971), (1985) and Domar (1989). A detailed comparative discussion of the buyers' and sellers' markets appears in Chapters 11 and 12 of Kornai (1992a).

6) In an open socialist economy the desire to increase production often runs up against constraints on the availability of hard foreign currencies.

circumstances as well. There is a complex mutual influence between recession and the switch of "market regime" (the change from a sellers' to a buyers' market), so that neither process can be plainly said to have *caused* the other.

In the countries moving away from the classical form of socialism before the political turning point – Hungary in the first place – the transition to a buyers' market began earlier. *Table 2.4* shows how the supply constraints (shortages of labour, materials, semi-finished products and components, for instance) eased steadily over a period of six years. Already it is rare for physical resource constraints to constitute a direct obstacle to production growth. The rarity with which production in Hungary runs up against input constraints can be found in any mature market economy as well. It can be established from this table (and from numerous other facts) that the shortage economy in Hungary has ceased; there is no longer a general, intensive and chronic shortage. Parallel with this very substantial change, the role of the demand constraint increases. The table shows clearly how this is now the obstacle that the desire to raise production encounters most often. (A very important role is additionally played by the financing constraints, which are discussed later.)

To simplify somewhat, this long period of transition in Hungary can be divided into two stages (*Table 2.5)*. In the first, repressed inflation that constituted one feature of the shortage economy turned into a moderate rate of open inflation. The gradual, increasingly widespread freeing of prices worked in this direction; a price level developed at which macro-supply and demand could reach equilibrium. This was also helped by supply factors: the emergence of the private sector, the easing of the conditions for entry into production, and the partial liberalisation of imports. The rate of inflation speeded up, reaching a peak in June 1991, when prices were for 39 per cent higher than a year before. These processes presumably soaked up the unspent purchasing power or "monetary overhang". In other words, there was an end to the macroeconomic situation that some economists characterise as a general excess demand.

The *disinflationary* efforts of the financial administration commenced in 1991 and became more perceptible in 1992. The rate of inflation reached its lowest level so far in July 1992, when the price level was 20 per cent higher than twelve months before. Since then it has fluctuated around 23-26 per cent a year. To some extent demand had actually been held in check even earlier by monetary policy. Though no orthodox monetarist economist would call the financial policy of the late 1980s and early 1990s "restrictive", as scope constantly remained for a very sizeable inflationary growth in the money supply, demand clearly did not "run away".[7] In fact it fell appreciably in volume terms, and the gap between demand and the earlier maximum supply, i.e. the potential GDP, steadily widened. Ultimately, the economy on the macrolevel tipped from excess to insufficient demand.

The "market regime" can be graphically demonstrated by a synthetic index that shows the composition of stocks. In a shortage economy, firms mainly accumulate stocks of inputs, while outputs are soon taken up by the buyers. When the shortage economy ends, the proportions change; there is no more need to hoard inputs, but output stocks build up due to sales difficulties. This change is shown in *Table 2.6*. The index in Hungary stood earlier at around 6 – input stocks were six times as big as output stocks. This compares with a value of around 1 in the mature and developed market economies. The present value (early 1993) of the index shows a dramatic fall to below 3, but it has yet to reach the figure typical of a mature market economy.

From all this can be drawn a range of conclusions important to our subject, recession. The recession cannot be explained solely in terms of insufficient demand. Even now, only half the firms consider the insufficiency of demand as the obstacle to production.[8] We currently face a "half-Keynesian" situation, for whose treatment a doctrinaire Keynesian therapy is not suitable *by itself*. But the other half of the comment must be added immediately: precisely because the situation is already half-Keynesian, demand plays a very marked role in determining output. So the second Part of the study analyses this in detail. In this transformational recession, the "brake" has not been applied by central controls on supply, as it was when investment and production were curbed in the socialist economy. Although we are not faced with a recession produced *exclusively* on the demand side, the demand side has assumed the primary role.

---

7) A part was played in curbing demand by the institutional reforms and the changes that took place in the behaviour of the economic actors as well. To some extent the budget constraint became harder, and that was accompanied by a lessening of the investment hunger; firms, and even the state budget, became less prodigal in their spending.

8) Nor does inadequate demand become the sole obstacle to production in a mature, developed capitalist economy, even during the downward phase of the trade cycle. The frequency there is at most 70-80 per cent. See Laffont (1985, p. 354).

When I first asked myself, 23 years ago, how a supply-constrained sellers' market would turn into a demand-constrained buyers' market, I hoped this could be accomplished without a fall in production.[9] I thought the supply would continue to grow, while the growth in demand would decelerate (but still remain positive) to an extent that finally tipped the situation from excess demand to excess supply. The idea, or rather hope, that I had at that time is shown in *Figure 2.2a*, taken from my 1971 book. Unfortunately the transition has been different in practice, for a number of reasons. Well before the change of system in Hungary, the growth of production had decelerated and been followed by a long period of stagnation. To transfer from excess supply to excess demand in such circumstances, the curbing of the growth of demand and (in volume terms) its absolute reduction inevitably drag down the supply as well, and interact in a vicious circle to deepen the recession. When the postsocialist economy shifts from one secular market regime, a sellers' market, to the other secular market regime, a buyers' market, it *tips over too far*, instead of arriving at an ideal state of equilibrium. The actual trend of supply and demand appears in a stylised form in *Figure 2.2b*. The actual volume of production falls back steeply from its previous peak; the state of the economy resembles in this respect the trough in the customary fluctuation of the capitalist trade cycle.[10]

In fact I have a bad conscience about using the expressions *general* excess demand and excess supply, because they over-simplify the situation. I have been campaigning for a long time against rash use of aggregate macro categories in this subject-area. Unsold goods also existed under the conditions of the shortage economy. Cases of excess demand and excess supply can coexist at the microlevel. Some producers run up against supply constraints, while others meet with demand constraints. This caution is now more apposite than ever before, but it leads on to the next factor, the transformation of the real structure of the economy.

---

9) See J. Kornai, *Anti-Equilibrium* (1971, p. 325). At that time I used other terminology ("suction" and "pressure"), but in later works, and in this study, I adopted the more widespread expressions.

10) The 1992 annual Survey of the UN Economic Commission for Europe considers it a mistake not to recognise the alteration in the macroeconomic conditions in Eastern Europe. "Emerging unemployment, the elimination of shortages and restoration of the basic monetary equilibrium are all symptoms of transforming the Kornai-type, supply-constrained economies into Keynesian-type, demand-constrained ones." (p. 51)

2.2 The transformation of the real structure of the economy

When we were looking at the restoration of macro monetary equilibrium just now, one question was left open: why does the change of market regime, the development of the sellers' market into a buyers' market, have recessionary effects?

Prices are gradually (or in some countries suddenly) freed, which brings a new system of relative prices. The greater the extent to which this is accompanied by liberalisation of foreign trade (which in Hungary took place in parallel to a substantial extent), the more strongly and immediately the effects of *foreign* relative prices are felt. It suddenly emerges that there is insufficient demand for a range of products and services at the earlier high prices or even at slightly lower ones; but if the prices plummet, the firms producing them make a loss. If the firms are deprived (either gradually or suddenly) of their state subsidies at the same time, they are forced to cut or completely cease their production. Meanwhile the prices of other products rise due to the appearance of hitherto suppressed demand, so that it becomes profitable to produce or import them. So the new relative prices and the concurrent new product composition of demand generate an adjustment in the supply, i.e. a transformation of the real structure of production. But the adjustment of the quantities to the new prices always takes time, and for several reasons it is particularly sluggish during the period of transition. (Some of these reasons will be returned to later.)

The strategy of forced growth under socialism gave rise to a production structure unadjusted to user requirements, including domestic consumption, but use of these products was imposed on buyers by central allocation and shortages. In the reform period a gradual change in the product composition of output took place. This transformation has accelerated in the last few years. At branch level, this primarily consists of a fall in the share and absolute volume of industrial production and a rise in the share and absolute volume of services (*Table 2.7*). Within this process, thousands of alterations, great and small, take place on the micro level in the specific product composition of output.

In this respect the transformational recession has characteristics that are far more Schumpeterian than Keynesian. It is not simply that aggregate demand is insufficient. The demand for the output of some sectors of the economy falls dramatically, while the demand for other sectors may actually grow. Let me give just two examples. Long-postponed demand led to an almost explosive development of businesses concerned with personal computers, electronics, modern information systems and telecommunications, so that for a long time this broad sector experienced a positive boom in the midst of the recession. The new relative prices and the new structure of demand caused the catering industry and services connected with tourism to flourish.

The change in the product composition and branch structure is connected with two other processes of change. First, property relations alter. The proportion of the sector in purely state ownership falls and the purely privately owned sector and the mixed-ownership sector with various combinations of state and private ownership, expands. This occurs in such a way that the production of the purely state-owned sector decreases in absolute terms, while that of the private and mixed-ownership sectors increases.

Second, a change takes place in the size distribution of firms. The small and medium-sized enterprises were almost totally eliminated under the classical socialist system. Small and medium-sized firms began to return during the period of reform socialism between 1968 and 1989, but they have only begun to multiply rapidly since the change of political system. The proportion and absolute production volume of the large firms are falling, while those of the small and medium-sized firms are rising.

These three kinds of restructuring do not overlap completely, but they coincide to a significant degree. It is not far wrong to say that the two most characteristic actors in a postsocialist economy are the large, contracting, state-owned industrial firm and the small, expanding, privately owned service firm. A more general and accurate way of putting it is to refer to contracting and expanding segments of the economy, without specifying their ownership, scale or product classifications. The desirable state would be an expansion faster than the contraction, so that the balance between them yielded a positive increment. The opposite is unfortunately the case: the contraction of the first segment is faster than the expansion of the second, not because anyone intended it should be, but because a number of factors retard the expansion of the growing sector. More will be said about these retarding factors later.

A painful process of "natural selection" takes place, but the trauma has a healthy, cleansing effect. In fact a similar process occurs during the normal capitalist trade cycle; the idea features large in the cycle theories of A. Spiethoff and J. Schumpeter.[11] In the transformational recession, this process is far more intense and comprehensive. At the end of a capitalist trade cycle, the real structure of the economy has changed comparatively little since the beginning of the cycle, whereas it can be assumed (or rather hoped) that the situation after the transformational recession will be drastically altered.

2.3 Disruptions in coordination

Many people had the naive idea that the elimination of central planning and bureaucratic coordination would be followed immediately and automatically by the appearance and operation of market coordination. In fact there is a curious "no-man's land", where bureaucratic coordination *no longer* applies and market coordination does *not yet* apply, and economic activity is impeded by disintegration, lack of coordination, and anarchy.[12]

The lack of coordination assumes various forms, of which I will pick out a few:

– The old behavioural norms of the economic actors have gone, but they have not yet learnt the new behaviour patterns for the new situation.

– Certain earlier institutions of bureaucratic coordination (organisations and legal regulations) have ended, but the erection of the new market institutions has either not begun yet, or is progressing very slowly. The network of market connections is still very loose, and it will take time before a dense network has been woven.

– The information structure of bureaucratic coordination has gone, but the new system of signals has not yet developed, or the economic actors are not yet sufficiently capable of assessing and processing the new kind of information.

– Bureaucratic coordination, especially in its more consolidated periods before the final disintegration, supplied a kind of order and predictability. The market by its nature involves its participants in a lot of uncertainty and risk. This,

---

11) See A. Spiethoff's (1902) and J. Schumpeter's (1934), (1939) works. An excellent account of these two cycle theories can be found in A. Hansen's well-known summarising work (1964).

12) G. A. Calvo and F. Coricelli refer in their study (1992) to a trade "implosion". The trade relations are destroyed by the absence of market institutions. The phenomenon they describe is an important constituent of the wider group of phenomena referred to above as the yawning gap and lack of coordination between the two kinds of coordination mechanism.

however, is multiplied in the present unsettled situation. Most of the actors are at a loss, anxious, and hesitant about their decisions.

This phenomenon takes its ultimate form in many of the republics that have replaced the Soviet Union, but it also plays a major part in other countries like Albania and Bulgaria. This in my view is one of the main causes (possibly *the* main cause) behind the recession in these countries.

In Hungary the supplanting of bureaucratic coordination began much earlier, in 1968, after which gradual progress was made, with successive relapses. So the phenomenon just described appears in less dramatic forms than in countries which jumped almost directly from classical socialism to postsocialism. But it is worth recalling that there were areas of "no-man's land" throughout the period of partial reforms implemented under the socialist system, a state described at the time by Tamás Bauer as one that was "neither plan nor market".[13)]

The process of transformation has not yet been completed in Hungary. The confusions of coordination, and the phenomena of "no-man's land", still appear from time to time, at least in certain branches, and they contribute greatly to the recession. Two examples follow.

One is agriculture, where production has taken a real nosedive. Cooperative production based on collective ownership, complemented by private farming on dwarf household plots, was not efficient in many respects, but nonetheless it worked and scored some successes. All the elements of coordination were adjusted to these property forms at the time: the central administration, the allocation of investments, the credit and tax system, the setting of prices, the commercial relations between producers and users etc. The old property forms have been shaken, but mature new property forms have not arisen in their place. Everything is in a fluid state. The old institutions and organisations of coordination cease to function under these conditions. But the requisite new system of coordinating institutions – an up-to-date new wholesale and retail network to link smallholders with consumers, a new credit system for smallholders, and a stability-enhancing price and subsidy system in line with European practice – have still not developed. All these factors gravely impede production. They are compounded by a succession of big government mistakes, above all over the compensation of formerly expropriated land-owners and the reorganisation of the cooperatives.

---

13) See Bauer (1983).

The other example is the building industry, and in connection with it, housing construction and urban planning. Although this sphere was relegated and neglected under the socialist system, it still had an established organisation and system of institutions. There were periods when the performance was relatively good, at least in terms of the number of housing completions, even though the quality of the housing completed was poor. Now the sector is in a state of collapse, despite the great demand for housing. The market institutions have not yet developed, a credit system to suit the specific features of the housing market still hardly operates, the network of real-estate agencies is rudimentary, developers able to undertake the development of whole neighbourhoods have not yet appeared, and there is confusion in the system of rents and social subsidies. There is an undoubted need for state supervision over the market processes in this field, and in certain respects for state regulation as well (for instance in applying urban planning and social policy criteria). Instead of a harmonious combination of bureaucratic and market coordination, one encounters repeated confused conflicts between them. As a result of all this, housing construction has fallen back seriously, whereas it might have been one of the leading sectors in the postsocialist transition.

The development of market coordination takes time, which is one reason why the recession is protracted in many fields. But the period of development can be shortened by appropriate legal regulations and state initiatives. The government has committed many sins of omission in this respect: it dawdled over drafting and implementing the legislation to support market coordination, over organising supervisory agencies in conformity with the market economy, and over supplying a system of state guarantees in certain areas requiring it.

2.4 Financial discipline and enforcement of efficiency

A hardening of the firms' budget constraint can be observed in the Hungarian economy.[14)] The most tangible manifestation of this is the forceful implementation of the bankruptcy legislation, even if this originally very strict piece of law has since been partly modified. A large number of insolvent firms are undergoing reorganisation through bankruptcy proceedings, and many of them are being liquidated. A private firm is under a hard budget constraint from

---

14) This process is analysed in greater detail in Kornai (1993).

the outset. Although there are attempts to soften it here as well, the growth of the private sector entails the spread of a hard budget constraint.

What effect do these changes have on the recession? Some firms go bankrupt and exit, which means lay-offs and an end to the firm's demand for inputs. The survivors, which from now on are truly profit-maximising firms that use market instruments to fight for their survival, economise more on their expenditure, which means that their demand for inputs decreases. They try to use up swollen stocks from the past, which also has a demand-reducing effect. They dismiss workers who have become redundant; the unemployed usually generate less consumer demand than the employed.

Even if the managers of state-owned firms bring themselves to dismiss workers, they remain somewhat disinclined to undertake a radical reduction of their excess labour. *Table 2.8* shows that employment in industry falls much more slowly than production, so that labour productivity deteriorates. Presumably there is still a great deal of "unemployment on the job". Once state-owned property is privatised, the situation changes. Experience in many cases confirms what would be expected in theory: the first thing the new owners do is to dismiss the workers they judge to be superfluous.

Privatisation is widely considered to be the main means of overcoming the recession and inducing growth, but this is a simplified misconception of the real relationship. *In the long term*, efficiency really will be increased by the spread of private ownership, by the privatisation of assets previously owned by the state, and by the enforcement of financial discipline and a hard budget constraint, in all sectors of the economy; and that will speed up the growth trend. *In the short term*, however, privatisation has a different effect, because it raises unemployment, reduces demand and so contributes to the recession. Choosing between a short-term, anti-recessionary goal and a long-term growth goal is one of the gravest dilemmas to be faced during the postsocialist transition.

The backwardness of the financial sector

The problem to be discussed now deserves separate treatment because of its special importance. Only now, when the financial sector's backwardness has become one of the obstacles to growth, can the full significance of the difference between a wholly monetised capitalist economy and a semi-monetised socialist economy be appreciated.

Let me return to the column in *Table 2.4* showing the proportion of firms that consider insufficient financing to be one of the obstacles to growth. It is worth noting that while this factor was mentioned by 20-30 per cent of the respondents in 1987, the frequency is 45-50 per cent nowadays.

The banking system under classical socialism did not operate as a real bank. Its actual function was to provide a nationwide bookkeeping and cashier service, coupled with some aspects of the supervision of producer firms. Its guiding principle was that if a real action was declared necessary by the plan or the state bureaucracy, they would provide the money for carrying it out. When a start was made to reforming the economy before the change of political system, as in Hungary, transformation of the banking system also began, so that it came somewhat to resemble its counterpart in a true market economy, although the development can certainly not be taken as complete. This study does not set out to make a comprehensive analysis of the financial sector, and so only a few problems directly related to the subject of recession and growth will be dealt with here.

One problem is the rash and irresponsible way in which credit risks are assumed when they are motivated by non-commercial considerations. This problem is linked with that discussed in the previous section, the lack of financial discipline which still appears very sharply in the successor states of the Soviet Union. There thousands of loss-making firms are being kept alive with bank credits, thus fuelling inflation and impeding the enforcement of financial discipline. This phenomenon does not occur on a mass scale in Hungary, since we have passed that stage. But not even in Hungary has the special relation between the state-owned commercial banks and the large state-owned firms ceased altogether. The owner of both is the state, and in a sense a "personal union" applies. The banks are at times more indulgent with their old customers than they are with their new customers, the private entrepreneurs, when it comes to pressing their claims. Sometimes a similar partiality can be seen in the extension of new credit as well.[15)] Settlement by unrecoverable loans was a very long time coming. This "soft" behaviour by the banks towards the state-owned firms hinders the process of natural selection described earlier. The

---

15) The bias is not shown exclusively to state-owned firms. The banks have also rashly extended vast credits to a good many large private firms, and find it hard to bring themselves to take harsher measures to force repayment.

situation is further exacerbated by the fact that from time to time a high-ranking figure in the government and political life will intervene in the activity of the commercial banks in state ownership, usually in an informal way, exerting pressure on their credit-extension decisions.

In some credit relationships there is a disregard for risks, and in others there is excessive caution and real cowardice about extending credits, particularly when the applicant is a small or medium-sized private firm or a household. It must be admitted that there is a real dilemma here. The banks are just beginning to get used to the idea that they must pursue *commercial* activities, which taken as a whole will yield a profit. They should learn that a bank is not an institution for distributing money on orders from above or friendly recommendations from politicians. That may be so, but they now apply the lesson they have learnt with eager zeal and are inordinately averse from risks. They have yet to master the second part of the lesson: a bank, as a commercial undertaking, must live and prosper by extending credit. No venture in a market economy can make lasting profits by "holding goods back".

So a paradoxical situation has developed. A huge stock of liquidity has accumulated in the banking system, but got stuck there. On the one hand the commercial banks are shy of lending it on a broad scale, but on the other, entrepreneurs are shy of drawing credit, because they think it is too risky as well.

For a long time the nominal rate of interest was very high, and it only began to fall quite recently. The real interest rate was less alarming because of the steep rate of inflation, but still high enough to deter many entrepreneurs from borrowing. There is a debate taking place about the present role played by high interest rates in decisions to borrow. For want of a strong enough argument to support a decided opinion, I can only give my impression. It seems that at the real rate of interest prevalent at the time of writing even a moderately successful business could service a loan on such terms. I tend to agree with those who say the *main* cause of the reluctance to borrow is the uncertainty.[16] There are too many unpredictable aspects of the future legal situation, property relations, taxation and other public levies, the future trend in relative prices and inflation, and not least the forecasts about the general state of the economy. On the creditors' side, the interest rate has probably come down enough to make

---

16) See, for instance, Valentinyi (1992).

the banks even less inclined to lend, precisely because of the uncertainty about the economic conditions.

To follow up this line of argument, I can point to the continued absence of a whole range of institutions and organisations very necessary for the general operation of a market economy, and especially important for stimulating Hungary's transitional economy. Let me give just a few examples. There has not yet emerged a system of collaterals and guarantees that does not just copy the rules and conventions of the mature market economies, but allows for the immaturity typical of the Hungarian economy and the initial problems of the entrepreneurial stratum. There has not yet developed fully one of the elementary tools of all modern financial systems: a system of current (checking) accounts. Transfers and payments of claims through the banking system are still very slow and expensive. Credit cards are not widespread. The network of various kinds of investment funds, venture-capital companies, pension funds and other financial intermediaries has still not consolidated. The development of the capital market is at its early stage.[17)]

Mention must again be made of the two branches referred to earlier: agriculture and housing construction. Throughout the world, both of these employ special credit and investment schemes. In Hungary, the development of these proceeds very sluggishly, which has greatly contributed to the grave recession in these two branches.

Development of the financial sector inevitably takes a long time, but a great many omissions by the government can be blamed for the slow progress. This applies to all the phenomena used to demonstrate backwardness. Yet another typical example of government neglect was the delay and procrastination before access was widened to the so-called "E-credits" for entrepreneurs. (This is a specific credit-scheme, which grants loans to private entrepreneurs for investment at favourable terms with government assistance.) Hesitation and

---

17) It is particularly worth noting that the country is facing problems of immaturity not only in the banking sector in a narrow sense, but in the broader financial sector. It would be a mistake for credit to play an excessive role in financing the firms, and so relegate their own capital to the background. Difficulties appear in assembling initial capital and obtaining investments needed for capital injections. A very high degree of uncertainty about the chances of value-preserving, profitable investments, and the underdevelopment of the organisations managing investments are deterring many holders of money from bringing their savings to the capital market.

a lack of imagination have been shown in a field where there is a real need for constructive governmental initiative.

Calvo and Coricelli,[18] take the disturbances in the credit system and the scarcity of credit to be one of the main causes of the recession. This statement seems to be correct, but at least in Hungary's case it needs some refinement. I do not think the main problem is the tightness of the total credit supply permitted by central monetary policy. In my view the problem lies in the excessive friction and low efficiency with which the financial system operates as an intermediary between the possessor of money – the depositor-saver – and the borrower of loans.

To sum up so far, it can be stated that the postsocialist transformation necessarily gives rise to processes that tend towards a reduction in aggregate production. This painful consequence of the transformation has been examined in five "dimensions". These five processes, intertwined with and reinforcing each other, hinder growth and retard production. Their negative effects are compounded by mistakes on the government's part.

2.5 The components of macrodemand

Attention was drawn to the conspicuous and constantly expanding role played by the demand side in determining output during the transition. So let us consider each of the principal components of demand, employing the categories customarily used in macroeconomics. (A summary of the changes in these is provided by *Table 2.9.)*[19] But I would like to stress in advance that I do not confine myself to examining the demand (utilisation) side; mention will also be made of some aspects of the supply (production) side. Although in each case I take a macro approach as the point of departure for examining the phenomenon, I will also refer to the microeconomic and institutional aspects.

---

18) Calvo and Coricelli (1992).

19) The text of this study uses the customary categories of macroeconomics: investment, private consumption, government consumption, and export surplus or net exports. The classification of the official statistics for the utilisation of GDP differs somewhat, as can be seen in *Table 2.9,* for instance. The macroeconomic categories can each be made to correspond more or less with a statistical category. Since I am not at this point making a quantitative analysis, it can be hoped that the deviations between the two classifications will not cause confusion.

(a) Fixed investment

Let us begin with the most important category from the point of view of medium- and long-term growth: fixed investment. The volume of investment has seriously declined (*Table 2.10*), in fact to 29 per cent below its peak in 1987. The proportion of investment in the utilisation of the steadily declining GDP has also fallen (*Table 2.11*).

Under the classical socialist system a constant and insatiable investment hunger prevailed: The investment stimulus of what Keynes called "animal spirits" never flagged. The decision-makers at every level from the works manager to the prime minister were driven by the expansion drive. The fact that the bill for the investment was always paid in the end out of public funds, so that the financial failure of the investment was ignored, guaranteed permanent optimism about growth.

This attitude, already dulled by the quasi-reforms, was completely eradicated by the political turn and the institutional changes that followed it. The investment hunger came to an end, to be replaced by caution, and even by cowardly fear in many people.[20)]

In the *government* sector, in which I am not including state-owned firms, investment activity has declined. This is connected, of course, with the troubled fiscal situation. Similar tension under the socialist system would not have deterred the top leadership from undertaking great investments, as the decision could be taken behind closed doors; however great the investment, it could be covered by taxes levied indirectly on the public. There can be no question of this now, because Parliament decides how the taxpayers' money will be spent in the full glare of publicity.

To overcome the recession, the investment proportion of government spending should be increased. The state needs to play a bigger part, especially in infrastructural investment.

Those *state-owned firms* which are likely to remain in long-term or permanent state ownership need investment to secure their survival and to modernise. The trouble is that many of these firms are also meeting serious

---

20) Looking at the behavioural motives, this phenomenon relates to the one described earlier in connection with credit. A strong aversion to risk is apparent in both spheres. The two spheres are not identical, although they overlap. Some investment is not financed from credits, and some credits are not extended for investment purposes.

financial difficulties and are not sufficiently creditworthy. If an investment project shows a loss, they cannot count on automatic assistance. So their old self-confidence has been lost; their managers are hesitant and do not dare to invest. This must change. The decision-makers, of course, have a responsibility for these investment decisions, which they cover out of public money after all. But this should not stop such decisions being made at all; public opinion in the business community should also encourage the state sector to invest.

The situation is even worse with *firms that are still in state ownership* but known to be destined for privatisation in the future. Here almost all investment activity has been paralysed; no one dares to initiate anything while waiting for the new owners. In fact there is quiet disinvestment – depletion of the assets invested earlier. Several practical conclusions can be drawn:

– An acceleration of the change of ownership is also urgent from the investment point of view. The immediate proceeds of the sale should not be the main criterion. Consideration should be given, alongside the general objectives of social transformation, to the likely results of the investment and job-creation programme promised by the new owners.

– Before the privatisation takes place there must be assurance at least that the assets will reach the new private owners in the best possible condition. A fundamental element of this is the conservation and careful maintenance of assets. Many firms need reorganising, which usually entails investment as well.

– The firms' managers must be given a far bigger incentive to carry out these tasks, so that the assets privatised are as valuable as possible, and not in a run-down condition.

In the *private firms,* in fact, the "animal spirits" referred to by Keynes are alive, as the large number of entries and firms being founded shows. They are alive, or rather would be if the propensity to invest were not cooled by several unfavourable circumstances. Two have already been mentioned when the financial sector was discussed: the uncertainty, which in fact is much greater than is usual in a market economy, and the financial sector's backwardness and reluctance to lend to private firms. Coupled with these are the weakness of the capital market and the fact that the tax system is not friendly enough towards investment. Many would also include the high level of interest rates (as noted above).

To overcome these unfavourable circumstances is the key factor in recovering from the recession.

A major figure in the investment sphere is the *household,* which can finance the construction of an owner-occupied dwelling from its own savings and from credit. Let me repeat that housing construction in general, including construction financed by households, has seriously declined. Its stimulation, for instance by more easily accessible credits and tax concessions, could play an important part in recovery.

(b) Private consumption

As *Table 2.9* showed, the volume of private (household) consumption has fallen, but to a less extent than GDP and total real income.

Under central planning, the predominant part of household incomes was regulated by the state, and the savings proportion was fairly stable, so that the central managers of the economy could accurately forecast consumer demand. There is no question of this now. We may take the determinants of the demand in turn:

– A smaller part of incomes derives from the state budget, while the greater part depends on agreement between employers and employees. Although this is influenced by collective bargaining and interest reconciliation at the highest level, on which the government has a great, though not exclusive influence, the actual wage agreements are decentralised. The central agreement is at most regarded as a suggestion.

– Once households possess a cash income and some stock of previously accumulated savings, the decision on how much to spend and how much to save is in their own hands. This may be influenced by government action (for instance by a monetary and fiscal policy that tries to affect the interest rate), but the strength of this influence is doubtful.

Although future spending intentions, i.e., aggregate demand of households, will have a great effect on the recession, they remain hard to predict. Households themselves are just getting acquainted with the new situation and learning to make savings decisions of a new kind. No economist can yet know the result of that learning process or yet recognise its regularity, and what represents a one-off departure from some future pattern.[21] A few hypotheses seem to apply not merely to the present situation in Hungary, but to have a more general validity:[22]

– Citizens who can rely less and less on the assistance of the state build up a safety reserve against illness or unemployment, and for their old age.

– Also appearing as "household savings" is the accumulation of the operating business capital for new private ventures (including unregistered, grey or black businesses).

– The savings-to-earnings ratio of the higher-income strata is generally higher than that of the lower-income strata. So it can be assumed that the income differentiation that took place in recent years tended to raise the average savings rate. All these tendencies can be expected to continue.

What can be the conclusions for an economic policy aimed at overcoming the recession? It would be a mistake to work for a growth in consumer demand through unbridled wage rises. Though perhaps popular initially, it is a dangerous weapon that can easily overshoot the target. There could also be an unexpected change in the spending-saving ratio, so that a still greater volume of intended spending spills onto the market from the excessive surplus of income. This would not only boost production, but price rises as well, leading to a big inflationary push. There is still a great need in the future for moderation and sobriety on the part of employees and organisations representing them. But if excessive wage pressure should appear after all, let us hope the employers (including the biggest, the state) will put up resistance.

---

21) Household savings can be described by a variety of stock and flow indices. Let us take here just one stock indicator, used in Hungarian financial statistics: the "net financial position" of the general public, i.e., the household sector. The indicator is calculated by subtracting total debt from accumulated gross savings (whose main components are cash, savings deposits and securities). This index suddenly grew in 1991 and in the first part of 1992; a contribution was certainly made by the strong incentive given to pay back housing loans immediately. Even after an easing of the sharp rise, the net position of the general public in real terms shows a great increase over the last three years: it was 71 per cent higher at the end of 1992 than at the end of 1989. (Source: communication from the National Bank of Hungary and Magyar Nemzeti Bank, 1993, p. 122.)

22) Some hypotheses that seem convincing are advanced in this respect in Király (1992), and I make use of these in what follows.

Rash handling of wages would affect employment unfavourably as well. There is a generally recognised macroeconomic connection here. Very many firms would be obliged to dismiss workers if they were burdened by too high a wage bill under the present cost and labour productivity conditions. Although there is still a need for caution and discipline over wages, there are some well-aimed measures that could help households as well to contribute by their economic decisions to overcoming the recession. The government and the financial sector, which is still mainly in state hands, have not shown enough initiative in this respect either. Let me give just a few examples.

– More should be done to ensure that the banking system is not the exclusive route by which private savings can flow into investment. Households should be involved to a greater extent in the capital market, primarily through the mediation of investment funds, insurance companies and decentralised pension funds. This would tie down and so stabilise a high proportion of savings.

– Let me repeat that it is desirable for a sizeable part of household savings to be used for financing housing construction.

– As a legacy from the socialist economy, too little scope is left in all the postsocialist countries, including Hungary, for consumer credit, which is far more limited than in the mature market economies. The spread of consumer credit can provide an easily controllable increase in demand, with favourable effects on production.

(c) Government consumption[23)]

The state budget, from which government consumption is financed, has become a constant topic in day-to-day politics. This study is not a contribution to these debates. I deal exclusively with the relationship between the budget and the recession. Looking beyond the immediate situation, I examine a few more general problems concerned with this relationship.

Hungary is in a vicious circle. Declining production is necessarily joined by declining state revenue, while most state expenditure is not related directly

---

23) The "government consumption" category (i.e., total government spending, minus governmental investment expenditures) does not coincide exactly with the statistical category "collective consumption" (see *Table 2.9)*, although there is a large overlap between them. A third category, "total budgetary expenditure", differs from both, for one reason because it includes the investment financed from the budget as well.

to the quantity of production. So a recession may produce a budget deficit in all economies. But once the deficit is there, it becomes hard for a government to bring itself to inject into the economy a fiscal stimulus, which is the most obvious method of overcoming the recession quickly. It has been a truism since Keynes's day to suggest that it is advisable in times of recession to take fiscal measures to raise macrodemand, even at the cost of a budget deficit. Policies of raising taxes and cutting spending during the contraction phase of the trade cycle were subsequently described in economic histories, written in a Keynesian spirit, as gravely mistaken, because these measures reduced total demand.

This line of thinking suggests the following statement. If the deficit had been lower in past periods (if spending had been less and revenue more) and all other circumstances had been equal, the fall in production would have been greater than it actually was. The budget deficit acted as an anti-cyclical stabiliser.

The same line of thinking gives rise in the short term to the following conclusion: it would be dangerous now to reduce the deficit quickly and to a large extent (even if the administration were capable of doing so). A rapid and drastic cut (for instance by a sharp increase in taxes) would suddenly reduce macrodemand and abruptly push an already deep recession even deeper. I do not want to ignore all the well-founded arguments about the seriously damaging nature of a budget deficit. It entails an inflationary risk; moreover the financing of it squeezes out the investment so necessary for recovery and growth. I merely want to draw emphatic attention to the existence of a direct connection between these two grave diseases in the Hungarian economy: the recession and the budget deficit. Treating one problem without sufficient circumspection will have harmful side-effects and may hinder recovery from the other.

It is far from my intention to encourage an increased deficit. On the contrary, the goal must be to take concerted measures to whittle down the main totals in the budget, i.e. to reduce expenditure, revenue and the deficit concurrently. But an eye must be kept on the following: the reduction must happen in such a way that the demand lost from government consumption is replaced, if possible in full, by investment demand. The hope is that this desirable reallocation of resources will be ensured from a future reduction in the need for credit to finance the budget, in other words the mitigation of the crowding-out effect. This must be combined with a rise in the proportion of investment spending within total budgetary spending. In this case there will be a favourable rearrangement of the composition of aggregate demand. Total investment demand of all sectors (government, business and household) will have more beneficial multiplier effects than the demand from government consumption.

(d) Exports and imports

The logic of the discussion has left foreign trade until last, although there is no doubt that of all the events inducing the recession, the serious decline in trade with the former Comecon countries, including the breakdown of the former Soviet market, has caused the greatest upheaval.[24)]

Some of the authors dealing with the question have described this occurrence as an "external shock". In my view this is not an apt name for it. It is certainly true that the shock from foreign trade is external to each country concerned in a geographical sense, but all the characteristics of Comecon trade can be traced back to the fundamental features of the socialist economic order; its effect is deeply imbedded in the regularities of the system. The sellers' market was able to work because there was a Comecon buyer even for the articles least desired at home; if all else failed, the sale could be forced by a tie-in. The expression "external shock" is normally applied to an event that suddenly appears and then vanishes again, so that the economy, after some adjustment, gets over it and continues from where it left off before the shock. The collapse of Comecon trade, however, has lasting, definitive effects. The structure of these economies must be altered once and for all before they can prosper without it.

Table 2.9 shows plainly that of the main components of macrodemand, exports fell back the most, even more than investment. The Hungarian economy successfully took the first steps of adjustment, proving capable of redirecting a very high share of its export potential to the OECD markets (*Table 2.12).* This made sure that the Hungarian economy stayed on its feet, that the fall in production did not assume catastrophic proportions and that the country's international payments position was consolidated.

Unfortunately this cavalry attack cannot be sustained; the growth rate of exports has already slowed down, and the first warning signs of a decline can be discerned. We are unlucky, because a recession (far milder than ours)

---

24) An attempt to quantify this effect numerically was made by Rodrik (1992).

appeared in the Western world just at the time when we had the greatest need to expand onto their markets.

Moreover the first great advance was made according to the old formula: "export at any cost". Many firms, particularly in the state sector, shouldered great losses in forint terms just to be able to export and not have to shut down production. But this cannot continue in the future, as the budget constraint hardens. Instead the struggle now must be for all possible additional exports that are really profitable without a state subsidy. On the other hand, the restriction of domestic demand has eased somewhat, so that firms sense to a lesser extent that they have to export or perish. On top of all this are the serious problems with agricultural exports, caused by several factors: not merely the unfavourable weather, but the growing tendency to protectionism shown by importing countries, and the crisis in agricultural production discussed earlier in the study.

I agree with those who say that exports constitute one of the growth-inducing branches for small open countries in the long term. But it is another matter to decide to what extent exports can contribute in present circumstances to the urgent short-term task of overcoming the recession as soon as possible. Some of the ways mentioned earlier in connection with the stimulation of investment can self-evidently be applied to exports as well. Particular attention should be paid to private investments aimed at producing for export.

Detailed analyses do not support the proposition that imports always squeeze the domestic producers out of the domestic market. There are examples of this, but it is far from general. Many firms without an import rival have sunk into deep crisis, while many manage to carry on producing and selling successfully in spite of competition from imports. None of this is an argument against giving temporary protection to some domestic product or group of products on a considered basis of economic rationality, not under pressure from lobbies. This can contribute to curbing the recession. But the protection must only be temporary, until the necessary adjustment has been made, and in line with the rules of GATT, so that it does not lead to protectionist retaliation by foreign trading partners.

The concerns about both imports and exports make it necessary once again to rethink exchange-rate policy. If the present policy of allowing real appreciation of the Hungarian currency is continued, the chances for exports and domestic production facing import competition may deteriorate further, which will tend to deepen the recession. The campaign against recession must include a revision of exchange-rate policy.[25)]

Devaluation is known to give a boost to inflation.[26)] Whichever way Hungary goes, either one problem (recession) or the other (inflation) will get worse. This dilemma arises in connection with most of the measures to be considered, and so it must be faced also in its more general form (see the final section of this study).

To sum up, it can be established that the contraction observable in all four components of macrodemand is largely the result of the transformation process itself. But a role in the development of macrodemand is also played by the economic policy of the state; the severity of the recession is partly attributable to errors and mistakes on the part of the government.

2.6 Conclusions

Priorities

In my view there are now grounds for reorganising the priorities. Around 1989-90, there were very strong political and economic arguments in favour of the following priorities:

(a) The increase in indebtedness had to be halted; the country's international liquidity position had to be improved.

(b) Inflation had to be slowed down as much as possible.

(c) Unemployment had to be "handled" from the point of view of welfare policy.

Neither the political statements and government programmes nor the writings of economists at that time included among the urgent priorities the need to guard against recession, or later the need to halt or combat the recession.

I now propose the following new priorities:

(a) We must forestall any further recession. Recovery from the recession must be promoted. The economy must be diverted onto a growth path. As a likely by-product of this, perhaps after some delay, unemployment will cease to increase, and employment will then start to grow.

---

25) This idea is argued in detail in a study by Obláth (1993); I agree with his conclusions.

26) The inflationary effect is particularly serious if nominal wages are allowed to rise to compensate for the devaluation. So a condition for the success of the exchange-rate policy is that it should be based on a social consensus.

(b) We must prevent a renewed acceleration of inflation. The inflation rate must be gradually brought down to the 12-18 per cent band known as the range of "moderate inflation".[27] The attainment of single-figure inflation must be taken off the agenda for the time being. Preparation for this will become opportune once the economy is on a growth path again.

(c) We need not work for a further sharp reduction in the total stock of foreign debt or rise in the foreign-exchange reserves.[28] A slight deficit on the current account is tolerable temporarily, although any marked deterioration on the balance of payments must be prevented, and we must not enter a new spiral of debt accumulation.

I have tried to phrase these new priorities as accurately as possible. On the basis of bad experience in the past, I would like to protest in advance against the eventuality of any opponent of mine in debate twisting one or other of these a little and leaving out some qualification, in order to take issue with a distorted form of my proposals.[29]

There is no justification for relaxing attention to inflation and the balance of payments. In fact the danger of inflation and accumulation of debt will be greater than ever before, precisely because measures are taken against recession. Countries that have to cope with only one of these three painful problems – inflation, or recession and the accompanying unemployment – are in an enviable situation. The Hungarian economy is suffering from several grave problems at once, which makes it extremely difficult to decide what to do, because whichever way we take, the desired beneficial effect will be accompanied by undesired side-effects. It is impossible to find a solution

---

27) Experience in many countries shows that an economy can remain within this band for several years without reaching single-figure inflation, but still avoid the danger of a renewed acceleration of inflation. See Dornbusch and Fischer (1993).

28) This last proposal should be understood as follows. The yardstick is not the absolute size of the exchange reserves, but the ratio between them and the volume of imports. Point (c) suggests that it is not worth increasing this ratio further.

29) Inaccurate interpretations have not been confined to my opponents in debate. When I presented this line of argument in public in Budapest, one daily paper in a short report interpreted the priorities I put forward as a *temporal sequence*. According to the report, I was proposing that growth should be achieved first, then after that had happened, we should defend ourselves against inflation, and when that had been done, we should tackle the balance of payments. In fact these are simultaneous tasks.

satisfactory in every respect. The only choice before us is to decide which disease we should devote most attention to treating in the immediate future – which disease we consider most acute.

I should say a separate word about the problem of inflation, where some disquieting phenomena are appearing. There is a danger of inflationary pressure in the rapid rise in the money supply (notably high-powered money, i.e., "monetary base") and the accompanying "surplus" of money building up in the banking system. The rate of inflation is easing more slowly than expected and promised by the government. So the emphasis throughout this study is on "growth-friendly" measures that might give a boost to production *without* causing a general rise in aggregate demand, i.e. ones less prone to have side-effects that speed up inflation.

My proposal is a *half-turn* towards growth, not a U-turn in which our backs are turned to the earlier priority tasks of tackling inflation and the growth of indebtedness. This cannot be confined to adopting "half-turn" as a slogan. To make it will require a convincing, detailed, practical programme whose implementation must begin at once.

What justification is there for rearranging the priorities? It would be a shame to commit the big mistake of rigid thinking. These economic-policy tasks, whether expressed in the earlier or the present set of priorities, are not among the *ultimate* goals and primary values of economic activity that must be stuck to at all times. They are *intermediate* goals and instrumental values that need choosing in a way appropriate to the specific situation and rearranging if the situation alters. No universally, eternally valid order of priority can be established between production growth, reduction of unemployment, curbing of inflation, or improvement of the international payments position. So the question at the beginning of the paragraph could be put more specifically like this: what alterations in the *situation* justify reappraising the priorities? Let me pick out a few.

First, as I pointed out, the recession has proved much deeper than anyone expected around 1989-90, and protraction of it cannot be ruled out. This is causing very serious damage. The country is suffering from a variety of problems: technical backwardness, widespread poverty, with the threat of further worsening of the financial position of the poor, neglect of the health service, education and infrastructure, and so on. None of these problems can be solved satisfactorily by redistribution, by transferring from elsewhere resources to carry out tasks that have been put off or neglected. Only a growing economy can slowly but surely resolve these and many other problems.

Secondly, while the private sector is the force for overcoming the recession on which we can most rely, insufficient demand is already holding back private-sector development. It is increasingly hard for many private firms coping with the difficulties of start-up to keep their heads above water.[30] If the total volume of the private sector's production should start to decline, the prospects for recovery would become almost hopeless.

The third (and possibly most weighty) factor is that the reduction in real income of a sizeable proportion of the population, and the previously unknown phenomenon of mass unemployment, have produced broad economic discontent. If the strength and extent of this discontent reaches a critical threshold, it will pose serious dangers for the young Hungarian democracy. Politicians have several times warned that there could be a "Weimarisation" of the postsocialist region, including Hungary.[31] It should be remembered that it was mass unemployment and waves of inflation in Weimar Germany that led to mass disillusionment and rejection of the institutions of democracy and the parliamentary system. This economically-induced disillusionment provides a fertile breeding ground for demagogy, cheap promises and desires for iron-handed leadership.

We must guard against Weimarisation in the political and ideological sphere. Not as a substitute for political action, but as a parallel effort conclusions need to be drawn in terms of economic policy. This is what the half-turn proposed in this study sets out to do.

Confidence and credibility

There are political and social-psychological requirements for an economic recovery. This is not an assumption suggested only by politicians or experts outside the economists' profession, like psychologists or sociologists. The truth

30) This concern was voiced by the heads of the biggest private companies in Hungary, who referred to "the private sphere contracting because of the recession" and drew attention to the fact that the economic decline was making it impossible to attain the turnover required to finance the debt stock of the large firms which had rapidly expanded. (See Hámor, 1993)

31) I first encountered this expression in an article by Tamás (1990).

in this realisation has penetrated fully into modern economics as well. It is worth drawing attention to the following connections:

– Study of expectations has come to the fore in modern macroeconomics. In the first wave of studies concerning the Phillips Curve, it was thought that all disinflation was plainly accompanied by a specific rise in unemployment. Since then, however, a modification of the theory has been devised. There is already general acceptance for the view that the Phillips Curve can shift depending on the inflationary expectations.[32)] The more the actors in the economy expect the inflation to continue, the greater the unemployment sacrifice required to overcome that expectation. The more they believe that inflation will decelerate, the smaller the sacrifice required. Applying this line of thinking to our case, the following can be established: parallel progress in both growth and the macro-equilibrium can only be made if the government programme to achieve this has credibility in the eyes of the actors in the economy.[33)] But if people expect that the recession and the inflation will continue whatever the government may promise, the expectation will be self-fulfilling.

– Keynes and other economists underlined that optimism – confidence that the economy will pick up – is required to reinforce the propensity to invest. In this sense it can be said that either optimism or pessimism will be self-fulfilling.

– A feeling of stability, a knowledge that the existing laws and institutions are lastingly stable not fickle or arbitrarily changeable, is needed to strengthen the propensity to invest, and in general for business activity on a private-ownership basis.

Unfortunately these socio-psychological phenomena present great difficulties. For the sake of illustration, I mention only one study. From *Table 2.13,* showing some results of an international opinion poll organised by Western researchers, the Hungarians emerge as the most pessimistic group of respondents.

---

32) This theory was first expounded in articles by Friedman (1968) and Phelps (1968). New impetus to the examination of the connection between inflation and unemployment has been given since then primarily by the theory of rational expectations.

33) The statement that the credibility of a stabilisation programme plays a decisive part in its success has been proved not only theoretically, but historically. This was proved with a force that swept all counter-arguments aside in a famous study by Sargent (1982) entitled "The Ends of Four Big Inflations".

Can this public attitude be reversed? Could a convincing government programme backed by a broad political consensus emerge? This study was written in June 1993, nine months before the next parliamentary elections are due. It would be self-deceptive to count on this consensus in the months ahead, when political divisions and rivalries are likely to become sharper than before. It would be much more sound to expect (and even this is far from certain) that the situation will at least not deteriorate further, and that the political configuration after the elections will provide conditions more favourable to implementing a credible, confidence-inspiring programme.

The role of the state[34)]

In theory there are two ways out of the recession: forward or back. *Back* means to restore the old structure of the economy with subsidies, support inefficient exports, sustain state-owned firms in financial crisis artificially and many jobs along with them, defend all domestic producers from import competition by protectionist means, and maintain unemployment on the job in the surviving firms and the low productivity that goes with it. This constitutes overcoming the recession by abandoning further transformation and partially restoring the old economic system. If we now ignore the political conditions, this is certainly a programme that in an economic sense can be realised by a combination of "hyper-Keynesian" demand-inflating monetary and fiscal policy with bureaucratic interventionism. Ideas of this kind appear in several places, tinged with the various colours of the Hungarian political spectrum.

The way *forward* out of the recession is to try and get over the gravest difficulties, in other words to eliminate the loss-making jobs and concentrate our energies on ensuring that the private sector expands, new, efficient jobs are created, the necessary structural adjustment takes place, and profitable exports develop.

---

34) Here and elsewhere in the study, I mean by the "state" the ensemble of all the branches of state power (the legislature, government and judiciary). I underline this because many readers will follow ingrained habits and immediately identify the "state" with the government of the day, not taking into account the roles of Parliament, the head of state and the courts, including the Constitutional Court, as "checks and balances" on the government. These have great powers, and share responsibility for the development of the country with the government.

But even among those who agree with the progressive line requiring a consistent transformation, two views can be found on the strategy to be followed. In one, the confidence in the spontaneous force of the market and private initiative is very strong. We need only to wait before the internal forces of the economy lift the economy out of the trough. These forces are so strong that they can prevail even against an incompetent government that makes repeated mistakes. I myself inclined to this view for a good while, all the more because I share the attitude of those whose past experience leaves them with little confidence in governmental wisdom. But I am now obliged to adjust this perhaps too doctrinaire position somewhat. I am induced to do so by awareness of the political danger of "Weimarisation" just mentioned. Another argument is a recognition that simply to await a spontaneous, self-engendered movement in the present political and economic situation in Hungary could set what is known in economics as a "low-level equilibrium trap". This state in Hungary's case would bear the following characteristics:

There would be a prolonged slackness of the propensity to invest. Mass unemployment would stabilise at a high level and the utilisation of other resources would also be low. The growth of the private sector would stick at its present level for lack of entrepreneurial spirit. Foreign capital would lose interest in investing in Hungary. The fiscal crisis would be perpetuated; there would be insufficient money for infrastructural development, education, medical care and welfare services. The budget deficit could not be overcome without production growth, but production would be unable to grow because of the high taxes and the crowding-out effect of the budget deficit. There would be repeated surges of inflation, followed by repeated painful measures to slow it down. Although the slump in the economy would halt, it would be unable to climb out of the trough. This is no mere nightmare. There are countries in the Third World where this kind of stagnation has persisted for a long time. Whatever happens we must climb out of the trough, and economic activity by the state is essential for doing so.

I am no advocate of superabundant state intervention and bureaucratic micro regulation. This would lead to the very endeavour from which I strongly dissociated myself just now: combatting the recession by partially restoring the old system.

It is worth referring, in my view, to two forms of justified and desirable state engagement. The first grade, in fact, is no more than what the state should do in a modern market economy even according to a libertarian concept: introduce laws and ensure they are enforced, pursue a fiscal and monetary policy, and exert supervision where this is essential (for instance over the financial sector or the natural monopolies). It must do all these things in such a way that they serve the priorities of the present day.

Under the second form, more than this is expected from the state during the postsocialist transition. It must *initiate and actively assist* the development of the new institutions required by a market economy, establish new organisations and abolish others, and transform property relations. The study has put forward plenty of examples of these as well.

So I do not support those who propose that the state should do nothing. That would relieve both the legislative and executive branches of responsibility. Within a well-defined field, the state should certainly do its job. If the recession accompanying the transformation proves too protracted and involves too great a loss, the government is responsible also for this.

The responsibility of the economists' profession

In a time of sharpening political struggles, there is a danger that politicians in government may opt for measures which are harmful in the long term but popular in the short term. There is similarly a danger that opposition politicians may try to turn public opinion against the government by making extravagant promises. At times like this, an even greater responsibility devolves on research economists, who have a professional duty to speak out against both these threats.

During the public debates on the recession and the country's economic situation in general, many politicians and political journalists, along with some researchers as well, have "dug themselves into ideological trenches," as Tibor Erdős so graphically put it.[35] An atmosphere of mutual suspicion prevails. Those who talk about "stimulation" are suspected of supporting the government, while those who mention "restriction" are classed as liberal oppositionists. Erdős emphasises that researchers should not climb into any ideological trenches, but retain their objectiveness and express views in accordance with their convictions. A similar opinion is expressed by Rudolf Andorka as well, who points

---

35) See Erdős (1992, p. 1000).

out that "there is no single redeeming economic-policy recipe. Pragmatism is required; ideologies and dogmas cannot be allowed to determine economic policy."[36)]

I fully agree with this position. Many of us feel fed up to the back teeth with the "labelling" that has become prevalent in economic debates. The dogmatic application of half-digested economic theories and in addition the habit of classifying various theoretical schools around the present party structure in Hungary (this party is Keynesian, that party is Friedmanite), have a toxic effect on objective research. The problems that have to be solved are extremely difficult and unprecedented. We can all make mistakes. That means there is all the more need for composure and rational argument.

References

Andorka, Rudolf (1993), "Gazdaság és társadalom dogmák nélkül" (Dogma-free Economy and Society), *Népszabadság,* 15 May, vol. 51, no. 112, pp. 17. and 19.

Bauer, Tamás (1983), "The Hungarian Alternative to Soviet-Type Planning", *Journal of Comparative Economics*, vol. 7, no. 3, pp. 304-316.

Blanchard, Olivier, et al. (1991), *Reform in Eastern Europe*, MIT Press, Cambridge.

Calvo, Guillermo A., and Coricelli, Fabrizio (1992), "Output Collapse in Eastern Europe: The Role of Credit", manuscript, presented at the conference "The Macroeconomic Situation in Eastern Europe" organised by the World Bank and IMF, 4-5 June 1992.

Commander, Simon, and Coricelli, Fabrizio (1992), "Output Decline in Hungary and Poland in 1990/1991: Structural Change and Aggregate Shocks", manuscript, presented at the conference "The Macroeconomic Situation in Eastern Europe" organised by the World Bank and IMF, 4-5 June 1992.

Domar, Evsey (1989), "The Blind Men and the Elephant: An Essay on Isms", in Domar, E., *Capitalism, Socialism, and Serfdom*, Cambridge University Press, Cambridge, pp. 29-46.

Dornbusch, Rudiger, and Fischer, Stanley (1993), "Moderate Inflation", *The World Bank Economic Review*, vol. 7, no. 1, pp. 1-44.

Erdős, Tibor (1992), "A gazdaság stabilizálásáról" (On the question of stabilising the economy), *Közgazdasági Szemle*, vol. 39, no. 11, pp. 985-1000.

Friedman, Milton (1968), "The Role of Monetary Policy", *American Economic Review*, vol. 58, no. 1, pp. 1-17.

36) See Andorka (1993, p. 17).

Gomulka, Stanislaw (1991a), "The Puzzles of Fairly Fast Growth and Rapid Collapse Under Socialism", Socialist Economies Reform Unit, Country Economics Department, World Bank, *Research Paper Series*, no. 18.

– (1991b), "The Causes of Recession Following Stabilisation", *Comparative Economic Studies*, vol. 33, no. 2, Summer.

Hámor, Szilvia (1993), "Tőke nélkül ma már nincs előrelépés" (Today there cannot be any progress without capital), *Népszabadság*, 19 May, vol. 51, no. 115, p. 17.

Hansen, Alvin H. (1964), *Business Cycles and National Income*, Expanded edition, W. W. Norton and Company, New York.

Király, Júlia (1992), "Tartós tendencia vagy pillanatnyi robbanás?" (Is it a lasting tendency or a temporal explosion?), *Napi Gazdaság*, 17 October, vol. 2, no. 240, p. 4.

Kolodko, Grzegorz W. (1992), "Stabilisation, Recession and Growth in Postsocialist Economy", *Working Papers*, Institute of Finance, Warsaw, no. 29.

Kornai, János (1971), *Anti-Equilibrium*, North-Holland, Amsterdam

– (1989), (1990), *The Road to a Free Economy. Shifting from a Socialist System: The Example of Hungary*, W. W. Norton and Company, New York.

–(1992a), *The Socialist System. The Political Economy of Communism*, Princeton University Press, Princeton, and Oxford University Press, Oxford.

–(1992b), "Visszaesés, veszteglés vagy fellendülés" (Recession, stagnation or recovery), *Magyar Hírlap*, 24 December, vol. 25, no. 302, pp. 12-13.

– (1993), "The Evolution of Financial Discipline under the Postsocialist System", *Kyklos*, forthcoming.

Laski, Kazimierz (1990), "O niebezpieczenstwach zwiazanych z planem stabilizacji gospodarki narodowej", *Gospodarka Narodowa*, vol. 1, no. 2-3, pp. 5-9. Also published in German in *Wirtschaftspolitische Blätter*, no. 5.

Laffont, Jean-Jacques (1985), "Fix-Price Models. A Survey of Recent Empirical Work", in *Frontiers of Economics*, Arrow, Kenneth J., and Honkapohja, Seppo (eds.), Basil Blackwell, Oxford and New York, pp. 328-367.

Obláth, Gábor (1993), "Economic Transition: Exchange Rate Policy, Real Exchange Rate Changes in Central Eastern Europe", in: *International Trade and Restructuring in Eastern Europe*, ed. by J. Gács and G. Wincler, IIASA, Vienna, forthcoming.

Phelps, Edmund (1968), "Money-Wage Dynamics and Labor-Market Equilibrium", *Journal of Political Economy*, Part 2, July-August, pp. 678-711.

Rodrik, Dani (1992), "Making Sense of the Soviet Trade Shock in Eastern Europe: A Framework and Some Estimates", manuscript, presented at the conference "The Macroeconomic Situation in Eastern Europe" organised by the World Bank and IMF, 4-5 June, 1992.

Sargent, Thomas (1982), "The Ends of Four Big Inflations", in *Inflation: Causes and Effects*, Hall, Robert (ed.), National Bureau of Economic Research, University of Chicago Press, Chicago.

Schumpeter, Joseph A. (1934), *The Theory of Economic Development,* Harvard University Press, Cambridge.

– (1939), *Business Cycles,* McGraw-Hill Book Company, New York.

Scitovsky, Tibor (1951), (1971), *Welfare and Competition,* Irwin, Homewood, Ill.

– (1985), "Pricetakers' Plenty: A Neglected Benefit of Capitalism", *Kyklos*, vol. 38, no. 4, pp. 517-536.

Spiethoff, Arthur (1902), "Vorbemerkungen zu einer Theorie der Überproduktion", *Jahrbuch für Gesetzgebung, Verwaltung und Volkswirtschaft.*

Tamás, Gáspár Miklós (1990), "Weimar", *Beszélő*, 12 February, vol. 1, no. 5, p. 5.

United Nations Economic Commission for Europe (1992), *Economic Survey of Europe in 1991-1992,* New York.

Valentinyi, Ákos (1992), "Stabilizáció és növekedés Magyarországon – néhány elméleti megfontolás" (Stabilisation and growth in Hungary – some theoretical considerations), *Közgazdasági Szemle*, vol. 39, no. 10, pp. 908-923.

Sources of Statistical Tables and Data

Dervis, Kemal, and Condon, Timothy (1993), "Hungary: An Emerging 'Gradualist' Success Story?", in *The Transition in Eastern Europe*, Blanchard, O. J., Froot, K. A., and Sachs, J. D. (eds.), NBER, Cambridge, forthcoming.

Kaaze, Max (1992), "Political Culture and Political Consolidation in Central and Eastern Europe", manuscript, presented at the conference "Democratic Governments and the Transition from Plan to Market", organised by Twente University, NL.

Kopint-Datorg (1992), *Konjunktúrajelentés* (Report on the trade cycle), no. 3.

– (1993), *Ipari konjunktúrateszt eredmények* (Results of the survey on the industrial trade cycle), 1st quarter.

Központi Statisztikai Hivatal (Central Statistical Office) (1989), *Statisztikai évkönyv 1988* (Statistical Yearbook 1988), Budapest.

– (1991), *Magyar statisztikai évkönyv 1990* (Hungarian Statistical Yearbook 1990), Budapest.

–(1992a), *Magyar statisztikai zsebkönyv 1991* (Hungarian Statistical Pocketbook 1991), Budapest.

– (1992b), *StatisztikaiHavi Közlemények* (Monthly Statistical Report), no. 8.

– (1992c), *Statisztikai Havi Közlemények* (Monthly Statistical Report), no. 12.

– (1992d), *Magyar statisztikai évkönyv 1991* (Hungarian Statistical Yearbook 1991), Budapest.

– (1993), *Magyarország nemzeti számlái 1988-1991* (Hungary's National Accounts, 1988-1991), Budapest, forthcoming.

League of Nations (1939), *Statistical Yearbook of the League of Nations, 1938/1939*, Geneva.

Magyar Nemzeti Bank (National Bank of Hungary) (1990), *Éves jelentés 1990* (Annual Report, 1990), Budapest.

– (1993), *Havi jelentés*, January, Budapest.

Mitchell, Brian R. (1976), *European Historical Statistics 1750-1970*, Hazell Watson and Voney, Aylesbury, England.

National Bank of Hungary (1991), *Annual Report*, Budapest.

Times–Mirror (1991), *The Pulse of Europe: A Survey of Political and Social Values and Attributes*, Times–Mirror, Center for the People and the Press, Washington DC.

United Nations Economic Commission for Europe (1993), *Economic Bulletin for Europe*, vol. 44 (1992), New York.

Vigh, Judit (1993), "Jelentés az 1991. évi bruttó hazai termék alakulásáról" (Report on the Gross Domestic Product in 1991), *Gazdaság és Statisztika*, vol. 5, no. 2, pp. 18-23.

Table 2.1

Indices of GDP and industrial production in Hungary, 1980-1992

year	GDP	industrial production
	(1989 = 100)	
1980	86.5	89.8
1981	89.0	94.3
1982	91.5	98.7
1983	92.1	100.4
1984	94.6	103.0
1985	94.4	100.9
1986	95.8	100.4
1987	99.7	103.6
1988	99.6	102.1
1989	100.0	100.0
1990	96.7	92.3
1991	85.2	74.8
1992[a]	80.9	63.8

a) Preliminary calculations of the Central Statistical Office of Hungary.

Source: GDP, period 1980-1990: Központi Statisztikai Hivatal (1992a, p. 94). Industrial production, period 1980-1984: Központi Statisztikai Hivatal (1991, p. 56); period 1985-1990: Központi Statisztikai Hivatal (1992a, p. 94). Data for 1991 and 1992 from Central Statistical Office of Hungary.

Table 2.2

Vacancies and unemployment

	number of registered vacancies	number of registered unemployed	unemployment rate (per cent)
1990/03	34,048	33,682	0.7
06	37,859	43,506	0.9
09	26,969	56,113	1.2
12	16.815	79,521	1.7
1991/03	13,583	144,840	3.0
06	14,860	185,554	3.9
09	15,351	292,756	6.1
12	11,529	406,124	8.5
1992/03	15,124	477,987	8.9
06	25,346	546,676	10.1
09	25,634	616,782	11.4
12	24,097	663,027	12.3
1993/01	26,471	693,983	13.3
02	32,432	705,032	13.6

The statistical definition of the unemployment rate has been adjusted, beginning in January 1992, to the definition used in Western labour statistics. The data for 1990 and 1991 are calculated according to the old definition, since no recalculation was made. The unemployment rate would be somewhat lower in this period on the basis of the new definition.

Source: Reports of the National Labour Centre, Budapest, 1991-1993.

Table 2.3

Output, investment and employment indices in Hungary during the Great Depression

year	net national product	industrial production	capital formation	industrial employment
1929	100.0	100.0	100.0	100.0
1930	103.3	94.6	75.6	91.3
1931	101.0	87.4	59.1	82.9
1932	96.2	81.9	54.5	73.0
1933	93.6	88.2	43.5	73.6
1934	102.0	99.2	34.9	79.9
1935	102.7	106.8	34.5	85.9
1936	107.8	118.4	41.8	94.7
1937	115.1	129.5	54.3	104.0
1938	112.5	125.3	60.7	112.3

Source: Net national product and capital formation: B. R. Mitchell (1976, p. 786); Industrial production and employment: League of Nations (1939, pp. 67, 181).

Table 2.4

Impediments to production

Hungarian Survey Data (in per cent)

quarter	insufficient demand	shortage of labour	insufficient supply of raw materials and spare parts: domestic origin	insufficient supply of raw materials and spare parts: imported from rouble area	insufficient supply of raw materials and spare parts: imported from dollar area	financing problems
1987/1	26.0	22.2	41.2	42.6		31.2
2	27.4	23.7	42.3	46.7		24.3
3	21.3	24.1	46.6	50.4		22.1
4	24.1	15.8	39.4	41.8		20.4
1988/1	28.0	15.7	50.0	16.6	32.8	32.7
2	28.3	24.7	44.1	17.2	35.3	36.4
3	27.3	23.0	45.3	18.2	64.0	35.0
4	30.7	19.3	38.5	14.9	22.4	40.1
1989/1	38.0	21.5	37.6	14.4	17.9	49.6
2	40.1	22.0	28.7	11.0	11.8	46.1
3	40.4	21.9	27.5	10.3	8.9	46.8
4	51.2	13.4	21.4	8.0	6.3	49.4
1990/1	51.3	12.1	13.8	5.8	3.9	57.8
2	56.1	13.9	13.0	3.4	2.2	45.2
3	51.0	10.3	15.3	4.6	5.2	51.9
4	54.5	4.3	11.3	3.2	3.7	48.7
1991/1	60.6	4.3	9.4	2.3	2.6	53.2
2	70.1	4.0	7.1	1.5	2.4	54.1
3	66.8	3.3	6.2	1.2	2.0	52.7
4	65.9	3.0	7.2	0.5	1.0	47.3
1992/1	65.1	3.3	5.8	0.3	1.0	51.0
2	62.2	7.4	5.9	0.7	1.5	45.9
3	56.1	4.4	10.6	1.7	3.1	47.8
4	54.5	4.8	8.7	0.7	2.3	42.9
1993/1	57.7	2.2	6.1	1.3		45.5

The survey applies the methodology of the German research institute IFO and used in several other countries as well. Respondents are asked to mention "impediments to production". Each respondent can mention as many impediments as he likes. The figures refer to relative frequencies in percentage. (E.g. in 1987/1 out of 100 respondents 26 mentioned insufficient demand, beside mentioning other factors as well.) There are other impediments mentioned by the respondents but not included in this table. "Rouble area" refers to the former member countries of Comecon. The survey did not separate the "rouble area" and the "dollar area" in 1987 and in 1993; the data refer to the lack of imported raw materials and spare parts.

Source: Kopint-Datorg (1993).

Table 2.5

Consumer price indexes in Hungary, 1980-1993

year	average annual rate of change (in per cent)	year	average annual rate of change (in per cent)
1980	9.1	1988	15.5
1981	4.6	1989	17.0
1982	6.9	1990	28.9
1983	7.3	1991	35.0
1984	8.3	1992	23.0
1985	7.0	1993 January	25.9
1986	5.3	1993 February	24.7
1987	8.6	1993 March	23.4

Source: Period 1980-1990, Központi Statisztikai Hivatal (1991, p. 218); 1991: Központi Statisztikai Hivatal (1992b, pp. 62-63); 1992: Központi tatisztikai Hivatal (1992c, p. 63). 1993: Data from Central Statistical Office.

Table 2.6

Ratio of input to output stocks

capitalist countries, average 1981-1985		Hungary	
Austria	1.06	1981-1985	6.10
Canada	0.92	1988	5.16
Finland	1.92	1989	4.65
Japan	1.09	1990	3.50
Portugal	1.66	1991	2.67
United States	1.02		
West Germany	0.71		

Source: Data compiled by A. Chikán.

Table 2.7

Composition of GDP in Hungary by economic branches

(in per cent)

	1986	1988	1990	1991
Industry	36.7	34.1	31.8	30.7
Construction	6.6	7.7	6.6	6.3
Agriculture and forestry	20.7	16.6	16.2	14.8
Transportation, post and telecommunications	8.9	8.0	8.2	8.8
Commerce	9.4	10.1	11.5	11.1
Water management	1.4	1.4	1.3	1.3
Other material activities	1.2	1.1	1.3	1.4
Material activities	**84.9**	**79.0**	**76.9**	**74.4**
Personal and economic services	4.6	5.0	5.6	-
Services by financial institutions	-	1.5	2.0	-
Health, social and cultural services	6.2	8.7	9.4	-
Community, public administration and other services	4.3	5.8	6.1	-
Non-material activities	**15.1**	**21.0**	**23.1**	**25.6**

Sources: 1986: Központi Statisztikai Hivatal (1989, p. 57); 1988 and 1990: Központi Statisztikai Hivatal (1992a, p. 95); 1991: Központi Statisztikai Hivatal (1992d, p. 61).

Table 2.8

Gross production, employment and labour productivity in Hungarian industry[a], 1980-1992

year	output	average number of employed (1989 = 100)	gross production per employee
1980	87.0	116.1	74.9
1981	89.4	113.7	78.6
1982	91.6	111.4	82.2
1983	92.3	109.2	84.5
1984	94.8	108.6	87.3
1985	95.5	107.9	88.5
1986	97.3	107.1	90.9
1987	101.0	104.4	96.8
1988	101.0	101.7	99.3
1989	100.0	100.0	100.0
1990	90.8	94.5	96.0
1991	71.3	82.2	86.7
1992[b]	55.0	68.0	81.0

a)The output data for the period of 1980-1989 are based on the gross production of economic organisations belonging to the category of industry. The output indexes for 1990 and 1991 are calculated on the basis of industrial production. Data from 1990 refer to firms with legal entity employing more than 50 persons. The table does not cover the construction sector. - b) January-June, 1992.

Source: Period 1980-1991: Központi Statisztikai Hivatal (1992a, p. 122); 1992: Kopint-Datorg (1992, p. 193).

Table 2.9

Gross domestic product and expenditure

components	1988	1989	1990	1991	1989/ 1988	1990/ 1989	1991/ 1990
	GDP at 1988 prices, Hung. Ft mn				**volume indexes, %**		
Private consumption	873,814	893,586	861,112	811,591	102.3	96.4	94.2
Collective consumption	175,000	164,000	168,300	163,755	93.7	102.6	97.3
Final consumption	*1,048,814*	*1,057,586*	*1,029,412*	*975,346*	*100.8*	*97.3*	*94.7*
Gross fixed capital formation	310,801	332,529	308,800	272,925	107.0	92.9	88.4
Changes in stocks	49,941	32,685	40,947	-1,136	-	-	-
Gross capital formation	*360,742*	*365,214*	*349,747*	*271,789*	*101.2*	*95.8*	*77.7*
Total domestic use	*1,409,556*	*1,422,800*	*1,379,159*	*1,247,135*	*100.9*	*96.9*	*90.4*
Exports	530,395	536,815	508,132	430,345	101.2	94.7	84.7
Imports	491,738	500,737	479,425	437,038	101.8	95.7	91.2
Net exports	*38,657*	*36,078*	*28,707*	*-6,693*	-	-	-
Total GDP	**1,448,213**	**1,458,878**	**1,407,866**	**1,240,442**	**100.7**	**96.5**	**88.1**

Source: Központi Statisztikai Hivatal (1993, Table 1.3.2).

Table 2.10

Fixed capital formation in Hungary, 1980-1992

(constant prices, 1980 = 100)

1981	95.6	1987	99.4
1982	94.2	1988	90.3
1983	90.9	1989	95.0
1984	87.7	1990	86.8
1985	85.1	1991	76.8
1986	90.6	1992[a)]	71.0

a) Preliminary.

Source: Central Statistical Office of Hungary.

Table 2.11

Fixed capital formation in Hungary, as a percentage of GDP

(at current prices)

1980	28.8	1987	24.7
1981	26.5	1988	20.6
1982	25.2	1989	20.3
1983	24.5	1990	17.8
1984	23.0	1991	19.1
1985	22.5		
1986	24.0		

Source: Period 1980-1987: Magyar Nemzeti Bank (1990, p. 97); period 1988-1990: National Bank of Hungary (1991, p. 129); 1991: J. Vígh (1993, p. 22).

Table 2.12

Destination of Hungary's exports

	EC	(former) Comecon	other
	share of total exports (%)		
1987	19.8	50.2	30.0
1988	22.5	44.8	32.7
1989	24.7	40.8	34.5
1990	33.5	30.2	36.3
1991[a)]	40.3	25.7	34.0

a) Figures for 1991 through to the third quarter. According to the preliminary export data of the Hungarian National Bank, which are calculated on the forint value of Hungary's exports, the share of EC countries in the total Hungarian exports was 49.7 per cent in 1992. (Magyar Nemzeti Bank, 1993, p. 71.)

Source: Dervis and Condon (1992, p. 11). Data based on IMF Direction of Trade Statistics.

Table 2.13

Personal optimism/pessimism in Western and Eastern European nations in 1991[a)]

	progress[b)] %	neither %	decline %	optimism[c)] %	neither %	pessimism %
United Kingdom	43	28	29	51	37	12
France	36	34	30	42	39	19
Italy	41	34	25	51	32	17
Spain	34	43	23	39	48	13
West Germany	45	38	17	42	46	12
Bulgaria	16	24	60	56	20	24
Czechoslovakia	29	22	49	41	33	26
East Germany	34	33	33	62	29	9
Hungary	18	25	57	26	40	34
Poland	27	21	52	36	40	24
European Russia	21	22	57	40	36	24

a) Row percentages, Cantril-type, 0-10 ladder scale. - b) Progress/ Decline is based on a comparison of five years ago/today. - c) Optimism/Pessimism is based on a comparison of today/five years ahead.

Source: M. Kaase (1992, p. 23), on the basis of Times–Mirror (1991, 21-23, tabular appendix). Missing data for the past and present averaged one to two per cent. The future was not assessed by an average of 20 per cent. Cases with missing data were excluded from this calculation.

Figure 2.1

Indices of industrial output, 1975 = 100

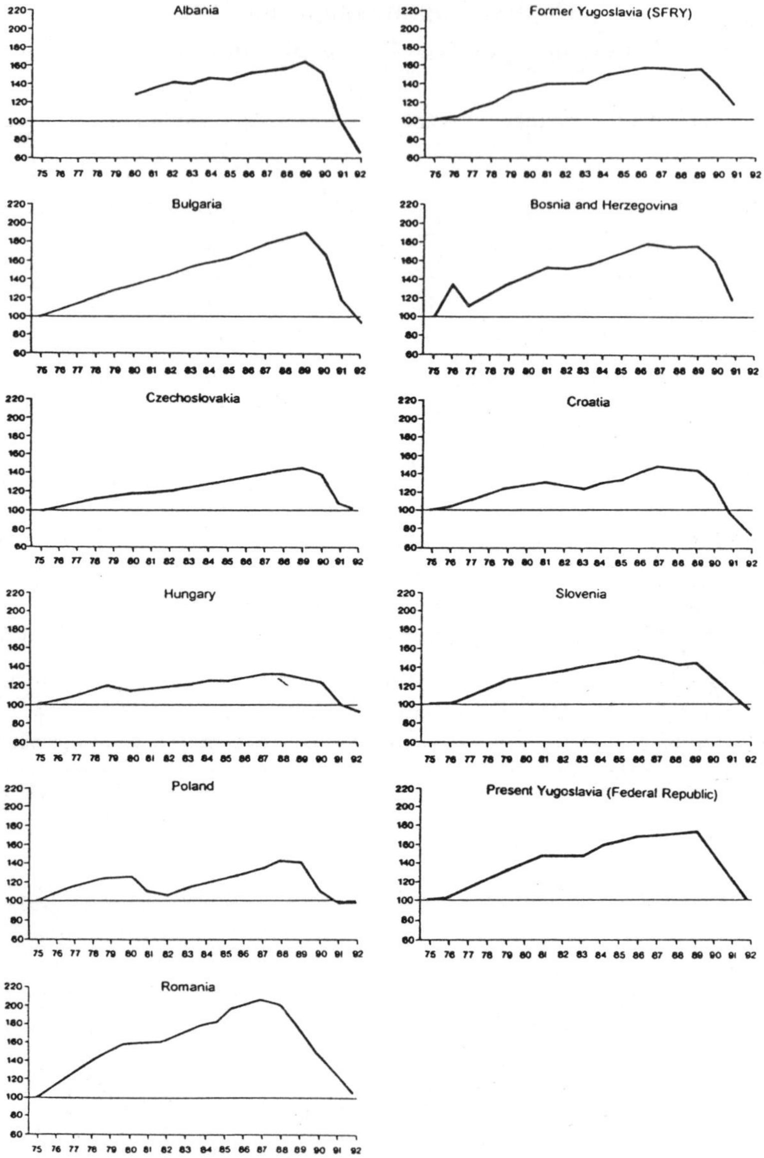

Source: United Nations Economic Commission for Europe.

Figure 2.2a

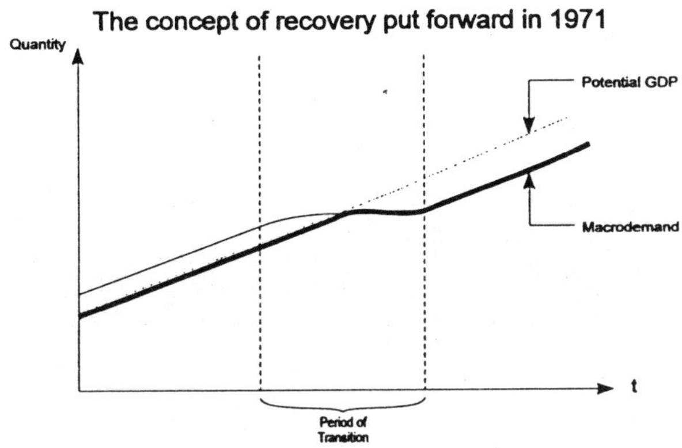

Figure 2.2b

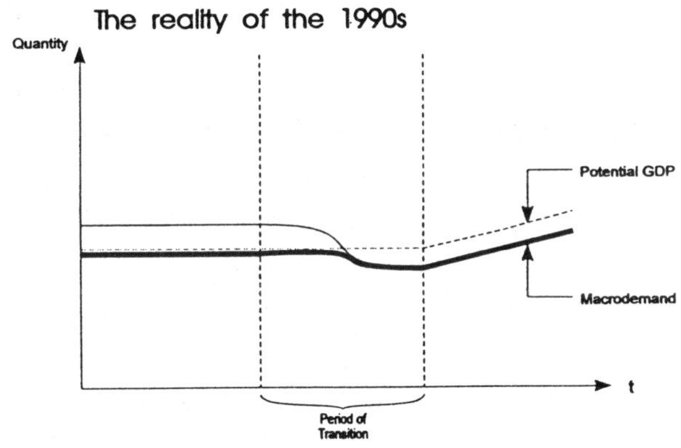

Note: The bold line represents the actual GDP. The actual GDP is the smaller of potential GDP and macrodemand. The curves in *Figure 2.2a* coincide with those of Figure 22.2 in *Anti-Equilibrium* (1971); I modified only the denominations of the variables as to follow the generally used terminology.

Chapter 3

LESSONS FOR THE EAST FROM STABILISATION IN THE WEST

G. D. N. Worswick*)

3.1 What is stabilisation?

Stabilisation is a portmanteau word, containing a wide variety of meanings. I begin by listing the principal ones.

(a) Stabilisation may mean simply "keeping prices steady". This is the way the word would have been used before World War I, when the economic "authorities" were principally central banks, and the ups and downs with which they were concerned were those in prices. An increase in monetary demand would cause prices to rise, and a decrease would cause them to fall. Price stabilisation might have deleterious consequences for other economic variables, but that would have been considered secondary. For policy, the rate of interest was the main stabilising instrument.

(b) It was precisely the observation that in the real world "inflation" and "deflation" might not be symmetrical – in particular, that deflation, brought about by reducing monetary demand, might reduce, not just prices, but real output as well – which preoccupied Keynes and others in the 1930s. We now have to be concerned with fluctuations in real output as well as in prices. Indeed, in many of the models of the "trade cycle" or "business cycle" which were produced in the 1930s, the centre of attention is the fluctuations in real output and employment, and prices enter in a subordinate manner. These models naturally gave rise to ideas for the stabilisation of output and employment: in particular, for the use of the balance of the budget (government revenue *minus* government expenditure) as a stabilising agent. The rate of interest continued to have a stabilising role, although the emphasis was now put on its effects upon real output as much as on prices. At the end of World War II, many countries committed themselves to policies of "full employment", and that objective was also written into the aims of newly created international organisations. The idea

*) Oxford.

of "demand management" by means of monetary and fiscal policy came into general use.

(c) The early business cycle models were "trendless". In real life, labour forces change, growing more often than declining, and advances in technical knowledge make possible higher output with an unchanged labour force. Stabilisation came to mean more than just steady output, with constant prices: it meant output steadily growing in line with labour force growth and technical advance, combined with constant prices, or prices rising at a slow, but not accelerating rate.

(d) Most theoretical models of fluctuations postulate a closed economy. Most actual economies trade in goods and services with the rest of the world. There are also, nowadays, in most Western countries, free movements of capital inwards and outwards. Although it is not always explicitly acknowledged, the expression "stabilisation" means more than securing the steady growth with non-accelerating inflation of paragraph (c). It requires that these objectives should be achieved in the context of a "steady" balance of payments. This need not be limited to exact balances on both current and capital account, but can include some combination of the two which can endure without requiring correction.

In this paper, we use "stabilisation" in the last and broadest sense (d).

The institutional and policy framework

There have been considerable differences in the institutional framework within which stabilisation policies have been conducted in Western countries at different times. For the most part, they have been market economies, the greater part of production of goods and services being undertaken by private enterprises. Some countries have had a substantial sector of public enterprises, or nationalised industries. Their relevance for stabilisation depends on whether the production and investment decisions of public enterprise follow "market" principles, and, if not, how far they deviate from them. In most countries, the nuclear energy sector has been governed by principles not obviously those of the market. (Some argue that if they had been, there would have been no nuclear energy!)

During World War II many Western countries were operated as "command" economies. Decisions concerning the allocation of labour and materials and other supplies were made by government, using controls which wholly or partially replaced the market. In varying degrees, food and other essentials were subject to rationing, though very often a "free" sector for non-essentials remained. In the post-war period the war-time control machinery was dismantled, albeit at varying speeds. The US economy was largely back to "normal" as early as 1948, whereas in Western Europe the dismantling of the control systems took much longer, with significant elements persisting into the 1950s. Some last remnants of exchange control continued into the 1980s. We shall have something to say about the lessons of the post-war "reconstruction" period in Western Europe later in this paper. But we will examine first the stabilisation policies being pursued when economies had returned to a state in which most economic decisions of detail were left to the market. Put differently, we want to examine the performance of "macroeconomic" policies, i.e. monetary and fiscal policies – and also, when appropriate, incomes policies – in stabilising GDP and the general price level. We are bound to resort to generalisations, and begin with a reminder that there were important differences between countries in institutions and in attitudes.

3.2 Before 1973

We consider the stabilisation question in two periods: from the early 1950s to 1973; and from 1973 until now. The characteristics of the first period were high growth rates of GDP and of productivity, low unemployment rates (not merely lower than in the Great Depression of the 1930s, but lower than had ever previously been experienced in peace-time), "moderate" inflation (between 1 and 5 per cent per annum and showing little sign of acceleration), and rapid and sustained growth in international trade. Although low by the standards of the next two decades, the inflation rates were high by the standards of previous peace-time history. What contribution did fiscal and monetary policy make to the maintenance of something like full employment throughout the period? For "deficit" finance, regarded by critics as the keynote of "Keynesian" policy, the answer is not very much. Investment was at a high level and growing. Once production facilities had been restored, consumers were anxious to spend, rather than save. An excess of demand was as likely to occur as a deficiency, especially in the earlier years. A proper understanding of "Keynesian" budgetary policy is not that the budget should always be in deficit, but the budget should be considered as a balancing item in the whole economy, being used to supplement, or to withdraw, purchasing power according to whether a deficiency, or an excess, of aggregate demand seemed likely. Fortunately, this point was well taken by finance ministers and their advisers. Whether the persistently high level of aggregate demand contributed to the exceptionally high rate of growth of productivity which was maintained throughout the 1950s and 1960s is more contentious. Certainly, industrial investment was almost everywhere above the long-term average, and several countries were encouraging the immigration of labour – the opposite of present-day attitudes, when growth has been slower, and unemployment much higher.

Although, on average, the pressure of demand was higher than it had been before World War II, there were still *fluctuations* in demand and output, not about an unchanging level of output, but about a rising trend. Most of these fluctuations were shorter and smaller in amplitude than before the war. Ironically, the fluctuations in GDP in Britain – whose policies were nick-named Stop-Go – were between 1958 and 1973 smaller than in any other industrial country of any size. One of the most thorough studies of fiscal policy was undertaken by Hansen (1969) for the OECD. Starting from a Keynesian model of national income determination, he attempted to isolate a "pure cycle" which would have occurred in the absence of both automatic and discretionary policy changes. The former were the automatic increases in tax revenue, and the falls in government expenditure on, for example, unemployment benefits, which occur when there is a change in national income. What remains of the total budgetary change, when these automatic changes are taken out, are, of course, the changes made at the government's discretion. Short-term stabilisation was measured by comparing the deviations from trend of the actual cycles and the pure cycles, with a value of 100 given to perfect stabilisation. According to this index, the best performance was USA, with 56; other countries had smaller figures and Germany zero. The UK index was small, but negative. The USA result came as a surprise to most people, who thought that Republican policy was one of the balanced budget, but it was pointed out that in times of deflation, the principle was not renounced, but quietly disregarded. (It was to be more spectacularly disregarded under Presidents Reagan and Bush!) Hansen did not deal with monetary policy. His test was also questioned for including public enterprise investment in general government expenditure, on the grounds that governments might not always exercise control over it, or did not always use such control for counter-cyclical purposes. When it was taken out, the Hansen test raised the stabilisation performance index for most countries, including turning the small negative index for UK into a small positive one. Carrying the modified test forward into the 1966-1971 period showed most countries' performance deteriorating (see Boltho 1981). It can be argued that by concentrating on year-to-year changes, the point is being missed that what really mattered was that businessmen came to believe that governments were (a) committed to the avoidance of serious slumps, and (b) knew what to do if they detected signs of one approaching. However, we cannot recommend without qualification to the Eastern countries that, once their transition problems are behind them, they can rely exclusively upon the effectiveness of conventional demand management policy. For, in other areas, this policy was less obviously successful – namely in inflation and the balance of payments.

Inflation: A.J. Brown (1955) said that the inflation of 1939-1951 was, by any test, one of the greatest, if not the greatest, in the history of the world. The rise in the cost-of-living over the period January-June 1939 to August 1948 varied enormously, from a low figure of 25 per cent in New Zealand to an increase of 305×10^6 times in China. Over the same period, the increase in UK was 67 per cent, and in USA 76 per cent. When Brown completed his study in the early 1950s, he was able to consider the great inflation as an episode in economic history which was over, and that it was possible to envisage a steady future rise in prices of around 1 per cent a year over a long period ahead. At least, he reckoned that this was conceivable for the United States, although he doubted whether such a low figure could be achieved in UK. This proved a good prognostication – perhaps a trifle optimistic for the United States, where the average annual rise in the GNP deflator between 1956 and 1965 was 2 per cent. This turned out to be the lowest rise among the major industrial countries, while that of UK was 3.5 per cent a year. In Brown's view, the high levels of employment which had become established in the post-war years would be accompanied by a persistent upward creep in factor and product prices, which would not be easily suppressed. As we now know, the upward creep did persist – well into the 1960s – but at rates which appeared in most countries to be politically acceptable. Concern was expressed in some quarters about rising prices. OECD, for instance, published a major report on the problem of *Rising Prices* in 1961. Some countries had also begun to develop "incomes policies", designed to moderate the annual increase in nominal wages and salaries, without resorting to a deflation of the economy by means of monetary or fiscal contraction. Thus, although the average rate of inflation in most advanced industrial countries was high, by historical standards, it remained "acceptable", and the assignment of demand management to securing low unemployment could continue.

This comfortable state of affairs had clearly come to an end by the mid-1970s. The rise in prices in advanced countries over the nine years from 1967 to 1976 was comparable in magnitude with the increases recorded over the period 1939 to 1948. Except that there were no significant hyper-inflations such as those in Hungary and China in the earlier period, this second "great inflation" of the 1970s and early 1980s was to appear as great as the first. But, even if similar in scale; were they also of the same nature? It is easy to see the main driving force of the inflation which followed on the outbreak of war in 1939. With all the leading industrial countries involved, there was a huge increase in expenditure on arms and armed forces, which first sucked in the large reserves of unemployed labour still remaining from the Great Depression, and then took an increasing share of capacity output. While demand for war output continued to rise, demand for civilian output had to be curtailed, through rising prices, or by means of controls and rationing. With so many countries involved, primary product prices, which had been in the doldrums in the Depression, soared. In his analysis, Brown distinguished two types of economy: in one the prices of factors and products were flexible, and changes in the composition of output were brought about by relative prices; in the other prices were sticky, so that they did not respond to changes in effective demand, but only to changes in costs. Switches in demand were expressed in changes in stocks and order books; workers moved from one industry to another less in response to wage differences than to changes in job availability. In this kind of economy, prices rose only when there was an increase in costs. These two types of economy are, of course, abstractions, actual economies being likely to be some mixture in different proportions. In 1939, USA was of the former type, and UK more of the second. The distinction, introduced to explain the events of the wartime inflation, remains useful in tracing the origins of the second inflationary surge. Here, there is no single factor, like a war, to point to. Instead, one can pick out a number of factors, which occurred between the mid-1960s and the early 1970s. First, there began in the United States in 1961 the longest sustained expansion in a hundred years. At the beginning, unemployment stood at as high a rate as at any time since the Second War, nearly 7 per cent. By 1969, unemployment was 3.5 per cent, below the rate considered by many economists at the time to constitute "full employment" in the United States context. Fiscal policy played an important part in this expansion: there were very large tax cuts in 1964 and 1965, and later on the Administration refused to raise taxes to cover the rising expenditure on the Vietnam war. To begin with, there was little effect on prices, but eventually the annual rate of increase in the Consumer Price Index was pulled up from 1.5 per cent at the end of the 1950s to 5 per cent at the end of the 1960s. By the European standards of the time, this might not seem so great, but the dollar was the anchor currency of the Bretton Woods system, and, given the weight of the United States in world trade, the rise was bound to be transmitted in various ways to other countries, whose inflation rates normally stood above that of the United States itself. This was an inflationary impulse on the demand side. One can also characterise the great rise in primary product prices which occurred in 1972 as demand induced, derived from the simultaneous boom conditions in virtually all industrial countries. The other inflationary impulses came from the side of costs. The first was an intensification of the pressure for increases of wages, heralded by the "events of May" in France in 1968, and followed in Germany, the United Kingdom and other European countries. The rise in world commodity prices, though derived from the expansion of demand in industrial countries, presented itself to the individual industrial country as a rise in costs. OPEC 1, at the end of 1973, quadrupling the price of crude oil, and OPEC 2, in 1979, were clearly exogenous "supply side" shocks.

The combined effect was to push up the annual rate of inflation to new heights. The large cost impulses, in particular, placed monetary authorities in a dilemma. If they held on to the existing monetary stance, there was a danger that, if prices were "sticky", there would be a sharp fall in output and employment. On the other hand, if they allowed monetary expansion, to "accommodate" the cost increases, not only would the price level rise, but, because of the powerful feedbacks from prices to wages and wages to prices, a higher *rate* of inflation would be consolidated. After OPEC 1, the response of the monetary authorities was mixed, and it is interesting to compare the extreme cases. In Italy, there was accommodation, and prices between 1973 and 1975 rose by 40 per cent; in Germany, there was not, and prices rose by only 13.4 per cent. But, between the two years, unemployment in Germany rose from 0.8 per cent to 3.6 per cent, while in Italy it actually fell slightly, from 6.2 to 5.8 per cent. After OPEC 2, in 1979, which gave a further kick to prices in many countries, the stance of monetary policy became restrictive in virtually all countries. By the mid-1980s, inflation had been brought down to levels as low as those of the 1950s, but, apart from recessions in the mid-1970s and again in the early 1980s, the average level of unemployment remained higher than ever before since World War II, especially in the European Community. This should not have come as a surprise. The objective of macroeconomic policy in the 1950s and 1960s had been to maintain employment. By the early 1980s it had been switched to the reduction of inflation, and in some cases the objective of full employment had been explicitly abandoned. One cannot use demand management in expansionary and contractionary modes at the same time. The lesson of this experience for Eastern Europe is that to rely on demand management to keep unemployment low is feasible only if the rate of "creeping" inflation which is delivered is "acceptable", or there exists some machinery of government for holding the growth of nominal wages and prices within bounds. We shall have a little more to say about this later.

The balance of payments: The trend of exchange rate policies in the post-war period was from the initial situation of inconvertible currencies towards one of general convertibility. We shall not trace the successive stages in any detail, but pick out those features which may have lessons for the East.

The breakdown of the gold standard in the 1930s had not been followed by any effective world-wide system, and, when the war broke out, besides the great division of the world into two belligerent blocs with a neutral area, individual countries operated exchange controls of varying degrees of severity. While the war was still being waged, the Allied nations, led by the United States and Britain, in a conference at Bretton Woods, set up the new International Monetary Fund whose objective was to create an orderly system of international payments to replace the disorderly patchwork of pre-war. It was to provide rules of good behaviour, and some credit facilities to help members keep the rules. The dollar would become, in effect, the anchor currency for the system. Other members spoke of their "gold and dollar reserves". Other currencies were related to the dollar at fixed parities. The Monetary Fund was to be used for the settlement of current transactions, and it is worth noting that it was a *requirement* of the Fund that member countries exercised control over capital movements. Parities would normally remain unchanged, but could be altered in conditions of "fundamental disequilibrium". Although some of its American sponsors had hoped that the Bretton Woods system could get going very soon after the end of the war, and although an attempt was made to introduce sterling convertibility in the summer of 1947, which failed dramatically, it was not until 1958 that the scheme could become fully operational. Meanwhile, piecemeal arrangements to finance trade were negotiated on a bilateral basis, and then, after the Marshall Plan was launched, multilateral settlements through the European Payments Union became possible. This experience does have lessons for the East, but they will be more conveniently held over to the last section of this paper. Meanwhile we shall look at the Bretton Woods system, as it operated from 1958 to its final demise in 1972.

During the period in which the Bretton Woods system was operating much as had been intended, world trade, and in particular, world trade in manufactures grew, year in year out, at record rates. If one is critical of the Bretton Woods system, and we shall be pointing out its flaws, yet when one compares trade performance with the 1930s, it may be that any order, even a flawed order, is better than disorder. The arrangements of the International Monetary Fund were designed to facilitate trade in goods and services and other current transactions, and were not to be used for capital transfers. A country running a deficit on current account could respond by taking a series of steps. First, it could simply allow its gold and dollar reserves to fall. Next it might reduce aggregate demand, by raising interest rates, or moving the budget further into surplus (or less into deficit): reducing aggregate demand would reduce imports. If the external deficit persisted, the country could make use of the Fund and borrow, up to a prescribed amount. If none of the above measures worked, the member could claim that its external balance was in "fundamental disequilibrium", and lower the parity of its currency in the Fund, i.e. devalue; the effect should be to reduce imports and increase exports. The way in which the IMF was set up meant that the onus of correcting external imbalances fell entirely upon deficit countries; there was no pressure on surplus countries to take any steps to reduce them, so that persistent surpluses could, and did, exist. This, in turn, would mean a persistent tendency for some countries to lose reserves and was the first of the weaknesses of the IMF, bound to tell in the long run. Another was that the original stock of reserves was expressed in gold, and nothing had been built into the scheme for the regular expansion in that stock. Before World War II, the *trend* in prices in the US and UK had been, in peace-time, virtually zero. No-one had envisaged that in the post-war world there would be continuing, albeit "acceptable", inflation. In the US itself, in the late 1950s, when the Bretton Woods scheme came into full operation, US prices were rising annually at 2 per cent or less, while in Europe, figures of 3, 4 or even 5 were more common. In addition the *volume* of world trade was rising at a rate faster than ever before. Thus the *value* of trade was bound to rise in relation to the reserves intended to cope with fluctuations of one kind and another. The growing stringency of reserves was partially relieved by the accident that the US was running a persistent deficit in its own current balance. Since dollars were directly linked to gold, this annual supply of additional dollars was virtually an increase in reserves of the Fund. But this means of replenishment depended on the goodwill of the other members of IMF. If they began to complain that it was wrong for "the Americans to finance their war in Vietnam" simply by printing dollars, then the US would correct the over-valuation of the dollar, which, in fact occurred in 1971. Meanwhile the first agreement on Special Drawing Rights came into effect in 1970. This creation of "paper gold" was the first time in history that internationally acceptable reserves had been created by international agreement. Thus, it was a significant event. But its immediate contribution to the growing difficulties in international payments was small. By the end of 1972, the original Bretton Woods system had broken down, and the major currencies were allowed to float against one another.

One ought not to write off the whole Bretton Woods system of fixed, but adjustable, exchange rates as a failure, simply because, in the end, it was abandoned. It was in effect for twelve years and accommodated different national stabilisation policies by permitting a number of exchange rate adjustments. The lessons to be learned concern more the regulation of exchange rates than national stabilisation policies as such.

3.3 The period after 1973

Soon after floating began, the industrial world experienced the great inflation exacerbated by the quadrupling of the price of crude oil at the end of 1973. The oil price rise also exerted a powerful *contractionary* effect on the output of oil consuming countries. Payment of the higher oil price involved a huge transfer of funds to the oil producing countries, funds which those countries were unable to spend on additional imports for some months, or even years, until their economies could be adapted to absorb higher imports. Meanwhile, the payment of the higher price in the consuming countries was equivalent in its impact on effective demand to the imposition of an indirect tax. A commonly accepted estimate of this effect made at the time was some 2 per cent of GDP. Thus the surge of price inflation was accompanied by a recessionary contraction (or slowing down in the growth) of output. When price inflation began to subside, many countries were still faced with balance of payments deficits, which inhibited any domestic expansion of effective demand. This led to the agreement at the Bonn Summit in 1978 that the leading surplus countries, Germany and Japan, should engineer demand expansions, which would spill over into increased imports, so that these countries would act as locomotives to pull the rest of the world out of recession. Before the world could test the efficacy of this cooperative effort, it was overtaken by the second oil price rise in 1979. This second surge in prices caused virtually all industrial countries to abandon any idea of full employment, and to throw the whole weight of demand management into bringing down inflation.

If we review the 1980s as a whole, we can say that demand management, both fiscal policy and higher interest rates, was successful in bringing back price inflation to the rates of the 1950s. But, there has been a cost, in the form of higher unemployment, in most, though not all countries. Average unemployment in the United States, for instance, in the 1980s was no higher than in the 1970s, which, in turn, was only 1.5 per cent higher than in the 1960s. In European Community countries by contrast, the rise in unemployment was much greater, from rates of 2 or 3 per cent in the 1960s, to 4 or 5 per cent in the 1970s, to 9 or 10 per cent in the 1980s. It is notable, however, that in EFTA countries, the rise in unemployment was not so great, although inflation has also come down; an obvious explanation is that, for many years, these countries have operated some kind of incomes policy. This reinforces our view that fiscal and monetary policy alone cannot secure high employment without the risk of inflation. We could leave it at that, but we cannot overlook certain developments in economic theory which occurred in the 1970s and 1980s and which purport to demonstrate that macroeconomic policy cannot have the effect of improving prospects for employment or growth.

From demand management to monetarism – and unemployment

The ideas which became known as "monetarism" began with Milton Friedman's Presidential Address to the American Economic Association in 1968. There were two key elements in the argument. First, inflation followed changes in the supply of money "with long and variable" lags. Secondly, there was a "natural rate" of unemployment. Monetary expansion might cause a temporary increase in output and fall in unemployment; but if the rate of unemployment was already at, or below, the "natural rate", the reduction would only be temporary, and the final outcome would be higher, and accelerating, inflation, while unemployment returned to the "natural rate". These ideas were seized on by governments, faced with *both* high inflation *and* unemployment, and persuaded of the failure of conventional demand management. In many countries, "targets" were set for the money supply, in the confident hope that inflation would, in a year or two, be brought under control. Monetarists claimed that any loss of output and rise in unemployment consequent upon adhering to the targets, would be small and not long lasting. There was a debate between those monetarists who believed in gradual reduction in inflation over a period of years, and advocates of the short sharp shock. That the policies derived from monetarist thinking "worked", in the sense that inflation did come down, cannot be disputed. But two things did not go according to plan. On the technical level, it was soon observed that there were numerous possible measures of "money", and that these measures did not always move in harmony with one another. Moreover, no sooner had a particular measure been singled out as the key instrument, than any relationship previously observed between this particular measure of money and the price level broke down. More important than this technical failure was the fact that the unemployment increases proved to be much greater and much longer-lasting, than the theorists had suggested. A Keynesian economist has no difficulty in accepting that monetary policy can have lasting real effects. Monetarists, however, cannot accept this: those who wish to stay in the faith say that the "natural rate" has increased!

Some economists have raised more fundamental objections to the kind of macroeconomic management which is being discussed here. This approach, they say, postulates that there is an economy "out there", whose behaviour can be observed by econometricians and incorporated in a set of equations linking the different economic variables: e.g. consumption is a function of income, wealth and rates of taxation, and so on. Once a model has been estimated, the econometrician can conduct simulations, e.g. of the effect of higher taxes on consumption, or of lower interest rates on investment. The results of these simulations enable the econometrician to inform the policy maker what changes he should make in policy instruments, such as tax rates, interest rates, or whatever, in order to bring about a desired end. This picture, it is argued, is seriously misleading. The variables the econometrician uses as raw data for the estimation of his equations are the outcome, not only of other parts of the economic structure, but also of all past policy changes. One cannot know what the true model of the economy is. This is so, but how much does it matter? Driving on the left, or the right, of the road was once a policy decision, but in most cases no harm comes from treating it as part of the structure. Some policy instruments are changed often, some only rarely. The next objection is that, just as governments study the behaviour of economic agents so as to be able to steer the economy as a whole, so economic agents study the behaviour of governments, so as to find out the rules of their behaviour. In such and such a situation, they might conclude, the government will let the exchange rate fall: in which case sell the currency now. This, so it is argued, alters the data set on which the government takes its decision. These two types of argument are not consistent. The first says that the observer cannot separate the influence of other parts of the economy from past policy decisions. The second implies that clever economic agents can do just this, in order to deduce the policy rules. Some economists believe that these arguments, consistent or not, are powerful enough to rule out the feasibility of rational management. The writer of this paper is not so sceptical, though he would not question that in certain markets, at certain times, the arguments can be significant.

There is now more than a quarter of a century's experience of systematic econometric forecasting, using a variety of models. Whatever may have been the hopes of the originators of this development, experience has shown that this is not an exercise in which the practitioners get better and better, more and more exact in their predictions. This leads many economists to express a preference for the "medium term" in the framing of policy. Politicians may go along with this in the aftermath of elections, but as the next election approaches, the time scale of their thinking gets shorter and shorter. There is a lesson here for the Eastern countries in seeking consensual rather than partisan economic policies.

From Bretton Woods to the European Monetary System

Since 1973 no new world-wide system of international payments has emerged to replace Bretton Woods. Initially, there was much enthusiasm for floating, which was expected to remove constraints on national policies. This enthusiasm began to wear thin when it was realised that some of the old problems, such as persistent balance of payments surpluses and deficits continued to appear. It also became clear that exchange rates did not move smoothly towards the levels suggested by the "fundamentals", notably purchasing power parity, but could stay at the "wrong" levels, and move in the "wrong" direction, for considerable periods. EC members tried to reduce exchange rate variability among themselves by establishing a European Monetary System in 1979. All members, other than Britain which stayed out, agreed to maintain their exchange rates within ± 2 ¼ per cent of their declared parity, with Italy negotiating a wider band of ± 6 per cent. This system was organised around a composite currency – the ECU – in terms of which the central rates were expressed. Realignments of the central rates, singly, or as part of more general movement, were permitted. Between 1979 and 1987, there were 11 realignments, two general and the remainder on a more limited scale. The evidence is that during this period exchange rate volatility was reduced, and not, as some feared, at the expense of increased variability of interest rates. The system of fixed, but adjustable, rates seemed to be working, and there was no obvious reason why this should not continue, so long as it was operated in the same way.

Towards the end of the 1980s, attitudes towards the ERM began to change. Some members began to regard their parities as fixed, and to indicate that they would no longer favour realignments. When Britain joined ERM in the autumn of 1990, at a rate which the government and some, though not all, outside observers regarded as competitive, with a band of 6 per cent, the view quickly took hold that this was a rate which would have to be held, and if necessary defended. There were two principal reasons for this shift of emphasis. Exchange controls were being dismantled throughout the 1980s, and, with capital increasingly free to move, discrete realignment became increasingly difficult to manage. Realignments immediately after a shock would not present a problem; but if the need for realignment grew gradually over a period, the markets would begin to move all one way, and the movement of speculative funds might swamp the counter-speculation of central banks aiming at maintaining the parity (or, at any rate, keeping it within the pre-assigned band). The view of ERM as the precursor of a fixed exchange rate system was embodied in the Maastricht Treaty, signed in February 1992, which set out a three-stage time-table for the establishment of a single currency in the Community by January 1997, or January 1999 at the latest. It was envisaged that all new members of EC, such as the EFTA countries and some of the East Europeans, would, when they joined, accept the single currency. Various "convergence" conditions were laid down before members could join.

Within eighteen months of Maastricht, the ERM was in disarray. In the course of 1992, it became increasingly apparent that the parity of sterling had been set too high, pointing to the desirability of a devaluation. The British government used massive reserves in an attempt to keep the exchange rate within its band, but to no avail, and in September sterling was withdrawn from ERM and allowed to float. At the same time the Italian lira was also allowed to float. Less than a year later, it was the turn of the French franc to come under speculative attack. This time, France did not leave ERM: instead the machinery of the system was kept in being by widening all the permitted bands to ± 15 per cent. In the view of many economists, the French franc was nearer to the rate indicated by "fundamentals" before it was obliged to devalue, than sterling had been the previous September.

At the time of writing (September 1993) the ERM bands are so wide that, effectively, all EC currencies are now floating with respect to one another, and, of course, with respect to the dollar and the yen. Whether a new attempt will be made to restore ERM on the 1979-1987 basis, or if another initiative will be taken in the direction of a single currency, is too early to say. There are no very obvious lessons for the East to draw from the exchange rate experience of Western countries since 1973, except to point out the unwisdom of becoming involved in over-ambitious schemes for fixed rates in a world of free capital movements.

3.4 Lessons from the transition from war to peace in Western economies

So far in this paper such lessons as we have been able to draw for the East have been taken from the experience of Western countries when they had already passed through their own transitions from war-economies to "normal" peace-time economies. That is, we have been dealing with capitalist economies, predominantly run by private enterprises. Some had quite substantial publicly owned sectors, such as energy, including nuclear energy, railways, steel, and in some countries, automobiles. Although public ownership of industries has sometimes featured in the literature of socialism and of planning, as key elements in securing such objectives for the whole economy as full employment, it is doubtful whether these enterprises played more than a minor part in macroeconomic policies after, say, the mid-1950s. (A possible exception might be France, where macroeconomic policy remained largely dirigiste.) In general these industries responded to market forces. Some markets could be manipulated, or controlled: for instance, a nationalised electricity industry might be required by the government to burn coal in its generators, not necessarily because it was the cheapest fuel, but because the government wished to maintain a certain level of output of coal over a long period. On the wisdom, or otherwise, of organising production in this way we say nothing in this paper. We have dealt only with those policies, be they monetary or fiscal, whereby governments endeavour to influence the performance of the economy, not by issuing commands or directives to individual firms or workers, but by working through markets, e.g. imposing taxes on consumption, or reducing company taxation, which may raise investment, and so on. It may, in fact, be many years before some Eastern countries find themselves with economic structures to which lessons drawn from the experience of stabilisation in well-established capitalist countries can usefully be applied. However, some of these capitalist countries were themselves turned into "command" economies during World War II, and themselves went through "reconstruction" or "transition" periods, in some cases lasting several years, before they returned to "normal" market capitalist economies. The "transition" is not of course, the same as that being attempted in the East. The wartime Western "command" economies had previously been market economies and had the institutions and experience of how such economies functioned; whereas in most Eastern countries very few people remain in industry and government who have had any such experience of working in a market economy, nor are there many of the essential institutions in place: they have to be built up from scratch.

Transitions in the West

Even so, a brief examination of these post-war transitions may throw up one or two ideas worth considering by the East. We shall give a short account of the "reconstruction" in only two countries, the United Kingdom and West Germany, and will add a few words on the Marshall Plan.

Of the major belligerents, Britain, at the end of World War II, was probably the most highly mobilised. Early in the war, the Coalition government had taken sweeping powers over persons and property. The primary aim was to secure the greatest possible share of total production for the armed forces and arms production. This was secured, in the main, by conscription of persons, and by the requisitioning of land, buildings and plant. Current production was secured by controlling the flow of raw materials to industry. The size of the war sector was limited only by the need to provide an acceptable minimum output for the civilian sector. The controls released the necessary raw materials, while demand was subject to extensive consumer rationing and price control. After World War I, there had been a brief inflationary boom, followed by a sharp slump. There was virtual unanimity at the end of World War II that this pattern should not be repeated. The problem, as seen by the government's economic advisers, was how to move from huge excess demand, fed by the vast unspendable liquid balances of the company and personal sectors, which could be contained only by the continuation of controls and rationing, to an economy managed by fiscal and monetary policy alone; individual production decisions would then be returned to the market. The transition period was likely to be prolonged by two special considerations. During the war, the financing of UK imports had been very much eased by the Lend-Lease arrangements with the United States, and exports had been allowed to run down to 30 per cent of pre-war. It was estimated that by 1950, exports would have to be at least 50 per cent higher than pre-war to pay for necessary imports. During the war, there had been much destruction by bombing of industrial buildings and plant and of housing: priority would have to be given to investment to repair war-damage, to replace plant and to create new capacity. Between 1946 and 1952, total GNP rose by 15.3 per cent. Exports increased by 77.3 per cent and investment by 57.9 per cent, which left room for an increase in consumption of only 5.9 per cent.

The controls in any sector could be removed once it became clear that there was no longer too large a gap between demand and supply in the conventional sense. The rate of decontrol can be indicated by the fact that by 1951 the proportion of industrial materials controlled had fallen from 94 per cent at the end of the war to 41 per cent, and the proportion of consumers' expenditure subject to rationing had come down from 25 to 10 per cent. The Korean war brought a temporary reversal of the smooth process of decontrol, but the process was largely complete by the mid-1950s; some controls, however, were to continue for many years more in the domestic economy, in the regional location of new plant, and externally in the control over capital movements. Exchange control was not to be finally abolished until 1979.

Was this gradualism in de-control justified? During the war, the cost-of-living index had been stabilised with the aid of price control and judiciously selected subsidies. An index of prices covering all consumers' expenditure rose on average by 3 per cent a year from 1942 to 1945. From 1945 to 1950, this average had risen to 4 per cent, and from 1950 to 1955, which included the Korean episode, the average was 4.5 per cent a year. The sharp rise and fall in prices experienced after 1918 had been ironed right out. The same contrast is apparent if we look at unemployment. In 1945 it was 0.8 per cent: three years later it was 1.3 per cent, and in only one year of the next nine did it touch over 2 per cent. By contrast, unemployment in 1918 was 0.8 per cent: three years later it was 11.3 per cent, and in the next nine years the lowest figure achieved was 6.8 per cent. As for production, the growth of output from 1948 to 1973 was the highest ever in a period of this length in Britain's industrial history. All this suggests that the policy of gradual de-control was fully justified.

The programme of gradual de-control has not been without its critics, especially in the light of the experience in West Germany after the war. Immediately following the war, there was a complete breakdown of all transport and public utilities, and, at the same time, there was a huge influx of refugees from Soviet occupied territories. Starvation was avoided only with the help of the armies of occupation. When transport, electricity and other services were restored, industrial production was resumed at some 25 or 30 per cent of pre-war levels. The system of rigid price and wage controls developed by the Nazis continued, although black markets began to develop. There was a huge overhang of monetary balances in the hands of persons and companies. The economy limped slowly and painfully into recovery. Then, in June, 1948, there was a major currency reform, and a reorganisation of private and public debt structures. The former was an exchange of 10 old reichsmarks for 1 new deutschmark, but when the less generous treatment of savings was taken into account, the conversion ratio was nearer to 100 old to 6.5 new. The currency reform was accompanied by the removal of many controls. Price control and rationing were maintained for basic foodstuffs, rents and some other essentials, but price and other controls were removed in manufacturing. At the time this drastic programme went against the dominant thinking among economic experts in the West. But it had one instant success. On 1 June 1948, goods reappeared in shops, and money resumed its normal function. Some contemporary economists are apt to see in the success of the German programme a vindication of the rapid introduction of market forces in the East today, almost as though a switch had been thrown and the German "miracle" began. This is a somewhat oversimplified account of what actually happened.

Immediately after the reform, industrial production began to rise sharply. But there was also a worrying rise in the cost-of-living. The tight fiscal and monetary stance ensured that the rise was reversed in the following year, but, while industrial production continued to rise, so also did unemployment. By 1950 an important debate developed whether the government should pursue a more expansionary policy, in order to make inroads into the very large unemployment (see Wallich 1955). Then the German economy had a stroke of good fortune. The rearmament necessitated by the Korean war was particularly awkward for the British economy, which was at full stretch, since it meant diverting materials, especially steel, away from exports and back to rearmament. But Germany had no rearmament commitment, and, in addition no supply constraint, with adequate industrial capacity and heavy unemployment. The Korean war boom gave a great impetus to its exports, especially of capital goods, and established the export surplus which was to be one of the most striking features of the German "miracle". It is interesting to speculate whether, had Germany adopted a domestically based "full-employment" policy in the early 1950s, it would have been handicapped later by the same balance of payments constraint that beset the British economy. But we cannot pursue the matter here. The point we wish to make is that the West German experience from 1948 onwards did not prove that the policy of gradual decontrol was wrong. Those who followed it had moderate inflation *and* full employment. Which policy was better, therefore, turns among other things on the value placed on low unemployment.

The lesson from the Marshall Plan is more straightforward. International trade had been drastically curtailed by World War II. Many European countries had lost most, if not all, of their gold and dollar reserves. To get trade restarted, a whole network of bilateral agreements was constructed, in which pairs of countries gave one another lines of credit on each other. Many of these agreements were between Britain and continental countries. Initially, such agreements were expansionary, restarting trade virtually from zero in some cases. But, when the value of net trade reached a credit limit, they could become restrictive. Further imports into the deficit country would now have to be paid for in gold or dollars, something which countries were anxious to avoid so as to keep precious reserves for imports which could not be obtained in any other way. The Marshall Plan has often been praised for the injection of dollars into

Europe. But it also led to the establishment of the OEEC (precursor of OECD), and it demanded the practice of mutual co-operation. For scarce goods and materials, the Americans said to the OEEC members: before you try to buy this or that from us, see whether you can get it from a non-dollar source (including the Soviet bloc). This mutual discrimination was assisted by the Intra-European Payments Schemes, the fore-runners of the European Payments Union set up in 1949, which was accompanied by the liberalisation of trade by the removal of quantitative import restrictions. The lesson for the East lies not in the details of the EPU, but in the manifest gains for all members to be derived from mutual co-operation.

3.5 Conclusion

We took the purpose of stabilisation in the West to mean the achievement of high employment, steady output growth, moderate price inflation and a sustainable balance of payments in foreign transactions. We put off to the end of the paper the transition of Western countries from war-economies to normal market economies in which the main instruments of stabilisation were fiscal and monetary policy. We examined their experience of stabilisation in the normal conditions of two periods: from the mid-1950s to 1973, and 1973 to date. We concluded that, in the first period, when full employment was included in the agenda of many governments, "demand management", mainly relying upon fiscal and monetary policy, achieved considerable success. Some increase in the rate of inflation was already beginning to appear towards the end of this period, and in late 1973 the first of the two OPEC oil price rises imparted great impetus to inflation which reached much higher rates in the 1970s – a decade in which Western governments struggled with simultaneous inflation and unemployment. By the 1980s, most had abandoned the objective of full employment, concentrating upon reducing demand to try to bring down inflation. They succeeded in this, but only at the expense of much higher average unemployment as well as deep recessions. Any lessons for the East, therefore, must be qualified by the observation that the Western economies themselves have not been performing optimally, and, in particular, have not found a means of sustaining high employment without unacceptable inflation. The other qualification, of course, is that many Eastern countries do not have the institutions, or the experience, to be able to operate successfully with fiscal and monetary policy alone in a market context. Accordingly, the final section of the paper gave a brief look at the experience of two Western countries – Britain and West Germany – in organising the transition from the command economy of war to a normal peace-time market economy. The transition was not identical with that being attempted by Eastern economies, since for the Western countries the period of command economy was comparatively short, and the institutions and experience for running a market economy still existed, whereas many Eastern countries have to create (for them) new institutions and to learn how to operate them. Nevertheless, consideration of these two Western countries at least illuminates the choices between "shock-therapy" and a more gradual approach to the transition. It also demonstrates the gains to be made by mutual co-operation among a group of countries in restoring the flows of international trade and payments.

References

Boltho, A. (1981), "British Fiscal Policy – Stabilising or Destabilising", *Oxford Bulletin of Economics and Statistics*, November.

Brown, A.J. (1955), *The Great Inflation*, Oxford University Press.

Hansen, Bent (1969), *Fiscal Policy in Seven Countries, 1955-1965*, OECD.

OECD (1961), *The Problem of Rising Prices*, Paris.

Wallich, Henry C. (1955), *Mainsprings of the German Revival*, Yale University Press.

COMMENTS ON PART I:

Wlodzimierz Brus*)

There are, in my opinion, two major aspects of the problem under discussion: assessment of previous stabilisation policies, i.e. those undertaken at the outset of the post-communist era in Eastern Europe, and policy conclusions relevant to the present stage of the transformation process.

---

*) Emeritus Professor, University of Oxford, UK.

On the *first aspect*, I share, by and large, the position presented (in Chapter 1) by *Levcik* and the *Vienna Institute* (WIIW), particularly when taken in conjunction with *Kornai's* "multi-causal explanation" of the "transformational recession" (Chapter 2) which provides a welcome moderating factor to the WIIW conclusions. There were differences in the economic situations of the individual countries as they entered the post-communist era; but the policy makers in all of them committed in the initial phase the same serious mistake of neglecting the question of aggregate demand and its implications for output and employment. Combined with lack of concern for the state sector of the economy, and overoptimistic expectations of the restructuring abilities of spontaneous market forces – both internal and external, with a widely opened door for the latter – this mistake was mainly responsible for the severity of the "transformational recession". It is not necessary to repeat the evidence. It seems to me clear that recession as such was unavoidable, but by far not so pronounced as it turned out to be. I also support strongly the view that criticism of the conventional stabilisation policy applies not to the aims – transformation into a market economy – but to the means: how to accomplish this transformation most effectively, from both economic and socio-political points of view.

It goes without saying that the *second aspect* of our problem deserves to command our paramount attention. Bygones are bygones, and whatever the lessons of the past, the present realities are, or should be, the determining factor of the policies ahead. This is true not only for the countries which made progress in the transformation process; it also applies to those which made little advance in marketisation, e.g. the Ukraine; but even there the situation is different from that in Poland, Czechoslovakia and Hungary in 1989/90.

In the light of the severe decline in output and of the rise in unemployment, a clear *shift of objectives* of economic policy is required: growth of GDP and effective fight against (or prevention of) mass unemployment ought to become the priority objectives, with inflation as a constraint. It may sound a purely verbal change, but explicit policy objectives matter in practice, as we are reminded by *Worswick's* paper (Chapter 3) on the lessons from stabilisation in the West.

The *aggregate demand approach* should be given the appropriate pride of place as a general *framework* for any policy measures: no sustained recovery would be possible if aggregate demand failed to match effective productive capacities.

Having stressed the importance of the aggregate demand approach, I think we should recognise however that the *supply-side* must be much more carefully scrutinised than in a classical "Keynesian-Kaleckian" situation of obvious demand-deficiency as in the Great Depression. True, critics of the aggregate demand approach exaggerate the price adjustment reaction to demand-stimulation and underestimate the role of cost-determined prices, but the realities of the economies in transition have shown that the problem of *unmarketable output* cannot be underestimated either. Under conditions of increasing financial discipline one can hardly expect a way out in the form of increased inventories, not to mention the undesirable macroeconomic consequences of such a "safety valve". This means that any demand-stimulation must be selective (which presents a whole set of systemic problems), and be clearly linked to restructuring productive capacities. One of the most promising avenues for this is to create conditions favourable to the process of "privatisation from below", i.e. promotion of new private businesses, particularly in manufacturing and construction.

The need to combine demand-stimulation with structural change on the supply-side leads to the obvious conclusion that the main area of active government policy must be *investment*. The selection of sectors or individual projects need not be made simply by bureaucratic whim; cooperation between the state and industry (private, domestic and foreign business) can be achieved as the Japanese and Korean experience has shown. I cannot go into detailed enumeration of instruments of government activity, but I should like to mention loan guarantees and preferential credit conditions as likely ones. The same goes for the areas of investment; some are widely regarded as rather obvious (housing construction is one; retraining, broadly understood, is another – particularly important for greater flexibility in the labour market), and the regional aspect must be kept closely in mind. Coherent and well-coordinated government activity in investment should not "crowd out" private capital. On the contrary, it would help to raise funds on the capital market, including internationally.

In *external economic relations,* the principal direction towards *greater openness* of the economy ought not to be interpreted, in my opinion, as excluding the possibility of selective protection. One could say that the standard "infant industry" argument applies to vast areas of the transitional economies which need time to gather strength before finding themselves exposed to the full blast of international competition.

I should like to end with two brief remarks. First, I am fully aware that under conditions existing now in the transitional economies, the room for manoeuvre is by no means broad, leaving hardly any scope for spectacular reversals of economic policies; nevertheless what can be done to influence a change in policy seems important enough to make a tangible difference. Secondly, a more economically active state requires that the government and the state apparatus in general must be capable of fulfilling such a role; this is, obviously, not only a technical but rather a political condition.

Robert S. Dohner*)

Both the paper by *Levcik* and colleagues from WIIW (Ch. 1) and that by *Kornai* (Ch. 2) address the most puzzling, and most disturbing questions of the transition in Eastern Europe: why was the drop in output so steep, what blame can be assigned to economic policy during the transition, and what set of policies are appropriate now. My remarks will be addressed primarily to the paper by *Levcik,* since it makes the most forceful argument against the macro policies that were recommended for and adopted by the economies in transition.

Although there is some question about the extent of unmeasured activity in the Eastern countries and the true extent of the drop in activity, there is no disputing that a sharp fall in output has taken place simultaneously with the reforms establishing a market economy. The immediate effect of the reform process was an acceleration of inflation and a substantial erosion of sources of government revenue, leading to adoption of policies addressed to macro-economic stabilisation. There is a tendency in both papers, but most strongly in the *Levcik* paper, to identify the drop in output as resulting from stabilisation policy, e.g.: " ... in every single case the economic depression, characterised by a fall in output during stabilisation, turned out to be significantly more severe than was predicted ... In practical terms this means that the massive social and political costs of stabilisation were miscalculated."

---

*) Economist, Central and Eastern European Division, OECD. The opinions expressed here are the author's, and do not necessarily reflect those of the OECD Secretariat or the OECD Member governments.

Although stabilisation was an essential part of the reform process, I hesitate to call the recessions in Eastern Europe the result of stabilisation policy. In my view, the key events were rather the liberalisation of prices and trade, the establishment of current account convertibility, the opening of entry in domestic activity and external trade, and the reduction in subsidies and progressive hardening of firms′ budget constraints – all parts of what both papers refer to as the "shift from a sellers' to a buyers' market". The sharp falls in output that followed the beginning of the transition process were more a result of these shifts than they were of the adoption of over-stringent stabilisation measures.

As a recent paper by Winiecki argues, the characteristics of enterprises under the previous regime of central planning were such that one should expect drops in output during the process of adjustment to a market environment.[1] I will mention two. The first of these characteristics was very large holdings of inventories, reflecting strong precautionary demand and little or no effective cost for stockholding. Inventory-to-sales ratios in the former centrally-planned economies were often two and one-half times Western levels, and may have accounted in aggregate for 60 to 80 per cent of a year's GDP. In a market environment, and particularly in recession, locating supplies has greatly diminished as a problem, while the real cost of holding inventories (evaluated at bank loan rates) has skyrocketed. Sharp reductions in inventory holdings have aggravated the output decline.

A second characteristic that Winiecki identifies is the excessive level of investment in the formerly centrally-planned economies. Incremental capital-output ratios (ICORs) in these countries were two to two and a half times as high as in the West, even when the centrally-planned economies were still growing, which again was a reflection of the fact that enterprises bore little of the cost of investing. With the liberalisation of imports and an increase in enterprise discipline a desirable *reduction* of investment and an increase in investment efficiency will occur.

There is a further characteristic of the transition that leads one to expect a fall in output, and that is the extent of the structural shift in demand with the

---

1) Winiecki, Jan (1993), "'Heterodox' Stabilisation in Eastern Europe", Working Paper no. 8, EBRD, London. Published as Winiecki, Jan (1993), "Knowledge of Soviet-Type Economy and 'Heterodox' Stabilization-Based Outcomes in Eastern Europe", *Weltwirtschaftliches Archiv*, vol. 129, no. 2, pp. 384-410.

opening to the world market. In the industrial sector alone, the average absolute change in industry output prices relative to the overall producer price index was 18 percentage points in Poland between 1988 and 1991. Hungary had a system of relative prices that was much closer to those of the world market, but still had an average absolute change in relative prices of 12 percentage points. This, incidentally, was about the same extent of relative price change as occurred in the United States over the course of the first oil crisis.[2)] As a part of this structural shift, there were goods for which demand for domestically produced output virtually disappeared – consumer electronics and other durables, military goods, and goods to East-bloc specifications. At the same time there was growth in demand for selected industrial goods, and particularly strong growth in demand for services, as *Kornai's* paper (Ch. 2) emphasises.

The extent of the structural change that takes place during transition makes me very uncomfortable with the use of aggregate "output" as a main indicator. A more accurate representation would be a two-good model, with what I'll call "East goods" and "West goods". In the transition there is a strong shift in demand from East goods to West goods. In addition, East goods appear to have very low, or perhaps even negative, income elasticities of demand. As a result, attempts to stimulate aggregate demand risk running up against capacity constraints in the West goods industries, particularly non-traded West goods, without appreciably raising the production of East goods. To put the point more colourfully, no amount of aggregate demand stimulation would have supported the production of East German Trabants.

Thus even though the output drop is large and there appears to be substantial excess capacity during the early phase of the transition, this observation is deceptive. Policies to stimulate aggregate demand may in fact achieve little in terms of stimulating activity, and are likely instead to have a high leakage into either inflation, imports, or both.

In addition to the probably limited effects of aggregate demand stimulation from the theoretical side, there are also problems on the operational side. I will not dwell on the problems confronting fiscal policies. The rapid erosion of tax collection during the transition has confronted almost all of the transition economies with soaring budget deficits (the Czech Republic is the exception) despite sharp cuts in real government expenditure. Budgetary stringency will

---

2) OECD (1993), *Economic Survey: Hungary,* Table 22 (p. 94).

constrain the transition economies from using fiscal policy as an expansionary tool.

It is argued in Chapter 1 that monetary policy has also been too tight. This point is debatable, but there are real limits to the use of monetary policy as a tool of demand stimulus in the transition countries. The first of these limits is external. Although formal exchange control varies across the countries, in each there is *de facto* currency convertibility. As a result, monetary authorities must maintain (near) positive real interest rates for depositors. Given the risk of large depreciations (what economists refer to as the "peso problem") this may require a large uncovered premium in favour of domestic currency assets. In Hungary between March 1991 and November 1992, ex post US$ returns on three month Hungarian forint bank deposits averaged 19.3 per cent, 14.6 percentage points above Eurodollar rates during the period.[3)]

The second limitation on monetary policy is the large spread between deposit and loan rates in the economies in transition; in Hungary this spread reached 11 percentage points during 1992. The spread comes from several sources, including high taxation of financial intermediation through the requirement to hold reserves at low interest rates, the perceived need to cover non-performing credits with high returns on good loans, and the importance of (still state-owned) commercial bank profits as a source of government revenue.[4)] If one adds to this the fact that producer prices have generally grown at a rate well below that of consumer prices, then real loan rates, measured in terms of producer prices, have been extremely high while real deposit rates, measured in consumer price terms, have been barely positive.

The final limitation on monetary policy is the weakness and lack of competition within the banking system itself that limits the effect of monetary policy on credit terms. Thus in Hungary when interest rates fell in early 1992 the initial effect was to widen loan-deposit spreads; it was not until the third

---

3) *Ibid.*, pp. 62-63. The ex-post dollar rate is defined as the rate of return from purchasing forints with dollars, depositing them in Hungary, and converting the proceeds back into dollars three months later.

4) In Hungary, reserve requirements were estimated to have added 2 percentage points to the spread between bank loan and deposit rates, while generating sufficient income to cover non-performing loans was estimated to have added an additional 4 percentage points. See *Ibid.*, pp. 137-139.

quarter that loan rates began to fall. The high degree of bank liquidity and the preference for government securities of the commercial banking system may reflect inadequate demand for loan credit, but the failure of loan rates to fall reflects the lack of competition among commercial banks, as does the fact that banks can charge good customers high rates to cover the losses on bad loans. However there is one characteristic of commercial banking that contributes to the cost of tight monetary policy in countries in transition. The lack of developed loan assessment skills, weak markets for collateral, and perhaps a lingering feeling that the government will stand behind loans to large firms, have limited the extension of credit to newly emerging firms, while maintaining credit to state-owned firms. As a result, monetary tightening is likely to be felt disproportionately by the emerging private sector, to the extent that they are able to obtain bank loans at all.

The weaknesses in the financial sector are a constraint on the process of structural transformation as well as on monetary policy, a point that Chh. 1 and 2 both emphasise. I agree with the argument advanced by *Kornai* that the role of the state is actively to assist the development of new institutions required by the market economy. In the financial sector, this means a solution to the bad debt problems of commercial banks, the restoration of positive net worth of the banks so that their own money is truly at risk when they make loans, and the encouragement of competition among banks for depositors and borrowers. It also means creating the legal/institutional mechanisms that facilitate borrowing by new entrepreneurs – in particular, rules on collateral and foreclosure – as well as rules on accounting and disclosure that would induce portfolio equity investment. The result would not only be a financial system that more efficiently channels funds from savers to investors, but also one where the tools of monetary policy are more effective.

Egon Matzner*)

Kornai (Ch. 2) presents a number of interesting insights as well as statistical observations on the reduction of output which Eastern European economies have experienced on their road from centrally planned to market type economies. I do not have serious objections to any specific argument; and yet I have to make a reservation with respect to *Kornai's* main thesis; that a fall in output is inevitable in the transformation process. The evidence of the performance of the People's Republic of China provides a clear falsification of the general validity of *Kornai's* position (see Perczynski 1994). This evidence may be questioned on the ground that the great differences in culture and size discredit the relevance of any kind of analogue with Eastern European countries. Therefore I should like to give examples to a second argument. What if the drop in output observed, at least its size, is due to the specific road to capitalism chosen? It can be argued, and there is evidence for it, that this has been the case. I shall try to present my view in brief drawing upon the work of the AGENDA-group (see Kregel et al. 1992 and 1993 and Perczynski et al. 1994).

The essence of the road to capitalism in the former communist countries so far has been the belief that a market economy comes into being spontaneously once a number of key conditions are fulfilled. Among them figure prominently:

(1) the abolition of central planning and state regulation,
(2) the stabilisation of the currency and the abolition of state subsidies,
(3) the liberalisation of prices (including foreign exchange) and
(4) rapid privatisation of collective production capacity.

This was and, to a great extent, still is the dominant orientation of transformation strategies. The differences between countries refer mainly to the speed, the sequence and the decisiveness of the efforts to be mobilised for ending up at capitalism. The greatest efforts undoubtedly were employed in transforming the economy of the former GDR into a market economy. It happened indeed on Monday, 3 July 1990. Thus East Germany represents the purest case of shock-therapy. The consequences have been the greatest

---

*) Professor of Public Economics and Head of Research Unit for Socioeconomics, Austrian Academy of Sciences.

fall in production observed by a single country in history (including periods of war).

Why so?

There are two main reasons for an event which is better named transformational catastrophe than recession:

The *first* is the immediate consequence of the abolition of the central planning agency. Its very function under the old regime was to link the producing units with the purchasing units (firms, retail chains and, ultimately, the private and collective household units). By eliminating central planning these links are immediately interrupted. The dominant transformation strategy did not provide for this situation. In market economies it is the business of wholesale trading firms and merchant banks (or a combination of both) to establish these links and to make a profit out of the spatial and temporal arbitrage of output bought on contract and financed by credit extended to the producing firm. In the days immediately after the birth of the market economy, this driving force of a market economy capable of producing additional output and assets is not yet in existence and will not fall from heaven. The intermediaries who connect the sellers with the buyers on the basis of contracts for future output financed on credit are the very *market-makers.* There is no market economy without market-makers. And, since market-makers do not emerge spontaneously, they have to be created.

The shock-birth of the market economy in the former GDR again provides illuminating evidence. The absence of market-makers connecting East German producers with domestic as well as West German and foreign buyers caused the catastrophic drop in output. The needs of the East German private and public households, which benefitted from massive income transfers from Bonn, were immediately met by West German wholesalers and chains: They established the links between the Western producers, thus absorbing part of their excess capacity, with the East German buyers. The consequences of the omission of the market-maker became dramatically visible in agriculture. The East German cooperatives whose contracts, established under central planning, became invalidated on 3 July 1990, had to kill thousands of pigs, cattle, geese and so on or had to throw away tons of milk within three weeks. German TV at that time was full of embarrassing pictures. This and other omissions in the prevalent transformation strategy are far too important to be understated by a term like "transformational recession".

The proponents of the dominant transformation strategy in general and the vanguards of shock therapy – sometimes called "radical reformers" – have forgotten three important lessons taught by those who have a profound understanding of the functioning of market economies. The *first* lesson tells the student that the provision of markets is an entrepreneurial activity (as taught by a recent Nobel Laureate (Coase 1988, p. 8)). Therefore markets where already existing goods are traded (as in flea markets) do not to contribute to making market economies.

The *second* lesson is taught by the English classical liberal political economists who stressed the role of the law-giver in making markets function in the private interest of economic man and yet in line with the public good. They were certain that the pursuit of self-interest unrestrained by suitable institutions carries no guarantee of anything except chaos.

The *third* lesson, taught especially by the WIIW authors (Ch. 1 in this volume), refers to the fact that market-making is not independent of effective demand. For demand to become effective market-making is necessary and for market-making to be successful sufficient effective demand is needed. In this sense I am, like *Kornai,* a half-way follower of Keynes (Matzner and Streeck 1994).

References

Coase, R. H. (1988), *The Firm, the Market and the Law,* University Press, Chicago.

Kregel, J. A., Matzner, E., and Grabher, G. (1992), *The Market Shock. An AGENDA for the Socio-Economic Reconstruction of Central and Eastern Europe,* Michigan University Press, Ann Arbor.

Kregel, J. A., Lushin, A. S., Matzner, E., and Specht, L. (1993), *The Post-Shock AGENDA: How to Make the Market – Forms of Property and Control. Peace and the Sciences,* ed. by the International Institute for Peace, Vienna, September.

Matzner, E., and Streeck, W. (1994), *Beyond Keynesianism. The Socio-Economics of Production and Full Employment,* Edward Elgar, Aldershot. (First published 1992)

Perczynski, M., Kregel, J.A., and Matzner, E. (eds.) (1994), *After the Shock,* Dartmouth Press (forthcoming).

Hans Seidel*)

Let me start by asking: What can be regarded as a successful transition? One criterion, although not the only one, is economic growth. In the last years a few renowned economists tried to find out if and how the Solow production function has to be changed in order to fit the stylised facts of world-wide economic development. As a by-product the empirics of economic growth are better known than before. From the evidence gathered, a baseline scenario of convergence can be sketched in which the gap in per capita income between the market economies of the West and the countries in transition will be closed at a rate of 2 per cent per annum. This implies that the growth differential will be large at the beginning and is expected to diminish as the gap becomes smaller. Assuming a growth rate of 2 per cent in the OECD area, 5 per cent growth in the Eastern countries over a period of years could be regarded as normal. Rates between 5 and 10 per cent would be classified as excellent even if they are still below the rates which China did achieve in recent years.

Up to now, the economic performance of the East Europeans lagged far behind this baseline scenario. Therefore the question is warranted: what can be done to facilitate the "take-off"?

Some doubt that anything can be learned from the transition period in Western Europe after Word War II. I agree to a certain extent. What worked reasonably well under specific historical circumstances might not be appropriate under different conditions. However, many reformers and their advisers from the West did not even try to understand what shaped the economic miracle of Western Europe after World War II. Or, perhaps they just picked up one example which seemed to fit into their preconceived ideas of how capitalism works.

Therefore, *Worswick's* paper (Ch. 3) fills an important gap. He gives a very competent and even-handed overview on stabilisation policy in the West. I shall underline two main points.

As *Worswick* tells us, after World War II wartime controls were in some countries abolished only gradually. The reason seemed to be obvious for the policy makers at that time: prices determine both the income distribution and the allocation of resources. If supply is very inelastic undesirable income effects

---

*) Austrian Institute of Economic Research (WIFO), Vienna.

dominate. Moreover, if demand drives prices up in one sector cost-push effects in other sectors are liable to follow. Since the monetary authorities must contain inflation an inflationary slump is likely to develop.

Worswick furthermore reminds us that the US urged the Europeans to buy in Europe what can be produced in Europe. They allowed European trade and exchange rate policy to discriminate against the US and against the dollar. The reason was the same as in the first case: low price elasticities of domestic supply tend to boost the price for scarce foreign currencies, and at that time only the US dollar was scarce. International economic policy accepted a "dollar shortage" rather than allowing market clearing exchange rates.

Judging from the mainstream economic thinking of the time the sequencing of economic reforms in Eastern Europe after the systemic change was ill-designed. The institutions of capitalism should be developed first before prices are liberalised. Imports from the West should only be allowed if no comparable goods can be bought in the former Comecon area. In any case, imports from the West should be confined to essentials; no fancy Western consumer goods like cars or even Coca Cola should be admitted.

It stands to reason that such a strategy requires an efficient bureaucracy, close co-operation between firm managers and civil servants as well as a high degree of solidarity among the individual economic agents. It might very well be that these conditions could not be established in the East. However, a more balanced approach might have caused less hardship. It is interesting to note that in some cases (e.g. for technical assistance) old concepts of the Marshall Plan era are resurrected.

For better or worse, different strategies were chosen. The important question today is not what should have been done in the past, but rather what can be done in the future to overcome the present stalemate and to bring the Eastern economies on to a reasonably steep growth path.

Kornai (Ch. 2) is one of the pioneers in transition economics. His views deserve special attention. I shall pick up from his paper what at first sight appears to be a minor point. *Kornai* told us that according to business surveys almost 60 per cent of the Hungarian firms in manufacturing are demand constrained. They could produce more with the given capacity and labour force. To bring this figure into the right perspective two facts should be mentioned:

(a) A probably significant number of the firms with excess capacity will be unable to use their present capacity, irrespective of the level of aggregate demand.

(b) A figure of 60 per cent does not necessarily indicate a recession. At present, in Austria, according to the same type of enquiry, 80 per cent of the firms in manufacturing report unused resources. Only during the last unexpectedly strong upswing at the beginning of the 1990s did the share of firms with demand constraints decline to 50 per cent.

Does that mean that supply in the Eastern economies is not as elastic as one is inclined to believe in view of the sharp reduction in overall production? I leave this question open. But I strongly recommend that economic policy should concentrate its efforts at removing the obstacles confronting the supply-constrained firms (which in Hungary amount to approximately 40 per cent of the firms if those with financing difficulties are included). During 1993 I visited about fifty firms in Eastern Europe as a member of an OECD mission. The sample of firms probably was biased. Nevertheless, one could draw some general conclusions. Especially in the former Soviet Union, the firms were slow in picking up opportunities for profitable business. Big differences between local costs and international prices were not exploited, partly because the firms had no experience of exporting to Western countries. Firms who could sell more than they produce told us that they do not plan to expand their capacity because the future is too uncertain.

If the East European governments supported by donor countries or international institutions can induce potentially healthy firms to expand and invest, aggregate demand would be stimulated without the risk of bottlenecks at an early stage of expansion.

That, of course, leads back to *Levcik* and the WIIW team. I agree that measures should be taken to stimulate aggregate demand in order to overcome the equilibrium of pessimistic expectations in which the Eastern countries are trapped. I would not attach too much importance to the now prevailing view among Western economists that demand shocks can stimulate production and employment only temporarily while raising permanently the rate of inflation. But an expansionary policy should be planned very carefully. Just increasing the budget deficit and printing money is not enough, and eventually may fail. A programme of investment promotion for viable firms supplemented by much needed infrastructure outlays would be a step in the right direction.

My views are, of course, shaped by my own experience. In Austria, investment promotion was always given a high priority, and I think with some success. At present, in the East, investment is not only hampered by pessimistic expectations but also by high user-costs of capital. Real interest rates may not look excessive ex-post. But high nominal interest rates are clearly prohibitive in an unstable inflationary environment. Furthermore, the prices of foreign investment goods are extremely high in terms of product prices. Many Eastern firms bought Western equipment before the systemic change at a very favourable exchange rate. Since that time the terms of trade have deteriorated dramatically. Much higher profits are necessary to allow a reasonably short pay-off period.

A selective programme for stimulating investment should aim at picking the winners, making strong firms even stronger. It should not be used to bail out big state-owned industries with no future but should aim at assisting mainly (but not exclusively) private firms to develop new markets, new products and new production processes.

The role of fiscal policy

Let me add a few words about fiscal policy, which for a long time has been regarded as the cornerstone of stabilisation policy. Contrary to some beliefs, fiscal policy does work. It has the power to influence aggregate demand and consequently output and employment. This proposition has been confirmed in many cases. Prominent examples are: the so-called Reaganomics at the beginning of the 1980s, the German reunification ten years later and even Austro-Keynesianism in the mid-1970s.

However, fiscal policy should be used with great care. To begin with, a fiscal stimulus may be costly in terms of national debt and interest payments. Especially in small countries with a high propensity to import, multipliers are low (and balance-of-payments constraints narrow the room for manoeuvre). Furthermore, recessions are usually connected with structural problems. Desirable and ultimately unavoidable structural adjustments might be delayed if aggregate demand is booming. The European car industry and the nationalised industries in Austria are often quoted in this context. Finally, a boost of demand may only temporarily stimulate output and employment but raise permanently the rate of inflation. One should not dismiss this argument solely on the ground that one distrusts neo-classical economics. The recent OECD-study on unemployment relies very heavily on the concept of equilibrium unemployment towards which actual unemployment converges.

This is a rather pessimistic view about demand management via fiscal policy. I accept it, only reluctantly, because during my whole career I believed in what 50 years ago Lord Beveridge called "full employment in a free society". But not all dreams of mankind become true. The employment programme under consideration in the European Community might alleviate the problem of unemployment, but is unlikely to solve it. Nevertheless, it deserves strong support. In the countries in transition of Eastern Europe, there are clear signs of demand deficiencies. The old system wasted resources: inventories were much too high and investments badly chosen. The new system avoids these and other inefficiencies, but does not employ the available resources fully. Obviously, a trade-off between inefficient use and underemployment of resources is only acceptable in a short transition period. Repeated reference has been made to the post-war period in Western Europe. Perhaps one point was not stressed sufficiently. The transition of Western Europe after World War II was achieved in a high-pressure economy; the present transition in Eastern Europe takes place in a low-pressure environment.

But although there seems to be scope for stimulating demand, economic policy should proceed very carefully. For one thing, the rate of inflation is still too high even in those countries which were able to keep inflation under control. Because the structure of production is still very unbalanced, bottlenecks might develop in an early stage of recovery. Therefore output responsiveness should be improved in line with any demand stimulus. Governments should encourage those predominantly private firms with good medium prospects and refrain from bailing out large state-owned firms with no future. Finally, if medium-term growth prospects are considered, perhaps something can be learned from those East- and Southeast Asian countries which manage to grow fast even under unfavourable external conditions.

Jože Mencinger*)

After three years, it has become evident that transition in Eastern Europe started without a clear picture of the actual situation, without a fully worked-out scheme of a new economic system, and without suitable economic and social arrangements in place. Instead, there were illusions that introduction of a market economy combined with macroeconomic stabilisation and privatisation would transform former socialist countries rapidly into welfare states. All countries declared firm commitment to full scale privatisation and uncompromising faith in capitalist market mechanisms; the firmer the commitment, the fewer market institutions they possessed. Unwarranted expectations did not materialise; production declined, unemployment increased, standards of living of most people fell, and distribution of income worsened. The enthusiasm of Western countries for political freedoms and economic transition in the former socialist world faded as well. It is thus not too surprising that the nostalgia for communism's cradle-to-grave social benefits has reappeared in many countries and in many different forms.

Three papers: by *Worswick* (Ch. 3), *Kornai* (Ch. 2) and by the WIIW team (Ch. 1) untangle the observed phenomena from very different angles; but they do constitute an entity.

Worswick (Ch. 3) draws "lessons for the East from stabilisation in the West" based on many relevant similarities and differences in circumstances, institutions and economic policies; they unfortunately remained neglected by policy makers in Eastern countries and, more surprisingly, by their Western advisers and international institutions. The most striking differences between the two "transitions" (in the West, after World War II) seem to be as follows. First, the institutions and know-how of a market economy were in the West only suspended during the war, while they were abolished by the Communist regimes in Eastern countries. The return in the West from a command economy to a "normal" economy after World War II nevertheless varied in speed and content among countries; some administrative restrictions remained in power for quite a long time. By contrast a "pseudoliberal" introduction of capitalism by decree prevailed

---

*) Professor of Economics, EIPF (Institute of Economics, Faculty of Law), University of Ljubljana, Slovenia.

in the transition. While, formally, market institutions can be established by decree and most Eastern countries have been more than willing to copy them from the West; the gap in social behaviour created by forty or seventy years of socialism cannot be simply overcome. It is therefore unlikely that market institutions with the same names and roles would operate as they do in the developed market economies where their creation was a gradual process of interaction between economic development, politics, and the institutions of civil society. It may take decades before some countries in transition will have an institutional structure to which one could fruitfully apply economic policies drawn from experiences after World War II.

Second, successful transition and good economic performance in the West after World War II relied upon the generally favourable circumstances – an unprecedented growth of world trade, and helpful political developments. These circumstances have not prevailed in the period of Eastern transition.

Thirdly, belief that governments were both committed and able to prevent serious slumps was shared by business. Such confidence in government has not abounded in the newly-born capitalist countries. The lessons after World War II also proved that demand management cannot be used at the same time in expansionary and contractionary modes, which also appears not to be believed in the East.

The decline of measured output has gone far beyond "the macroeconomic stabilisation" expectations. The disappearance of Leszek Balcerowicz's "pure socialist production" (unwanted) goods, the trade shock, the macroeconomic policies, and statistical overstatements have been blamed for it; the estimates of their relative importance, however, differ. The differences among the countries in transition are also enormous; their abilities to convert into "normal" market economies differ even more (see *Annex).* Two groups can be distinguished. In the first, comprising the less developed countries of Eastern Europe and the former Soviet Union, production more than halved, there are no signs that it has reached bottom yet, and the countries have been struggling with hyperinflation. Economic analysis of the present situation and prospects in these countries appears to be premature; economic prospects depend too heavily on future political developments.

The Visegrád countries (the Czech Republic, Hungary, Poland and Slovakia) with Slovenia, or "the Austro-Hungarian group", have probably reached the bottom of *Kornai's* "transformational recession". They exhibited quite similar economic performances during the transition; GDP fell by one fifth, industrial output by one third, the countries managed to get inflation under control, and they were, at least initially, successful in penetrating the world market. Indeed, the similarity of macroeconomic and systemic developments in these countries is a little surprising considering the differences in circumstances, starting positions, and approaches to transition. The mechanisms of depression also seem to be similar, and general factors inducing recession, elaborated by *Kornai,* apply to all. The weights of various elements in the mechanism however differ considerably depending on the size of the country, formerly established links with the world market, the stage of economic reforms before transition started etc. A continuing fast revival of economic activity also seems unlikely because of the nature of the recession, which cannot be cured by standard anti-cyclical policy tools. Instead, all must engage in a "parallel process of destruction and creation, eliminating unprofitable product lines and unproductive jobs while encouraging the evolution of profitable ones" (Kornai 1993).

Among these countries, Slovenia was, probably, the least affected by the disruption in coordination and by transfer from the sellers' market towards a buyers' market. The coordination of the economy has been for many years decentralised, the impacts of insufficient demand prevailed over those of supply shortages already in the mid-1980s, and the notion of "monetary overhang" was unknown. Hungary and Poland seemed to follow while Czechoslovakia should have more problems. The effects of the transformation of the real structure of the economy have been severe in all, but again for very different reasons. In Slovenia, they were produced more by the secession from the rest of former Yugoslavia and its economic collapse than by transition itself. The hardening of firms' budget constraints, i.e. enforcement of financial discipline, has been so far the most important element of transition in Slovenia.

It seems that in general the impacts of privatisation on economic efficiency were overestimated both in the short and in the long run. Private property is a necessary condition for economic efficiency emerging from "the incentive superiority of private property rights in guiding efficient economic behaviour" (Urban 1990, p. 36). But it is not sufficient. Ownership "restructuring" alone, by transferring property rights to formally private institutions established by the state and/or giving away the shares of these institutions to citizens at large, are only a grandiose administrative operation which could be envied by central planners but which does not help much. It reflects the specific distribution of political power in a particular country and the ideas of randomly chosen western "privatisers". The first round of privatisations in Eastern Europe based on such "paper privatisations" will most likely not produce any efficiency impulses in the economy; it will not create owners responsible for the proper use and maintenance of capital assets. The development in Slovenia, where internal "owners" have prevailed, confirms the findings for Poland by Pinto, Belka and Krajewski (1993) that hardening of the budget constraint, increased independence, and managers' loyalty to the firms, are what matter. However, warnings over the adverse effects of privatisation in the process of transition because it would affect existing property rights, particularly those of managers (Bajt 1992), have so far been disregarded. Instead of relying on the step-by-step construction of the institutions of a market economy on the legacies of the past, capitalism is "created" by fiat as communism once was.

The WIIW team (Ch. 1) concentrates on macroeconomic stabilisation in the economies of the Visegrád group: Poland, former Czechoslovakia and Hungary. While agreeing with most of the analysis, let me comment on some of the messages.

The paper correctly questions the stabilisation programmes pursued in transition which tend to be uniformly based upon: credit restraint, reduction of fiscal deficit, insistence on "price rationing" of credits, devaluation of domestic currency, liberalisation of trade regime, and introduction of two nominal anchors: exchange rate and nominal wages. First, such programmes overlook the characteristics of the transformational depression. Second, empirical evidence does not confirm what is implied by such stabilisation programmes, namely, that credit restrictions affect prices rather than output and that velocity of circulation is constant. It seems that policy makers were too overwhelmed by the "monetary overhang" which had presumably existed in the former socialist countries and which proved to be a bubble. The decline of economic activity which might have resulted from such policies was therefore underestimated; the programmes neglected the already existing low level of capacity utilisation, adverse effects of other factors on output, and the fact that prices have been determined predominantly by costs rather than by demand.

A highly simplified "vicious circle" of the mechanism of transformational depression is depicted in *Figure A.*

Figure A

The transformational depression

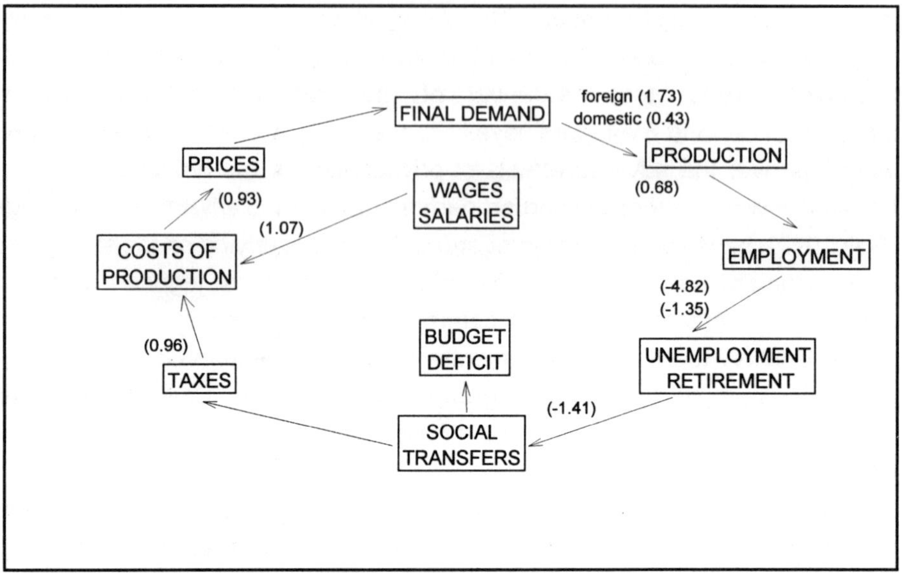

Note: The numbers in parentheses are constant elasticities in the Slovene economy estimated by monthly data for the 1991/1-1992/12 period, with the adjustments for auto-correlation. The mechanisms of depression in other countries of the group might differ considerably from those observed in Slovenia with elasticities being country specific.

According to it, the depression starts with the drop in aggregate demand. This might be the joint outcome of very different factors such as the collapse of the CMEA or the Yugoslav market, the disappearance of the "pure socialist production goods" that nobody wants any more, the competition of foreign goods by trade liberalisation etc. The decrease of demand accompanied by enforced financial discipline affects output in different ways: by forced reduction of inventories, by lowering capacity utilisation, bankruptcies etc. These affect employment and increase unemployment and retirements which in turn necessitate massive social transfers that can be collected by increased taxes or deficit financing. The latter is ruled out by a reduction rather than an increase of the budget deficit by which the countries try to fight inflation. However, even to keep budget revenues unaltered during a severe decline of economic activity implies increases in the tax rates and in the costs per unit of output. But due to the feeble market conditions, the increased costs cannot be shifted to price increases, which leads to new reduction of inventories, capacity utilisation, bankruptcies. If, however, prices are increased, demand is reduced again; the circle starts anew.

Formally, there are possibilities for economic policies to intervene at different stages of the vicious circle depicted in *Figure B.* Monetary policy could, for example, intervene by softening the credit constraint; this would however affect price stability and might also prolong the life of the industries which produce "pure socialist production goods" and which are distressed borrowers. Or it could finance the budget deficit; all the adverse effects of such a policy would follow. The role of fiscal policy is also limited; savings of domestic non-government sectors are low, borrowing abroad is expensive or even unavailable. Trade restrictions would increase domestic demand, but would also adversely affect export demand. In short, there are not many alternatives for actual economic policies in these countries. They depend heavily on the characteristics of the country in question. This is illustrated by Bole-Taylor's diagram depicted in *Figure B.*

The figure relates capacity utilisation to real wages (which are external in the vicious circle of transition) using aggregate "demand" and "supply" curves. The "demand" curve is composed of two parts; above C domestic demand prevails over foreign demand, the opposite is true below C. The "supply" curve is backward bending; the increases of real wages reduce capacities of the economy because more and more firms collapse if wages and costs of production increase. Transition shifted the demand from A to C which denotes the situation in the bottom of the transformational recession; the distance between C and full capacity or "supply" curve indicates the underutilisation of capacities. There are two possible avenues to move from point C: by increasing domestic demand or by increasing foreign demand. In the former case demand moves from C to A, in the latter from C to B. The first avenue is adversely affected by the factors that distinguish transformational depression from the "normal" depression. On the other hand, the reduction of wages and thus the movement towards B is socially and politically unacceptable, and also lessens domestic demand. Thus, a kind of Bermuda triangle in which output would

Figure B

Bole-Taylor's diagram

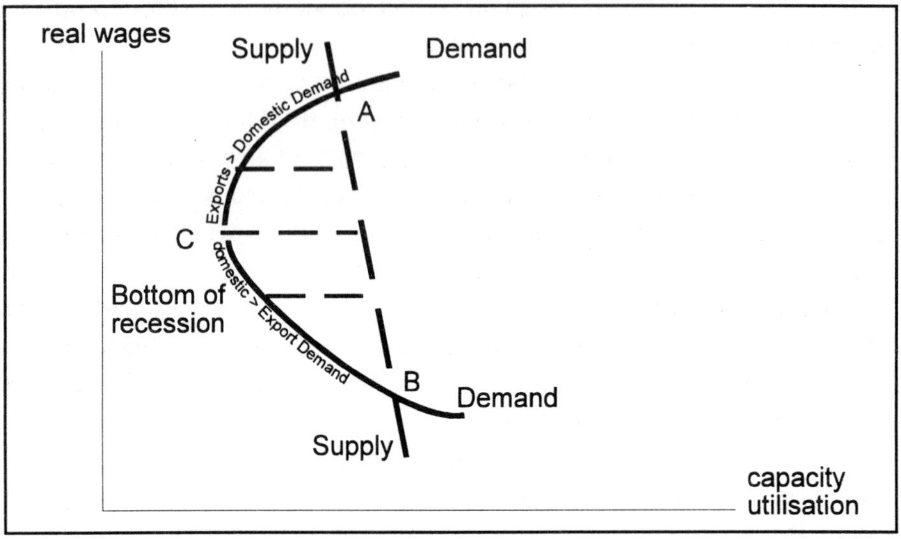

repeatedly shift back to position C develops. In short, the size of the country, the corresponding relative importance of foreign and domestic markets, the characteristics of the labour market, social conditions etc., determine the ways in which demand policies can be used. The capacities of demand policies in Poland with a population of 38 millions differ considerably from those in Slovenia with a population of 2 millions; the latter is too small and too open, and the structure of supply too adapted to the former Yugoslav market for the classical Keynesian cure. The increase of domestic demand would only marginally affect economic activity; it would trigger inflation despite low capacity utilisation. The "take off" is bound to be generated by export demand which however implies lower real costs of production, thus lower real wages and social transfers. In short, there does not seem to exist a once-and-for-all answer to "what went wrong and what to do now?".

References

Bajt, A. (1991), "Irrelevance of the Soft Budget Constraint for the Shortage Phenomenon", *Economics of Planning,* no. 24, pp. 1-12.

Bajt, A. (1992), *A Property Rights Analysis of the Transition Problems in the East,* Institute of Economics, Ljubljana, p. 26.

Gomulka, S. (1985), "Kornai's soft budget constraint and the shortage phenomenon: A criticism and restatement", *Economics of Planning,* no. 19, pp. 1-11.

Kornai, J. (1980), *Economics of Shortage,* North Holland, Amsterdam.

Kornai, J. (1993), "Anti-Depression Cure for Ailing Postcommunist Economies" (interview), *Transition,* February.

Mencinger, J. (1989), "The Quagmire of Socialism", *Communist Economies,* no. 1, pp. 385-393.

Pinto, Belka, Krajewski (1993), "Transforming State Enterprises in Poland: Evidence on Adjustment by Manufacturing Firms", *Brookings Papers on Economic Activity,* pp. 213-270.

Urban, L. (1990), "Objectives, Methods and Problems of Privatization", in *Privatization in Eastern Europe,* Proceedings of the Conference "Privatization: How to Use This Instrument for Economic Reform in Eastern Europe", Vienna, 17-18 November 1990.

ANNEX

(to comments by J. Mencinger on Part I)

The differences in the former socialist countries' capabilities for successful transition are indicated by the ranking, summarising recently published data by the *Emerging Market Economies Report 1993* (World Economic Forum, 1993).

The ranking of countries by their transitional ability

	(1)	(2)	(3)	(4)	(5)	(6)	(7)	(8)	(9)	(10)
				middle size economies						
Czechoslovakia	3	1	1	3	1	1	1	6	17	2.12
Poland	1	4	2	4	4	2	2	2	21	2.63
Hungary	2	2	3	5	7	3	3	3	28	3.50
Romania	4	6	4	2	8	4	4	4	36	4.50
Ukraine	6	8	7	7	5	7	5	1	46	5.75
Bulgaria	9	5	5	1	3	5	9	8	47	5.88
Kazakhstan	8	3	9	9	2	6	8	5	50	6.25
Byelorussia	5	7	8	8	6	8	6	7	55	6.88
Uzbekistan	7	9	7	7	9	9	7	8	63	7.88
				small economies						
Slovenia	1	4	1	2	4	1	1	2	16	2.00
Croatia	2	3	2	8	1	2	3	5	26	3.25
Estonia	5	1	3	6	2	5	4	3	29	3.63
Lithuania	7	2	7	3	3	8	5	1	36	4.50
Moldova	4	5	4	5	6	6	2	6	38	4.75
Macedonia	3	7	5	1	5	3	7	8	39	4.88
Armenia	8	8	6	4	7	7	6	7	53	6.63
Kyrgyzstan	6	6	8	7	8	4	8	4	53	6.63

The ranking is based on 192 economic, social, and political indicators which are grouped into eight determinants of competitiveness: (1) domestic economic strength, (2) degree of internationalisation, (3) proficiency of government, (4) quality of financial structure, (5) quality of infrastructure, (6) managerial skills, (7) science and technology, and (8) peoples' characteristics. Sums of ranks (column 9) and average rank (10) are calculated for each group separately.

PART II – FINANCIAL SECTOR REFORM

Chapter 4

THE BANKING SYSTEM IN RUSSIA

Carlo Boffito*)

The recent evolution of the banking system in Russia is further evidence of both the government's inadequacy in managing the national economy and of the chaotic and primitive process by which the private sector of the economy has emerged in a spontaneous fashion. The management skills of the Russian central authorities are limited by the difficulties of using traditional structures or creating new ones. As a result, the Russian banking system has evolved in the absence of an adequate legal framework and without the central authorities being able to provide adequate direction and supervision.

The prevailing radical view is that each inch lost by the state in withdrawing from economic involvement has been a gain for economic reform and liberalisation. This view seems to be based on the recognition of necessity – i.e. inability to manage the economy from the centre, at least for some time – and on the spontaneous movement of the market's expansive forces, rather than on the radical political camp's ability to take action. And this can be substantiated in several ways, for example by looking at the progress of the banking system.

---

*) University of Turin, Italy.

4.1 The banking structure

By year-end 1993, some 1,900 banks had been registered at the Central Bank of Russia. By western standards, this number still appears to be far less than adequate if compared with the population numbers. Yet if branches are accounted for, the banking-to-population ratio tends to come closer to the branch density figures usually found in the industrial countries of the West.

Furthermore, the banks are highly concentrated geographically. At the end of June 1993, almost 40 per cent of them had their head offices in Moscow. As a result, a banking marketplace with multiple competitors has blossomed in the capital, while competition between banks is almost entirely lacking in the rest of the country. Just one bank is operating in many cities – often after turning the local branch of the Promstroybank of the USSR into a commercial bank. Other inhabited centres can lie a thousand kilometres away from the nearest bank. Even if the issue of banking competition is viewed in terms of branches, the picture remains unchanged. Of the 42,570 branches of the first 100 largest Russian banks, 40,278 (94 per cent) were branches of the Sberbank – the savings bank of the Russian Federation – at end of June 1993. As a result, wide areas of the country are deprived of any banking services except those provided by the savings banks.

Table 4.1

Percentage shares of the different types of banks[a)] as of 1 July 1993

types of bank	number of banks	assets	capital	loans	deposits	profits	branches	employees
APB	12	16.2	17.1	24.3	9.3	12.8	53.9	34.2
PSB	37	25.0	22.1	21.0	22.0	44.8	27.2	34.9
ZHSB	12	16.1	11.3	8.6	14.6	19.0	8.2	43.1
SB	14	10.0	13.9	7.0	9.6	8.4	4.0	6.8
NB	23	32.7	35.6	39.1	44.5	15.0	6.7	11.0
Total	98	100.0	100.0	100.0	100.0	100.0	100.0	100.0

a) For notes see *Table 4.2*.

Russian banks are classed according to their origins, which have greatly shaped the direction of, and opportunities for, their growth (*Tables 4.1* and *4.2*).

Three major groups of banks can be identified, though a few special cases should also be accounted for. The first group includes the banks – 38.5 per cent of all banks registered in early May 1993 – that emerged as spin-offs of the three big specialised banks originating from the reform of the Soviet banking system in July 1987: the Agroprombank, the Promstroybank, and the Zhilsotsbank of the USSR, whose initial tasks were to finance the agro-industrial, manufacturing and construction sectors, and the local economy and residential building, respectively. The banks in this first group have been incorporated as joint-stock companies mainly owned by large enterprises, and, to a minor extent, by government entities. The second group includes "sector banks", i.e. those set up by applying funds formerly in the hands of government departments or other sector-specific agencies. The third group is made up of new banks, whose equities have been contributed by large enterprises or groupings of large enterprises, or through investments by new private or cooperative businesses the so-called "new commercial structures". Finally, a few cases should be viewed in isolation, outside the general classification, such as the Vneshtorgbank, the Vnesheconombank, the Sberbank, and the foreign banks. The Vneshtorgbank of the Russian Federation was set up in 1991 as a state bank for foreign trade by using some of the former Zhilsotsbank's facilities. Thereafter, Vneshtorgbank has taken over most of the Vnesheconombank, which will only continue in operation as an agency for the rescheduling and service of the Soviet Union's external debt. Twelve banks partly owned by foreign financial institutions have been registered so far with the Central Bank of Russia, and the two former-Comecon government-owned banks could be added to this group. Yet, only three of them were in operation at year-end 1993, and only one, the Mezhdunarodnyi Moskovskii Bank (MMB), has adequate built-up experience since it was first established in the time of the USSR.

MMB has performed outstandingly, and it ranked second by asset value among Russian banks in June 1993. (See *Table 4.3)* The negotiations for its formation were started by Banca Commerciale Italiana back in September 1986, even before the former Soviet Union's Joint-Venture Companies Act was published in January 1987. It was later incorporated as a joint bank owned by five western and three Russian banks, and it was started up as such in October 1989. The former Comecon's two banks, the International Bank for Economic Cooperation (IBEC) and the International Investment Bank were turned into joint-stock companies, the shareholders of which are the governments of the former Comecon countries. These banks have performed very poorly out of their shareholders' neglect, and Hungary even disposed of its share in IBEC in April 1992.

Two preliminary points must be made before reviewing the figures about the Russian banks' operations. First, there is ample evidence that the balance sheet and income statement figures furnished by these banks can hardly be relied upon, blemished as they are by far too much accounting duplication. For example, insider lending by a bank's head office to its branches often inflate the amount of its assets, a bank's own shares re-purchased by it and in its possession are not deducted from its share capital, or a bank's reserves are frequently manipulated in many ways in order to present a more attractive image of the bank than it is in fact. The first banks to publish correct figures have been the Unikombank, the Sberbank, the MMB, and the "Delovaya Rossiya" bank.

Table 4.2

Average ratios for the different types of banks[a)] as of 1 July 1993

types of bank	IB/L	K/A	R/A	Lo/A	D/L	A/E	D/E
APB	49.2	4.8	19.3	68.4	29.7	126.3	32.5
PSB	23.7	5.8	23.4	48.2	39.5	203.4	75.0
ZHSB	8.1	7.8	35.2	37.4	51.5	791.2	350.4
SB	10.7	8.3	39.6	36.2	50.4	816.4	421.0
NB	6.4	11.5	43.1	33.9	57.1	837.8	611.7

Notes to Tables 4.1 and 4.2: a) Covering the 98 largest commercial banks.

APB Banks created by using spin-offs of Agroprombank of the USSR
PSB Banks created by spin-offs of Promstroybank of the USSR
ZHSB Banks created by using the Zhilsotsbank of the USSR (except for Vneshtorgbank)
SB Sector Banks
NB "New Banks", i.e. all other banks (except for the Sberbank)

IB/L Liabilities to other banks (including CBR) as % total liabilities
K/A Capital as % assets
R/A Reserves (cash, funds on correspondence accounts with other banks and CBR) as % assets
Lo/A Loans as % total assets
D/L Deposits as % total liabilities
A/E Assets per employee (million roubles)
D/E Deposits per employee (million roubles)

Source: Ekonomika i zhizn', no. 41, 1993.

Second, because of a highly devalued exchange rate – especially in 1992 and in the first half of 1993 – the figures of foreign exchange transactions can be dramatically misleading. Rather than being recorded as separate entries, foreign exchange transaction amounts are added to those of transactions in roubles after translation at current exchange rates. For example, foreign currency transactions accounted for five sixths of the total transactions of the Inkombank, which ranked sixth among the largest Russian banks, was rated as one among the healthiest new banks, and operated 19 branches with 2,039 employees at the end of June 1993. Another, even more astounding, example of the distorting nature of foreign exchange transactions is provided by the MMB, which, though not an offshore bank, virtually makes no transactions in roubles. Without branches – the one in St. Petersburg having only been opened in October 1993 – and with less than 400 employees (among whom the number of those engaging in ancillary services far exceeded international standards), it was ahead of the Sberbank, which employed 185,500 at the end of June 1993, in the Russian banks' ranking by asset value. One final example is the Vneshtorgbank, the bank for foreign trade – by far the topmost Russian bank in terms of asset value, with 10 branches and 1,229 employees at the end of June 1993. (See *Table 4.3)* In the aggregate balance sheet figures of Russian commercial banks at the beginning of June 1993, foreign transactions accounted for 48.1 per cent of assets, and 40.4 per cent of liabilities.

Once again, the increased ability of the new banks (MMB, Inkombank, Tokobank, Kredobank, etc.) to attract deposits and make loans despite the smaller number of branches and employees is the net result of the distorting effects of exchange rates. By far the greatest part of foreign-currency deposits are re-deposited with the international banking industry, while an almost negligible proportion is offered in the Russian inter-bank market and used to make loans to non-institutional customers. Obviously, through the reputation of its incorporators and its higher efficiency, the MMB can comfortably attract huge foreign-currency deposits (in excess of $ 3 billion in its balance sheet as of 31 December 1992), most of which are placed with major international banks.

Table 4.3

The Top 30

end of

Bank		headoffice	assets[a)]	authorised capital[a)]	credits[a)]
1.	Vneshtorgbank RF	Moscow	7.545	486	56
2.	Intermosbank	Moscow	3.010	152	2.898
3.	Sberbank RF (Savings bank)	Moscow	2.605	315	1.524
4.	Rossel'khozbank	Moscow	2.486	252	1.858
5.	Mosbuzinesbank	Moscow	2.008	75	198
6.	Inkombank	Moscow	1.038	36	218
7.	Promstroybank	Moscow	---	---	252
8.	Imperal	Moscow	867	106	104
9.	Tokobank	Moscow	726	162	378
10.	Moscow Industrial Bank	Moscow	---	---	162
11.	Unikombank	Moscow	489	37	217
12.	Kredobank	Moscow	448	31	39
13.	Promstroybank	St. Petersburg	440	21	94
14.	AKIB NTP "Menatep"	Moscow	---	---	184
15.	Elektrobank	Moscow	342	36	275
16.	Zapsibikombank	Tyumen'	327	11	87
17.	Vozrozhdenie	Moscow	315	16	132
18.	Stolichnyy	Moscow	309	61	19
19.	Yugorskiy	Nizhnevartovsk	307	18	147
20.	Mezhregionbank	Moscow	300	30	120
21.	AvtoVAZbank	Tol'yatti	286	57	64
22.	Neftekhimbank	Moscow	280	17	106
23.	Bashprombank	Ufa	268	18	113
24.	Sankt-Petersburg	St. Petersburg	267	12	48
25.	Chelindbank	Chelyabinsk	---	---	94
26.	Narodnyy	Moscow	233	13	105
27.	Konversbank	Moscow	220	15	31
28.	Enisey	Krasnoyarsk	220	12	98
29.	Kuzbassprombank	Kemerovo	191	11	118
30.	Mezhkombank	Moscow	188	17	48

a) In billion roubles. - b) Debts vis-à-vis other banks/liabilities, per cent. - c) Capital/assets, per

Source: Ekonomika i zhizn', no. 41, 1993.

Russian Banks

June, 1993

deposits[a]	profit[a]	IB/L[b]	K/A[c]	number of branches	number of employees
2.804	40	0.43	6.44	10	1229
2.840	29	0.00	5.05	0	310
1.959	---	0.00	12.08	40278	185500
700	63	50.13	10.15	1087	21852
813	47	10.82	3.71	36	3000
719	14	1.60	3.50	19	2039
---	30	---	---	42	2304
449	15	1.21	12.25	0	180
422	9	2.80	22.34	17	648
---	30	---	---	---	---
203	34	11.04	7.66	59	3534
171	9	0.58	6.90	20	1500
195	23	0.58	4.70	36	3033
---	8	---	---	---	---
46	11	34.69	10.44	25	540
151	15	8.28	3.36	29	1510
150	15	20.15	4.99	48	2524
66	5	2.31	19.89	1	324
192	5	3.86	5.76	5	550
155	26	4.43	10.10	43	1143
156	17	5.74	19.85	18	2006
200	4	1.64	6.16	8	200
162	16	1.21	6.78	30	1370
135	13	2.10	4.65	18	1505
---	19	---	---	---	---
179	10	2.16	5.73	0	250
191	6	4.38	6.87	7	495
113	9	20.52	5.52	32	1119
67	12	18.09	5.78	64	1317
88	7	4.41	9.22	3	253

cent.

4.2 Banking operations

By mid-1983, rouble-denominated deposits from enterprises and organisations on current accounts (on which no interest is accruing) and accounts of other kinds were eight times larger than those from households. A significant proportion of these deposits is collected by banks originating from the restructuring of the Promstroybank of the USSR (*Table 4.1),* which resulted in the creation of the Moscow-based central Promstroybank and a number of regional Promstroybanks (*Table 4.3)* more or less closely linked with the central Promstroybank.

As *Table 4.2* shows, the least heavily capitalised banks – those spun off from the Agroprombank and the Promstroybank of the USSR – are also those showing the largest share of loans among their assets, and being forced to resort most heavily to the inter-bank market (including centralised credit) to raise funds. They are also the least liquid (see the R/A (Reserves/Assets) ratio in *Table 4.2)* as well as the least efficient of all banks. Largely because of misleading exchange-rate effects, the new banks appear to be the most efficient ones in terms of assets and liabilities per employee. Yet, a deeper scrutiny would place them below international efficiency standards – at least twice as high as the Russian level. The high profits reported by the banks spun off from the re-organisation of the Promstroybank of the USSR have been the result of its low cost of funding, and possibly even of accounting standards not fully reflecting the degree of risk and performance of its loans and advances.

As no limitations are imposed by law on the maturity dates of the transactions Russian banks are allowed to make, the stage is set for the development of universal banks. Yet, this description should be regarded more as a desired outcome than a reality. Most rouble-denominated deposits from the households are collected by the Sberbank, which accounted for 75 per cent of total household deposits in early August 1993, thanks to its pervasive branch network. Because of the other banks' competition, this percentage has dramatically declined since early 1993 (90.4 per cent) and even more so since 1990, when the Sberbank was the only bank with which households were allowed to deposit money. Because of the highly concentrated deposits from both the households and the enterprises, and the somewhat unrefined tools the central bank applies to its monetary policies, the inter-bank market has come to the forefront to play a major role (*Table 4.3).*

The interest rates applied by the Sberbank to household deposits ranged (1 October 1993) from 40 per cent on sight deposit to 180 per cent on savings deposits exceeding 5 million roubles with one-year maturity. Unlike those with the other banks, household deposits with the Sberbank are fully guaranteed by the state.

In the other banks, deposits from the households are very rare. Though the interest rates on household deposits with commercial banks are 40 to 50 percentage points higher than those applied by the Sberbank, this interest rate differential between the Sberbank and the other banks is obviously justified by the easier access one can have to Sberbank branches, the households' established habit to go to the Sberbank, and the services the latter has often to offer on an exclusive basis (e.g., payments to public entities) as well as – though to a somewhat lesser extent, it seems – the state guarantee of deposits with the Sberbank.

Because of inflationary pressures, under which Russian banks are led to take the returns on their investments at the earliest possible time, and because of the uncertainties surrounding the borrowing firms' future solvency or their very existence, commercial banks offer loans almost exclusively short-term. At the beginning of July 1993, the short-term share of the banking system's total lending was 96.4 per cent. Average maturity is around two months. Not entirely for fun, it is often said in Russian banking circles that short-term credit is one month, medium-term three months, and long-term six months. The only sources of medium and long-term credit are directed loans made by the central bank or under the state budget. The interest rates applied by commercial banks were (November 1993) 240-250 per cent on a yearly basis. As a large share of deposits come through non-interest-bearing checking accounts, the spreads between average deposit and lending interest rates are very wide. Annual interest rates appear to be comparatively low relative to the inflation rate, but a far higher level would be arrived at if the compounded rate were computed on a monthly or quarterly basis.

As the Sberbank incurs higher funding costs, its profitability must be based on the volume of transactions. Accordingly, it has split its investments into loans to households (around 25 per cent of total assets) and "commercial loans" (more than one-half of its assets), which include loans in the inter-bank market (90 per cent of commercial loans) and loans to enterprises. Commercial loans are mainly intended for large firms because financing start-up enterprises is looked upon as involving exceedingly high risks. The Sberbank's lending interest rates are 235 per cent a year (230 per cent for shareholder borrowers) in the inter-bank market, and 245 per cent (240 for shareholders) on enterprise loans. Average maturities are less than three months. Household loans are largely granted for the building, purchase or re-structuring of town dwellings or dachas.

The Russian monetary authorities and foreign consultants have recently discussed several possible approaches to re-organising the Sberbank, including the establishment of new thrift institutions to introduce more competition into the industry, the preservation of traditional functions to provide the bank with some characters of a postal savings bank, or the development of the Sberbank into a universal bank. The Sberbank seems to have, by now, grown into a somewhat independent business (though 50 per cent of its shares are owned by the Central Bank) strong enough to impose its own plan: to reinforce its present structure while moving towards the strategic goal of using its widespread branch network to serve the needs of large firms operating throughout the national territory, such as Aeroflot, large retail chains, and companies distributing oil products.

The new commercial banks' loans are primarily directed to financing the banks' own incorporators and shareholders and, secondarily, to trade, an area in which private firms thrive very successfully. Strategically, the new banks tend to move, in the medium term, towards raw-material extraction and processing operations and in the longer term towards technologically advanced industries.

The significance of foreign-currency lending is related to the growth of the private trade sector, which retails mainly imported goods. The interest rates on foreign-currency deposits ranged (early November 1993) from 3 per cent to 2 to 3 percentage points above market rates for large-size deposits. Interest rates on short-term foreign exchange loans are in excess of 14 per cent a year – the minimum rate in the inter-bank market – and can attain 25 per cent or more. The trade sector is also served by money-lenders offering foreign-currency loans at 20 per cent a month, and rouble loans at 1 per cent a day.

The high interest rates on foreign-currency loans is not due only to the detachment of the Russian banking market from the international market; other factors are the moratorium on the country's external debt and the risk of exposure to start-up enterprises, and also the high profits that can arise from the sale of imported goods. Foreign currencies flow into the Russian system mainly from the exporting firms' retention quotas and from funds illegally deposited abroad and repatriated. Foreign-currency deposits of the former Soviet Union's banks – including the Central Bank of Russia – with the international banks reporting to the Bank for International Settlements grew from $ 7.9 bn at end-1991 to $ 12.2 bn at end-1992, and $ 15.9 bn at end-June 1993.

Funds for investment

The banks' rouble-based activities are mainly supported by centralised and directed credit (*tselevye kredity*) – the only instrument by which the Russian monetary policy is effected at present. The total amount of the Central Bank's credit is split by the Credit Policy Commission on a quarterly basis into funds to finance the state's budget deficit at a 10 per cent annual interest rate, inter-state credits intended for other former Soviet republics, and credits directed to the economy at large, 70 per cent of which from the Central Bank and the remaining 30 per cent from the budget. The credits in the third class are further split into several programmes – rural programmes, programmes for military enterprise conversion, programmes aimed at the Northern Territories and at the development of the energy industry, etc. – and issued to commercial banks for delivery to target-sectors or enterprises. It would seem, therefore, that the central authorities have a powerful industrial policy instrument they can use to direct productive resources towards investments better matching the new demand breakdown. In fact, according to many observers, it has been found that the targets to which centralised credits are directed are the result of inconsistent, fragmented negotiations between the various government departments, groupings of enterprises, and individual enterprises.

Directed loans, which take up the whole supply of high-powered money to banks, are mainly issued to the banks originating from restructuring the Agroprombank and the Promstroybank of the USSR, and to sector-banks (both usually referred to as "channel banks") at the official rate of discount. Channel-banks are then allowed to charge only a 3 per cent spread. Yet, since these funds are already directed, they require no particular risk assessment – this being an added defect of this form of lending – so that no significant costs are involved in their management. In theory, a bank may withhold centralised credits from an enterprise considered not creditworthy, but this is a very rare occurrence. Enterprises, and often banks (which are supposed to take the risk), tend to treat centralised credits as transfers. As the situation further progresses towards the economy's stabilisation and the conduct of a normal monetary policy, complex rehabilitation programmes – of which there is no sign for the time being – will have to be set up to restore operational health to the banks that have funnelled centralised credit to enterprises.

4.3 Pressures for modernisation

Through its new independence, sanctioned in the Constitution (Article 75) adopted following the referendum of 12 December 1993, the Central Bank of Russia will try to eliminate directed lending, which is expected to become the state's full responsibility in the form of budgetary subsidies. The Central Bank will then be left free to conduct its monetary policy with more appropriate instruments. In 1994, after several postponements, credit is scheduled to be auctioned to banks for the first time, and a re-financing scheme is now being prepared.

The Central Bank is also expected to improve its supervision activities. A supervision department and an inspection department have been set up, and, as early as April 1991, Directive No. 1 defined capital adequacy, liquidity, and lending risk standards, along with minimum capital requirements and maximum exposure to single borrowers. Yet Mr Gerashchenko, the President of the Central Bank of Russia, curtly stated in a recent interview to the *Nezavisimaya Gazyeta* (28 October 1993) that "there exists no firmly established bank control system at the Central Bank". In fact, the Central Bank's departments determine supervisory ratios without being able to audit the accuracy of the figures furnished by its peripheral offices.

In 1993, the Central Bank has tried to limit the creation of new banks and to strengthen existing ones by raising minimum capital requirements to 100 million roubles – though not without some resistance on the part of the Association of Russian Banks. In January 1993, only 12 per cent of the banks had a share capital in excess of 100 million roubles, and the proportion had risen to 24 per cent by early June. It should be pointed out, however, that this 24 per cent accounted for 77.7 per cent of the banking system's entire capital. Most banks easily increased their capital by the appointed date (1 July 1993), some merged, and others even obtained a postponement of the deadline by which their re-capitalisation was expected to occur. In November, 25 per cent of all banks had not yet met minimum capital requirements. The Association of Small and Medium-sized Banks was created in the same month to strengthen the lobby of ailing bankers.

Russian banks have tried to bar foreign banks from entering the Russian market out of fear that the MMB experience (see above) might be repeated and themselves be deprived, as a result, not so much of their most highly skilled personnel – as they have alleged – but of the ability to collect profitable foreign-currency deposits. In March 1993, in the face of repeated liberal statements, the Central Bank restricted foreign banks' equity commitments to 12 per cent of the overall capital of the banks operating in Russia. Finally, on 17 November 1993, a presidential decree was issued which was gladly received by Russian banks. It inhibited all banks whose capital was held by foreign entities in excess of 50 per cent that had not began to serve resident customers by 15 November from doing so until 1 January 1996, even if they were already licensed by the Central Bank. Citybank, which was licensed in October 1993, opened its Moscow branch in January 1994. According to its representatives' statements to the press, it seems to rely on the sympathy of the Central Bank of Russia – which criticised the President's decree of 17 November – in its resolve not to restrict its operations to off-shore transactions.

The Russian interbank clearing system is backward, though its operations have been improved through the reduction of the average lead-time for inter-regional transfers from two months to two weeks. Such delays result in a large float giving banks exceedingly large resources obtained at no cost. In this area, banks and other financial institutions have shown considerable initiative by using advanced technologies (some brand-new; others inherited, such as the "Iskra" line originally installed to provide communication links between the Communist Party of the Soviet Union's local and central governing bodies), to open correspondence accounts and create local clearing houses – the latter not always approved by the Central Bank, whose responsibility is to develop a nation-wide communication network for clearing purposes.

The building-up of payment arrears between enterprises which begun immediately after the liberalisation of trade in January 1992, has not yet been addressed. This is in part the result of the commercial banks' extreme caution in lending anything above directed loans to enterprises.The use of commercial paper is hindered by the absence of an adequate legal framework – merely consisting of the Soviet government's decree of 7 August 1937 – which has resulted in the banks' reluctance to guarantee bills of exchange.

The improvement in banking activities is expected to progress considerably faster through the implementation of the International Standard Bank Programme which the World Bank developed in 1993. In 1994, the World Bank and the EBRD are expected to grant loans to the Russian Federation for $ 300 and $ 200 million, respectively, as a part of international finance assistance programmes. These amounts are expected to be loaned through an Apex agency to some 20 banks identified so far (but the number is still open) as complying with international rules on banks' financial reporting and operations. These 20 banks are to be responsible for making loans at their own risk for production re-structuring.

Under the original project, the Central Bank of Russia was intended to be the initiator of the International Standard Bank Programme. That the World Bank, jointly with the EBRD, has decided to take independent action is further evidence of the difficulties Russian monetary authorities are facing in pursuing a consistent policy of close supervision and guidance of the Russian banking system.

4.4 Long-term investment: financing problems

The area in which the slowest advances have been made – and stronger efforts are required – is that of long-term lending institutions. Because of its past experience with other countries, the World Bank firmly opposes the creation of government-controlled investment banks. The two existing investment banks in Russia – the Russian Bank for Reconstruction and Development, and the Russian Project Finance Bank – will be reinforced with some venture-capital funds; these are to be set up under the programme adopted by the Tokyo G-7 summit in July 1993 to provide support to the Russian economy. The original project was far more ambitious, but western countries' budget difficulties have resulted in its being down-sized to three or four funds of $ 20 mn each, two to be financed by the United States, one by the European Bank for Reconstruction and Development, and possibly one by the International Finance Corporation.

In view of the difficulties of financing production activities, particularly investment and reconstruction, international aid ought to be focused on the establishment of financial institutions able to supply long-term credit facilities and to perform investment banking functions. Though the International Standard Bank Programme and the provision of venture-capital funds are major efforts, they are still inadequate to meet actual needs. To set up long-term lending and investment banks with sufficient capital to allow appropriate funding and retain their shareholdings long enough would be a more viable approach. The World Bank's worries arising from its unfavourable experience with developing countries can be entirely understood. But investment banks created through western aid could be managed by a shareholding mix of multilateral organisations, national entities, and foreign private financial institutions (whose equity contributions could be in part guaranteed) in order to curb or restrict the political influence of the host countries – Russia, in this instance. This appears, however, to be a belated approach in that most available Western financial aid has already been earmarked for other uses.

References

"Banking reform in central and eastern Europe" (1993), *Current Economic Issues. EBRD Economic Review*, July.

"Ekonomicheskii obzor: finansovo – kreditnaya sfera" (1993), *Ekonomika i zhizn'*, no. 39.

"Iz otchëta Tseutral'nago banka RF" (1993), *Den'gi i kredit*, no. 8.

"K obsuzhdeniyu proekta dolgosrochnoi kontseptsii razvitiya denezhno-kreditnoi sistemy Rossii" (1993), *Den'gi i kredit*, nos. 1, 2 and 3.

"Russia. The banking system in the transition" (1993), The World Bank, 26 May.

"Tekushchie tendentsii v denezhno – kreditnoi sfere" (1993), *Statistiko-analiticheskie operativnye materialy*, Central Bank of Russia, September.

"100 krupneishikh bankov. Kommentarii eksperta" (1993), *Ekonomika i zhzn'*, no. 41.

Chapter 5

MONEY DEMAND, BANK CREDIT AND ECONOMIC PERFORMANCE IN THE FORMER SOCIALIST ECONOMIES[1)]

Guillermo A. Calvo[*)]
Manmohan S. Kumar[*)]

Abstract

This paper examines factors determining the allocation of bank credit to the enterprise sector, and the implications of this allocation for aggregate supply and macro-economic performance, in the former socialist economies. It first develops a model to explain how changes in demand for money by the household sector directly influence the availability of working capital, which in turn determines aggregate output and employment. It then examines factors influencing the allocation of bank credit between enterprises and other borrowers, in particular the government. Finally, the paper discusses relative merits of bank finance and equity capital in financing medium- and long-term investment, and constraints on the development of efficient equity markets.

5.1 Introduction

A salient characteristic of former socialist economies is the strong and persistent fall in (measured) output, which has taken most economists and policy makers by surprise. Although initial output disruptions were expected, their size and persistence were not. In fact, it was expected that the better incentive mechanisms of a market-oriented system would quickly unleash productive power by pushing the economy to its "production frontier".

---

1) This paper was prepared for The Vienna Institute for Comparative Economic Studies Workshop (Vienna, 21-25 November 1993) on "Transformation of the East European Economies 1989-1993: Critical Assessments and Ways out of the Crisis". The paper was published in IMF Staff Papers, June 1994. The authors are grateful to Gérard Bélanger, Adrienne Cheasty, Ajai Chopra, Fabrizio Coricelli, Eduard Hochreiter, Mark Lutz, Donald Mathieson, John Odling-Smee and Mark Stone for helpful comments and suggestions, and to Nadine Orosa for excellent research assistance.

*) Research Department, International Monetary Fund, Washington DC.

One possible explanation for the output collapse is that the necessary economic transformation is so profound that sizable destruction is needed before construction takes place. For this to be so, however, the output fall must be concentrated in sectors and activities displaying negative value added. Thus, if aggregate output were correctly measured GDP should rise, not fall. Berg and Sachs (1992), for example, argue that the output fall in Poland in 1990 was substantially less than that recorded, but still conclude that the fall was of the order of 7 per cent. Thus it appears that this type of explanation is insufficient.

Another explanation is "market failure". The main argument in that respect is that political events have overtaken economic reforms. There has been very little time to develop the institutions, the information base, and the expertise required for the normal operation of a regular capitalist economy. Market failure has been reflected in a number of interrelated areas such as trade and the provision of credit. Following the onset of the reform process, trade – particularly domestic trade – slowed down markedly, exacerbating the consequences of the collapse of trade among the CMEA partners. Bruno (1992) notes, for instance, that the size of the output decline in Eastern European countries in 1991 was directly related to their dependence on the CMEA market. According to this explanation, the proximate cause for the output decline has been trade implosion.

Given the rudimentary nature of the bond and equity markets, commercial banks, mostly state-owned, continue to dominate the financial sector in the East, and enterprises are heavily dependent on bank credit for both working capital and investment. A common characteristic has been a massive fall of real credit at the beginning of their transformation programmes and, as argued in Calvo and Coricelli (1994), firms resorted to informal and/or illegal devices like cutting wages below the statutory minimum or, falling into arrears with one another, with banks, or the government. Despite these efforts, weak credit may have been an element in output declines, and may continue to be important in the sluggish recovery underway in some of Eastern Europe.

In this paper we will pursue the "market failure" line and, in particular, focus on issues related to the operation of credit markets in the reform process. We examine the conditions under which output declines may reflect inadequate credit, not only at the beginning of the reform process, but also subsequently, and explore two key factors influencing the provision of credit to the enterprise sector: first, demand for bank deposits, which determines the availability of loanable funds; and second, constraints upon the banking sector, both endogenous and exogenous, limiting the credit which banks may want to extend to productive firms, whether in the state or the private sector, for a given amount of deposits.

These two explanations are complementary in that even if the banks are able to provide credit, a number of factors may constrain their willingness to do so. In the context of providing direct subsidies to the enterprise sector as a way of making up for the inadequate credit provided by the banking sector, the paper also explores the policy trade-off between inflation and output. Such a trade-off is particularly important in the early stages of the transformation process when the liberalisation of prices and trade, together with an inherited monetary overhang, leads to serious problems of inflation stabilisation and in the balance of payments. In addition to the provision of working capital, the paper also briefly notes the constraints on the banking sector in providing longer-term finance. These constraints are in addition to those likely to inhibit lending in the short run and arise mainly because of the nature of lending contracts. The paper notes the role that equity funds could play in this context.

The following section provides a brief overview of the performance and policies in former socialist economies during the transition and notes the salient structural features of the economies. Section 5.3 sketches the basic conceptual framework that identifies some key characteristics of imperfect credit markets, paying special attention to their short-run macroeconomic effects and the trade-off between inflation, employment, and output. 5.4 explores implications of the model for the relationship between interest on bank deposits, money demand, and bank credit. 5.5 discusses the relationship between the provision of liquidity to the enterprise sector and the financing of public sector deficits. 5.6 examines more closely both the incentives and the constraints on the newly created commercial banks, most of which are still state-owned. 5.7 briefly discusses the relative merits of debt and equity capital for the longer-term financing needs of the enterprise sector, and a final section summarises the main conclusions of the paper. Tables and Figures will be found at the end of this chapter.

5.2 Policies and performance: a synopsis

Recent performance

There are four striking aspects of the performance of East European economies in the transition to a market-based system. First, as noted above, output has declined sharply, in several of the East European countries ranging cumulatively between 20 and 40 per cent over 1990-92 (*Table 5.1*). While output has begun to recover in Poland and former Czechoslovakia, it continues to decline, at a much reduced pace, in other countries. The decline in output has been accompanied by sharp increases in unemployment – in several countries close to 15 per cent of the work force – compared with virtually negligible *open* unemployment before the reform process. In the states of the former Soviet Union, which embarked on the transformation process in early 1992, the declines in output appear to be just as marked, if not greater, although open unemployment is so far limited.

Second, in the period immediately after price liberalisation – but not only then – inflation increased sharply. In some Eastern European countries inflation has been markedly reduced, but it still remains above 20 to 30 per cent a year in most countries. In Russia and the Ukraine, inflation rates have exceeded 25 per cent a month, and a move toward hyperinflation has appeared possible.

Third, in most countries large fiscal deficits have emerged, or persisted. A key feature has been the dramatic decline of tax revenue, largely because of the steep drop in output, which has cut tax revenue on turnover and business profits (Tanzi 1993). Business tax revenue was also adversely affected by the collapse of the former arrangements whereby the government had direct access to state enterprises' profits. The pronounced fall in government revenue has not been matched by an equal drop in public spending, despite the large cuts in public subsidies and in government infrastructural investment implemented in almost all countries (*Table 5.2*).

Fourth, although the external current account position improved initially owing both to a sharp decline in imports and an increase in exports of goods diverted from the former CMEA markets, it has subsequently worsened in several countries. A deterioration in the current account has, in general, not been offset by any marked increase in capital inflows. The real effective exchange rate of most countries has appreciated significantly since the onset of the reforms, adversely affecting the competitiveness of the industrial sectors.

These stylised features of performance reflect, and have been affected by, the stabilisation and structural reform policies pursued in many countries. The initial focus of macroeconomic policies was on containing the inflationary consequences of price liberalisation and what was considered to be a significant monetary overhang. Hence, the policy package consisted of a tight monetary and fiscal stance, with strict credit ceilings especially on credit to the enterprise sector. In addition, to reduce inflationary expectations, extensive use was made of nominal anchors including a fixing, or a pre-announced crawl, of the nominal exchange rate, and ceilings on nominal wages.

The macroeconomic policies were complemented by major structural reforms to increase competition, improve the micro-economic efficiency of the economies, and to hasten the way to a market-oriented system. Major reforms were envisaged, and implemented, in the trade sectors, making the economies more open, and in the fiscal sector, reducing the direct involvement of government in the economy. However, the restructuring and privatisation of industrial enterprises, as well as of the financial sector, has in general made little headway. The privatisation of large enterprises, in particular, is proceeding slowly, in part because of the concerns about the further rise in unemployment that would result.

Nevertheless, the structure of the economies is changing, although not nearly as fast as had been anticipated. The share of the private sector in total output has expanded sharply in, e.g., Poland and Hungary, accounted for mainly by newly created, rather than privatised, firms.[2)] Despite this, the bulk of industrial output still originates in the state sectors. Similarly, the financial sector continues to be dominated by the commercial banks, which, having originated in the mono-bank system, are mostly state owned, and despite a number of significant measures, continue to be saddled with a high proportion of unserviceable loans.[3)] There is an active and rapidly growing government

2) In Poland, for instance, the private sector share of GDP increased from under 30 per cent in 1989 to nearly 45 per cent in 1992, while in former Czechoslovakia and Hungary respectively, the share increased from under 5 per cent to 20 percent, and from 39 to 45 per cent. (See Schwartz et al. 1993.)

3) In Poland, while there has been a proliferation of private banks, they collectively account for a very small share of banking activity.

securities market in several countries, while equity and commercial bond markets are in their infancy. As shown below, the weak loan portfolio of banks, combined with the growth of securities markets, appear to have significant implications for the volume of credit channelled to the enterprise sector as a whole.

5.3 Basic conceptual framework

In this section, a simple model is developed to emphasise the role of working-capital credit in the determination of employment and output. It is motivated by the observation that the transition to the market economy entails a switch from a regime where credit is independent of the demand for money, to a regime in which it is dependent on it. The reason for this switch in regime is elaborated in the model and hinges on the fact that the bulk of credit in the transition economies is provided by the banking sector. The model also illustrates the likely short-run macroeconomic consequences of attempts to increase output by increasing government subsidies to firms.

A model of money demand and credit

Consider the case in which output is produced by labour alone under constant returns to scale. Labour is applied at time t and output is obtained at time $t + 1$. Firms have no initial liquidity, and wages have to be paid at the beginning of the production process (i.e., at time t).[4] Thus, under this assumption, credit is essential for the firm to be able to operate; if credit is not available output collapses even though the firm may be perfectly viable from an economic point of view.

We will denote the average (= marginal) labour productivity by γ.
Thus, profits per unit of employment at $t + 1$ are given by the following expression:

$$(1) \quad \gamma P_{t+1} - W_t (1 + i_t) = P_{t+1} [\gamma - w_t (1 + r_t)],$$

where P, W and i are the nominal price of output, wage and bank interest rate on loans, respectively; and r and w is the real interest rate on bank loans, i.e., $1 + r_t = (1 + i_t)P_t / P_{t+1}$, and the real wage respectively.

---

4) Equivalently, one can think of production occurring at time t, when labour has to be paid, but sales revenues do not accrue until time t + 1.

We assume initially that firms are price-, wage-, and interest rate-takers. Therefore, if profits are positive, profit-maximising firms will try to expand without limit, which would not be consistent with labour-market equilibrium.[5] On the other hand, if profits are negative, no production will be carried out. Therefore, equilibrium with positive and finite production requires that the square-bracketed expression in equation (1) be equal to zero; or, equivalently, that

$$(2) \quad \gamma = w_t (1 + r_t) \quad (\textit{factor-price frontier}).$$

Let B_t denote bank loans, in nominal terms, granted at time t. The liquidity-in-advance constraint referred to above takes the following form:

$$(3) \quad B_t = W_t N_t,$$

where N denotes employment at firms.

To close the model, we assume that labour supply is perfectly elastic at real wage $\underline{w}$. Thus, total output, y, satisfies:

$$(4) \quad y_t = \gamma N_t$$

The infinite-elasticity assumption captures a situation in which workers have employment opportunities outside the enterprise sector – the "informal" sector, say. The informal sector is not subject to the liquidity-in-advance constraint because production techniques are more primitive (i.e., labour productivity is lower than in the enterprise sector) and output is obtained within the period in which inputs are applied.[6] Thus, total output (at steady state) falls when resources are shifted away from the enterprise sector (i.e., when N falls).[7] (Below we will offer another, perhaps more plausible, interpretation.)

---

5) For the time being, we will assume that firms intend to honour their contractual obligations.

6) Thus, the informal sector may not appear to be an adequate way of modelling the emerging private sector in these economies, since the latter is supposed to be more efficient than traditional enterprises. However, in the context of the present model, since the informal sector is more labour intensive, labour productivity might fall (even though total factor productivity might increase).

7) Under this interpretation, total output should also include output from the informal sector. However, given the productivity differentials between the formal and informal sectors pointed out above, output as given by equation (4) is positively correlated with the all-inclusive output measure (which includes informal-sector output).

By liquidity-in-advance equation (3) and the labour-supply equation, we have

$$(5) \quad \frac{B_t}{P_t} = \underline{w}N_t .$$

Consequently, by (4) and (5), real credit determines employment at enterprises and output: the larger is real credit, the larger is employment at enterprises and national output.

Another scenario that would give essentially the same relationship between real credit and output is one where total employment at enterprises is constant (= 1, say), but effort is variable and proportional to the real wage. Thus, equation (5) would become $B_t/P_t = w_t$. Moreover, we would interpret variable N as effort, and assume $N = w/\underline{w}$ (i.e., proportionality between effort and the real wage). These assumptions, in conjunction with equation (4), would yield

$$y_t = \frac{\gamma B_t}{\underline{w}_t P_t} ,$$

which is also implied by equations (4) and (5). This alternative interpretation is attractive, because it implies a low (here, zero) response of employment to a fall in output, which is a salient characteristic of transition countries during the first stage of the transformation process. Also, if less effort is equivalent to more shirking, equation (4) would fully capture the standard GDP concept.[8)]

We will now endogenise real credit. Assuming, for simplicity, that commercial banks hold no wealth or foreign assets, we have

$$(6) \quad B_t + H_t = M_t ,$$

where H and M are bank reserves (held in the form of high-powered money) and deposits (assumed to be entirely held by households). Thus, assuming that neither households nor firms hold cash, M can be identified with money supply. Moreover, at equilibrium, H equals total high-powered money.

We assume that the minimum-reserve requirement, δ, is binding. Thus, $\delta M_t = H_t$, for all time t. Moreover, by (6),

$$(7) \quad \frac{B_t}{P_t} = (1 - \delta)\frac{M_t}{P_t} = (1 - \delta)\ L(\cdot) ,$$

where $L(\bullet)$ denotes the demand for real monetary balances, M/P.

---

8) For a more explicit shirking model with variable effort, see Calvo and Wellisz (1979).

Implications of the model

We can illustrate the main implications of the model in the special case in which the demand for real money is a constant, ℓ. Combining equations (5) and (7), we get the following employment-determination equation:

$$(8) \quad N_t = \frac{1 - \delta}{\underline{w}} \ell .$$

Thus, a fall in the demand for money, ℓ, provokes a fall in employment at enterprises and, by (4), in GDP. Notice that we get a contractionary effect from a decrease in the demand for money even though prices and wages are assumed to be perfectly flexible. The fundamental reason for such a relationship is that credit is essential for undertaking production at enterprises, and the real value of credit is intimately linked to the demand for real monetary balances by the public.[9)]

One way the government may try to increase output is via inflation. For instance, the government could increase subsidies to firms, and finance these simply by printing high-powered money, H. Recalling that $\delta M_t = H_t$, we have

$$(9) \quad P_t = \frac{H_t}{\delta \ell} .$$

Therefore, in the present setup, inflation is proportional to the rate of growth of high-powered money, H. The liquidity-in-advance condition (normalising the total number of enterprises to unity) is now

$$(10) \quad \frac{B_t}{P_t} + \frac{H_{t+1} - H_t}{P_t} = \underline{w}\, N_t ,$$

where $H_{t+1} - H_t$ is the subsidy. Thus, under inflation, the employment-determination equation becomes

$$(11) \quad \underline{w} N_t = (1 - \delta + \delta \pi_{t+1}) \ell ,$$

where $\pi_{t+1} = P_{t+1}/P_t - 1$ = inflation rate between periods t and $t + 1$. The second term on the right-hand-side of equation (11) reflects the fact that government is using the inflation tax to "finance" the enterprise sector.

---

9) The analysis does not assume that there was a shift in the demand for money. Rather, the main argument is based on the fact that there was a decline in M/P at the beginning of the transition process owing simply to the sharp increase in prices following their decontrol combined with monetary restraint.

Equation (11) illustrates an important policy tradeoff between inflation and employment and output. The tradeoff is more relevant in the short run when the demand for money, ℓ, is inelastic with respect to inflation. Eventually, however, the demand for money adjusts in a direction opposite to inflation. Thus, lower inflation eventually results in higher ℓ and possibly, recalling equation (8), *higher* employment and output. Notice, incidentally, that the employment-maximising inflation rate (at steady state), for $\delta < 1$, is less than the rate that maximises revenue from inflation (i.e., the value of π that maximises $\delta\pi L(\bullet)$); moreover, if the reserve requirement, δ, is low enough, the employment-maximising inflation rate (at steady state) could be zero or negative.[10)]

5.4 Banks and arrears

We will now examine the operations of commercial banks more closely, in particular the constraints and the incentives facing them. For simplicity, we assume that the operational costs of running banks are negligible. Therefore, if loans are fully serviced, nominal bank profits in the period from t to $t + 1$ are

$$(12) \quad i_t B_t - s_t M_t = [\, i_t (1 - \delta) - s_t]\, M_t \,,$$

where s_t is the nominal deposit interest rate for the period from t to $t + 1$. By factor-price frontier (2), if, as assumed, $\underline{w} < \gamma$, then the real interest rate on bank loans, r, will be positive. Consider now the realistic case in which inflation is non-negative. Then, the nominal interest rate on bank loans, i_t is also positive (since $1 + i_t = (1 + r_t)(1 + \underline{\pi}_{t+1})$). Thus, if the deposit interest rate, s_t, is zero, banks will display positive profits, unless the reserve requirement is 100 per cent (i.e., $\delta = 1$). Therefore, there is room for banks to offer positive interest rates on deposits without violating their budget constraints (zero bank-profits $s_t = (1 - \delta)i_t$). Since the demand for real monetary balances is an increasing function of the deposit rate, a possible employment-increasing policy is to pay interest on bank deposits. The tradeoff here is that if banks' profits are subject

---

10) Russia has recently been the paramount example of trying to employ the inflation strategy to prop up output, with no visible success.
This discussion has disregarded the fact that the existence of positive government subsidies to enterprises implies that firms will now exhibit positive profits. The latter would help to relax the liquidity constraint in future periods. This topic will be picked up in Section 5.4.

to taxes, higher interest on deposits by reducing bank profits would reduce tax liability and increase the fiscal deficit.

As noted above (5.1), firms in transition countries reacted to the credit crunch by falling into arrears with each other, the banks, or the government. Thus, in our example above, firms may choose not to repay their bank debts, implying that the liquid funds available to enterprises at the beginning of period $t + 1$ – assuming that no new credit is extended to the delinquent firm – will be $B_t(1 + i_t)$, which may well exceed the amount of credit received by firms if they had repaid their bank debt in full. However, firms' nonpayment may be counterproductive because it may fuel inflation and firms' *real* liquidity may fall, undermining enterprises' ability to increase employment and output.[11] We will expand on this point in the following discussion.

Consider first the case in which interest on bank deposits, s, equals zero. Then default on B_t drives bank profits to $-B_t$. However, banks would not go bankrupt in period $t + 1$, as long as the demand for bank deposits does not decline (i.e., if $M_{t+1} \geq M_t$). The latter condition is likely to be satisfied if inflation is non-negative and no panic (specifically, bank run) is produced. In this scenario, banks make "bad" loans, but the ultimate claimants (i.e., depositors) do not, on average, call them (by not withdrawing their bank deposits). However, even under these extremely favourable conditions, macroeconomic difficulties may occur. In the first place, it is unlikely that banks would have incentives to lend any further to enterprises, since they are likely to expect firms also to default on *new* bank credit.[12] Besides, normally bank profits are heavily taxed. Therefore, default on bank credit lowers fiscal revenue and increases fiscal

---

11) Although massive default may be counterproductive for enterprises, the individual firm may still find it optimal to default. This is so because the price level is determined by the market, not by the individual firm. The latter takes prices as given by the market, and in that context failing to repay bank debts adds to the firms' liquidity and ability to employ labour. This rationalises the possibility that atomistic firm behaviour may result in massive default on bank credit, even though, at the end of the day, no firm benefits from such action.

12) This issue is discussed in detail in Section 5.6 below where additional constraints on bank lending to firms are discussed. Here notice that even if, in principle, banks are capable of "riding the storm", they would run against bank regulations. Experience shows that banks are likely to try hiding their "bad" loans from the regulator, but they are eventually caught (by the regulator or by reality).

deficit. The latter, if monetised, increases inflation, undermining the firms' benefit from default, as noted earlier.

We will now consider the polar case in which the interest rate on bank deposits is set so that bank profits are zero (this would be their equilibrium level if banks operated under perfect competition and with no risk of default). In these circumstances, banks may run into difficulties if depositors fail to increase their demand for money (i.e., deposits) in period $t + 1$ to at least $M_t(1 + s_t)$, i.e., to its level in period t plus interest accruals. Moreover, the same argument shows that if the situation remains unchanged, deposits will have to keep increasing at a rate at least equal to the interest rate on bank deposits. Thus, in order for this to happen, the rate of inflation will also have to be equal to s_t – if the demand for real monetary balances remains constant – or higher if the demand for money falls with inflation – thus tending to invalidate the employment-enhancing effects of default in period $t + 1$, and causing a deterioration of the firms' real liquidity position later on.

The central policy dilemma is whether government intervention is called for under these circumstances. Not intervening probably implies higher inflation and lower output, as suggested by the above discussion. Furthermore, eventually banks are likely to sue delinquent firms, threatening to paralyse the enterprise sector and provoking a sizable fall in output and employment in the short run.

Alternatively, government may intervene by bailing out banks saddled with nonperforming loans. For example, this may take the form of the central bank lending new money to banks in exchange for their nonperforming loans. This is directly inflationary. Thus, if firms are not restructured and banks refuse to lend new funds to them, real liquidity at enterprises will fall, giving rise to higher unemployment. Therefore, to be successful, the bailout operation must also involve some kind of debt forgiveness that initially lowers enterprises' incentives to default. However, the main drawback of this rescue operation is that it entails "moral-hazard" – it may lead firms to expect similar operations in the future, resulting in a loss of control of money supply. The latter, in turn, by fuelling inflationary expectations, lowers the demand for money and, by (11), lowers employment at enterprises even further.

To recapitulate, our discussion has revealed that if enterprises are heavily dependent on bank credit for their day-to-day operations, then output is likely to be very sensitive to changes in the stock of real monetary balances. Thus, this approach helps to rationalise the fall in output that occurred in conjunction with price liberalisation. As shown in Calvo and Coricelli (1994) real bank credit suffered a precipitous fall immediately such reforms were implemented. Moreover, as the evidence in the following sections illustrates, real bank credit to firms has continued to decline even during the last year or two, although the reasons for this decline are somewhat different.

Our approach also sheds light on why it may be so difficult to improve output performance without igniting hyperinflation. Even though, in our interpretation, one cause for low output is low enterprise liquidity, injecting more liquidity through central bank credit could be counterproductive. Conceivably, more *nominal* credit could result in more *real* enterprise liquidity and, thus, output; however, more nominal credit implies higher inflation, which reduces the demand for money and the *stock* of real bank credit and, thus, output. The latter effect of higher inflation is likely to swamp the first beyond relatively low inflation rates. It is, of course, the case that in the short run, an increase in output because of higher nominal credit could lead to an increase in the demand for money, thus dampening the inflationary consequences. Nevertheless, even in this scenario, the effect on inflationary expectations could be substantial. Thus, inflation does not seem to be a promising strategy.

An unrealistic feature of the above example is that firms would (at equilibrium without default) exhibit zero profits. If profits were positive, reflecting in part the continuing oligopolistic structure of industry, then firms would be able to accumulate liquidity over time which, as argued in Calvo and Coricelli (1992), would help output recovery. As noted in Calvo and Coricelli (1994), however, this process of recovery could be slow if *inter alia* inflationary expectations remain high. Firms themselves may prefer to operate at low output levels if the opportunity cost of holding liquid assets is high, and, in addition, uncertainties are engendered by the speed and the extent of the privatisation process.

The process of enterprise liquidity accumulation could be enhanced in a noninflationary way by endowing firms with an initial stock of liquidity. However, if a further rise in the initial price level is to be prevented, simultaneously households' liquidity will have to shrink. This could be achieved, for example, by an initial partial confiscation of households' bank deposits. The main difficulty with such policy is that if not swiftly carried out, it may give rise to high inflation (which, as argued above, does not bode well for an output-recovery programme). As soon as the public anticipates a sharp price rise or deposit confiscation, it will try to get rid of most of its monetary balances.

The latter difficulty explains the general reluctance to increase enterprise liquidity at the beginning of reform programmes. However, our discussion suggests that the government should avoid burdening firms with liquidity-using transactions in the short run. For example, if firms start with a stock of debt (possibly acquired in the period of central planning) that has to be serviced in the short run, a case could be made for debt rescheduling.

5.5 Bank credit and fiscal deficits

The above analytical framework can readily be extended to help shed light on an important but puzzling feature of recent economic performance in several East European countries: that is, how, despite increasing fiscal deficits, inflation stabilisation has been relatively successful. As discussed below, the answer to this puzzle lies mainly in increased private saving, or perhaps more accurately, a rechannelling of private saving into the financial sector. That is, an increase in money demand led to an increase in loanable funds. However, the increased availability of funds was not used to provide increased credit to the enterprise sector but was used instead largely to finance fiscal deficits. Thus, as the analysis below shows, the availability of loanable funds is a necessary but not sufficient condition for the provision of credit to the enterprise sector.

The factors behind the increase, or continuation of, fiscal deficits are similar across countries. In all countries the share of government revenue in GDP has fallen considerably following tax reforms, which lowered tax burdens. In addition, falls in consumption squeezed consumption tax revenues, and the plummeting activity in the enterprise sector reduced revenues from state enterprise profits taxes *(Table 5.2)*.[13] Tax liabilities of the emerging private sector have been, in any case, difficult to monitor, and avoidance and evasion have been common. With regard to government expenditure, although subsidies and current and capital expenditures have been cut, social safety net expenditures (including pensions, unemployment benefits, and social assistance) have increased rapidly.

---

13) In Poland in 1990 and the former Czechoslovakia in 1991 enterprise profits were artificially inflated by the revaluation of inventories, and, as there was little or no inflation adjustment in the profits tax, most of these paper profits were transferred to the government. As Schaffer (1992) shows, about half of the swing in Poland's budget position, from a surplus of 3 per cent of GDP in 1990 to a deficit in 1991 of over 5 per cent of GDP, was accounted for by the fall in profit taxes (due in large part to a decrease in the inflation bias).

Therefore, in general, the share of expenditure in GDP has remained rather stable. The net result has been a marked increase in fiscal deficits in, for example, Poland and Hungary where in 1992 they exceeded 7 per cent of GDP.

Although the countries differ considerably in their access to foreign financing, the key to the above puzzle lies in the surge, or quite likely a rechannelling, of private saving intermediated through the banking sector. Private financial saving increased in part due to an increase in precautionary saving, and cessation of subsidised mortgage loans (Schwartz et al. 1993). For instance, household financial saving as a share of disposable income in Hungary rose from 6 per cent during 1989-90 to 14 per cent during 1991-1992, while in former Czechoslovakia money incomes minus expenditures increased to 7 per cent of income in 1991-2, from about zero in 1990.

As money remains by far the most important financial asset and instrument of saving, the increase in saving manifested itself not so much in direct lending to the government but through a growing demand for broad money, intermediated through the banking system.[14] There has been a noticeable decline in money velocity in several countries during the last year or two *(Figure 5.1)*. The fall in inflation in Hungary and Poland, together with interest rate deregulation, initially pushed up deposit rates in real terms and played an important role in inducing larger holdings of financial assets *(Figure 5.2)*.

However, these financial assets were by no means denominated only in domestic currency. As *Table 5.3* illustrates, at end-1991, in both Poland and Hungary foreign currency deposits accounted for around 30 per cent of total deposits, with this ratio declining somewhat over the following year or so. From the perspective of public finance, such dollarisation has a number of offsetting implications. On the one hand, dollarisation would be expected to reduce the domestic monetary base and aggravate inflationary impact of government deficits. On the other hand, as Rostowski (1992) suggested, such dollarisation may actually increase total money supply (domestic plus foreign) which, in the framework of our model, could help maintain the level of output and hence be beneficial from a fiscal perspective.

However, as Calvo and Végh (1992) point out, dollarisation also has important implications for the banking sector. At the limit, banks will be forced

---

14) Even where the public can directly subscribe to government bonds, as for instance in Hungary, the share of government securities in total household savings remains very small.

to operate without a lender of last resort, and would be particularly vulnerable to a mismatching of assets and liabilities in terms of currency or maturity. Moreover, to the extent that dollar deposits have higher reserve requirements, or have to be paid higher interest, lending rates would increase. Higher lending rates would, in turn, increase the problems of moral hazard, and the probability of default. To counteract these factors, banks may prefer relatively liquid, and safe assets, which in the context of the Eastern European countries, would essentially amount to investing in government securities.[15)]

In terms of the analysis in Section 5.3 above, equation (6) can thus be extended to include lending to the government, so that

$$B_t + H_t + G_t = M_t,$$

where G_t denotes purchase of government securities by the banks. This, of course, raises a number of additional questions relating to the factors determining the distribution of bank credit between government and the productive sector.[16)] These factors are discussed in the following section where several specific constraints on bank lending to firms are examined.

Whatever the reasons for those constraints, there is now, as part of the transition to a market economic system, a sharper separation between government and state enterprises than under central planning. Therefore policies that channel bank credit to central government could end-up having a negative effect on enterprise liquidity and output. This would obviously be the case if, as at present, the government finances a larger share of its deficit, or accumulates international reserves, through the issuance of public debt. Public debt instruments are guaranteed by the state and are therefore likely to be more attractive than enterprise debt – particularly in the circumstances while enterprises are in a legal limbo and ownership is still to be properly defined.

As *Table 5.4* shows, in Hungary credit to the government has increased noticeably relative to credit extended to the enterprise sector; a similar development has taken place in the other East European countries. Specifically,

---

15) In Russia too, similar factors have led to the banks keeping a large proportion of their assets liquid, but in the form of holdings of US dollars (see Easterly and da Cunha 1993).

16) Quite apart from the distributional concern, there is a concern about the sustainability of current saving rates, especially given that some of the factors underlying the initial increase in private saving may now be waning. (See, for instance, Gomulka 1993).

there has been an increase in both Poland and Hungary in the share of government securities in banks' asset portfolio. *(Figure 5.3)*[17] This evidence probably understates the relative decline in real credit to the enterprise sector since a proportion of the nominal increase in enterprise credit consists of a capitalisation of interest arrears. Moreover, although there is no detailed evidence, it also appears that the relative share of the newly emerging private sector in total credit may have declined the most (see Varhegyi 1993).

Redirecting credit from enterprises to government could actually give rise to tax arrears. The initial effect of such redirecting will be lower output, which will increase the firms' incentive to default on any obligation they may have as, for instance, taxes.[18] Tax arrears, in turn, worsen the fiscal deficit and – if money supply is kept under control – induce further public debt growth, possibly setting the economy on a vicious cycle. Large amounts of tax arrears have already accumulated, particularly in the state enterprise sector. As of early 1993, these arrears are estimated at 3 per cent of GDP in Hungary and 2 1/2 per cent of GDP in Poland. As illustrated by *Figure 5.4,* in Poland tax arrears as a proportion of total enterprise liabilities increased by nearly 50 per cent between August 1991 and December 1992.[19]

5.6 Portfolio problems and credit allocation

A key feature of the banking sector in the Eastern countries is that the state banks, which dominate the banking sector, are undercapitalised, and their asset portfolios contain a large proportion of nonperforming loans (see Calvo and Kumar 1993). A large number of the bad loans stem from the pre-reform system when credit was extended without regard to the performance of enterprises or their ability to service debts. Moreover, the subsequent collapse of CMEA trade, declines in output, and significant changes in relative prices adversely affected

---

17) The data for Hungary in *Figure 5.3* are adjusted for various credit consolidations and changes in classification which inflated outstanding credit to government.

18) Section 5.6 below provides some impressionistic evidence on the positive relationship between the lack of availability of credit and declines in output in Poland in 1992, consistent with the evidence provided for an earlier period by Calvo and Coricelli (1994).

19) The irony here is that quite recently the development of government securities markets was regarded as likely to bestow significant benefits for financing fiscal deficits. (For a discussion of the issues, see Calvo and Kumar 1993.)

the profitability of enterprises and compounded the difficulties for the banks' balance sheets. Some of the bad loans also stem from the extension of new credits to unviable enterprises, resulting partly from the banks' own inability to distinguish between the riskiness of different enterprises in a rapidly changing economic and financial environment and partly from external pressures on them to lend to specific enterprises for essentially political reasons.[20)]

Although the precise magnitude of the portfolio problem is difficult to assess, there is a general consensus that it is substantial and that, instead of diminishing over time, it may actually have increased.[21)] In Poland, for instance, at the end of 1992, some 20 per cent of the large banks' assets were estimated to be "substandard", a somewhat higher figure than at the end of 1991. Similarly in Hungary, some 30 per cent of bank loans were regarded as unserviceable at the end of 1992, markedly more than two years earlier, while in Bulgaria, the share of bad loans, which was already high, is also considered to have increased.[22)]

The balance sheet difficulties of banks are related to the problem of interenterprise claims. These claims, which derive largely from arrears in payments to suppliers, have accounted for a sizable proportion of enterprises' debt; in Romania and Russia, for example, the arrears have exceeded overall bank credit or broad money. (For a discussion of the arrears problem in Romania, see Clifton and Khan 1993.)[23)] The beginnings of the reform process brought about a sharp increase in these arrears, essentially as a result of attempts by enterprises to increase their liquidity and circumvent the strict credit ceilings. Although a large proportion of the debts could be netted out within the enterprise sector, a considerable share corresponded to an increase in the

---

20) There is by now a considerable literature on the portfolio problems of banks, and the policies which have been, or should be, adopted to deal with them. In addition to Calvo and Kumar (op.cit.), see Fries and Lane (1993), and Varhegyi (1993).

21) The difficulties in accurately assessing the bad loan problem arise, in part, from inadequate information about the current and prospective performance of enterprises, as well as simply from inadequate bank auditing procedures.

22) These estimates are derived from Hogan et al. (1993) for Poland; Buyske and Vogel (1993) for Hungary; and Davis et al. (1993) for Bulgaria.

23) For a broader discussion of issues relating to interenterprise arrears, see Calvo and Coricelli (1992), Clifton and Khan (op.cit.), and Rostowski (1993).

enterprises' net debt to banks; if one enterprise did not repay another, the latter was not able to repay interest on its bank credit, increasing further the share of nonperforming loans.

It is worth emphasising that the problem of these arrears is not simply that of separating out "good" from "bad" firms, that is, firms with and those without high net arrears. Given the chain links between enterprises, with most firms having both debts and credits of similar magnitudes, the enterprise sector as a whole is affected (see Calvo and Coricelli 1994). Moreover, as the experience of Romania and Russia illustrates, unless the incentives and constraints facing enterprises change in a credible way – that is, unless expectations of a bailout change, even if the constraints are eliminated through money creation – arrears can reappear very quickly.

The low quality of loan portfolios, exacerbated by the arrears problem, has led to an understandable concern about the broader impact of insolvent banks on the transition process. This concern, together with the desire to prepare banks for eventual privatisation, has led several countries to implement major policy initiatives towards recapitalising banks and consolidating loans. Although some of these policies may appear to yield short-term specific benefits for improving banks' books, the implications for the banks' performance, for the allocation of credit to the enterprise sector, and for government finances have not received adequate attention.

The policies adopted by different countries for strengthening bank balance sheets vary considerably, but all entail a fiscal burden. In general, while no resource flows may be involved in the balance sheet clean-up, the replacement of bad loans by government debt does imply an ensuing debt servicing burden.[24)] In Poland, for instance, which has recently adopted a "decentralised" approach to the portfolio problem (noted below), the recapitalisation plan

---

24) It is worth noting that replacing bad loans by government bonds may not necessarily have any short-run implications for liquidity to the enterprise sector (banks would now receive interest which they may then use to buy more bonds) but it would have significant fiscal implications in the long-run.

currently under consideration would nevertheless be financed largely by domestic bond issues.[25)]

In addition to this direct government effort, the banks are, to varying extent, also required to make provision against bad loans, and as a result are paying markedly less in profit taxes. For instance, in Hungary, where bank provisions are greatest *(Table 5.5),* the impact on the budget in 1992 has been estimated at 2 per cent of GDP. This implication is not, of course, that adequate provisioning is undesirable or unnecessary – especially from a longer term perspective – but that in the short term it can have considerable effects on both for output and the budget which should be taken into account in assessing the cost of bank restructuring.

The process of recapitalisation and loan consolidation appears to have made banks excessively cautious in lending to enterprises for a number of reasons. First, as in Poland, state banks have been required to complete restructuring of their loan portfolios by March 1994. To this end, banks have been warned and discouraged against extending credit to enterprises with bad or doubtful debts, unless such credit is given as part of a "conciliation" agreement to reschedule claims, write-off part of them, or convert them into equity.[26)] Given banks' limited expertise in assessing riskiness of enterprises, complicated by the problem of interenterprise arrears, these exhortations have essentially led to a dampening of banks' overall lending to the enterprise sector and in particular to the small and medium-size firms. Instead of distinguishing between the degree to which firms would be potentially profitable, and solvent, and adjusting the terms of the loans accordingly, banks appear to have retrenched in terms of their lending.

In Poland, the above process could have been exacerbated by the new incentives given to banks' managements. Generous stock options have been provided to bank executives to be exercised upon privatisation, which would in turn depend on the health of banks' balance sheets. This action has further propelled banks into holding an increasing proportion of their assets in government securities and into building up liquidity.

---

25) The plan aims to increase capital/asset ratios for large banks to 12 per cent or more. In addition to the bond issue, the plan may also draw on the $ 1 billion stabilisation fund instituted in 1990 by bilateral donors.

26) For details of this restructuring strategy, see Hogan et al. (1993).

A similar development appears to be evident in Hungary, where the 1992 bankruptcy law (which has since been amended) led to a large number of small and medium-size firms, which may have had short-run liquidity problems, being declared insolvent. However, this outcome, far from benefitting the banks, actually exacerbated their portfolio problem given the inter-linkages between firms, and was an element in the sharp increase in provisioning noted above. To the extent that credit in nominal terms has increased, it reflects largely the capitalisation of interest arrears, and some new lending to a few, not necessarily the most efficient, large enterprises. At the same time, the above factors, combined with limited competition in the banking sector, have led to marked increases in lending margins. As *Figures 5.5 and 5.6* suggest, while deposit rates of interest in real terms have declined, there has been virtually no equivalent decline in the loan rates, resulting in high or increasing margins. High loan rates may exacerbate the adverse selection problem whereby inefficient firms or essentially insolvent firms, which are most likely to default, are the ones which end up obtaining credit.

As shown by the model in Section 5.3 above and by the evidence in Calvo and Coricelli (1994), lack of credit has an adverse effect on firms' output. Some further illustrative evidence on this is provided in *Table 5.6,* which examines the relationship for Poland in 1992 between bank credit, profitability, and output across 25 major sectors of the economy. It shows a positive relationship between changes in real credit and in output, taking into account differences in profitability. Although this evidence can not be regarded as conclusive, given the methodological problems inherent in this type of analysis, it nevertheless provides some support for the argument concerning the importance of bank credit for sustaining activity in the economies in transition.

What are the options for increasing credit and output? As shown above, a macroeconomic policy of loosening monetary policy stance is likely to be counterproductive. An increase in inflation which such a policy will entail would end up by reducing, not increasing, real credit. To the extent that inflation generates uncertainty, and makes it even more difficult to assess firm creditworthiness, it could further exacerbate the credit crunch. A reduction in fiscal deficits could, of course, lead to less credit being pre-empted by the public sector, but for the reasons noted earlier, it may not automatically lead to any corresponding increase in credit to the enterprise sector.

A possible solution could be to modify the strategy for reform of the banking sector to encourage banks to lend to enterprises, so long as that does not lead to excessive risk for themselves. Thus, while the resolution of the portfolio problem should certainly not be neglected, the specific policies for such resolution should be re-examined. More important, policies should be implemented to encourage banks to become much more adept at assessing risk than they have been until now. Both these aspects of the problem could be tackled by privatising the state-owned banks, allowing much greater participation by foreign banks, and by obtaining additional external expertise in assessing and pricing credit risk.

5.7 Credit, equity capital, and investment

The analysis of bank credit as a source of working capital can be extended to the use of such credit by firms for finance investment and undertake product and market diversification in the medium and long term. Bank loans in the short run are virtually the only formal source of credit, but other sources of finance such as venture and equity capital may also be available over a longer time horizon. Over such a horizon, the relative merits of these alternative sources of finance become important and are briefly discussed below.

At present, as the earlier discussion has emphasised, given the banks' reluctance to lend even for short-term working capital, credit for longer term investments in several of the Eastern European countries seems virtually unavailable. However, it has been argued that once the commercial banks are fully restructured and placed on a sounder footing, they could actively participate in the provision of long-term finance (Brainard 1991). As banks build up information and expertise in evaluating operations of firms borrowing from them, they could be active role in screening, monitoring, and restructuring these firms. This is especially so since the equity-ownership of firms being privatised is likely to be highly diffused and the individual owners may have neither the information nor the incentive to corporate governance, the banks' role could be especially important.

Even if the current constraints on banks are removed, however, it is uncertain that they would be able to oversee management decisions in a constructive way. More fundamentally, there could be internal constraints in credit markets, resulting from asymmetric information, adverse selection and incentive problems, which would prevent banks from providing investment finance. These constraints have been analysed at length in the existing literature on financial sector liberalisation in developing countries. They are contingent, in part, on the possibility that a bank's return from lending to a specific group of borrowers may not be a monotonically increasing function of the interest rate it charges to borrowers (see Stiglitz and Weiss 1981 and Cho 1986). This is so for two reasons: first, the adverse selection effect – higher interest rates discourage the safe borrowers which the banks prefer; second, the incentive effect – if borrowers have choice of projects, they will tend to favour projects with higher probability of default when the interest rate is increased. These two effects could discourage banks from raising their interest rates in response to an excess demand for credit.

The above constraints imply that banks avoid financing a new, productive groups of borrowers, who may be perceived to be risky even when the banks are risk neutral and free from interest rate ceilings. The difficulty that new productive customers have in obtaining finance from banks comes essentially from the fixed-fee contract nature of bank loans (see Stiglitz 1991 and Diamond 1991). The borrowers are concerned about the upper tail of the distribution of investment outcome while the lenders are concerned with the lower tail of the distribution. In this situation, banks may completely avoid lending to specific groups of potential borrowers unless they have information that enables them to rank each borrower and charge appropriate interest rates according to each borrower's riskiness so that they can ensure a profitable expected return.

The issue then is whether, in the absence of this information, equity markets could play a role in supplying investment capital to enterprises. It could be argued that precisely because of the above constraints and the risk-return trade-off, enterprises might be more able to raise capital from equity markets since equity holders would be concerned with the entire distribution of returns. In addition, for the privatisation of enterprises or banks to make any headway, development of equity markets is essential. However, in practice, as the experience to-date has shown, the development of equity markets is proceeding at a much slower pace than had been anticipated. For instance, at end-August 1993, despite a sharp increase in equity prices, market capitalisation of the Polish Stock Exchange was less than $ 1 billion, with only 20 firms quoted and very limited active trading. Similarly, the Hungarian exchange had a capitalisation of less than $ 0.5 billion and also limited activity.[27)]

Equity markets in East European countries have not developed rapidly enough for a number of reasons. First, the slow development is due to the slow pace of the privatisation programme itself, which has severely limited the supply of equity.[28)] Second, the regulatory regime, in particular the enforcement of legal requirements and regulations, remains weak, engendering uncertainty and imposing high transactions costs. This is exacerbated by the weak accounting, and opaque reporting standards of firms' financial information. There is not enough reliable information about the current, much less the future, prospects of quoted companies to enable the potential domestic investor to take rational decisions about investing in equities. These factors also explain why the inflow of foreign portfolio capital has also, in general, remained limited.

If it is accepted that banks may not be able to provide adequate investment finance and that the equity markets can make a contribution in this regard, a number of policy measures need to be implemented to encourage the growth of these markets: in addition to speeding up the privatisation process, accounting and reporting standards of firms need to be improved dramatically; initial public offerings need to be priced realistically; and finally, to increase confidence in the market operations, regulations against insider trading should be stringent and laws ensuring that private contracts are honoured should be enforced.

5.8 Concluding remarks

The main focus of this paper has been on analysing factors in former socialist countries that are likely to determine the volume of bank credit allocated to the enterprise sector, and the implications of this allocation for aggregate supply, and macroeconomic performance. The paper developed a model to explain how changes in the demand for money by the household sector directly

---

27) For a discussion of issues relating to the role of equity markets in East Europe, see Brainard (1991), Borensztein and Kumar (1992), and Calvo and Kumar (1993). For a discussion of the issues relating to the importance of equity markets in developing markets see, for instance, Singh and Hamid (1992).

28) The important exception in this regard is the Czech stock market where since June 1993 shares have been traded in a large number of companies following their privatisation through the voucher schemes.

influence the volume of loanable funds and credit, which in turn determines output and employment in the productive sectors. If firms cannot obtain sufficient working capital, production will be cut back. The model showed, however, that attempts to increase credit by inflation may actually exacerbate the credit crunch because of the effect of inflation on the household demand for deposits.

The paper also examined factors which determine the *allocation* of bank credit between enterprises and other borrowers, in particular the government. The reasons why banks may prefer to finance government deficits rather than make potentially more profitable loans to enterprises include limited information about enterprises' current performance, considerable uncertainty about their future prospects, lack of expertise in evaluating risk, and pressure from the government to improve the quality of banks' asset portfolios. These reasons for preferring credit to government, while perfectly rational from the perspective of individual banks, may end by creating a vicious cycle of low output, low enterprise profits, high fiscal deficits, and, again, low credit to enterprises. Empirical evidence for a number of Eastern European countries seemed to be consistent with the analysis. A number of policy options for increasing the provision of credit to potentially viable enterprises were noted.

Finally, the paper considered the relative merits of bank finance and equity capital in financing medium- and long-term investment. In a credit market with imperfect information, liberalisation of the banking sector would not necessarily lead to efficient allocation of long-term capital: adverse selection and moral hazard effects arise when debt contracts are used in the presence of asymmetric information. Equity contracts, however, are free from the adverse selection effect and thus could overcome inefficient allocation of capital when the same degree of imperfect information about borrowers exists as in the case of debt contracts. However, a number of important constraints exist on the development and efficient functioning of equity markets, and the paper noted some policies that might be implemented to overcome them.

References

Berg, A., and Sachs, J. (1992), "Structural Adjustment and International Trade in Eastern Europe: The Case of Poland," *Economic Policy,* no. 14 (April), pp. 117-173.

Borensztein, E., and Kumar, M. S. (1991), "Proposals for Privatization in Eastern Europe," *Staff Papers,* International Monetary Fund, vol. 38 (June), pp. 300-326.

Brainard, L. J. (1991), "Strategies for Economic Transformation in Central and Eastern Europe: Role of Financial Market Reform", in *Transformation of Planned Economies: Property Rights Reform and Macroeconomic Stability,* Bloomenstein, H., and Marrese, M. (eds.), OECD, Paris, pp. 95-108.

Bruno, M. (1992), "Stabilization and Reform in Eastern Europe: A Preliminary Evaluation", IMF Working Paper, WP/92/30, International Monetary Fund, Washington DC.

Buyske, A., and Vogel, R. (1993), "Hungary's Financial System: Status and Prospects", *Report of the Agency for International Development,* Agency for International Development, Washington DC, August.

Calvo, G. A., and Wellisz, S. (1979), "Hierarchy, Ability, and Income Distribution", *Journal of Political Economy,* vol. 87, October, pp. 991-1010.

Calvo, G. A., and Végh, C. (1992), "Currency Substitution in Developing Countries: An Introduction", *Revista de Analisis Economico,* vol. 7, June, pp. 3-28.

Calvo, G. A., and Coricelli, F. (1992), "Stabilizing a Previously-Centrally-Planned Economy: Poland 1990", *Economic Policy,* no. 14.

Calvo, G. A., and Coricelli, F. (1994), "Credit Market Imperfections and Output Response in Previously Centrally Planned Economies", in *Building Sound Finance in Emerging Market Economies,* Caprio, Gerard, Folkerts-Landau, David, and Lane, Timothy D. (eds.), International Monetary Fund, World Bank, Washington DC, pp. 257-294.

Calvo, G. A., and Kumar, M. S. (1993), "Financial Markets and Intermediation", in *Financial Sector Reforms and Exchange Arrangements in Eastern Europe,* Occasional Paper 102, International Monetary Fund, Washington DC.

Cho, Y. J. (1986), "Inefficiencies from Financial Liberalization in the Absence of Well Functioning Equity Markets", *Journal of Money, Credit and Banking,* vol. 18, May, pp. 191-199.

Clifton, E., and Khan, M. S. (1993), "Interenterprise Arrears in Transforming Economies: The Case of Romania", *Staff Papers,* International Monetary Fund, vol. 40, September, pp. 680-96.

Davis, P., Hogan, D., and Vogel, R. (1993), "Bulgaria's Emerging Financial System:Progress and Prospects", *Report of the Agency for International Development,* Agency for International Development, Washington DC, August.

Diamond, D. W. (1991), "Monitoring and Repudiation: The Choice Between Bank Loans and Directly Placed Debt", *Journal of Political Economy,* vol. 99, August, pp. 689-721.

Easterly, W., and da Cunha, P. V. (1993), "Financing The Storm: Macroeconomic Crisis in Russia, 1992-93", Policy Research Working Paper 1240, World Bank, Washington DC.

Fries, S., and Lane, T. (1994), "Financial and Enterprise Restructuring in Emerging Market Economies", in *Building Sound Finance in Emerging Market Economies,* Caprio, Gerard, Folkerts-Landau, David, and Lane, Timothy D. (eds.), International Monetary Fund, World Bank, Washington DC, pp. 21-46.

Gomulka, S. (1993), "On the Design of Economic Policy: The Challenge of Eastern Europe", World Bank Transition and Macro Adjustment Division Working Paper no. 5, Policy Research Department, World Bank, Washington DC.

Hogan, D., Rhyne, E., and Dod, D. (1993), "Poland's Emerging Financial System: Status and Prospects", *Report of the Agency for International Development,* Agency for International Development, Washington DC, August.

National Bank of Hungary (1993), *Monthly Reports,* various issues.

Rostowski, J. (1992), "The Benefits of Currency Substitution During High Inflation and Stabilization", *Revista de Analisis Economico,* vol. 7, June, pp. 91-107.

Rostowski, J. (1993), "The Inter-Enterprise Debt Explosion in the Former Soviet Union: Causes, Consequences, Cures", *Communist Economies and Economic Transformation,* vol. 5, no. 2, pp. 131-159.

Schaffer, M. (1993), "The Enterprise Sector and Emergence of the Polish Fiscal Crisis, 1990-1991", Policy Research Working Paper 1195, World Bank, Washington DC, September.

Schwartz, A., Stone, M., and Van der Willigen, T. (1993), "Beyond Stabilization: The Economic Transformation of Czechoslovakia, Hungary and Poland", International Monetary Fund, Washington DC (unpublished).

Singh, A., and Hamid, J. (1992), "Corporate Financial Structures in Developing Countries", IFC Technical Paper no. 1, World Bank, Washington DC.

Stiglitz, J. E., and Weiss, A. (1981), "Credit Rationing in Markets with Imperfect Information," *American Economic Review,* vol. 71, June, pp. 393-410.

Stiglitz, J. E. (1991), "Government, Financial Markets, and Economic Development", NBER Working Paper no. 3669, National Bureau of Economic Research, New York, April.

Tanzi, V. (1993), "Fiscal Policy and the Economic Restructuring of Economies in Transition", IMF Working Paper WP/93/22, International Monetary Fund, Washington DC.

Varhegyi, E. (1993), "Key Elements of the Reform of the Hungarian Banking System: Privatization and Portfolio Cleaning", CEPR Discussion Paper no. 826, Center for Economic Policy Research, September.

Table 5.1

Eastern Europe: Output, investment, and inflation

(percentage change or as indicated)

	1989	1990	1991	1992
Bulgaria				
GDP	-0.5	-9.1	-11.7	-5.7
Gross investment	-6.2	-13.6	-58.6	-16.4
Stocks (change in % of GDP)	-1.5	0.6	-1.0	-4.1
Fixed investment	-2.3	-19.0	-72.7	23.9
Gross investment (% of GDP)	32.1	31.5	12.8	14.5
Unemployment rate	0.0	1.6	15.6	15.0
Consumer prices	6.4	21.6	333.5	82.0
Former Czechoslovakia				
GDP	4.5	-0.4	-15.9	-8.5
Gross investment	29.7	9.0	-31.6	-15.0
Stocks (change in % of GDP)	-0.2	2.6	-1.7	-5.1
Fixed investment	32.7	0.0	-29.9	5.1
Gross investment (% of GDP)	27.7	30.7	26.8	23.1
Unemployment rate	--	0.8	3.2	5.7
Consumer prices	1.4	10.8	59.0	11.0
Hungary				
GDP	-0.7	-3.5	-11.9	-4.4
Gross investment	-0.4	-7.9	-17.0	-24.7
Stocks (change in % of GDP)	-1.0	-0.3	-3.0	-4.5
Fixed investment	5.1	-8.7	-5.5	-4.7
Gross investment (% of GDP)	26.1	25.4	20.8	19.0
Unemployment rate	0.4	1.7	7.7	12.3
Consumer prices	17.0	28.9	36.4	23.0
Poland				
GDP	0.2	-11.6	-7.6	1.0
Gross investment	-10.7	-37.6	-14.2	-2.8
Stocks (change in % of GDP)	-2.7	-7.5	-1.6	-1.0
Fixed investment	-2.1	-10.6	-4.5	2.5
Gross investment (% of GDP)	28.7	27.5	21.5	17.7
Unemployment rate	2.6	6.2	8.4	14.0
Consumer prices	251.1	585.8	70.3	43.0
Romania				
GDP	-5.8	-7.4	-13.7	-15.0
Gross investment	-11.4	-3.5	-0.3	-24.1
Stocks (change in % of GDP)	-3.1	10.2	5.7	-7.7
Fixed investment	-0.4	-37.6	-28.8	...
Gross investment (% of GDP)	26.7	27.8	33.5	25.6
Unemployment rate	3.4	5.7	2.8	6.4
Consumer prices	0.9	4.7	161.1	210.3

Source: IMF World Economic Outlook Data Bank.

Table 5.2

Eastern Europe: Government balances and monetary variables

(percentage change, or as indicated)

	1989	1990	1991	1992
Bulgaria				
Government revenue (% of GDP)	57.9	52.5	42.9	36.8
Government expenditure (% of GDP)	58.5	65.1	50.5	43.3
Capital expenditure (% of GDP)	5.5	6.6	1.9	1.9
Fiscal balance (% of GDP)	-0.6	-12.6	-7.6	-6.5
Domestic credit	9.6	25.0	148.3	54.2
Broad money	11.6	79.2	44.6	47.8
Short-term deposits	1.0	4.0	54.0	65.0
Exchange rates (US$/NC[a])	-8.2	-13.7	-88.4	-22.1
Real effective exchange rate	...	...	...	...
Former Czechoslovakia				
Government revenue (% of GDP)	49.3	47.6	51.8	47.0
Government expenditure (% of GDP)	52.8	54.0	52.0	50.7
Capital expenditure (% of GDP)	7.9	7.0	6.3	6.0
Fiscal balance (% of GDP)	-3.5	-6.4	-0.2	-3.8
Domestic credit	2.7	9.7	20.3	16.9
Broad money	3.5	0.5	26.8	16.9
Short-term deposits	3.0	5.0	11.0	11.0
Exchange rates (US$/NC[a])	-4.5	-16.1	-38.1	3.5
Real effective exchange rate	...	...	...	...
Hungary				
Government revenue (% of GDP)	59.6	57.4	57.9	52.6
Government expenditure (% of GDP)	60.9	58.2	61.1	60.7
Capital expenditure (% of GDP)	6.6	5.9	4.2	6.7
Fiscal balance (% of GDP)	-1.3	-0.8	-2.7	-8.0
Domestic credit	15.2	11.1	7.2	11.1
Broad money	14.4	29.6	34.5	27.4
Short-term deposits	...	...	...	...
Exchange rates (US$/NC[a])	-14.6	-6.6	-15.4	-4.8
Real effective exchange rate	1.3	4.1	13.3	7.9

(continued)

Table 5.2 (continued)

Eastern Europe: Government balances and monetary variables
(percentage change, or as indicated)

	1989	1990	1991	1992
Poland				
Government revenue (% of GDP)	30.8	33.3	25.8	27.1
Government expenditure (% of GDP)	36.9	32.7	32.1	34.4
Capital expenditure (% of GDP)	3.3	2.8	2.4	1.7
Fiscal balance (% of GDP)	-6.1	0.7	-6.3	-7.3
Domestic credit	222.7	2,746.9	-80.2	72.9
Broad money	236.0	121.9	36.9	57.5
Short-term deposits	85.0	145.0	48.0	35.5
Exchange rates (US$/NC[a])	-70.1	-84.9	-10.0	-22.5
Real effective exchange rate	12.9	-15.7	54.3	0.6
Romania				
Government revenue (% of GDP)	51.1	37.7	34.3	37.6
Government expenditure (% of GDP)	42.7	37.6	35.4	39.6
Capital expenditure (% of GDP)	17.6	7.8	4.3	3.9
Fiscal balance (% of GDP)	8.4	0.1	-1.0	-6.1
Domestic credit	8.5	19.5	110.2	-1.2
Broad money	5.6	17.4	100.8	48.7
Short-term deposits	2.5	3.0	18.0	60.0
Exchange rates (US$/NC[a])	-4.3	-33.5	-77.7	-71.7
Real effective exchange rate	-3.2	-31.6	-5.2	-37.9

a) National currency.

Table 5.3

Domestic and foreign currency deposits – Poland and Hungary

	Poland [a)]			Hungary [b)]		
date (end of period)	**domestic currency**	**foreign currency**	**foreign as a % of total**	**domestic currency**	**foreign currency**	**foreign as a % of total**
December 1991	139.8	57.4	29.1	302	130	30.1
March 1992	159.1	69.3	30.4	317	136	30.1
June 1992	178.1	71.9	28.8	352	140	28.5
September 1992	199.5	79.0	28.4	398	153	27.8
December 1992	230.6	90.8	28.2	430	152	26.2
March 1993	287.1	108.8	27.5	478	170	26.3

a) Data, in 000 billions of zlotys, relate to deposits of the nonfinancial sector. - b) Data, in billions of forints, relate to savings deposits of the household sector.

Source: Narodowy Bank Polski Information Bulletins, and National Bank of Hungary Monthly Reports.

Table 5.4

Hungary: Composition of lending portfolio of commercial banks

(in per cent of total)

Dates	enterprise sector	general government	house-holds	non-residents	total
1 January 1992	73.8	7.2	9.9	9.1	100.0
31 December 1992[a)]	62.5	22.0	8.0	7.5	100.0
1 January 1993[b)]	51.2	26.5	15.2	7.1	100.0
31 July 1993[c)]	51.9	29.1	12.0	7.0	100.0

a) Without credit consolidation. - b) These data differ from those of 31 December because of credit consolidation and changes in classification. - c) Preliminary.

Source: National Bank of Hungary: Monthly Report, various issues.

Table 5.5

Hungary: Bank profits and provisions 1991

(billion forints and percentages)

	operating profits	provisions		pre-tax profits	
			%		%
Five large banks	52.2	35.6	68	16.6	32
Medium-sized banks	13.9	2.6	19	11.3	81
Large and medium-sized banks	66.1	38.2	58	27.9	42
Total	75.3	41.1	55	34.2	45

Source: Varhegyi (1993).

Table 5.6

Poland: Changes in output, credit, and profitability[a)]

Equation: $\Delta\ \text{output}_{ti} = \alpha + \beta\Delta\ \text{Credit}_{ti} + \gamma\ \text{Profit}_{t-1i} + \epsilon_{ti}$

Sectors	α	β	γ	R^2
All	0.007	0.261		0.149
(25)	(5.330)	(2.008)		
	0.007	0.261	0.001	0.151
	(5.192)	(1.962)	(0.189)	
Sectors with	0.008	0.272	0.002	0.150
moderate inflation	(5.231)	(1.947)	(0.210)	
(21)				

a) Dependent variable is the change in real output in 1992 in 25 (or 21) major sectors of the economy. The explanatory variables are change in real credit and the average profit rate in 1991; t-statistics are provided in parentheses.

Figure 5.1

Money velocity in Eastern European countries, 1987-1993[1)]

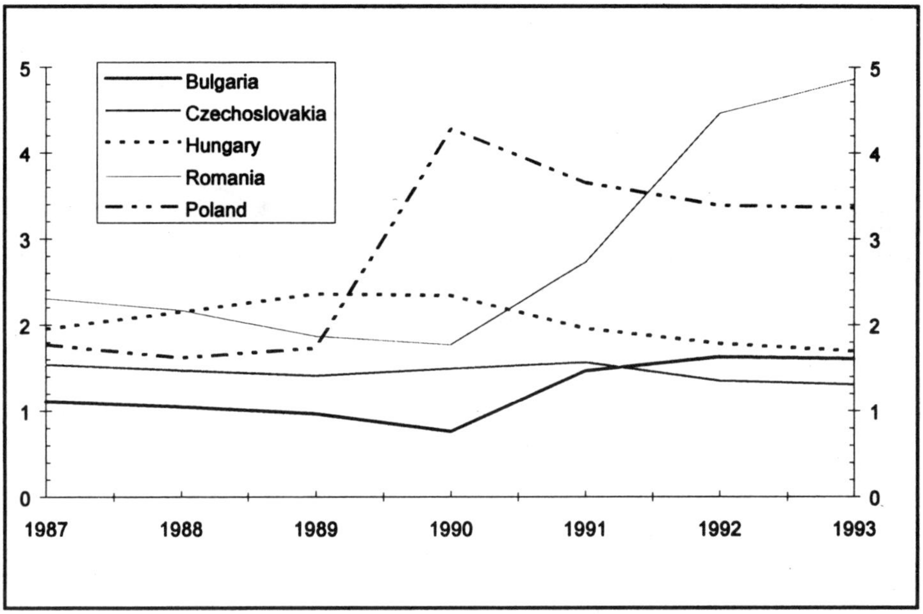

1) Velocity is measured as nominal GDP/average of broad money (M2).

Source: IMF World Economic Outlook.

Figure 5.2A

Household deposits in Poland

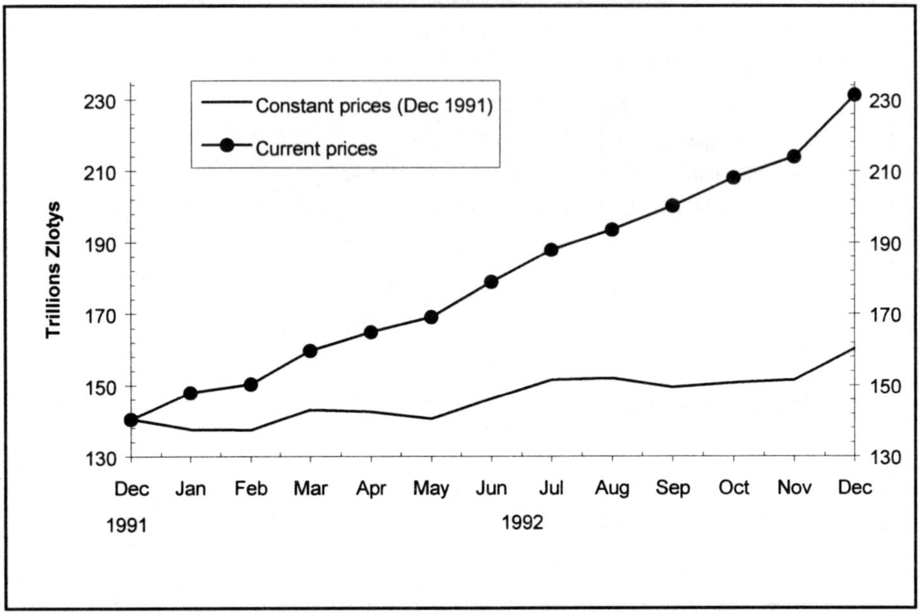

Source: Narodowy Bank Polski, Information Bulletin, various issues.

Figure 5.2B

Household deposits in Hungary

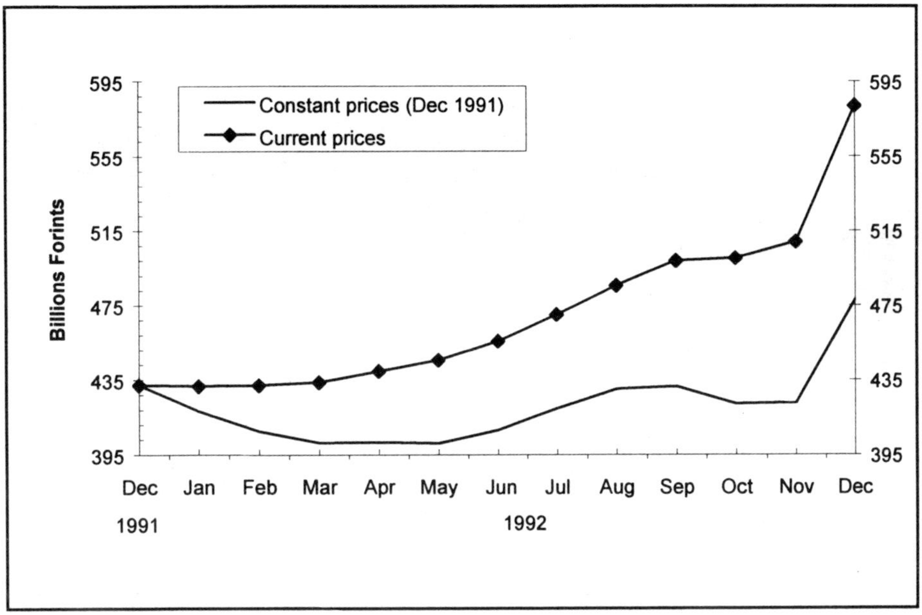

Source: National Bank of Hungary, Monthly Report, various issues; and Monthly Bulletin of Statistics.

Figure 5.3A

Bank credit to government and enterprises in Poland

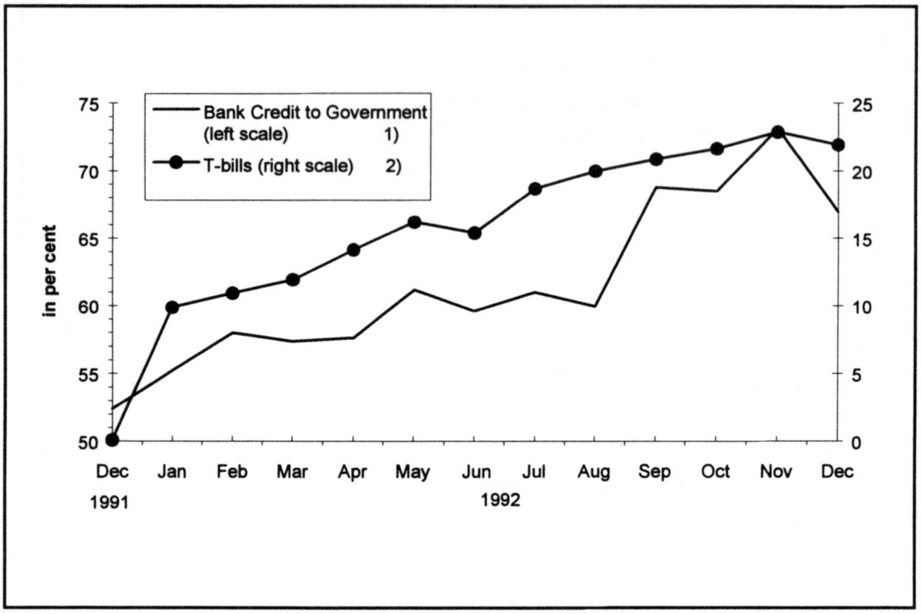

1) Bank credit to government as a per cent of credit to enterprises. - 2) T-bills held by banks as a per cent of credit to enterprises.

Source: Narodowy Bank Polski, Information Bulletin, various issues.

Figure 5.3B

Bank credit to government and enterprises in Hungary

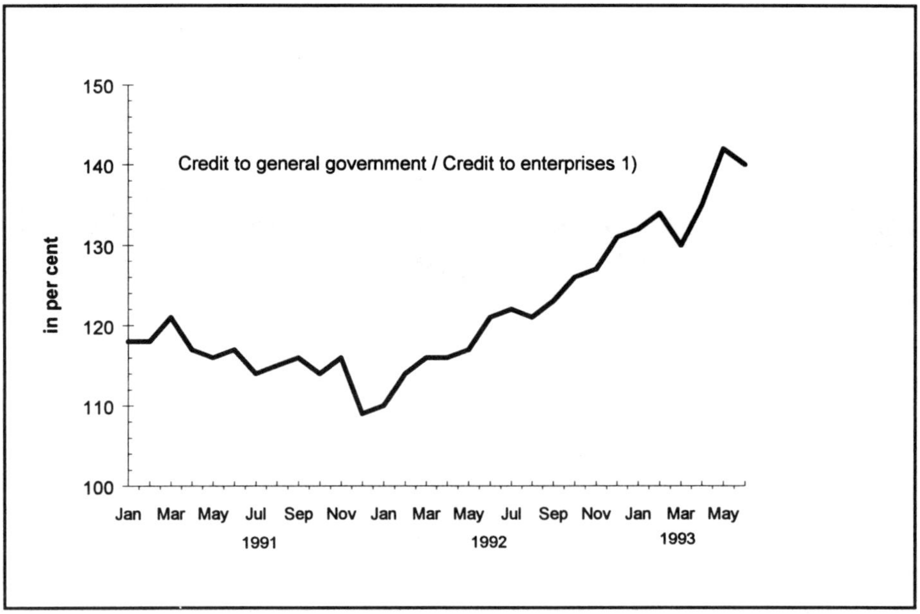

1) Data are adjusted for loan consolidation and reclassification of loans to the government in April 1991, December 1992, and March 1993.

Source: National Bank of Hungary.

Figure 5.4

Poland: Enterprise liabilities to the budget

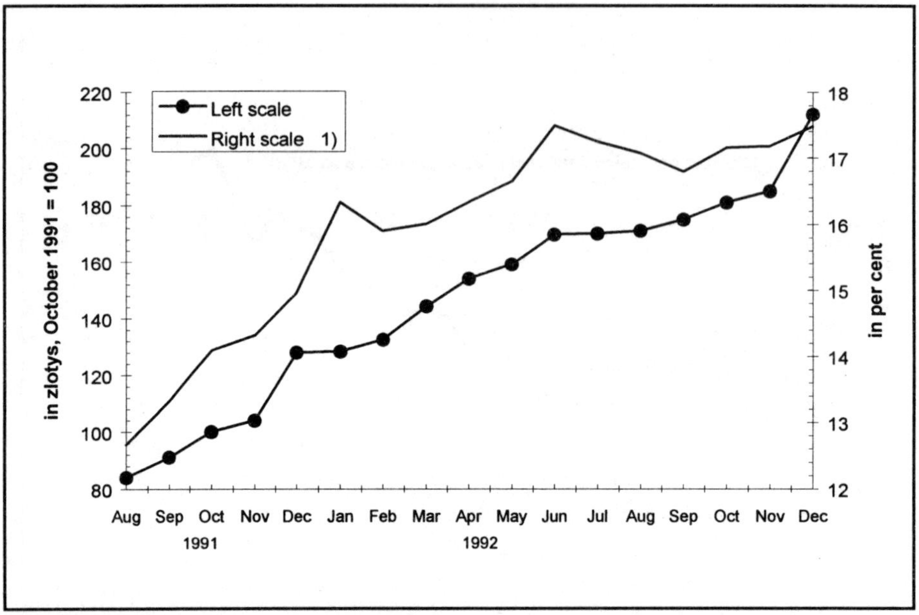

1) Liabilities to the budget as a percentage of total liabilities.

Source: Biuletyn Statystyczny, various issues.

Figure 5.5

Poland: Real interest rates

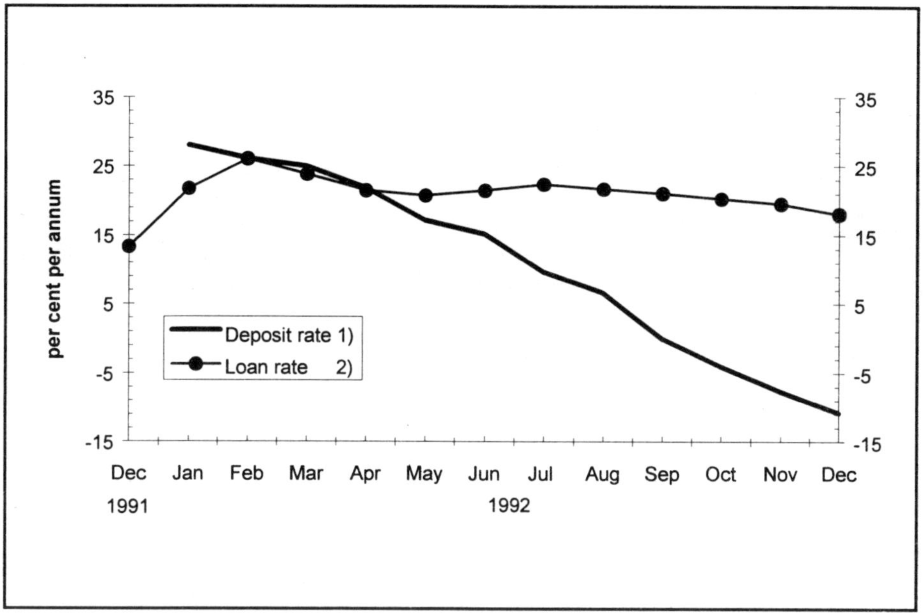

1) Nominal deposit rate adjusted for changes in consumer price index. - 2) Nominal loan rate adjusted for changes in producer price index.

Source: Narodowy Bank Polski, and Biuletyn Statystyczny, various issues.

Figure 5.6A

Commercial bank interest rate spread in Poland[1)]

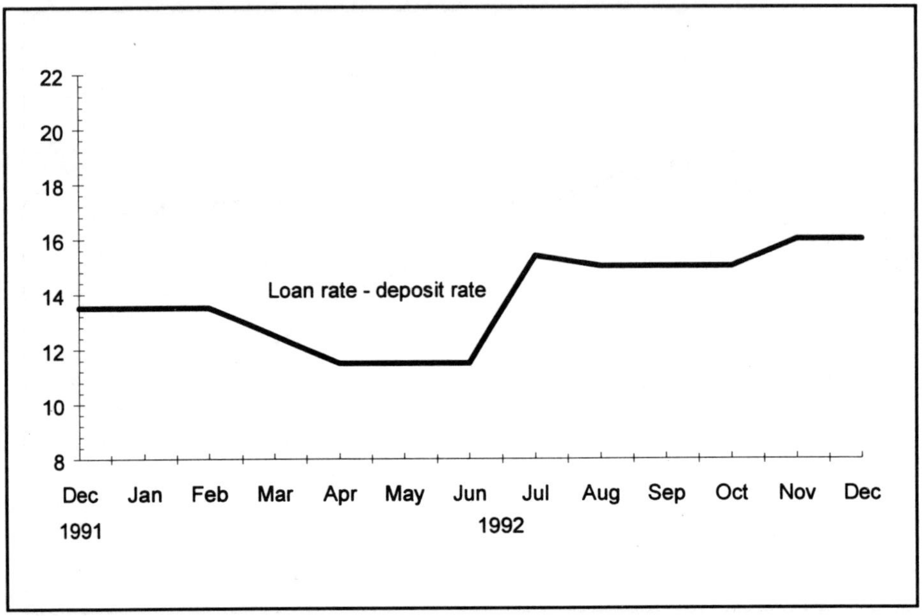

1) Rate on lowest risk credit less 3-month deposit rate.

Source: Narodowy Bank Polski, Information Bulletin, various issues.

Figure 5.6B

Commercial bank interest rate spread in Hungary[1)]

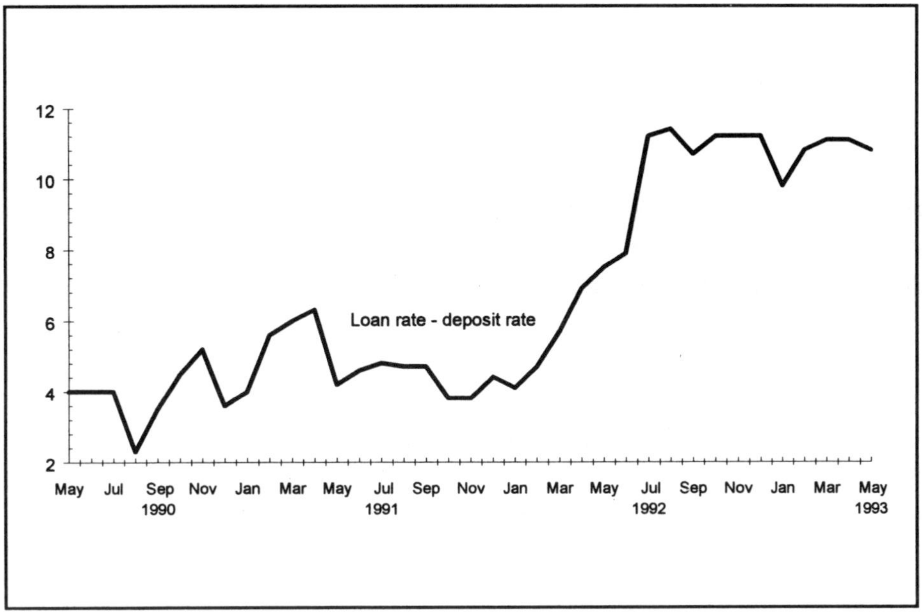

1) Rate on one-year or less enterprise credit less one-year deposit rate.

Source: National Bank of Hungary, Monthly Report, various issues.

Chapter 6

WESTERN FINANCIAL MARKETS OFFER CHOICES FOR THE EAST

Peter R. Haiss*)

During the first wave of financial market reform, the old monolithic banking systems in East Europe were broken into two-tier structures, and various schemes were devised to create capital markets. *Boffito* (Ch. 4) and *Calvo/Kumar* (Ch. 5), among others, argue that structural reform of the financial sector must continue. The role which the capital markets are supposed to play in the reforming countries, especially in the context of enterprise restructuring, however, is controversial (Schmidt-Chiari 1993). For the second stage of reform, Calvo/Kumar and Boffito advocate equity markets in preference to commercial banks for efficient capital supply for enterprises. Given the current economic and structural features of these economies, it is argued below that priority should instead be given to the creation of a universal banking system. Implications of an answer to this issue are of importance to foreign investors (progress in company restructuring and privatisation), banks (progress and type of financial sector reform) and banking supervision (priority of reforms).

The task of a financial market is to establish, in an efficient manner, the equilibrium between supply (funds offered by savers) and demand (funds desired by investors). The institutions involved play an important role as transformers of capital in mobilising money and by transforming size, maturity and risk (Corbett 1990). Financial systems in market economies, however, differ greatly from country to country in their capital allocation mechanisms. Thus, in developing financial markets in East Europe, one of the most important questions to be addressed is: which type of financial system should be adopted to fulfil the country's specific needs?

---

*) Secretariat to the Managing Board, Bank Austria and Lecturer at Karl Franzens University, Graz. The opinions expressed are the author's personal views and do not necessarily reflect the policy of Bank Austria.

6.1 The menu available from the West

In general, transfers of capital from savers to those who need capital can take place in three different ways (Brigham and Gapenski 1988). First, this can be achieved by *direct transfers of money against securities* (when a business sells its stocks or bonds directly to savers without going through any type of intermediary). Second come *transfers through an investment banking house* which serves as a middleman (when a company sells its stocks or bonds to the assisting investment bank, which in turn sells them to final savers). The third mode available is through *commercial banks or mutual funds* which obtain funds from savers and then issue their own securities in exchange (e.g. through issuing savings passbooks, mortgage loans and bonds).

All market-based financial systems are a mix of these three modes, but the emphasis is different. The prevailing modes depend partly on historic reasons for national legislation (e.g. the 1930s depression gave rise to the McFadden Act imposing regional restrictions on banks and to the Glass-Stegall Act separating commercial from investment banking in the US (Gruson and Herndl 1992)); partly on the size distribution of industry; partly on ownership structures (private vs. publicly owned); partly on different degrees of market imperfections (Corbett 1990). In some countries, large enterprises dominate, whereas in others small and medium enterprises are more important. Only the former use the equity markets to a significant extent. Small- and medium sized firms, on the other hand, rely mostly on bank loans. Another difference lies in the incentives faced by state-owned companies, which face a lower probability of bankruptcy, but for which the pressure to show an adequate return on equity is also less important. That is, the type of financial system established in a market economy depends on the structural features of the real economy which it is supposed to serve. This has to be kept in mind when advocating the creation of certain financial systems in reforming countries.

Figure A
Capital market systems

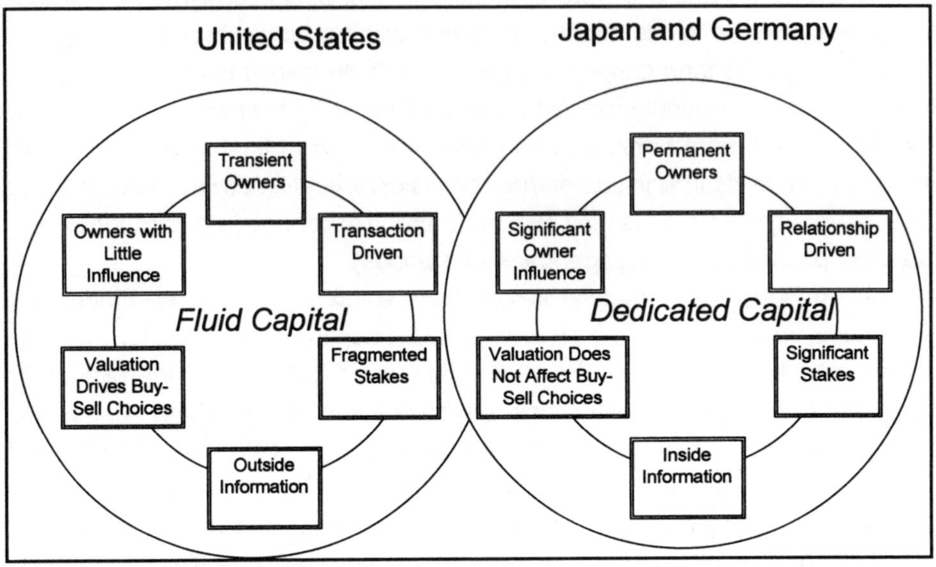

Source: Porter 1992.

Independently from the prevailing mode, a variety of providers of financial services are involved in allocating surplus capital to those needing funds: commercial banks, investment banks, savings & loan and retail institutions, mutual funds, stock and bond exchanges, etc. Together, they play an important role as "transformers" of capital in mobilising money and by transforming size, maturity and risk, i.e. in overcoming market imperfections. In different financial systems, however, different types of financial intermediaries perform these functions. That is, the allocation and risk assessment mechanisms, by which capital moves from its holders to investment projects, differ.[1)] The major distinction can be drawn (Porter 1992) between financial systems with capital-market-orientation ("fluid capital") and those with universal banking systems ("dedicated capital"). The prevalent capital and risk allocation mechanism determines how the available pool of capital in a nation is distributed among industries, companies, private and public investors and forms of investment.

Systems with fluid capital

In *"fluid capital systems"* strong legal barriers separate investment banking from other types of financial services, commercial banking in particular, as well as from owning non-banking businesses on a large-scale basis (Gruson and Herndl 1990). Typical examples are the US and the UK financial markets, where companies' financial needs are covered mainly on stock and bond exchanges (high stockmarket capitalisation as a percentage of GDP), a quarter of the population holds securities but the personal savings ratio is low. Banks are rather asset-driven, are privately held and are not allowed to hold stakes in industrial and commercial conglomerates (except up to 5 per cent of equity in the US). Hence, bank managers do not sit on corporate boards and have virtually no direct influence on management behaviour. Publicly traded companies instead rely on institutional investors (pension, insurance, and mutual fund managers) which hold highly diversified portfolios with small stakes in many of these companies.

The ownership of firms in such a system has become increasingly fragmented and transient, also more adept at reallocating capital rapidly from unprofitable industries to profitable ones. In the US, institutional investors have increased their share of total equity from 8 per cent in 1950 to 60 per cent in 1990. As pension funds are judged by their quarterly or annual gains in relation to the market-share indices, they tend to shift rapidly from one company to another (Pozen 1994). The goals of these institutional investors are rather financial and short-term oriented and thus lead to "fluid" capital markets" (Porter

---

1) There clearly is a trend towards convergence on both ends of the spectrum. Interstate-banking and branching as well as securities business are more accessible to US banks now than ten years ago. Competition-driven disintermediation from banking systems into securitised money and capital markets is gaining ground in continental Europe. Still, the differences are highlighted because these are still important for the creation of new financial markets.

1992). Thus, through the higher "hurdle rates" American firms use for evaluating projects, they seem to face higher cost of capital (Thurow 1992). With small stakes, held only briefly, carrying out in-depth research into firms' prospects is not worthwhile.

With regard to risk assessment, the capital market reduces the direct financing risk for suppliers of capital by broadly dispersing investments. Monitoring investments and disciplining of the managers (by change of management or ownership or by winding up a business) as part of that risk management function (Rybczinski 1992) is mainly performed through rating agencies, the managers of pension and mutual funds, investment banks and other capital market players; firms are valued by shareholders, not by credit officers. At the same time, restrictions on institutional investors sitting on company boards deny them access to "inside" information. Institutional investors therefore decide whether to buy or sell shares on the basis of limited information. To combat this, disclosure rules are rather harsh. Legal barriers, not only company-internal codes of ethical business conduct, are intended to keep banks from sharing the know-how gathered during credit approval with capital market decision-making.

Figure B

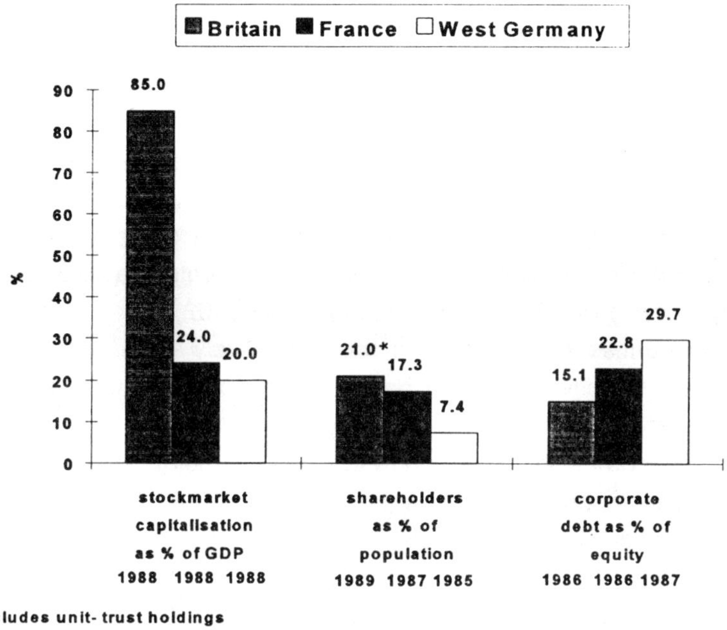

Source: Stevenson (1989).

Systems with dedicated capital

Universal banking systems in Austria, Germany, the Netherlands, Belgium and Switzerland, on the other hand, permit banks a much wider range of activities in the financial services arena, as well as owning trade and industrial companies. Banks tend to be liability-driven, have devoted relatively more resources towards the development of deposit-taking networks and can engage in deposit taking and lending, but also engage in securities and insurance activities (Kingsley 1993; Frazer and Orton 1990). Companies' financial needs are covered mainly through bank credits (i.e. low stockmarket capitalisation as a percentage of GDP), private share ownership is rather low (only 5 per cent of the Austrian population holds securities), the majority of savings are held in bank deposit accounts (the private savings rate is at about 11 per cent in Austria); high local savings led to high local investments (Thurow 1992).[2)]

Unlike the US, Austrian banks are partly owned by the government or municipalities, and also hold large stakes in industrial and commercial conglomerates on a long-term basis. In such systems of *"dedicated capital"*, the dominant owners are principals rather than agents; they hold significant stakes, rather than small, fragmented positions. These owners (private, banks or governmental) are rather permanent; they seek long-term appreciation of their shares (Porter 1992). Suppliers and customers often own stakes in each other, not to profit from the share ownership itself but to cement their business relationship. Bank ownership helps firms to plan corporate strategies and to raise the money to carry out these strategies (Thurow 1992).

While securities markets have remained relatively illiquid in these financial systems, the respective universal banks enjoy close institutional ties to the corporate sector (in terms of both equity stakes and their membership on corporate supervisory boards) and often play a major role in helping the corporate sector resolve debt problems (Goldstein et al. 1992). In addition to longer-term credits, short-term wholesale payments also flow across the banks' balance sheets. Banks derive their important role from imperfections of capital markets and from the possibility of achieving returns to scale by organising money and capital transactions. Their considerable placement power allows universal banks to exercise strict quality control over which potential borrowers obtain access to the respective debt markets. Risk assessment is mainly performed by commercial banks through their credit screening; hence rating agencies, mutual funds and capital market institutions are of lesser importance. Thus, there is less need for harsh disclosure rules. Bank-internal "chinese walls" between credit and investment banking departments, however, are built against the sharing of insider information.

Both modes of financial systems have their advantages and disadvantages. They are the outcome of respective legislative, historic and structural circumstances and the resulting needs of the real economies. Every nation setting up

---

2) While in the early 1990s the differentials narrowed substantially, in 1989 the corporate cost of capital for twenty-year investment in plant and equipment in the US was 60 per cent above that in Germany, using stock-market multiples, adjusted for taxes and depreciation. See Thurow (1992, p. 43) for details.

a new financial system therefore has to decide which of these two fits better its specific needs; its macroeconomic and cultural environment as well as the current structural conditions surrounding investment projects.

6.2 Semi market-driven financial markets in Eastern Europe

The first steps towards financial reform were straightforward. All Eastern European countries have moved away from the single centralised state bank channelling resources to public sector enterprises on the basis of plan requirements. Two-tiered banking systems have been created, new banks are being established to take over the commercial banking operations of the former monolithic state bank which thereupon reverted to the classic central bank roles of conducting monetary policy and supervising the banking system (Debs et al. 1991; Vanek 1993). Such a change is one of the major prerequisites for reforms in the real sector of the economy (Filc and Winkler 1991, p. 186). The *new commercial banks* were empowered to operate as universal banks with the freedom to undertake a wide range of lending and deposit-raising activities. What is important to understand about these banks is that they were created by transferring existing loans from the portfolio of the central bank (Brainard 1993). Thus, these banks started life with an inherited overhang of troubled assets, in most cases concentrated by industry or enterprise. In addition, new local, foreign and joint venture banks were permitted.

Capital markets, not banks, gained priority

In spite of the efforts during the first stage of financial sector reform, competition in the financial sector remains limited. Much attention, however, focused on the *re-creation of formal stock exchanges,* and several have been set up in recent years. Various privatisation procedures and a growing private sector (generating about 45 per cent of Poland's GDP, 35 per cent in Hungary and roughly 25 per cent in the Czech and Slovak Republic (Debs et al. 1991; Haiss 1992; Hunya 1993) served as triggers for re-establishing these capital markets. While the issuing and trading of bonds started in Hungary at the beginning of the 1980s on a very limited scale, the Budapest Stock Exchange reopened in June 1990. Initial euphoria at the political and economic changes led to a bull market. With corporate profits in Hungary under severe pressure, average multiples of Budapest traded equities, however, had exceeded 15 times earnings by the end of 1992 with over half of the 21 listed companies making losses. Capitalisation of shares increased from Ft 38 billion to Ft 47 billion in 1992. The Ljubljana Stock Exchange held its first exchange trading session in March 1990. At the end of 1992 a total of 10 shares were traded, with 8 quoted on the unlisted securities market only; total equity capitalisation of the Ljubljana exchange was at DM 41,494,000. In April 1991, the Warsaw Stock Exchange was reopened. After two years of operation, 23 banks and brokerage firms were registered members. The shares of 16 companies were listed together with seven government bond issues; market capitalisation was $ 263 bn by the end of the first quarter of 1993. The Bratislava and Prague stock exchanges were opened officially on 6 April 1993, but the delay in allocating shares meant that only three unlisted securities changed hands in Prague, and only one in the Slovak capital (Meth-Cohn 1993). This is a welcome development, but to function effectively, these exchanges require financial instruments (shares issued, listed and traded), and investors, traders and dealers with the necessary resources and skills – and, most important, banks and companies with clean books and appropriate asset/liability management and earnings potential (Debs et al. 1991; Filc and Winkler 1991).

Old and new problems for Eastern financial systems

Economic structures in East European countries are still different from Western standards. Weak banking systems act as a drag on the economies of the region, because the continued misallocation of scarce capital slows down the overall transformation process. Having broken the old monolithic banking system into two-tier structures, the governments have directed their energies to macroeconomic stabilisation and privatisation of the industrial sector. The second phase of banking reform – restructuring and consolidation – is still in its infancy: old problems inherited from the previous planning systems, and new problems that accrued since the inception of reform, need to be addressed:

– *Ballooning grey economy:* while the grey economy accounted for about 10 per cent of GDP and employment in Hungary and Poland in 1989, its share rose to about 30 per cent in 1992 (Dallago 1993; Gábor 1993). The coexistence of controlled official markets for credit and foreign exchange with the informal financial markets affects the operation of macroeconomic policies in fundamental ways (Montiel et al. 1993). In the absence of efficient secondary securities markets, the monetary authorities retain certain instruments of policy,[3] but lack the option of open market operations. In those circumstances, the (high) level of insider information is unbearable for a fluid financial system.

– *Size of the financial sector:* In 1991, total financial intermediation in Hungary, Czechoslovakia and Poland was at a level of about one tenth of that in Austria and only one twentieth of that in Switzerland, both countries of comparable size (Haiss and Fink 1993).

– *Poor-quality loan portfolio:* The new commercial banks were created by transferring existing loans from the portfolio of the central bank (Brainard 1993). Thus, these banks started life with an inherited overhang of troubled assets, in most cases concentrated by industry, region or enterprise. The scale of the problem is such that in 1992 the collective bad debts in the balance sheets of Hungarian, Czech, Slovak and Polish banks amounted to $ 12 bn (more than enough to pay off Czechoslovakia's foreign debt at the time). About 25 per cent to 40 per cent of outstanding bank loans across the region are considered as "contaminated," causing a severe need to recapitalise banks (Brainard 1993; Podkaminer 1994; Pick and Turek 1993; Štiblar 1994). Thus, the structure of banks' equity capital, deposits and credits is still highly irregular; in real terms, Polish commercial banks actually decapitalised (Podkaminer 1994).

– *Fresh debt:* While the bad debt problem is frequently considered a financial legacy of the Communist past, the biggest increase in bad debt has occurred over the last two years; mainly as a result of structural problems in the financial and enterprise sector, still to be addressed (Bloomenstein and Lange 1993, p. 14).

– *Lack of privatisation and skewed client structure:* The financial intermediation operations were taken over mainly by the old specialised banks. Many continue to be state-owned, and a significant proportion of the existing loans include credits to essentially insolvent enterprises as well as loans at highly concessional rates (Calvo and Kumar 1993, p. 8). In addition, the "nomenklatura" tried – often successfully, e.g. in Poland – to become de facto owners of nominally state-owned banks by using their insider knowledge (Podkaminer 1994). The one-dimensional customer structure, i.e. banks' customers all

---

3) The level of administered bank interest rates, the required reserve ratio, the amount of credit extended by the central bank to the commercial banking system, and intervention in the parallel exchange market; Montiel et al. 1993, p. 85.

belonging to one business sector, which came about at their foundation, means a lump risk – something to be avoided at all costs according to western schools of thought – clearly reflected in the respective banks profitability (Móra 1994).

– *Skewed competition:* New local, foreign and joint venture banks were permitted. However, competition remains limited. Most newly-licensed local and foreign banks are small and concentrate on a limited range of activities. In part this is due to the fact that the former state bank's commercial banking activities were hived off to relatively few banks, only one each in Romania, the Czech and Slovak Republics, for example (Vanek 1993).

– *Separate financial circuits:* The structure of the major banks remains badly skewed as local household and industrial financial circuits are still substantially separated (Timewell 1993). The commercial banks are still heavily dependent upon central bank refinance while local savings banks prefer to deposit their surplus funds in the emerging wholesale money markets rather than develop their own corporate banking operations (Thieme 1991, p. 28). Therefore, the cost of central bank re-finance continues to dominate the setting of interest rates, borrowers and savers are faced with a restricted choice, the cost of financial intermediation remains high and the efficiency of the banking system is still low.

– *No adequate risk assessment:* Few state-owned banks in the region price risk by market criteria yet. To a certain extent, the banks are not only unable to operate on the basis of commercial criteria, but even have to operate uncommercially, rolling over or even increasing credits to uncreditworthy industrial customers while denying commercially-priced funds to promising startup companies (Jones 1992). The newly created banks, therefore, cannot currently play a role in the allocation of capital similar to the role played by sound banking institutions active in regular capital markets (Brainard 1993). Hence investment funds have developed and take over some of the banks' regular functions.

– *Skewed bank lending and interest rate-structure:* Given the governmental pressure, the lack of risk control know-how and the shaky situation of many medium-sized private companies, the banks now lend more to each other and the state than to firms in need of investment capital. Faced with the choice between risky private borrowers and risk-free government paper, banks have opted for the latter. The easy returns diminish the need to form a new client base, causing a credit crunch. Thus firms often criticise the banks' lending policies, arguing that banks do not lend or lend only at very high rates (in Hungary, for example (Móra 1994)). Due to credit ceilings limiting the expansion of individual banks in Bulgaria, those banks with a comparatively small share of bad loans follow the debt-ridden in their pricing by charging the same high interest rates (Dobrinsky 1993).

Table 6.1

Developments in credit and monetary aggregates

(% changes in year, at year-end)

	Bulgaria			Czechoslovakia			Hungary		
	1990	**1991**	**1992**	**1990**	**1991**	**1992**	**1990**	**1991**	**1992**
Domestic credit: total	25.6	148.0	50	9.7	18.0	16	11.8	7.1	11
To non-government sector	10.7	112.5	31	1.4	20.3	18	20.1	0.1	5 a)
Broad money	14.8	124.8	50	0.1	27.3	20	28.9	27.7	29
Real broad money	-7.3	-60.6	-16	-15.2	-17.1	8	-5.9	-3.4	6

	Poland			Romania		
	1990	**1991**	**1992**	**1990**	**1991**	**1992**
Domestic credit: total	193.9	97.5	60	22.7	116.5	33
To non-government sector	262.6	62.3	26	-15.6 b)	101.1	39
Broad money	155.5	44.4	58	22.0	101.2	71
Real broad money	-26.9	-10.0	9	-13.0	-37.7	-43

Note: Credit to the non-government sector includes state enterprises, broad money is essentially equivalent to M3 and real broad money is deflated by prices.

a) Estimate. - b) Not comparable with total domestic credit (break in series).

Source: Bank for International Settlements.

– *Disintermediation:* Companies increasingly postpone credit and business activities, or turn to the grey market, or to direct foreign financing, because loans intermediated by local banks remain expensive compared to these sources. Disillusioned with paying high interest rates on loans, companies are also turning to commercial paper to finance working capital instead. The market for credit is dominated by a few big state-owned banks which are willing to grant credit only if they are guaranteed fat mark-ups (Valencia 1993, p. 48). In 1992, Hungarian banks charged 30 per cent on average for short-term loans to companies but paid less than 20 per cent for deposits. Hence, companies issue short-term promissory notes to provide themselves with working capital.

– *Lack of financial control:* The combination of decentralisation with limited private ownership has resulted in self-management of capital within firms at the outset of reform (Fischer and Gelb 1991). As a result of government commitment to the preservation of existing jobs, balance-sheet constraints on firms proved ineffective. In the absence of tight budget constraints, firms may simply refinance growing interest charges or further increase payment arrears. The disintermediation of credit flows through the growth in inter-enterprise credit has reached significant proportions (Brainard 1993).

As pointed out above the banks may have to operate uncommercially in allocating or extending credits. However, the prolongation of existing bank credits and the growth in inter-company credits were initially necessary for three reasons: the vitality of export markets was unknown, prices and companies' accounts were distorted, and insolvency rules were non-existent (BIS 1993). As a credit crunch, as well as fast privatisation, often proved inappropriate, there is rising urgency to install sound financial management practices in companies. Financial services reform thereby is of key importance. The failure to give top priority to monetary reform in general and to bank reform and re-capitalisation of the banking system in particular has become a major hindrance to reforms in the real economy and to foreign investment (Brainard 1993; Filc and Winkler 1991).

6.3 Creating a banking system for funding investment

Market economies and sophisticated financial systems are mutually dependent, which means that a market system cannot function without an efficient banking system. Therefore, the development of a sound financial system is imperative for economic progress, especially in view of the lack of domestic institutional investors and the need for transforming "credits" (i.e. former governmental allocations) into long-term equity relationships. Only a smoothly functioning financial system – efficient banks or stock markets or both – can allocate capital to the right enterprises. In the second phase of restructuring, however, the architects of reform need to decide whether to establish a primarily stock-exchange oriented financial system with liquid capital or a primarily universal banking system with dedicated capital.

Advocates of creating a capital-market driven financial system should keep in mind that bank loans remain by far the most important source of external funds for non-financial companies – independently of the "prevailing mode." Even in the US, the world's most securitised market, loans account for around 60 per cent of the external funds of non-financial businesses (Boonstra and de Jong 1993; Corbett 1990). Although direct access to the capital markets is of major and growing importance for large companies, small and medium-sized companies do not have direct access to the capital markets and therefore have no real alternative to a bank loan. Moreover, in the early stages of re-industrialisation, when per capita income and wealth are relatively low, capital markets play only a very limited role in channelling newly generated savings and in monitoring and disciplining the use of savings (Rybczynski 1992).

The key issues in creating a sound, efficient and competitive financial sector are to ensure that domestic savings are mobilised and efficiently allocated to their most productive users, that the backbone of every economy – small and medium-sized companies – can finance its inventories and production facilities, and that an efficient payment system is readily accessible. These are tasks typically performed by commercial and retail banks, not by investment banks and stock exchanges. Moreover, the East European countries, which are trying to privatise their economies, will need banks to perform a multitude of roles connected to the privatisation process. While the voucher/mass privatisation programmes currently in place prove that commercial banks can be by-passed to a certain extent in the transfer of ownership rights, yet without a strong and efficient banking system, the long-term objectives of privatisation cannot be achieved (Bloomenstein and Lange 1993). Banks may, in practice, be the only financial institutions that can enforce financial discipline on the state-owned corporate sector through the imposition of hard-budget constraints. Efforts of East European governments to develop investment funds, and bond and stock markets, as critical components in the ultimate success of the privatisation process, cannot succeed without the range of financial services provided by an efficient commercial and retail banking sector. Hence, an efficient universal banking system may be a prerequisite for the development of a viable, liquid and more sophisticated capital market. In the light of the East European countries' current macroeconomic situations and the individual companies' specific situations, priority should thus be given to the development of a universal banking system with dedicated capital and less emphasis should be devoted to stock-exchange driven financial systems.

Under the privatisation methods applied in the Czech and Slovak Republics, large sectors of the economies have been handed over to mutual fund managers. Of the 1,491 companies on offer, 75 per cent of all the shares designated for voucher purchase were attracted by the over 300 funds available (Meth-Cohn 1993). The top 14 funds now control almost 70 per cent of voucher shares and just over a quarter of the entire equity of these companies. (These top 14 funds are: Obchodní banka, CS Fond, Živnobanka, Agrobanka, Bohemia, YSE, Creditanstalt, PPF, VÚB Bratislava, Česká pojištovna, Komerční banka, Harvard, Investiční banka, and Česká spořitelna. Some funds, such as Harvard, chose to concentrate shares in a few key companies; at the other extreme, funds such as PPF went for a wide spread with less control.) (*Business Central Europe;* Meth-Cohn 1993) As many of the mutual funds are under the control of commercial banks,[4)] the result could be a financial structure of "dedicated capital" in which banks are owners, creditors, directors and advisors to big companies.

Prerequisites for such a universal banking system with industrial affiliations are, however: (a) *Allocation of credits* according to market (i.e. efficiency) criteria; (b) a *recapitalisation of banks,* and corporate governance rules that ensure strong and independent *supervision of banks* (Corbett 1990);[5)] (c) progress in *company privatisation,* with careful attention to sequencing the transfer not merely of ownership, but even more significantly, of control (Carlin and Mayer 1992); (d) establishment of credible *insolvency regulations* for companies;

---

4) The banks' directly held investment funds attracted over 30 per cent of all the voucher points. Bloomenstein and Lange 1993, p. 33.

5) The recapitalisation of the banks could be achieved by first lifting the bad loans out of their portfolio and then providing a mechanism for injecting new capital. The portfolio of bad loans can be sold to the government with long-term bonds paying a positive interest spread over the banks' cost of funds (Brainard 1993). Alternatively, spinning off a bank's bad loans into a separate entity managed by a special work-out team from the bank while feeding fresh money from governmental bonds, venture funds or stabilisation funds (set up with governmental and Western help) directly into the banks may be applied (BIS 1993; Brainard 1993). Transferring certain types of sour credits into special "consolidation fund banks" was done in the Slovak and Czech Republics, while other companies remain to be restructured by their respective banks. The monetary overhang on the deposit side, however, still remains to be cut (Filc and Winkler 1991, p. 191; Thieme 1991, p. 23).

(e) until tight budget constraints and, thereby, a credible threat of bankruptcy can be introduced, a range of *direct controls* will be needed to reinforce indirect measures (Fischer and Gelb 1991). These can include the elimination of subsidies that offset the losses of firms, public sector wage controls, and credit ceilings administered by the central bank. "Dedicated" capital systems fit the current needs better and thus should be given priority.

References

Bank for International Settlements (1993), *63 Annual Report,* Basle, June.

Bloomenstein, H., and Lange, J. (1993), "Balance Sheet Restructuring and Privatisation of the Banks", OECD (1993), *Transformation of the Banking System: Portfolio Restructuring, Privatisation and the Payment System,* Paris, pp. 13-33.

Bloomenstein, H. (1993), "Transformation of the Payment System and the Development of Money Markets", OECD (1993), *ibid.,* pp. 151-155.

Brainard, L. (1991), "Eastern Europe: Creating a Capital Market", *The AMEX BankReviewPrize Essays,* no. 4, pp. 1-22, Oxford University Press, Oxford, UK.

Brigham, E., and Gapenski, L. (1988), *Financial Management,* Dryden Press, New York.

Boonstra, W., and de Jong, H. (1993), "The Future of European Banking", in *European Monetary Integration and the Financial Sector,* Eyffinger, Sylvester, and Gerards, Johan (eds.), DeGruyter, Amsterdam, pp. 84-115.

Carlin, W., and Mayer, C. (1992), "Restructuring enterprises in Eastern Europe", *Economic Policy,* no. 15, pp. 311-352.

Calvo, G. A., and Kumar, M. S. (1993), "Financial Markets and Innovation", *IMF Occasional Paper No. 102, Financial Sector Reforms and Exchange Arrangements in Eastern Europe,* Washington DC.

Corbett, J. (1990), "Policy issues in the designing of banking and financial systems for industrial finance", *European Economy,* no. 43, March, pp. 225-237.

Dallago, Bruno (1993), "Measurement of the Irregular Economy", IIASA Working paper, Vienna.

Debs, R., Shapiro, H., and Taylor, C. (1991), "Financing Eastern Europe", Group of Thirty, Washington DC.

Dobrinsky, R. (1993), "Banking in Bulgaria", *WIIW Members' Information Bulletin,* no. 12, pp. 7-17.

Filc, W., and Winkler, A. (1991), "Monetäre Voraussetzungen marktwirtschaftlicher Reformschritte in den Staaten Osteuropas", *Kredit und Kapital,* no. 7, pp. 174-197.

Fischer, S., and Gelb, A. (1991), "The Process of Socialist Economic Transformation", *Journal of Economic Perspectives* no. 5, pp. 91-105.

Frazer, P., and Orton, I. (1990), *Financial Revolution in Europe*, Lafferty Publications, London.

Gábor, I. (1993), "Schattenwirtschaft in Ungarn", *Transit,* no. 3, pp. 159-168.

Goldstein, M., Folkerts-Landau, D., El-Erian, M., Fries, S., and Rojas-Suarez, L. (1992), "International Capital Markets", *IMF World Economic and Financial Survey,* Washington DC.

Gruson, M., and Herndl, T. (1990), "Prinzipien des US-Bankrechts", *Bankarchiv,* no. 1, pp. 6-18.

Haiss, P. (1992), "Notwendige Randbedingungen für die Reformen in Osteuropa", *Wirtschaftspolitische Blätter,* no. 5, pp. 327-335.

Haiss, P., and Fink, G. (1993), "Strategic Patterns of Western Companies Entering Eastern Europe", Proceedings of the *Fifth International Conference of the Eastern Academy of Management,* Berlin, pp. 97-100.

Hunya, G. (1993), "Foreign Direct Investment and Privatization in Central and Eastern Europe", *Communist Economies and Economic Transition,* no. 4, pp. 501-511.

Jones, C. (1992), "The Cultivation of a Creed", *The Banker,* no. 12, pp. 41-43.

Kingsley, S. (1993), "European Banking and Capital Markets", *Andersen Consulting and Economist Intelligence Unit,* London.

Manasian, D. (1991), "Business in Eastern Europe", *The Economist* (Survey), 21 September.

Meth-Cohn, D. (1993), "Directors in Waiting", *Business Central Europa,* no. 5, pp. 58-59.

Montiel, P., Agénor, P., and Ul Haque, N. (1993), *Informal Financial Markets in Developing Countries*, Blackwell, Oxford.

Móra, M. (1994), "Banking in Hungary", *The Vienna Institute Monthly Report* no. 1, pp. 23-31.

Pick, M., and Turek, O. (1993), "Banking in the Czech Republic", *WIIW Members' Information Bulletin,* no. 12, pp. 18-24.

Podkaminer, L. (1994), "Banking in Poland", *The Vienna Institute Monthly Report,* no. 1, pp. 10-22.

Porter, M. (1992), "Capital Disadvantage: America's Failing Capital Investment System", *Harvard Business Review,* September-October, pp. 65-82.

Pozen, R. (1994), "Institutional Investors: The Reluctant Activists", *Harvard Business Review,* Janunary-February, pp. 140-149.

Rybczynski, T. (1992), "The role of finance in the restructuring of resource allocation in Eastern Europe", in *The New European Financial Marketplace,* Steinherr, A. (ed.), Longman, London, pp. 253-270.

Schmidt-Chiari, G. (1993), "The Role of the Banking System in the Transformation Process", in *Towards Global Banking,* Winckler, G. (ed.), IBSS Austrian Bankers Association, Vienna, pp. 9-24.

Stevenson, M. (1989), "Europe's Capital Markets", *The Economist* (Survey), 16 December.

Štiblar, F. (1994), "Banking in Slovenia", *The Vienna Institute Monthly Report,* no. 1, pp. 32-39.

Thieme, H. (1991), "Reformen des monetären Sektors in sozialistischen Ländern: Ursachen, Transformationsbedingungen und institutionelle Voraussetzungen", *Kredit und Kapital,* no. 1, pp. 1:15-35.

Thurow, L. (1992), *Head to Head,* William Morrow and Co, Inc., New York.

Timewell, S. (1993), "Catch a falling star", *The Banker,* no. 7, pp. 27-41.

Valencia, M. (1993), "The Paper Chase", *Business Central Europe,* no. 7/8, pp. 7-8.

Vankek, Z. (1993), "Tschechische Banken im Privatisierungsprozeß", *Die Bank,* no. 8, pp. 85-488.

Zwass, A. (1986), *Money, Banking and Credit in the Soviet Union and Eastern Europe,* MacMillan Press, New York.

COMMENT ON PART II:

Eduard Hochreiter*)

Two papers in this Part are conceptually very different so that it is difficult to deal with them under one heading. *Boffito* (Ch. 4) is, in effect, rather descriptive. However, his paper contains a wealth of factual information. Therefore, I recommend it for study. *Boffito's* detailed figures on Russian banks show how their development sprang out of a spontaneous privatisation process.

Calvo and *Kumar* (Ch. 5) explore the possible role of weak credit expansion in explaining the sharp output decline in reforming countries. In doing so the authors touch an important area of research. Their findings are very relevant to policy advice, especially in view of the economic take-off needed in these countries.

The basic problem, as the authors see it, is that financial markets in Eastern Europe (and elsewhere) are still in their infancy and continue to be dominated by banks (in many cases still state-owned) which – on average – prefer low risk-credit to the government and which are constrained by (the given)

---

*) Senior Adviser and Head, Foreign Research Division, Austrian National Bank, Vienna. The views expressed in this comment are those of the author and need not represent the opinion of the Austrian National Bank.

demand for bank deposits. As a result there is a severe crowding-out problem. Because of the immaturity of the financial markets, firms are forced to rely on banks for liquidity. The problem – in a nutshell – is: no funds, no production, no employment.

Calvo and *Kumar* develop a simple model which rather neatly shows that a fall in real credit provokes a fall in employment because firms have to rely on banks for working capital while the supply of credit depends on the demand for money. Without going into the details, I have one rather basic problem: what is it that causes the initial fall in the demand for money? Customarily, the demand for money is seen as a function of, *inter alia,* real income, interest rates, inflationary expectations, etc. Thus, if, as the paper argues, a fall in the demand for money leads to a fall in loanable funds and therefore in credit extended and, subsequently, to a fall in production, I wonder about the causes which induce the initial fall in the demand for money. The authors need to be clearer in this respect.

The arguments lead to some very important policy implications:

First, *institution-building has to be speeded up* and, even more important – but not mentioned by the paper – these new institutions must function. An efficient banking sector has to be created and financial markets have to be developed quickly to make firms less dependent on bank credit. In effect, slippage in this sector has to be seen "as the single most important error in sequencing, with the greatest cost to restructuring and to output" as has been noted in a recent paper by Nuti and Portes (1993).[1)]

The second policy implication concerns the ways that have to be found to *induce banks to increase lending to firms,* i.e., to raise the supply of bank credit. It is clear that the central bank cannot be called upon to take such measures because of the moral hazard implied. To achieve an increase in bank lending, solutions both to the bad debt problem and payment arrears have to be found. *Boffito* points out that in Russia the tackling of these problems had not even started. When looking at the bad debt problem one might profitably also take into account the solutions found in Chile and elsewhere. It is regrettable

1) Nuti, D. and Portes, R. (1993), "Economic Transformation in Central Europe: a Progress Report", CEPR and European Community.

that the paper only touches upon these important issues (although *Calvo* has worked on them). More details would be helpful.

In addition, credit interest rates reflecting risk might be helpful to increase bank lending to private enterprises. In this context it should also be pointed out that without rigorous training bank staff will not be in a position to assess adequately credit risks and hence are likely to continue to prefer extending riskless credit to the government.[2)] Finally, accelerated privatisation of firms might induce more bank lending because of the elimination of the "ownership limbo".

The third policy implication is that measures have to be found to *raise the demand for bank deposits.* We have two issues here: First, in many reform countries citizens are free to choose between domestic and foreign currency deposits. There is a potential currency substitution problem, if confidence in the domestic currency sags. The need to induce citizens to hold deposits in domestic currency is an additional argument for a stability-oriented monetary policy. The other aspect refers to the need to raise interest rates for deposits so that they are positive in real terms. *Calvo* and *Kumar* note this possibility but then go on to argue that raising interest rates on deposits will reduce profits and, therefore, increase the budget deficit which in turn raises the rate of inflation. While the logic of this argument is clear, it seems to be rather farfetched because in the authors' own reasoning more deposits will result in more credits, higher output and lower unemployment.

Perhaps the most important conclusions of *Calvo* and *Kumar* relate to macro-economic policy. While they show that the credit crunch has had some limited effect on the output decline, this credit crunch was not due to restrictiveness of monetary policy but rather to micro-economic reasons specific to reform countries. Therefore, a more expansionary monetary policy to increase the supply of credit and to overcome the decline in output would be counter-productive. Their paper rather points to the need for stability-oriented monetary policy in order to reduce uncertainty about the future and to speed up the micro-

---

2) In passing I would like to mention that the Austrian National Bank has singled out practical training as one of the most lasting contributions to the reform process a small country can make. Up to now, the Austrian National Bank has trained more than 3,000 central bank and bank staff from Central and Eastern Europe and the FSU in one-week seminars covering all aspects of central and commercial banking.

development of the banking sector. Furthermore, fiscal consolidation policies are called for, because of the various linkages between the fiscal deficit and inflation spelled out in the paper. *Calvo* and *Kumar* make an important contribution to the current discussion about the reasons for the output decline and their paper is highly recommended for study.

PART III – THE LIBERALISATION OF FOREIGN TRADE

Chapter 7

TRADE RELATIONS OF THE EASTERN EUROPEAN COUNTRIES

Patrick A. Messerlin[*)]

Unlike macroeconomic policies, trade policies generally evolve progressively and slowly. After a short period (from mid 1990 to late 1991) of dramatic changes, the trade relations of the Eastern European countries have returned to this typical pace.

These trade relations make a lengthening story of illusions and missed opportunities. After the collapse of the Berlin Wall, many Western institutions and governments hoped that something could be salvaged from the CMEA. These institutions only reluctantly recognised that very few trade flows imposed by the CMEA principles could be applied under market forces and that the CMEA was doomed. The view that trade flows between the former CMEA members will be important in the future (especially when higher incomes generate strong intra-industry trade) is certainly correct. But it does not mean that the trade specialisations developed in the late 1980s could evolve gradually to those sustainable under market forces and that the CMEA could carry on the transition.

---

*) Institute d'Etudes Politiques de Paris.

Similarly, hopes to create an equivalent of the Payments Union[1] established in Western Europe during the 1950s did not pay enough attention to crucial differences between the Europe of the 1950s and the Europe of the 1990s. Last but not least, the 1990s are quite different from the 1950s under one aspect crucial for trade policies (which always tend to be narrow-minded and captured by import-competing industries). The 1950s were dominated by one country which was able to blend its trade policy with strong political views about the necessity of taking into account the long-term interests of partners – hence imposing substantial sacrifices on the dominant country's domestic interests. There is no such situation in the early 1990s.

As a result, the trade relations of the East European countries are slowly dragged into a vicious circle – each lack of openness or protectionist drift by one group of trade partners being an incentive for protectionist drifts by partner countries. This is particularly true when one focuses (as this paper does) on Eastern trade relations with the EC and EFTA countries.

The paper is organised as follows. Section 7.1 presents the global picture which can be drawn from aggregate trade flows and relates it to a broad description of trade policies between 1989 and 1992 (with a special attention to the EC trade policy which has dominated the scene). It also aims at explaining why things were going wrong – in particular why the mere prospect of increased imports from Eastern countries (which could be only of modest proportions by the standard of the gigantic EC economy) faced such an opposition in the EC (and to a smaller extent in the EFTA countries). Section 7.2 describes the major sources of disputes during the two last years, the improvements that countries hoped would suffice to correct the initial errors, and the inadequacy of these measures. Lastly, Section 7.3 looks at what could be done. It suggests a few improvements which could minimise the consequences of the past errors made by both East and West. The paper covers six Eastern countries (Bulgaria, the Czech and Slovak Republics, Hungary, Poland, and Romania) with a focus on the countries which founded the Central European Free Trade Area (hereafter the Visegrád group, that is, the Czech and Slovak Republics, Hungary and Poland). Emerging trade issues which involve Russia and the successor states

---

1) The European Payments Union, established by West European countries in 1950 as a multilateral clearing home for balancing bilateral surpluses/deficits of members.

of the former Soviet Union have been left aside. However, lessons for this group of new countries may be drawn.

7.1 A global picture

The ambitious hope of a "Free Trade Europe" was quickly wrecked on a multitude of apparently minute trade issues. This sharp contrast between political hopes and trade considerations has created a situation where trade barriers maintained by the EC and EFTA countries against Eastern exports have been accompanied by a deep feeling of guilt in Western Europe. This feeling has led the EC and EFTA countries to introduce hasty changes in trade policies – but without looking at the real blocking factors, that is, the domestic policies which in some respect dominate trade issues. As a result, the EC and EFTA countries have corrected only marginally their initial errors. In fact, substantial changes in the EC and EFTA trade policies vis-à-vis the Eastern countries would require profound changes in EC or EFTA domestic "industrial" policies – which include the Common Agricultural Policy (and their even more monstrous EFTA equivalents) and the implicit anti-competition policies pursued in crucial sectors (autos, textiles and apparel, and steel).

This section examines first the evolution of trade flows and relates it to changes in trade policies. Second, it provides a brief presentation of the Association Agreements which are now well known. Lastly, it explains why the EC (and to a lesser extent, EFTA) trade concessions have been so small – when compared to the challenge of the evolution in the East.

Trade flows and trade policies

Table 7.1 presents the trade of the Eastern countries in 1989-1992.[2] It displays three major results. First, trade flows to the non-OECD countries have declined whereas trade flows with other OECD countries have considerably expanded. Second, the EC has been the main beneficiary of this new trade

---

2) Three different problems in collecting trade data make difficult the analysis of the impact of trade policies: (i) the system of official exchange rates chosen by the CMEA system makes difficult time series before 1990; (ii) the shift to the Harmonised System plus new customs procedures have created large problems about the quality of trade data in most of the Eastern countries; (iii) the creation of the Single Market has made more complex and less reliable the collection of trade data in the EC.

Table 7.1

Trade flows of the East European countries, 1989-1992

million US dollars

	Exports to				Imports from				EC share		EC-EFTA share	
	World	OECD	EC	EFTA	World	OECD	EC	EFTA	exp.	imp.	exp.	imp.
ex-CSSR												
1989	14109	5082	3625	1170	14118	5448	3676	1522	25.7	26.0	34.0	36.8
1990	11654	5243	3733	1244	13700	6626	4265	2109	32.0	31.1	42.7	46.5
1991	10896	5643	4436	953	10240	4862	3287	1209	40.7	32.1	49.5	43.9
1992	12320	7799	6093	1303	12681	7871	5323	1707	49.5	42.0	60.0	55.4
cgr[a)]	-4.4	15.3	18.9	3.7	-3.5	13.0	13.1	3.9				
Hungary												
1989	9674	3904	2390	1026	8883	4124	2534	1207	24.7	28.5	35.3	42.1
1990	9407	4864	3214	1151	8621	4412	2662	1322	34.2	30.9	46.4	46.2
1991	9972	6723	4654	1517	11420	7301	4481	1815	46.7	39.2	61.9	55.1
1992	10705	7382	5297	1575	11066	7606	4693	2281	49.5	42.4	64.2	63.0
cgr[a)]	3.4	23.7	30.4	15.4	7.6	22.6	22.8	23.6				
Poland												
1989	13533	6473	4339	1462	10328	5426	3495	1503	32.1	33.8	42.9	48.4
1990	13627	8815	6371	1862	8160	5202	3469	1367	46.8	42.5	60.4	59.3
1991	14913	10918	8290	2059	15531	10671	7750	2260	55.6	49.9	69.4	64.5
1992	14046	9615	7811	1221	18738	12875	9946	1996	55.6	53.1	64.3	63.7
cgr[a)]	1.2	14.1	21.6	-5.8	22.0	33.4	41.7	9.9				
Bulgaria												
1989	2141	730	543	70	4148	2655	1803	453	25.3	43.5	28.6	54.4
1990	2107	914	713	109	3043	2084	1608	291	33.9	52.8	39.1	62.4
1991	2160	1047	849	88	2584	1761	1316	239	39.3	50.9	43.4	60.2
1992	2592	1290	1059	102	2973	2027	1583	286	40.8	53.2	44.8	62.8
cgr[a)]	6.6	20.9	25.0	13.2	-10.5	-8.6	-4.3	-14.3				
Romania												
1989	10642	4089	2838	365	8380	1030	511	123	26.7	6.1	30.1	7.6
1990	6027	2593	1894	217	9358	2849	1838	371	31.4	19.6	35.0	23.6
1991	4193	1848	1433	247	5146	2000	1412	352	34.2	27.4	40.1	34.3
1992	4469	1883	1454	248	5582	2800	2093	363	32.5	37.5	38.1	44.0
cgr[a)]	-25.1	-22.8	-20.0	-12.1	-12.7	39.6	60.0	43.4				

a) Cgr: annual compound growth rates.

Source: International Monetary Fund, *Direction of Trade Statistics Yearbook,* 1993. Author's computations.

pattern – because EFTA countries (in particular Finland and Switzerland), which had privileged trading relations with Eastern countries before 1989, have experienced trade declines. Lastly, during this transition, ex-Czechoslovakia and Hungary (and Poland in 1991) have tended to exhibit positive balances in world trade – mirroring sound macroeconomic policies – and this evolution has protected the choice of open trade policies from the politically powerful (but economically wrong) argument about the need of protection when trade balances are negative.

This global image of profound changes in trade patterns mirrors the new economic forces reshaping the Eastern economies (from comparative advantages as defined by the CMEA to advantages determined by the markets). It also mirrors changes in trade policies.

Table 7.2

Market shares of East Europe's exports in European OECD countries, 1988-1993

monthly % growth rates

Period[a)]	**ex-CSSR**	**Hungary**	**Poland**	**Bulgaria**	**Romania**
			Eastern exports to EC		
Before the EC elimination of QRs	-0.04	0.62	0.28	0.41	-1.49
From the QR elim. to the AA[b)]	4.41	1.31	1.73	1.23	-0.05
Since the Association Agreements	1.79	0.41	1.69	---	---
			Eastern exports to EFTA		
Before the Gotheburg Declaration	-0.09	-0.30	0.28	1.17	-2.89
from the G.D. to the FTA[b)]	1.61	1.34	0.33	2.31	1.04
Since the FTA	0.83	-2.13	-1.80	-2.36	-1.68

a) For the dates, see text. Initial month: January 1988. – b) QR elim.: EC unilateral elimination and suspension of quantitative restrictions; AA: East-EC Association Agreements; G.D.: Gotheburg Declaration; FTA: East-EFTA Free Trade Agreement.

Source: OECD, *Monthly Trade Statistics,* various issues. Author's computations.

Indeed, the 1989-1993 period has witnessed remarkably rapid and strong reactions of Eastern exports to changes of EC trade policy and of their own trade policies when significant. Between 1989 and the signature of the Association Agreements, the significant change in the EC trade policy has not been the Association Agreements, but the EC's *unilateral* decision to eliminate or suspend quotas on most products (except agriculture, coal, iron and steel, textiles and apparel). During the same period, *unilateral* changes in the trade policies of the

Visegrád countries have been even more dramatic. Before these significant changes, *Table 7.2* shows that compound monthly growth rates of shares in total EC imports were negative or small for all the Eastern countries. After them (and before the signature of the Association Agreements and the new trade policies adopted by the Eastern countries) these monthly growth rates were positive and large.[3)]

That trade policies of both sides do matter is underlined by the fact (shown by *Table 7.2*) that the East-EFTA trade flows have had the same evolution as the East-EC trade flows, but with a lag of almost one year. This lag was due to the fact that the EFTA countries took the conscious decision to let the EC lead in trade policy (in order to minimise trade distortions).

By contrast, trade figures do not suggest that the EC Association Agreements with the Visegrád countries (implemented since March 1992) constitute another significant change in the EC trade policy.[4)] In 1992, the compound monthly growth rates of the shares in total EC imports have been much lower than during the period ranging from the EC unilateral elimination of the quantitative restrictions and the Association Agreements.

The Association Agreements

Detailed examinations of the East-EC Association Agreements show that these Agreements suffer from three limits which can be briefly summarised as follows.[5)] Similar observations could be made for the East-EFTA Free Trade Agreements.

First, the Agreements contain few new trade concessions by the EC (compared with the unilateral elimination and suspension of quantitative restrictions) which can be valuable in the short run for the Eastern countries. The Agreements maintain substantial tariffs and quantitative restrictions on

---

3) These growth rates are based on OECD monthly trade data (from OECD, *Monthly Statistics of Foreign Trade*, Series A, various issues) which are not always consistent with the IMF trade data used for *Table 7.1*.

4) Figures for period after the East-EFTA FTA given by *Table 7.2* should be taken with caution since they cover only a few months. No data are available for Romanian and Bulgarian trade flows with EC during this third period.

5) For instance, see Rollo (1991), Sapir and Prusa (1991), Messerlin (1992), Portes (1992) and Winters (1992).

agriculture and on textiles and apparel – two out of the four major Eastern exports. Moreover, the EC liberalisation commitments contained in the Agreements are weakened by the introduction of safeguard provisions which allow the EC to escape very easily from its obligations – raising a permanent and high risk of "reversibility" of EC trade policy. In the summer of 1992, these risks have materialised in steel – another major Eastern export – with the introduction of EC tariff-quotas on steel products exported by ex-CSSR and the re-establishment of EC surveillance on Eastern steel exports.

Second, the Eastern countries have used the Agreements as an opportunity unilaterally to raise their own trade barriers vis-à-vis the non-EC countries (sometimes with the support of EC officials). These changes are likely to have long-lasting economic effects – to increase the likelihood of increasing trade distortions during the process of European regional integration – with their associated costs.

Lastly, the Association Agreements contain provisions which tend to reduce competition in crucial exports markets for Eastern exporters. In particular, this applies to textiles and apparel where special quotas are granted to Eastern exports using EC inputs, making Eastern firms more dependent on EC firms than they would have been in a free market context. That is also now the case in steel (tubes).

Why have the Association Agreements been so limited?

The gap between the expectations raised by the fall of the Berlin Wall and the Association Agreements (which cover ten years) is so large that it raises the following question: what have been the motives for such narrow-minded and short-sighted Agreements?

During the negotiations of the Agreements, it was easy to realise that Eastern countries' exports could not be a serious threat to EC and EFTA industries. The Eastern economies are simply too small to be expected to have a large impact on the EC's gigantic (in relative terms) economy. As shown by *Table 7.3*, the order of magnitude of the difference in terms of size between the EC GDP and the total GDP of the six Eastern countries is a multiple of 29 (based on current exchange rates) or 9 times (based on PPP-based exchanges rates) and the total GDP of the six Eastern countries is smaller than the Dutch GDP (at current exchange rates) or twice this GDP (at PPP-based rates).

Table 7.3

Population and GDP: Regional groups

	population million	GDP a)	GDP b)		population million	GDP a)	GDP b)
Argentina	32.3	76.6	151.2	EFTA countries	32.7	808.1	555.5
Bolivia	7.2	4.5	13.8				
Brazil	150.4	403.1	718.9	Bulgaria	8.8	19.8	69.5
Chile	13.2	25.6	81.7	Hungary	10.6	29.5	65.6
Colombia	32.3	40.7	159.9	Poland	38.2	64.6	173.0
Ecuador	10.3	11.3	38.3	Romania	23.2	38.0	157.3
Mexico	86.2	214.6	515.5	ex-CSSR	15.7	49.3	97.2
Uruguay	3.1	7.9	18.6	East Europe	96.5	201.2	562.7
Venezuela	19.7	50.4	132.8				
Total	354.7	834.8	1830.6	Ex-USSR	250.0	625.0	1132.5
Korea	42.8	231.1	314.2	Germany[d)]	79.5	1774.4	1295.1
Hong Kong	5.8	66.6	94.1	Belgium	10.0	155.4	129.5
Indonesia	178.2	101.6	418.8	Denmark	5.1	112.6	78.4
Malaysia	17.9	41.5	105.6	Spain	39.0	429.8	422.8
Philippines	61.5	44.9	142.7	France	56.4	1099.2	857.3
Singapore	3.0	33.5	44.8	Greece	10.1	60.5	74.1
Taiwan[c)]	20.0	118.9	172.4	Ireland	3.5	33.4	32.0
Thailand	55.8	79.2	257.2	Italy	57.7	971.1	839.5
Total	385.0	717.4	1549.7	Netherlands	14.9	258.1	217.5
				Portugal	10.4	51.0	82.7
China (PR)	1133.7	419.5	2210.7	United Kingdom	57.4	924.1	858.7
Total	1518.7	1136.8	3760.5	European Community	344.0	5869.6	4887.6
Regions "Asia-Pacific"				**Regions "Europe"**			
Japan	123.5	3140.6	2093.3	Community & EFTA	376.7	6677.7	5443.1
Asia-Pacific	1642.2	4277.4	5853.8	EC, EFTA & East Europe	473.2	6878.9	6005.8
Regions "America"				EC, EFTA, East Europe & ex-USSR	723.2	7503.9	7138.3
United States	250.0	5447.5	5340.0				
NAFTA	362.7	6204.6	6396.1				
Americas	631.2	6824.8	7711.2				

Indices (EC and EFTA = 100)

Regions "Asia-Pacific"				**Regions "Europe"**			
Japan	32.8	47.0	38.5	Community & EFTA	100.0	100.0	100.0
Asia-Pacific	435.9	64.1	107.5	EC, EFTA & East Europe	125.6	103.0	110.3
Regions "America"				EC, EFTA, East Europe & ex-USSR	192.0	112.4	131.1
United States	66.4	81.6	98.1				
NAFTA	96.3	92.9	117.5				
Americas	167.6	102.2	141.7				

a) Billion US dollars, 1990, at official exchange rates. – b) Billion, US dollars, 1990, at estimated PPP exchange rates. – c) GDP based on the average of Singapore and Hong Kong. – d) GDP based on the Western German GDP.

Source: World Bank, *Development Report,* 1992. Author's computations.

In these circumstances, it could not come as a surprise that Eastern exports could capture very modest shares of EC consumption – even in the sectors where Eastern countries were expected to have comparative advantages. Simple computations (Aghion et al. 1991) suggest that Eastern exports would capture roughly 0.5 (in the most likely scenario) per cent of EC consumption (with peaks in sensitive sectors of about 1.5 per cent, except for agriculture where the Eastern countries' share could capture 3.5 per cent of the EC consumption).

Rollo and Smith (1992) reach similar global conclusions about the modest impact of the Eastern countries on the EC economy. Moreover, their much more sophisticated model is very interesting because it allows an additional hypothesis for explaining the narrow-minded Association Agreements: could the answer lie in an unequal distribution of the global impact of Eastern exports among EC regions? Rollo and Smith do not find evidence of regional concentration of losses in the EC – even for the "sensitive" sectors. For instance, they look at intra-EC changes related to the expected ECU 2 bn increase of Eastern exports of agricultural (raw and processed) products. They show that the global impact on the EC of such an increase in imports can be a small cost or a small gain. It would be a small cost if the existing CAP prices were kept unchanged: then the expected increase of Eastern exports will lead to an ECU 2 bn transfer to the Eastern countries by EC tax-payers. But it would be a small gain if EC prices were allowed to react to imports from the Eastern countries: then, EC farmers would lose ECU 3.7 bn in lost revenues, EC consumers would gain ECU 3.9 bn and EC tax-payers would save ECU 1.8 bn of budgetary burden – thus leaving a net gain of roughly ECU 2 bn (allowing the EC Commission to compensate EC farmers if politically necessary). Looking at the distribution of these gains and losses among EC Member states, Rollo and Smith found no concentration of losses in specific EC regions – with, maybe, the exception of Greece.

A last explanation could be the budgetary costs associated with the prospective EC membership of the Eastern countries – in particular the costs of the EC regional policy which consists in "structural funds" transferred from EC "rich" regions to EC "poor" regions (thus splitting Member states between net donors and net receivers). An EC enlargement to the Eastern countries would exhibit a substantial impact in terms of the "structural funds" (indeed, much larger than the impact related to CAP transfers) as shown by a CEPR (1992) simulation. *Table 7.4* which presents the results of the CEPR report shows that the total transfers related to structural funds would amount to roughly ECU 13 bn

Table 7.4

Estimated contributions and receipts of the EC structural budget and CAP[a)]

ECU million

EC Member states	contributions	receipts b)	receipts c)	net contributions
Belgium	1657	95	446	1116
Denmark	991	105	544	342
Germany	10477	1335	4219	4923
Greece	477	1080	893	-1496
Spain	3704	3135	2539	-1970
France	8589	1470	4436	2683
Ireland	363	700	460	-797
Italy	7848	1305	4269	2274
Netherlands	2272	0	2950	-678
Portugal	531	1060	558	-1087
United Kingdom	6619	595	2009	4015
Total				9325

EFTA countries (if candidates)	contributions	receipts b)	receipts c)	net contributions
Austria	1364	145	558	661
Finland	1110	40	809	261
Norway	1059	0	391	668
Sweden	1751	0	684	1067
Switzerland	1832	0	977	855
Total				3512

East Europe: central estimates (1989 output)	contributions	receipts b)	receipts c)	net contributions
ex-CSSR	617	1360	446	-1189
Hungary	341	1255	544	-1458
Poland	817	4600	1409	-5192
Bulgaria	263	1205	516	-1458
Romania	396	3190	809	-3603
Total				-12900

East Europe: low estimates (75% of 1989 output)	contributions	receipts b)	receipts c)	net contributions
ex-CSSR	478	1415	335	-1272
Hungary	253	1285	418	-1450
Poland	628	4675	1062	-5109
Bulgaria	202	1225	391	-1414
Romania	304	3225	613	-3534
Total				-12779

East Europe: high estimates (double 1989 output)	contributions	receipts b)	receipts c)	net contributions
ex-CSSR	1161	1190	893	-922
Hungary	641	1195	1088	-1642
Poland	1534	4500	2818	-5784
Bulgaria	493	170	1032	-1709
Romania	743	3195	1618	-4070
Total				-14127

a) CAP: Common Agricultural Policy. A zero entry is assumed when estimates are negative. – b) Structural funds. – c) CAP funds.

Source: CEPR, *Is Bigger Better?*, 1992.

(based on the 1989 output level for the Eastern countries). Moreover, the CEPR study provides two more results which are very interesting because they lead to conflicting conclusions. On the one hand, almost 70 per cent of these funds would go to two Eastern countries (Poland and Romania). If the budgetary problems of the EC enlargement are so limited finding some compromise is likely to be easier than expected. On the other hand, the Eastern net receipts are relatively insensitive to their outputs: when these outputs double relative to their 1989 levels, the Eastern net receipts *do* increase but only by roughly 10 per cent (because the EC mechanism is such that the new members' contributions are increased but so are their receipts). This result suggests that the budgetary problems of the EC enlargement to the Eastern countries will not be removed by Eastern growth in the next few years – if the EC rules about structural funds are not revised.

7.2 Sectoral trade disputes

The conclusion to be drawn from the previous section is that the economic impact of the Eastern countries may be small *per se,* but sufficient to oblige the EC to revise large chunks of its domestic rules. In these circumstances, sectoral trade disputes need attention, more especially as they show a similar feature: in each sector, the interests directly concerned are small but Eastern exports change the cosy ways of doing business that thirty years of EC policies have created. The section looks at the latest developments in the four familiar sectors – agriculture, textiles and apparel, steel and chemicals – which represent the bulk of Eastern exports.

Agriculture

Agriculture is one of the most bitter fields of dispute. EC trade concessions in the Association Agreements have been minimal and they have been accompanied by a host of regulations imposed by the EC on the Eastern countries that subsequent events have shown to be insufficient for shielding these countries from EC protectionism. For instance, Eastern meat can *de facto* be exported to the EC only if processed in a limited number of establishments accepted by the EC authorities and listed in the EC *Official Journal.* However in early 1993 this strong constraint did not stop the EC from imposing an immediate ban on Eastern meat exports on sanitary grounds – though it was not proved that the contaminated meat was related to Eastern production.

The EC is debating again a new package of concessions, the suggestion being to offer trade concessions defined at the highest level of disaggregation in terms of products. However, it does not seem that this approach can go very far: concessions are likely to be small, and their economic impact is likely to exacerbate distortions caused by the fact that certain agricultural products will have a low protection whereas other agricultural goods will have a very high level of protection.

This sector suggests problems which will emerge also in the following sectors. If a unilateral EC initiative (aiming at dismantling EC trade barriers in agriculture) is out of reach, there is little hope that a satisfactory solution could be found at a bilateral (East-EC or East-EFTA) level. The Eastern countries have a small bargaining power and the potential deals are very limited. In such circumstances, the solution lies (as has been proposed in GATT): in lower barriers to agricultural trade and more direct support to farmers. This solution implies a considerable change of approach for the Eastern countries – looking less to Brussels and more to Geneva – as examined in Section 7.3.

Textiles and apparel

The EC liberalisation in textiles and apparel undertaken since 1990 has been conducted *outside* the framework of the Association Agreements and *within* the traditional Multi-Fibre Arrangement (MFA) based on quotas for various categories of products. Quotas granted by the EC to the Eastern countries have been increased, but the fact remains that the EC has taken no firm, definitive and precise commitment to a complete liberalisation.

Until 1989, Eastern exporters faced an EC protection which strongly discriminated against them. Their exports were concentrated in product categories which faced the highest EC tariffs in these sectors: the average EC tariff on Eastern exports of textiles and apparel was 12.4 per cent – to be compared with 8.8 per cent for all EC MFA categories. EC quotas on Eastern exports followed a very peculiar distribution: the Eastern countries have been granted either very small, or very substantial, shares of the EC global quotas for the products concerned. As a result, Eastern exports represented a very modest portion of EC imports – less than one per cent, except in a handful of cases.

Since 1990, the EC trade policy in textiles and apparel has been an ambiguous mix of trade liberalisation and trade management. On the trade liberalisation side, the tight net of import quotas on Eastern textiles and apparel has been relaxed in 1990, 1992 and 1993. As a result, EC quotas granted to Eastern exporters have been almost doubled between 1989 and 1993: in 1989, quotas granted (for all textiles and apparel products) to each Eastern country (excluding Bulgaria) ranged from almost 3 to 5 per cent of the EC global quotas whereas, in 1992, they ranged from 4 to 7 per cent. These large increases have eliminated the EC discriminatory stance *against* Eastern exports which existed before 1990 but they have not led to a strong preference *in favour* of these exports since 1990. In particular, that the system of quotas is maintained may simply mean that the removal of tariffs may have no or little impact on the quantities exported by the Eastern countries and that the relaxation of the EC quotas may essentially lead to a shift from EC tariff revenues to private rents for the exporters, traders or EC producers which are in the best situation for manipulating quotas. It seems unlikely that Eastern exporters will be the main beneficiaries of these quota rents.

On the trade management side, the relaxation of some quotas has been counterbalanced by three measures. First, quotas have been introduced on new products (flax products). Second, quota increases to be expected after 1993 (for the period 1993-1997) are small: their compound annual growth rates range from 2 to 6 per cent in the regular quotas (that is, quotas not granted under the outward-processing traffic regulations). Last but not least, the relaxation of the EC quotas has been accompanied by the introduction of a new type of quotas at the EC level: the quotas on outward processing traffic (OPT).[6)] OPT quotas concern roughly two thirds of the MFA categories involving Eastern exports. Their average share in the total quotas (total being defined as regular plus OPT) is 40 per cent and it has been systematically increased since 1990. Moreover, between 1993 and 1997, OPT quotas will experience annual growth rates systematically 1.5 times higher than the rates for the corresponding regular quotas. OPT quotas can be seen as an instrument of pure managed trade because they make Eastern exports *conditional* on decisions by EC firms. As a result, such OPT quotas give to EC firms a strong bargaining power. They can be analysed as equivalent to a quasi-vertical integration beneficial to the EC firms (since these firms have the initiative) and their anti-competitive impact on trade and investment (in the EC and in Eastern countries) is likely to be large.

In 1993, this already complicated EC trade policy has been even more complicated by the implementation of the EC Single Market. According to this programme, "regional" quotas (that is, quotas decided by EC Member states) have been eliminated since January 1993. However, it is still not clear whether this "communitarisation" of the quotas will lead to more open EC markets. The

---

6) OPT rules specify the conditions under which EC producers can export textiles to an Eastern country for processing and reimport apparel into the EC under specific quotas and at lower tariffs.

current procedure allows "communitarised" licences to be monitored in such a way that "regional" markets could not be too much disturbed (as explicitly stated by the MFA-related bilateral agreements signed in December 1992).[7] In other words, it is not clear whether the step of regional quotas has been really eliminated or whether it is merely hidden or triggered in *ad hoc* cases.

Description of recent events leads to the following crucial question from an economic point of view: do the quota increases granted by the EC in 1990-1993 correspond to a *de facto* elimination of the quota system (because the new EC quotas would be much larger than the actual shipments of the Eastern countries)? *Table 7.5* aims at answering this question and it gives three results.

First, it reveals the ambiguities of the EC trade liberalisation. On the one hand, it shows that fewer categories are covered by quotas (that the 1993 import quotas are lower than the 1992 import quotas is caused by the elimination of quotas for some categories, generally pertaining to Group III). It also shows that the quantities pertaining to the categories still subject to import quotas in 1993 have been roughly doubled (as shown by the indexes). On the other hand, it illustrates the irresistible rise of the OPT quotas since 1992 (in 1989 the few OPT quotas were imposed by EC Member states, hence marginal and not comparable to 1992 or 1993 OPT quotas).

Second, the utilisation rates of the quotas in 1992 suggest that the Eastern countries have adjusted very rapidly to the increased quotas granted by the EC. The average utilisation rate of the total quotas is 73.3 per cent, that is, close to the utilisation rates usually observed in the textiles and apparel trade.[8] In particular, the Visegrád countries exhibit export performances equal to or better than their performances for the much smaller quotas of the 1985-1989 period.

---

7) In particular, there is still the possibility to have tariff (and product) lines in the Harmonised System specific to EC Member states on a product by product basis.

8) The high rates for Bulgaria and (to a lesser extent) for the ex-CSSR should be treated with caution (due to still preliminary and partial data).

Table 7.5

EC Multi-Fibre Arrangement quotas and East European export performances, 1989-1997

	EC regular import quotas			EC "OPT" quotas[c]				total EC quotas			
	tons	index[a]	util. rate[b]	tons	index[a]	OPT ratio[c]	util. rate[b]	tons[d]	index[a]	share[e]	util. rate[f]
Bulgaria											
1989	4819	60.1	na	g)	g)	--	--	4819	g)	0.7	52.4
1992	7765	87.4	220.2	5113	95.1	39.7	74.0	12878	90.5	0.8	162.1
1993	8022	100.0	na	5378	100.0	40.1	--	13400	100.0	--	--
1997	h)	h)	--	h)	h)	--	--	h)	h)	--	--
ex-CSSR											
1989	35864	38.7	na	g)	g)	--	--	35864	g)	4.1	60.1
1992	67531	85.7	105.6	19996	73.7	22.8	48.7	87527	82.2	5.7	92.6
1993	66544	100.0	--	27119	100.0	29.0	--	93663	100.0	--	--
1997	79071	118.8	--	36126	133.2	31.4	--	115197	123.0	--	--
Hungary											
1989	23662	43.4	na	g)	g)	--	--	23662	g)	3.5	44.5
1992	35023	87.9	77.7	26383	68.8	43.0	52.8	61406	76.0	4.0	67.0
1993	23479	100.0	--	38363	100.0	62.0	--	61842	100.0	--	--
1997	28317	120.6	--	52153	135.9	64.8	--	80470	135.9	--	--
Poland											
1989	21461	32.6	na	g)	g)	--	--	21461	g)	3.0	63.2
1992	49684	86.4	75.0	39936	85.7	44.6	69.8	89620	86.1	5.9	72.7
1993	44412	100.0	--	46599	100.0	51.2	--	91011	100.0	--	--
1997	53383	120.2	--	63728	136.8	54.4	--	117111	128.7	--	--
Romania											
1989	56195	60.6	na	g)	g)	--	--	56195	g)	5.0	39.1
1992	63650	95.1	32.9	13514	95.1	17.5	86.9	77164	95.1	5.1	42.4
1993	66297	100.0	--	14151	100.0	17.6	--	80448	100.0	--	--
1997	h)	h)	--	h)	h)	--	--	h)	h)	--	--
All above countries											
1989	142001	45.7	na	g)	g)	--	--	142001	g)	16.4	49.4
1992	223653	89.1	77.7	104942	79.7	31.9	63.9	328595	85.5	21.5	73.3
1993	208754	100.0	--	131610	100.0	38.7	na	340364	100.0	--	--
1997	h)	h)	--	h)	h)	--	--	h)	h)	--	--

a) Indexes (1993=100) are computed on the basis of the categories subject to quotas in 1993. – b) Estimates based on total imports for the full year 1992 and on OPT imports from Jan. to Sept. 1992. – c) OPT: outward processing traffic. OPT ratio is the percentage of OPT quotas in total quotas. – d) Quantities for 1989 do not include OPT quotas granted by EC Member states. – e) Tonnage of all the quotas granted to an Eastern country as a percentage of total tonnage (from all EC trading partners) under EC import quota. – f) Total imports of textiles and apparel as a percentage of total quotas. – g) Only OPT quotas granted by EC Member states. – h) Information not published.

Sources: World Bank MFA Database; EC *Official Journal;* Eurostat; European Observatory for Textiles and Clothing. Author's computations.

Third, the utilisation rates for the OPT quotas are lower than the rates for the total quotas. However, the EOTC Report (1993) underlines the fact that the Eastern countries are fulfilling their OPT quotas more than the other exporters to the EC and that they have increased considerably their exports under OPT quotas in 1992, in particular Bulgaria (90 per cent), the Czech Republic (43 per cent), Romania (32 per cent) and Poland (15 per cent).[9)] That these four countries seem to have rapidly adjusted their export capacities to the expanded EC quotas implies that the EC quota system is likely to be still binding and to remain so in the near future.

As a result, the future discussions on trade in textiles and apparel between the EC and the Eastern countries are likely to continue to be dominated by performances in terms of utilisation rates – with low utilisation rates for a given exporter as an argument for not increasing the quotas allocated to this exporter. This last observation leads to the following question: could the EC procedure (based on successive rounds of negotiations) of relaxing quotas be a source of problems for the Eastern countries in the future? The close examination of what happened between 1989 and 1993 suggests that an approach based on such a procedure tends to generate the risk of a "stop-and-go" phenomenon which would unduly stop the liberalisation process. In particular, if larger quota shares can increase the risk of lower utilisation rates for the benefiting countries, they can also reduce transaction costs – hence generate higher utilisation rates. If these two effects do not occur simultaneously (one would expect the second effect to be slower than the first) the Eastern countries could see their negotiating positions in the forthcoming negotiations weakened by getting larger quota shares during the present negotiations. This last result – compounded by the concerns on OPT quotas and by the fact that the EC provisions on price constraints (contained in the bilateral agreements and unused so far) can be a substitute to eroded quotas – leads to the suggestion of an alternative approach which would consist in unconditional annual enlargements of quotas (but at rates lower than the increases adopted in the 1992-1993 liberalisations) during the period of transition and in an unconditional complete removal of all

---

9) However, the EOTC report stresses the fact that the breakdown between imports under OPT quotas and under regular import quotas may be subject to errors at the level of customs declarations. As a result, these comparisons should be manipulated with caution.

the quotas at the end of the transition period. This point will be taken in Section 7.3.

Iron and steel

The EC trade liberalisation in iron and steel has been short-lived: EC steel markets were opened in March 1992 and *de facto* closed again (though at a higher level of trade) in August 1992 for (at least) the two next years. This failure can be explained by three reasons.

First, until 1988, the EC steel industry was truly a "command" industry based on domestic production quotas and protected by strictly binding trade barriers. Eastern steel exports to the EC were subject to quotas and basic (minimum) prices which have kept the Eastern share in the EC steel market to a constant 3 per cent. EC protection combined with their domestic problems have led Eastern producers to adopt a strategy of downgrading in terms of product mix and quality during the 1980s, the negative consequences of which will be perceived for a long time.

Second, between 1988 and 1992, the EC adopted a cautious but more market-oriented approach. That has been possible largely because the EC has maintained a substantial level of protection against steel exports from the East: EC quotas on Eastern steel exports have been maintained (though at increased levels) whereas the EC restrictions on exports from other non-EC sources (in particular, from the EFTA countries) were largely removed. As a result, EC trade liberalisation during this period has been (despite appearances) a discriminatory trade policy against Eastern steelmakers.

Lastly, the Association Agreements impose the total elimination of all the existing quotas and state that the protection of the EC markets will be based only on moderate and declining tariffs. Moreover, the Association Agreements specify that the necessary rules for the implementation of the provisions on competition and state aids shall be adopted within three years of the entry into force of the Agreements – opening a transitional period particularly uncertain in terms of rules.[10)]

---

10) Interestingly, "exceptional circumstances" are not defined by Article 5. In the Association Agreements signed with Bulgaria and Romania, Article 5 of the Iron and Steel Protocol state that in "exceptional circumstances", quantitative restrictions can be immediately imposed by the EC.

Table 7.6

EC steel quotas under the arrangements, 1989-1995

Limited quantities imposed (1000 tons)

Year[a]	Czechoslovakia b)	Czechoslovakia c)	Hungary b)	Hungary c)	Poland b)	Poland c)	Total	Other East Europe[d]	Grand Total	East Europe total exports 1000 t	East Europe utilis. rates %[e]
Export programme imposed by Germany											
1989	245.6	222.3	60.9	94.4	133.4	153.4	910.0	342.3	1252.3	890.0	7.1
1990	245.6	229.1	60.9	97.4	133.4	158.1	924.5	346.3	1270.9	998.0	78.5
1991	359.0	236.2	89.0	100.4	195.0	163.0	1142.6	474.5	1617.1	1620.0	100.2
1992[f]	292.4										
Export programme imposed by Benelux (Belgium, Luxembourg, Netherlands)											
1989	39.4	1.6	7.7	1.6	14.0	1.6	65.9	50.7	116.6	182.0	156.1
1990	46.7	1.7	8.8	1.7	16.5	1.7	77.0	59.6	136.7	178.0	130.3
1991	46.7	1.7	8.8	1.7	16.3	1.7	76.9	59.7	136.6	120.0	87.8
Export programme imposed by Italy											
1989	116.8	40.7	111.2	0.0	15.5	14.4	298.6	178.1	476.8	815.0	170.9
1990	138.4	42.0	128.6	0.0	36.5	14.8	360.3	205.4	565.7	1117.0	197.4
1991	138.4	43.3	128.6	0.0	16.5	15.3	342.0	206.1	548.1	946.0	172.6
1992[f]	36.4										
Export programme imposed by the other EC Member States											
1989	0.0	260.3	0.0	117.7	0.0	127.9	505.9	224.7	730.6	761.0	104.2
1990	0.0	268.4	0.0	121.3	0.0	131.9	521.5	231.6	753.2	833.0	110.6
1991	0.0	276.7	0.0	125.0	0.0	135.9	537.6	238.8	776.5	754.0	97.1
1992[f]	55.7										

Export programme imposed by the whole European Community											
1989	401.8	524.9	179.8	213.7	162.9	297.3	1780.4	795.8	2576.2	2648.0	102.8
1990	430.6	541.2	198.3	220.3	186.4	306.5	1883.4	843.0	2726.4	3126.0	114.7
1991	544.0	557.9	226.4	227.1	227.7	316.0	2099.2	979.1	3078.3	3440.0	111.8
1992 f)	384.5						384.5			--	--
1993 g)	134.2						134.2			--	--
1994 g)	135.0						135.0			--	--
1995 g)	155.0						155.0			--	--

a) Figures for "liberalised" steel in 1989 and 1990 are estimated. – b) E. Europe export programme under steel quotas. – c) E. Europe export programme of "liberalised" steel. – d) This column adds the three other East countries (Bulgaria, Romania and the ex-USSR) to quotas granted to the former GDR in 1989 and 1990 (quotas on GDR steel were eliminated in 1991). – e) Imports as a percentage of the Grand Total for limited quantities. – f) Quotas imposed by Germany, Italy and France under the "safeguard" action (see text). – g) Tariff-quotas imposed for the years 1993-1995 (see text).

Source: EC *Official Journal* (various years) and interviews. Author's computations.

Taking into account the large excess capacities existing in both the EC and Eastern steel industries in 1991, this sudden opening of the ECSC steel markets could lead only to price falls. As shown by *Table 7.6*, the 1991 utilisation rates of the steel quotas for the whole ECSC (and for the largest national market, Germany) were close to, or even higher than, 100 per cent – despite the increased ECSC quotas; thus Eastern steelmakers could easily export more to the ECSC. Indeed imports from the East increased and reached 4 per cent of the ECSC steel consumption for the year 1992.

Immediately, the EC "loose" cartel Eurofer requested safeguard measures. In June 1992, Eurofer made representations to the EC regarding rising steel imports from Czechoslovakia. In July 1992, the usual mechanism of *a posteriori* surveillance was reintroduced on exports from "all the countries except the EFTA countries", a diplomatic wording for the Eastern countries. In August 1992, two stronger decisions of the Commission were published. The first decision imposed quotas on Czech exports of welded tubes to Germany and reinforced the surveillance scheme on Czech exports of the same products to Italy. The second decision imposed quotas on a much wider set of products (hot rolled coils, cold laminated plates and wire rod) and three EC Member states (Germany, France and Italy): these quotas were defined as the 1991 deliveries plus 20 per cent. All these decisions were valid only for 1992.

Since Summer 1992, two types of measures have been taken. First, the anti-dumping actions against tubes exported from the ex-CSSR, Hungary, Poland and Croatia, which were initiated before the signature of the Association Agreements, have continued. In November 1992, anti-dumping measures were taken against the products investigated after December 1991 (when Eurofer made clear that it did not accept the trade liberalisation). Ex-CSSR exports were put aside (the margin of dumping was 49.6 per cent, whereas the next margin of dumping was 25.5 per cent). These provisional measures were renewed in March 1993 and final anti-dumping duties were imposed in May 1993: they ranged from 10.8 to 21.7 per cent. Meanwhile, undertakings from nine firms were accepted by the EC Commission. Moreover, in December 1992, an anti-dumping case on cast iron from FSU exporters was extended to exports from Poland (and Brazil).

Second, new safeguard measures on ex-CSSR steel exports were introduced for 1993, 1994 and 1995. In December 1992, the *a posteriori* surveillance was extended to 1993 and an *a priori* and automatic surveillance mechanism was introduced on a long list of steel products from "all the countries except the EFTA countries". In January 1993, quotas on steel exports from Bulgaria, Romania and the former Soviet Union were published. In April 1993, a new list of basic prices was published (for the first time since 1988). Lastly, in May 1993, new measures were taken concerning the Czech and Slovak steel exports in order to expand the 1992 quotas. The instrument used by the EC is tariff-quotas over the two next years: EC imports at regular tariffs are limited, and additional imports are subject to additional tariffs of 25 to 30 per cent according to the products. These measures concern a wide array of steel products (under both the EC and the ECSC regulations). Clearly, managed trade is back in the iron and steel sector.[11)]

EC contingent protection against Eastern exports

Contingent protection is defined as the set of protectionist tools the use of which is conditional on a specific situation. It includes anti-dumping measures (conditional on dumping), countervailing measures (conditional on subsidies), and the various safeguard measures (which are conditional on import surges or export displacements and which range from measures taken under GATT Article XIX to the so-called EC "new trade policy instrument").

Until 1992, the Eastern share of EC anti-dumping actions (by far the most important component of EC contingent protection) was much larger – two to four times – than the Eastern share of EC industrial imports, a feature which is likely to depend upon permanent economic forces more than upon some hypothetical bias against state trading countries. The Eastern chemical industries have been particularly targeted by these EC anti-dumping actions. EC anti-dumping actions are estimated to have covered from between 3 (the lower bound) and 15 (the higher and probably the most likely) per cent of the total manufacturing trade between the EC and the Eastern countries. The high *ad valorem* equivalents of the EC anti-dumping measures – estimated on average at 20 per cent – have left the Eastern exporters with no alternative but to curb their exports to the EC – on average by 20 per cent five years after the case initiations.

---

11) In May 1993, press reports mentioned the fear among EC independent steel users about price increases (of up to 40 per cent) following these new trade barriers (*Financial Times*, 4 May 1993). It would be interesting to look at recent price developments.

The Association Agreements are not likely to improve the situation substantially for two reasons. First, they contain no provisions which could slow down the EC anti-dumping activity – more especially as Eastern exports are concentrated on products traditionally facing anti-dumping actions, such as chemicals. Second, the Association Agreements contain safeguard provisions much looser than the anti-dumping provisions. These provisions make safeguards conditional on only two elements: an increase of imports and the existence of injury which is defined by such loose criteria that proof appears to be practically certain (as already seen, the safeguard provisions have already played an important role in the steel dispute between the EC and Czechoslovakia).

From March 1992 to late 1993 seven new anti-dumping cases have been initiated against the Eastern countries.Three have been initiated under the Association Agreements: Portland cement (Romania), cast iron (Poland) and ammonium (nitrium) fertiliser (Bulgaria and Poland). The other cases have been initiated against former Soviet Union countries: ammonium fertiliser (Belarus, Lithuania, Russia, Turkmenistan, Ukraine and Uzbekistan), ferrochrome (Russia, Ukraine, Kazakhstan), isobutanol (Russia), potassium chloride (Belarus, Russia, Ukraine), ferro-silicio-magnesium (Russia, Georgia, Ukraine, Brazil and South Africa).

During the same period, anti-dumping duties have been imposed in six cases initiated before March 1992: steel tubes (ex-CSSR, Hungary, Poland and Croatia), synthetic fibres (Romania) and ferrosilicium (Poland). Apart from the steel cases mentioned above, duties range from 14.1 per cent in synthetic fibres to 32 per cent in ferrosilicium. Undertakings – probably in the form of minimum prices – have been accepted in the ferrosilicium case (and in the steel cases).

This rapid survey leads to five observations.[12)] First, EC anti-dumping activity has not slowed down since the Association Agreements. Second, the new cases deal with traditional products: cement, cast iron, fertilisers, ferrochrome and ferrosilicium, synthetic fibres (and welded steel tubes, as already seen) are all among the best clients of the EC anti-dumping procedure. That confirms the expectation that anti-dumping actions in the future will be

---

12) One wonders how the EC anti-dumping authorities are able to make such clear distinctions between the various Republics of the former Soviet Union (though Russia and Ukraine are generally involved).

similar to those in the past (in particular, the increasing difficulties of the EC chemical industry are likely to nurture a new wave of anti-dumping actions in this sector, for goods such as fertilisers, polypropylene, polyethylene). Third, anti-dumping duties imposed recently have been no lower than those imposed before. Fourth, it happens that two new anti-dumping actions faced by Eastern exporters are "regional" (that is, related to one Member state) such as cement (Spain) and ammonium fertiliser (United Kingdom). This is a new feature which – if repeated – could also be a worrisome drift. Lastly, there is no case which shows a clear shift from procedures based on indirect price estimates (that is, the use of proxies, such as the prices in other countries) to direct price comparisons. In particular, the status of market economy had not been granted (it was granted to Croatia but denied to other Eastern exporters) before the last case of ammonium fertiliser.

That the protectionist measures taken against Czech steel exports have been based on the safeguard provisions supports the view that the safeguard provisions of the Association Agreements could be an active instrument of EC contingent protection in the near future.

7.3 What can be done?

What kind of improvements could be introduced in a situation characterised by a slow – and barely controlled – drift to more protectionist policies (relative to 1991)? Before suggesting a few changes, this section briefly describes the Eastern trade policies during the two last years.

The evolution of East European trade policies (1991-1993)

The scanty information on these policies leave little doubt about the trends: tariffs have been increased and tend to become more discriminatory, and the "delicatessen" of contingent protection are spreading – opening the back-door to non-tariff protection.

The best information available shows the evolution of the Polish tariff schedule (Warsaw School of Economics, 1993). In August 1992, Polish tariffs were increased from less than 10 per cent to 18.4 per cent on average. The new tariff schedule is based on ten basic tariff levels (the highest being 35, 40 and 45 per cent if one excepts duties of up to 145 per cent for goods such as tobacco and alcoholic beverages). Export sectors such as textiles got relatively high protection – about 25 to 30 per cent. However, Poland is by no means atypical. A similar evolution occurred in Czechoslovakia. In late 1991, Romania introduced a new tariff schedule which was higher than the schedule initially considered and in 1993 eliminated the tariff reductions introduced in 1992 in this schedule. Lastly, as underlined by the GATT (1991), Hungary has made more product-specific its global quota system.

All these developments have one common feature: they occurred during the negotiations of the Association Agreements with the EC. It was largely perceived by the Eastern countries (and by the EC) that to introduce higher tariffs was a way to improve the "asymmetry" to be incorporated in the Agreements. To start from higher tariffs was seen by the Eastern countries as a way to enjoy a longer real tariff protection during the transition period of the Agreements (again, this view was supported by EC officials).

However, the economic cost of this approach (which will inevitably increase as time goes on) is that protection vis-à-vis the rest of the world has been substantially increased. As well known, customs unions generate costs to the extent they reduce or stop imports from the rest of the world and to the extent that efficient countries exist in the rest of the world. The impact of this evolution towards a more country-discriminatory protection is compounded by an MFN provision included in the Association Agreements which states that tariff concessions to be granted by an Eastern country to the rest of the world should be immediately granted to the EC. In the next few years, this provision reduces the incentive of the Eastern countries to reduce their tariffs vis-à-vis the rest of the world because such a measure will have an immediate impact on the "benefits" of the asymmetry.

The revision of the Association Agreements: proposals

In early 1993, the EC Commissioner in charge of trade – Sir Leon Brittan – proposed that the EC should unilaterally improve the concessions embodied in the current Association Agreements. Changes proposed concentrated on four points. First, all EC tariffs on non-sensitive industrial goods (including chemicals) should be removed by the end of 1994, that is, two years earlier than scheduled. Second, the removal of tariffs on industrial sensitive goods (textiles and apparel, iron and steel) should be accelerated, the complete elimination being reached one year earlier than scheduled (1996 instead of 1997). Third, existing tariff quotas and ceilings should be increased for sensitive goods, including food products (meat, fruit, dairy goods and vegetables). Lastly, the EC should transform as many tariff quotas as possible into tariff ceilings.[13)]

These proposals leave one with mixed feelings. Without any doubt, the EC decision to act unilaterally was encouraging. However, these proposals followed the general approach taken before: they focus on tariff liberalisation and contain no firm commitment on the complete elimination of the quotas on textiles and apparel nor on the elimination of the newly re-established tariff-quotas on steel. They also remain silent on the crucial weaknesses of the constitutional provisions of the Association Agreements. As a result, these proposals may well lead to a perverse outcome: they may increase the risk of reversibility of EC trade policy because they increase the risks of using safeguard or anti-dumping actions by speeding up trade liberalisation under a too loosely constructed legal apparatus (and at a time of economic recession and protectionist mood among several EC Member states).

These fears suggest a proposal inspired by the Treaty of Rome and the first years of its so successful implementation. This proposal consists in four recommendations.

First, the focus of the revised Agreements should shift from tariff liberalisation to quota enlargement. Annual unconditional quota enlargements should be adopted in steel as well as in textiles and apparel and there should be a firm commitment to the complete elimination of the quotas at the end of a transitional period of ten years. The enlargement rates could be moderate until 1997 (the mid-term review of the Agreements) and higher during the second period of five years of the Association Agreements. As an Eastern response to these EC quota enlargements, tariff decreases could be slowed down.

Second, OPT quotas in textiles and apparel could be directly subject to an enlargement procedure leading to a total elimination at the end of the period of transition. Or they could be transformed into regular quotas according to a precise time schedule (and then be eliminated).

Third, these first two proposals represent an explicit recognition of the existence of quotas and a more gradual reduction of EC protection in the short run than is currently scheduled. As a result, they represent concessions to EC

---

13) Tariff ceilings require a request to come from one EC member state for enforcing the highest tariff (after the fulfilment of the quota). As a result, a tariff ceiling is less strict than a tariff quota (under which the tariff increase is automatic as soon as the quota is fulfilled).

firms. These concessions should be compensated by a considerable tightening of the safeguard provisions. First, there should be a unique safeguard provision, instead of several alternative versions as today. Second, the use of safeguards by EC firms should be conditional on *domestic* (that is, in the EC markets) behaviour of EC firms.[14)] For instance, EC steel firms should not be able to request the use of safeguard measures if they did not comply with the reductions of capacities or if they do not respect the EC disciplines in terms of subsidies.

Lastly, anti-dumping rules should also be tightened by the introduction of a "boomerang" provision (similar to Article 91:2 of the Treaty of Rome which was so successful in limiting the use of anti-dumping actions in the intra-EC trade; there were only twenty or so cases during the first years of the implementation of the Treaty). A boomerang provision would stipulate that goods exported from an Eastern country to the EC (and conversely) should be admitted for reimport in the partner country without any duty, quantitative restriction or equivalent measure.

All these measures have one objective: to make more economically-sound, more complete and less reversible the EC trade liberalisation. Moderate and regularly declining tariffs – rather than quotas or safeguard measures – will become the core of protection during the transition period.

These new EC concessions could be granted on a unilateral basis. They could also be accompanied by Eastern concessions in terms of the existing Association Agreements. There are three valuable concessions the Eastern countries could offer: the elimination of the infant industry provisions embodied in the Association Agreements; the adoption of trade liberalisation measures between themselves; the reduction of their discriminatory protection vis-à-vis non-EC countries.

The options for Eastern Europe

Economists have recently suggested initiatives aiming at reducing trade barriers *within* the Eastern countries. These suggestions range from these countries joining the EFTA organisation (Baldwin 1992) to the Eastern countries

14) Legal improvements (such as a better definition of the import surge, the product and the injury) could also be introduced. But experience shows that safeguards and anti-dumping provisions cannot be fought efficiently by a better legal wording (any wording can be circumvented).

creating their own common market by "importing" the Treaty of Rome (Messerlin, 1992). It is not necessary to repeat these suggestions.

It seems more important to mention that these suggestions have generally been badly received by the East. They smack of a past too recent to be completely left aside. This reaction is understandable: in the EC, it has been necessary to wait for six years after World War II before the move to the Community could start. Thus, it seems reasonable to wait until 1995 or 1996 for the Visegrád countries, for example, to emerge as a serious trade anchor for the Eastern countries.

This intra-East option should not eliminate two other options as alternatives or as complementary.

The first option is unilateral liberalisation. Countries which have chosen this way have greatly benefited from it. A good example is Chile which has chosen this option in difficult circumstances (though in a better worldwide economic environment) and which has been able to use this option as a device to solve serious economic and political problems. From purely economic aspects, relatively small countries (and this applies to all the Eastern countries) will gain more from worldwide liberalisation than from accession to the Community.

The second option for the East is to focus on GATT (that is, non-EC and non-EFTA) issues which have been left aside during these three years of intense re-orientation to Western Europe. Many issues with the EC are also major issues in the GATT arena: agriculture, textiles and clothing, steel, anti-dumping, services, etc.

It is important to stress that neither of these two options limits the strengthening of East-West European trade relations. In fact, there is a strong argument for looking at the GATT arena as a joint option for the Eastern countries and the EC – that is, regarding Eastern countries and the EC as "natural allies". In the 1990s, the EC faces a completely different world. Until the mid or late 1980s, the EC had the choice between the GATT road and the regional road, whereas the US was limited to the GATT path (because no Latin American country was then following open trade policies). As a result, the US was the natural support of the GATT rules. Now, the situation is completely inverted. The benefits of the regional road are more or less exhausted for the EC, whereas they are open for the US (and for the Asian countries). As a result, US support for GATT rules is likely to become weaker, whereas EC support is likely to become stronger. A more GATT-oriented option for the East European countries will thus be consistent with these new circumstances.

References

Aghion, Philippe, Burgess, Robin, Fitoussi, Jean-Paul, and Messerlin, Patrick A. (1992), "Towards a European Continental Common Market: A Preliminary Assessment", in *Trade Payments and Adjustment in Central and Eastern Europe,* Flemming, John, and Rollo, Jim (eds.), Royal Institute of International Affairs and European Bank for Reconstruction and Development.

Baldwin, Richard (1992), *An Eastern Enlargement of EFTA: Why the East Europeans should join and the EFTAns should want them,* Graduate Institute of International Studies of Geneva, mimeo.

Centre for Economic Policy Research (1992), *Is Bigger Better? The Economics of EC Enlargement,* Report no. 3 on Monitoring European Integration, CEPR.

EOTC (European Observatory for Textiles and Clothing) (1993), *Factual Report,* Prepared at the Request of DG III of the EC Commission, EOTC, mimeo.

GATT Trade Policy Review Mechanism (1991), *Hungary,* GATT.

– (1993), *Romania,* GATT.

Messerlin, Patrick A. (1992), "The Association Agreements between the EC and Central Europe: Trade Liberalization vs Constitutional Failure?", in *Trade Payments and Adjustment in Central and Eastern Europe,* Flemming, John, and Rollo, Jim (eds.), Royal Institute of International Affairs and European Bank for Reconstruction and Development.

– (1993), "The EC and Central Europe: The missed rendez-vous of 1992?", *Economics of Transition,* vol. 1, no. 1, pp. 89-109.

Portes, Richard (1992), *The Impact of Eastern Europe on the European Community,* Centre for Economic Policy Research, mimeo.

Rollo, Jim (1991), *Integrating Eastern Europe into a Wider Europe,* Royal Institute of International Affairs, mimeo.

–, and Smith, Alasdair (1993), "The Political Economy of Eastern European trade with the European Community: why so sensitive?", *Economic Policy,* vol. 16, pp. 141-181.

Sapir, André, and Prusa, S. (1991), *EC Trade with Eastern and Central Europe: Trade rather than Aid?,* The EC Commission, mimeo.

Winters, Alan (1992), *The Europe Agreements,* Université Libre de Bruxelles, SCH Consultants and Centre for Economic Policy Research, mimeo.

Warsaw School of Economics (1993), *Poland: International Economic Report (1992/1993),* World Economy Research Institute.

Chapter 8

FOREIGN TRADE IN THE PROCESS OF ECONOMIC TRANSFORMATION; WITH SPECIAL REFERENCE TO CZECH EXPERIENCE

Judita Štouračová[*)]
Alojz Neustadt[**)]

8.1 Foreign trade liberalisation in the reform process

Foreign economic relations of individual countries and their groupings play a key role in all the economic processes taking place in contemporary Europe towards the turn of the century – the processes of integration, disintegration, transformation and stabilisation.

For many years traditional theoretical discussions sought a solution of the fundamental dilemma: trade liberalisation versus protectionism, open economy versus autarkic development. In earlier decades (under the influence of world economic development and its problems), discussion shifted to the basic models of *liberalisation* of foreign trade, above all with respect to developing countries; at present, the discussion concentrates on trade liberalisation as a component of the transformation processes in the post-communist countries.

For the developing countries, the discussions concentrated on the analysis two basic models: the import substitution and export promotion models of development. Theoretical as well as practical approaches preferred the export promotion model (and its application). Mainly because of the serious debt problems of the developing countries (reaching even debt crises), the analyses of development opportunities concentrated recently on solving the problems of structural adjustment. In this connection, the importance of *liberalising foreign*

---

*) Managing Director, Centre for Foreign Economic Relations, Prague, Czech Republic.

**) Deputy Managing Director, Centre for Foreign Economic Relations, Prague, Czech Republic.

trade as well as opening economies to the external environment, became stressed once again, with a view to implementing desirable structural changes.[1)]

The present transformation processes in Eastern Europe challenge both economic theory and empiricism with the new, practically unknown problems of transition from the so-called developed socialist, non-market system, to a market economy.

Although these processes are taking place within different transformation models (at times widely different models), they always include the *liberalisation of foreign trade* as one of the key objectives, but also as a major instrument, of the economic policy of transformation. This is quite understandable because a *complete state monopoly* of foreign trade prevailed in most of the then socialist countries, with implications both for the institutional set-up of foreign trade and for the *impermeable economic boundary* that separated (to an extreme) the domestic economies from the development of the world economy.

This economic isolation, like the high degree of state *dirigisme* in all spheres of the national economy, is being eradicated in the early stages of economic reform by radical liberalisation measures. In practically all these countries, the liberalisation of foreign trade is being presented (at least in proclamatory form) as a key element of the move to a market economy.

A number of essential questions may be posed (see also Ch. 1):

- Should trade liberalisation be understood as an objective, or as an instrument, of economic policy?
- What should be the sequence and speed of various liberalisation measures?
- What is the causal relationship between the liberalisation measures adopted (speed, scope and depth, gradual introduction) and their influence on the behaviour of domestic producers (especially in structural, technological and performance terms)?
- In what direction and to what degree may the liberalisation of trade influence the position of transforming economies in the world economy?
- Is there any, and if so what, kind of conditionality between trade liberalisation and the application of industrial, restructuring and export-promotion policies?

---

1) See Goldin, Ian, Krudsen, Odin, and van der Mensbrugghe, Dominique (1993), *Trade Liberalisation: Global Economic Implications,* OECD, Paris.

Answers are now being given by the actual development of the economies in transition. As said above, trade liberalisation – as a set of specific measures – has been included in all reform programmes from the very beginning of their implementation.

The following facts should be stressed as a point of departure for theoretical and economic policy discussions on trade liberalisation:[2)]

- The transformation of Eastern Europe represents a dramatic, revolutionary change of the economic system;
- The reform-based transformations are very genuine; they cannot be compared with the current reforms in countries which are (and have always been) market economies;
- The former socialist countries execute their reform procedures by overcoming the inherited deformations of practically all basic components of their former economic system – characterised, in particular, by:
  - the absence (or virtual insignificance) of the private sector,
  - the artificially deformed, uniform industrial structure,
  - nearly total monopolisation of individual spheres of national economies,
  - the deformed structure of prices and price relations,
  - the underdeveloped domestic market,
  - the absence of capital and labour markets,
  - extensive centralisation and regulation of foreign trade activities, including exchange rates, customs, monetary, credit and other policies.

In this context of specific conditions for the formation of market economies, the implementation of one of the corner-stones of the reform process – trade liberalisation – becomes connected with the need to design, in *Rosati's* words, "... a specific package of trade liberalisation measures".[3)] Here is a dilemma between the need for the fast opening of the national economy (through massive liberalisation of foreign trade) on the one hand, and the legitimate need for temporary protection of the national economy on the other hand. He points to four major questions:

---

2) The issues in Eastern Europe are discussed in considerable detail and deep insight (both from the point of view of economic theory and policy) in Rosati, D.K. (1993), "Foreign Trade Liberalisation in the Transition to the Market Economy", *WIIW Research Reports,* no. 193, March.

3) Rosati, op. cit.

- the timing for introducing currency convertibility,
- the level of protection during transition,
- the level of exchange rates,
- the speed of liberalisation.

To expect an unequivocal answer to these questions would be unrealistic. Because of the specific conditions of economic development and economic standards (in the broadest sense of the word) prevailing in individual countries, their reform processes and, within them, the trade liberalisation processes, are genuine (but not universal) transformation models, differing in many respects.

Only analyses of the individual models in the form of case studies could lead to the formulation of general findings. As one of such miniature case studies, I will give some information on how these questions have been solved in the Czechoslovak, and now Czech, variant of economic transformation.

8.2 Trade policy in the Czech Republic: aims and instruments

The abolition of the state monopoly of foreign trade, of the foreign exchange monopoly and indeed of the central planning system as a whole – involving the gradual liberalisation of the external Czechoslovak economy – shaped new conditions for trade policy. In the continuing transformation of the economy, the principles of free trade have become the foundation of trade policy, with resulting changes in its objectives and instruments. Autarchic instruments for protection of the domestic market and for export promotion have receded to the background. Contractual instruments were aimed mainly at the opening of markets for Czechoslovak manufacturers and at the geographical re-orientation of foreign trade towards the markets of Western Europe and other developed market economies. Another major objective of the new instruments is to create adequate conditions for the desired inflow of foreign capital, particularly of foreign direct investments. Stress is laid on multilateral arrangements, as shown by the activities in the Uruguay round of trade negotiations within the GATT.

The instruments of policy

The foreign trade policy of the Czech Republic follows closely that of the former Czech-Slovak Federation (the CSFR): it maintains the consistent orientation towards free trade as well as the main priority: accelerating effective incorporation of the Czech Republic into European integration structures.

The liberalisation of foreign trade culminated with the enactment of the Commercial Code (Act No. 513/1991 Coll.). From 1992, foreign trade activities have become a normal part of business activities. The Commercial Code also set out new regulations for business activities of foreign persons in the former CSFR and, as a receptive Act, in the Czech Republic, too. Foreign entities and persons thus enjoy the same rights and have the same obligations as the Czechs.

For influencing foreign trade activities of the growing number of companies and entrepreneurs, in view of the increasing private share of foreign trade, the Czechoslovak Government had at its disposal only commonly used autonomous instruments. It was only in late 1991 that the Federal Government adopted an export promotion programme and established the Export and Guarantee Insurance Company (EGAP) in the form of a joint-stock company. The Company began its activities in the middle of 1992. After the division of the CSFR, EGAP a.s. was transformed into separate institutions of the Czech Republic and Slovak Republic. The Czech Government decided to increase EGAP's funds (in 1993 by half-a-billion Kč, in 1994 by one billion Kč) to enable it to increase its insurance and credit services. An act on export promotion is under preparation. The basic aim of export policy is to create for Czech exporters conditions comparable with those enjoyed by exporters of other countries. No direct export-supporting instruments are envisaged that clash with GATT rules or with obligations undertaken under other international agreements. Actual support of Czech exports remains underdeveloped as compared with that in other developed countries and, as yet, does not represent comparably coherent measures, services and institutions.

In recent years, customs policy has been activated, the customs system rebuilt and the customs tariff restructured to become closer to EC standards. The customs policy concentrated on protection of the so-called sensitive domestic products which satisfy a major portion of domestic demand, are produced on the basis of local raw materials or represent traditional Czech manufactures. Wholly or mainly imported raw materials, semi-finished products and finished products are either subject to the lowest possible duties or efforts are being made to abolish import duties altogether. The average incidence of customs tariffs amounts to only 5.8 per cent.

Through the Reception Act, the Czech Republic took over the legal provisions of the existing licensing system. Goods and services subject to licensing may only be exported and imported to the extent and under the conditions stipulated in the licence. Automatic licences are granted for the import of 86 agricultural and food products, mineral raw materials and metallurgical products.

Under the Reception Act, the Republic also took over the compensatory charges levied on imports of agricultural and food products. The charges are levied exclusively on imports of a limited number of selected products, provided that their import price falls below the cost of domestic production. The charges are expressed either as a percentage of the customs value of the goods or as a specific amount in crowns per unit. The charges represent income of the state fund for market regulation in agriculture.

The 10 per cent import surcharge levied in 1992 on imports of consumer goods was abolished on 1 January 1993. In the transition to the value added tax (rates 5 and 23 per cent), the import tax was also abolished. Imported goods are subject to the value added tax, while exported goods are exempt. The rendering of services and transfers of rights abroad are, for taxation, treated on the same basis as the export of goods. If exempt from import duties, imported goods are exempt from the tax, too. However, this principle is not applied to goods exempt from import duties under the General System of Preferences or under international agreements on customs unions, free trade areas or other arrangements. The same holds true of the exemption of consumer taxes which are levied on certain selected products (hydrocarbon fuels and lubricants, spirits and alcohol, beer, wines and tobacco products).

The introduction of the internal convertibility of the crown in 1991, allowing access to foreign currencies by entrepreneurial legal entities and, later on, natural persons, as well as the exchange rate policy maintaining a stable level of the Czech crown vis-à-vis the currency basket, form a basis for the trade policy of the Czech Government. The Foreign Exchange Act in force continues to limit capital transactions with foreign countries. Export and import of Czech currency (and of values denominated in that currency) is admissible only with permission from the Czech National Bank (CNB). Similarly, a foreign exchange account may be opened by a Czech legal entity or natural person, and capital interest abroad acquired, only with permission from the CNB.

Czechoslovakia and the European agreements

Of the contractual trade policy instruments, the most significant is the Association Agreement concluded between the former CSFR and the EC, which made it possible for the provisions on free trade to enter into force as early as 1 March 1992; their validity for the two successor states was prolonged to cover 1993. The Free Trade Agreement with the EFTA countries is derived from the Agreement with the EC. Thanks to a certain asymmetry and successive provisions to the benefit of the former CSFR and, at present, of the Czech Republic, the two agreements offer more advantageous conditions for the activities of Czech entrepreneurs. In March 1993 the Central European Free Trade Agreement between the Czech Republic, Slovak Republic, Polish Republic and the Republic of Hungary entered into force (the Visegrád group). Under this agreement, a free trade area is to be formed among these countries within eight or, in certain areas, five years.

In 1993, the contractual practice of the Czech Republic concentrated mainly on the succession to the contractual acts concluded by the former CSFR, including agreements on mutual protection and promotion of investments and agreements on the prevention of double taxation. For trade with Slovakia, the most significant contractual acts include the Agreement on Customs Union between the Czech Republic and the Slovak Republic (signed on 29 October 1992); and, following the division of the common currency and the termination of the Agreement on Monetary Arrangements, the Payments Agreement (4 March 1993) and the agreement on the settlement of certain types of payments in the foreign exchange field.

In its industrial and trade policies, the Czech Government does not consider it necessary or desirable to promote the inflow of direct foreign investments by tax concessions or other preferences. Nor does it make use of selective instruments to orient foreign investments to certain sectors or regions.

A problem faced by the Czech Government, with its markedly liberal foreign trade policy, is the protectionist measures applied by partner countries. In this connection, representatives of Czech industry point to insufficient protection of the Czech market, in particular from unfair foreign competition, and call for a more efficient support of Czech exports. Especially burdensome are imports of subsidised commodities (e.g. apples from the EC countries). Under the pressure of these facts, the Government intends to initiate in such cases anti-dumping proceedings. However, the legislation that would allow these procedures does not (at the time of writing) exist. The preparation of an anti-dumping act is under way.

Besides its principled liberal orientation, Czech foreign trade policy is based more consistently on the actual conditions prevailing in European and world trade. It is already, and will be more, pragmatic than was Czechoslovak trade policy during 1990-1992. Under the conditions of the sluggish negotiations within the Uruguay round of GATT, growing protectionism and neo-protectionism, it will more consistently aim at the assertion of trade policy interests of the Czech Republic. It can therefore be expected that the Czech trade policy will make adequate use of the protection of the domestic market and of more efficient measures to promote Czech exports.

Internal convertibility of the crown

Internal convertibility of the Czechoslovak crown, introduced on 1 January 1991, represented one of the important measures in the approved programme of economic transformation of the CSFR. It was a fundamental change, conceptually based on the mandatory sale of acquired foreign currencies to the respective banks, on the one hand, and on the possibility of buying for crowns, from such banks, foreign currency needed for payments abroad. This limited convertibility made it in principle possible to link the hitherto separated currency and price systems – the crown system and the foreign exchange system, domestic and foreign trade prices – and to establish the interbank foreign exchange market, to liberalise the transactions on current account of the balance of payments and to regulate the required equilibrium by means of instruments influencing the demand for and supply of foreign currencies.

By contrast with the previous situation, it became possible to make use of the instruments of budgetary and monetary policies to influence foreign exchange demand, the exchange rate, the development of the balance of payments and foreign exchange reserves, and to increase the efficiency of these instruments in regulating the quantity of money in the economy. At the same time, the prerequisites for application of exchange rate policy were created: the exchange rate of the crown vis-à-vis convertible currencies started to play a decisive role in balancing supply and demand for foreign currencies.

The introduction of internal convertibility was not, however, feasible without devaluation of the crown. The devaluation rate was derived from the over-valuation of the existing official rate of exchange and the excess of demand over supply for foreign currencies, on the one hand, and on the other hand from the prognosis of future trends; in this prognosis, the main factors were on the demand side – the then expected increase of oil prices and the anticipated increase of domestic price levels as a result of the liberalisation of prices. Determination of the rate of exchange that would allow introduction of internal convertibility was also influenced by estimates of the equilibrium level fluctuating between 30 and 35 CSK/US$, as well as by the black market rate and the rates reached at foreign exchange auctions. That is why there were understandable fears of possible overvaluation that would lead to unjustifiable increase in foreign indebtedness, to the need for extensive administrative controls or to excessive restriction of domestic credits. There was also a danger of successive devaluations that would strengthen inflation expectations and undermine confidence in the currency.

Under the influence of these facts and of the trends experienced in the course of 1990, the initial rate of exchange was set at a level close to the upper limit of the range (24 to 30 CSK/US$) considered, in the Government's "Scenario of the Economic Reform", the alternative to a higher initial rate. The selection of this alternative naturally intensified the effect of devaluation on the price level (estimated at 20 per cent overall rise of consumer prices following the liberalisation of prices in early 1991). However, it made possible, as the actual trends show, stabilisation of the exchange rate, strengthening confidence in the crown and credibility of the monetary as well as the exchange rate policies. Although analyses of the sensitivity of foreign trade to the changes in the exchange rate suggested that this degree of devaluation would bring about only a small growth of exports[4)], the devaluation was well founded. It allowed the introduction of internal convertibility without any major new burden of foreign loans, further liberalisation of foreign trade through successive elimination of temporary foreign exchange controls, and broader domestic access to the foreign exchange market as well as subsequent relaxation of its regulation.

---

4) For more detail, see Mandel, M. (1992), "Prognóza vývoje kursu čs. koruny na rok 1992" (Prognosis of the trend in the rate of exchange of the Czechoslovak crown in 1992), *Finance a úvěr*, no. 2, pp. 85-86.

8.3 The Czechoslovak exchange rate system

On 28 December 1990, the third devaluation of the Czechoslovak crown in that year was accomplished and its rate of exchange was set at 28 CSK/US$ in terms of the currency basket composed of five convertible currencies; at the same date, the composition of the basket as well as the weights of individual currencies were adjusted to match their shares in the turnover of the Czechoslovak balance of payments.[5] Initial basic rates of exchange for other currencies in the basket were then established at these levels.

Under the IMF classification, the Czechoslovak crown was classified as a currency with fixed rate of exchange, fixed to a basket of currencies. At the same time, the crown continued to be classed as a currency whose external purchasing power was not formed under the influence of international market forces – a currency which lacked external convertibility.

With the shift in trade with the successor states of the USSR to payments in freely convertible currencies, the share of US$ in Czechoslovak foreign transactions considerably increased, while that of the DM decreased. Consequently, the composition of the currency basket was adjusted on 2 January 1992. The share of US$ increased to nearly 50 per cent, while the shares of other basket currencies decreased (DM by 9.37 percentage points), and the £ was replaced by the French franc. The combined weight of the AS, Sfr and FF amounted only to 14.78 per cent. Hence, it was a basket with two dominant currencies. In 1992, the crown's rate of exchange thus reacted less markedly to the fluctuations in the US$, but more substantially to the changes in the DM vis-à-vis other currencies.

However, subsequent developments during 1992 showed that the increase of payments in US$ was only temporary, and that their share in the turnover of the current account again declined in favour of the DM, especially in the balance of services. That is why another adjustment was considered in 1992 in the composition of the currency basket, together with the simplification of the calculation of the crown's exchange rates. As the share of other currencies kept steadily declining, but without any marked differences from DM fluctuations, it was considered advisable to limit the currency basket to the two major

---

5) The composition of the CSK currency basket (in percentage shares of individual currencies) was as follows: DM – 42.52; US$ – 31.34; AS – 12.35; Sfr – 6.55; £stg – 4.24.

currencies, which recorded an identical exchange rate trend. Although the share of DM in the total turnover of the current account amounted in 1992 to approximately 45 per cent, it was decided to increase the share of the DM to 65 per cent, and to decrease the share of the $ to 35 per cent.

The introduction of internal convertibility changed not only the crown's rate of exchange with respect to the currency basket used but also the method of exchange rate determination. As opposed to previous practice, the rate of exchange started to reflect the ratio between supply and demand for convertible currencies on the Czechoslovak interbank foreign exchange market, based on daily purchases and sales of foreign currencies between commercial banks and the Czechoslovak State Bank SBCS as well as among the commercial banks themselves. From the very beginning, the SBCS aimed at the stabilisation of the rate through interventions, and was authorised to adjust the rate in the range of ±10 per cent if it was unable to maintain the balance between supply and demand for convertible currencies. The bank gradually acquired the resources necessary to accomplish such interventions through loans from international financial institutions. The daily announced rate of exchange is thus used for all payments. After the currency separation, the existing level of exchange rates of the former Czechoslovak crown vis-à-vis convertible currencies was taken over, without any adjustments, by the newly introduced Czech and Slovak crowns.

The interbank foreign exchange market

The establishment of the interbank foreign exchange market provided for the functioning of the internal convertibility of the Czechoslovak crown. In 1991-1992, those participating in the market were the commercial banks authorised for transactions with foreign countries as well as the SBCS. By the end of 1992, the number of participating banks was 27 (22 Czech and 5 Slovak banks).

The development of the foreign exchange market made it possible to relax certain restrictions as early as 1991. The restrictive monetary, fiscal and wage policies together with the relatively high rate of inflation eliminated excess demand by households as well as by the business sector and resulted in a decline of demand for foreign exchange. The exchange rate vis-à-vis the currency basket was maintained at the established level without any major interventions in the course of 1991. In October 1991, the SBCS was able to abolish the regulation of payment conditions for imports. The import surcharge was also gradually cut down to 10 per cent (to 15 per cent for imports for personal consumption); these values were valid for 1992. The limit for purchases of foreign currencies by the population in 1992 was increased from Kč 5000 to Kč 7,500. In April 1992, the range of entrepreneurs having access to foreign exchange resources was broadened to include natural persons as well. Trading at the foreign exchange market became enriched by the so-called swap operations, widening the range of services rendered by the commercial banks. From May 1992, the new trading rules made it possible to effect deals among the participating commercial banks at mutually agreed exchange rates.

The objectives of exchange rate policy

Linked to the system of internal convertibility, the exchange rate policy aimed at stabilising the realistic exchange rate of the Czechoslovak crown. Such a policy was considered more appropriate than an entirely free exchange policy. A stabilised rate of exchange eases implementation of the transformation programme, particularly at the early stages when market price structures are being established. It contributes to the restoration and strengthening of confidence in the local currency. At the early stages, major exchange rate fluctuations would greatly increase uncertainty in foreseeing trends. Calculations of returns would thus become very difficult, the risks and, consequently, the costs of various foreign trade activities would be high, becoming a barrier to trade as well as to investment.

The realistic exchange rate level is maintained by the central bank's interventions on the interbank foreign exchange market; thus, it is an interventionist exchange rate policy. Its more long-term goal is to reach full convertibility of the Czech crown (the same path has so far been followed by the Slovak crown). It is only in a more distant perspective that the transition to a floating rate of exchange acquires practical significance. It should not be forgotten, however, that the future decision will be predetermined, to a considerable degree, by the anticipated membership of the successor states in the EU and, consequently, by the need to create prerequisites for a closer link with the European monetary and exchange rate system now under development.

The results achieved in the implementation of the exchange rate policy in 1991 created favourable prerequisites for its extension in 1992. Thus maintaining a stable exchange rate of the crown vis-à-vis the currency basket continued to represent the basic aim of this policy for the year 1992, too. This was helped by the low inflation rate (in mid-year 6.2 per cent over the corresponding period of 1991) as well as by the development of the balance of trade and payments. Due to the inflation rates at home as well as abroad, the exchange rate did not lose its ability to stimulate exports. The changes in the dynamics of exports and imports in the second half of 1992 led gradually to a shift of the balance of trade from a surplus to a deficit, to the decline in the surplus of the current account, and to a fall in foreign exchange reserves (becoming steeper in late 1992). The interventions by the SBCS on the foreign exchange market were able to resist the pressures on the crown. The continuing inflation, the annual rate reaching 11.5 per cent, contributed to the crown's value and, thus to the weakening of export stimulation and import discouragement. However, the forces making for valuation and devaluation remained in balance so that there was no need in 1992 to abandon the objectives of exchange rate policy followed so far. On the other hand, the calls for revaluation of the crown by certain entrepreneurial circles proved unsubstantiated in the light of actual developments of foreign trade.

Czech exchange rate policy should contuinue to aim at maintaining the stabilised rate of exchange of the Czech crown against the newly adjusted currency basket. The achievement of this objective has become easier after the separation of the Czech and Slovak currencies as it no longer calls for strict coordination of their exchange policies. However, achievement depends even more on the growth of exports. The steeper the decline in Czech exports to Slovakia (no reliable data on Czech-Slovak trade have so far been available), the more difficult it will be to replace these losses by increased exports to other markets. The shift of imports to other sources and the declining dynamics of Czech exports may thus lead to a markedly stronger pressure towards a further depreciation of the Czech crown against convertible currencies. Moreover, the recovery of economic activity will generate increased imports. The expected rate of inflation, estimated at 15-17 per cent per annum, will most probably exceed the growth of prices on dominant foreign markets; the real rate of exchange of the Czech crown will thus increase and price competitiveness of exported Czech products will tend to decrease. This pressure might be weakened by increased trade in services and the flow of foreign investments. It would then become realistic to maintain a stabilised rate of exchange without additional loans for supplementing the foreign exchange reserves.

8.4 Possible lessons from the Czech experience

In seeking answers to the questions formulated above, it has been found, for the Czech economy, that:

- The liberalisation of foreign trade was accomplished as a once-for-all massive measure and was understood as one of the foundation stones of the reform process, rather than as one in a series of successive steps. This means that liberalisation, in the conditions of the Czech economy, was from the very beginning of the reform process, and still is, approached in two forms: as an *objective*, and also as a set of economic policy *measures* in the economic reform.
- By the liberalisation of Czech foreign trade, the openness of the economy has even been turned into an extreme threat by the external environment, so that one can perhaps speak of an ultra-liberal system; regulatory instruments are being consistently restricted to the operation of the market mechanism and state interventions are excluded from the model adopted as inconsistent with its other components.
- The Czech model of liberalisation of foreign trade is transparent, fully compatible with the liberal, or even ultra-liberal, models prevailing in developed market economies.
- The results of almost three years' functioning of the model for liberalising foreign trade are indeed remarkable.

Chapter 9

THE TRANSFORMATION OF EAST-WEST TRADE RELATIONS

Joseph E. Smolik*)

This paper deals with the transformation of East-West commercial relations since the political changes and economic reforms in Eastern Europe and the former Soviet Union began. The former network of trade relationships represented an accommodation between two fundamentally different economic systems, market economies on the one hand and centrally planned economies (CPEs) on the other. Given the political cleavage between East and West, their trade also took on a strategic dimension reflected, above all, in export controls on goods with military applications. Overall, East-West economic relations were fraught with discriminatory practices.

Section 9.1 of the paper discusses the normalisation of trade relations, involving the removal of discriminatory measures specific to East-West commerce. Then it addresses the development of preferential trade arrangements, which originated in the decision taken by the Group of 24 Western countries (G-24) to give the transition countries more access to their markets and thus to provide support for the economic reforms. An overview of current negotiations on new trade agreements follows. Section 9.2 summarises the progress made in opening Western markets to Eastern goods and sets out the prospects for the further extension of preferential agreements in the region. It also mentions some of the specific implications of these agreements for the trade of the CIS (former USSR) republics with Western Europe, which according to the current timetable will not take place on a preferential basis until the end of the decade, at best. Section 9.3 draws attention to three current problem areas:

---

*) United Nations Economic Commission for Europe, Geneva. The opinions contained here are the author's and do not necessarily reflect those of the United Nations.

He would like to thank Mr. P. Rayment for his comments and Mr. C. Majernik for his research assistance.

The material presented here draws in part upon section 4.2 of the UN/ECE, *Economic Bulletin for Europe,* vol. 45, 1993. This source should be consulted for details and additional references.

the apparent increase in the frequency of Western anti-dumping actions against Eastern goods, the rise in the level of protection in the transition economies and the slow pace at which the Eastern countries have promoted trade among themselves.

9.1 The transformation of trade relations

Trade under the former system of central planning is well understood so that only certain key elements need be briefly mentioned here. Planners decided the types and quantities of goods to be traded and individual trade partners. In general, the Eastern countries were price takers, reflecting their comparatively small presence in world markets and the poor quality of their goods. Often export prices would not fully cover production costs,[1] which, in any case, were based on internal prices frequently bearing little relation to relative scarcities. In short, the economic system created a large potential for trade discrimination (actually applied for political and economic goals in the form of strong CMEA preferences) and for the arbitrary pricing of exports.

Western trade policies vis-à-vis the East contained a political element as well. However, they were also designed to offset the particular consequences of the administered trade systems of the East. Western Europe and Japan applied quantitative restrictions (QRs) which originated in the system of quotas and bilateral agreements introduced after World War II.[2] The US practised tariff discrimination through denial of MFN treatment to Eastern countries. The process of dismantling these obstacles to trade got under way in the late 1960s. By the late 1970s the bulk of QRs affecting Eastern exports had been removed by the EC. Among those which remained were the so-called "specific" (i.e. discriminatory) QRs applied exclusively to selected imports from the East European and other state trading countries (other "non-discriminatory" quotas, such as those applying to steel and textiles, also remained). For its part, the US granted MFN treatment to Hungary (1978), Poland (1970), Romania (1975),

---

1) At the old overvalued accounting exchange rates, exports often incurred a loss in domestic currencies and were subsidised by the "profit" made on imports.

2) "The Determinants of East-West Trade", UN/ECE, *Economic Bulletin for Europe,* vol. 33, no. 4, p. 574.

and Yugoslavia, more for political than economic reasons.[3)] These four countries also became GATT members in the 1970s, although they acceded under special conditions intended to take into account their non-market systems.[4)]

In 1988 and 1989 the EC concluded Trade and Cooperation Agreements with Hungary and Poland.[5)] These were non-preferential agreements which reaffirmed mutual MFN treatment, created the framework for mutual trade concessions, and foresaw the removal on the EC side of certain specific QRs over several years. Similar agreements were subsequently concluded with the former Czechoslovakia (1990), Romania (1991), and the former Soviet Union (1990). These accords could be seen as a further step toward eliminating the discriminatory elements of Western policies in return for promises of increased trade by the Eastern partners.

The decision taken by the new Eastern authorities to transform their economies from centrally planned to market-based systems paved the way for the full normalisation of East-West trade relations. Reform of the external sector has involved the replacement of the administered system of trade and payments by economic instruments compatible with decentralised decision-making: foreign trade rights for enterprises, tariffs and explicit quotas in the trade sphere and internal convertibility of the domestic currency in the payments sphere.[6)] Indeed the foreign sector played an early and leading role in the economic reform (in retrospect, it proved the easiest of the sectors to restructure). In consequence, many Eastern countries ended up with relatively liberal trade systems early in the transition, in some cases (eg. the former Czechoslovak Republic) more open than those of most market economies. It should be stressed, however, that progress in reforming the external sector varies considerably among the Eastern

---

3) For more detail on the relations between East European countries and the GATT, see Lindén, Åke (1989), in *East-West Economic Relations in the 1990s*, G. Bertsch and C. T. Saunders (eds.), Macmillan (vol. 11 in the present WIIW series).

4) The other East Europeans had failed to apply for GATT membership for economic and/or political reasons.

5) A summary of unilateral trade policy measures and economic agreements between the Western market and the transition economies and the dates of their entry into force are given in UN/ECE (1993), *Economic Survey of Europe in 1992-1993*, New York, table 4.2.1, pp. 254-255.

6) Reform of the foreign trade sector is discussed in detail for the Czech Republic by *Štouračová* and *Neustadt* in Ch. 8 of this volume.

economies. As will be seen below, this has affected the development of Western trade policies toward these individual countries.

Western responses

Western policy responses to the reforms initiated in Hungary and Poland date back to the 1989 Paris Summit, when the Group of Seven industrialised countries (G-7) initiated a plan of economic support based on improved market access for Eastern goods and financial assistance.[7)] Henceforth, the Eastern countries were to be treated increasingly as market rather than centrally planned economies. In line with this new policy, the West eventually took four actions:

(a) The EC temporarily suspended all specific QRs affecting East European exports (which under the trade and cooperation agreements were to be phased out over several years). Later, in the wake of the dissolution of the USSR and Yugoslavia, the EC concluded trade and cooperation agreements with the three Baltic states (1992), Slovenia and Albania. The Commonwealth of Independent States (CIS) countries, on the other hand, accepted the obligations of the original trade and cooperation agreement concluded with Russia. All these agreements stipulate the eventual removal of discriminatory QRs.

(b) By November 1993 the US had extended MFN treatment to all Eastern countries, including all republics of the former Soviet Union, but excluding the FR Yugoslavia. Prior to the reform movement, only Hungary, Poland, Romania[8)] and the former Yugoslavia had benefited from this status. All West European countries and Canada had previously accorded MFN to their Eastern trade partners and have now extended it to the new states as well.

(c) In their legislation governing the relations with the Eastern countries, the West has begun to drop its Eastern partners from the "state trading (or non-market) category". By end-1993, the EC had made this change with respect

---

7) Coordination of the support efforts of the Western countries, the G-24, was entrusted to the EC Commission. One of the first actions taken by the G-24 involved extension of GSP privileges to most Eastern countries (see below).

8) The US suspended MFN for Romania in November 1987, after the then Romanian government unilaterally renounced these privileges. Legislation restoring MFN for Romania was signed by President Clinton in November 1993.

to Bulgaria, the Czech and Slovak Republics, Hungary, Poland and Romania. Among other things, the reclassification has potential implications for the way in which anti-dumping investigations are carried out. Anti-dumping actions have long been a key instrument to control imports of Eastern products. Although it was generally impossible to determine whether or not dumping had actually occurred (because of the problem of internal prices and exchange rates), Eastern goods were particularly susceptible to complaints because they often competed on the basis of (low) prices rather than non-price factors (quality, marketing, after sales service, etc.).

(d) Perhaps most symbolic of the change in East-West commercial relations is the decision taken in November 1993 to abolish COCOM (Coordinating Committee on Multilateral Export Controls).[9)] Established in 1951 during the Cold War, the 17-member organisation (consisting of NATO members plus Japan] was intended to prevent the transfer of Western technology to Eastern Europe and the former Soviet Union. COCOM lists of proscribed exports included not only military goods but also civilian technologies with potential military applications (so-called "dual-use" technologies). In its concern about the buildup of the East's military capacity, COCOM also hindered the Eastern area's efforts to modernise the civilian sector (although the controls were not the major reason for its technical backwardness). The lifting of the regime should facilitate the badly needed upgrading of certain sectors.

For their part, virtually all of the Eastern economies have initiated steps to modify their relations with the GATT. Hungary (1973), Poland (1967), and Romania (1971), which had become members, had been obliged to accept special terms which reflected the administered nature of their economies and are renegotiating their terms of accession to reflect their ongoing market-oriented reforms. Those countries which are seeking membership for the first time (e.g.

---

9) According to the original announcements, COCOM is to be dissolved no later than 31 March 1994. It is to be replaced with a new expanded organisation which would include Russia, other Eastern countries and industrialised Western countries not currently members of COCOM. Its basic objective will be to discourage exports of technology for producing atomic, bacteriological and chemical weapons. National export control regimes are to remain in place although these are to be liberalised.

Bulgaria) will be required to show their commitment to market principles as will also other countries now only at the stage of applying for observer status.

A cooperation agreement concluded between the EC and Yugoslavia in 1980 was the first arrangement involving preferences in East-West trade. With the demise of the old Yugoslavia in 1991, the EC made available equivalent trade preferences to Bosnia-Herzegovina, Croatia, Slovenia, and the Former Yugoslav Republic of Macedonia.[10)] A trade and cooperation agreement concluded between the EC and Slovenia in November 1992 placed these trade arrangements on a contractual basis.[11)]

Grant of General System of Preferences (GSP) privileges (i.e. favourable treatment of imports from countries recognised as "developing") by most G-24 member countries, first to Hungary and Poland in 1989 and then to other transition economies, constituted the next development of preferential trade arrangements.[12)] These were unilateral concessions granted by the Western partners, implementing the decisions of the G-7 (Paris) Summit in July 1989.

However, bilateral and multilateral economic agreements, aiming ultimately at free trade in industrial products, have been the chief instruments for the extension of preferences in East-West trade. In concluding these agreements (and, to a lesser extent, in granting GSP privileges) the Western partner has generally sought to differentiate between the individual economies, linking the degree of market liberalisation with progress in economic reform. This graduated approach is reflected in the fact that the most liberal arrangements – the EC Association Agreements (European Agreements)[13)] and EFTA free trade agreements – were concluded in 1991 with the countries furthest advanced in

---

10) In view of the civil war in Yugoslavia, the EC Council of Ministers decided in November 1991 to denounce the application of the agreement. In the following December it made available equivalent trade preferences to these four successor republics. EC Commission (1993), *Overview, EC-East Europe,* Brussels, 29 January.

11) Underthese arrangements, almost all industrial products originating in Slovenia will eventually enter the EC duty-free and almost one-third of its agricultural exports will receive preferential access. *Ibid.* A separate protocol deals with textiles and ECSC products (i.e. steel and coal).

12) Romania had already received limited GSP privileges from the EC in the 1970s, chiefly for political reasons.

13) The EC Association Agreements supersede trade and economic cooperation agreements, which contain much more modest provisions for the reduction of trade barriers.

reforms i.e. first with the Czech and Slovak Republics (then Czechoslovakia)[14), Hungary, Poland, and then with Bulgaria and Romania in 1992.[15)] The goals of the trade component of the agreements are the eventual elimination of all import duties and non-tariff barriers affecting industrial goods[16)] and improvement of access for agricultural products.[17)] The trade provisions are asymmetric in the sense that the EC and EFTA grant their East European partners immediate duty free access upon entry into force of the agreements (although exceptions are made for "sensitive" goods on which tariffs are to be reduced according to separate timetables). By contrast the Eastern partners have transition periods of up to ten years before having to grant full reciprocity. The aim of the agreements is gradually to link the economies of the EC and EFTA member states and those of their East European partners so as to prepare for the latters' eventual membership of the Community.

EFTA has generally followed the lead of the EC in reshaping its economic relations with the East, taking into account constraints imposed by the European Economic Area (EEA) and aiming at a certain compatibility between the EC's agreements with the individual Eastern countries. However, in relations with the Baltic states, Finland,[18)] Norway, Sweden and Switzerland have set the pace by concluding a network of bilateral FTAs. All of these accords have been in force since May 1993 or earlier.

With the reunification of Germany, the EC granted duty-free treatment to certain imports from Bulgaria, Czechoslovakia, Hungary, Poland, Romania, the

---

14) The dissolution of the former Czechoslovakia at the beginning of 1993 required the two successor states, the Czech and Slovak Republics, to renegotiate the original Association Agreement.

15) The trade components of the Association Agreements (Interim Agreements) with the former Czechoslovakia, Hungary and Poland came into force on 1 March 1992, with Romania on 1 May 1993, and with Bulgaria at the end of 1993. The FTA agreement between the former Czechoslovakia and EFTA countries came into effect in the second half of 1992, while those with Bulgaria, Hungary, Poland and Romania were not implemented until 1993.

16) The timetables for the reduction of tariffs and dismantling of quotas contained in the agreements with the former Czechoslovakia, Hungary and Poland can be found in UN/ECE (1992), *Economic Survey of Europe in 1991-1992*, New York, pp. 187-188.

17) By contrast with the provisions of EC Association Agreements, trade in agricultural products between EFTA members and their Eastern partners is subject to bilateral arrangements.

18) Finland's FTA with the former Soviet Union was extended to the Baltic Republics.

former USSR and Yugoslavia to the limits foreseen in trade agreements entered into by the former German Democratic Republic. Such preferences are important to the transition economies since the former GDR was one of their major markets. The EC had been authorised to accord such treatment to these countries since 1990 under a waiver from GATT rules on transitional trade measures taken in connection with the unification of Germany.[19] In 1993 the EC requested another year's extension of the waiver.

Recent Western initiatives

The unilateral measures and agreements discussed above have given the Eastern countries greater access to Western markets. However, the current arrangements have been criticised for not going far enough, for leaving too many actual and potential barriers in place. Already in the early stages of the formulation of the Association Agreements, the perceived restrictiveness of the trade provisions came under criticism from different directions,[20] especially as regards the treatment of "sensitive goods". In particular, it was pointed out that agricultural products are excluded from the proclaimed objective of free trade (although some liberalisation in this sector is foreseen), and concessions in other sectors are spread over long periods (instead of being heavily concentrated in the early years). Hence the agreements might not provide the necessary policy support for Eastern exports when it is most required. Moreover, some observers were concerned about the potential scope for both parties to apply contingent protective measures (anti-dumping and safeguard actions). Indeed, the various anti-dumping and safeguard actions initiated against Eastern exporters in 1992-1993 (see below) drew critical responses in both East and West and provoked questions about the strength of the West's commitment to open markets and support for the transition.

---

19) GATT (1993), *Focus*, no. 99, May/June. The original waiver from GATT rules, for a period of two years, was sought by the EC at the end of 1990. GATT (1990), *Circular,* L/6730.

20) On several occasions it was even proposed that the Association Agreements be scrapped and that the East European transition economies be incorporated into a free trade area centred on the European Economic Area (EEA).

The relevance of this for the transition countries is, of course, that large shares of their Western exports are concentrated in the sensitive sectors.[21) By virtue of their apparent competitiveness and production capacity, these sectors are counted on to provide the bulk of export growth in the next few years. Thus, the Association Agreements in their original form may not provide the needed policy support early in the transition, when it is most required. This argument was reinforced when the depression in the East turned out to be much deeper and longer than expected and the growth of exports to the West became virtually the sole support to domestic production. It was against this background that the EC officially addressed the issue of strengthening ties with East European countries at its Edinburgh Summit of December 1992 and then decided at the Copenhagen Summit in June 1993 to accelerate the schedule contained in the Association Agreements for improving access to its markets.[22)]

The decision involves shortening the timeframe of liberalisation of EC market access across broad product groups. It includes an accelerated reduction of EC customs duties on imports from associated countries of: *sensitive basic industrial products* (certain base metals) on which tariffs were abolished at the end of the second year after the entry into force of the Agreement (instead of at the end of the fourth year); and of *industrial products affected by the consolidation of GSP*,[23)] for which quotas and ceilings were increased by 30 per cent (for Poland, the Czech and Slovak Republics, Bulgaria, and Romania) and 25 per cent (Hungary) per year, starting from the second half of the second year after the entry into force of the Agreement (instead of by 20 and 15 per cent, respectively). In addition, levies/duties on *agricultural products* subject to quotas

---

21) In 1990 the combined export shares of the "sensitive products" (textiles and clothing, iron and steel, and agricultural products) ranged from 32 per cent for the former Czech and Slovak Federal Republic to 41 per cent for Hungary. The shares are even higher if certain bulk chemicals are included. In all three countries, sensitive goods accounted for around 40 per cent of the incremental value of the growth in their total exports to the West from 1988 to 1990. See UN/ECE (1992), *Economic Survey of Europe in 1991-1992*, New York, pp. 78-81.

22) *Agence Europe*, Documents nos. 1844/45, 24 June 1993, p. 6. This is Annex II of the Commission's report.

23) This refers to the annual Community tariff quotas or ceilings which are raised progressively. The products concerned are contained in Annex III which covers certain sensitive products such as textiles (not Multi-fibre Arrangement products), footwear, iron and steel (not ECSC products), glassware, motor vehicles and furniture.

were reduced by 60 per cent six months earlier than foreseen in the Agreements. The 10 per cent increase in the quotas, foreseen from the third year onwards, has been applied six months earlier than scheduled. Finally, *outward processing operations* have been exempted from customs duties as from the beginning of 1994.[24)]

EFTA has discussed formally granting similar concessions within the framework of the FTAs. However, some EFTA members maintain that the FTAs are somewhat more liberal than the Association Agreements and that some of the new EC concessions are already covered by liberal EFTA member GSP schemes.[25)]

Rules of origin[26)]

Another initiative to further liberalise access to Western markets involves the harmonisation of the rules of origin in the existing free trade agreements (FTAs).[27)] An aspect of these agreements which is often overlooked is that they constitute a network of essentially independent (parallel) preferential free trade zones rather than a free trade area. Although the contents of these agreements are similar and their goal is the elimination of duties and quantitative restrictions,

---

24) In other sectors, the rate of tariff reductions is somewhat slower: for *industrial products* subject to consolidation of GSP, tariffs are to be abolished at the end of the third year (instead of at the end of the fifth year); on *textile products* tariffs will be eliminated at the end of five years instead of six years; on *ECSC steel products* tariffs are to be abolished, at the latest, by the end of the fourth year instead of at the end of the fifth year, subject to compliance with specific decisions relating to trade in steel products.

25) Personal communication with the EFTA secretariat.

26) This section is based in part on material presented by H. Tschani of the EFTA Secretariat at the Second EFTA Parliamentary Colloquium with Central and East European countries, Geneva, 21 and 22 April 1993.

27) This relates to the (bilateral) Association Agreements and FTAs between six East European countries and EFTA, respectively (often described as wheel-spoke arrangements in which the EC and EFTA are the hubs); bilateral FTAs between Finland, Norway, Sweden and Switzerland and the individual Baltic countries; and two multilateral FTAs, the Central East European Free Trade Association (CEFTA, comprising the Czech and Slovak Republics, Hungary and Poland, concluded at Visegrád on the Danube, in 1993: see also note 57 to this chapter) and the Baltic FTA (signed June 1993). In Eastern Europe, only Albania, Bulgaria, Romania and the successor states of Yugoslavia do not belong to any multilateral trade group; all of their economic ties are bilateral.

they are established on bilateral lines and therefore are not linked to each other. According to their rules of origin, material originating in one free trade area is regarded as third-country material when exported for processing to another free trade area.[28] If such imported material exceeds certain limits, it fails to qualify for cumulation purposes. Put differently, such imported material disqualifies the product into which it is incorporated from benefiting from trade preferences offered in another trade area.

For certain products exported from an Eastern country to qualify for trade preferences (i.e., lower or zero tariffs) granted in a particular trade area (e.g., EC and EFTA), those products must be produced from inputs which are either: wholly obtained in the exporting country; imported from the country or group of countries granting the preferences; obtained from a third country (or trade area), but only within limits set out in the trade accord between the contractual parties. In practice little use of material coming from the outside is allowed. Material inputs which exceed specified limits have to undergo sufficient domestic working or processing for the final product to qualify for area treatment.

Thus exports from any one Eastern economy must be produced chiefly from domestic inputs or from materials originating in the respective free trade zone (EC or EFTA, but not both taken together) to qualify for preferences in either of them. Basically, no material originating in other Eastern economies can be used. The exception to this otherwise restrictive system, governed by a special protocol attached to the Association Agreement, is that materials from the Czech and Slovak Republics, Hungary and Poland (the CEFTA countries) cumulate (but only bilaterally) for export to the EC or EFTA.[29] However, this arrangement excludes Bulgaria and Romania, which individually, are able to use only domestic materials or materials from the EC and EFTA for exports to either of these groups of countries. That is to say, cumulation is bilateral between EC-Bulgaria and EC-Romania as is the case between EFTA-Bulgaria and EFTA-Romania, but no cumulation is possible between Bulgaria and Romania.

---

28) The implications of rules of origin attached to GSP schemes are similar.

29) Similarly, an EC or EFTA country is able to use for cumulation purposes materials of CEFTA origin for export to the CEFTA countries (but not to Bulgaria or Romania). It might be noted that cumulation between the CEFTA countries is bilateral under the provisions of the CEFTA Agreement, i.e., only domestic material and material originating in the country of destination qualify for cumulation purposes.

The implications of these restrictions are, first of all, that producers have an interest in selecting suppliers of inputs in countries qualifying for cumulation rather than purely on the basis of price, quality, reliability, etc. Second, the East European countries may be unable fully to utilise preferences available to them.[30)] Third, various cooperation projects involving partners from third countries may be discouraged. Finally, the application of different systems increases the administrative burden on producers, traders and the authorities involved. Thus the current systems inhibit the very regional integration which has been one of the recent key policy objectives of Eastern and Western governments. A simplification of cumulation rules is essential, so that a manufacturer can use material from any country in Europe and still be able to profit from the trade preferences. EFTA has made a proposal for a coherent pan-European system of cumulation of origin rules and a report by the EC on its possible application is due in April 1994.

Agreements in the pipeline

Albania, Estonia, Latvia, Lithuania, and Slovenia currently conduct their trade with the EC within the framework of trade and cooperation agreements (which in the case of Slovenia already provide for some preferential access, as noted). For most of these countries, negotiations are under way or planned to conclude new accords which would lead to greater, preferential access to the EC market. A full Association Agreement between Slovenia and the EC (and a FTA with EFTA)[31)] could enter into force in early 1995. In the current discussions between the EC and the Baltic states, consideration is being given to accords which are at least comparable with free trade agreements but not as comprehensive as full Association agreements. Such an outcome would provide greater access to the EC market than exists at present and would be compatible with the bilateral free trade agreements already in force between

---

30) For example, a recent EC study in part attributes the limited use of GSP by East European countries to restrictions imposed by rules of origin. See "EC trade with Central and Eastern Europe: a new relationship" (1993), section II.B, in *European Economy: The European Community as a World Trade Partner*, no. 52, pp. 38-40.

31) Negotiations between EFTA and Slovenia are to proceed in parallel with the EC-Slovenia talks. Currently, trade between EFTA members and Slovenia are conducted on an MFN basis, except for Slovene products which receive GSP treatment.

the Baltic States and the Nordic countries. The issue of compatibility between future arrangements is of concern to the EC because, under the current accords, goods originating in the Baltic States could circumvent EC tariffs by entering the EC via the Nordic countries. Ultimately, Estonia, Latvia and Lithuania hope to conclude full Association Agreements. This is also the objective of the Community "as soon as the necessary conditions have been met [by the Baltic States]."[32]

Trade relations between the CIS and the EC also continue within the framework of trade and cooperation agreements (originally concluded with the former Soviet Union). The maintenance of this arrangement reflects, *inter alia,* the EC's reservations about the degree to which these economies are functioning according to market principles. In the near future, EC-CIS economic relations are to be governed by non-preferential Partnership and Cooperation Agreements. Among other things, they are to include MFN treatment for trade in goods (except for products qualifying for GSP, which is granted separately). It appears that separate sectoral agreements are to cover agriculture, ECSC goods (steel and coal), and, possibly, uranium and aluminium.[33] Quotas in these sectors are to be set periodically, probably annually, in bilateral negotiations.[34] Until these are decided, it will not be possible to determine the extent of any additional access that these countries will receive to the EC market.

The European Commission's original mandate for negotiating a Partnership Agreement with Russia was broadened on a number of occasions in 1993 in order to strengthen support for Russia's economic reforms. Although the agreement was not completely finalised by the end of 1993, a "Joint Political Declaration" was signed in December 1993 which contains most of the main principles envisaged for the Partnership Agreement.[35] In the economic sphere these include:

---

32) European Council of Copenhagen, 21-22 June 1993, *Agence Europe,* Documents no. 1844/45, 24 June 1993.

33) Communications with officials of the EC, Russia and the Ukraine.

34) These new agreements would appear to replace sectoral accords between the EC and the USSR which were extended to the new republics. EC quotas on imports from the USSR contained in these agreements are allocated to the individual successor republics.

35) *Agence Europe*, 10 December 1993.

– improved market access on the basis of mutual MFN treatment and reductions in quantitative restrictions;

– recognition that Russia is no longer a state trading country, but an economy in transition;

– creation of more stable and predictable trade conditions. *Inter alia,* the agreement will include references to safeguard and anti-dumping procedures and to the establishment of conditions for fair competition;

– agreement to examine the possibility of creating a free trade area between the EC and the Russian Federation[36)] and a promise to work together for the gradual liberalisation of services and capital movements.

The terms of the prospective agreement reflect the progressive enlargement of EC's mandate during the negotiations, intended as a demonstration of support for the Russian government's programme of economic reform.[37)] Initially, the EC had resisted Russia's demand to be treated like a GATT member and to have incorporated in the agreement the objective of the free movement of goods, services, capital (with some restrictions) and persons. The EC argued that Russia did not yet comply with market economy rules, notably with respect to the relationship between costs and prices of goods.[38)] Instead, the EC had insisted on a special safeguard clause which would remain operational until Russia complied fully with GATT rules. This clause would permit the EC to block imports it considered were being "dumped" on its market, especially in "sensitive" sectors such as aluminium, steel and textiles.[39)] According to the prospective agreement, it appears that Russia will be removed from the EC's list of state trading countries and be treated like GATT members in the application of the safeguard clause, anti-dumping and anti-subsidy regimes, etc.

By the end of 1993, the EC had concluded at least one round of negotiations with Ukraine, Belarus, and Kyrgyzstan on a Partnership Agreement. Ukraine and Belarus have sought reference in their agreements to the creation of a free

---

36) It appears that the timetable for discussions on a free trade area will not be decided until 1998. *Agence Europe*, 10 November 1993.

37) This was also the motivation for the US' decision to grant GSP privileges to Russia.

38) *Agence Europe*, 10 June 1993.

39) Ibid.

trade agreement as a future goal, but such a request was beyond the EC's current negotiating mandate.

9.2 Future evolution of Eastern access to Western markets

The removal of or reductions in standard measures of protection (i.e., tariffs and quotas) in the West has improved the East's access to Western markets.[40] Trade between the transition countries and the Western market economies is now on a MFN basis and the Eastern countries generally enjoy GSP privileges.

In other respects, progress toward the removal of barriers has and will continue to be uneven. The most significant steps taken so far involve the preferential agreements (i.e., Association and free trade agreements) concluded by the EC and EFTA with six East European countries and between individual EFTA countries and the Baltic states. Even in these agreements, however, trade barriers remain in place. While some restrictions were lifted at the time of their entry into force, in the "sensitive" manufactures sectors (eg textiles) tariffs and quotas will be eliminated completely only over a number of years. Most assessments are that improvements in market access in the agricultural sector have not been -and will not be – large, although this sector is of current or potential importance to several transition economies. At the same time, Western subsidising of agricultural exports is said to have hindered Eastern Europe's ability to compete, even in traditional Eastern markets, and to have harmed the agricultural sector in these countries.

Reduction of EC trade barriers facing other Eastern economies – those with which trade is conducted within the framework of non-preferential, trade and cooperation agreements – has proceeded more slowly. However, accords currently under negotiation (or planned) will extend the EC-EFTA-based preferential zone Eastward over the next decade.[41] EFTA-EC agreements with Slovenia may be ready for implementation in early 1995 and the EC-Baltics FTAs probably somewhat later. In Russia and probably the Ukraine (the most

---

40) The impact of the liberalisation of Western markets vis-à-vis Eastern products is discussed in more detail in UN/ECE (1993), *Economic Bulletin for Europe*, vol. 45, New York and Geneva, pp. 112-114.

41) EFTA member countries which have applied for EC membership will presumably adopt EC external policy toward the Eastern countries, although no specific provisions or timetable for this currently exist (except in the EFTA country-Baltic bilateral FTAs).

advanced members of the CIS in their negotiations with the EC), however, discussions on a FTA are not to begin before 1998. The willingness of the EC to conclude preferential agreements has depended on its perception of the partner's degree of commitment to market principles, and this is likely to continue.

This timetable, together with the (typical) six-year transition period for the elimination of EC tariffs and quotas on Eastern industrial products, implies that the transition economies will receive unequal treatment into the next century. By 1997 the industrial exports of the first group of East European countries[42] to have concluded Association/FTAs will enjoy free access to the EC market (and EFTA). In that year, the Baltic states and Slovenia will be about half way through their transition period and will have reaped most of the benefits of trade liberalisation.[43] However, Russia, Ukraine and presumably other CIS republics will still be subject to MFN tariffs (except for GSP products) and face sectoral quotas (although the degree of restrictiveness cannot be determined yet).

Clearly, the frontrunners in this process will derive the greatest benefits, and the CIS will be at a disadvantage through at least the remainder of the decade.[44] However, the value of tariff preferences will be reduced by the one-third cut in MFN tariffs agreed under the Uruguay Round accord (which will be implemented over a period of years).

9.3 Some problem areas

Although considerable progress has been made eliminating barriers in East-West trade, several developments give some cause for concern: in the West, an apparently growing (although perhaps temporary) willingness to resort to

---

42) Tariffs and quotas facing Bulgaria and Romania will be phased out somewhat later, since their interim agreements came into force after those of the Czech and Slovak Republics, Hungary and Poland.

43) The terms of these agreements provide for the removal of a large share of the Western partners' trade obstacles in the early years of the accord.

44) The importance of these differential gains is difficult to assess due to the complexity of the schedules for tariff and quota liberalisation in the Association Agreements and EFTA FTAs and, also, the large differences in the commodity structures of the transition economies' exports. Moreover, whether a country benefits or not depends on its capacity to supply additional goods to the relevant market.

contingency measures of protection to control imports from the East; in the East, a tendency to raise domestic barriers and, also, lagging efforts by these countries to promote trade among themselves by liberalising their intra-trade.

Protectionist tendencies in the West

When the Western countries started at the turn of the decade to improve market access for Eastern goods, their domestic output and trade growth were buoyant. The favourable environment at that time facilitated domestic acceptance of this liberalisation, although even then the modest actions proposed were resisted by sectoral interests.[45] In 1991-1992, however, the Western market economies slid into recession and, as in past periods of economic difficulty, pressures built up for protection from imports. In Western Europe, there has been a tendency to blame Eastern exporters for a whole range of sectoral problems, even though officially it has been recognised that the latter account for only a small (although growing) share of the Western market.[46]

Against this background, there was a steady stream of complaints against imports of certain Eastern goods in 1992 and the first half of 1993 which eventually culminated in import restrictions. Thus the transition economies' gains in access to Western markets through the reduction in standard measures of protection (tariffs and quotas) has been partially offset by new contingent protection measures (anti-dumping and safeguard actions). The EC took such actions even against those countries with which Association Agreements were in force. Thus, one of the earliest concerns voiced about the Association Agreements – the large scope they allowed for the application of contingent protection – appears to have been justified. The new measures also raised the question whether Western governments would be able to resist further calls for protection as the recession persisted, leading to an intensification of protective measures which could endanger Eastern export growth at a crucial time in the transition. Some observers have stressed the potential risks for the transition countries of becoming engaged in sectoral, managed trade arrangements which

---

45) On the efforts of Western protectionist lobbies, see Hindley, B. (1993), "Helping transition through trade? EC and US policy toward exports from Eastern and central Europe", *EBRD Working Paper,* no. 4, March, p. 3.

46) For example, see Sir Leon Brittan, *Financial Times,* 20 March 1993.

often arise as a "solution" to actions initiated by domestic interests against imports.[47)]

The ECE secretariat has compiled an inventory of some of the measures taken against Eastern exports during the course of 1992-1993.[48)] Twenty actions were noted during the period, most of which were taken in the first seven months of 1993 and affected mainly East European products. Most of the restrictions were imposed by the EC. In many of these cases, imports from the Eastern partner(s) had risen substantially, often by between 100 and 500 per cent, over periods ranging from one to three years. Their market shares rose rapidly, but rarely exceeded 10 per cent (although in two cases it rose to about 30 per cent). Overall, however, the transition countries still account for only a small share of the Western market: in 1992 Eastern Europe and the former Soviet Union accounted for only 1.5 per cent and 1.1 per cent of total Western imports, respectively.

The inventory also shows that all of the restrictions affect the sensitive sectors (agriculture, steel, certain metals (including aluminum from the former Soviet Union) and bulk chemicals) in which the transition countries are considered to be most competitive and where much of their exports are concentrated. The latter two product groups have traditionally been the subject of Western anti-dumping or safeguard actions. It is difficult to gauge the loss of export revenues since, among other things, shipments may have been diverted to other markets.

It is perhaps useful to recall that, in general, measures of contingent protection constrain not only the exports of those enterprises directly targeted by the measures but also the exports of other sectors. The magnitude of this indirect impact is uncertain. If Eastern exporters are persuaded that the authorities in the importing area are willing to take at least occasional action against foreign goods, they are likely to take steps to reduce the probability of a formal complaint being lodged against them.[49)] This may involve, at least, a voluntary reduction in the growth of their sales. A sufficiently large number

---

47) See, for example, Ostry, Sylvia (1993), "The threat of managed trade to transforming economies", *EBRD Working Paper,* no. 3, March.

48) See section 4.2, UN/ECE (1993), *Economic Bulletin for Europe*, vol. 45, New York and Geneva.

49) The literature stresses the high cost of legal proceedings and the possibility of a permanent loss of market share.

of exporters behaving in this way may perceptibly affect the overall level of exports.[50)] These restrictive measures may also discourage foreign direct investment in the East. Foreign companies contemplating investing in the East often do so with the intention of exporting at least part of the output to the West. However, they may forego making investments if, among other reasons, they think that their goods, too, will become a target for protectionist actions.

The inventory indicates that new Western actions against certain goods from the CIS continued to be initiated in the second half of 1993, but that actions against other East European exports virtually ceased. A number of possible reasons may be suggested for the latter. The competent Western authorities may have been more successful in resisting demands for additional protection, especially after earlier actions had provoked criticism and raised questions about the strength and consistency of Western support for the transition process. Second, the pressure from East European exports has diminished. The East European export boom of 1991-1992,[51)] which is likely to have contributed to some of the Western actions in the first place, tended to peter out in 1993. Third, for the reasons mentioned above, Eastern exporters may have become more cautious as a result of the active Western anti-dumping policy during the previous year. However, even if the frequency of new actions subsides, the restraining effect of the threat of contingent protection may remain unchanged.

In contrast with Eastern Europe, economic activity in the CIS continued to decline sharply in 1993. In consequence, further quantities of certain products may have become available for export, increases which could have contributed to the Western decisions to take the new restrictive measures. The CIS may be particularly susceptible to anti-dumping actions since many Western governments still regard them as state trading countries, due to their lagging reform programmes. It appears that under the provisions of the prospective

---

50) It may be doubted, however, whether the application of contingency protection in some of the Western countries can explain the cessation or decline in the exports of several, but not all, East European economies in 1993. See UN/ECE (1993), *Economic Bulletin for Europe,* vol. 45, p. 114.

51) The rapid growth of East European exports to the West in 1991-1992 is explained in part by the collapse of domestic demand (including the metals-intensive military sector) and of the CMEA trading system, which prompted Eastern exporters to channel goods to the West. The weakening of East European exports in 1993 may reflect the stabilisation of economic activity in this area.

Partnership Agreement between the EC and Russia, the latter would be treated as a GATT member in the application of the anti-dumping clause. In principle, the EC would look at the price of the good in question in the Russian market to determine a possible dumping margin (i.e., as opposed to taking the price of a similar product in a surrogate country). It is difficult to determine the implications for Russia – indeed for all economies entitled to GATT treatment – of this and other prospective changes in anti-dumping procedures. It has been pointed out that classification of a country as a market economy (instead of a state trading economy) does not necessarily imply that it will be subject to fewer actions.[52)] The new anti-dumping code incorporated in the Uruguay Round Agreement is likely to offer the transition countries some additional protection.[53)] Positive results may also come about from the introduction of a greater degree of transparency in the EC's new anti-dumping procedures, but the net impact of the overall streamlining of these procedures remains to be seen.

Protectionism in the East

Another problem area concerns the growing tendency for Eastern countries to raise the level of their domestic protection.[54)] No one factor appears to explain the reasons for the measures taken so far, but they appear to include:

---

52) See Hindley (1993), op. cit.

53) In a number of respects the draft agreements on the new codes go beyond, but in other respects fall short of, a special regime advocated for the Eastern countries during the transition period. Elements of this proposal include the adoption of selective safeguard measures in place of anti-dumping and countervailing actions; an international (GATT) review of any request for relief from imports; limitations on the magnitude and duration of any corrective action; and a mechanism for reviewing the economic impact of such restrictions on the country's transformation process. See Ostry (1993), op. cit., pp. 21-22.

54) A partial inventory of these measures was presented in UN/ECE (1993), *Economic Bulletin for Europe,* vol. 45, pp. 111-112. It may be noted that under the EC and EFTA FTA agreements, Eastern partners benefit from a slower reduction of trade restrictions on their industrial imports than do their Western partners (i.e. the asymmetrical reduction provision).

adjustment of trade instruments to meet current needs of the transition,[55] domestic pressures arising from the deep and persistent recession, reinforced by the appreciation of East European currencies (in real terms), balance of payments considerations, and demands from sectoral interests, including foreign investors, for greater protection of their products. Since these investments are generally made in oligopolistic markets an important element of potential competition may be sacrificed. Although the restrictive moves may be justified, the danger remains that the policies will become entrenched, as they have in the West. The Eastern authorities often point to restrictive Western policies, but it is uncertain whether any of the Eastern actions have been taken specifically for this reason.

Decline and neglect of intra-Eastern trade

The final problem area raised here involves the relative lack of attention which the transition economies have given to the promotion of intra-Eastern trade. Despite the major domestic economic repercussions of the collapse of CMEA and, especially, intra-CIS trade, few steps appear to have been taken to promote these trade links.[56] This is reflected, for example, in the limited preferential trade arrangements which have emerged among former CMEA

---

55) There are grounds for believing that in certain cases the reforms resulted in excessively open systems which prematurely exposed domestic industries to foreign competition. While liberal trade regimes have undoubtedly conferred certain benefits on the transition economies, the costs have included precipitate losses in production. The impact was exacerbated by the pronounced shift in consumer preferences toward Western goods early in the transition. Although Eastern consumers have partially reverted to domestic goods, local industry is likely to have been weakened. See UN/ECE (1992), *Economic Bulletin for Europe*, vol. 44, United Nations, New York, p. 75.

56) Arguments against concerted actions to strengthen intra- Eastern trade centred on the risks of recreating the CMEA under a different guise, although this attitude now appears to be changing. Eastern Europe, however, has retained its interest in the republics of the former USSR as major markets for manufactured goods (now limited by shortages of convertible currency) and as a source of raw materials.

partners in conjunction with the reform of their trade and payments regimes[57] and in policies which give priority to the development of trade with the West.

So far only a few Eastern economies have taken steps to liberalise their intra-trade. The Czech and Slovak Republics, Hungary and Poland have created the Central European Free Trade Agreement (CEFTA)[58] and they are now in the process of concluding bilateral FTA's with Slovenia. The Baltic Free Trade Agreement has been ratified by the governments of Estonia, Latvia and Lithuania and it was to come into force on 1 April 1994. Trade between Russia and the other CIS republics is carried out within the framework of bilateral free trade agreements, most of which date from 1992. However, exchanges of many products are subject to quantitative restraints, implemented through a system of indicative and obligatory lists, and Russian exports are subject to export taxes. A CIS summit on 24 September 1993 agreed in principle to set up a CIS Economic Union. The preliminary agreement on the Union posited the gradual reduction and eventual elimination of all customs duties and other trade barriers. However, no further action appears to have been taken.

Despite these limited initiatives, there are powerful economic arguments for promoting the development of intra-Eastern trade, or at least placing it on an equal footing with exchanges with the West. Economic reforms have created the preconditions for new trade patterns in the East based on comparative advantage reflecting world prices of traded goods, enterprises operating according to commercial principles, outward-looking trade policies and so on (i.e., all the economic conditions which were absent under the old system).[59] The new domestic conditions need to be complemented by a reduction in external barriers affecting their intra-trade and an upgrading of the business-

---

57) The CEFTA Agreement came about primarily to correct the incongruity that arose after the Czech and Slovak Republics, Hungary and Poland signed Association Agreements with the EC and free trade agreements with EFTA. Without CEFTA, goods traded between any two of these Eastern countries would have met less favourable tariff conditions than goods traded between one of them and the EC or EFTA.

58) The CEFTA Agreement went into effect 1 March 1993.

59) For intra-Eastern trade, the new comparative advantages of the transition countries are likely to better reflect cost advantages due to their geographical proximity and a greater exploitation of scale economies. Better use of the latter can result from producing (similar) goods for export to all markets. Under the former system, costs were often high because products were tailored for particular markets.

supporting infrastructure. Such policies would also foster the development of intra-industry trade, an important form of economic growth in the West, but underdeveloped in the former CMEA.

All of the above points apply to the republics of the former USSR as well. The rejuvenation of trade between the new republics takes on special importance in that context. The high degree of specialisation built into the production system of the former USSR resulted in a strong interdependence among the successor republics. As a result, the disintegration of these trade links contributed to the massive fall in output throughout most of the area. Overcoming these difficulties will require an improvement in the current inter-republican payments system, alleviating convertible currency shortages of the republics running large trade deficits with Russia, and the adoption of effective structural and macroeconomic policies throughout the area.

COMMENT ON PART III:

Vít Bárta*)

Before the revolutions in 1989 there was a "Chinese Wall" between the East and West in trade relations. After the wall had fallen, the process of mutual convergence started. This was a result of two factors. Firstly, the shifting away from trade priorities defined by the CMEA allocation principles towards the comparative advantages generated by the markets. Secondly, came changes in trade priorities, mostly in western countries, which were and are closely related to their domestic industrial policies.

Two observations can be made:

(a) The trade relations of East European countries went through rapid changes during 1990 and 1991. Since 1992 the intensity slowed and they now display a steadier evolutionary pace.

---

*) Economic Transition and Integration Project, International Institute for Applied Systems Analysis (IIASA), Laxenburg, Austria.

(b) Expansion of foreign trade represented an area for big initial hopes for the transition countries but later, after a period of disillusion, they became a "vale of tears". It is now apparent that there is a big difference between the declarations and rhetoric of Western countries on the one hand, and their actions on the other. Their actual policy is characterised by selfishness and growing protectionism in some trade niches. It is evident that the breakdown of communism is a challenge for developed market economies of a scope which was not originally anticipated.

The general pattern is that many Eastern countries opened up trade excessively to begin with. As a result, the trade volume between OECD countries and Eastern countries expanded substantially. But while the EC area benefited, the EFTA countries were losing. For the East, the growth of trade with market economies was a good success: it helped to offset the losses incurred on the former CMEA market. Understandably enough, after the initial expansion we are witnessing a stabilisation (or even a remarkable decline as in Hungary during 1993). It is a matter for deeper analysis to find out the reasons for both the initial expansion and for the current stagnation.

The expansion was definitely conditioned by the liberalisation of trade on both sides: Western countries abolished or liberalised quantitative restrictions and concluded Association Agreements with Eastern countries; Eastern countries dissolved the monopolies of foreign trade and liberalised both exports and imports, accompanied by the introduction of current account convertibility.

Messerlin (Ch. 7) provides an interesting table (7.2) which shows the relationship of trade development between the East and EC or EFTA on one side, and the trade agreements on the other. It looks as if the institutional framework is a powerful explanatory variable. However, this view should be completed by an analysis of national economic policies, namely the impacts of devaluations and other export promotion measures. Similarly, the extinction of export growth from the East to OECD cannot be attributed to flaws or limits of Association Agreements or to an ambiguous mix of trade liberalisation and trade management by Western countries. It is, rather, that national incentives to export and upward-creeping tariffs (for example in Poland, Bulgaria, Hungary) should be taken into account. Special attention should be given to the increase of the Hungarian real exchange rate although some experts assert that exporters disregard the real exchange rate.

Let me briefly mention some issues which arise.

(a) Strong protectionism in agriculture, textiles and apparel, steel, chemicals and others is agreed to be a shameful feature of the anti-competitive behaviour of western countries. Although liberalisation of the import of these items could bring some difficulties for developed countries, the impact should be limited. Despite some progress a significant liberalisation cannot be expected in future. In any case, foreign trade policies of Western countries are closely related to deeply rooted domestic policies. So progress in foreign trade relations calls for reconsidering domestic policy priorities.

(b) Some retreat of Eastern countries on the path to liberalise foreign trade (especially imports) is understandable and can be excused if they keep to tariffs rather than quotas. We must be sure that this process does not end with barter trade.

(c) We cannot claim to understand fully the structural changes in Eastern countries as reflected in export and import figures. In spite of numerous statistical shortcomings and discontinuities (even OECD and IMF statistics differ) it appears that trade expanded more or less across the board. But export incentives seem to have a one-shot character, implying that without new investment few Eastern surpluses can be expected in future – even in industries which are now quite successful in export performance.

(d) What is the way out from the current unsatisfactory situation? One short-term measure could be increased protection in the East in order to equalise tariff protection vis-à-vis Western countries. More promising seems to be the renegotiation of Association Agreements. Another improvement could consist of further developing Free Trade Zones within East Europe. More active export policies are also advisable.

(e) Western countries themselves should clarify their trade and economic policy strategies towards the East. They should realistically assess what can be expected from Eastern countries during their transition to market economies.

PART IV – PRIVATISATION AND INDUSTRIAL RESTRUCTURING

Chapter 10

WHO WILL OWN "NOBODY'S PROPERTY"? PRIVATISATION PROBLEMS IN RUSSIA

Oleg T. Bogomolov[*)]

At the beginning of Gorbachev's *perestroika,* a number of economists expressed the idea that so-called "socialist property" essentially belonged to no one – it lacked a subject. But the well-being of those who managed this property in the name of the state directly depended neither on the size of the property under their authority nor on its effective use. Complete or partial property losses due to bad management did not lead to those severe consequences that an entrepreneur experiences in the West. The state simply registered the losses. In a word, the changing of property rights was put forward even at that time as the principal item of an economic reform designed to make the incentive of profit the motive force of development.

Today it seems that society and its ruling powers firmly associate transition to the market with privatisation of state property. For the most part, one cannot prove that market mechanisms are beginning to function and guarantee the

---

*) Academician, Director, Institute of International Economic and Political Studies, Russian Academy of Sciences, Moscow.

progress of the economy simply by virtue of the fact that producers and consumers of goods and services are now free to behave as they please. In other words, market mechanisms will really function only when the state ceases to be a monopoly property owner of land, minerals, forests, enterprises, residential housing, roads, and so on, and when a majority of independent property owners, acting at their own risk and competing among themselves, comes into being.

But just who will become the owner of "nobody's" property, and how? Theoretical arguments on the issue continue, but practice often takes an unexpected and far from optimal turn. What arose in other countries in the course of lengthy historical development must be reconstructed in postcommunist Russia, as in the other successor states of the USSR, with the aid of social engineering, and in a fairly compressed time period. The process in question is not about the privatisation of individual state enterprises located in a sea of private business, as in Great Britain or France, but the transfer of the predominant share of national wealth into various forms of private property: individual, cooperative, corporate stock, and so forth. The task is practically unprecedented. The experiences of Hungary, Poland, and former Czechoslovakia – who are outdistancing Russia in the implementation of privatisation – are perhaps worthy of study, but do not lend themselves to simple reproduction. These countries chose dissimilar models of privatisation, and, more important, it has yet to be proved which of them is best. What is more, the psychological and social atmosphere of these countries hardly resembles that of Russia. Therefore, it is up to us to find our own path.

10.1 Privatisation policies evolve

The government of Ryzhkov believed that the purchase of state property by citizens would become the most acceptable method of privatisation. This same approach essentially underlay the "500 Days" plan for economic stabilisation and market reform. Gorbachev repeatedly spoke out in favour of selling enterprises to worker collectives or leasing them to collectives with the option to buy. Early on, the Gaidar team also preferred the sale of state property, since it considered any free distribution of property to carry the danger that people would not value and multiply such property. "What the wind brings", declared Minister Chubais, "the wind also takes away".

Thereafter the Russian government changed its position and developed a new plan of privatisation, taking into account the social mood and the lack of money for purchasing state property. The comparatively limited savings at the disposal of the population and, likewise, the resources available to enterprises (amortised deductions, technical reconstruction funds, and so on) turned out to be almost completely worthless in 1993. One can hardly expect a strong propensity to save in order to purchase enterprises in the future, given raging inflation and the negative real interest rate paid on savings accounts. In such conditions, the disposal of state property could drag on for decades or fail to take place at all.

Moral and ethical considerations must also be added to this picture. The idea that the country's riches – with the exception as a rule of the modest belongings that became personal property – belonged to the people was firmly established in social consciousness over the decades. This idea was strengthened by the constitution of the Soviet Union. Call it naiveté by virtue of the prevailing idealism, but each citizen believed that some part of the general wealth belonged to him or her. And now it is very difficult to convince those citizens of the necessity to buy their own property. This challenges a keenly felt sense of social justice and is forcing the architects of reform to turn to the idea of a partially free distribution of state property.

Specialists in Eastern Europe and the former Soviet Union alike have long recommended free distribution, or free distribution in combination with sale and purchase, as the principal method for privatising state property. A number of my articles have been dedicated to the economic and social reasons that make this method expedient. The notion of social justice speaks in favour of the idea of a combined distribution – free and paid – of state property. Possessed of enormous riches, the state, it would appear, must compensate the population for the enormous losses due to inflation and the fall of real income. Other arguments are similarly convincing. In order to create a social base for market reforms, the state should facilitate the acquisition of property by broad sectors of the population in the form of apartments, houses, and plots of land, or in the form of shares of enterprise stock and allotments of joint (cooperative) property. Property ownership will awaken in millions of people an interest in increasing the production of goods and services for the market, and accumulating and effectively using property.

In my view, the economy can be revived if people's attitude toward work changes. But in order to guarantee their motivation, effective material stimuli, adequate salaries in a sound currency, and the transformation of the masses into property owners are needed.

The limitations on consumption have reached a critical point beyond which endurance may run out and a popular revolt (*smuta*) ensue. Fiscal measures alone will not succeed in stabilising the rouble; in order to make the rouble sound, it is necessary to increase the supply of goods on the market and to find ways rapidly to widen and encourage entrepreneurial activity. Here the privatisation of state property acquires a fundamental meaning. The principal wealth of Russia – its productive and intellectual potential and natural resourses – was withdrawn from market circulation, nationalised, and then, instead of being subject to purchase or sale, was subject only to administrative redistribution between users. This removal of wealth from monetary circulation limited the supply of goods in the extreme and deprived the rouble of the guarantee so essential to it.

Valuation issues

State property (land, forests, minerals, enterprises, housing, and so on) – valued at market prices and in hard currency – could become an anchor securing the stability of the monetary and banking systems, if a considerable part of this property becomes the object of trade on the open market. Unfortunately, the government has considered privatisation least of all from this point of view. The spontaneous division of property that has begun among state authorities at various levels and among the heirs of state structures that are being liquidated, and the subsequent sale or lease of this property, have not provided for a determination of the real value of this property.

Under current conditions in Russia, only small enterprises can be privatised by sale at genuine market prices. Other means are needed for the privatisation of all other state property, including free distribution and the sale of property to Russia's citizens, or to foreigners. It seems to me that the most intelligent method of free distribution of property is the distribution of vouchers to the adult population assigning each person a portion of the value of state property. This method, however, has met and will continue to meet with a number of objections, the most important being the surge of inflation caused by the issue of vouchers.

Vouchers a source of inflation?

I believe this danger has been greatly exaggerated. The vouchers can, of course, be considered an additional means of payment entering into circulation, but this means of payment has a particular purpose: the purchase of shares of an enterprise, perhaps, or of land or apartments, that is, that part of state property that can be transformed into a market good. And it is this property that will serve as real security for people. The relation between the population's demand for means of payment and the supply of goods should not, therefore, worsen as a result of the issue of vouchers if, it stands to reason, the supply of shares, land, and so on does not excessively lag behind the supply of vouchers. Finally, the vouchers will be destroyed after their exchange into shares.

The sale of vouchers for cash should also not be considered an additional inflationary factor, inasmuch as the amount of money in the hands of the population will not increase as a result. Money will simply pass from one hand to another.

The weakness of this form of privatisation lies elsewhere. Enterprises that offer their shares in exchange for vouchers receive nothing in return that would allow them to renovate their equipment or make new investments. Only assistance in sound money and hard currency will do that. However, one must not disregard the social effect of an enterprise making an offering of its shares. The personnel, having become partial owners of their enterprises with the aid of vouchers, acquire a stimulus for more productive work and better use of the firm's plant. I will not mention the generally favourable influence this type of privatisation will exert on the political climate of the country which, in the end, will help it overcome its economic difficulties. One can be sure of this social effect only when voucher privatisation has been sufficiently well thought out in all of its details and answers on the whole to the population's conception of social justice.

This last proviso is absolutely essential, for in practice reasonable ideas are often transformed into their opposite. Such a threat is very real in Russia, where transforming enterprises into shareholder corporations and privatisation through vouchers is being forced at a fast pace. Under small-scale privatisation, small firms in retail trade and the service sector as well as local industrial firms are selling their shares at market prices at open auction. These firms' shares are redeemed either by worker collectives, which enjoy certain advantages, or with capital pulled together by private entrepreneurs. In 1992, more than 14,000 small enterprises were privatised. Altogether, this accounts for only 11 per cent of their total number. It is significantly less than the government had projected and is proof of buyers' lack of confidence in future business as well as of the difficulties of obtaining credits for purchases.

Urban apartments in a number of cities (for example, Moscow and St. Petersburg) and modest garden and dacha lots are passing into the ownership of their users free of charge. Here again, the legalities are vague and there is a great deal of red tape in registering the property rights, but for millions of people this kind of privatisation has the most tangible effect. Such privatisation does not correct, but rather reinforces the unfair distribution of goods that took place in the past. The future, however, offers the prospect of a new distribution of property according to market, and no longer administrative, laws.

At the moment, the Russian population regards the chances for using vouchers warily. Every citizen of Russia, regardless of age, possesses the right to receive a voucher of 10,000 roubles. Great uncertainty exists as to which enterprises will put their shares up for sale in exchange for vouchers; very likely, only the workers of an enterprise are certain to succeed in becoming its shareholders. Thus, not all people are inclined to wait until they can exchange their vouchers for shares – many prefer to sell vouchers for cash at a price significantly lower than face value. At the end of December 1992, the price of a voucher on a number of exchanges had sunk to 6,000 roubles. Recalculated in dollars according to current exchange rate the value of the voucher increased from $ 6-7 in December 1992 to $ 20 in November 1993.

Risks of social conflict

The sceptical attitude toward "voucherisation" has serious foundations. First of all, privatisation through vouchers applies only to a small part of the national wealth: medium- and large-scale industrial enterprises primarily in the civilian economy, and, even then, not all of these enterprises. This privatisation does not encompass military factories. The value of the land and its minerals, the forests, the state housing fund, communal facilities, intellectual potential, and much more have not been considered. The face value of a voucher was determined by dividing the highly artificial book value of the above-mentioned rather small range of enterprises by the total number of the population. The book value was calculated in already out-of-date prices even before the price liberalisation and inflation explosion. In current prices at the end of 1992, and even more so in 1993, the face value of the 10,000-rouble voucher can only be seen as a pathetic offering to people who have been robbed. If shares were to be put on the market at an amount corresponding to the book value of enterprises in pre-January 1992 prices and could be obtained at face value in exchange for vouchers, then the value of the vouchers would increase in number by 50 to 100 times. Obviously, only workers who acquire a portion of the property of their own enterprise receive this advantage; the shares remaining after this initial distribution will be sold at market prices having little in common with their face value.

It is foolish to approach privatisation without having determined beforehand the real value of the property being privatised – even if only roughly. Under conditions of rapid inflation, this valuation can only be in hard currency and using international prices. Technically, of course, this task is extremely complicated, but, as the trusteeship of East Germany by the *Treuhandanstalt* agency demonstrates, not impossible. Obviously, the assistance of Western specialists and consulting and auditing firms is required.

10.2 The privatisation process

The complexity of such an appraisal and lack of time have impelled the Russian authorities to start privatisation without bothering about the real price for which state property will be put on the market. In this situation, one can expect that some people will become undeservedly rich, while others will receive almost nothing from the sale of the state's goodies. It is difficult to know what social discontent this process bears within itself, but it is already clear that privatisation of this sort is in the hands of the former and new *nomenklatura* – that is, it is in the hands of those who control information, possess influence, and stand at the levers of management.

According to the laws adopted in Russia, all state enterprises with more than a thousand workers or a book value greater than fifty million roubles as of 1 January 1992 are subject to an obligatory reorganisation into shareholder companies and the creation of a board of directors made up of managers, workers, and government officials. In other words, these enterprises will remain state property, but must switch over to working under market conditions and competition, covering all their own expenses (including capital investment) from proceeds derived from the sale of products and services and the use of bank credits. This approach to privatisation sometimes goes under the name of "commercialisation". After this commercialisation, privatisation in the proper sense ought to begin, as the enterprise will receive the right to choose one of two possible privatisation plans.

According to the first plan, a quarter of a company's capital is to be transferred free of charge to its workers in the form of nonvoting shares of stock, with up to 10 per cent of the voting shares available for their purchase at a 30 per cent discount from the face value. Under favourable conditions, managers will receive 5 per cent of the total stock package. The remaining shares are reserved for the state and may be sold to any willing buyer.

According to the second plan, workers and managers together have the right to purchase up to 51 per cent of the enterprise's entire capital stock, estimated at its book value as of 1 January 1992, multiplied by a factor of 1.7.

The procedures for acquiring shares in exchange for vouchers at open auction in which all willing buyers participate have not yet been definitely determined. An experiment with the large-scale enterprise *Eleks* in Vladimir, which produces televisions and computers, is noteworthy. In the government's opinion, this experiment can become an example for other privatisations and will demonstrate to many citizens how to use their vouchers. Those who wish to acquire shares of *Eleks*, but choose not to name an acceptable price for these shares, hand in a demand to the State Property Administration (*Goskomimushchestvo*) indicating the number of shares they wish to buy. These people make up the first group of buyers. Those who are bolder and prepared to suggest a price form the second group; they turn in a bid indicating the number of vouchers they are prepared to exchange for a certain number of shares.

The State Property Administration then determines a base price for the shares by dividing the face value of the total number of shares demanded by the first group by the number of shares being offered for sale. Next, all bids of the second group lower than the base price are thrown out. The final price is established by calculating the mean of the weighted value of the total number of demands at the base price and the total value of bids exceeding the base price. Practice will show how workable these procedures are and whether or not they allow for the real price of the shares to be determined.

By the middle of 1993, the more than 6,500 privatised enterprises received the necessary legalisation by the government. Employees of three-fourths of all privatised enterprises have chosen the second plan. Characteristically, the workers of the largest auto factory in Volzhsk were in favour of the second plan, which gave them control of the enterprise and provided considerable profits derived from the difference between the book and real value of the enterprise. The advantages received by workers of the most modern and more or less efficiently functioning enterprises when they trade their vouchers for shares explains why they are buying up vouchers from the rest of the population. The industrial élite's acquisition of vouchers on the cheap is becoming a more widespread phenomenon and is troubling public opinion.

Privatising land – special problems

The most disputable aspect of the privatisation programme concerns land. 95 per cent of the arable land belongs to the state and collective farms, which got it free of charge for permanent use. In 1991 individual farmers got the right to lease land or to buy it as private property. But a ten-year moratorium was introduced before the privately owned land could be sold.

In October 1993 the President of Russia abolished this moratorium and introduced some new rules for land privatisation. Now members of collective or state farms will each get equal allotments of the joint property at their disposal (land and fixed capital). These allotments can be withdrawn by each member of the collective farm for the establishment of a family farm, sale or organisation of a joint farm with other families.

There are still many unclear technical details about implementation of the new legislation on land. Some additional clarification will be needed to prevent the destruction of the effective and profitable state cooperative farms and the possible misuse of land. The new legislation allows peasants to acquire land as their property free of charge (within the limits of their allotments) or to buy it at auctions. How the land reform will affect agricultural production is hard to foresee. But one can hope that the right to sell, buy and mortgage land will prod the transition to a market economy.

10.3 Criticism of the programme

The practical realisation of the government's privatisation programme is subject to intensifying criticism of both its conception and implementation. Correction of the government's chosen course is becoming more and more urgent. Ideal solutions are altogether impossible, yet it is highly desirable to reduce the social and economic costs of so cardinal a reform to a minimum. Otherwise a struggle for the next redistribution of what was once "nobody's" property will break out.

Above all, the aspiration to do away with state property in one fell swoop in a short period, using two or three standard privatisation plans, must be called in question. This process does not account for the diversity of concrete working conditions of different types of enterprises in various branches of the economy. Critics adopt a common theme in the government's plans for all-out stock issue and "avalanche" privatisation: they perceive excessive curtailment of state participation in economic activity and too much deregulation of the economy. In their opinion, it is a mistake to suppose that state property is in all conditions absolutely inefficient, that the state must relieve itself of a maximum of regulatory functions in a period of market transformation, and that one must get rid of state property as quickly and completely as possible, regardless of the price. In confirmation of this argument, they refer to the experience of privatisation in Germany, France, Italy, and Hungary. In these countries it is precisely the government and not market forces or worker collectives that implements privatisation and regulates the economic activity of the firms subject to the privatisation process. As a result of hasty and poorly prepared privatisation, Russian enterprises have lost their status as state property but have not begun to work better – they have only raised the prices on their goods and services.

The Russian government's plan of using vouchers for privatisation has many hidden dangers. By this I do not mean only the reinforcement of social inequality and the redistribution of property in favour of certain groups of the population at the expense of others (for example, workers in public health, education, culture, employees of various institutes). The present injustice can probably be alleviated by broadening the use of vouchers or by issuing additional vouchers for the acquisition of land, apartments, and other property not yet involved in privatisation. The dispersion of property and the preservation of control over its use is becoming the more serious problem. When property is dispersed among numerous, and often random, owners, the tendency to use income for consumption at the expense of future savings and renewal of fixed capital is reinforced.

The sketchiness of many of the economic, legal, and technical details of voucher privatisation arouses serious doubts about its success. Meanwhile, the social gravity of the problem, and the threat that many enterprises will be disrupted by a change in owners, force us to consider more considered and carefully elaborated methods of privatisation.

However paradoxical it may sound, one must be concerned with state property – property that, within fixed limits, needs to be preserved and that in many cases does not lend itself to rapid privatisation. In Russia the state does not carry out the functions of a property owner in the generally accepted sense of Western practice. Russian state enterprises do not bear those responsibilities of an owner borne by enterprises belonging to the state in, say, France or Italy. The government appears powerless to restrain these enterprises' group egotism, to compel them strictly to follow established rules, or accurately fulfill their budgetary obligations. The destruction of the central industrial ministries that formerly controlled and managed the state enterprises, and the rise of "concerns" and similar structures with sloppily defined functions and rights in their place, has pretty well left state enterprises to their own devices. Not yet possessing ownership rights, these enterprises have begun nevertheless to pursue their own interests. Thus even before formal privatisation according to one or the other plan, directors and managers have taken control of the enterprises.

Even in its most consistent and democratic forms, privatisation runs up against the determined opposition of old structures. This was distinctly visible in the agonising passage through the suppressed Parliament of recognition of the right to private ownership of land and authorisation of its sale and purchase. Chairmen of collective and state farms (*kolkhozy* and *sovkhozy*), having received land for free and indefinite use in the past, are very reluctant, even opposed to let this land slip out of their hands. They used to act as the effective owners of the land, often leasing it to farmers on crushing terms while allotting the worst lands and often arbitrarily abrogating the lease agreements.

Other circumstances also impede mass privatisation. Specifically, the demarcation of state property between federal and local levels has dragged on. Skirmishes between officials over what property should be left to the autonomous republics, regions, and cities, over what will become municipal property and whether or not the latter should be privatised last, continue to this day.

With intelligent methods, privatisation in Russia can strengthen the market and the monetary system, as it will increase the supply of goods and distribute property to broad sectors of the population. The newly arising middle class – interested in the development of market relations and, in the future, in increasing production and accumulating property – will guarantee the irreversibility of reform.

Unfortunately, privatisation in post-totalitarian societies often acquires perverted forms. The former *nomenklatura*, who aspire to exchange the political power now escaping them for property (the power of which is far more durable), find it increasingly easy to learn the technique of partitioning state property. If "*nomenklatura* privatisation" achieves a massive dimension, or if criminals get hold of a great deal of former state property, it is capable of engendering acute social conflicts and impeding democratisation. At the moment, we are still far from the optimal solution to the problem of privatisation.

Chapter 11

A PROGRESS REPORT ON PRIVATISATION IN EASTERN EUROPE

Gábor Hunya*)

11.1 Introduction: more questions than answers

Experience of privatisation in Eastern Europe for almost four years (1990-1993) has left many questions open. Political debate about the basic aims and results of privatisation has been uninterrupted despite the remarkable increase of the private sector's share in GDP. Most of the discussion described here will be confined to the transfer of ownership rights of state-owned enterprises (SOEs) to private hands. It will be kept in mind, however, that privatisation in its broader sense does not mean only this "top-down" process, but also covers a "bottom-up" process – the simultaneous growth of genuine private business. We shall look at the interrelationship between the two processes determining the growth of the private sector.

Another subject of this paper is to sum up the available, often most controversial, *data on the results of privatisation,* following strict methodological rules. Only firms with a 50 per cent plus one share in private hands will be considered privatised. Attention will be paid to the depth of privatisation[1]: "corporatisation" (converting a state-managed enterprise into the legal form of a joint-stock, but still state-owned, company) will not be treated as privatisation, only as a preparatory step for the sale of shares; primary stock owners in the wake of voucher privatisation, privatisation investment funds, and social

---

*) The Vienna Institute for Comparative Economic Studies (WIIW).

1) For the introduction of the notion of deep and surface privatisation see Hunya, G. (1991), "Speed and level of privatisation of big enterprises in Eastern Europe – General concepts and Hungarian Practice", *WIIW Research Reports,* no. 176, November, reprinted in *The Transition from Command to Market Economies in East-Central Europe* (1992), Richter, S. (ed.), Westview Press, Boulder.

insurance funds and also employee share-owners, will not be classed as fully-fledged private owners.

The progress of privatisation must be connected with results in other areas of transformation; its speed cannot be separated from progress in hardening the budget constraints on enterprises, from the development of the financial system and from the formation of capital market institutions. Differences between countries regarding the achieved level of privatisation are basically in line with their achieved *level of economic transformation.*[2] The interrelationship with transformation tasks was not sufficiently stressed in early privatisation projects which concentrated on the method of selling or distributing property rather than on its functioning.[3] More recent analyses concentrate more on the weak environment of privatisation: recession, weak financial and bureaucratic systems, etc.[4] Some questions still remain: Should and could privatisation be accelerated and in what ways? Are the governments in power able to work out and implement such acceleration?

There is by now some experience of various *techniques of privatisation,* but there is little knowledge of the change of entrepreneurial behaviour in the wake of privatisation. Thus substantial reservations have emerged about the speed and depth of voucher privatisation. Czech and Slovak companies privatised by vouchers are still without strong owners carrying out restructuring. After privatisation by various forms of sale (direct sale, public offering, auction, management-employee buyout), emerging new owners show a great variety of behaviour. On the average privatised companies are more efficient than before, but examples of disinvestment and hostile takeover are numerous. Meanwhile there are also examples that non-privatised but corporatised state-owned units show positive changes of behaviour and increased efficiency.

---

2) For comparative studies on economic transformation see: UN Economic Commission for Europe (1993), *Economic Survey of Europe in 1992-1993,* New York; Grosser, I. (1993), "Shared aspirations, diverging results", *WIIW Research Reports,* no. 191, February; Hunya, G. (1993), "Frictions in the economic transformation of Czechoslovakia, Hungary and Poland", *WIIW Research Reports,* no. 190, February.

3) Lipton, D., and Sachs, J. (1990), "Privatization in Eastern Europe: The case of Poland", *Brookings Papers on Economic Activity,* no. 2; Třiska, D. (1990), "Privatization in post-communist Czechoslovakia", mimeo.

4) Borensztein, E. (1993), "The Strategy of Reform in the Centrally Planned Economies of Eastern Europe: Lessons and Challenges", *IMF Papers on Policy Analysis and Assessment.*

Intermediary stages in privatisation and the management of state assets call for more lasting solutions than expected earlier.

While the debate on privatisation goes on, the state sector shrinks as assets are sold and companies *liquidated.* Liquidation is possible in countries where the budget constraints on SOEs have hardened and they consequently adjust capacities to the feasible volume of production or undertake a variety of restructuring measures. One may find that this unorganised process happens on a larger scale than the sale of enterprises. Assets not locked in SOEs are easily accessible to the genuine private firm not interested in taking over more complicated structures. The *restructuring* of SOEs, whether at enterprise or national level, remains a lasting subject of discussion.

11.2 Why privatise?

Liberalisation, stabilisation and privatisation are the basic steps for introducing the market economy in the formerly centrally planned economies of Eastern Europe. As a result, markets for commodities, labour and capital replace the redistributive role of the state. New legal and institutional environments must be created in which autonomous economic actors can strive to maximise profits. In the early stage of transformation the aim of privatisation is to reach the minimum requirement of market economies, i.e. the predominance of private property in the economy. It is generally expected that the dominance of private property will increase the efficiency of production and provide a long-term growth incentive for enterprises. There are three main features of privatisation:

- It creates the autonomous enterprise as the basic unit of exchange relations.
- It contributes to the hardening of budget constraints of enterprises, thus pushing them to adapt to market conditions and give up rent-seeking attitudes characteristic of socialist enterprises.
- It is expected to give owners control over management, thus giving profit-maximisation a long-term character.

Enterprise independence, hard budget constraints and effective management control are interlinked, but do not come into being simultaneously. Discrepancies depend on the timing and sequencing of reforms, and on the method of privatisation applied.

In the course of liberalisation, state-owned enterprises received the freedom to conclude contracts with one another according to their own interest, choose their domestic and foreign business partners and set their prices. At the same time the creation of genuine private businesses was liberalised. Dependence on state administration was radically reduced, and enterprises became responsible for their own economic activity. They faced an increasingly competitive environment, since the number of economic units active in national markets exploded through disintegration of monopolies, new entries of genuine private businesses and the appearance of foreign firms.

Countries able to introduce the initial liberalisation and stabilisation package (regardless whether as a "shock" as in former Czechoslovakia and Poland or in two or three years as in Hungary) arrived at functioning commodity and labour markets, although their capital markets still remained underdeveloped. Market distortions that can be related to systemic inertia (e.g. manipulation of prices by the state through discretionary subsidies or credits) considerably hinder the emergence of functioning markets in Russia, Romania and Bulgaria. The lack of successful stabilisation has led to rather chaotic conditions in Russia and many other former Soviet republics. In these countries privatisation is lagging behind, but also the functioning of privatised companies is doubtful because of the contradictory and unstable economic framework.

If administrative control over state-owned enterprises is not replaced by budget constraints and by strong owners, the rent-seeking attitude of company managers increases when some sort of superficial privatisation is carried out. If, as a step towards a more liberal attitude, the state transfers some property rights to the managements of state-owned enterprises, their rent-seeking attitudes are left intact while allowing them to make decisions according to personal interests. One can sell more lucrative parts of a company to friends or clients. "Spontaneous privatisation" in Hungary, "nomenklatura privatisation" in Poland (both during 1989-1990), and "quiet privatisation" in Bulgaria (in 1990-1992) all involve asset-stripping. Managers frequently prepare the enterprise for a management-buyout by reducing its value. Thus although enterprise autonomy is a necessary precondition for developing markets, control over management by the owners is also vital.

The problem of tight control by the owners can be solved by inviting private companies and individuals to invest in SOEs, but also by allowing the capital market to act as a constant check on the value of firms. Both bring about control over management and may provide access to additional financing either though direct investment, or by issuing new stocks. Strategic investors, emerging as new owners in privatisation by sale, usually improve the management of companies by providing management strategies. When institutional investors and dispersed owners emerge in the course of voucher privatisation, importance is attached to the stock exchange leading to more concentrated ownership, and to the activity of investment funds helping to find strategic investors.

The arguments of budget constraint and control by the owners lead to the conclusion that the state cannot be a strong owner, because of its diverse social and political responsibilities. Nevertheless there are certain public goods, the scope of which may change, that can best operate under unified national control. The issue in Eastern Europe is just the opposite to that underlying the emergence of SOEs in market economies. In the West the state is called upon to correct market failure; while in the East the market is called in to correct public failure. However, there may be temporarily successful cases of state ownership in the West, where the public sector must basically fit into the market environment and its decisions must be justified by cost-benefit-analyses. If the budget constraints on these enterprises are softened, this is to fulfil social aims agreed upon in the decision-making process of parliamentary democracy. The current privatisation wave in market economies is justified, as in former socialist countries, both by organisational inefficiencies of the state as owner and by the once-and-for-all government revenue earned by privatisation.

Problems of privatisation often have their political aspect. Governments and enterprises must be strongly interested in privatisation; workers and the population generally must at least not be hostile to such an extent as to hinder privatisation. The process in every country is subject to changing political coalitions, especially well demonstrated by the example of Poland (see 11.5 below).

11.3 Methods of privatisation

There are basically two approaches to privatisation: the sale of state-owned assets and their distribution among the population by vouchers. In the first case, the state as owner sells assets and businesses to private persons or groups selected in the process of sale. In the second case, the state relinquishes its control over property rights in the hope that new owners will be selected by equity market operations. While the first method aims at complete privatisation one unit at a time, the second initiates a process of privatisation on a massive scale. In a sale, enterprises are valued before the deal. In a voucher distribution, valuation takes place after the initial divestiture so that all assets can be included. While individual sales benefit persons who have accumulated capital, distribution gives the chance of an ownership decision to a wide range of people and allows them to decide whether they want to become long-term proprietors.

Without going into more detail concerning the benefits and shortcomings of the two main ways of privatisation it is worth noting that the political and economic environment can be decisive in making the choice. If political support for transformation is small and there are strong forces trying to block it, a mass-scale divestiture may be necessary to initiate the process. This is basically the argument of Russian liberals in favour of their voucher scheme.[5)] In Czechoslovakia and Hungary the supporters of voucher privatisation also came from the liberal ranks. If the market environment develops with no major opposition, direct sales are possible, as in Hungary. Although privatisation is not popular, there are also no forces opposing the necessity for it and the population at large is indifferent. The basically political choice of way of privatisation should not of course prevent its critical analysis from an economic point of view.

Ways of privatisation differ in their influence on the emergence of strong owners. With direct sale, strong owners emerge immediately, while in the case of voucher privatisation the emerging stock market must take over this role. The stock market will constantly value firms and provide access to additional financing.

The notion of employee ownership emerged at the very beginning of privatisation programmes. Vested interests of workers, who in some countries had quasi-property rights under socialism, and ideological considerations arising from the idea of a "workers' state", made this idea quite popular. Its political support varied according to the influence of workers' organisations: quite strong in Poland and Slovenia, weak in other countries. Workers' ownership received strongest legal support in the Russian privatisation decree and more political backing in Romania. In the two latter countries it has both ideological support and can be taken as a "better than nothing" approach. There is no proof that

---

5) A. Chubais at the conference "Privatisation of Large State Enterprises in the Russian Federation", IIASA, Laxenburg, Austria, 9-11 July 1993.

workers behave in an entrepreneurial spirit rather than being motivated by job security. Nevertheless, minority employee ownership does not harm restructuring, increases political support for privatisation and lessens some conflicts of interest between workers and management.

Despite much general theoretical discussion and the similarity of the problems involved in the individual countries, detailed discussion is impossible at a comparative level. Their legislations are very different and even more so their practice. This necessitates a country-by-country description of privatisation results.

11.4 Poland

The fate of state-owned enterprises

Poland, next to Hungary, has the longest experience of privatisation. It is reported that more than half of its GDP is produced by companies in the private sector. The figure for end-1992 was 45 per cent of GDP. In employment, the private sector's share reached 60 per cent by mid-1993. These figures include in the private sector the large proportion of agriculture not collectivised during the communist era and the cooperative sector of all branches having undergone legal transformation. (It is not clear from the available sources whether SOEs that had only begun to be privatised are included in the private sector.) The dynamism of the private sector is not confined to trade and services (its share in retail trade turnover was over 86 per cent in 1992 already). In the first half of 1993 the output of private *industry* increased by 32 per cent from the year before while the output of the public sector shrank by 1.2 per cent (both in comparable prices).[6] Thus the private economy's share in industrial production reached one third. The private sector's share in the industrial workforce increased to 45 per cent, which means that the labour-intensive, small and medium-sized establishments are predominantly private. But it does not appear from the evidence that privatisation of the large state-owned enterprises has played the decisive part in this changing balance of ownership.

Table 11.1 summarises available data on the distribution of firms by type in the Polish economy. The growth of the genuine private sector has vastly overtaken the decline in the number of firms in the public sector. The strength

---

6) Half-year statistical report in *Rzeczpospolita,* 7-8 August 1993.

Table 11.1

Poland: Extent of privatisation by different methods

number of firms[a)]

	end 1990	end 1992	mid 1993
Public sector	.	9,436	8,605
of which			
State-owned enterprises (SOE)	8,347	7,344	6,327
State-owned companies (SOC)	.	764	842
joint ventures of SOEs and SOCs	.	794	799
communal		534	637
Private sector	37,643	89,505	96,942
of which			
domestic	33,239	59,002	63,498
foreign	2,507	10,847	13,486
cooperative	.	19,372	19,534
Started privatisation[b)]	130	2,052	2,265
Commercialised	10	484	490
Undergoing liquidation	97	1,568	1,764
of which based on			
corporate law	(49)	(833)	(967)
privatisation law	(48)	(715)	(797)
Started privatisation in agriculture	.	539	1,092
Privatisation completed			
Privatised by public and private offering	5	53	74
Privatised by liquidation	14	617	710 [c)]
of which based on			
corporate law	.	(104)	(132) [c)]
privatisation law	.	(513)	(578) [c)]

a) Excluding private ventures and farms without corporate form. – b) Excluding agriculture. – c) By end March 1993.

Sources: Jermakowicz, W. (1993), "Privatisation in Poland 1990-1992: Methods and Results", mimeo, Evansville, based on *"Dynamika Priwatyzacji"*. For 1993: Half-year statistical report in *Rzeczpospolita*, 7-8 August 1993.

of bottom-up privatisation is quite obvious, although the genuine private sector is dominated by small firms. Privatisation figures include 2,265 started cases but only 784 finished ones, which reveals how long and cumbersome the process of privatisation is. Started cases include some corporatised enterprises which have been waiting to be included in the mass-privatisation project for two years now.[7)]

The direct sale of SOEs through the "capital way" of privatisation has had meagre success; only 74 companies were sold in three years. Twenty-three of them were offered through the Warsaw stock exchange, the rest were offered privately. Foreign companies are involved as buyers in many of the more important cases but the numbers are not specified.

Privatisation by liquidation

There are two reasons for liquidating enterprises: because of bankruptcy, and after privatisation was initiated. It turns out that although 60 per cent of the liquidation cases initiated are due to insolvency, they constitute only 17 per cent of the completed cases. Insolvent companies, even if they underwent financial restructuring, are not very attractive for private investors and tend to keep on as SOEs.

The second way of liquidation is a simplified form of standard privatisation, in which the SOE does not undergo corporatisation, but ceases to exist and a new company takes over its assets. This process, open to small and medium-sized enterprises above all, has nothing to do with the financial standing of the enterprise. Enterprises involved in privatisation by liquidation are either auctioned or leased. Management or employee organisations are the typical new owners.[8)]

Employee and management interest play a crucial role in Polish privatisation. State-owned enterprises operate by self-management, which means that there is little outside control over management. The managers would lose autonomy if a strong owner appeared and employees, too, would be deprived of some of the ownership rights they possess. It was therefore crucial that a compromise between government and trade unions was reached in February 1993 which laid down the conditions for the corporatisation and privatisation

---

7) Even the simple way of privatisation by liquidation takes six to nine months. See Blaszczyk, B., and Dabrowski, M. (1993), "The Privatisation Process in Poland", paper read at the conference "Privatisation of Large State Enterprises in the Russian Federation", IIASA, Laxenburg, Austria, 9-11 July.

8) Slay, Ben (1993), "Poland: The role of managers in privatisation", *Radio Free Europe/Radio Liberty Research Report,* 19 March.

of SOEs. Unfortunately, parliament was not able to pass the respective law, so the enterprise pact could not be enforced.

However, there have been certain incentives for self-managed enterprises to become private, as the state sector was subject to taxes on wage increases and had to pay "dividends" to the budget, not as a profits tax but as fees for using state-owned assets. The significant role of privatisation by liquidation shows that these incentives seem to have worked mostly when the managements of enterprises were able to become shareholders. There are few studies about the behaviour of SOEs privatised by internal investors. Common sense suggests that low efficiency of state-owned enterprises cannot be improved unless internal coalitions are broken.[9)] General data put the profitability of privatised companies higher than that of those only starting privatisation[10)]. Quite possibly, small and medium-sized enterprises can improve their efficiency more dynamically than larger ones, even if internal structures are not much disturbed.

Mass privatisation

Mass privatisation, planned since 1991 and enacted in April 1993, will not start before 1994. Some 400 state-owned companies (corporatised enterprises) will be selected for privatisation through investment funds. Twenty investment funds set up by the state but hopefully operating on a commercial basis will become majority shareholders. The funds themselves will be privatised by issue of vouchers to the citizens at a later stage. It is assumed that the funds will be interested in trading the shares and will also promote the value of their portfolios by initiating restructuring of the companies they control. Critics of the idea doubt that the managers of the funds will be politically independent.

It seems reasonable to assume that the number of funds is big enough for competition among them. They may be efficient in managing assets of companies not privatised by standard methods if they can really be stimulated to increase the value of their portfolio and if they retain the possibility of selling companies to outside owners. At present the selection of state-owned companies to be included in mass privatisation is a problem because no loss-

---

9) Keren, M. (1993), "A Dynamic-Evolutionary Perspective on Transformation", paper read at the conference "Bottom-up Transformation in Eastern Europe", Freiburg, 9-11 September.

10) *Rzeczpospolita,* 7 August 1993.

making ones, which comprise a large share of state-owned firms, are to be chosen in order to ensure a good starting position for the funds.

Even if mass privatisation is implemented, there remain some 6,000 SOEs with vaguely defined ownership rights and not involved in the privatisation process at all. Steps to speed up corporatisation at least would be possible if the enterprise pact were implemented. On the other hand, the value of assets and the contribution to GDP by the state-owned sector is decreasing, meaning that enterprises are being streamlined. This implies a sale of assets, mostly to private owners, i.e. a contribution to privatisation without change in the number of SOEs.

11.5 Hungary

Size of the private and public sectors

A recent survey by the statistical office[11)] provides information about the size of the private sector originating both from privatisation of state-owned enterprises (SOEs) and from private start-ups. At the end of 1992, the share of the business sector in GDP amounted to 85 per cent (the rest being the non-profit government organisations). Within the business sector 52 per cent was produced by companies with majority private ownership, which means that the private sector's share in total GDP was 44 per cent. In contrast to Poland and the Czech Republic, these shares do not include cooperatives, because they had not, at the time of reporting, undergone legal transformation.

The same survey found that 38 per cent of the equity capital of firms was in private hands: 25 per cent represents the value of privatised capital and the rest (13 per cent) is the share of the genuine private sector. The share of foreign owners in equity capital amounts to 10-12 per cent, that is about 30 per cent of the private sector.

These data seem not to consider corporatised or minority state-owned companies as private. Nevertheless, some exaggeration of the private sector's share in equity capital could not be avoided, because state-owned enterprises could be valued only at their "historical" book-value, while corporations, private firms and state-owned companies (SOCs), were valued on their new equity

11) The survey processed tax declarations of companies and was reported in *Napi* and *Magyar Hírlap,* 23 August 1993.

capital. On the average, revaluation during corporatisation puts equity capital at twice the earlier book-value. If all SOEs were converted into joint-stock companies with revalued equity capital, the public sector's share would be increased.

Most remarkably, the share of the private sector in production is higher than that in equity capital. Taking into consideration the undervaluation of the public sector for equity capital, the difference is even greater. This can prove that the operation of the private sector is more efficient than that of the public sector, but also that it is mostly the less efficient enterprises that have been left in public hands.

In 1990 there were 2,363 state-owned enterprises in Hungary awaiting privatisation. 1,728 of them were put under the supervision of the State Property Agency (SPA) with the aim of privatisation, restructuring or liquidation. About 400 state-owned enterprises belong to the municipalities and others to the branch ministries – mainly those active in infrastructure. In autumn 1992 the government set up the State Asset Holding Company (SAHC) with the aim of keeping 163 companies partially in state hands. Only those companies of the business sector selected for privatisation in full were left with the SPA. Owners other than the SPA should also privatise, but they are not keen on selling their property.

The number of state-owned enterprises has been decreasing for two separate reasons: corporatisation and liquidation (*Table 11.2).*[12] Both processes received momentum in 1992. To start with the latter, the SPA wound up over 500 SOEs during the last three years, some that were in unsolvable financial difficulties and those that had been "emptied out" in the process of "spontaneous privatisation" in 1988-1990. (SOEs were allowed to set up several companies in corporate form for running actual business, and also to partially privatise them, while the SOE itself remained as an assets management holding company without productive activities.) Under the bankruptcy law of 1992, 62 SOEs were liquidated up to the end of April 1993.

---

12) The State Property Agency cannot give a clear report on the number of companies and amount of assets transformed and privatised in the course of the last three years. Split-offs, liquidations, partial sales, joint ventures and cross ownership have made the enterprise scene so complicated that it can hardly be compared with earlier stages.

Table 11.2

Hungary: Basic data on privatisation

	end 1990	end 1992	mid 1993
A/ Number of firms			
Total [a]			
State enterprises (SOE)	2,363	1,733	1,465 (May)
State corporations (SOC)	27	602	924 [f]
Under the State Property Agency			
Still State-owned[c]:			
SOE	1,728 [b]	.	562 [b]
SOC	.	.	541
Formerly under SPA			
Privatised	n.a.	n.a.	253 [g]
Liquidated	n.a.	n.a.	251 [h]
Transferred to other owners	n.a.	n.a.	174 [h]
Under the State Assets Holding Company [f]			
State-owned:			
SOE	.	110	62
SOC	.	53	101
B/ Value of assets supervised by the SPA, Ft bn, 1990 book value			
SOE and SOC	2,000	.	800 [b]
Transferred to SAHC	.	.	700 [d]
Owned by SOC-banks	.	.	60-80 [f]
Privatised	.	.	200 [h]
Liquidated	.	.	300 [e]

Sources and remarks:

a) *Statisztikai havi közlemények*, no. 5, 1993. - b) SOEs not under SPA belong to local authorities and to branch ministries, and have not been privatised; *Figyelö*, 8 June 1993. - c) *Heti Világgazdaság*, 25 June 1993. - d) *Magyar Hírlap*, 3 June 1993. - e) Only those liquidated under bankruptcy; *Magyar Hírlap*, 28 May 1993. - f) *Napi*, 16 August 1993. - g) *Napi*, 17 August 1993. - h) *Napi*, 23 August 1993; transfer to other authorities includes mostly those transferred to the SAHC. The value of totally privatised companies amounted to Ft 46 bn.

Preparations for privatisation

Enterprises undergoing privatisation must first face *corporatisation* by transformation into joint-stock companies. The sale of their shares is a subsequent step taken either immediately after corporatisation, or later. Hungary has favoured selling, because the authorities wanted to find strategic investors in order to establish strong owners able to restructure former SOEs, and to raise public revenues.

Corporatisation was preceded by the evaluation of SOEs by foreign or domestic consultants. The value of shares thus established became the basis for bargaining with investors. Evaluation and corporatisation was a rather long process, often lasting more than a year. Outside investors could get access to a firm only afterwards. The SPA hoped to arrive at an economically and politically acceptable price. Although in the majority of cases the selling price proved to be realistic, there has been a long history of political controversy about its acceptability.

In 1990-1992, 602 SOEs were transformed into corporations[13]. In 296, transformation was initiated by the management or outside investors, 257 smaller SOEs were transformed in the framework of self-privatisation during 1992, and only 49 in the framework of privatisation projects initiated by the SPA. In 1993 all SOEs had the task of changing into corporations. About 200 of them had not made the first steps at the end of June, so the SPA put them under direct state supervision. Accelerated transformation became possible, because private consulting firms and law offices contracted by the SPA had gained experience in such activities during the past three years.

Transformation increased the transparency of property rights. The changes can be summarised as follows:

- Corporatisation produced a realistic evaluation of the firms as a basis for sale to private investors. The previous aggregate book value of Ft 645.5 bn was revalued to Ft 1,364 bn. Corporatised companies are obliged to have balance-sheets audited.
- Property relations of state-owned firms were clarified. The self-governing management structure was replaced by a supervisory board, with the SPA or SAHC representing the main owner and with the participation of banks

---

13) Sources of all data as in *Table 11.2*.

that may have swapped part of the property. Employees also received legal representation. Some minor part of the shares was transferred to municipalities as they had been the owners of the land occupied by state-owned companies.

- The management lost its quasi-property rights and came under stricter supervision. Loss-making managers are replaced by SPA more often than when they had been appointed by the enterprise councils. More pressure is put on the management by the new owner to look for investors. Nevertheless, the management of corporatised companies is still in a state of pre-privatisation uncertainty, with a very short-term interest in survival.
- The performance of corporatised enterprises is better than that of SOEs, although this may be the result of selection and not only of higher efficiency. Nevertheless, in 1992 the majority of SOEs operated with losses, while most of the SOCs were in the black. Better financial results enabled SOCs to reduce their labour force less rapidly (by 12 per cent in 1992) than SOEs (by 30 per cent)[14). This suggests that as a step towards privatisation, corporatisation has not been responsible for much unemployment.

Methods of privatisation

Sales of companies have taken place mostly in the form of open or closed bidding, where the SPA was obliged to sell to the highest bidder. Decisions were quite often contested and winners were not always able to pay on time. The selling process has been accelerated by the decentralisation of decision-making in small and medium-sized companies, which gave some impetus to privatisation in early 1993. Companies that could not be sold even under preferential terms are offered for lease (a dozen cases until now).

Unlike in former Czechoslovakia, no restitution in kind and no distribution of vouchers took place in Hungary, but preference was given to certain groups of domestic investors: former owners, employees, domestic investors, citizens.

- Those deprived of their property in the course of nationalisation and collectivisation after 1948 received restitution vouchers as compensation which they can use for buying state property. If not used for buying

14) Source: the survey cited in footnote 11.

agricultural land or a municipal flat, vouchers can be invested in minority shares of selected companies.

- Employees of privatised companies can get up to 15 per cent of shares under preferential conditions. Employee buyout is also possible, and the employee organisation can rely on preferential credits, but its offer is usually considered second best by the SPA compared with cash payments.
- Domestic investors can take out heavily subsidised credits (so-called E-loans) after a down payment of 15 per cent of the price for acquiring even majority stakes in SOEs. Skilful application of the subsidised credit scheme, together with compensation vouchers quoted on the stock-exchange at 50-60 per cent of face value, enables domestic investors to acquire an SOE in exchange for 7-8 per cent of the sales price.[15)] Supported by preferences, E-loan holders compete side-by-side with cash-payers and foreign investors.
- For the population at large the government will issue interest-free credit vouchers in 1994, which can be invested to buy selected minority shares and repaid from the dividends.

It is a peculiarity of the Hungarian way of privatisation that free vouchers (compensation- or credit-vouchers) remain secondary; their holders can buy residual shares left over by strategic investors. Vouchers have more political than economic importance. The government has not gained much of the expected popularity so far, because issuing of vouchers is in delay, their use is complicated and the returns obscure.

Results of privatisation

A statement of the State Property Agency refers to 253 companies privatised under its jurisdiction by the middle of 1993. In many cases a minority of the shares is still state property; only 64 companies have been fully privatised.[16)] Strategic investors often have an option on minority shares. The SPA has recently started selling residual shares without option on the stock exchange and in exchange for restitution vouchers.

---

15) *Figyelö,* 8 April 1993.

16) Companies with majority private owners are classified as private.

It is especially difficult to trace back the history of the 1990 book-value of state-owned enterprises. At the outset Ft 2,000 bn came under the authority of the SPA. In the middle of 1993 there were Ft 800 bn with the SPA, while SAHC took over Ft 700 bn (see *Table 11.2*). This means that Ft 500 bn went to other, non-public owners. Of this sum, Ft 300 bn was the book-value of liquidated enterprises, and Ft 200 bn can be calculated as the value of privatised enterprises. The latter figure is more or less in line with the reported Ft 120-130 bn revenues of SPA (also taking into account the costs related to privatisation, and the capital retained by privatised companies). Money from direct sales to foreigners made up 80 per cent of privatisation revenues in 1991, 70 per cent in 1992[17)], and only 45 per cent in the first five months of 1993[18)].

Comparing the data on privatisation with those on liquidation, we see that by mid-1993 10 per cent of the state property was privatised directly, by selling the company, while 15 per cent was liquidated, that is privatised in an indirect way. Liquidation meant, that SOEs were sold in the form of individual assets, not as a company. Even if not called so, "privatisation by liquidation" (also the most widespread, though in somewhat different form, in Poland) is the major form of privatisation in Hungary.

A recent SPA statement suggest that about half of the property still in the hands of SPA will have to undergo liquidation; 40 per cent of the SOEs under the SPA in mid-1993 were making losses. Most of the heavily indebted ones will have to sell their assets or undergo liquidation in order to satisfy creditors.

New methods of privatisation

Due to mass-scale corporatisation, socialist-type state-owned enterprises will disappear from the Hungarian scene in 1994, but the privatisation of most of them will be pending for quite a while. Nevertheless it seems to be important that corporations in the economy should operate under equal legal status, regardless of their ownership structure.

In the future, SPA will have to dispose of companies worth Ft 800 bn. Of SAHC's assets 25 per cent will remain in public hands on the average, so that this agency must privatise Ft 525 bn. If 40 per cent undergo liquidation, the value

---

17) *Magyar Hírlap,* 22 June 1993.

18) *Magyar Hírlap,* 11 June 1993.

of assets to be privatised can be put at Ft 800-1,000 bn. This means that about half of the privatisation task is still ahead. One cannot realistically assume that this amount of assets can be sold; the demand for property will need to be enlarged.

Future plans concerning the more than Ft 800 bn of assets managed by the SPA are taking shape. Non-conventional methods of privatisation are gaining momentum especially for minority shares. The following methods are proposed:[19)]

- Assets will be offered in exchange for compensation vouchers worth Ft 80-90 bn from the assets of SPA and Ft 60-70 bn from the assets of SAHC, i.e. Ft 150 bn in total by the end of 1994. (The face value of the total amount of vouchers concerned is about Ft 200 bn, part of which is used for buying land and apartments.)
- Mass privatisation through privatisation credits is planned to need about Ft 100 bn until the end of 1994.
- Shares are to be transferred to the social insurance fund worth Ft 300 bn over two years.
- Ft 1.3 bn is to be transferred to the obligatory car insurance fund.

Half of the property to be privatised in these projects will be divested to non-strategic investors. For the other half strategic investors are sought. This will certainly be possible for many of the efficient companies under the SAHC, like those of the pharmaceutical industry and hopefully also for the major banks. In these cases it is mostly foreign investors who will qualify. In the majority of cases the cumbersome process of hunting for investors will go on for some years. E-loans, bank loans, and leases may become more widespread which will lead to problems. The new owners will be under pressure to repay credits, even if the interest rates are preferential. Profits will be drained and credit lines exhausted before investment in restructuring can be made.

Meanwhile the government has prepared projects for the financial consolidation of viable but heavily indebted SOEs. Thirteen large SOEs were separated in mid-1993 to undergo credit-restructuring and relief. In that very limited number of cases the state as owner has stepped in for its companies, but is aware of both the political and financial limits of such a bail-out.

---

19) *Magyar Hírlap,* 11 June 1993.

Restructuring before privatisation is also done by the SPA, although it has very limited means for this purpose because of the transfer of most revenues to the state budget.

Conflicting priorities of the Hungarian government complicate privatisation and restructuring. The aim of maximising revenues has become more difficult to pursue as sales prices decline, windings-up proliferate and political pressure to subsidise domestic investors grows. Maximisation of revenues also hurts the interests of the corporatised state-owned companies, if the SPA or SAHC channel dividends to the central budget and do not leave them with the companies for investment. (In a recent example, the SAHC deprived the best Hungarian pharmaceutical company of its profits by paying itself a dividend of 40 per cent, thus undermining the company's research activities). This attitude should remind us again of the inefficiency of public ownership and be an argument for accelerated privatisation.

The Hungarian government seems unable to choose between fast sales at a low price in a time of recession and waiting to sell until an economic upswing drives prices higher. If it tries to sell fast, it loses possible revenues, or would have to favour non-strategic investors who would not be able to restructure the companies. If privatisation is held back, the conditions for an economic upswing become less favourable. It is rather unrealistic to expect that this dilemma will find a clear answer before a new government comes to power in spring 1994.

11.6 The Czech Republic[20)]

Although most of the analysis of Czechoslovak privatisation has been based on privatisation by vouchers, it must be stressed right at the outset that real success has been due to other methods: small privatisation, restitution, sale to foreigners, together with the spontaneous growth of private enterprises, which comprise the genuine private sector. The share of the private sector (excluding cooperatives) in Czech GDP increased from 10.6 per cent in 1991 to 21.5 per

---

20) Although this chapter refers to the Czech Republic, procedures until recently have been almost identical in the Slovak Republic. The time since the split has been too short to elaborate on diverging practices.

cent in the last quarter of 1992.[21] This increase does not include voucher privatisation but only small privatisation, restitution and the increase in the growth of the genuine private sector – all quite successful operations. The development has been impressive keeping in mind that before 1989 the private sector was almost non-existent.

Of the 3,841 state-owned enterprises existing in 1992, voucher privatisation affected 965 firms[22] that is one quarter of the total.[23] In mid-1993 the shares of these companies have been transferred to the new private owners, individuals and privatisation investment funds (PIFs) (70 per cent of the shares). These firms have thus undergone pro-forma privatisation. At the same time, also the cooperatives (including agriculture) were transformed into business cooperatives. Due to these developments, the share in GDP of the non-public sector (private and cooperative) reached 44.2 per cent in the first half of 1993.[24]

The future of enterprises privatised by vouchers is controversial. The time has come for concentration of ownership, assumption of control over management and harder budget constraints on privatised firms. When and at what pace these changes will take place is the question. Trade with shares started rather slowly, both the Prague stock exchange and the over-the-counter trading system ("RM-System") is characterised by excess supply and small turnover. First meetings of shareholders are just about to be organised. PIFs are beginning to consider whether to act as active or passive owners towards companies. If budget constraints on enterprises are really hardened, a massive wave of bankruptcy and lay-offs is to be expected.[25] The government wants

---

21) *Hospodářské Noviny,* 15 March 1993.

22) For the source of data on voucher privatisation see: Mejstrik, M. (1993), "A rapid enterprise privatisation as a vital part of Czech transformation", paper presented at the conference "Privatisation of Large State Enterprises in the Russian Federation", IIASA, Laxenburg, Austria, 9-11 July.

23) The split of Czechoslovakia has caused confusion in the statistics concerning the number of economic units so that time series are not available.

24) *Bulletin Českého Statistického Úřadu,* June 1993.

25) The *Economist* of 19 June 1993 quotes expected rates of unemployment ranging between 40 per cent and 10 per cent for mid-1994 against the current 2.5 per cent. The first scenario is based on the current financial position of enterprises, the latter estimated by the Czech National Bank which realistically assumes a slower pace of hardening budget constraints.

to slow down the process so as to tackle the social consequences, so that the future relationship between PIFs and government may also become strained.

11.7 Romania[26)]

Methods and progress of privatisation

There are 6,291 state-owned corporations (SOCs), with a total capital of lei 11,000 bn, to be privatised in Romania.[27)] (The other 900 state-owned enterprises ("régies autonomes"), representing more than half of the total state-owned capital (railways, energy generation, mining, etc.), have been excluded from privatisation. The value of state-owned corporations to be privatised is approximately equal to one year's GDP, while private savings amount to about lei 400 bn only. Presumably most SOCs could only be sold for much less than book value. As liquidation has not yet started, "phantom companies" are also registered as privatisable. The transfer of public property to private hands is in its early stages: the total value of privatisation sales up to mid-1993 amounts to lei 50 bn.

A basic element of the privatisation law is the free distribution of 30 per cent of the state property. The 16 million adult citizens have become, by the distribution of vouchers, owners of five Private Ownership Funds (POFs), which control 30 per cent the of shares of all SOCs. Citizens who are shareholders of POFs receive no dividends for a period of three years, and it is still unclear how they can buy shares in SOCs with their vouchers.

The remaining 70 per cent of the shares of each state-owned company was assigned to the State Ownership Fund (SOF). This organisation should act independently of daily political struggles as it is not subordinate to the government (its supervisory board is appointed by parliament and by the president). The SOF has the task of representing the state's property rights, and of selling the shares it controls within seven years. Although the SOF and

---

26) This chapter is based on research done together with Zsolt Virág from Cluj, Romania. An earlier version appeared in *WIIW Members' Information Bulletin,* no. 8, 1993.

27) This is the number of SOCs registered by the State Ownership Fund. The National Agency for Privatisation quotes the number as 7,093, while the commercial register includes 8,140 state-owned companies, probably including subsidiaries with legal status not registered separately by the SOF. Some observers quote these discrepancies as proof of negligence by state authorities (*Romania Libera,* 15 July 1993).

the POFs were created in July-August 1992, their activity in 1993 was limited because of administrative problems: by the middle of 1993 the process of transferring property rights from the government to the SOF had not yet been completed.

The National Agency for Privatisation (NAP), which is an organisation supervised by the government, must (according to the privatisation law) co-ordinate and control the entire privatisation process, distribute the Certificates of Ownership (by the end of 1992), and carry out a pilot privatisation programme (by mid-August 1993) and manage a small privatisation (sales of assets) programme.

This Agency selected 32 companies for privatisation in the framework of a pilot programme before the ownership funds started operating. Most of the companies had less than 500 employees and were quite profitable by Romanian standards. By mid-July 1993 the privatisation of 22 of these SOCs was completed. The valuation was done by domestic companies, except for SOCs bought by foreign investors which were valued by foreign consulting firms. There is more information about the sale of 19 companies with an aggregate value of lei 12.1 bn; in most of them the sales price was very close to the estimated value.

The most widespread privatisation method was the management-employee buyout (MEBO), which was used in 14 cases. Foreign investment took place in six, and in two a public offering was made. In privatisation by MEBO, the NAP and the MEBO agreed on 30 per cent cash payment and instalments for two years. Supplementary conditions often prescribed investments at a higher value than the sales price, and an engagement to maintain the number of employees for two years. The MEBO method was preferred to direct sales: employees could buy their company without competing with other potential investors. Foreign investors were accepted where SOCs had fairly stable markets but needed a great deal of additional investment to become profitable.

In public offerings, the shares of SOCs could be bought only by domestic physical or legal persons. An investor could buy only a maximum 6 per cent of shares; even the major domestic private bank was not allowed a larger share. There is no functioning stock exchange yet, but shares can be traded privately.

At the same time the NAP started a separate small-scale privatisation programme, i.e. *auctions of assets* which could be utilised directly (shops, hotels, restaurants, workshops, etc.). One third of the selected assets have been sold.[28)] Over 11,000 employees worked in these enterprises. More than 80 per cent of the selected assets belonged to companies in trade and tourism.

The *State Ownership Fund* started its privatisation activity in December 1992, but until May 1993 it sold only 6 companies, increased to 51 by mid-June 1993.[29)] The total book value of companies sold was lei 5.4 bn which was sold for lei 6.9 bn mainly in the framework of MEBO. The number of employees was over 11,000, which means that the average number of employees was only 200.

Inter-agency conflicts may paralyse privatisation

The government's decree number 10/1992 has redefined the tasks of privatisation authorities: 3,120 small enterprises, which own only 2.6 per cent of the total capital, will be privatised by NAP; about 2,500 medium-sized ones will be privatised by POFs, and the remaining large enterprises by the SOF. The recent privatisation activity of the SOF conflicts with this agreement since most of the companies privatised were small ones. It shows that the SOF is eager to prove its competence by becoming the main agent of privatisation.

The 1993 privatisation programme, which the State Ownership Fund brought to parliament in April, includes 379 small, 106 medium-sized and 6 larger companies. In an advertisement[30)], 40 companies were offered to domestic and foreign investors, mostly in trade, the food industry, and light industry, as well as four large construction companies and the national airline TAROM. These companies are medium-sized or large: each has a book value of at least lei 500 mn, and most of them employ more than 500 people. Strangely, the method of privatisation will be decided only after offers have been received.

The NAP and the POFs declared that the SOF's 1993 privatisation programme was contrary to the principles laid down by the government, and that the SOF intends to monopolise privatisation. The NAP elaborated a counter-proposal which would put this organisation in charge of privatisation and the SOF under government control.[31)] At the same time the POFs are outraged

---

28) Data base of the National Agency for Privatisation.

29) *Tineretul liber,* 21 June 1993.

30) *Economistul,* 29 June 1993.

31) *Economistul,* 27 May 1993.

by the fact that their interests are in a minority position vis-à-vis the SOF.[32)] They would welcome an amendment of the privatisation law which would protect minority interests. Views also differ inside the SOF. The executive manager was replaced in May 1993 because he opposed the softening of MEBO conditions as well as government interference in the SOF.[33)] The present leaders seem to be more obedient to the government, but they are still interested in expanding the power of the SOF.

The Vacaroiu government, in office since November 1992, does not agree with the principles of the privatisation law elaborated by Petre Roman's government in 1991. They cannot accept even the limited independence of the privatisation process from government interference. Some sources believe that the government wants to impose its control over the SOF. Prime Minister Vacaroiu suggested[34)] creating a privatisation ministry. The opposition fears that both solutions would lead to further centralisation and the slowdown of privatisation. They claim that parliament has not fulfilled its duties in the field of privatisation: it has not discussed the SOF's privatisation programme, has not accepted the appointment of the POF's board and has not even tried solving the conflict between different state organisations.

Privatisation in Romania guided by competing state bodies is an obscure, unpredictable and rather slow process. Nevertheless, compared with other south-east European countries, the sheer existence of organised privatisation can already be regarded as a success.

11.8 Bulgaria

Reform delayed

Almost all the major issues of privatisation (enterprises, small-scale privatisation, agricultural land) are still pending in Bulgaria. The share of the private sector in GDP was 15.6 per cent in 1992. The private sector increased its contribution to sales, excluding agriculture, from 17 per cent to 20 per cent between the first halves of 1992 and 1993, mostly due to the decline of the public

32) *Economistul,* 16 July 1993.

33) *Economistul,* 30 June 1993.

34) TV discussion on 15 July 1993.

sector.[35)] The private share was highest (about 50 per cent) in retail trade and agriculture, but only 2.5 per cent in industry. Most of these shares are due to genuine private business and not to the privatisation of state-owned assets.

The first privatisation law was passed as late as April 1992. The establishment of the privatisation agency and legal amendments lasted until the end of that year so that the law became operational only in 1993. The Bulgarian law is quite similar to the Hungarian, preferring sales to other forms of privatisation, while the staff of SOEs are offered 20 per cent of the shares for half the price.[36)] In the first half of 1993, a few smaller and two larger deals were concluded as a result of auctions. Auctions starting with an estimated book value of companies are often unsuccessful, because most enterprises are in a bad financial situation, indebted and with shrinking markets. Unless the state and the general public accept that state property is sold off very cheaply, no success can be expected.

The country's political situation can be blamed both for the delay in enacting the privatisation law and for its sluggish implementation. Influential lobbies are not interested in clear rules, preferring cheaper ways of taking over property rights, through spontaneous or illegal privatisation.[37)] Between May and August 1990 when state property belonged to the enterprises themselves, they could transfer assets to outsiders and insiders, which was a very widespread practice. Such sales were later prohibited, but well-known cases also happened later without being prosecuted.

The idea is gaining ground in Bulgaria that government institutions are unable to direct the sale of state-owned assets, and that a voucher scheme would speed up privatisation and increase its popularity. In fact, the example of Bulgaria supports the political argument for voucher privatisation which dismantles state interference as fast as possible.

---

35) National Statistical Institute (1993), *Current Economic Business,* Sofia, June.

36) For details see Grosser, I. (1992), "Bulgaria: Recent legal developments of interest to foreign investors", *WIIW Members' Information Bulletin,* no. 7.

37) Gradev, T. (1993), "Bulgaria: Slow pace of privatisation discredits reform process", *WIIW Members' Information Bulletin,* no. 7.

11.9 Russia

By mid-1993, in 18 months, the number of privately owned or managed shops and small enterprises increased from 30 to 61 thousand. Besides, 4,500 state-owned enterprises were privatised, mostly to voucher holders. Of the three methods of privatisation allowed by law, more than half of the enterprises opted for handing over most of the shares to the employees and managements of companies. There are 20 million shareholders involved either directly or through investment funds, and privatised companies employ 35 per cent of the workforce in Russia. As pointed out by Deputy Prime Minister Anatoly Chubais,[38)] the popularity of vouchers is a major source of support for the government's reform programme against conservative forces in parliament. This mass-scale, bottom-up privatisation strategy has avoided political dispute on individual cases and opened up a lively security market beyond the control of state organisations. Foreign investors can now approach either the new owners, or the stock exchange to acquire a stake in Russian companies.

Very little is known about the composition of the new class of proprietors. The tradeability and anonymity of vouchers allowed strategic investors to obtain controlling shares. There are hints that the money earned by corruption and by the mafia was white-washed and turned into property. Participants in a IIASA workshop stressed the need for strong owners who can protect their property. They were concerned about the lack of proper control over management since minor shareholders cannot organise. Majority ownership by employees in privatised companies promotes interest in wages rather than in profits and investments.

Case studies found no striking difference between the behaviour of state-owned and privatised companies. Both tend to rely on a very limited number of traditional suppliers and purchasers. Competition is small not because of monopoly positions but because contracts without personal connections do not function. Rent-seeking is a typical attitude; managers can successfully lobby for cheap credits, subsidies, and licences. The present system has given considerable autonomy to the managers of state-owned enterprises, without requiring financial responsibility. The purpose of bargaining with the state is no

---

38) Paper presented at the conference "Privatisation of Large State Enterprises in the Russian Federation", IIASA, Laxenburg, Austria, 9-11 July 1993. This is also the source of data about the process of privatisation.

longer access to physical inputs but to preferential financial conditions. Under soft budget constraints, enterprises are not induced to change their behaviour and increase efficiency. Most of them have adopted a policy of pure survival.

A precondition for deeper privatisation is stabilisation, because with the present inflation and soft budget constraints no positive adjustment can be expected. Privatisation and deregulation should be continued and the banking sector consolidated, which would put an end to the rent-seeking attitude of enterprises.

11.10 Conclusions

The country-by-country analysis has highlighted the main approaches to privatisation and their interrelationships. It was impossible to find countries with strict adherence to a single approach; the complexity of approaches is growing even as time passes.

Four basic approaches to the privatisation of state-owned enterprises could be identified:

(a) The privatisation of SOEs as companies by sale. Most of the available information refers to the methodology, institutional framework and results of this form of privatisation. Its underlying assumption was that there would be a big supply of SOEs for sale and a matching demand on the part of private investors, and also that some state authority would be able to mediate a great number of deals. As most of these assumptions did not hold, the sale of SOEs has been a rather cumbersome process. Nevertheless, expected positive results of this approach did materialise: hardening budget constraints, imposing better corporate management; and restructuring of production. Financial and organisational restructuring sometimes preceded sales to make SOEs more attractive, but most of the task of restructuring was left to the new owners. After the sale of the more lucrative SOEs, partial restructuring before privatisation is gaining ground.

(b) Sale of assets as units or parts of companies after liquidation of an SOE. By this method, a widespread practice, assets were made available to private investors without obliging them to take over the historical burden of a state-owned organisation. The case of SOEs in financial difficulties selling off part of their assets to maintain streamlined operations also falls under this approach, which is important for increasing the supply of assets for investors.

(c) Both the sale of companies and of individual assets can take place under preferential terms, payments by instalments, low-interest credits or leasing. Special conditions can apply to former owners, employees, the population at large. This approach increases domestic demand for state-owned assets, and at the same time reduces the risks to new owners.

(d) Apparent privatisation, usually by vouchers, was used when denationalisation as such, and not stable corporate management, was the primary objective. This approach was also favoured when political support for privatisation appeared to be the crucial problem. As a result, the state would be deprived of its operational control over enterprises, and a broad dispersion of property rights was expected. The problem of a lack of demand does not apply when privatisation takes place through vouchers, but supply difficulties and organisational constraints slow down implementation. As both good and bad companies participated in voucher privatisation, financial and physical restructuring was generally postponed.

The coincidence of growth of the genuine or spontaneous private sector with the decline of the public sector can make the private sector dominant in an economy, even when only a minority of state-owned enterprises are actually privatised. While privatisation of SOEs has proved to be a lengthy process, the value of the SOEs' assets, and also their contribution to GDP, have fallen quite rapidly. This was especially the case when assets were not frozen inside SOEs, but could be privatised piece by piece – a matter of legal and practical possibility and of budget constraints. Enterprise autonomy allows SOEs in the Czech and Slovak Republics, as well as in Hungary and Poland, to sell assets up to a restricted value, above which authorisation by a state agency is necessary. In the Czech and the Slovak Republics budget constraints on SOEs were not effectively hardened before privatisation; moreover, enterprises included in the two-year process of voucher privatisation had to maintain their book value until the end of the process; therefore they were not obliged to get rid of redundant assets, such as the redundant workforce in the Czech Republic. In Hungary, budget constraints on SOEs have been hardening, especially because of new accounting and bankruptcy regulations, and changes in banking practice, since early 1992. A constant streamlining of production capacities has been practised in Hungary. The State Property Agency did not usually object to the sale of parts of SOEs if the price was in line with expectations. In Romania only, the assets-privatisation programme, started in late 1992, transferred some workshops and hotels from SOEs to private hands. In Bulgaria, where both small and large-scale privatisation are pending, there is no legal possibility for assets-privatisation. In all countries semi-legal or illegal practices occur.

Restructuring and privatisation

The sale of assets and liquidation are not only the most wide-spread, but also the most controversial methods of privatisation. Those favouring restructuring of capacities by public investment may object to this process, and those who regard SOEs as the main organisational barrier against restructuring should approve it. There are also physical difficulties in streamlining capacities without dismantling technologically viable production lines.

Restructuring can apply to several aspects of company operation: its financial standing, its production technology and sales strategies, as well as management and organisation. Some organisational changes, such as splitting up SOEs which are little more than holding companies have been widely practised, but other restructuring steps were mostly left to the firms themselves. Debt relief was organised for privatised Czechoslovak SOEs. Financial restructuring of SOEs and banks has recently been launched in other countries, because problems emerging in the financial relations between firms, as well as in the relationship between firms and state-owned banks, could not be solved in a decentralised way.

Physical restructuring of SOEs, with public investment to make them efficient in the market economy, would keep SOEs as intact as possible during the adjustment shock. Such government programmes have existed for infrastructure, mining and energy generation all over Eastern Europe, but in other business sectors bottom-up adjustment has been prevalent. Traditional industrial policy targets, like branch adjustment programmes, could not as a rule overcome the constraints of public budgets.

A huge restructuring of capacities must follow the restructuring of markets – the changes in foreign and domestic demand patterns. In many traditional branches this requires a shrinkage of productive capacities.[39)] Improving the efficiency of existing production in the lasting absence of markets makes little sense. Only if there are hopes for new markets, viable products and ingenious management is the retention of capacities justified. Usually the private sector is successful in making such discoveries; nevertheless its chances for success would improve with public backing. The possibility of bringing about the restructuring of SOEs through public investment has been doubted by analysts of enterprise behaviour.[40)] The SOEs' inherited links to the bureaucracy, and their internal coalitions of workers and management, have both been seen as major obstacles to needed investment decisions and to hardening budget constraints.

Public services, directed credits, and a functioning macroeconomic framework can considerably improve the conditions for private economic adjustment. In many countries, serious operational frictions in the functioning of institutions can be seen as major obstacles to the development of the private sector.[41)] Privatisation by the release of assets from SOEs, and their sale to private investors, seems to be the task most successfully performed by governments in transition economies – especially if combined with policies facilitating bottom-up growth of private entrepreneurship.

---

39) A Hungarian government official quoted the chicken meat processing industry, once a successful branch producing for Soviet and Middle Eastern markets. Out of a capacity of 740 thousand tonnes only 200 thousand could be used during the past two years. All experts exclude the possibility of re-utilisation of excess capacities. This means that most of the companies in this branch can neither be restructured nor privatised before undergoing liquidation (*Napi,* 23 August 1993).

40) Keren, M. (1993), "A dynamic-evolutionary perspective on transformation", paper presented at the conference "Bottom-up Transformation in Eastern Europe", Freiburg, Germany, 9-11 September; Swaan, W., and Lissowska, M. (1992), "Enterprise behaviour in Hungary and Poland in the transition to a market economy: routines as a barrier to change", *Tinbergen Institute Research Memorandum,* The Hague, TI-1992/84.

41) Hunya, G. (1993), "Frictions ...", *op. cit.*

Chapter 12

RESTRUCTURING, PRIVATISATION AND INDUSTRIAL POLICY MAKING

John A. Kennerley*)

Abstract

The paper questions the effectiveness of some aspects of the processes of privatisation and restructuring in achieving the objective of transforming state enterprises into modern successful companies. It focuses on the role of foreign investment in these processes, and it underlines the crucial importance of coherent national industrial policies or strategies. It draws extensively on the work undertaken within the secretariat of the United Nations Economic Commission for Europe, in particular, the Economic Survey of Europe in 1992-1993[1)], its studies relating to foreign direct investment and privatisation in the countries of eastern Europe and the results of a number of workshops which have been organised with the assistance of the ECE and which have dealt with strategies for enterprise restructuring, privatisation and industrial policy.

For many countries in eastern Europe, the processes of privatisation, restructuring and attracting foreign direct investment are not new. Indeed they are processes which have been going on for three or four years, and as a result of the experience gained, perhaps a saner and more rational approach is now being taken in the ways in which they are being applied. It is also now recognised that these processes, although of crucial importance, are only part of the overall process of reform which is going on in these countries in their efforts to move to market-driven economic systems.

The effective operation of market economies calls for a complex integrated national framework of legislation and regulatory authorities as well as administrative institutions and infrastructure, property rights and corporate and non-corporate law. It calls for an extensive system of banking and financial institutions, an efficient operational service sector and well developed infrastructures

---

*) Deputy Director, Industry and Technology Division, United Nations Economic Commission for Europe, Geneva, Switzerland.

1) United Nations Economic Commission for Europe (1993), *Economic Survey of Europe in 1992-1993,* United Nations, New York, June.

to handle transport and communications. It also calls for change in cultural and social attitudes, traditions, business practices and behaviour patterns at the level of central, regional and local governments and administrations and at the level of enterprises and individuals. The political revolutions which have taken place over the last few years in the countries of eastern Europe have effectively made redundant much – if not most – of the institutional and organisational capital of the former centrally planned economies. However, the building up of the new institutions and infrastructure which are required for the effective functioning of a market economy cannot be done overnight and making the necessary changes in attitudes and behaviour patterns at the level of governments, institutions, enterprises and individuals takes time. Furthermore, "the ability of a country to change – and to adjust to change – depends crucially on the nature and strength of its economic, political and legal institutions, on its social cohesiveness and traditions, and on the conditions prevailing at the start of the process of reform".[2] If one lesson has been learned from the experience of the last few years, it is that one cannot afford to throw everything of the past out. One has to build on the past, restructure and transform, without, if possible, wreaking social havoc.

12.1 Privatisation and foreign investment

Since 1989/90, we have seen a major effort by the governments of a number of countries in eastern Europe to privatise. This has been done in the belief that it would be the quickest and most efficient way of moving to a market economy. However, it is also worth recalling that the principal or underlying motive behind a government's wish to privatise state enterprises is not merely for the government to divest itself of state assets, but rather to make the enterprises more efficient and provide them with the independence and the capability to take initiatives; innovate; undertake research; develop markets; improve quality and productivity; and compete on both domestic and international markets. The process of privatisation and, for that matter also restructuring, is or should be one which governments can use to allow industrial enterprises to achieve these goals. Accordingly, it should not be viewed as a policy objective in itself, but rather as an instrument which can be used to achieve specific goals. Privatisa-

---

2) *Op. cit.*, p. 7.

tion, while offering side benefits, may have disadvantages in particular for the labour force, and thus it needs to be used with a full understanding of the short- and long-term consequences and not as an *ad hoc* panic move to overcome short-term problems.

In the light of the experience which has been gained, it is timely to ask whether the processes of privatisation of the medium to large industrial enterprises in eastern Europe are really achieving the principal underlying objective – to make industrial enterprises more efficient. To answer this question, we need to look at the ways in which it is being undertaken.

A distinction needs to be made between "small" privatisation and what one might call "big" privatisation. "Small" privatisation, which can be considered as "government actions to divest itself of such assets as service work shops, retail outlets, catering establishments, taxis, car rentals, etc.",[3] has gathered momentum in almost all eastern Europe and is proving very popular. However, "the difficult problems arise with the privatisation of the large – and by western standards extremely large – state enterprises",[4] where the pace has been slower and where there has been more opposition, problems and obstacles than might have been expected. In these countries, "a majority of the population is by and large in favour of the market economy but when questions get closer to their personal situation the responses are more guarded".[5] A succession of polls in Hungary suggest that "those who support privatisation and are willing to accept the costs (in terms of unemployment and increased inequality of incomes) are in a minority which is getting smaller,[6] and whereas so-called "small" privatisation is generally popular, "there is considerable opposition to the transfer of ownership of large enterprises, large estates and other items of wealth".[7]

---

3) *Op. cit.*, p. 199.

4) *Op. cit.*, p. 10.

5) *Op. cit.*, p. 11.

6) Hann, E., and Laki, M. (1992), "The Hungarian Public on the Advance of Private Economy", *Acta Oeconomica*, vol. 44, no. 1-2, pp. 191-300.

7) Ibid.

It can be observed that privatisation is taking two forms. First there has been privatisation without an injection of new capital and second, there has been privatisation resulting in the acquisition of state enterprises by foreign interests.

(a) Privatisation without capital injection

One way of undertaking privatisation has been the process of "mass" or "wild" privatisation, notably the Czech and Slovak approaches involving schemes such as the distribution of vouchers or employee share option programmes or worker participation ventures. These schemes have essentially meant a dissipation of share ownership and they have not given the enterprises the necessary concentration of ownership with a vested interest in performance, and needed to ensure good management and sound decisions. For small enterprises, especially those in the service sector, this may not pose a serious problem, but for the larger industrial enterprises it is of crucial importance. Where a large industrial enterprise has been privatised and is in part owned by the workers or the labour force, serious problems can be expected when decisions have to be taken which mean loss of jobs and downsizing, or when major capital investments have to be made which may adversely affect short-term profits. Even where national investment funds are being established, as in Poland, and where a certain concentration of ownership is being developed, this is not resulting in the creation of the meaningful corporate decision-making and management structures which are essential for the effective running of modern industrial enterprises.

Another aspect of the privatisation process is what sort of agents are being used to privatise. "One of the most striking observations that a cross-country comparison of privatisation practices reveals is the similarity in institutions"[8) which are being used. These rest on three main pillars. At the government level there are the privatisation ministries which set out privatisation policy. Then there are the privatisation agencies which have the responsibility for planning and implementing privatisation programmes. Finally, there are the privatisation funds or asset management agencies. However, these are still at an early stage of development in most of the countries and are not yet exerting the necessary pressure and authority on the enterprises in which they have invested to improve

---

8) *Economic Survey of Europe in 1992-1993*, section 3.6, p. 193.

the organisational and management structures. The question also needs to be asked whether or not the agents which are now being used to implement the programmes of privatisation are focusing undue attention on the process of privatisation and not enough on creating viable enterprise organisational and management structures. It could be argued that the government authorities which have been made responsible for the privatisation of state assets were not set up with the idea of ensuring that the privatised enterprises ultimately became successful private companies; but that was the original goal of the exercise.

(b) Privatisation with capital injection, in particular foreign direct investment

An important adjunct in the process of privatising and restructuring is the need for injection of new capital, especially of foreign direct investment; at least in the medium to large industrial enterprises, there is inevitably going to be a need for capital regardless of whether they are privatised or restructured. "While it is true that enterprises have been privatised in eastern Europe by methods which have not involved the raising of finance for the enterprises, e.g. voucher privatisation schemes or employee share option programmes or worker participation ventures, new private enterprises ultimately must secure finance to overcome debts accrued in the past or to restructure for the future."[9] It is possibly where foreign companies and/or investors have taken a controlling interest in or outright ownership of eastern enterprises that the process of privatisation of medium/large industrial enterprises has been most successful in creating viable private companies. Capital can come essentially from three main sources: government or private investment funds, the commercial banking system and foreign companies or investors. If an enterprise is privatised, it has essentially to fend for itself on the financial markets. In contrast, when an enterprise is being restructured as a state enterprise, it should be made accountable for the way it uses the credits it receives regardless of the source, and this applies especially to government subsidies or assistance programmes, which unless tied to strict restructuring schedules may mean a misuse and waste of public funds and loan guarantees. It is also important to face squarely the issue of how to attract foreign capital.

---

9) United Nations Economic Commission for Europe (1993), "Guide on Financing East-West Trade and Privatisation in Central and Eastern Europe. Note by the Secretariat" (TRADE/WP.5/R.11), September.

In October 1993, the total number of foreign investment projects established in eastern Europe had reached over 75,000, a rapid increase from barely three years earlier (end 1989) when less than 2,500 projects had been registered. The value of these investments totalled US$ 14.6 billion. The most successful countries in the region in attracting foreign investment have been Hungary ($ 3.8 bn), Russia ($ 2.9 bn), the Czech Republic ($ 2 bn) and Poland ($ 1.8 bn).[10] Romania has been the most successful in terms of the number of foreign investment projects, with over 25,000 established to date, as compared with fewer than 1,000 registered in 1991.

To put into perspective the relative performance of the countries of eastern Europe in attracting foreign investment compared with other countries, it can be noted that the total stock of foreign direct investment (FDI) worldwide now stands at some $ 1.7 trillion, with annual flows amounting to $ 225 billion.[11] Average annual FDI inflows in two of the most successful European countries in attracting inward foreign investment, the United Kingdom and France, are of the order of $ 22 and 15 bn, respectively. The rather modest figure of $ 14.6 bn representing total investments in the countries of eastern Europe reveals that, despite the rapid rise in the number of projects being established, these countries have a long way to go to emulate the performance of the developed market economies.

An interesting development in the growth of FDI is the shift in the proportion which is now attracted by the privatisation process in eastern Europe. Up to 1991, foreign investment came, with few exceptions, in the form of joint ventures – separate entities set up by foreign companies in cooperation with domestic enterprises – and occasionally greenfield investments. With the implementation of ambitious privatisation programmes in a number of countries, FDI has begun to be channelled through western enterprises either by acquiring a stake or by purchasing a company outright. A profile of the nature of these investments can be gathered to some extent from the information contained in the two tables

---

10) These figures may be inflated since they correspond to investments recorded when the projects were originally registered by the authorities, and in some cases the projects never became operational and the capital was not transferred into the country. In addition, domestic companies may register as joint ventures in order to benefit from tax advantages.

11) United Nations (1992), *The World Investment Report 1992: Transnational Corporations as Engines of Growth,* New York. Figures are for 1990.

annexed to the present report. Estimates of the total value of foreign investments attracted through privatisation in a few of the countries are as follows:

Czech Republic and Slovak Republic	$	5,873 million
Poland	$	4,274 million
Russian Federation	$	703 million
Hungary	$	689 million

In contrast to the figures on overall foreign direct investment referred to above, the Czech Republic and the Slovak Republic along with Poland are by far the most attractive destinations for western FDI through the process of privatisation, and Hungary appears to have been much less successful. In other countries, such as those of the CIS and the Baltic republics, the number of significant cases of FDI through privatisation has, so far, been negligible. When these figures are compared with the capitalisation figures for each country referred to above, it can be observed that in Poland and the Czech and Slovak Republic most FDI is now coming through privatisation rather than through joint ventures. In Hungary, where statistics distinguish between the type of investment by foreign companies, 60 per cent of the total foreign capital that came into the country during 1991 was invested in companies which had been privatised. At the end of the first quarter of 1993, about 80 per cent of privatisation in Hungary involved foreign capital. However, it also appears that foreign investments through privatisation in Hungary are already diminishing as a proportion of total investment, representing only some 25 per cent of all investment from abroad.

In terms of country of origin, the main investors through acquisitions (as is the case for joint ventures) are, without doubt, the United States and Germany. The world's other large foreign direct investors are relatively under-represented: France, the Netherlands, Sweden, the United Kingdom, and Japan have thus far not been active participants in the purchase of corporate assets in eastern Europe.

In contrast to investments in the form of joint ventures, the main preference for foreign enterprises in their acquisitions has been in the field of manufacturing. There are a few large projects in the primary sector, but almost none in the financial services sector (covering banking and insurance), or in retail trade. Within manufacturing, it appears that FDI through privatisation is focused on the following four main branches:

- fast-moving, low-priced consumer products, most notably cigarettes, confectionery, food and beverages and detergents;
- transport (automobile manufacture);
- power generating equipment; and
- telecommunications equipment.

Although it is difficult to extrapolate from the cases listed in *Annex 12.1,* it is possible to make certain observations on the type of enterprises which have been favoured by foreign investors in the countries of eastern Europe in their privatisation programmes. An analysis of this information suggests that foreign investment in privatisation is tending to be focused on:

- low rather than high technology enterprises – investments are focused on companies operating at the low end of the technology spectrum, e.g. food, tobacco, rather than specialty chemicals, pharmaceuticals, microelectronics, etc.;
- with the exception of a few cases, notably Volkswagen's acquisition of Skoda, domestic rather than foreign markets – goods produced by the acquired company are intended for the domestic market;
- both private and public customers: in both power generating and telecommunications equipment, the state will be the main customer for the goods manufactured;
- monopolistic or oligopolistic markets where competition is limited to a small number of players; and
- a highly visible product range – the domestic companies acquired tend to be well-known in the domestic market.

It appears that when making investments in industries in eastern Europe, major multinationals and foreign corporations are looking for one or all of three things: they want to penetrate safe, low-risk local or regional markets, establish low-cost manufacturing operations and/or complete global marketing and sales networks.

Over the past forty years in eastern Europe, and over seventy years in the countries of the CIS, the large state industrial enterprises dominated at least their own domestic markets, if not the whole of the former CMEA. Thus, a western corporation or multinational that buys into an industrial enterprise in eastern Europe stands to gain rapid market penetration in the local domestic market if not the regional market, especially if it comes with modern technology and know-how. This is especially important for industries which are or could be manufacturers of consumer goods where there is significant pent-up demand, or in high-growth specialised fields, such as producers of electronics, computing and telecommunications equipment. Thus, the real trick is to convince foreign companies to move in with capital, know-how and technology – something which again needs to be addressed within the framework of a country's industrial policy and the instruments/incentives it uses to attract foreign investors. It is also recognised that there is a very significant market in the countries of eastern Europe and whereas there has been a breakdown of the traditional trading patterns between these countries, the links still exist, albeit in a tenuous way, and could be rebuilt with relatively little effort to open up significant possibilities for increased sub-regional trade. Here again, governments of these countries need to exploit the potential for intra trade to attract foreign investors.

A second factor influencing foreign corporations in making investments in eastern Europe is the possibility of establishing low-cost manufacturing operations in these countries where labour costs and to some extent energy and raw materials are considerably cheaper than in the west. Under the present economic conditions in the west, with labour costs very high compared with the east, a transfer of manufacturing operations from the west could be particularly attractive for many profit-hungry western corporations. But the eastern countries have to do a real selling job to exploit some of these national competitive advantages. By the same token, however, western corporations which invest in these countries are unlikely to be interested in industries which have a large hidden unproductive work force, and lack a sound organisational and management structure. That means essentially that the majority of the medium and large industrial enterprises will probably not be in a position to attract foreign investors until they have been restructured, down-sized and stripped of their unproductive work force.

A more specialised case can be made for the interest of foreign investors in pockets of the former defence and military equipment manufacturing industries of eastern Europe which may provide centres of excellence and research bases at significantly lower cost than those in the west and which could make a significant contribution to overall corporate R and D programmes.

Foreign investors and entrepreneurs in general, however, are always looking at the bottom line. They are looking for profits. They are also looking for a climate which is politically stable, where there are sound legal, judicial and financial systems, where there are good transportation and communications facilities and where there is reliability in supplies of raw materials and energy.

12.2 Restructuring

As already indicated, the really difficult problems arise with the privatisation of the large state enterprises; progress here has been very slow and has confronted serious problems. In part, this can be attributed to the heritage of the past. To overcome vested interests and entrenched behaviour patterns takes time, good will and much patience on the part of governments, enterprises and the general public. Further complicating the picture are the problems posed by claims for compensation and the restitution of property to former owners of enterprises. There are a myriad of environmental problems faced by many of the large state industrial enterprises, in particular, the large steel and chemical industries. Then possibly the most important problem concerns the corporate or enterprise organisational, decision-making and management structure; this has not yet been adequately solved through the process of privatisation and must be addressed, especially, for the medium and large industrial enterprises.

If a large enterprise cannot be privatised, then the government or a government agency, as owner, has a clear responsibility to launch the process of restructuring. For the important large state industrial enterprises, the short-term prospects probably favour restructuring as a short/medium-term expedient in preference to privatisation. However, the one does not necessarily rule out the other in the long term. "In many respects 'large' privatisation (large state-owned enterprises) is the core of the restructuring problem and one of the most crucial stages in the transition to the market economy. But a rapid change in ownership of these enterprises will not automatically solve their problems or even assist in the creation of an efficient market economy. To sell such enterprises without restructuring them would undermine the creation of a competitive environment, although there are doubts that many of them would actually interest private buyers" let alone foreign investors "in their present state.[12] Questions of competitive structure, of effective corporate governance etc., all need to be settled before privatisation takes place, otherwise the private owners will probably resist any belated attempt to correct market failure. A slower

12) See also, *Economic Survey of Europe in 1992-1993,* section 3.6, section (viii).

pace for 'large' privatisation, giving time for such questions to be settled, as well as for the improvement of managerial skills, the corporatisation of enterprises, and the adoption of commercial patterns of behaviour, may thus be more effective in achieving the ultimate objective of an efficient and sustainable market economy."[13)]

Restructuring ultimately has, or should have, the same objective as privatisation – to transform an existing, possibly unproductive and inefficient enterprise into a viable and profitable company. In this process of transformation, the first and possibly most difficult question to be addressed is whether the state enterprise or parts thereof has the ghost of chance ever to become a viable and profitable company. If not, then a government, or the government agency which is responsible for the enterprise, has to decide to phase it out, since it is pointless to pour public funds down the drain. If it is determined that the enterprise has a chance to survive in a market economy, then the real process of restructuring must begin. This means establishing an effective management structure for both developing and implementing the restructuring plan. It also calls for setting up a competent management structure, the engagement of a senior executive officer who should be under contract with a specific mandate, and the provision of a package of incentives both for the management of the enterprise and the work force. The restructuring programme for a large industrial enterprise or sector of industry should include specific plans during the period of the restructuring for the reorganisation and refinancing of the enterprise or sector, and, where necessary, the provision of training and retraining programmes, social safety nets for the workers who are made redundant, and a programme of government assistance, including financial guarantees or loans, agreements on the write-off of certain debts and protective programmes.

For the vast majority of the large state owned industrial enterprises in eastern Europe, the process of restructuring represents an enormous job. These enterprises, many of which are also monopolies, are characterised by a large work force, much of it unproductive, obsolete equipment, poor product quality, huge inventories, poor or non-existent marketing systems, and little if any after-sales servicing systems. In addition, organisational structures, management, costing and accounting practices are in need of a complete overhaul. Painful decisions have to be made on downsizing and breaking up enterprises into

---

13) Ibid., p. 10.

smaller manageable companies, and sizeable staff cuts are almost inevitable in the majority of the enterprises. In most cases, the restructuring will also call for significant injections of capital, which may call for the development of financial packages with commercial banks.

For the labour force which is made redundant, social safety nets have to be put in place and training programmes launched in order to retrain workers for other jobs. "Placing retraining in the context of the social safety net emphasises the need for an integrated set of policies designed to assist the process of structural adjustment rather than just to provide a static net to catch the casualties. Coordinating safety net and active labour-market policies in coherent programmes of industrial restructuring should make it easier to attract western financial assistance to ease the pressures on the pace of government deficit reduction and would provide a sharper focus and a clearer set of priorities for foreign technical assistance. But this also raises the larger issue of industrial policy",[14] referred to below. The mobility of the labour force is also a critical factor which needs to be taken into account especially in municipalities where a large state enterprise is the dominant employer, if not the sole employer, and special programmes may have to be set in place at the municipal and local levels in order to help workers adjust to new conditions and create new sources of employment.

12.3 Industrial policy

During the early stages of the reforms, almost no word was spoken about industrial policy. It was too close to central planning or "sinning" against the purist concept of a free market economy. To some extent even in the west, where *de facto* every country has an industrial policy or strategy, there is, even now, a rather ill-defined role for governments in elaborating national industrial policy. More recently, however, and certainly in eastern Europe, it is now recognised that privatisation and market forces alone will not be sufficient to transform the industries of those countries and make them competitive and profitable in the domestic and international markets. Thus an active supportive role of governments in the process of transformation is essential.

---

14) Ibid., p. 10.

A country's industrial policy should be one which encourages market forces in industry in a way which makes best use of national resources and endowments and fully exploits the potential for economic and industrial growth. Among other things, it should be designed, for example, through a comprehensive system of multidisciplinary programmes and policies, to encourage and facilitate investment; R and D and innovation; development, introduction and diffusion of technology and know-how; the process of industry privatisation and restructuring; the introduction of modern management, costing and pricing practices; and the establishment of new small- and medium-size enterprises. Experience in the west, in particular in the United States, suggests that industrial policy could well be focused "on the externalities that might encourage growth rather than on the spotting of "winners" or "national champions" in specific industries or products. In particular, positive externalities are believed to exist in business investment, especially in machinery and equipment; in public infrastructure investment which can raise the productivity and rate of return of private investment (a "crowding-in" effect); in research and development; and in education and training (or human capital investment).[15] At the same time governments, within the framework of their national industrial policy, have to ensure that the necessary infrastructure on which modern industries depend is developed – modern road, railway, transportation and communications networks; that appropriate banking and financial institutions are set up and that the necessary laws, regulations and regulatory and administrative bodies are created which safeguard property rights and allow companies to operate efficiently, unhampered by unnecessary administrative and bureaucratic procedures.

A country's industrial policy must of necessity be embedded in a whole series of related policies and programmes relating to industry standards and trade; the exploitation of natural resources, including mining and the utilisation of raw materials and energy. Thus, for example, a country's trade policy should be one which will encourage domestic industries to be more competitive on international markets. Similarly, its environmental policy should be one which will encourage industry to protect the environment, reduce waste and move towards sustainable patterns of industrial behaviour. Its labour and social programmes should take into account the process of industrial restructuring

---

15) Ibid., pp. 15, 16.

and/or privatisation which is going on. Its educational and training and retraining policies and programmes should take into account the future needs of industry. Its finance and tax policies and programmes should include economic instruments and incentives which provide the "right" messages for industry and encourage it to be successful in a modern market economy.

As observed earlier in this paper, industrial policy must face the issue of how to attract foreign direct investment and put it to optimal use in the process of both the privatisation and the restructuring of state industrial enterprises.

From the observations made above, it can be seen that in comparison with FDI attracted through joint ventures, FDI attracted through privatisation is both qualitatively and quantitatively different. It tends to be large-scale rather than small-scale, focused on low technology manufacturing rather than services, making finished goods for both the domestic private and public market. Is this pattern of investment in a country's best interest and if not how can a country's industrial policy change the pattern? Foreign investors appear to be seeking overwhelmingly market access or market share in their acquisitions, and in some cases, where markets tend to be near-monopolies or oligopolies, a guaranteed market for their products. This appears to be a *sine qua non* for large-scale purchases in eastern Europe at present. It has both positive and negative implications for the current or planned restructuring in a number of the very large industrial enterprises in the east, which suggests a trend towards the break-up of the monopolistic position of the major industrial enterprises. To date, the process of privatisation has not tended to attract FDI to industries where investment could raise the technological level of the company to good effect or where it could increase the capability of the company to sell its products on international markets. In a number of companies which have been acquired by foreign investors, there is neither the necessity nor the possibility to achieve greater investment (the company has already got a guaranteed market for its products); or to carry out significant technological developments either with the products being manufactured or the processes being used; or to capture foreign markets. For eastern Europe, experience so far in attracting FDI as a support to the process of privatisation and restructuring has been disappointing; these investments have, rather, tended to constitute a means for easing the financial difficulties of the countries. To do more, governments must seek to attract FDI into industries where the effects will be more tangible as well as to use industrial and other policy measures to direct the existing investments into areas where the benefits to the national economy will be greater and have a longer-term positive impact.

Finally, a country's industrial policy must fit into the context of what is happening in other countries of the region and in the world at large and in Europe to adapt to what is going on within the framework of the European Community.

Suffice it to say that a country's industrial policy is a web of interlocking policies and programmes all of which should work in a coherent way to support industry. This suggests that in developing industrial policy in the countries of eastern Europe, measures should be taken to ensure that there is a clear institutional and consultative framework for its elaboration. That is to say, effective arrangements should be put in place to allow the ministries responsible for the development of sectoral polices, together with industry and society in general, to play their role in the development of a coherent national industrial policy or strategy and thereby ensure coherence at the national level in all policy-making and coordination in its application. A country's industrial policy should also be a detailed and transparent programme of action and it should be subject to parliamentary scrutiny and to independent audit.

Annex 12.1

Acquisitions with foreign capital

Date	Company name	Foreign partner country	Initial foreign investment US$ mn	Total foreign investment US$ mn	FII type
May 1993	Amylum	B	100.0		equity stake
June 1993	Total (F); AGIP (I); CONOCO (US)	F/I/US		2500.0	equity stake
May 1992	Philip Morris	US	226.2	398.0-413.2	equity stake
March 1992	Coca-Cola, AMATIL	A	28.0	82	acquisition
June 1992	Kathreiner	D	9.6	35.1-40.8	acquisition
Aug. 1993	TRW	US	9.6	15.6	equity stake
unknown	Siemens	D	170		acquisition
Feb. 1992	Air France	F	60		equity stake

participation in East European Enterprises

Host country	Local partner	Product line	Stage	Additional information
Bulgaria	Maize Production	production of starch products	negotiated	Belgian company is seeking a majority stake
The Czech Republic	Two oil refineries (Chemopetrol in Litvinov and Kaucuk in Tabak)	oil refining	negotiated	the two plants have the capacity of 8 mn tonnes of oil per year; western partners will be allowed to buy 49% of shares
The Czech Republic	Two oil refineries (Chemopetrol in Litvinov and Kaucuk in Tabak)	production of tobacco products	agreed in May 1992	Philip Morris was to pay initially 226.2 mn US$ for 77.4% of equity of 5 eastern partner factories; subsequently it will invest 187 mn US$ in modernisation bringing its stance to over 80%
The Czech Republic	KYJE Soft Drinks	production of soft drinks	agreed	
The Czech Republic	Druzba Department Store, Prague	retail trade	agreed	in addition to acquisition cost of 15 mn DM (9.6 mn US$), western partner will invest 40-50 mn DM (22.5 mn-31.2 mn US$) next year
The Czech Republic	DAS Dacice	production of automotive parts	agreed	western partner will transfer a part of its west European production to the Czech Republic
The Czech Republic	Skoda Plzen; Skoda Praha	manufacture of energy-generating machinery	awaiting Gov. Approval in Feb. 1993	western partner took over the turbine, generator and nuclear arms of Skoda; Siemens will own 57% of joint venture stock
The Czech Republic	Ceskoslovenske Aero-line/CSA	provision of expertise in engineering, maintenance and catering	negotiated	foreign partner will acquire 49% stake in carrier airline valued at 150 mn US$

(continued)

Date	Company name	Foreign partner country	Initial foreign investment US$ mn	Total foreign investment US$ mn	FII type
June 1992	Leykam, Mürztaler Papier und Zellstoff	A	53.0		equity stake
Aug. 1993	Ford Motor	US	45.0		acquisition
June 1992	Charbonnages de France	F	30.1		acquisition
1993	ASEA, Brown Boveri	CH, S			equity stake
March 1993	OSPAG (Subsidiary of Keramik Holding, CH)	A			equity stake
May 1992	K Mart Corp.	US	120.0		acquisition
June 1993	Marketcraft International	US	15.0		equity stake
June 1993	South African Breweries (SAB)	ZA		100.0	equity stake
Oct. 1989	General Electric	US	150		equity stake

Host country	Local partner	Product line	Stage	Additional information
The Czech Republic	OSAP	production of paper	agreed	western partner acquired 53% stake in OSAP; OSAP produces 90 thousand tonnes of paper a year
The Czech Republic	Autopal, NOVY JICIN	production of head-lamps and heating equipment for motor cars	negotiated	western investment is spread over 3 years and includes cost of acquisition
The Czech Republic	Ostravskokarvin Ske Doly	mining of bituminous coal and lignite	agreed	
The Czech Republic	Prvni Brnenska Strjirna (PBS)	production of energy-generating equipment	agreed	ASEA Brown Boveri acquired a 67% stake in PBS
The Czech Republic	Hotelovy Porcelan, Karlovy Vary	production of porcelain fixtures	agreed	western partner acquired a majority stake; local partner is the sole supplier of porcelain fixtures to hotels with the production capacity
The Czech Republic/ Slovakia		development of K Mart retail chain	negotiated	western partner purchases and refurbishes 13 large department stores in the CSFR; in 1993 19 mn US$ will be invested in modernisation
Estonia	Potato processing plant in Kaagjarve	processing of potatoes	negotiated	Estonian side will contribute the site and building worth about 5 mn US$; financing may be provided from the EBRD, IFC and OPIC
Hungary	Kobanyai Sorgyar Brewery	production of beer	agreed	western partner will acquire over 75% of stock; the sum of investment includes the initial purchase price, initial investment and further investment over the next 5 years
Hungary	Tungsram	production of lighting equipment	agreed in Oct. 1989	General Electric acquired a stake of 51% in Tungsram

(continued)

Date	Company name	Foreign partner country	Initial foreign investment US$ mn	Total foreign investment US$ mn	FII type
March 1993	Pepsico	US	115.0		equity stake
Dec. 1992	Alitalia, Simest Investment Group	I	71.7		equity stake
June 1992	Danubia AG (sub-sidiary of Mautner Markhof AG)	D	52.4		equity stake
1992	Atex Foreign Trade Company/CEIC	RU/CAN	50.0+2.0		equity stake
June 1992	Stollwerck	D	47.8		acquisition
June 1992	Scholler Lebensmittel	D	36.4		acquisition
1992	Mautner Markhof AG	A	34.0		equity stake
June 1993	Universal Leaf tobacco	US	22.0		equity stake
Jan. 1992	Group International	US	10.0		equity stake

Host country	Local partner	Product line	Stage	Additional information
Hungary	FAU	production of soft drinks	agreed	Pepsico will acquire 79% of company stock from government; during first two or three years profits will be reinvested
Hungary	Malev Airlines	operation of an airline	negotiated	two western partners will acquire 30% and 5% stakes in Malev; government will retain control of 51% of equity
Hungary	Budapest Distillery PLC	production of spirits	agreed	Danubia holds 75% of voting shares
Hungary	Ikarus PLC	production of buses	agreed	Atex (Russian Federation) bought 30% of shares and CEIC (Canada) 7%
Hungary	Budapest Edesipari Vallalat	production of candies		50 tonnes of chocolate will be produced annually; western partner has committed itself not to reduce a 3000 work force by more than 10% through 1995
Hungary	Budatej	production of ice cream	agreed	
Hungary	State Property Agency, Municipalities, individuals	production and distribution of food products and soft drinks	agreed	foreign partner holds 51% of equity; enterprise produces baker's yeast, fine alcohol, vinegar, carbonated soft drinks, wheat starch, alchoholic drinks, electric energy
Hungary	Nyidofer Tobacco Enterprise	production of tobacco products	negotiated	western partner will acquire a 76% stake in the enterprise; value of investment includes the purchasing price, initial and further investment
Hungary	Csepel Automotive Works	manufacture of vehicles and spare parts	initial agreement signed; negotiated	assembly of cumins diesel engines and truck cabs is considered; Hungarian state liquidation agency estimated that some 60 mn US$ were needed to modernise works

(continued)

Date	Company name	Foreign partner country	Initial foreign investment US$ mn	Total foreign investment US$ mn	FII type
27 Sept. 1993	Philip Morris	US		400.0	equity stake
March 1993	Philip Morris	US	30.0-40.0		equity stake
20 May 1992	Fiat	I	810	1980.0	equity stake
Feb. 1992	CONOCO subsidiary of Du Pont de Nemours	US		1000	equity stake
11 Aug. 1992	International Paper Company	US	150.0	325.0	equity stake
May 1992	Kay Universal	US	6.3	131.3	equity stake
Aug. 1993	Cimenteries CBR (Unit of Generale De Belgique)	B	55.7	122.2	equity stake

Host country	Local partner	Product line	Stage	Additional information
Kazakhstan	Alma-Ata Tobacco Factory	production of tobacco products	agreed	western partner will acquire 49% of factory to be privatised to be increased to 90% by the end of next year; production of cigarettes will rise from 12 bn to 20 bn a year
Lithuania	State Tobacco Company, Klaipeda	production of cigarettes	negotiated	western partner will acquire (earlier: 55% of stock for 30 mn US$) 65.2% of stock for 40 mn US$; it is the first privatisation for convertible currency; support is to be increased from 3 bn cigarettes a year
Poland	FSM	plant to produce "Cinquecento" small cars ("500" model)	agreed on 20 May 1992	output of 160,000 cars a year is projected to be mostly exported (100,000) to Italy and other west european countries; projected expansion to 240,000
Poland	Gdansk Refinery	oil refining	final decision pending, negotiated	western partner plans to invest 1 bn US$ over a 10-year period to modernise and expand the refinery; state retains control over the refinery
Poland	Kwidzyn Paper Mill, Elblag Province	production of paper, printing paper and coated cardboard for packaging	agreed	western partner bought 80% of the shares for 150 mn US$ and made a commitment to invest 175 mn US$ by the end of 1996 in modernisation, product quality and environmental protection
Poland	Budimex	construction industry	agreed	Kay Universal has a 42% stake in Budimex; western partner considers investment of 125.0 mn US$ over the next two years
Poland	Zaklady Cementowo-Wapie nnicze Gorazdze Plant; Cementownia	production of cement	agreed	western partner paid 90.4 mn DM for 30% stake in the first and for 42% in the second plant; 76 mn DM and 32 mn DM will be invested in new equipment, respectively; in 1997 western partner will buy additionally a 21% stake in the first plant

Date	Company name	Foreign partner country	Initial foreign investment US$ mn	Total foreign investment US$ mn	FII type
3 March 1992	Peugeot	F	32.0	102.0	equity stake
April 1993	ALCATEL Standard Electrica (ES) subsidiary of ALCATEL Alsthom	E/F	37.3	97.3	equity stake
Oct. 1993	Siemens AG	D	38.5	95.5	equity stake
1993	AT&T	US	28.0	84.0	equity stake
1993	Pepsico	US	29.0	81.0	equity stake
unknown	Unilever	GB/NL	29.7	49.0	equity stake
Aug. 1993	Linde	D	16.1	46.1	equity stake
April 1993	Jacobs Suchard (CH), affiliated with Philip Morris Group (US)	CH	11.3	26.3	equity stake
16 June 1993	Bahlsens Keksfabrik	D	10.2	26.1	equity stake

Host country	Local partner	Product line	Stage	Additional information
Poland	FSC Truck Factory in Lublin	assembly of "405" models and modernisation of the plant	agreed	output of 2000 "405" model cars as from mid-1993; and 10,000 as from the fourth year
Poland	PZT Telecom Factory	manufacture of transmission and switchboard equipment	negotiated	western partner will purchase 80% equity stake in two plants for 37.3 mn US$; and will invest further 60 mn US$
Poland	Zwut Telecom-munications equipment producer; Elwro Electronic	production of telecommuni-cations equipment	agreed	western partner will invest in two enterprises 57 mn US$ in the next six years
Poland	Telfa Bydgoszcz	construction and operation of tele-communication network	agreed	western partner acquired 80% of equity in Telfa Bydgoszcz
Poland	Wedel S.A.	production of sweets	agreed	western partner acquired 40% of equity
Poland	Pollena Bydgoszcz	production of soap and detergents	agreed	western partner holds 80% of equity in Pollena Bydgoszcz
Poland	Polgaz Enter-prises in Mielec and Pszczyna	distribution of gas	agreed	western partner purchased a 70% stake and will invest some 33 mn US$ in upgrading production facilities
Poland	Olza Chocolate-wafer Enterprise	production of chocolate products	agreed	western partner paid 5 mn US$ for 80% equity stake, initial investment will amount to 11.3 mn US$, and 15 mn US$ will be invested subsequently
Poland	Konzentraty Spozywcze Wskawinie near Krakow	production of baked goods, coffee and noodles	agreed	western partner acquired 80% of the local factory for 10.2 mn US$; it will invent 15.9 mn US$ in new equipment and production facilities by the end of 1996

(continued)

Date	Company name	Foreign partner country	Initial foreign investment US$ mn	Total foreign investment US$ mn	FII type
Aug. 1993	Mieback Projekt-gesellschaft (a member of Mieback Group)	D	3.7	22.8	equity stake
Aug. 1993	AGA	CH	4.9	21.3	equity stake
March 1993	Unilever	NL/GB		17.5	equity stake
June 1992	CPC International	US	25.8		equity stake
Jan. 1993	Unilever	NL/GB	25.0+14.0		equity stake
Aug. 1993	Forum Maritime	GR	355.0	650.0	equity stake
Nov. 1991	Madrina AG	D		300	equity stake
April 1992	Star Technology system	A		250.0	equity stake

Host country	Local partner	Product line	Stage	Additional information
Poland	Odra cement factory in Opole	production of cement	agreed	western partner bought an 80% equity stake for 6 mn DM; in addition 31 mn DM will be invested; 1/5 of output will be exported
Poland	Polgaz Koscian	production of industrial gas	agreed	western partner bought a 70% stake in Polgaz and promised to invest 120 mn SFK in the next 5 years
Poland	Roma, Banin near Gdansk	production of ice cream	agreed	majority stake was bought out from local owners; western partner will cover debts and invest 17.5 mn US$ to expand operations (current production is 15 tons of ice-cream per day)
Poland	Amino	production of food products	agreed	western partner acquired 80% stake in the company for 8.8 mn US$ and agreed to invest 17 mn US$ over five years
Poland	Slaskie Zaklady Przemyslu Tluszczowego	production of margarine, edible oils and fats	negotiated	western partner will pay 25 mn US$ for a 70% stake and 14 mn US$ in subsequent three years
Romania	Petromin shipping company	maritime shipping	negotiated	western partner will acquire a 51% stake; 355 mn US$ will be invested in cash and the remainder in modernisation and building of 20 new ships
Russia	Elektrosila	production of electrical generating, power equipment and consumer goods	agreed in Nov. 1991	Madrina AG acquired a 30% stake in Electrosila
Russia	Lenzsoloto	development of Sukhoi Log gold mine	agreed in April 1992	western partner obtained a 31% equity stake in Lenzsoloto; total reserves of Sukhoi Log are estimated at 500 tons or 5 bn US$; Russian partner will invest 640 mn SUK (at Nov 1992 prices). Gold will be sold exclusively to the State

(continued)

Date	Company name	Foreign partner country	Initial foreign investment US$ mn	Total foreign investment US$ mn	FII type
Feb. 1993	Philip Morris	US	4.95	65.0	equity stake
Sept. 1993	Henkel	D		23.6	equity stake
July 1993	Sherson, Leeman Brothers	US	40.0		equity stake
Aug. 1992	R.J. Reynolds Tobacco International Inc.	US	25.0		equity stake
June 1992	Sabrio	E	88.0		equity stake
June 1992	Rhone Poulenc	F	90.0		equity stake
June 1992	Jacobs Suchard affiliated with Philip Morris	US	21.4		equity stake
Sept. 1992	RJR Nabisco Holdings	US			equity stake

Host country	Local partner	Product line	Stage	Additional information
Russia	Krasnodar Tobacco Factory	production of cigarettes	negotiated	western partner has purchased a 20% stake in the factory's capital and wishes to increase it to 75-80%; output is to be increased from 6.8 bn to 12 bn
Russia	ERA detergent and adhesive factory	production of detergents and adhesives	agreed	Henkel will invest 39 mn DM including the purchase price of 39% of shares; it will be responsible for management and will provide the know-how to upgrade existing products
Russia	Inkombank	financial services	agreed	at a later stage shares of the local partner may be quoted by western partner on world markets
Russia	Uritski Tobacco factory	production of cigarettes	agreed	R.J. Reynolds bought 52% of the stock; RJR-Petro (new company name) will be producing 22 bn cigarettes a year
Slovenia	Papirnica Kolicevo	production of cardboard	agreed	production will be increased from 100,000 tonnes to 180,000 tonnes a year; remaining 24% of shares are held by Slovenia's development agency
Slovakia	Chemlon Plant in Humenne	production of polyamide yarn	agreed	western partner has the right of increase its stake in chemlon to 63% (initially 52%)
Slovakia	Figaro	production of chocolates	agreed	10.7 mn US$ will be invested in acquisition and 10.7 mn US$ in modernisation, marketing and training
Ukraine	Ukrainian cigarette plants in Lvov	production of cigarettes	agreed	western partner has taken 70% interest in the two plants; plans to renovate plants and raise annual output to 22 bn cigarettes a year (25% of national consumption)

(continued)

Date	Company name	Foreign partner country	Initial foreign investment US$ mn	Total foreign investment US$ mn	FII type
28 March 1991	Volkswagen	D	309.0	2470.0	equity stake

Source: UN/ECE SECRETARIAT

Host country	Local partner	Product line	Stage	Additional information
The Czech Republic	AZM¨(automobilove Zavody Narodni Podnik)	joint venture to manufacture Skoda-Favorit cars	agreed on 28 March 1991	500 mn DM (309 mn US$) were invested in 1993; about 4 bn DM (2.5 bn US$) will be invested over next 10 years; output of 400,000 cars a year as from the middle of 1990s is projected; foreign stake will increase from 31% in 1991 to 70% by 1995

Annex 12.2

Growth of foreign investment registrations in countries of Eastern Europe and former Yugoslavia

(cumulative total and estimates of foreign capital in US$ mn at dates indicated)

	1 January 1992		*1 January 1993*		*1 April 1993*		*1 July 1993*		*1 October 1993*	
	number	**foreign capital**	**number**	**foreign capital**	**number**	**foreign capital**	**number**	**foreign capital**	**number**	**foreign capital**
ex-Soviet Union, of which:	4208	4462.2	15290	5566.5	18562	5777.0	20290	5918.5	21750	6155.0
Commonwealth of Independent States:	2593*	4300.0	8007*	5250.0	9600	5400.0	10900	5500.0	12000	5700.0
Russia	2022*	2827.4	3252*	2850.0	4424*	2885.7	5249*	2916.9	5800	2950.0
Ukraine	400	440.0	2000*	480.0	2200	500.0	2400	515.0	2600	550.0
Belarus	283*	---	714*	265.5*	850	275.0	944*	281.6*	1050	310.0
Estonia	1100	84.2	2662*	142.0*	4012*	177.0*	4052*	188.5*	4100	200.0
Lithuania	220	33.0	2000	90.0	2300	100.0	2638*	110.0	2900	120.0
Latvia	295	45.0	2621*	84.5*	2650	100.0	2700	120.0	2750	135.0
Hungary 1)	9117*	3137.0*	13218*	3680.6*	14287	3818.2	15311	3875.5	15800	3950.0
Poland 1)	5583*	479.5*	5740*	1545.6*	6000	1650.0	6300	1800.0	6500	1900.0
The Czech Republic	4000 2)	1076.0 2)	3120	1573.5*	3400	1700.0	3700	1965.5*	3900	2028.5*
Slovakia			2875*	231.2*	3200	260.0	3948*	320.4*	4200	360.0
Bulgaria	900	130.0	1200	170.0	1300	180.0	1400	195.0	1500	210.0
Romania	8022*	268.7*	20684*	539.8*	23453*	646.3*	26249*	678.8*	27000	700.0
Subtotal	**31830**	**9553.4**	**62127**	**13307.2**	**70202**	**14031.5**	**77198**	**14753.7**	**80650**	**15303.5**
ex-Yugoslavia, of which	---		---	---	---	---	---	---	---	---
Slovenia	1000	650.0	2815	962.2	2950	1000.0	3050	1050.0	3169*	
1106.2*										

1) Revised estimate. - 2) Including Slovenia.

Note: Values in national currencies converted to US$ at current (historical) exchange rates. Figures with an asterisk are official data, while other figures are secretariat estimates.

Source: United Nations Economic Commission for Europe.

Chapter 13

POTENTIAL LESSONS FROM AUSTRIA FOR THE RESTRUCTURING PROCESS IN EAST EUROPE[1)]

Karl Aiginger[*)]

This paper is about the role government and non-private institutions played in shaping the environment of industrial firms in the market economies after World War II. It touches upon aspects of the legal framework, property rights, taxes and subsidies, and reports mainly the experience in Austria. The paper does not intend to present a balanced review of the post war economic development, but focus on specific aspects which could be interesting for the restructuring process in Eastern Europe today.

13.1 Economic preconditions and policies

At the end of World War II industrial production in Austria collapsed to about one third of pre-war level. This was partly due to physical destruction and to the lack of energy and raw materials. Demand from the industrial-military complex in Germany collapsed, while questions of ownership, property rights and management hampered production.

The war regime could be described as a planned economy with decentralised production. Prices and output goals were fixed, but firms had some leverage in fulfilling the goals. Investment was centrally planned. The Nazis had deliberately built up a few large firms for steel production, aluminium and basic chemicals to make use of Austria's natural resources as well as to diversify the location of basic goods needed for the war machine. Compared with the final

---

1) I express my gratitude to many colleagues who discussed this paper and related work with me, among them Kurt Bayer, Felix Butschek, Gernot Hutschenreiter, Annamaria Inzelt, Michael Landesmann, Michael Peneder, Wolfgang Pollan, Sándor Richter, Kurt Rothschild, Hans Seidel, Jan Stankovsky, Erich Streissler, Alena Zemplinerova.

*) Professor of Economics, University of Linz, Austria, and Austrian Institute of Economic Research (WIFO).

period of socialist planning in Eastern Europe, the efficiency of the planning bureaucracy as well as that of the managements was definitely superior. Political and military obsessions on the part of the planners, and fear and repression from the point of view of the workers, were substitutes for direct financial incentives.

Pre-war output was reached in 1949. But even then Austria was lagging behind other European countries in GNP per head and productivity.[2)]

Today Austria is among the leading industrial nations in Europe measured by such indicators as GNP per head, share of the industrial sector in GNP and labour productivity in manufacturing. GNP per head is above the EC average (and higher than in Germany after unification). 27 per cent of gross national product originates from the industrial sector. Among the leading industrial countries this share is larger only in Japan and Germany. Net output per worker is about the same as, or slightly higher than, in the former West Germany.

A gradual approach to price liberalisation

In today's terminology we would say that Austria chose the gradual approach. In the first years after the war Austria had quantity and price controls for important products (food, clothing, housing). Quantity controls (for industrial products) and rationing schemes for consumer goods were gradually removed over the years 1946-1949, and food stamps finally disappeared in 1950. Prices were first set directly by government, but afterwards subject to upper ceilings on the absolute price. In the 1950s price governance shifted from government to the social partners.[3)] Starting in 1957 a voluntary price commission (the *Preis- und Lohnkommission),* fixed "maximum rates of price increase" for important manufacturing products and for consumer goods. The association of employers guaranteed the compliance of the firms with the agreed price increases, while

---

2) Austria's GNP per head (measured in terms of purchasing power) was one-third of Switzerland's in 1950; today it is 80 per cent of Switzerland's (Butschek 1993).

3) The development was not so smooth if we watch the details. The system of government-led price control (including tripartite negotiations which were moulded into government price regulation) ended about 1950 (with exceptions for bread, raw materials and energy prices). In the following liberalisation period price controls seemed to be unnecessary. Later in the 1950s the voluntary system of price and wage negotiations (with maximal rates of price increase) was created.

the trade union monitored wage discipline. Both associations were organised in quite a central manner, giving power more to the top than to the sectoral branches.

The approach was pragmatic and comprehensive. In judging which prices should be fixed and which could be determined by market forces, demand and supply conditions were considered. The commission judged whether prices exceeded average costs by more than an adequate mark-up for "normal" profits. Price ceilings (more exactly limits for price increases) were negotiated for important industrial goods.

In some industries the (threat of) trade liberalisation was used as an instrument to dampen prices in industries suspected of pushing prices up. Eventually, import competition reduced the importance of price monitoring.

A late revival of price negotiation came in the 1970s in the wake of the oil shock. In the 1990s the system has been phased out, although some price monitoring remains. A department in the Ministry of Economics, e.g., watches the response to oil prices on the world market of gasoline prices in Austria (if they differed too much it could still set maximum prices). The social partners no longer fix maximum price increases, but agree to watch supply and demand conditions for important industrial goods and may propose new upper ceilings in case of monopolistic price hikes.

It is not easy to assess the performance of this gradual approach. The inflation rate has been low in Austria over the whole period, but this may be due to incomes policy or to the high productivity growth. The variability of inflation is definitely lower in Austria than elsewhere at least from the 1950s. The largest price increases could be capped, which is usually credited to the voluntary price regime. However prices for many consumer goods are rather high; competition is softened by a lot of restrictions and rules which have to be regarded as consequences of the relatively small domestic market with few competitors, but also as by-products of economic codetermination by the social partners. Restrictions on entry and competition can be in the common interest of incumbent firms and of trade union members in existing firms. As regards competitive pressure, a vested interest version of the social partnership cannot be rejected, even if it is agreed that in general the social partners gave priority to general economic goals even at the expense of short-term interests.

Patience threatens to run out: crisis and new credibility

There was no smooth economic development in post-war Austria. The wage aspirations of workers had to be disappointed to allow firms to accumulate internal cash (self financing) for new investment. Five tripartite wage price agreements *(Preis- und Lohnabkommen)* tried to combine moderate wage increases with sensible price reforms. Fixing a direct link between wages and productivity provided the correct signals and incentives – as we would say in today's terminology – to workers. The employers' and employees' negotiators exhibited a high degree of general responsibility and the direct involvement of the Austrian Institute of Economic Research (WIFO) provided not only the statistical facts but also the economic expertise necessary for the difficult compromises.

Nevertheless the efficiency of the agreements decreased successively; firms learned to "play against the agreements" as rational expectations theory predicts, and prices increased before and after the agreements. Workers' disappointment with the slow increase in living standards rose; the necessity to restrict aspirations today to get a better outcome tomorrow was no longer accepted. The climax was reached in October 1950, with demonstrations and an attempt to call a general strike. The prestige and the political sensitivity of the trade union leaders were at that time high enough to cope with the problem (more information for members was offered, communists were the scapegoat). The employers' side of the social partnership helped by announcing a voluntary absolute price decrease ("breaking inflationary expectations"). Government announced a strict budgetary and monetary policy and made it "credible" by putting a liberal hard-liner into the Ministry of Finance and by committing itself to stricter liberalisation rules (by membership in OECD).

What can we learn from this?

At least under the Austrian post-war conditions a gradual approach was feasible. Quantity and price controls as well as import restrictions were phased out gradually without distorting the remaining system too much. The pace of the internal liberalisation was pragmatic, depending on sensible economic factors like demand, prices and conduct. Under the pragmatic approach, controls were sometimes eliminated for a trial period with the possibility of return to the old system. Firms were not afraid of arbitrariness or coercion since their representatives had a say in the process. The anti-inflationary stance of the system (social partnership plus government) was considered credible, at least after the new stabilisation policy in the early 1950s. To effect this credibility took seven years, and the danger existed that time might run out.

Some conditions were very specific. The determination to work together between government, trade union and firms' representatives was extraordinary (due to Austria's pre-war experience of the outlawing of conservative as well as of social democratic politicians under the Nazi regime and of the post-war occupation). The orientation of the social partners towards general economic performance (instead of vested interests) has rare parallels. The information and the economic expertise available for this planning process were better than can usually be expected. The institutions were centralised and their representatives were highly respected internally and externally.

Increasing the relevance of the future

Time inconsistency means that the government has too high a discount rate and overvalues present revenues at the expense of long-term success. Among the multiple equilibria that an economy can reach, some "bad equilibrium" may be attained instead of a better one (see Calvo et al. 1992, p. 114). The social partners helped to insert a longer time horizon into economic policy and implicitly reduced the time discount of policy makers. Making economic policy predictable and stabilising demand, prices and profit shares are important parts of a strategy to reduce future risks. Production is higher under reduced uncertainty (Aiginger 1987).

Another important instrument was *accelerated depreciation.* For investment goods (especially machines) an extra proportion of the purchase value (up to eighty per cent) could be deducted from profits in the first year. This greatly reduced the payoff period and therefore the riskiness of investment. This instrument also decreased ex-post profit tax rates in the case of investment chains (if one investment followed the next). Continuously rising investment was the rule rather than the exception in a period of fast growth.

Accelerated depreciation is an unbureaucratic instrument for discriminating between firms which use profits for consumption and firms which use them for reinvestment. It is secondly a way to favour successful firms (since the subsidy effect is conditioned by profitability). It is thirdly an instrument to promote manufacturing at the cost of distribution. It can be additionally used to discriminate between machinery and building (this was done) or between domestic and exporting industry (this was not done and may now be incompatible with international trading rules).

No instrument works too long. In the course of time additional schemes came into effect. Tax depreciation as high as 120 per cent of the purchase value became possible (favouring capital-intensive firms with long periods of depreciation), tax-free reserves (for firms which did not see urgent investment opportunities), and finally tax credits for unprofitable firms all eroded the tax base. Finally the system was thought to favour capital-intensive firms and new domestic monopolies while discriminating against investments in research, human capital, young firms and entry. The system was scrapped, the subsidies were cut and the nominal tax rates reduced to offset the profit squeeze. In the period when capital markets did not work properly and firms had to rely on self-financing, it was an *important investment resource for profitable firms* in manufacturing. It was an instrument to reduce the rate of time discount and a guarantee to employees that profits would be reinvested.

Another way of reducing the time discount was the creation of *special financial institutions.* A special bank for industrial investment *(Investkredit)* was founded, following the perception that commercial banks did not supply long-term credits and provided capital only to firms with tangible assets. Other financial institutions specialised in supplying guarantees for long-term projects in risky markets *(Kontrollbank, Finanzierungsgarantiegesellschaft).* Of course these institutions were imperfect substitutes for a well-functioning capital market, but they did an important job over many decades (and are now either private banks or institutions providing guarantees and soft loans).

Discriminating between sectors

Besides the general tax credits there is an extended system of cheap loans and subsidies. It started with the European Recovery Programme and a major part is still the revolving funds originating from the Marshall Plan. The amount of subsidies increased over time with a peak in the late 1970s. Its Net Value is estimated as 2 per cent of value added in manufacturing – neither larger nor smaller than in other west European economies.

Direct subsidies in general are intended to discriminate between firms (otherwise cheaper instruments like lower tax rates are available). Whether they discriminate according to sectors, size, regions or performance varies. Whether the discrimination is made *explicit* or implicit is *crucial*.

It is not easy to find out ex post which firms were targeted by the ERP credits. To my knowledge, this was never made explicit. The programme was intended to promote reconstruction, technical progress, and competitiveness of Europe in a growing world economy. The participating countries were obliged to submit plans for short-term and medium-term investments. In Austria a special department of the Ministry of Economics (up to 1949 in the department for planning and reconstruction), together with experts from the Austrian Institute of Economic Research, combined investment plans proposed by firms with some industry-specific information into so-called "annual programmes". These annual programmes can be understood as something like "soft sectoral plans". The proportions of credits allotted to the sectors did not deviate too much from the investment structure of the large enterprises. Examination of plans and statistics does not reveal much distortion; nor does the sectoral structure differ between submitted and approved credits. What is evident is that the nationalised sector got a larger proportion of the money than its output share. The veil over the actual decision process may one day be lifted by historical research; but casual evidence and discussions with the participants in the process did not reveal any consistent method of discrimination.[4)] Nevertheless only one-third of investment in manufacturing was financed by this scheme. So the programme looks, with hindsight, as a cheap method of finance, disciplining firms to make articulate plans and forecasts. The international source of the money required that projects should make sense and would be judged critically (the US ERP agency was the outside agent guaranteeing credibility and solving the domestic prisoner's dilemma).

---

4) A strict discrimination between manufacturing sectors (neither planned nor actual) was not remembered. Some of the answers were: "Every sensible programme was approved", "sometimes there were discussions whether basic industries or consumer industries should be favoured". One remark which shows that policy considerations existed was the following: "the paper and pulp industry was forced to propose investments by the threat of import liberalisation". And definitely there was a discussion how large the capacities should be in the firms inherited from Nazi-Germany (the Ministry of Planning and Reconstruction worked out four sectoral plans, but they were not directly related to the ERP programme). It was also controversial whether Austria should get a car production facility.

Later on, the subsidies increased in Austria along different lines and in different agencies. Some schemes discriminated between sectors, usually favouring mature and declining industries (textiles, apparel, paper and pulp). From the published intentions it appears that most schemes focused on productivity increase or export promotion (environmental aspects and energy saving were added in the 1970s). The volume of subsidies reached its maximum in the 1970s when used to combat recession, stabilise employment and counteract a rising market interest rate.

Though usually no ex ante sectoral discrimination was planned, ex post analyses showed that the schemes in general favoured capital-intensive, basic goods industries and other mature sectors. The system discriminated in favour of large enterprises, and slow-growing firms.

What can we learn from this?

Schemes which propagate rather general and partly conflicting goals ("productivity increase", "employment stabilisation", "export promotion" or "import substitution") are found ex post to discriminate in favour of branches in which large firms exist and vested interests are well organised.

This finding initiated two reform approaches in the late 1970s. The first was a scheme focusing specifically on innovations and investment in firms in the most sophisticated market segments (called *TOPINVESTITIONEN),* the second a scheme promoting the application of three generic techniques (technology promoting programme, *Technologieförderung).*

The idea of *TOPINVESTITIONEN* is that, while government does not know which industrial sectors will be the most important and profitable ones in future, *there is a consensus about the characteristics of firms a with competitive edge in the most sophisticated market segments.* Firms could get a cheap credit if their own past performance and their planned innovations got a high score according to specific criteria. The criteria referred partly to the *firm*, partly to the *project* and partly to the *market* they were engaged in: Benchmarks were fixed, translating firm data into grade points.

Among the criteria were:

- past *performance of the firm*: growth, cash flow, exports
- *the use of specific inputs*: qualified labour, research personnel, low energy intensity

- *project impact*: increase in exports, in unit value of product, innovative content (own research), market growth in EC, positive specialisation of leading countries in the specific industry.

The list included 30 variables; an expert group set quantitative limits for each. If a firm passed a limit of pre-fixed points cheap money had to be granted.

The economic philosophy behind this scheme was the product cycle theory; firms in advanced industrial countries should produce a certain mix of products in the first and second phase of the product cycle. Doing this, a firm has to use sophisticated inputs and specialise in rapidly growing, diversified markets, in which leading countries have a comparative advantage. The subsidising of "excellent firms" is justified in a market economy by the external benefits of innovations and the spillovers from innovating firms to the non-innovating ones. On a less philosophical level, this scheme should counteract the tendency of "traditional" schemes to bias the interest rate in favour of mature, non-profitable firms. Banks were suspected of aggravating this bias by the use of conservative credit rules.

To implement this programme the expertise and independence of the rating group was decisive. The final decision was made by an independent commission, not by some political decision unit. Usually final decisions had been made by a government department after getting advice from experts or a commission.

Between 1982 and 1993 AS 30 billion were allotted to the *TOP-FIRMS* and several ex post analyses (by the author of this paper and his colleagues from WIFO) have shown that the scheme was a success, in the sense that the composition of the credits was consistent with the goal of rewarding above average performance and that the firms performed even better after getting the credit.

In the 1980s the volume of credits under this scheme was decreased for three reasons. First, subsidies were curtailed in general. Secondly, special interest groups complained that it was very hard to get credits from this scheme (above all, politicians could not guarantee *ex cathedra* that a specific firm would get cheap money). And public opinion complained that it made no sense to give money to firms in good financial positions.

Though I myself was one of the promoters of this scheme, and helped to implement and monitor it, I feel that the gradual phasing out may not be that bad. The capital market has improved in this decade so that risky and innovative firms now have a better chance of equity financing. Secondly, the core of the ideas has spread among firms and institutions. The largest source of subsidies – the ERP fund – is now using similar criteria, though not with the same rigour and independence from political pressure. The firms have learned to assess their own performance according to some of these criteria.

The Technology Promoting Programme focused on three "generic" technologies, namely microelectronics (incl. CAD, CIM etc.), biotechnology and genetic engineering. These programmes are continued as technology promotion programmes with annually shifting goals (*TECHNOLOGIEFONDS*). There is also a well developed scheme to promote research and development.

What can we learn from this?

New programmes in the 1980s focus specifically on innovation, on the transfer of research into the production process. They make it attractive to invest in sophisticated markets, in which a country with increasing wages will continue to be competitive in the future. This attempt comes near to a "picking the winner strategy", but it differs from it in so far as its information requirements are much less than in similar attempts. No governmental agency knows which sectors and which products will be successful. But economists are confident of knowing some of the prerequisites of success. The use of qualified labour, an own research base, the positioning in diversified markets and in market segments in which prices deviate from marginal costs, are all crucial for success. Our innovative subsidy scheme *(TOPINVESTITIONEN)* focused on these firms. Schemes to promote implementation of new technologies and research and development are other methods for promoting structural change, recognising the limited knowledge of government.

Regulating monopolies and investing in infrastructure

Austria has no clearly elaborated policy for regulating monopolies. Dominant private firms in manufacturing industries had to submit their planned price increases to the voluntary system of price control. For natural monopolies like electricity, railways, telecommunications (postal service, telephone), Austria chose public ownership plus supervision by a government department. (This is a good field for economists who want to study capture theory.) The double grip of ownership plus control leads to an intermixture of interests in which the objectives of state ownership and the special interests of managers, employees and bureaucrats became entangled. With the exception of disagreement on the rate of price increases, the firms and their regulators agree on almost all issues, while consumer demands about quantity and quality of service are poorly monitored. Ecological concerns are usually rejected by both the regulated firms and their regulators.

Austria has not much experience in antitrust policy. Government usually favoured the collaboration or even the merger of firms. Its own price regulation procedure and that of the social partners facilitated or even required collusion and parallel behaviour. Defining the preconditions for entry (including the "local need criterion") comes near to a substantial entry barrier.

The technical performance of the state monopolies had been quite good for a long time, and investment is very high. Economic efficiency (productivity per head) is reported to be low (public transport, information services); allocative efficiency (no marginal cost pricing where it is feasible), and innovations in the 1980s are lacking (telecommunications). Reforms are on the way, inter alia looking for the reforms proposed by the EC.

There is now the criticism that inefficiency of the infrastructure hurts the competitiveness of manufacturing due to high prices (telephone, data transmission) and insufficient speed and service (trains). But the first steps to reform of the public sector proper, as well as of schools and hospitals, have not so far been very successful.

What can we learn from this?

Double grips (ownership plus regulation) seem neither necessary nor successful. There should be a strict division of labour between the regulator who sets the targets and monitors the performance and the agent who tries to meet these objectives. The Anglo-American system of an independent and highly esteemed regulatory body (with judicial power) seems superior to the responsibility of a department in some ministry, particularly when moderated by a commission in which the special interests of the regulated firms dominate.

The principal agent problem in nationalised industries

Fifteen per cent of Austrian industry, especially large firms in the basic goods sector, was nationalised after World War II (partly due to the lack of owners, partly following a political vision). The nationalised industries were quite successful in the first phase. Reconstruction was speedy, the basic production goods were supplied to Austrian firms at low prices and of high quality. In the early 1960s there was some political debate about whether nationalised firms should be allowed to expand into the final goods sector, which was eventually agreed. Until the late 1970s sales and exports grew faster than in the private sector.

As product markets became diversified, multinational firms were divisionalised; as commodity markets turned into excess supply, the nationalised firms started to make losses. Several government bailouts and structural reforms did not help and the story of nationalised Austrian industry effectively ends in November 1993. The government decided to sell the majority of the nationalised industry groups (as soon as possible, in some cases after a reconstruction period).

This is not the place finally to assess the reasons for the failure of nationalisation nor to rank them. The determinants of the failure include the *industry problem* (too much concentration in basic goods), the *organisational problem* (too bureaucratic organisation), the *soft budget problem* (no withdrawals from unprofitable sectors) and the *monitoring problem* (how to judge the performance of firms).

The principles for management, or the objectives which nationalised firms should pursue, have never been defined explicitly. The goals actually pursued have varied; the organisation and the management structure were changed frequently.

Whether the goals of nationalised firms should differ from those of private firms has been controversial. In good times some people (and politicians) expected the nationalised firms to be the spearheads of the technological progress and/or innovators in shop floor democracy and codetermination. In bad times politicians expected nationalised firms to stabilise employment. But neither of these aims was defined explicitly or written into any law or charter.

The decision process in the nationalised sector and the degree of interference by government changed over time. Sometimes a government department was responsible directly for firms' decisions (including investment plans); usually some intermediate agency (holding company) was constructed. The recruitment process for top management favoured political selection.

What can we learn from this?

Probably nationalisation has to be assessed differently in the 1950s when excess demand, homogeneous products and domestic markets dominated, from the 1990s when excess capacities in sophisticated, heterogeneous and internationalised markets prevail. If something can be learned from Austria's failure it is that the goals of nationalisation should be made explicit. Yardsticks for positive performance should be set and monitored, if the goal is not profit maximisation. If nationalised firms have to carry excess burdens, they should be quantitatively specified. Ideally the government should offer a reward for a specific task and then ask whether some private or some nationalised firms would be willing to perform this extra task (by auction).

Rules for foreign capital

Austria has a liberal policy on investment of foreign capital. More than one-third of the manufacturing industry is owned by foreign firms. They were helpful in promoting technical progress and new organisational techniques. The foreign-owned firms showed superior performance according to several economic criteria (productivity per worker, growth of sales, profits). Over many decades, the amount of capital inflow was larger than the investment of Austrian firms abroad. This has changed in recent years; Austrian outward investment is now larger than foreign investment in Austria.

Austria never dropped its favourable attitude towards capital inflow, but some problems arise from a dominant role of foreign investment. The first is that foreign investors get the signal that cheap labour and big subsidies are not the inputs in which Austria will continue to have a comparative advantage. Investment should draw upon the qualifications of Austrian workers and high productivity. The second comes from the fact that there are few multinational firms with a homebase in Austria. This is a problem since multinational firms often concentrate productive services, including research, near their headquarters. Austria therefore encourages firms to choose headquarters, or at least a regional or divisional centre, in Austria. Austria also tries to persuade existing firms (and made this explicit in the privatisation law of 1993 for the nationalised industry) to keep their headquarters in Austria (sometimes by keeping a majority of assets in Austria). The main strategy, however, is to make the tax system and economic environment in general favourable for establishing headquarters.

13.2 Has there been an industrial policy in Austria?

I have so far reported on the Austrian experience without using the term "industrial policy".

If one defines as industrial policy the totality of *measures relating to and influencing manufacturing,* then there has been a very comprehensive industrial policy in Austria.

If one defines as industrial policy *a coherent attempt to influence the development of industry in a specific direction, into specific sectors etc.,* then there exists no industrial policy. This does not mean that policy did not implicitly sometimes favour specific sectors or activities. The impact of government intervention tended to favour mature, capital and energy intensive industries and in some cases also those employing cheap labour. Sometimes the economic strategy and subsidy schemes favoured innovation and structural change. The overall impact is unclear.

What can we learn from this?

My personal opinion is that governments in market economies should formulate an industrial policy strategy[5)], which could be used to assess the totality of actual policy measures and schemes. A government which officially claims to have no industrial policy usually has an implicit one. Half of GNP is redistributed, regulated, or monitored by government via taxes, tariffs, subsidies, rules, and regulation. *And if there is no industrial strategy, the short-term vested interests will shape one and no outside agent, analyst, political opponent will*

---

5) Recently the social partners defined the goal of the industrial policy as follows: "The goals of industrial policy are to promote dynamic structural change in the direction of higher value added, internationalisation, full employment and use of qualified labour. To reach dynamic competitiveness implies high and increasing incomes and high and increasing social and environmental standards" (Beirat 1991, p. 8). There are a lot of compromises incorporated in this definition, but it nevertheless gives priority to promoting change instead of slowing down structural change. The formula defines the priority of high value added, internationalisation and qualification and rejects a concept of short-run competitiveness at the expense of social and environmental standards.

be able to judge it. A macroeconomic research institute monitoring compliance with an explicitly formulated industrial strategy, the commitment of industrial policy to structural change and the behaviour of institutions and firms can be helpful.

In my opinion even the US have an implicit industrial policy. It favours industries needing cheap labour and low energy prices, and has insufficient incentives for on the job training compared with Europe and Japan. Education in schools and firms' investment in training is strongly influenced by government, be it directly in schools, training and retraining schedules or indirectly via the rules for hiring and firing. Within the high tech sector the military sector alone gets its positive external effects rewarded; risks are reduced by long-term stable contracts, thus twisting profitability away from consumer and investment goods to goods with military or at least double use. These are elements of an indirect industrial policy, maybe more harmful – but more difficult to judge – than an explicit one.

The rationale for government industrial policy in a market economy and in an economy in transition

Why should there be an industrial policy in a market economy? The uncontested arguments come from the following areas. Government should intervene if there are external effects, if there is monopoly power, if there are informational asymmetries and incomplete markets. Apart from these arguments government must help to provide public goods, infrastructure etc.

In all these cases government intervention does not distort the market process, but brings the economy nearer to the theoretical ideal, where consumer values and producer costs are equalised (at the margin) and efficiency is attained. The *external costs argument* calls for subsidies especially in research and development, but also for risky investment. The monopoly argument allows for monitoring prices for many industries and services, and for encouraging entry. It could induce the restructuring of existing monopolies (e.g. the break-up of AT&T in the US). The *asymmetry argument* allows for subsidising small and medium sized firms, but also gives government a stake in large enterprises as long as capital markets are underdeveloped or risk averse.[6)]

These arguments apply even to well developed market economies or – to use another model – for *economies near equilibrium*. Austria's economy after World War II and the countries in transition today are however quite far away from equilibrium. Remember that most economists agreed for a long time that the stabilisation of employment in case of cyclical or structural unemployment was an important goal for economic policy. Today's scepticism comes more from the feasibility side (in periods of inflation, rational expectations and accumulated deficits) than from the justification corner.

In periods of large structural disequilibria there is definitely a larger potential for a prudent industrial policy. I will discuss three additional arguments for guidance in periods of structural change

- The demand for investment will exceed the supply of savings in periods of structural change, even if macroeconomic saving and investment were in long-run equilibrium. The reason is that new firms and sectors have investment outlays equal to their total capital stock, while in equilibrium only gross investments are needed year by year. This argument is called the "fundamental stock-flow problem in the transition" by Landesmann 1993.
- Prices are still distorted. Capital is too expensive in relation to the prospective long-term equilibrium price (due to inefficiency of the financial system, which lacks criteria and experience to judge the credibility of firms, unclear property rights, and the stock-flow problem). Labour is too cheap compared with the long-run equilibrium. Firms which specialise according to current factor price relations will have to readapt some time in future.
- Some firms make losses today but are viable tomorrow. "Tomorrow" means after reconstruction and readjustment of factor prices in the growth period following today's slump, if intra-CMEA trade were resumed on a new base etc. Allowing these firms to go bankrupt destroys physical capital and human skills, which cannot be recovered if the capacities become profitable

---

6) Other arguments for government interventions come from the new trade theory. Rent shifting and protection of infant industries could be profitable for welfare in a specific country. But many arguments prove only that *theoretically* a country can be better off if it follows this strategy, while in the real world the distortionary effect may dominate and retaliation reduces the potential positive effect. See Krugman (1993) for scepticism about the conclusion of a discipline to which he has contributed a lot.

again. If firms were "correctly" discounting the future (with a very small discount for long-term benefits) and financial markets were complete, firms could cope with these problems without intervention.

These are additional arguments for industrial policy in periods of reconstruction, and these policies were heavily pursued in Western Europe after World War II and in sectoral crises thereafter (vide European activities in the steel industry, national support for coal, shipyards, textiles etc.).

The European experience calls for modesty in applying these arguments in favour of an industrial policy. The *feasibility of improving the market process* by government intervention does not guarantee *that actual intervention goes in the right direction.* The bulk of real world intervention has dampened structural change or was structured by lobbies or by chance rather than by external effects and a correct assessment of future risks and prospects.

Nevertheless it is important to stress that an active industrial policy is better than a reactive or passive one. We define as an active policy one which accelerates the structural change dictated by demand and consumer needs; a passive policy slows down the change to prevent abrupt changes in income and employment. But since government does not know too much about the specific sectors and products which will be demanded in the distant future, it is important not to pursue a very specific sectoral targeting, but to favour the transmission of information, knowledge and skills which allow structural change without having to define the products or sectors into which investment should go ("process oriented industrial policy").

Governance structures in market economies

Each western country has some governance structure for its large industrial firms. It is quite different from textbook economics, and rather different between Western countries.

- In the US, antitrust legislation had an important impact on the shaping of modern industry. While price fixing, concentration rates, price discrimination and pre-emption are highly suspect and violations were sometimes drastically punished, antitrust policy did not prevent the emergence of large and very large enterprises. Import duties and anti-dumping legislation are seen as justified exceptions from general principles of free trade (and not regarded as instruments misused by special interests). While low wages and low energy prices are seen as important for the competitiveness of the US economy, much lower wages and even lower pollution standards in Mexico justify special restrictions for imports from this country (see the discussions and the annex to the NAFTA treaty). Technology policy is effected more indirectly via military demand, but support for an industrial policy to foster the development of super computers etc. is growing. The governance structure changes over time, as seen in the increasing importance of the arguments about "competitiveness" of US vs. Japan. Note the decreasing threat to economic welfare regarded from mergers and the vanishing impact of consumer organisations and trade unions in recent years.

- In Germany a governance structure emerged with an important role for large banks. Antitrust policy had been more important than in other European countries, though it is sometimes softened by the strive for competitiveness in the world market. Industrial policy makes use of massive funds for research, and regional investment subsidies, subsidies for shipyards and the coal industry (and now for restructuring in the new Länder). In France industrial policy has included sectoral development strategies, the creation and promotion of large firms (including nationalisation to create "national champions"). Implicit governance follows from the education system, where the "élite" in government and in large firms passes the same management schools.
- The role of industrial policy in Japan is well discussed in the literature and includes the role of MITI, of banks and of *genkyokus.* Policy for structural change in declining industries as well as promotion of important sectors in the medium term plans (visions) should be kept in mind. Low interest rates, high investment quotas, long working time and lifetime employment are some features which could not be maintained without an implicit governance structure. The system is extremely efficient in promoting collusion (in prices, import restriction, technologies), but, in contrast to other similar attempts, is able to promote efficiency and competitiveness and even to enforce disinvestments. Korea, Taiwan, Indonesia, Singapore all have their own systems of industrial policy, each quite far away from textbook market economies and theoretically founded arguments for interventions. Some authors call these systems "managed market economies" (see Wade 1990, Bayer 1991).

- The European Community explicitly calls for an industrial policy (see Hutschenreiter 1993) on the community level as well as on the national level. It should help to increase the competitiveness of the countries by the promotion of "accelerators" and "multipliers". The approach should be horizontal (encouraging preconditions of growth, not targeting specific sectors). But there exist sectoral programs for specific mature sectors (steel, textiles, cars) and for generic technologies (biotechnology, electronics etc.).

What can we learn from this?

Industrial policy in the West is not a success story. Many interventions went in the wrong direction and slowed down structural change. Industrial policy as pursued would have needed information which government does not have. Industrial policy should have been immune to special interests, which it cannot be.

Nevertheless it looks as if an industrial policy is indispensable. As a very minimum the institutions of industrial production have to be shaped; at a very minimum, funds for research, future investment and restructuring in periods of rapid change are necessary. It is more honest and more successful to define a concept of industrial policy than to suffer from an implicit undisclosed industrial policy.

It is easy to understand that the first years after transition in Eastern Europe were not a good period to argue for an industrial policy. Any industrial policy run by the same institutions and persons as were in charge of the old planning system would have prevented structural change. And any industrial policy starting in the very first reform period would have been under enormous pressure to subsidise large firms even if they were not viable in the long term.

But maybe now is the time to confess that no catch-up process, and no real world industrial system, has ever worked or is performing today without a *system of formal and informal interventions* of state, government, and intermediate non-profit institutions. But while it is clear that a market economy works better than a planned economy, industrial policy can either help to *get a still better system* than a "pure market economy" or can aggravate the problems by slowing down structural change. Making the system of state governance explicit, and defining an active industrial policy, may help an economy to grasp the advantages of industrial policy while preventing a slip into some of its traps. The most important single element of a successful industrial policy is that it should be shielded from the pressure of strong special interests. If an institution or a person is able to decide about a subsidy for a large firm or an investment for a specific region *without clear-cut rules and without ex post control by an outsider authority, the system will sooner or later be captured by vested interests.*

A clear-cut goal, an independent operator of the subsidy scheme and objective ex post control opens the potential for industrial policy (being the necessary, if not sufficient conditions of its success).

13.3 Summary

The minimum of public intervention in a market economy is to *set the rules* for private production and consumption (property rights, legal structure, taxes) and to *provide infrastructure*. This intervention will not be called industrial policy by the majority of economists, though the specific set of property rights, and the quantity and quality of infrastructure, go far to determine industrial competitiveness. Even in shaping the property rights and providing infrastructure, a vision of current and future industrial development is of great help.

Interventions of government in coping with external effects, monopoly power and informational problems are rarely contested. How much intervention is needed may not be easy to define. Each type of intervention has different information requirements on the part of government. It may have side effects and be distorted by bureaucratic failure or special interests. Types of interventions which increase the response rates of agents or equip them with capabilities (Landesmann 1993, p. 2) or which decrease barriers to entry are preferred to interventions which need information about good products and profitable sectors. In general, *interventions which are robust despite informational errors and bureaucratic failures* are superior to those *targeting very specific sectors and firms.*

Industrial governance relies on an *intermediate layer of institutions* which are quasi-public (meaning non-private, not dominated by special interests, and with a stake in general economic development). Having such an *intermediate layer of institutions* helps in implementing more sophisticated macroeconomic or industrial strategies. *Social partnership* is such a layer in Austria, *financial non-commercial intermediaries* are another, MITI and *genkyokus* are such institutions in Japan; the *Deutsche Bank, Treuhand* and *Volkswagenstiftung* are some important ones in Germany. *These institutions enforce continuity in periods of political instability, and help to widen the time horizon of politics and firms.* And these institutions help to internalise external economies. It has to be guaranteed that these institutions remain flexible, incorporate market signals and are not captured by special interests. Of course they should not be the old planning boards in a new disguise.

References

Aiginger, K. (1987), *Production and Decision under Uncertainty,* Blackwell.

– (1993), "Schwerpunkte einer nationalen Industriepolitik in einem integrierten Europa", *WIFO Vorträge,* no. 60.

– (1993), "Determinants of Net Trade Flows between East and West", Paper presented at the European Association of Industrial Economics (EARIE), Tel Aviv.

– (1993), "Strategic Behavior of Austrian Firms towards Central and Eastern Europe", Paper presented at the Austrian Economic Association (Nationalökonomische Gesellschaft), Graz.

– (1993), "Collusion, concentration, profits", *Empirica,* vol. 20, no. 2.

– (1993), "Chancen und Gefährdungspotentiale der Ostöffnung: Konsequenzen für die österreichische Wirtschaft", *WIFO Gutachten,* 3 Bände (jointly with Geldner, N., Kramer, H., Peneder, M., Schnitzer, Y., and Stankovsky, J.), Vienna.

–, and Bayer, K. (1985), *Untersuchung der wirtschaftlichen Auswirkungen der TOP-Aktion, Teil 1,* Vienna; ibid. Teil 2 (1986).

–, and Clement, W. (1993), "Grundzüge einer Neuen Industriepolitik", *WIFO und IWI Gutachten,* Vienna.

Bayer, K. (1991), "Strategic planning for industrial restructuring", Austrian Institute of Economic Research (WIFO), Vienna.

Beirat für Wirtschafts- und Sozialfragen (1991), *Industriepolitik,* Vienna.

Butschek, F. (1993), *External shocks and long term pattern of economic growth in Central and Eastern Europe,* mimeo, Vienna.

Calvo, G. A., and Frenkel, J. A. (1991), "Credit markets, credibility and economic transformation", *Journal of Economic Perspectives,* vol. 5, no. 4.

– (1992), "Transformation of Centrally Planned Economies: Credit Markets and Sustainable Growth", in *Central and Eastern Europe. Roads to Growth,* Winckler, G. (ed.), IMF, Washington DC.

Fath, J. (1992), "Industrial Policies for Countries in Transition", *WIIW Research Reports,* no. 187.

Geroski, P. A. (1989), "European Industrial Policy and Industrial Policy in Europe", *Oxford Review of Economic Policy,* vol. 5, no. 2, pp. 20-36.

Grossman, G. M. (1990), "Promoting New Industrial Activities: A Survey of Recent Arguments and Evidence", *OECD Economic Studies,* pp. 87-125.

Hahn, F. R. (1993), "Theoriegrundlagen moderner Industriepolitik", *WIFO Working Papers,* no. 60.

Hilpert, H. G. (1993), "Japanische Industriepolitik", *IFO Schnelldienst,* no. 17/18, pp. 7-22.

Hummel, M. (1993), "Industriepolitik – kontrovers", *IFO Schnelldienst,* no. 17/18, pp. 3-7.

Hutschenreiter, G. (1993), "Industriepolitik der EG: Grundlagen und neue Initiativen", *WIFO – TIP,* Vienna, July.

– (1993), "Neue Ansätze zu einer Industriepolitik der EG", *WIFO Monatsberichte,* no. 5.

Klodt, H. (1993), "Europäische Industriepolitik nach Maastricht", *Weltwirtschaftliches Archiv*, pp. 263ff.

Kursch, D. B. (1993), "Zur Debatte über die Industriepolitik in den USA", *IFO Schnelldienst,* no. 17/18, pp. 23-25.

Landesmann, M. (1993), "Industrial Policy and the Transition in East-Central Europe", *WIIW Research Reports,* no. 196.

Laski, K. (1992), "Transition from Command to Market Economies in Central and Eastern Europe: First Experiences and Questions", *WIIW Research Reports,* no. 181.

Lindbeck, A. (1982), "Industrial policy as an issue in the economic environment", The Institute of International Economic Studies, Stockholm.

Meihsl, D. (1991), "Die Landwirtschaft im Wandel der ökonomischen Faktoren", in *Österreichs Wirtschaft – gestern, heute, morgen,* Weber, W. (ed.), Berlin.

Passeron, H. (1993), "Die Entwicklung der französischen Industriepolitik. Zur Debatte über die Industriepolitik in den USA", *IFO Schnelldienst*, pp. 30-33.

Streissler, E. (1972), "Investment stimulation and the hierarchy of individual plans", in *Convertibility, multilarism and freedom,* Schmitz, W. (ed.), Vienna, pp. 49-65.

Urban, W. (1992), "Economic Lessons for the East European Countries from Two Newly Industrializing Countries in the Far East", *WIIW Research Reports,* no. 182.

US Report of the President (1984), *Industrial Policy,* Washington DC.

Wade, R. (1990), *Governing the Market. Economic Theory and the Role of Government in East Asia Industrialization,* Princeton.

Weder, G. (1993), "Coase institutions", *Weltwirtschaftliches Archiv,* no. 3.

Winckler, G. (1992), "Central and Eastern Europe. Roads to Growth", IMF, Washington DC.

Zemplinerova, A. (1993), "The Demonopolization of the Previously Centrally Planned Economies", *EI CERGE,* Prague.

COMMENT ON PART IV:

Erich W. Streissler*)

Let me start by summarising what seem to me to be the main ideas of the four papers. *Bogomolov* (Ch. 10) recounts the difficulties facing privatisation in a political environment as chaotic as that of Russia and in an economic environment which is so highly inflationary. He expresses the hope that nevertheless "intelligent methods (of) privatisation" can be found that would "strengthen the market and the monetary system". *Hunya* (Ch. 11) summarises the varying privatisation experiences in six countries. His highly perceptive and important remark "'Markets' in non-homogeneous products are extremely complicated search processes" cannot be repeated too often or stressed too much. In consequence he finds that *liquidation* of state-owned enterprises by parts, i.e. selling them asset by asset, has frequently proved most effective.

Kennerley (Ch. 12) rightly pleads: "If one lesson has been learned from the experience of the last few years, it is that one cannot afford to throw everything of the past out." He then examines the amount of capital which countries could raise via privatisation and convincingly shows that "foreign direct investment attracted through privatisation is both qualitatively and quantitatively different" from that formerly acquired through joint ventures.

Finally, *Aiginger* (Ch. 13) reminded us that no market economy – or what I would prefer to call more appropriately, no *free enterprise* economy – is without an industrial policy. Usually, however, such an industrial policy is only implicit, haphazard and without well-defined goals. *Aiginger* pleads for a *conscious* and *explicit* industrial policy and is here in full agreement with *Kennerley*. If there is nationalisation its "goals ... should (also) be made explicit" and clear "yardsticks for positive performance should be set and monitored". All this reminds me, however, a little of the old rogue and roué advising on his death bed his young nephew to lead in contrast to himself an upright and virtuous life. For *Aiginger* has to conclude: "Industrial policy in the West is not a success story."

---

*) Professor, Institute of Economics, University of Vienna.

Now to my more critical comments. *Kennerley* remarks, and *Bogomolov* concurs, that one should not privatise in "an *ad hoc* panic move to overcome short-term problems". This sounds absolutely sensible. However, one has to remember that in countries in rapid transformation from a former state planning system the government frequently has already lost all effective control of *"its"* enterprises. It has already lost most of its "property rights" in a *socio-economic* sense though it still retains property rights in an abstract legal sense. Or, to quote *Bogomolov:* "The government appears powerless to restrain these enterprises' group egotism, compel them strictly to follow established rules, or accurately to fulfil their budgetary obligations." In this not infrequent situation, where, in fact, "wild-cat" privatisation is imminent, it will be best to find quick forms of drawing a clear line and of turning unorganised privatisation into a legally binding one rapidly, in spite of the fact that this might appear "an *ad hoc* panic move". Better cut your losses quickly than create a drawn-out period of costly uncertainty.

My second comment is supplementary. *"Commercialisation"* or *"corporatisation"* of enterprises, while retaining state ownership, may be a wise *intermediate* step, as *Kennerley* points out; but, of course, only in a social environment where managers of state firms understand market rules sufficiently to know what "commercialisation" or "corporatisation" imply.

My third point is again critical. It is a fallacy of vulgar Marxism that in a free enterprise economy capital will be of value just because it was costly to produce and just because it entails property rights. This is not true. None of the authors has addressed the problem explicitly of how to privatise firms of *negative value.* About ten years ago I had a very revealing discussion with an Austrian politician to whom I suggested that if one does not wish to let our large state-owned steel firm, the VOEST, go bankrupt, at least one should give it away to the workers for free. To which this politician immediately very correctly replied: "The workers won't take that firm." So what to do with the firms that even the workers won't take? A variant of this fallacy is expressed in a gem of a statement which I have now heard for the second time from *Bogomolov:* "The former nomenklatura ... aspire to exchange political power now escaping them for property (the power of which is far more durable)." The remarkable insight that *private property is far more durable than political power* stands in conflict with all the history of political nationalisation and other burglaries by the state, or by private criminals. Unfortunately, the insight is not correct in a free enterprise system in *rapid change.* The economic value of property frequently evaporates very quickly. And this brings us to the next serious social problem of the near future. How strong will be the social unrest of workers in the many enterprises which are going to *fail,* so that the workers lose not only their jobs, but their property, vested in the enterprise, as well. Privatisation of firms by giving them to workers appears eminently sensible from the perspective of a vulgar Marxist position. In a free enterprise society, however, it actually burdens them with an additional large risk.

Finally, my last point is again supplementary. In a rapidly changing market environment the value of a firm is not an objectively determined magnitude; much rather, it is *highly subjective:* it rests *solely in the entrepreneur* who can do something useful with that firm. It is part of *Hunya's* "extremely complicated search process" to find this person or persons. There is no unique real value of state-owned enterprises, at least without a perfect capital market. And this means that even in a perfect market for firms, but with very different abilities to manage firms, the successful bidder for a firm will seem to get an unjust bargain if judged from a wrong concept of objective values. For in a normal auction, the successful bidder gets the firm at the approximate valuation of the second highest bidder or a little above. If abilities to manage given firms differ much, the differences between the value to the highest and that to the second highest bidder can be very large. But one has to remember that a (perhaps high) *ex post* value of a firm may not have existed *ex ante* without the entrepreneur who created it out of thin air.

PART V – SOCIAL PROBLEMS OF TRANSFORMATION

Chapter 14

SOCIAL COSTS AND SOCIAL GOALS OF TRANSFORMATION POLICY: POLISH EXPERIENCE

Jolanta Supińska[*)]

14.1 Some basic notions

One has to be very cautious in using the term "social costs of transformation processes"; the term is abused and deceptive. What does "transformation" mean? What do "costs" mean? And what does "social" mean? We will attempt a brief approach to these terminological problems, not only because they are intellectually interesting, but also because all political thinkers in Poland must cope with them.

First, we cannot attribute to transformation itself all the phenomena emerging in society in the transformation period. We should distinguish the following potential or suspected economic determinants of the negative social phenomena studied:

(i) the long-term crisis rooted in the last two – or even four – decades of communist rule,

---

*) Institute of Social Policy, University of Warsaw.

(ii) changes in the international context (the loss of CMEA markets is the most important phenomenon in this area),
(iii) spontaneous activities of new businessmen trying to collect capital – in very different ways, not always honest, making use of all gaps and inconsistencies in the legal system and extracting profits from the socio-economic derangement,
(iv) the stabilisation programme undertaken by the government: such as the "Balcerowicz plan",
(v) the true transformation programmes (mainly privatisation).

To these factors must be added a variety of non-economic factors (we must leave them aside, without detailed analysis).

The only thing of which we are quite sure is that all these factors act in parallel; we should neglect none of them and we know little about their relative importance. In discussions on the reasons for the so-called social costs, politicians in power tend to overestimate the role played by factors independent of themselves and they stress how their own decisions at least diminished the negative phenomena. Their opponents tend to treat all worsening social indicators as the results of current government policy.

The complex character of the notion of the "social sphere"

The next question is: what does "social" mean? In reply, we may define the *social sphere* as a set of very different phenomena; some are "hard" – material, objective, quantitative – and some of them are "soft" – hidden in people's minds, subjective, qualitative. Therefore we shall understand the "social sphere" as comprising such matters as living standards, labour conditions, citizens' position in the regulations on law and justice, health and demographic trends, real life prospects and their perception in people's minds, attitudes, moods and unfulfilled desires, political behaviour.

These areas are full of negative phenomena. No one can deny that there are also numerous positive facts, although not so spectacular. It is very easy to get used to positive changes and it is very difficult to make people reconciled with their bad fate. It seems more and more obvious that positive trends are not – objectively and in people's minds – any counterbalance to the regression processes. Public opinion polls show the decline of social moods and the strength of social criticism in very sharp outline.

The public debate: where does the blame lie?

We should ask whether the term "cost" – which implies spending some reasonable outlays in order to gain our goals – is always adequate. So we come back to the question of what factors have played the most important roles – those independent of politicians or those dependent on them? We want to know further:

- What are the unavoidable costs of the economic strategy undertaken? And we should introduce the distinction between costs unforeseen by politicians, costs foreseen by politicians and recognised by society, and costs foreseen by politicians but hidden by them from public opinion;
- What mistakes (avoidable costs) have been made?
- What accidents, without any logical connection with the transformation process, can occur?
- What ideological choices are consciously made by the political élite, but are not accepted by the majority of society?

These questions are easy to ask but very difficult to answer. The difficulties are both intellectual and political. The answers can serve as a weapon for politicians fighting with each other (and the political scene is in Poland very segmented, very unclear, and actors seem to behave very nervously). On the other hand, ordinary people who are not involved in active political life, do long for simple answers, because simple answers arouse the hope of finding solutions that are simple and easy to implement. The more tired people are, the more often they tend to simplify socio-economic problems.

The only thing we are sure about is that both the extreme opinions are false. Can all the negative social indicators, events and processes be seen as "unavoidable social costs of a reasonably programmed economic order"? No. Are all the negative phenomena the result of activities of "enemies of the people"? No. The rest is open.

Anyhow, these questions are crucial for the future of the politicians' future, because their personal and historical responsibilities are involved.

14.2 Socially unwanted phenomena in the social sphere

(a) A decline in average living standards and a widening of income inequality

The greatest shock happened at the beginning of 1990. Rapidly, an average worker's family with two children had to face the need to spend more than 72 per cent of income on food; at the end of 1989 it was enough to spend 42 per cent of income on food. An old couple living on retirement pensions has been forced to increase food expenditure from 34 per cent to 59 per cent. The increasing share of food expenditure was a consequence of the decline of households' total real incomes, which dropped in the first half of 1990 to 68 per cent of previous income for workers' families, 79 per cent for farmers' and 73 per cent for pensioners'.

It has been estimated that in 1990 far more households found themselves below the *social minimum level* (33 per cent against 11 per cent in 1989 for workers', 42 per cent against 20 per cent for farmers', and 32 per cent against 22 per cent in pensioners' households, fell into a *low income* statistical category).

The situation of still poorer households, with income below the poverty line (30 per cent less than social minimum level was estimated as an *"insufficient income"),* is the most dramatic, their biological needs being at risk. In 1990, 12 per cent of workers', 19 per cent of farmers' and 11 per cent of pensioners' households fell below this level. We should add that at that time there were almost no unemployed workers; the decline in living standards was due to the liberalisation of prices, the essential element in the Balcerowicz plan.

Although the decline of living standards was so dramatic, in this first stage people were very patient, if not enthusiastic, for three reasons:

- they had still very deep confidence in the honesty and good will of the Solidarity leaders who had just come to power,
- they believed that a new era had begun, an era of professionalism in politics and economics, ending for ever the rule of incompetence; Balcerowicz, with his academic outlook and manner, has given much credibility to this image of a new kind of government,
- the first positive effects of the shock therapy came quickly, in a really short time; this was – as often described later – the famous effect of *full shelves* in Polish shops. It was distressing for the poor, but it was at the same time exotic and exciting: *"It works, it's efficient, it's professional",* people were saying. They did not expect then that these first positive results of the therapy would be its last positive results.

The following years come did not bring the promised rise in living standards for the majority of Polish families. Even if average real income per capita appeared in 1991 a little bit higher than in 1990 (apart from farmers, whose economic position still continued to decline), it was still far from reaching the level of 1989. Moreover, during the next three years the declining tendency in real incomes returned.

Month by month and year by year a new phenomenon has become increasingly noticeable: *nouveaux riches* have emerged into view in the streets and in new luxury shops and restaurants – even if they succeeded in hiding themselves from the Central Statistical Office. We have very poor statistical information about this category. According to the most representative research about household incomes, the top ten per cent of households get slightly more than 33 per cent of total incomes. That does not seem very provocative, even for people accepting the idea of egalitarian society (as most Poles do). Nevertheless, everybody knows that the richest refuse information for such research (so do the poorest, by the way) and are underestimated.

Generally, credibility of official statistics has declined in recent years. A new income-tax system was started in 1992; most Poles had never been paying taxes on their earnings and did not get used to it. In consequence, in the first year of its operation there were mistakes or simple swindles in 40 per cent of income-tax returns. It is fairly certain that the majority of tax swindles occurred in the growing private sector (private employers successfully avoided paying social insurance contributions as well). So we can acknowledge these developments as one of more important results of privatisation. This should also have an impact on income statistics.

(b) Unemployment growth and its darkest aspect

The growth of unemployment in Poland has had the character of a shock. In 1989 there was – as in preceding years – a shortage of labour and – at the same time – "hidden unemployment" among people employed in state-owned enterprises. There were only 10 thousand people registered as unemployed. In December 1990 there were already over 1 million (6 per cent of labour force) and in December 1991 over 2 million – 13.6 per cent. 1992 has brought the number to almost 2.5 million, 13.5 per cent of the labour force; and at the end of 1993 to about 3 million (16 per cent).

In the first stage, industrial managers tended to dismiss rather marginal employees: "peasant-workers", unskilled workers, women and older workers who could enter into new early retirement schemes (just created by the state); the core group of the labour force (males of 25-45 years) was more secure. Later, the situation changed and the "core" has begun to be threatened by real unemployment which has become more and more widespread. In 1992 about 90 per cent of unemployed persons were below 40. *Too young because below forty?* Women and youngsters have the most serious problems, while the *old and disabled* are "pushed" into social security schemes.

The share of women among the unemployed is higher than their share in the total labour force, although the role of the sex factor slightly diminished after 1991. Women also have a smaller chance of finding a job in the new private enterprises. Nevertheless, they struggle for survival and do not want to withdraw irrevocably out of the labour market, in spite of researchers' prognoses and conservative politicians' hopes. The reason is clear – the dramatic decline of earnings, or rising unemployment, of their husbands.

School leavers are the growing problem. According to varying estimations, each older unemployed worker (over 55) goes with between 1.5 and 3.2 unemployed person under 24 years. Some authors argue that the young unemployed have the best chance to find a new job in the private sector and to earn some income in the parallel or black economy. But these statements cannot change the general conclusion: the young generation happen to face a closed door at the beginning of their adult life. In January 1993, persons who had never been employed constituted 27 per cent of the newly registered unemployed. In July – just after examinations for the secondary-school and university – the never employed group has become predominant. Although unemployment is a new phenomenon in Poland, it begins to be inherited: young school leavers cannot find a job; neither can their parents with longer than one year off the labour market.

The share of long-term unemployed (searching for a job for longer than one year) in Poland is one of the highest in Europe – in February 1993 6.1 per cent of the labour force. The increase was very rapid – from 24 per cent in May 1992 to 42 per cent in February 1993 of the total of unemployed.

At the end of 1992, large groups of long-term unemployed people appeared who had lost their benefits due to the termination of benefit payments after 12 months unemployment. In January 1993 almost a half of the unemployed registered at labour offices had no right to benefits. Some of them cope with the difficulties, are stimulated to search more effectively for a job or are supported by their relatives. Yet most of them, especially those attached to small local labour markets (strictly attached by tradition and housing shortages), feel, and actually are, hopeless, and begin to drop into the well known "unemployment culture" losing their "human capital".

The living standards of households with an unemployed person fall rapidly. As early as in 1991 more than 50 per cent of those households have already fallen into the *low income category* (against 34 per cent of all households). Unemployment benefits were quite generous in 1990 and it was then easy – sometimes too easy – to get them. But the more the number of unemployed increased, the more difficult it was to get benefits and their level in real terms diminished.

Unemployment growth is due to different factors difficult to separate. However, in general terms, they can be regarded as deriving from weak active labour market policies. Most impressive is the estimate (by Urszula Sztanderska, one of the most prominent specialists): even if all expenditures from the central Labour Fund were spent efficiently, they could touch at the most only 1.75 per cent of the unemployed in 1992. (Sztanderska 1993) The majority of this fund is spent on benefits; the more unemployment grows, the less money is available for benefits. That is one of the most astonishing of Polish vicious circles.

(c) The housing crisis and its impact on the young generation

Life strategies for the young are paralysed, first because of the unemployment, second, because of restricted access to cheap housing credits and the deep and long-term decline in new building of flats.

Post-communist Poland inherited a disastrous housing situation. There were 14 per cent more households than housing units. Only 18 per cent of young families (below the age of 30) lived in their own independent flats, while 60 per cent had to share a flat, most often with their parents (perhaps alternately with his and her parents). A new phase, the "guest syndrome", has appeared in the life cycle.

Interest on housing loans, introduced in 1990 at a commercial rate (above two-digit inflation), has made these loans prohibitively expensive. This affected even those people who had contracted cheap credit many years earlier. As a result a completely new phenomenon has appeared in this sphere, comparable with the "full shelves" effect described above. More and more often, housing cooperatives could not find among their members people ready to take over new-built flats – though these people had waited for them usually for more than 10 years. People who had seemed able to afford the new prices quickly found themselves in the so-called "debt trap". In spite of having paid month by month 25 per cent of their total income to the bank (we might add that the current costs of maintaining a flat often took another 25 per cent) the debt was steadily increasing, exceeding after two or three years the market price of a new flat.

In such a situation no one can be astonished that housing cooperatives ceased new investments and housing construction – both in cooperative and private sectors – began to fall away. While the number of dwellings built in 1978 (the post-war record year) amounted to 284 thousand, in 1988 it was only 190 thousand, and in 1992, it was 127 thousand. But in 1993 only about 90 thousand new flats are expected (as in the early 1950s). In 1992, only 33 thousand new flats were started and only half that number were completed. These figures may be contrasted with the approximately 250 thousand newly married each year in Poland.

If we confront these facts with the brand-new act making abortion illegal and the strong pressure against sexual education in schools and the mass media, we have a broad image of the starting-point for the youth of today. To be honest and objective, we should acknowledge that it is among the young generation that we can the most frequently find people ready to meet the challenges of competitive society. Nevertheless, even there, people ready to compete in the market are in a minority, and only some of them can find favourable openings in the near neighbourhood (being *glebae adscriptis* – locally restricted by the shortage of flats).

The housing problem is not limited to the scarcity of new flats. A general reform of *rents* is needed; only 30 per cent of total housing maintenance and repair costs are now covered by rents; both rich and poor tenants benefit by the subsidies (however, prices of utilities increase rapidly because their subsidies were cancelled).

On the other hand, we observe a growing share of rents in family expenditures, more and more frequently exceeding capacity to pay.

Although this share is still much lower than in Western countries, it is beginning to be too high in comparison with the costs of food. In towns, almost twenty per cent of families, in both communal and cooperative buildings, fail to pay their rent. This fact has serious consequences (the deterioration of the housing stock and the erosion of the legal system).

(d) The decay of institutionalised social policy and the growth of voluntary services and charity

The growing impotence of the inherited institutions responsible for social benefits and public services provided under the Constitution (health service, education and culture, leisure, and – last but not least – social insurance) has become glaring. The vicious circle has appeared in social services. They need both money and reforms; the reforms cannot start for lack of money, and the diminishing funds are spent with worse and worse results due to the lack of reforms. More and more social institutions fail to meet human needs and more and more the state budget is overburdened by expenditure to support them. It seems that the only solution for the budget managers is to delay promised flows of funds to the social institutions.

All this explains why there are no new solutions or new institutions to meet the problems of public education, health services and social insurance after four years of rapid change in the Polish economy. Instead of their own "shock therapy", the social services have been offered only a slimming diet.

Average wages and salaries in health care and education institutions have gone from about 100 per cent down to below 90 per cent of the average industrial wage in the period 1990-1993 and are expected to fall to 82 per cent in 1994.

No one has the courage to propose repeal of the constitutional obligations, but everybody forecasts – through the mass media – that it will soon happen. More and more often people are asked to pay from their own pockets – voluntarily, of course – for supporting the basic activities of the supposedly free schools and free hospitals.

People notice at the same time the collapse of various institutions, regarded as "less important", meeting secondary needs (mostly cultural and leisure centres, kindergartens and day-care centres for children). The closing down of cultural and leisure services (free or cheap, totally or partly financed from public funds) deepens the tendency to withdraw from participation in culture and from healthy ways of life, a tendency perhaps irreversible during the life of a single generation.

In 1989-1992 the proportion share of children in infants' nurseries declined from 4.4 per cent to 2.6 per cent of the total number in the 0-3 years age group. The share of children in kindergartens was declining much more slowly – from 34 per cent to 33 per cent – but that was due only to the demographic situation.

The closing down of kindergartens and other services supporting mothers working professionally outside their homes, is apparently compatible with the growth of women's unemployment; but it is hardly beneficial; one must stress that the coincidence of the two trends may stabilise a high level of women's unemployment.

The number of retired and disabled pensioners (former employees and farmers) rose from 7.1 million in 1990 to almost 8.5 million persons in 1992 (more than one million of them are the relatively young "hidden unemployed").

Huge social groups are becoming increasingly dependent upon voluntary welfare benefits and services (social aid, social protection, philanthropy). In 1991 there were already 2.1 million people who had obtained some kind of welfare benefits and in 1993 the number had grown to 3 million. Many of them were employed or retired, but nevertheless needed the extra support. The excessive burden on social workers of trying to help people to solve their problems, which are obviously deep-rooted in macro social and economic strategies, makes individual therapy hopeless. The division between statutory and voluntary services is clearly wrong so that people lose their sense of security and feel stigmatised. I must say that social policy falls deeper and deeper into decay and charity is expected to fill in the gaps; such expectations are futile, of course.

(e) Popular attitudes and political behaviour

As the result of all these symptoms of social decline, many new psychological problems have emerged. These can be summed up as the refusal of confidence to political leaders with their origins in the trade union movement and who carried for a time the romantic charisma of *Solidarity.* One day, people started to feel that they had become victims of a swindle prepared by new leaders who inherited from the old communist élite both arrogance and ignorance of the basic needs of the common man. This general feeling was to some extent independent of material shortages; it was a well-founded conclusion based upon observation of the behaviour and statements of this new élite.

These attitudes are confirmed by research. An outstanding psychologist, Janusz Reykowski, comments in his research on the political mentality of the Poles:

> The fact that so many people became disillusioned with the present political power was the result not only of the social costs of the reforms but also, to a large extent, of the style in which policy was made. The style has discredited political élites, depriving them

of public confidence; it was only confidence in the leaders which could raise hopes that the chosen road was correct and that one day everything would be for the best. (Reykowski 1993)

We could add sceptically that Reykowski was not absolutely unprejudiced, being a former long-term communist party activist. But another prominent sociologist, Hanna Świda-Ziemba, who has been known for many years as one of the most independent oppositional intellectuals, expresses very similar opinions and goes even further. She has just completed research about a "silent majority" of Polish society – those who had never been active either in the communist party or in the Solidarity movement, nor in present political parties – and who have no clear political preferences. She remarks:

> The respondents say "they used to deceive us, and they are still offending us". When people demand decent pensions for themselves or fair wages for good work, the élite immediately call them people with a post-communist mentality. The same happens when instead of engaging in "business" they just want to work honestly in their professions, which are so poorly paid nowadays. This means they are not cared for, and are offered only basic social essentials (so-called "social protection"). And the term has always been irritating my respondents just because they consider social aid as something for the ill or disabled; if a man works and is efficient in his work, he is entitled to a wage which covers his needs". (Świda-Ziemba 1993)

Both researchers – so different politically – agree on the question of settling accounts with Poland's communist past and on people's attitudes to this issue. According to Reykowski:

> Speaking about (people's) longing for "the old good days", I think it is a reaction to the dichotomised presentation of the world which was typical of the previous power élites: either our unique liberal-capitalistic programme of reforms, or an obscure PRL (Polish People's Republic) type of socialism offering an apparent feeling of security. My opinion is that this is a false alternative, the effect of lack of imagination and lack of readiness to search for different, better solutions. (Reykowski 1993)

Świda-Ziemba gives delayed advice to the politicians:

> First of all the causes of (communist rule) bankruptcy should be revealed; it is not enough just to say that the communists ruined the economy which we are now trying to rebuild. It is necessary to analyse thoroughly the system which has built up many superfluities and collapsed, not because it was morally evil, but because it was an error. That is why it should be transformed. Still the transformation should be aimed at people. People should feel themselves actors in this transformation, not beggars for social assistance. The new power élites should also declare that they want to preserve the previous social gains, that they consider them morally correct though for the time being, unfortunately, impossible to realise. (Świda-Ziemba 1993)

If we trust the above statements – and there are many good reasons to trust them – we cannot agree with the opinion, frequently repeated in Poland, that the last government's greatest fault was the inadequate information policy. It was suggested that, "if people knew social costs were necessary, they would accept them so we have to explain, repeat and repeat, that the costs are necessary". The problem is that not all negative phenomena were costs of transformation, and especially that many of them were not *necessary* costs. And, it was not only the *methods* of informing people that were imperfect, but also that the *substance* could not satisfy. Communication of the political élite with society should not be one-way.

Consequently all these negative phenomena in Polish political life resulted in the worsening of moods revealed by the public opinion polls published from month to month, and, finally, in rejection of the political leaders who were rooted in the Solidarity movement. This rejection was expressed by a great number of voters in the September 1993 Parliament elections.

References

Bezrobocie – wyzwanie dla polskiej gospodarki (1993), Fratczak, E., Strzelecki, Z., and Witkowski, J. (eds.), Glówny Urzad Statystyczny (Central Statisticl Office), Warsaw.

Deniszczuk, L., and Żukowska, I. (1992), "Sytuacja materialna gospodarstw domowych w okresie wprowadzania programu stabilizacji gospodarki", *Ekonomista,* no. 4, 1992.

Emerytury i renty pracownicze, szanse i zagrożenia, budowa systemu (1993), Ministerstwo Pracy i Polityki Socjalnej (Ministry of Labour and Social Affairs), Warsaw, May.

Informacje o mieszkalnictwie, wyniki monitoringu za 1993 rok (1993), Instytut Gospodarki Mieszkaniowej, Warsaw.

Kuroń, J. (1993), "Rynek z ludzka twarza", *Gazeta Wyborcza,* 20-21 November.

Polityka Spoleczna (monthly), 1990-1994.

Polityka spoleczna i warunki spoleczne w Polsce w latach 1989-1993 (Social Policy and Social Conditions in Poland 1989-1993) (1994), Golinowska, Stanislawa, and Ochocki, Andrzej (eds.), report for UNICEF, Instytut Pracy i Spraw Socjalnych (Labour Institute), Warsaw, no. 5, January.

Program polityki spoleczno-gospodarczej na lata 1994-1997 (projekt) (1994), Centralny Urzad Planowania (Central Planning Office), Warsaw, 4 December.

Reykowski, J. (1993), "Obszar nadziei i margines ryzyka. Albo odwrotnie" (interview), *Trybuna,* no. 251, 26 October.

Rocznik Statystyczny 1993 (Statistical Yearbook of Poland) (1993), Glówny Urzad Statystyczny (Central Statistical Office), Warsaw.

Sztanderska, U. (1993), "Raport o rynku pracy 1990-1992 – wybrane wyniki", Instytut Pracy i Spraw Socjalnych (Labour Institute), (unpublished paper).

Świda-Ziemba, H. (1993), "Oszukani i obrażeni" (interview), *Życie Warszawy,* 7 October.

Wagrowska, M. (1994), "Apele o nowa solidarność, *Rzeczpospolita,* 3 January.

Zagrożenia i szanse polityki spolecznej w Polsce w okresie transformacji, (1993), Ksieżopolski, M., and Supińska, J. (eds.), Friedrich Ebert Stiftung, Warsaw.

Chapter 15

SOCIAL ASPECTS OF ECONOMIC REFORM IN RUSSIA

Vladimir Kollontai*)

In the great transformation taking place in Eastern Europe and specifically in Russia the limelight is on economic and political problems. The social aspects of this process receive much less attention. To the extent that they are studied the focus is on government expenditures for social welfare – viewed either neutrally or as a barrier to more rapid economic reform. But the transformations in Russia are creating very rapid and serious shifts in the whole social fabric of society. They are bringing about changes in social structures that cannot but deeply influence the whole process of reform, social stability, the context in which market formation takes place, the type of markets that emerge, etc.

It is not the object of this paper to try and analyse the entire interaction between the social and the economic aspects of the transformation taking place in Russia. The aim is much more modest – to try to define some of the problems arising from insufficient attention to social aspects of economic reform and market formation. Special attention will be devoted to the interaction between income and property redistribution and the type of markets that emerge in Russia. First, I propose to look into the changes in the social structures that economic reform has brought about. After that, I intend to look into the feedback effect that the dismantling of the old social security system is having on the process of market formation. And lastly I propose to explore the social and economic implications of privatisation as it is carried out in Russia.

15.1 The growth of inequality

Each stage of economic reform in Russia (starting with *perestrojka)* tended to increase economic inequality and stratification. The existing data on income distribution are very unsatisfactory, tending to reflect only the distribution of current wages, and neglecting the secondary and tertiary redistribution of income.

---

*) Institute of World Economics and International Affairs, Russian Academy of Sciences, Moscow.

Property income is mostly ignored. Income tax returns are just being introduced and they are still not aggregated and even a satisfactory static picture cannot be drawn, leave alone any comparable time series. The existing data also do not reflect the fact that previously on a large scale, and even now to a lesser degree, different social groups had access to goods and services at very different prices, so that a formally equal monetary wage income in practice signified access to very different amounts and qualities of goods and services.

Keeping these serious imperfections in mind, let us look into the comparative dynamics of existing wage (income) distributions by social groups and regions. Numerous surveys and studies covering the whole Russian Federation seem to agree that even in very aggregate terms during the one year of 1992 the gap between the richer and poorer parts of the population has grown by 20-50 per cent (if decile groups or large territories are compared). These same surveys show that if smaller 2-3 per cent groups are compared the gap has increased manifold.[1)] In 1993 similar trends quite evidently persisted. These changes – in very aggregate terms – reflect even more rapid and serious processes at an individual, sectoral and regional level. In circumstances of rapidly increasing prices (inflation bordering on hyper-inflation due to price liberalisation) nominal monetary incomes are increasing everywhere but their purchasing power is diminishing. Officially, in 1992 prices rose 30 times whereas wages and salaries rose 10 times. This trend persisted in 1993. On average real consumer spending – estimated in terms of fixed prices – fell during 1990-1993 by more than one half.[2)] For many social groups (especially those whose wages are paid out of the state budget) purchasing power has fallen to one-third, one-quarter or even one-fifth of what it was in the beginning of the 1990s.[3)] Previous accumulations (meagre by themselves since saving capacity under socialism was very limited) have quickly evaporated. Surveys in many towns and regions acknowledge that nearly one-third of the population is at or below the poverty line. And practically everywhere this share is continuing to grow.

---

1) *Izvestiya,* 13 February 1993, p. 4; *Rossiyskie Vesti* (Russian News), 18 April 1993, p. 2.

2) *Finansovye* (Financial News), no. 24, 1993, p. 4.

3) *Rossiyskaya Ekonomicheskoe* (Russian Economic Journal), no. 4, 1993, p. 21.

These average, aggregate figures smooth out much more heterogeneous, differentiated situations for individuals, sectors and regions. This is not only due to big differences in starting positions, natural endowment, accumulated wealth, skills, etc. During *perestrojka* and thereafter specific industries and regions have been able to appropriate for themselves numerous privileges which tangibly influenced the material status of various social groups. Different political stances and policies (of ministries and local authorities) accentuated these trends. Export industries, miners, the higher echelons in the civil service and army are usually among the more privileged. Transport areas and free trade zones have received numerous legal and tax privileges, which however have most often failed to materialise as substantial benefits, especially if the negative aspects of such developments – crime, disruption of communities, etc. – are taken into account. Enterprises of the military-industrial complex continue to attract various benefits (first priority supply, government financing, etc.) but these have tangibly evaporated. Predominantly agricultural areas continue to be among the most deprived, squeezed by diminishing government subsidies, falling prices for their produce and more rapidly rising prices on inputs, etc.

At an individual level the situation is even more highly differentiated. In an increasing number of cases workers are not paid even their nominal wages – postponements of payments for several months, obligatory vacations without pay, etc. Some people are locked into professional positions which make their nominal wages practically their only source of livelihood whereas others (even in the same profession) have much more room for manoeuvre. A case in point is the difference between taxi and bus drivers. Similar differences (but on a much broader scale) are emerging between workers in state and in private enterprises. There has been a marked shift into jobs with higher income opportunities, even by specialists moving to very different professions. Many people have opted for second jobs as a way to survival. According to some surveys the number of respondents who acknowledged having second jobs increased more than threefold during 1992.[4)] But such a solution is open to only a rather limited number of people due to shrinking job opportunities. Many more go for part-time and casual jobs as well as into semi-legal activities on the side (street-trading, building, moonshining). Fraud, swindling, theft, extortion, embezzlement as well as more serious crimes are on the increase all over the

4) *Sotsiologiskia Issledovaniya* (Sociological Researches), no. 7, 1993, p. 19.

country. Another major source of additional income is farming on small country and suburban *(dacha)* plots. Up to two-thirds of the Russian population (especially in rural areas) receive a supplementary income through semi-subsistence activities of this kind, which have substantially increased during 1992-1993. Some of these sources of livelihood are only inadequately reflected in income statistics; most of them are passed over unnoticed. For many individual cases this somewhat modifies the general trend towards impoverishment, by slowing it down.

At the same time the last years (and especially 1992 and 1993) have been marked by a very rapid growth of relatively small but exceedingly prosperous *nouveau riche* groups with undisclosed high money incomes.

15.2 Cutting down of social security

A major aspect of the economic reform process is the virtual scrapping of the previous elaborate social security system, and of most direct and indirect social expenditures. Ideologically this is justified by a desire to eliminate the basis of previous laxness and lack of initiative by the need to instal market methods of motivation (in a neo-liberal interpretation). Economically the dismantling of the old social security system was dictated by the escalating budgetary crisis and a growing shortage of resources (in a context of rapidly falling overall production). Less than two-thirds of government commitments to social expenditures are covered by real financial disbursements. E. Panfilova, the minister in charge of social policy, complains with some reason that the Federal government is giving ever lower priority to social issues.[5)]

Again the cuts of social security are not uniform by sectors and regions. The richer economic units usually counter the slashing of Federal funds for social purposes by additional injections of local resources. Poorer regions have far fewer such possibilities. Accordingly the dismantling of the social security system is aggravating the impoverishment of large masses of the poorer population. Previously people did not have to pay very much for medical care, medicines, education, transport, etc. Now this has become a growing item in the family budget. All these factors are increasing the highly differentiated pattern of material well-being between individuals, industries and regions.

---

5) *Argumenty i Fakty* (Arguments and Facts), no. 43, 1993, p. 3.

Economic reform has greatly accelerated economic and social stratification in Russia. An across-the-board redistribution of wealth and income is taking place. This is leading to an unprecedented polarisation of political forces and deep-rooted social instability (especially taking into account the recent prevalence of an inegalitarian ideology). The cleavages concern not only current power and wealth distribution but also the whole problem of what kind of society is to emerge as a result of the reform process and what system of values will prevail. Old ideological differences are surfacing in new forms and in conditions of a new and rapidly changing balance of forces. Given the deep splits in society on all these issues (and the lack of compromise culture in politics) extremism is rapidly growing. A major expression of the polarisation in society is the growth of separatist trends, increasing demands for decentralisation and for a geographical redistribution of power and economic functions. Another fallout from this situation is the rapid undermining of governance in society, a crumbling of moral and legal restrictions on many forms of societally dangerous activities, and a growth of crime.

This stratification is having a profound impact on the whole market formation process (elaborated later). At present we may just note that one of the major legacies of the socialist era is a wide gap between monetary income and real living standards. In the post-*perestrojka* years it has somewhat diminished but not disappeared. This gap (and the underlying subsidies, payments handouts and growth of semi-subsistence activities) have a serious impact on all aspects of market formation. All economic units – both households and enterprises – are now being thrown into market conditions with a flagrant shortfall of financial resources compared with current transactions and flows of material goods and services. Moreover most units have numerous outstanding obligations, which were camouflaged by state subsidies.

15.3 Inequality and the price and production structure

Social policy in the former Soviet Union was a major element in the whole strategy of transforming society on a non-market – indeed anti-market – basis. Initially the main thrust was to counter the inequality inherent in market relations by a system of social grants and subsidies, which were intended partially to equalise real incomes. Accordingly a social security system in its narrower sense was devised – payments to the elderly, sick and disabled. In a broader sense, this social security system encompassed free medical care, free education and other amenities. A prominent role in the socialist transformations implemented in the USSR was played by the subsidising of food, housing, transport. All this created an artificial network of free or low-priced goods and services (subsidised out of the budget). Such a strategy of development created in time a society with features which in various ways were incompatible with a market society. On the one hand this stimulated in the population a mentality of false security and laxity (free-riding on government amenities) which later translated itself into growing economic problems, diminishing productivity, disorganised production, overall inefficiency, etc. On the other hand this system tended to foster an atmosphere of subservience, since the distribution of (or access to) many "free" goods (or their quality) depended on management and higher-up decision-makers. The hope of better access made many people obedient instruments of the powers that be. Still another aspect of this system was the increasingly distorted (as compared with market economies) structure of the economy, of material goods and financial flows, a growing inconsistency between costs, demand, budgetary needs and availabilities, and a total distortion of all the relationships between essential economic indicators. In the final analysis the imbalances and other problems that have accumulated in an excessively welfare-oriented state to a large extent define the issues that reform in Russia has to overcome.

The magnitude of these imbalances and of the problems involved is often underestimated in the West. Here is one example of relative prices: in the West a trip in city-transport in almost any town will cost about $ 1; a personal computer – around $ 1,500. In Russia in the beginning of 1992 (before price liberalisation and run-away inflation) a city-transport trip would be 5 kopecks, and a computer 80,000 roubles. That means that in the West the relationship between the two was 1:1,500 whereas in Russia it was 1:1,600,000. In other words the difference in relative prices was more than a hundred times greater in Russia than in the West. We can find many cases of gaps in relative prices hundreds of times greater than in the West. Gaps and imbalances of similar scope can be found in many other economic areas – in productivity, in industrial structures, etc.

The size of the structural changes that have to take place (the magnitude of the imbalances that have to be overcome) before the Russian economy can function as a market mechanism is unprecedented. This inevitably warrants a rethinking of the type of solutions that can give the desired results. It is, for instance, far from certain that market forces can successfully cope with structural problems of such dimensions – and, if they can, what will be the costs, social, environmental, cultural, etc. When the oil crisis brought about a threefold increase in petroleum prices it took the West more than one and a half decades to overcome the consequences; and this was done with substantial government intervention. Market formation in Russia poses problems of much greater magnitude. Up to now, price liberalisation in Russia against a background of highly distorted (and monopolised) structures has only increased economic havoc, placed the country on the verge of hyper-inflation, and eroded the possibilities of success.

The reform process in Russia, especially after 1991, has taken extremist forms. A major example is the rapid cutting of the previous social policies and social security system as well as the elimination of a large part of existing budgetary subsidies. Together with price liberalisation, this has led not only to a serious impoverishment of most of the population, but also to very profound structural changes in the economy and to a growing disconnection between material goods and financial flows. Since a shift of priority from material goods criteria to financial ones is a basic component of any process of market formation, the implications of the cuts of the social security system deserve special attention.

The previous – rather egalitarian – pattern of monetary income distribution (after large price subsidies) defined a certain pattern of consumption and this in turn partially influenced the structure of production, at least in consumer goods industries. Moreover, even within the centrally-planned system (especially in the later years), there emerged a growing gap between production capabilities and consumer demand. But mass purchasing power was at a moderately differentiated but relatively stable level.

Economic reform (especially in 1992-93) has abruptly changed all this. The onslaught on social security and subsidised prices has hit most strongly the lower income groups of society. Their real standard of living (and real purchasing power) has fallen drastically. The pattern of their consumption has also changed substantially. In most family budgets many items had to be eliminated. A much larger share of family resources is now devoted to the bare essentials of survival – first of all, food. Expenditures that can be postponed are put off until later. The magnitude of the shifts involved can be judged from the following overall figures for the country. In 1992 the share of food in retail trade rose from 48 to 62 per cent and the share of light industry products fell from 33 to 20 per cent.[6] Between 1990 and 1993, per capita consumption of meat, dairy products and fish fell by 20-25 per cent whereas the consumption of bread and potatoes rose.[7] The shrinking of numerous markets brought about the curtailment of production in many industries which in pre-market conditions were not able to satisfy either real needs or purchasing power demand. In August 1993, production in the food industry of Russia was 65 per cent of its average level in 1989, and in the textile industry 43 per cent.[8] The drastic fall in purchasing power (caused by extreme price liberalisation policies) is one of the main factors in the present decline of Russian production (as in other CIS countries). Continued monetarist policies, with total disregard of the consequences for production, can only aggravate the situation.

At the same time an "enclave" market with very high purchasing power is emerging among a small minority of the population. Secondary redistribution of income somewhat enlarges this enclave. An increasing part of the income here is directed towards higher quality and luxury goods, most of which are not produced in the country. Hence a spate of imports of such goods from abroad irrespective of prices and conditions. This in turn becomes a prominent factor spiralling inflation. Moreover high incomes in this enclave increasingly translate into capital flight, which constantly depresses the national exchange rate.

As a result the type of market that is emerging in Russia – due to the prevailing, increasingly skewed, distribution of monetary incomes (and purchasing power) – is one which stimulates speculative and intermediary operations but strangles existing and potential future production in many fields. It is very indicative that in the total of bank lending operations between July 1992 and April 1993 the share of productive investments has fallen, and the share of loans to trade intermediaries has increased (according to a survey of more than forty large banks) from 45 per cent to 75 per cent.[9] Productive investments are diverted from consumer production for the internal market into exports, mining, and the production of high-cost prestigious goods. An outward-oriented develop-

---

6) *Ekonomist,* no. 4, 1993, p. 29.

7) *Ekonomika i Zhizn* (Economics and Life), no. 40, 1993, p. 1.

8) *Kommersant* (Business), no. 40, 1993, p. 6.

9) *Russian Economic Barometer,* no. 3, 1993, p. 23.

ment strategy will put heavy pressure on the world economy by disruptive exports, unpredictable movements of capital, spill-overs from conversion, unpredictable consequences of the enormous science and technology potential and violent shifts in competitiveness.

On a more general level, increasing differentiation and polarisation in society are fostering social and political instability and accordingly undermining the possibilities of normal market development. In situations of political instability capital tends to evade long-term, low-liquidity investments and to favour more speculative financial, real estate and intermediary operations. It is in this context that the forms and methods of privatisation should be examined.

15.4 Social consequences of privatisation

In the former Soviet Union, material status was defined primarily by current earnings (wages, salaries, etc. paid out by state enterprises and/or institutions). Formally, a spirit of egalitarianism prevailed (in ideology, theory, officially proclaimed value systems, etc.). In practice – especially in the later years – wage differentials were constantly widening and the *nomenklatura* was receiving increasing privileges – both official and *"sub rosa"*. Management and disposal of state property opened numerous avenues for robbery, extortion, embezzlement, corruption. This was reflected in burgeoning savings and hoarding, as well as in various semi-legal practices. Inequality – mostly inconspicuous – was prevailing in one area after the other. But all this was formally in the framework of an egalitarian society without private property.

Perestrojka brought a rapid introduction of private property and privatisation. This was viewed as an indispensable element in the creation of a democratic, market-oriented society. Deep-rooted Russian traditions were ridiculed. Against a background of very primitive notions about both the market and democracy, the idea was insistently propagated that unless everybody owned property no serious reforms could be carried out. The illusion was fostered that existing assets (in the creation of which all the population had taken part) would somehow be divided equally among all members of society. As soon as the notion of privatisation ceased to be unacceptable, numerous new difficulties were invoked to modify and transform the pattern of privatisation initially proposed. The impossibility of defining each individual's contribution to the creation of the existing economic potential was stressed. The interests of those working in specific economic units (and their reluctance to come under outside control) were emphasised. The problems of those (teachers, doctors, etc.) who do not produce physical assets was also stressed. At one stage the advisability of leasing as an alternative to immediate privatisation surfaced, but it was rather quickly discarded. A long and not very fruitful debate on the modalities of privatisation took up a lot of time and energy during several years. It has led to a few general legal acts which in principle sanction a process of privatisation and set forth – in rather vague terms – a few guidelines and possible models. The most important of these was the distribution of (free) vouchers which were supposed to represent a share in the overall assets of the country. These vouchers were made negotiable and tradeable. As a result they are today sold at a price only a little above their nominal value – set in the beginning of 1992 at 10,000 roubles (which now is equal to less than one third of a monthly wage).

In practice privatisation is taking numerous, often shady and unforeseen, forms. The old *nomenklatura* – directors of state enterprises and local governments – are using various devices to gain economic and/or financial control over privatised units. New financial assets (mostly acquired through intermediary activities) are partly being redirected towards speculation in vouchers, the buying up of old enterprises (often to acquire real estate) and also (to a lesser degree) into service and production facilities. In some cases privatisation is becoming a channel for laundering illegally accumulated resources. New investment trusts and holding companies are springing up to accumulate resources from the population and to gain control over lucrative enterprises. All this is leading to an escalating concentration of control over private property.

The main problem with privatisation is the fact that physical assets in nearly all branches of the Russian economy are to a large extent obsolete and in urgent need of replacement. Privatisation is being carried out at a time when the value of existing assets (especially in the sphere of production) cannot be realistically assessed. There are growing suspicions that the enterprises being put up for privatisation need tremendous new investments while the government is getting rid of assets that cannot function efficiently.[10)] In the not so distant future, when the implications of this situation become evident to numerous stock-holders, a wave of dissatisfaction can be expected.

---

10) *Kommersant* (Business), no. 39, 1993, pp. 6-7.

Privatisation broadens the scope of market relations by bringing important new items into the market. A real estate and housing market is emerging and growing very rapidly. But – given the massive impoverishment and constant market pressures – privatisation may often lead to the loss of assets previously in private property. In the old days, most people had secure rights to live in municipal apartments. Now, with privatisation and the growing economic squeeze, some are being forced to leave (sell) their privatised flats. Similar problems face the newly emerging farmers who have to operate in highly volatile and state-manipulated markets and credit conditions. (This is a major source of opposition to land privatisation.) The sale of vouchers by impoverished people is an even more common phenomenon. As a result the task of creating a mass property-owning, middle class as the social basis of reform in Russia has been far from successful. Property ownership is increasingly concentrated in a relatively narrow circle. The methods of privatisation employed have tended to create dissatisfaction and undermine the legitimacy of private property and market relationships (at least in the opinion of some circles).

Privatisation is changing the whole social structure of society, creating totally new cleavages and groups. If previously the state sector (together with a highly regulated cooperative sector) were all-prevailing, now a strong private sector is quickly growing in many branches of trade and industry. Both management and workers in the latter are as a rule materially much better off than those in the state sector. The private sector functions in quite a different framework and according to very different criteria. Accordingly, not only economic but also social conflicts are crystallizing between the state and private sectors are developing.

15.5 A new look needed at the integration of social policy with a reformed market economy

Historical experience in all countries shows that market formation is always accompanied by far-reaching social changes many of which tend to undermine social cohesion – differentiation and stratification of society, unemployment, rise in social tensions, separatist trends, etc. In Russia, at present an unprecedented (in scope and speed) process of redistribution of power and wealth is evolving, exacerbated by a broad scrapping of the old social security system. The elaborate network of social security in the former USSR was an important element in the then predominant command-administrative system of central planning. Its dismantling was an integral part of the general offensive against the old system. But the old social security network played an important role in the formation of economic structures and in the definition of material status, life styles, values, etc. What was needed was not its destruction at one stroke but its careful replacement with an alternative mechanism and institutions to fulfil the necessary functions. In reality, however, the previous system was abolished, in the hope that unregulated market forces would on their own fill in all the gaps and solve all the problems. This created a totally new context for further development. The problems that are emerging – the fall in production, the dislocation of many social units and the loss of social cohesion – constitute a real danger, which can be overcome only through active and well conceived strategies and policies, including social policies.

Disregard for social policy, especially for measures limiting excessive differentiation and stratification in society, tends to shape a disconnected, two-tier, "enclave" type of market in which speculative operations are prized and production disadvantaged. Consumption patterns are distorted. A large majority of the population is marginalised with its consumption limited to bare essentials, constituting at best a stagnant and at worst a shrinking market. On the other hand, a narrow segment of society indulges in luxury consumption satisfied predominantly through imports. Such a market tends to be excessively outward-oriented and constantly undercuts the potential for internal development. These are the processes which characterise the present stage of market formation in Russia.

Such a model of market formation places a country inside a mutually reinforcing spiral of development; social differentiation fosters social and political instability. The latter in its turn accelerates distorted market formation and economic degradation. Social policies aimed at mitigating stratification, creating more socially acceptable forms and rates of market formation, could become an important factor in overcoming the present economic and political crisis in Russia. This would mean a slower dismantling of some social institutions and policies, and more socially acceptable and broadly advantageous forms of privatisation (and other economic measures) could play a useful role.

Economic reform in Russia has shown how vague and fluid is the borderline between social and economic phenomena. There is a profound interaction between the two. If we distinguish them, this is only as a pretext for a more profound study of this interaction. The main impact of social policies on market formation comes through its influence on the distribution of incomes and the corresponding patterns of demand. In Russia, neo-liberal policies and the scrapping of previous social policies have also led to a very rapid and obvious shrinking of overall real purchasing power. Exchanges previously regulated by central planning are being replaced partly by market relationships, but also by a retreat into semi-subsistence activities and primitive barter. This is an inevitable consequence of attempts to force the speed of socio-economic change.

Social policy viewed as a set of measures aimed at minimising social inequality and fostering cohesion in society can and should be a very important element in the formulation of a viable strategy of market formation and transition to stable democratic societies. A more equal distribution of the burdens of transition must occupy a prominent place in all thinking on transitional problems. Otherwise there will be constant instability in society and markets will be deeply distorted. Unfortunately these questions do not receive the attention they deserve. At best pre-election promises and token measures can be expected from the now ruling parties. Very few people understand that the real difficulties of economic reform in countries like Russia lie not in the economic but in the social sphere. Excessively rapid and lopsided reforms threaten to undermine the legitimacy of what is happening in the country and lead to unpredictable upheavals and civil strife. The transition to a market economy in a country as large as Russia cannot be achieved except in the context of competent and democratic social policies.

COMMENT ON PART V:

Bernard Cazes*)

The interplay between the economic and social facets of development is a matter for perennial debate among economists, and is quite often expressed for lay persons in terms of the distinction between the size of a cake and the number of parts in which it is divided. For mainstream economists, the two dimensions are separable, with a one-way influence of global size (i.e. pro-

---

*) Former Head, Division of Long-term Studies, Commissariat Général du Plan, Paris.

duction) on the magnitude of the shares (i.e. distribution), while for political economists distributive considerations do feed back on productive efficiency.

Earlier chapters in this volume clearly provided an opportunity to replay this classical drama: on the one side, the neo-classical or supply-side players believed in market-oriented structural reforms; on the other side, the neo-Keynesians, or meliorists with a human face, were very sceptical about the way reforms are currently implemented. Unsurprisingly, the same pattern appears in these chapters on the social problems of transformation.

Some authors have no doubt about the validity of the reform strategies, while recognising that non-economic feedback mechanisms might harm them. The two papers under discussion here (*Supińska,* from Poland, in Chapter 14, and *Kollontai,* from Russia, Chapter 15) are more explicitly critical. Admittedly they recognise a number of important points, such as the facts that the former Soviet system of social protection "stimulated in the population a mentality of false security and laxity" as well as "an atmosphere of subservience" (*Kollontai),* that economic inequality was already present under *perestrojka*, and finally that "the previous social gains (are) for the time being, unfortunately, impossible to realise" (*Supińska). Supińska* also points to the vicious circle which inevitably makes social progress slow: social services "need both money and reforms; the reforms cannot start for lack of money, and the diminishing funds are spent with worse and worse results due to the lack of reforms".

At the same time the reader cannot help being impressed by the dramatic plummeting of living standards, and by the awareness that this happened *after* the introduction of systemic reforms, which suggests a kind of *post hoc, ergo propter hoc* inference.

What I personally read in the papers is a different lesson, namely that structural transformations might have been introduced with a greater consideration for their distributive implications without contradicting the underlying economic rationale. Let me give you two examples:

(a) Market logics does not preclude food or rent subsidies *per se*. What it suggests, rather, is that the best (economically speaking) redistributive strategy should be one that operates through transfers in cash rather than relying on "social" price-setting, with the dual benefit of not distorting relative price patterns and of increasing consumer power, but at the possible cost of the money being used for unintended purposes (e.g. more vodka instead of better housing).

(b) One of the most visible flaws of the transition countries' policy mix is the ease with which taxes can be cheated, particularly among the *nouveaux riches*. Again, this is not a market outcome proper, but rather the unfortunate implication of the current financial situation, including the fact that new wide-based taxes, such as the VAT, are quite recent.

The story looks strangely like similar controversies which raged in recent years concerning the structural adjustment programmes (SAP) implemented in many developing countries. In both groups of countries one sees the same tendency to blame the stabilisation policies for the very same critical situations which the policies were supposed to remedy. Another possible parallel is that the donors took some time before realising that SAPs should be complemented with some kind of social safety net and a hard core of infrastructural investments.

Three main points may be highlighted:

(a) The assessment of living conditions and their worsening should take into account the existence of palliatives such as home-production and the hidden economy.

(b) Analysis of the social budgets of the Czech Republic, Hungary and Poland, shows that, at least in relative shares, social protection expenditures are not neglected at all. What is missing is rather a careful evaluation of the outcomes derived from these expenditures.

(c) The fact that policy instruments in the East European countries are sometimes rather flawed, and that the magnitude of the task of creating property rights from scratch was underestimated, does not prove that market logic is wrong. What it does suggest is that a careful reading of what the Nobel prize winner Douglas North (a Czech government adviser, too) wrote on the institutional factors of development[1)] might have been a worthwhile intellectual investment. Nor does the inadequacy of policy instruments provide evidence that the former system of central planning was viable. After all, "it is not by accident", nor because of any policy prescription from the IMF, that the system fell to pieces so quickly.

---

1) Or the argument of Robert Putnam on the role of civic traditions in Italian development (see his *Making Democracy Work*, Princeton University Press, 1993).

PART VI – COUNTRY COMMENTS

Chapter 16

THE CONCEPT OF FINANCIAL PROGRAMMING CONFRONTED WITH RUSSIAN EXPERIENCE

Alexander Nekipelov*)

16.1 The general picture

The degree of austerity of monetary and fiscal policy has by no means been constant since early 1992 (see *Table 16.1).* The first two quarters of 1992 were characterised by a relatively modest increase in the value of nominal money and credit aggregates. A small surplus (0.9 per cent of GDP) in the balance of the general government was even achieved in the first quarter. However, in the third quarter a significant budget deficit emerged accompanied by a drastic increase in the growth of money supply. Later (in the last quarter of 1992 and the first half of 1993) some efforts were made to harden slightly both monetary and credit policy.

Retail prices have been advancing faster than producer prices (except in the fourth quarter of 1992). Inflation rose sharply in the third quarter of 1992 and has been fluctuating since then (to mid-1993) by between 20 and 30 per cent per month (measured either by retail or producer prices).

---

*) Deputy Director, Institute of International Economic and Political Studies, Russian Academy of Sciences, Moscow.

The economic slump was deepening throughout 1992 so that in the fourth quarter the annualised rate of GDP decline reached 25 per cent. During the first half of 1993 the recession continued, but there emerged some signs of a fall in the rate of decline in production. A catastrophic situation appeared in investment: after a 16 per cent fall in 1991 investment decreased by an additional 45 per cent in 1992.[1] In the first half of 1993 the investment-GDP ratio was only 12.7 per cent[2] against 25.7 per cent in 1991 and 31.8 per cent in 1989.[3]

Foreign trade (without the so-called inter-republican trade) fell in 1992 by roughly the same rate as that of GDP (-19 per cent), exports diminishing by 21.6 per cent and imports by 18.2 per cent.[4] In 1993 the rate decrease became ever steeper (-23 per cent) in the first half of the year, entirely determined by the massive fall in imports (-49 per cent). Exports even increased somewhat (+3 per cent), exports of machinery and equipment growing by 14 per cent.[5]

It is obvious that trade with former republics of the USSR has been much reduced, although there are no reliable data; Russia's indirect subsidies to these new independent states, resulting from deviation of contract prices for centrally supplied goods from world market prices, are estimated for 1992 at Rbl 2.4 trillion (15.3 per cent of Russia's GDP). In addition, Russia financed through the so-called corresponding accounts and technical credits imbalances in mutual trade with these states amounting to more than Rbl 1 trillion, or 6.6 per cent of GDP.[6]

The dramatic fall in the living standards of the population was another by-product of the reforming process, its negative social consequences being reinforced by rapidly growing differentiation of incomes. The real average wage after more than halving in the first quarter of 1992 increased a little during the rest of the year reaching in the fourth quarter nearly 60 per cent of the December 1991 level. But with the beginning of 1993 the opposite trend took over and this indicator quickly returned to 50 per cent. (*Table 16.1*)

---

1) IMF (1993), *Russian Federation,* IMF Economic Reviews, no. 8, p. 86.

2) *Ekonomika i zhizn'* (1993), no. 31, p. 21.

3) IMF (1993), op.cit., p. 91.

4) ibid, p. 107.

5) *Ekonomika i zhizn'* (1993), no. 31, p. 23.

6) IMF (1993), op.cit, p. 108.

Table 16.1

Russia: Major economic indicators (1992-1993)

	1992				1993	
	Q1	Q2	Q3	Q4	Q1	Q2
Real GDP index (%)[a)]	86.2	82.2	78.8	75.5	82-84	85.2-86.2
Nominal money supply index (%)[b)]	131.7	150.0	225.0	159.7	143.3	...
Domestic credit index (%)[c)]	145.8	173.0	265.7	138.1	145.6	...
General government fiscal balance (% GDP)[d)]	0.9	-7.8	-14.6	-6.5	-9.0	...
Producer price index (%)[e)]	1079.7	195.7	150.7	193.5	214.3	...
Retail price index (%)[f)]	618.9	162.6	135.5	193.7	193.6	178.5
Average real wage index (%)[g)]	46.8	49.2	55.4	59.9	50.1	...

a) In relation to the corresponding period of the previous year. For quarters I through IV indices are calculated on the basis of data published in *Rossija – 1993. Ekonomicheskaja kon'unktura* (1993), Centr Ekonomicheskoy kon'unktury i prognozirovanija, p. 11. The index for the first quarter of 1993 is taken from the official report of Goskomstat of Russia, *Ekonomika i zhizn'* (1993), no. 17, whereas the second quarter index is calculated on the basis of the semiannual index also presented by the official report of Goskomstat of Russia, *Ekonomika i zhizn'* (1993), no. 31. - b) End of quarter in relation to the end of previous quarter. "Broad money indicator", used by IMF experts, less foreign-exchange deposits is taken as a measure of money supply. Source: IMF (1993), *Russian Federation,* IMF Economic Reviews, no. 8, p. 100. - c) End of quarter in relation to the end of previous quarter. Source: IMF (1993), op.cit., p. 100. - d) Source: IMF (1993), op.cit., p. 93 (quarters I through IV, 1992); *Ekonomika i zhizn'* (1993), no. 17 (first quarter of 1993). - e) End of quarter in relation to the end of previous quarter. Source: IMF (1993), op.cit., p. 88. - f) End of quarter in relation to the end of previous quarter. Source: IMF (1993), op.cit., p. 88 (quarters I through IV, 1992); *Ekonomika i zhizn* (1993), no. 31 (first two quarters of 1993). - g) December 1991 = 100. Calculated on the basis of data published in IMF (1993), op.cit., pp. 88, 91.

16.2 Money, credit and prices

A reliable correlation is found (see *Table 16.2*) between changes in money supply, and changes within the same periods (quarters) of the following credit aggregates: domestic credit, net domestic credit of the Central Bank of Russia (CBR) and net domestic credit of the CBR to the federal government. Whereas changes in the first two credit aggregates accompany significant change in the money supply index (respectively 0.67 and 0.50 percentage points in response to a one-percentage-point change of each credit aggregate), the impact of changes in the CBR's credit to federal government is relatively small (0.28 percentage points in response to a one-percentage-point change).

There is a reliable correlation (r = 0.68) between changes in the monetary base and, with a lag of one quarter, changes in money supply. But the latter's degree of sensitivity to changes of the former – 0.9 percentage points in response to a one-percentage-point change – makes us to suspect an unusual weakness of the multiplying process. Data in *Table 16.3* confirm this supposition showing that:

- beginning from December 1991 through March 1993, the money multiplier was changing rather erratically, though the main tendency – towards reduction – was obvious. Its latest value is extremely low;
- the propensity to hold money balances in cash rather than in the form of deposits was steadily growing;
- the tendency to growth of bank reserves is clear.

In the first quarter of 1992 the rate of growth of nominal money supply was far behind that of both retail and producer prices. Later on this discrepancy naturally diminished: from the second quarter of 1992 through the first quarter of 1993 the nominal money supply rose by little less than retail prices but still much less than producer prices. Tentative calculations in *Table 16.4* show that the velocity of money circulation has increased sharply since December 1991 though in a quite erratic manner.

A certain correlation was revealed between dynamics of changes in money supply and in retail prices. Analysis showed that one-percentage-point change in the money supply index resulted, with a lag of one quarter, in 0.43 percentage points change of retail prices (coefficient of correlation – 0.59). At the same time, there existed no reliable and logically consistent linear dependence

Table 16.2

Russia: Some monetary/credit correlations

y	Retail price index		Producer price index		Nominal money supply index	
x	1*	2**	1*	2**	1*	2**
Indices of –						
1. Domestic credit	y=2.8-1.24x r=0.47	y=1.58-0.34x r=0.7	y=3.3-1.57x r=0.40	y=1.3-0.08x r=0.16	y=0.37+0.67x r=0.91	y=1.07+0.1x r=0.15
2. CBR net credit	y=3.47-1.76x r=0.75	y=1.03+0.1x r=0.19	y=4.46-2.48x r=0.70	y=1.47-0.19x r=0.39	y=0.56+0.5x r=0.5	y=0.99+0.34x r=0.5
3. CBR net credit to general government	y=2.12-0.65x r=-0.82	y=1.06+0.07x r=0.41	y=2.56-0.93x r=0.78	y=1.36-0.10x r=0.66	y=1.05+0.10x r=0.44	y=0.99+0.15x r=0.77
4. CBR net credit to federal government	y=2.84-1.25x r=0.87	y=1.12+0.03x r=0.11	y=3.59-1.78x r=0.83	y=1.39-0.13x r=0.48	y=0.82+0.28x r=0.70	y=0.92+0.21x r=0.58
5. Nominal Money supply	y=3.91-2.21x r=-0.63	y=0.69+0.43x r=0.59	y=5.1-3.14x r=0.59	y=1.11+0.10x r=0.16	–	–
6. Monetary base	–	–	–	–	y=0.66+0.41x r=0.49	y=0.05+0.9x r=0.68

*) Correlations between respective quarterly indices for the period 1.1.1992-31.3.1993.

**) Correlations between quarterly indices of x and y with a lag of one quarter. Correspondingly, quarterly indices of x for the period 1.1.1992-31.12.1992 and of y for the period 1.4.1992-31.3.1993 were used in calculations.

Source: Calculations are made on the basis of data in IMF (1993), *Russian Federation,* IMF Economic Reviews, no. 8 , pp. 88, 100, 101; *Ekonomika i zhizn'* (1993), no. 31 (RPI index for the first quarter of 1993). Money supply indices are based on the indicator "broad money" less foreign-exchange deposits.

Table 16.3

Russia: Changes in money multiplier

	c_p [a)]	c_b [b)]	Money multiplier[c)]
December 1991	0.201	0.170	3.23
March 1992	0.223	0.258	2.54
June 1992	0.294	0.533	1.56
September 1992	0.287	0.512	1.61
December 1992	0.355	0.746	1.23
March 1993	0.410	0.639	1.34

a) Desired cash-deposits ratio of economic agents. - b) Desired reserve-deposits ratio of banks. - c) Can be calculated in two ways: either as money supply to monetary base ratio or using the formula: money multiplier = $(c_p+1)/(c_p+b)$.

Source: Calculated on the basis of data in IMF (1993), *Russian Federation,* IMF Economic Reviews, no. 8, p. 100. Foreign-exchange deposits are excluded from deposits.

Table 16.4

Russia: Changes in velocity of circulation of money

	December 1991	1992 Q1	1992 Q2	1992 Q3	1992 Q4	1993 Q1
1. GDP (billion roubles)	104	1878	2910	4128	6636	15000
2. Money supply (bn roubles)						
2.1 beginning of period	...	998	1314	1972	4438	7086
2.2 end of period	998	1314	1972	4438	7086	10155
2.3 average	998 *	1156	1643	3205	5762	8620.5
3. Velocity of money circulation						
V=[(1).4]/(2.3)	–	6.5	7.1	5.2	4.6	7.0
V=[(1).12]/(2.3)	1.3	–	–	–	–	–

*) Data on money supply at the beginning of December 1991 are not available; the average level for this month is taken to equal the end-period value. As a result the calculated annualised velocity of money circulation in December 1991 should be regarded as slightly understated.

Sources: IMF (1993), *Russian Federation,* IMF Economic Reviews, no. 8, pp. 93, 100; *Ekonomika i zhizn'* (1993), no. 17; *Obzor Ekonomiki Rossii 1993* (1993), pp. 61-62.

between money supply or different credit aggregates, on the one hand, and producer prices, on the other (see *Table 16.2*).

On balance, one can argue that not only was the price movement determined by changes in money supply, but equally that the price rises themselves provoked some accommodation in the monetary sphere by modifyingthe velocity of money circulation. It is necessary also to take into account that the indicator calculated as a GDP-money supply ratio reflects, strictly speaking, not only the genuine velocity of money circulation but the scale of interenterprise arrears as well, because the value of GDP comprises all goods and services supplied whether they have been paid for or not.

The demand for money balances

The fact that inflation outstripped the growth of the nominal money supply means that, under conditions of money market equilibrium, demand for real money balances was reduced considerably. The reduction of demand for real money balances can to some (but a relatively small) extent be explained by the fall in production and income. Another traditional factor supposed to influence the demand for real money holdings is the movement of nominal interest rates. Standard textbooks on economics explain why the nominal and not the real rate should be considered as the opportunity cost of holding money (see Begg et al. 1991). Their arguments are perfectly correct but only in conditions which they presuppose as given. Critically important here is the idea that interest-bearing financial instruments (e.g. bonds) represent the best alternative to holding wealth in the form of money. This supposition is quite natural for a mature market economy where nominal interest rates and inflation increase, in accordance with Irving Fisher's hypothesis, simultaneously. This is, however, not so in the Russian case. A permanently and heavily negative real interest rate makes economic agents look for better alternatives to money than interest-bearing deposits. And such a practical substitute for Russian national currency as "a store of value" has been found – convertible currency (first of all US$ and DM). The resulting high demand for convertible currency has led to a massive depreciation of the rouble; its rate of exchange has deviated enormously from its purchasing power parity.[7] According to IMF data, the share of foreign exchange deposits in broad money increased from 16.9 per cent in December 1991 to 45.8 per cent in March 1993[8].

Production and prices

In 1992 industrial production decreased by 19 per cent. Employment in industry dropped by only 5.4 per cent.[9] Correspondingly, labour productivity fell by 14.4 per cent. The most significant recession took place in nonferrous metallurgy (-27 per cent), light industry (-26 per cent), production of chemicals (-25 per cent), construction materials (-22 per cent).[10] It is interesting that in industries distant from final consumers relative prices, as a rule, increased (in nonferrous metallurgy by 44 per cent, in the production of chemicals by 17 per cent), whereas in light industry and construction materials recession was accompanied by a fall in relative prices (respectively, by 52 and 17 per cent).[11]

It should also be noted that during the one-and-a-half years of reforms there existed an obvious trade-off between changes in the rate of inflation and in the depth of recession (*Table 16.5*): reduced inflation was accompanied by the deepening of recession and vice versa.[12]

---

7) It is significant that the GDP per capita level in Russia in 1992 calculated on the basis of PPP equalled 3430 US dollars whereas the same indicator determined at the interbank exchange rate was less than one-seventh as much – 492 US dollars (IMF (1993), op.cit., p. 85).

8) IMF (1993), op.cit., p. 100.

9) ibid, p. 89.

10) ibid, p. 86.

11) ibid, p. 86.

12) Such a trade-off between inflation and recession in the modern Russian economy is acknowledged by many specialists. Thus the report of the government Centre for Economic Reforms says: "During the third quarter (of 1992) the fall of production was stopped at the expense of massive credit emission." *(Obzor* 1993, p. 5)

Table 16.5

Russia: Production and inflation

	1992				1993	
	Q1	Q2	Q3	Q4	Q1	Q2
Changes in real GDP (% against corresponding period of previous year)	-13.8	-17.8	-21.2	-24.5	(-16)	(-13.8)-(-14.8)
Changes in retail prices (% from previous quarter)	+486.8	+47.5	+34.0	+108.8	+93	+78.5
Changes in producer prices (% from previous quarter)	+979.7	+95.7	+50.7	+93.5	+114.3	...

Sources: Calculated on the basis of data in *Rossija – 1993. Ekonomicheskaja kon'unktura* (1993), p. 11; *Ekonomika i zhizn'* (1993), no. 17 and no. 31; IMF (1993), *Russian Federation,* IMF Economic Reviews, no. 8, p. 88.

16.3 Interpretation

The way reforms have proceeded in Russia confirms many key ideas such as those presented by the WIIW in Chapter 1. The country has experienced an unprecedented economic slump deepening after the hardening of monetary and fiscal policy. A genuine threat of irrevocable loss of a significant part of industrial potential has emerged.[13] Contraction of aggregate demand, including that resulting from fast impoverishment of the major part of the population, naturally has a negative impact upon production. Cost-push inflation acquires a key role in the mechanism of post-socialist inflation.

At the same time the interpretation given by the WIIW to some of these theses does not seem fully convincing. One can see an obvious endeavour to link the slump in post-socialist countries almost exclusively with measures resulting from the concept of "financial programming". It is underlined that beyond

13) The threat of hysteresis during post-socialist reforms was also pointed out in the report published in February 1993 by the Institute of International Economic and Political Studies, Russian Academy of Sciences *(Uroki* 1993).

certain limits supply begins to fall faster than demand and as a result excessive demand even increases.

But what kind of fall in aggregate supply is meant? Do the authors have in mind the movement along the supply curve or its shift to the left? If we take into account that, according to the authors, an increase in the nominal interest rate is considered as one of the main factors determining the drop in supply, then we should accept the first answer: we have to do with the movement along the aggregate supply curve resulting from the shift of the aggregate demand curve to the left as a consequence of the increased interest rate. Then, however, there can be no increase in excessive demand and, correspondingly, in inflation, simultaneously with the deepening recession.

It also seems that by stressing the stimulation of aggregate demand by means of classical Keynesian recipes – increased budget deficit and softened monetary policy – the authors overlook the fact that they deal not with a mature market economy hit by a cyclical recession, but with a transformational crisis characteristic of the post- socialist economies.

To my mind, the analysis of economies in transition must pay attention to their following specific features:

- inadequacy, in terms of market economy criteria, of the production structure;
- whimsicality of motivation and behaviour of liberalised state enterprises;
- absence or immaturity of market institutions.

16.3 Structural problems

There is no need now to prove that the allocation of resources in socialist economies was not in conformity with market criteria and that relative prices were heavily distorted. That is why when market mechanisms are "switched on" through the liberalisation of economic activity, the production apparatus can no more function in its integrity. In macroeconomic language this can be expressed in the following way: the notion "potential output" no more coincides with that of "existing productive capacities". This means that the aggregate supply curve is shifted to the left (as compared with its position under a command economy!), which launches the mechanism of cost-push inflation and provokes the so-called stagflation trap. Hysteresis becomes inevitable: i.e. the change in the long-run path of economic development associated with the contraction of productive potential is the result not of cyclical deviations from an equilibrium position but a consequence of systemic transformation.

Confronted with strong supply-side shocks the western countries used to rely on an "accommodating" monetary policy to alleviate the production slump at the expense of a slightly more intensive inflation. In post-socialist countries the "price" of such policy is much higher because of the all-embracing character of the shock provoked by "structural collapse". Alleviation of the slow-down by monetary policy has to be paid for by much higher inflation. An extremely unfavourable trade-off between inflation and recession (see Nekipelov 1993a) is the main reason why efforts to base economic policy exclusively on the management of aggregate demand (either through its severe limitation or by artificial stimulation) are doomed to failure. To ignore this fact leads to alternating periods of hardening and softening of monetary and fiscal policy (and with them of government teams). Completion of this sinuous movement is possible only after the productive potential becomes more or less adapted to market economy criteria, as a result of its partial destruction, on the one hand, and its micro-economic adjustment. The more often the government is forced to use the "inflationary lubricant" to prevent social disturbance the more distant will be the prospect of stability. In practical terms this means that reducing the policy treatment of post-socialist economies to the choice between demand contraction or demand expansion can sink the economy for an uncertain period into co-existence of recession and high inflation.

16.4 State enterprises' reaction to market signals

It is now evident that simple decentralisation of control of the state sector does not automatically result in the appearance of economic agents capable of reacting appropriately to market signals.

a) The conditioned reflex of socialism manifests itself: it is more important to produce and deliver goods than to be paid for them. It is this reflex that underlies mutual delays in payment, which can be regarded both as the emergence of a special form of credit and as a decrease in money demand; it is clear in any case that official means of payment are far from serving the entire turnover. Moreover, in a situation of "non-obligatory" payments the demand-side limitation of the price level is dramatically reduced. This is one of the main reasons why producer prices move independently from money and credit aggregates.

b) The paternalistic nature of state-owned enterprises translates itself, in particular, into employment being reduced much more slowly than output. As a result, production costs grow, further aggravating the cost-push inflation.

c) A clear relationship between the owners, managers and wage earners is absent in the state sector.[14] Today, the managers are inclined to regard themselves more as members of the working collective than as representatives of the owner-state. From this results the almost unrestricted propensity of state-owned enterprises to increase expenditure (including both consumption and the spending of capital funds), which is conducive to higher inflation through acceleration of money circulation (investment funds are transferred to consumer expenditures, which involves a higher money circulation rate).

d) The high level of production concentration and the related problem of monopoly and monopolistic prices.

The first two features indeed alleviate the market shock, but by methods rather far removed from economic rationality. Moreover, all these features contribute to the aggravation of inflationary processes in a situation of economic liberalisation.

16.5 Some specific institutional problems

The absence or even immaturity of market economy institutions, quite natural at initial stages of transformation, have their impact upon both the results of normal (for western economies) economic decisions and the possibilities of executing some of such decisions.

a) The fundamental restructuring of the banking system inherited from socialism is accompanied by the emergence of serious problems relevant to the settlement of payments. This has several important consequences, among them:

– the demand of commercial banks for reserves in order to ensure that payments grow thus contributing to reduction of the money multiplier;

---

14) R. McKinnon is certainly right (McKinnon 1991, p.149) when he says: "The important caveat is that the state must assert its role as owner." The position of the author of this paper with regard to how this task could be carried out is presented in Nekipelov (1991).

– delays in settlements through banking transfers intensify the propensity of economic agents to hold their money balances in cash.[15] Besides the negative effect on the money multiplier this contributes to the very different attitudes to holding cash as against current accounts, and to the technological mystification of the process of printing money. To exemplify this attitude, rather natural for the command economy, but very strange for the market-based society, a survey of economic development of Russia prepared in July 1993, by the Institute headed by E. Gaidar, suggested that the Central Bank of Russia had pursued a restrictive policy but had not had a similar success in limiting the money supply (*Rossiyskaja Ekonomika* 1993, p. 5).

b) Financial markets exist only in embryo and the short-term prospects (slump, inflation) for their development are gloomy. The actual absence of a developed market for state financial instruments precludes non-inflationary methods of financing the state budget deficit as well as regulation of the money supply through open market operations.

The real interest rate is negative though its nominal level is high. The latter effectively precludes long-term credits. At the same time the negative rate increases the demand for money and makes the control of inflation more difficult. A positive real interest rate achieved by a simple increase of the nominal rate does not resolve – and here I agree with the authors of Chapter 1 – the long-term investment problem, because the possible sharp change in the level of inflation could in such conditions lead to numerous bankruptcies of banks or firms.

The absence of smoothly operating mechanisms for the formation of an equilibrium interest rate, that is the lack of financial markets, is by itself a serious factor in the economy's vulnerability to inflation while money supply is growing: the entire burden of balancing the demand for money with its supply is immediately placed on prices.

c) Uncertain property relations within the state sector are probably the most important cause of the undeveloped comercial law and absence of a working mechanism for bankruptcies, which in turn adversely affects the development of long-term credit.

---

15) There also exist other factors: endeavours to escape taxes, technical difficulties in transforming, when necessary, deposits into cash, problems in assessment of commercial banks' financial state etc.

Thus some specific institutional features of the monetary sphere in post-socialist economies are rather significant. They can generate contradictory forces with unforeseeable intensity. Here are rooted those unusual relationships between the money supply, the monetary base and different credit aggregates which have been described above. Many features of post-socialist inflation can also be found here.

While the deformed nature of the economic structure explains why a restrictive monetary and fiscal policy is extremely painful in the conditions of the post-socialist economy, because of institutional peculiarities the regulation of money supply becomes a much more complex task, from a purely technical point of view, than in a "normal" market economy.[16)]

References

Begg, D., Fisher, Stanley, and Dornbusch, Rudiger (1991), *Economics,* Third Ed., McGraw-Hill Book Company, London, p. 426.

International Monetary Fund (1993), *Russian Federation,* IMF Economic Reviews, no. 8.

McKinnon, Ronald J. (1991), *The Order of Economic Liberalisation: Financial Control in the Transition to a Market Economy,* The Johns Hopkins University Press, Baltimore and London.

Nekipelov, A. (1991), "Transition to a Market Economy: The Role and the Future of the State Sector", *Studies on Soviet Economic Development,* vol. 2, no. 4.

– (1993a), "Transformation in Post-Socialist Economies: Specific Features", *Reforma,* Monthly Newsletter, International Foundation for Economic and Social Reforms, no. 8, p. 8.

– (1993b), "Udastsja li zashtopat' Trishkin kaftan?" (Will it be possible to mend the hole in Trishkin's caftan?), *Rossija.*

Obzor Ekonomiki Rossii. Osnovnye tendencii razvitija (1993), I (1993) (Economic Survey of Russia: Basic trends of development in 1993), Moscow.

Rossija – 1993, Ekonomicheskaja kon'unktura (1993), Centr Ekonimicheskoy kon'unktury i prognozirovanija, Moscow.

"Rossiyskaja ekonomika v iule 1993 goda" (1993) (The Russian economy in July 1993), *Delovoy mir,* 4 September.

16) It is by no means by chance that in its current operations the CBR pays attention only to the two following indicators: net credit to the Federal Government and the volume of centralised credits.

"Socialno-ekonomicheskoe polojenie i razvitie ekonomicheskih reform v Rossiyskoy Federacii v pervom kvartale 1993 goda" (1993) (Socio-economic situation and development of economic reforms in the Russian Federation in the first quarter of 1993), *Ekonomika i zhizn',* no. 17.

"Socialno-ekonomicheskoe polojenie i razvitie ekonomicheskih reform v Rossiyskoy Federacii v pervom polugodii 1993 goda" (1993) (Social economic situation and development of economic reforms in the Russian Federation in the first half of 1993), *Ekonomika i zhizn',* no. 31.

"Uroki Vostochnoy Evropy. Analiz Instituta mejdunarodnyh ekonomicheskih i politicheskih issledovaniy pod rukovodstvom akademika Olega Bogomolova" (1993) (Tasks for Eastern Europe: Analysis of the Institute of International Economic and Political Studies, under the direction of Academician Oleg Bogomolov), *Nezavisimaja gazeta,* 9 February.

Chapter 17

IN QUEST OF LOST STABILISATION: REFLECTIONS ON HUNGARY IN 1993

Ádám Török*)

This short paper is meant to highlight some crucial issues in the stabilisation problem. Therefore it does not give a description of the current state of affairs (or of the Hungarian economy) but analyses only a few aspects of Hungarian stabilisation understood as an essential element of the transition.

Our starting point is more or less methodological, with some intention of provocation. Recent Hungarian experience has quite clearly shown that neither so-called monetarist-type, restrictive stabilisation efforts, nor modestly expansionary measures with the label "Keynesian" attached to them, could offer feasible solutions to the crisis. So we have to part with the conventional approach to macroeconomic stabilisation based on Pareto-optimality.

This approach suggests that a handpicked mix of aggregate macroeconomic indicators, including GDP growth, unemployment rate, consumer prices (or GDP deflator), budget deficit (as expressed in percentage of GDP) and balance of payments, could be used to describe the pre-stabilisation state of the economy. If the same set of indicators is used to describe the post-stabilisation state of the economy, at least one indicator should show improvement in the case of successful stabilisation, and none of them any deterioration.

The current state of the Hungarian economy, as well as of the consecutive efforts to stabilise it, seem to show a very low efficiency of all stabilisation policy mixes available – not only of those recently or currently used but also of those with some likelihood of feasibility at the moment. To show the size of the stabilisation problem in Hungary: the volume of GDP has shrunk by almost 20 per cent since 1989, the volume of investment by 35 per cent, R&D expenditure

---

*) Research Institute of Industrial Economics of the Hungarian Academy of Sciences, Budapest and LICOS Institute, Catholic University of Leuven, Belgium.

by more than 60 per cent, and the number of jobs by 13 per cent (Kádár 1993, p. 4).

The title of this paper is meant to be a reference to the following persistent problem: the necessity for an effective stabilisation policy has been obvious to successive Hungarian governments since 1987 but the original idea of macro-economic stabilisation as top priority was always lost somewhere on the road. Stabilisation-related economic policy priorities had to give way to more urgent reform steps in the years 1988 to 1990 or even later (an example is the liberalisation of imports which was introduced more quickly than would have been necessary from a stabilisation-oriented viewpoint). And in most recent years, the lack of a consistent policy framework for stabilisation resulted in some very contradictory economic policy measures.

For example: at a certain point in September 1993, the government had to make a clear choice between reversing the trend of (i) falling real interest rates (harmful for savings propensities and, therefore, indirectly for financing the budget deficit from household savings); or of (ii) the real appreciation of the Hungarian currency (unfavourable for the balance of payments).

Any interest rate increase would have increased the budget deficit almost immediately, whereas any further currency devaluation would have also immediately increased the state debt. Moreover, an interest rate increase would have worsened the anyway very fragile growth and investment climate, while a currency devaluation would have increased expectations of *both* inflation *and of* continued devaluation.[1)]

In the end, *both steps were taken,* but each of them only to a limited extent. This shows the awkwardness of the situation: *the lack of clear priorities in ranking the short-term targets of stabilisation policy* has led to a compromise

---

1) The view of the author on devaluation is quite strongly influenced by the theory of rational expectations and it seems to have been shared to a certain extent by some prominent central bankers in Hungary at least at one time. Devaluationary expectations probably could have been, or could be, calmed in not more than two, only seemingly contradictory, ways. Option 1: a very firm sticking to the "hard-currency" policy and to the corresponding reputation of the Hungarian monetary authorities with *no nominal devaluation at all* despite increasing pressures from exporters. Option 2: a one-step devaluation significant enough to convince present and future holders of foreign currency in Hungary that this was not just a *short-term corrective step* and is therefore unlikely to be followed by another devaluation in one year or so. This devaluation ought to have been around 10 per cent instead of 4.8 per cent.

"attacking" the budget from two opposite directions: higher interest on the state debt; a higher level of the state debt itself. This sent out very mixed signals, open to a wide variety of misinterpretations. The simultaneity of the two contrary steps also extinguished part of their eventually positive effects. For example: the currency devaluation ought to have improved the climate for exports, but the interest rate increase probably worsened it due to the increased costs of export financing.

The current Hungarian macroeconomic situation is very appropriately described by *Kornai* as a "transformational recession" in the title of Chapter 2 of this volume. My interpretation of this term would be "a recession which calls for stabilisation policies with a considerable structural component". In such a situation *any available mix of conventional stabilisation-aimed measures can have only a low level of efficiency.*

Three selected issues related to stabilisation in Hungary can help explain this statement. The first problem is that of the historical parallel with OECD countries raised by *Worswick* in Chapter 3. The second issue is the structural component of the stabilisation problem. The third subject is the persistent budget deficit as one of the key constraints on governmental action for stabilisation.

(a) The first stabilisation period of the industrialised Western economies lasted more than 20 years between the early 1950s and 1973 (*Worswick*). This could be called a "textbook" type stabilisation with high rates of GDP and productivity growth, low rates of unemployment, moderate inflation and rapid and sustained growth of international trade. The post-1973 stabilisation period was a period of structural adjustment serving to stabilise the new industrial, trade and financial structures much more than just macroeconomic stabilisation without any considerable structural content.

This post-1973 period was already more controversial as regards macroeconomic balances in the West, but the overall macroeconomic situation improved in most OECD countries. This happened, but not in a Pareto-optimal sense any more: many OECD countries had to accept relatively low long-term growth rates (except for Japan, Finland and the Southern countries of the EC). Moreover, inflation, unemployment and budget deficits could not be brought back to pre-1973 levels in most OECD economies.

The structural and conjunctural components of the two distinct stabilisation periods of the OECD economies were very different. Just one major difference deserves mention: in the 1950-1973 period *major new components were added to aggregate world demand* due to

– the post-war reconstruction of Europe,
– the Korean War (mainly for Japan),
– the Vietnam War (mainly for the USA) and
– the apparent modernisation boom of Eastern Europe and Latin America financed by credits in the 1960s and 1970s.

By contrast the post-1973 stabilisation period[2], especially after 1979 phase, could not benefit from any significant further expansion of the demand side of world trade. In the same time the supply side was substantially enforced by the rapidly increasing participation of Pacific Rim countries in manufacturing exports. Moreover, the absence of booms generated by major armed conflicts, as well as the debt crisis of Eastern Europe and Latin America, practically limited the growth of aggregate world demand to the OECD countries and Southeast Asia.

In such a comparative approach, it can be seen that

– the first stabilisation period of the West benefited from rapidly growing aggregate world demand, while
– the second had a regionally much more limited, but still not actually declining demand component.

In this time sequence, the post-1990 stabilisation period of East European economies can be considered the *third*, still more controversial, post-war stabilisation period in Europe. Its demand component, as opposed to the two former periods, is *evidently declining.* The volume of Hungarian industrial output was, for example, 37.5 per cent below its 1985 level in January 1993, the bottom point of its crisis (KSH 1933, p. 33).

While the Western stabilisation policies of the 1950s could capitalise on strongly increasing domestic and foreign demand, *Hungarian industry had to attempt stabilisation while losing more than one third of its markets.* Partly abroad, in the former COMECON area, and partly in the country, owing to the wave of bankruptcies, the sweeping liberalisation of imports and the formally

---

2) Or, to be more precise: the 1973-1990 stabilisation period. The post-1990 period is not only characterised by a market-oriented transition and stabilisation (or efforts in that direction) in Eastern Europe, but also by major changes in the conditions for growth of the major OECD economies such as Japan, Germany, the USA, more recently also in France, Canada, Italy and the Scandinavian countries.

very restrictive macroeconomic climate. This observation makes it necessary to dwell upon *the structural component of the stabilisation problem*.

(b) Industrial production has borne the brunt of the recession in Eastern Europe, with contractions of gross output substantially larger than those in GNP/NMP since 1989. Over the period 1989-1992 the fall of industrial output in Eastern Europe as a whole was over 40 per cent" (ECE 1993, p. 77). Calculated from the same source (ECE, Table 3.1.1., p. 73), the corresponding Hungarian figure for the period 1989-1992 was -31.3 per cent.

The ECE assessment refers to an overall growth crisis with industry as the major sectoral victim of the crisis. The logic of this approach says that if industrial growth could be restored macroeconomic stabilisation could reasonably be expected to start within a short time. Very recent experience seems to contradict even this modest optimism at least for 1993 and for Hungary.

Macroeconomic forecasts for the Hungarian economy in 1993, prepared in late 1992, gave more or less parallel assessments for GDP and for industrial growth. These forecasts were made in a conceptual approach not very far from that of the ECE referred to above. Industry was considered the "engine" of GDP growth by these forecasts in the sense that if industry could achieve at least some positive growth the persistently negative trend of GDP could be reversed as well.

Preliminary figures from the first months of 1993 did in fact show a modest growth in the volume of industrial output. This short-term trend was then called "positive stagnation" and considered an encouraging sign pointing to the end of the crisis. The pattern of the actual Hungarian growth performance in 1993 as a whole was completely unexpected. While the positive growth trend of industry gained even more strength the negative trend of GDP growth remained basically unchanged. The growth of the volume of industrial output reached 4 per cent in 1993, whereas GDP shrank further (in the sixth consecutive year) by approximately 1 per cent. The suddenly opening gap between the two formerly closely interrelated trends of GDP and industrial growth can be explained by a sudden collapse of agricultural production. In the first half of 1993, for example, the volume of sales of agricultural products was 31 per cent below the comparable figure for the previous year (KSH 1993, p. 45). This rapid change in the growth pattern of the Hungarian economy raises several important issues for analysis and discussion:

(a) *The nature of the agricultural crisis:* this crisis may be interpreted as a sign of structural adjustment to world economy trends. This would mean that the share of agriculture in Hungarian GDP (13.7 per cent in 1989 and 10.0 per cent in 1991) is approaching West European levels of the 1970s (except for France and Italy). If so, this would not be a problem related to stabilisation policy.

It must be remembered, though, that the structural role of agriculture rapidly diminished in a Western Europe still in a favourable growth environment, where the "employment overhang" of agriculture could be absorbed by industry and services. This is clearly not the case in Hungary. In so far as the collapse of agriculture makes governmental action necessary to help the sector to a "soft landing" (if its later expansion must be ruled out), *agriculture becomes a major issue in overall stabilisation.*

(b) *The role of the government in the collapse of agriculture.* This is the topic of a very heated debate now in Hungary not without strong political elements.[3] One side is stressing that the government sacrificed Hungarian agriculture to its own political interests and disorganised the ownership patterns and organisation of the sector. The other side claims that the shrinking of agriculture was inevitable anyway due to the loss of traditional markets, and only the speed of the process could be subject to discussion. In any event, to define the role of the government in agricultural development, and in the future of Hungarian agriculture in general, is essential for designing any future stabilisation policy mix in Hungary.

(c) *Agricultural development versus stabilisation.* The challenge to the designers of an efficient macroeconomic stabilisation policy mix is linked to the big difference between the demand management toolkits to be used for industry and those for agriculture. Industry is considered a growth sector. On the other hand, agriculture could be much more a terrain for an "organised withdrawal" of factors of production at best.

This dichotomy points to *the desirability of a sectoral component of stabilisation policies* hitherto neglected in Hungary. It would be very difficult if not impossible to elaborate any feasible stabilisation package without respect to the strongly different growth paths of the major sectors of the economy. For example: a "stop-go" approach should have not only a *temporal* dimension, as

---

3) This can be linked to the parliamentary elections where the rural electorate is expected to play an important role.

in the UK economy of the 1970s ("stop" in year X, "go" in year X+1), but also a *spatial* dimension – applying "stop" tools for one sector and "go" measures for another.

The persistent budget deficit (which was forecast at over 8 per cent of Hungarian GDP in 1993)[4] could no doubt be interpreted as a demand-side factor, helping growth to take off (Erdös, p. 731). The size of the budget deficit is a key factor in negotiating with the IMF and therefore in getting better or worse conditions for external financing. The budget deficit generates an increasing "crowding out" mechanism, draining off part the of capital necessary for investment.

This "crowding out" mechanism has been made overtly legal in Hungary by the taxation legislation. Exemption from personal income tax for investment was possible, but until 1994 only for participation in closed-end investment funds and some strictly defined types of shares. Government bonds were added to this list from 1994. Since the capital of the investment funds is mostly if not exclusively invested in government bonds and treasury bills, most forms of tax-deductible investment help to finance the budget deficit.

The correct interpretation of the role of the budget deficit in stabilisation requires several qualifications. In the first place, a budget deficit expressed as a percentage of *measured GDP* has an approximately 30 per cent upward bias because of the large part of GDP not registered by official statistics. This does not mean, of course, that the current level or, more important, the growth trend of the budget deficit could be deemed satisfactory. It is still true, however, that a more efficient functioning of the fiscal system would be one of the most effective measures for pushing down the relative level of the budget deficit.

A second problem: some hidden macroeconomic reasons for the big budget deficit (or resources to finance it) deserve more attention. So-called conventional stabilisation policies or, more accurately, such stabilisation efforts in Eastern Europe, have aimed at reducing the excess demand (monetary overhang) usual in shortage economies. The Hungarian case was special in this respect, since

---

4) The final figure for the budget deficit of 1993 reached Ft 200 billion (approx. US$ 2 bn), the equivalent of 6 per cent of GDP. This was Ft 13 billion less than forecast in the Amendment of the 1993 Budget Act adopted by Parliament in the summer of 1993. The relatively low budget deficit can be mainly attributed to one factor of importance: ahead-of-schedule receipts of the state from major privatisation deals such as the Hungarian Telecommunications Company.

monetary overhang had already ceased to exist a few years before the beginning of the transition process. Moreover, Hungary practically did not have a shortage economy from the mid-1980s.

In spite of these differences between the Hungarian case and its counterparts in the region, the Hungarian state budget seems to have had *a persistent component of excess demand.* A quite convincing argument, indirectly confirming this statement, has been offered by a working paper recently published in Hungary. This rather path-breaking analysis (Obláth-Valentinyi 1993) shows that *seigniorage-type revenues* had an important role in financing a significant part of governmental expenditures. Although the authors do not use this argument, their analysis seems to imply that seigniorage has been used to finance certain governmental expenditures *not included in calculating the recorded budget deficit,* even in periods of negative GDP growth.

For example: seigniorage-type revenue of the consolidated "state household" (budget) represented 2.8 per cent of the Hungarian GDP in 1990 (against a consolidated budget deficit reaching 1.1 per cent of GDP); at 5.1 per cent of GDP, state revenue from seigniorage covered 85 per cent of the budget deficit in 1991, and at 2.6 per cent of the GDP it still covered 35 per cent of the budget deficit in 1992 (Obláth-Valentinyi, p. 63).

Of course, the results of the Obláth-Valentinyi analysis could be interpreted differently if excess demand created by the budget is understood differently. But it seems very plausible that the excess demand from the budget deficit can be understood as its excess over the deficit financing allowed by the complete use of "classical" tools of generating budgetary revenue (including tax income, the issuance of bonds and treasury bills and the legally fixed annual maximum of deficit-financing credit from the central bank).

A third point for a better understanding of the budget deficit as a major stabilisation problem is the following. The budget proposals of the government, as adopted in the Budget Acts each year, regularly overstate the revenue side of the budget while the forecasts of the expenditure side are normally quite accurate. These miscalculations have repeated themselves each year from 1990. They are probably due to serious misinterpretations by the government of the growth climate of the coming year. The excessively optimistic macroeconomic forecasts have resulted in a regular overestimate of the tax base of the subsequent year. Moreover, these forecasts have tended to neglect the changes in the debt service component of the budget deficit. In fact, the Hungarian state budget would still show a slight surplus if the annual debt service were not included.

In addition to these problems, the generous tax concessions for joint ventures, as well as for private firms created in 1990 and 1991 with exclusively Hungarian ownership, have eroded that part of the tax base which would have corresponded to the most dynamic part of the economy. Since the negative impact of most of these tax concessions will be phased out from 1994 on, the corporate tax base can be expected to increase somewhat.

The efficiency of the tax system is probably strongly compromised by excessively high marginal tax rates for personal incomes (40 per cent, to be increased to 44 per cent in 1994), the abnormally high "upper" VAT rate (25 per cent) and the also high linear corporate tax rate (40 per cent, decreased to 38 per cent in 1994). All these elements of the tax system might make the "opportunity cost" of tax evasion lower than they should be.

A successful stabilisation policy package would make *a complete overhaul of the tax system* unavoidable. This is very urgent because any further governmental effort to squeeze out more tax revenue from an economy still in recession would create the danger of a "slump (or recession) spiral" (Erdös, p. 741).

As a crucial element of the tax reform, the tax system should be made more transparent and less complicated with fewer tax brackets and exceptions. Tax incentives should be offered for savings (these are missing from the current system) and the politically motivated progressive character of the personal income tax system[5)] should be weakened or eliminated.

Current high VAT levels are also undesirable for their evidently and only restrictionary character. Furthermore, they could become a major fiscal roadblock for Hungarian integration in the EC owing to their quite high share (22 per cent in 1992) in budget revenues and the significantly higher VAT levels than in Western Europe.

The current fiscal policy of the Hungarian government is much criticised because it leads to a large deficit without the recovery of growth that could at least partly justify a big deficit.

---

5) This is, among other things, responsible for the high costs and long delays in the annual processing of personal income tax returns.

The fiscal policy choice for the next government is not simple: one option would be an even tighter fiscal policy with even less hope for the long-expected recovery of the economy and thus with a further shrinking of the tax base. This would obviously be a short-sighted choice, but its main alternative seems also quite risky. That would involve some relaxing of fiscal policy in order to speed up investment-related spending. The feasibility of this alternative depends on whether the Laffer-curve works for Hungary or not. We must trust that it does work. Otherwise the recession would last long beyond the transition period and the stability of the economy could be seriously compromised. This would be very bad news for other former socialist countries embarking upon the transition experience.

References

ECE (United Nations Economic Commission for Europe) (1993), *Economic Survey of Europe in 1992-1993,* Geneva-New York.

Erdös, T. (1993), "Válságelmélet és válságellenes gazdaságpolitika" (Crisis theory and anti-crisis economic policy), *Közgazdasági Szemle,* vol. XL, September, pp. 729-744.

Kádár, B. (1993), "Gazdaságpolitika válságban" (Economic policy in crisis), *Külgazdaság,* vol. XXXVII, August, pp. 4-13.

KSH (Central Statistical Office of Hungary) (1993), *Statisztikai Havi Közlemények* (Monthly Bulletin of Statistics), CSO, Budapest.

Obláth, G., and Valentinyi, Á. (1993), "Seigniorage, inflációs adó és államadósság: néhány makrogazdasági összefüggés magyarországi alkalmazása" (Seigniorage, inflation tax and state debt: the application of some macroeconomic tools of analysis for the case of the Hungarian economy), KOPINT-DATORG Múhelytanulmányok 12, Budapest, October.

Chapter 18

TRANSITION IN POLAND

Witold Trzeciakowski*)

18.1 The Polish economy in the early 1990s

Poland was among the first of the East European countries to embark upon a comprehensive policy of economic and political reform in 1989 under the impetus of the mass movement inspired by Solidarity as well as by vigorous support for radical change in intellectual circles. Poland was also the first to feel the full impact of economic collapse following the reforms, with industrial production and total national output falling in 1990 by more than in any other of the former socialist countries. But it was also in Poland that signs of economic recovery first began to show: in 1992, and probably in 1993, Poland was the only East European country to record statistically any increase in production, although only a very small one against the previous almost catastrophic declines. In 1992, too, Poland suffered a severe reduction in agricultural output, but that was due in part to an exceptional drought.

The growth of the private sector

In Poland, the private sector at end March 1993 accounted for 58.6 per cent of overall employment including agriculture and for 44.5 per cent excluding agriculture (see *Table 18.1).*

More than 2,000 state enterprises have been privatised (see *Table 18.2),* mainly small-scale etablishments in trade and service sectors. But in addition more than 1.6 million *new* private business have been set up and form the most dynamic element of the private economy.

---

*) Professor, Institute of Economics, Polish Academy of Sciences, Warsaw.

Table 18.1

Poland: Percentage share of private sector in main non-agricultural branches

		1992 Jan.-March	1993 Jan.-March
Industry	a) sales	25.8	32.0
	b) employment	36.3	43.0
Construction	a)	72.8	83.0
	b)	61.0	75.0
Transport	a)	34.9	42.0
	b)	20.0	27.0
Trade	b)	88.1	91.0

Source: Central Statistical Office; *Rzeczpospolita,* no. 4, 8 May 1993.

Table 18.2

Poland: Number of enterprises privatised, by privatisation process

	Total	1990	1991	1992 iQ	1992 IIQ	1992 IIIQ	1992 IVQ	1993 IQ
Non-agricultural state enterprises privatised	2149	130	1128	315	185	117	177	97
of which –								
by capital transformation[a)]	491	58	250	123	33	11	9	7
by liquidation	1658	72	878	192	152	106	168	90
Agricultural state enterprises liquidated	873	-	-	-	10	231	298	334

a) i.e. converted into limited companies with mainly private shareholdings.

Traditional direct sales of large enterprises to private owners (privatisation through capital transformation) encountered many difficulties connected with the huge costs of assessing the market value of enterprises sold in an environment lacking a capital market, as well as with the lack of capital (domestic and foreign).

Staff and management buy-outs in the wake of what is called "privatisation through liquidation" has been widespread in Poland.

A quantitative breakthrough in privatisation of large state-owned enterprises is expected under the programme of so-called mass privatisation controlled by National Investment Funds. The long awaited act was finally accepted in 1993 by the Polish parliament just before its dissolution. It envisages the immediate restructuring of state enterprises into corporations whose shares are totally owned in the first place by the state. These enterprises are intended to be managed by specialists of the Investment Funds (including specialists hired from foreign countries). These National Investment Funds will take over around 600 state enterprises. 27 million adult Poles will be entitled to buy "participation certificates" for a symbolic sum (10 per cent of monthly salary). One third of the shares in some of these enterprises will provide for old-age and disability pensioners, and compensation to government sector employees (whose salaries were not indexed). These "participation certificates" will be later on exchanged for shares – after restructuring of the enterprises. After two years of functioning everybody will know better what he buys. The distribution of property rights will be split as follows:

25 per cent: shares owned by the state,
15 per cent: of shares distributed among the employees,
27 per cent: of shares distributed among the remaining National Investment Funds,
33 per cent: of shares of 200 enterprises will support old-age and disability pensioners and, partly, compensation to government sector employees claiming lack of adequate indexation of wages,
33 per cent: shares of 600 enterprises will be distributed to adult Polish citizens. Additionally, some of the stock will be kept to finance expenditures on restitution of the property of expropriated former owners.

Various conventional and non-conventional schemes of privatisation are being tried in other East European countries: coupon-schemes, privatisation bank-accounts; they are still at an experimental stage. (See *Hunya* (Ch. 11) in this volume, reviewing methods and progress of privatisation in individual East European countries.) It remains to be seen, whether they will result in improvements in the behaviour of the managements and in efficiency.

Foreign trade and the balance of payments

According to the statistics of the National Bank of Poland, foreign currency earnings from exports in 1992 amounted to $ 14.0 bn and import expenditures to $ 13.5 bn, yielding a surplus of $ 0.5 bn. However, the situation deteriorated in the first quarter of 1993 (see *Table 18.3*).

Table 18.3

Poland: balance of payments

$ million

	I/1992	**I/1993**
Current account	+133	-680
Foreign trade balance	+385	-370
Services	+75	-2
Capital account	+21	+24
Interest due	-1375	-1487
Transfers	+1027	+1155

The deficit of the current account ($ -680 mn) is large by comparison with the $ 133 mn surplus in the first quarter of 1992. On the other hand, it is to be stressed, the deficits declined in the consecutive months: January – $ 269 mn, February – $ 76 mn, March – $ 25 mn. Optimists draw attention to the fact that the foreign currency reserve has been maintained (at the level of three months imports). They conclude that there is no need to devalue the zloty above the normal pegging rate (attached to the rate of inflation of producers' prices). Pessimists warn that the deficit may grow, because of the increase of agricultural prices, the introduction of VAT and import duties.

The recent growth of production – if maintained – will result in an increase of imports. To maintain the balance of trade in equilibrium requires an adequate export expansion; hence depreciation of the zloty may be unavoidable. What really matters is improved access to Western markets for Polish exports.

Indebtedness at the end of January 1993 in convertible currencies amounted to $ 47.7 bn, two-thirds of it with the Paris Club countries. In accordance with the agreement reached a 50 per cent reduction of indebtedness is envisaged: in the first stage till the end of March 1994 a reduction by 30 per cent, in the second stage, after the fulfilment of a three year programme agreed upon with the IMF, further reduction by 20 per cent. Negotiations with the London Club continue for a reduction of debt similar to that with the Paris Club. Poland's debt in transferable roubles is TR 4.8 bn and in $ 1.8 bn; Russia's debt to Poland in transferable roubles is 7 billion. Recently the Poles proposed the "zero" option settlement.

Inflation, stabilisation and unemployment

Shortages of goods – typical of the communist economy – have vanished. Equilibrium has been achieved despite considerably reduced spending on goods and services.

Increased propensity to save proved possible even under two-digit inflation. There was a strong increase in private deposits (even long-term), as a result of a policy of a real positive interest rate and of zloty savings being more attractive than foreign currency deposits. These savings were mostly intended for spending on consumption, and the government is trying to encourage their redirection to investments. These attempts have limited chances of success so long as the interest rate must be set at the present level, determined by the actual rate of inflation.

Economic decision-makers – facing the danger of hyperinflation – concentrated their attention on the fight with inflation as their highest priority. Together with the liberalisation of prices, the introduction of internal convertibility of the zloty, the elimination of most subsidies, and the liquidation of the budget deficit, the government imposed a tight monetary policy, a credit squeeze, a positive real rate of interest, a highly progressive tax on wage increases and a temporarily fixed exchange rate. All these drastic stabilisation measures resulted in the following rates of inflation (average annual percentage change of consumer prices against preceding year):

1990: 586	1992: 43
1991: 70	1993: 35 (prov.)

Hence the fight with hyperinflation was successful; however, the actual rate of inflation – in Western European terms – is still too high.

The success of stabilisation policy depends to a large extent on the state budget. Tough monetary policies imposed in 1990 connected with drastic cuts in subsidies for producers resulted in a small surplus on the 1990 budget.

However, tight monetary policy constrained overall demand a deep and long recession. The liberalisation of prices ("corre a still highly monopolised economy resulted in accumulatic state-owned enterprises. But the cumulated reserves melted rap fall in production, leading to a deterioration of rentability and profitability Table 18.4).

Table 18.4

Poland: profits of enterprises

		Rentability[a)]	Profitability[b)]
1991	December	4.8	-13
1992	Jan.-Feb.	2.9	..
1992	Jan.-Dec.	2.1	..
1993	Jan.-Feb.	3.5	-1
	public sector	4.5	-1
	private sector	1.1	0

a) Rentability: ratio of gross profit to overall costs. - b) Profitability: ratio of net profit to 1000 zloty of income.

The budget for 1993 provides for a deficit of Zl 81 trillion (5 per cent of GDP) on a total expenditure of Zl 511 trillion. The newly introduced VAT system functions from July 1993. The pegging rate of the US$ is supposed to end in December 1993 at Zl 19,000. The expected rate of interest is 28.7 per cent.

At the end of March 1993 there were 2.6 million registered unemployed (14. per cent of the total labour force), expected to reach 3 million (around 16 per cent of the labour force) by the year-end. There are regions heavily affected, where unemployment surpasses 20 to 25 per cent, and such regions become socially explosive. For Poland these are alarming figures. The system of safety nets requires restructuring. Out of the total Social Safety Fund 88 per cent was devoted to unemployment benefits; hence there remained very small funds for active forms of fighting unemployment: creating new jobs, re-training in new occupations, public works, credits for small entrepreneurs. Developing the ability to target transfer payments better to the poor must be a vital component of efforts to limit the growth of poverty. In short, unemployment has become the most dangerous political and social issue in Poland.

The expansion of direct foreign investment in Poland is crucial for the enforcement of the privatisation processes and for the further development of the economy. By mid-1991 a new law on joint ventures had been passed by parliament. The rules for foreign investors have been liberalised. Foreigners are invited to buy shares in Polish firms (including 100 per cent ownership). Full transmittal of profits was granted with the convertibility of the zloty. In 1989-1992, more than 10,000 joint ventures were registered; several transnational corporations bought shares of privatised enterprises; foreign banks and foreign insurance companies settled in Poland.

The inflow of foreign private capital to Poland is assessed at $ 2 bn; the total engagement is assessed at $ 4 bn.

These figures fall short of our expectations.

18.2 Problems of transformation – goals and strategies

Setting Poland's basic goals

Any political-social and economic transformation policy – if it is to succeed – must start with a clear formulation of its basic goals. "Solidarity", as an opposition movement, elaborated its strategy in a completely different political situation; hence the first democratic Solidarity-led government could not formulate its policy on the basis of former programmes which had been elaborated in a political environment dominated internally and externally by communist regimes. The speed of change in the political set-up surpassed the most revolutionary expectations. As a result, the opposition was unprepared to take over the political power and had to improvise its strategy and tactics.

"What are our basic goals?" – the answer to this questions seemed to be simple: *democracy – market economy – integration with the European Communities.* However, in reality these supposedly simple answers are enmeshed in complex problems:

- There are differing views as to the kind of democracy we want,
- What kind of market economy are we aiming at?
- To what extent is our political and economic independence limited by the integration at which we are aiming?
- What social cost is Polish society ready to accept in order to transform the communist economy into a market economy and to fulfil the requirements for admission to the European Union?

Difficult decisions on these issues should be clearly formulated from the start of the transition and should get the full support of the parliamentary majority. As experience shows, reaching consensus in these matters is not easy in practice, and takes much more time than initially expected

The choice of strategy

The strategic choices must take into account:

- that there is no ready-made theory of transition from communism to a capitalist market economy; the pragmatic approach of learning from our own experience, and from the experience of others, seems to be the best indeed the only feasible approach;
- that we have to deal with a society that is unconsciously indoctrinated by the communist mentality: a society that disapproves of open unemployment, but tolerates disguised unemployment, that accepts the concept of justice as tantamount to equality in distribution of wealth. Forty five years of communist indoctrination cannot be erased at once; in other words, the government must spend a great deal of effort in elaborating a conscious information policy at explaining the rationale for political, social and economic decisions. None of the previous "Solidarity"-led governments seemed to be convinced about the importance of such a policy;
- that we inherited a collapsed economy with huge external and internal debt, worn-out productive capacities, a devastated natural environment; all this means that there are no easy economic improvements in sight, and that those politicians who promise quick successes are irresponsible demagogues;
- that we are facing a disintegrated COMECON market and painful constraints in our access to Western markets; hence we must be aware that we are living in a protectionist world, where free access to foreign markets is – to a large extent – an illusion.

The policy of the consecutive governments in the 1990s was successfully concentrated on stabilisation, curbing inflation and maintaining the convertibility of the zloty. On the other hand, we lacked a strategy for development, a programme for its sequential transformation and progress in the carrying-out of restructuring. Too many decisions were left to be solved by the "invisible hand of the market".

The transformation of a post-communist economy starts while there is no market infrastructure, i.e. in systemic vacuum. Not yet existing market forces were believed to lead automatically to their full and quick development. It is true, that under conditions of freedom of decision-making human relations would lead to a "normal" market. However, two principal elements were lacking, namely: the time needed to remove obstacles on the road to transformation, and capital. The time required to build a fully fledged market economy was historically measured in decades rather than in single years. But in Poland capital was lacking and there was no net inflow of capital from abroad; consequently, expectations that the stabilisation policy would automatically result in structural adjustment processes, characteristic of the "normal" capitalist economy, proved unrealistic.

Shock or evolution?

The often raised question whether the "shock therapy" should be applied or rather the "evolutionary approach" has no unequivocal answer. Both methods should be applied, but in different spheres of economic activities. Activities linked with the policy of stabilisation could be performed within a shock therapy, and brought in practice positive results in the form of curbing hyperinflation, introducing internal convertibility of the zloty and in eliminating shortages of goods.

However, the remaining activities connected with restructuring required the creation of market infrastructure institutions, the transformation of the banking system and development of the capital market, the privatisation processes and commercialisation of state enterprises, as well as the initiation of investments, proved unsuitable for the shock therapy.

The weaknesses of the shock approach become evident in the sphere of demonopolisation and in opening of the Polish economy:

- demonopolisation processes require time and capital; they constrain privatisation, as privatisation of monopolies resolves nothing;
- the opening of our economy in 1990/91 proved to be excessive, as competitive imports seized the Polish market, causing a drastic recession, a drop in revenues of state firms and falling revenues of the state budget. The error lay not in the policy of opening the market intself, but in the pace of the shock process (domestic producers had no time to prepare themselves for the competitive struggle). At the same time, the Polish

market was opened without first securing equivalent access to the EC markets.

Privatisation of large enterprises and role of the state

There is a general consensus that privatisation is the really crucial factor determining in the long run the stability of democracy and the rise in efficiency. However it creates a very sensitive political problem. The workers and trade unions in large state-owned enterprises were expecting implementation of the initial programmes of Solidarity, based on the selfgovernment principle. In order to get their consent to privatisation they had to be given 10 to 15 per cent share of the ownership. Privatisation implemented according to traditional Western rules appeared extremely expensive and slow. In view of the magnitude of our task the use of this traditional method would take a few decades.

Attempts at mass-distribution of property rights, intended to give dynamism to privatisation and to cheapen it, are still in the experimental stage and arouse a number of questions and fears with regard to effective results. Still, we are searching for methods that would enable us to privatise as much and as quickly as possible.

Similar political problems arise with the restitution of property rights of former owners. No one can question their rights, but there are complicated legal cases which block the restitution of property in its physical form; on the other hand, there are no resources in the state budget to pay the financial indemnities that could compensate the losses incurred. After four years of parliamentary discussions the claims of former owners are not settled and the restitution issue blocks privatisation.

An illusory belief in the reality of shock therapy for privatisation has caused a systemic neglect of state enterprises: the cure of their inefficiency (commercialisation in the fashion of Western state-controlled firms) was not worth the money, as quick privatisation was expected.

The theory of constructive destruction has been strongly advocated by some influential advisers. The theory may appeal to countries disposing of large reserves of capital investments. The FRG's financing of huge investments in the former GDR illustrates the point. However, for all the remaining post-communist countries the theory is not applicable. Production can be stopped, but only within certain limits. Massive bankruptcies can endanger the functioning of the entire economy. It is equally dangerous to tolerate unemployment surpassing socially acceptable limits. The deeper and quicker the structural changes, the more serious the problems. Generally speaking the pace of bankruptcies has to be correlated with the volume of investments (domestic and foreign) creating new enterprises. Similarly the level of unemployment should be synchronised with development policies creating new jobs. The state cannot allow the market to settle these processes automatically. Therefore implementation of the theory of constructive destruction has to be centrally steered if it is not to cause social outbursts.

The active role of the state, as well as the idea of industrial policy, was charged with all the vices of communist directive planning – hence it was seen as anathema to any kind of transition towards a market economy. Some influential economists preached that: "The best industrial policy for Poland is to have no policy at all." They overlooked the fact that industrial policies form an integral part of the set of policy instruments used by leading Western economies, as well as the fact that these policies are especially important for developing countries which embark upon successful catching-up.

In the West, the argument for industrial policies is based on what the market cannot achieve because of externalities, economies of scale, information constraints or capital market imperfections; however, in a post-communist economy the gradually emerging market institutions are still weak and the rules of the "normal" market mechanism are not yet strong enough to enforce the adjustment processes in enterprises. In such circumstances the question is not whether the state should or should not intervene, but rather what kind of state intervention is able to increase the response rate of agents (firms, households, workers) to a newly emerging market environment and equip them with "capabilities" that allow them to respond flexibly to market signals (Landesmann 1993).

State intervention is especially needed if there are fundamental changes in the direction of trade, heavy external indebtedness and drastic internal imbalances. Hence the function of industrial policy in the new context is to make sure that the state becomes sensitive towards operating in an evolving market environment and develops policies designed to assist the development of a competitive market economy (Landesmann 1993). There is no modern state in which the government can be relieved from responsibility for the development of the economy.

The fight against inflation is as important as the fight against recession. The Polish democratic governments concentrated their attention on the stabilisation programme, insufficient attention being paid to the fight against recession.

Adjustment processes were supposed to be taken care of exclusively by the mechanism of the market. Since the "invisible" hand of the market did not appear in a visible way, the government had to change its attitude towards industrial and agricultural policy. The state must also take the responsibility for the regional problems caused by mass-unemployment.

Equally, only the government can take responsibility for incomes policies, playing the role of a mediator between employers and employees. The situation looks normal in the private sector, but in the still dominant state sector the situation resembles the past, where the government is forced to play the role of owner in bargaining with the trade unions. This direct involvement at the micro level should disappear as soon as possible.

On the other hand the state must be responsible for macro policies in the social sphere, in the overall level of employment, investments, etc. The state must be also responsible for investments in infrastructure and in the protection of the environment.

The state must be responsible, too, for training and education, R & D activities and technology dissemination policies. Interaction between the economic reform and education, which supports such processes, is evident. Though highly skilled workers are seen as the main comparative advantage of the Polish economy, the utilisation of this competitive potential is hampered by the lack of complementary skills in management, advertising, accounting, and the like.

The state should support the setting up of financial institutions promoting small and medium-sized enterprises with venture capital and assist in the emergence of financial markets. In this situation there is strong economic justification for the government to step in and provide credit insurance (Svejnar 1991). The government should encourage the creation of banks holding equity and performing part of the control over enterprises, solving the problem of accumulated bad loans and facilitating restructuring.

Export orientation is a fundamental condition for a successful implementation of catching-up processes. In Poland the very heavy burden of indebtedness and the permanent shortage of hard currency make dynamic export expansion the basic element in the overall strategy of development. Successful export performance will result also in upgrading quality standards and thus in recapturing the markets invaded by foreign expansion in recent years in a naive – too quick and one sided – opening of the Polish market.

The lack of a consistent restructuring policy for adjusting the pattern of industrial and agricultural development to the long-term requirements of foreign markets is still one of the weakest points in the overall strategy. The policy of integration with the European Union should directly and immediately affect the economic strategy of growth and foreign economic policy; unfortunately in spite of all the achievements in implementing the stabilisation programme, our results in restructuring policy are limited; there are no essential improvements in adjusting the structure of our exports to the requirements of the international division of labour: in 1992 the value of per capita exports was $ 365 and of imports $ 338, a very slight improvement in comparison to 1989. The shares of Polish exports and imports in total world exports and imports were unchanged at 0.36 per cent and 0.40 per cent respectively. The abrupt fall of industrial production requires radical changes in the whole economy; the dominance of extractive industry and of heavy, especially military, production must be eliminated; huge investments must be financed in order to adjust to Western competition.

The magnitude of the needs for funds are characterised by the strategy of the FRG devoting around $ 100 bn a year to modernise the former GDR. Poland cannot mobilise such resources; hence it must select its priorities carefully and elaborate a cautious trade policy introducing competition from abroad, but at the same time allowing sufficient time for domestic producers to adjust to foreign competition with a defined time horizon.

Basic dilemmas: reconciling stabilisation, growth and tolerable unemployment

One must frankly admit that neither theory nor practical experience allow satisfactory answers to these basic questions. By satisfactory answers I mean firm rules setting out procedures for the transformation from stabilisation through restructuring to economic growth with unemployment within tolerable limits. The restrictive policies of stabilisation, aimed at improving the balance of trade and at lowering the rate of inflation, in certain conditions hinder supply adjustments in enterprises; on the other hand, stimulative policies, aimed at promoting growth of production, in an environment dominated by monopolies, lead to rising inflation, with all its destabilising effects.

There was no doubt that transition from a communist to a market economy must involve high political, social and economic costs; but these costs proved to be much higher than initially expected. Restructuring of the ownership system, together with restructuring the branch composition of the economy so as to make it compatible with the requirements of the domestic and foreign market, requires huge capital outlays and takes time.

If democracy is to be maintained the society must be informed about the expected costs of the change of system, and must accept the main directions of the reforms and the resulting consequences. In the light of experience of the years 1989-1993 we must admit, that in spite of unquestionable achievements, many mistakes have been committed.

- Politically, the successive change of governments proves that none of them was able to gain lasting support of the majority of the population for the reforms implemented. Without political consensus for a sustained transition strategy the democratic system is unstable.
- Socially: the rising costs of the reforms and their impact on various social strata were not approved by the population, creating the danger of social eruption.
- Economically, divergences arose about the extent of the necessary demand reduction, the choice of policy instruments for compressing demand, the methods for stimulation of growth, the methods of privatisation and the consistent strategy of fighting unemployment.

Conventional stabilisation assumes that the restriction on credit affects basically the level of prices but not of production. However, recent experience of transition, not only in Poland but also in other post-communist countries, shows how the fall in production and employment during the stabilisation period turned out to be much deeper than initially expected.

Theoretically, there may occur two extreme cases: that of pure quantity adjustment, and that of pure price adjustment. In practice we have a combination of the two in varying proportions. The supporters of conventional stabilisation rightly point to the fact that micro-incentives operating in still dominant state-owned enterprises are inconsistent with the profit maximisation criterion. Their preference function is the maximisation of wages; on the other hand, as monopolists they are interested in maximisation of prices. Hence, the expansionary policies of increasing budgetary deficits would lead to the rise of inflation. This reasoning was correct in the very initial stage of the reform. However, with the growing share of the private sector in overall output, the growth of commercialised state enterprises and the opening of our economy to foreign imports both arguments lost their exclusive validity. The very imperfect market was changed into a more normal buyers' market, where the level of production tends to be increasingly demand-determined. Which pattern of adjustment prevails in reality depends on factors determining prices, as well as on the level of capacity utilisation: quantity adjustments would prevail at low capacity utilisation and price adjustments if the capacity utilisation is high.

In the light of the above arguments the general assumption by the supporters of conventional stabilisation that a balanced budget is the basis of a "sound" fiscal policy "under all circumstances" seems to deprive the government of an important policy instrument for fighting recession. Of course, the budget deficit should not be used for stimulating demand in the long run. The policy of stimulating investment and reaching a trade surplus seems to play a crucial role in stimulating growth. However, these policies are much less under direct control of the government by comparison with budget policy. Conventional stabilisation policy assumes that quick privatisation is the best way to fight recession. However, privatisation does not necessarily improve overall employment. Hence the improvement in efficiency may coexist with a further deterioration of unemployment. If the rise of efficiency is accompanied by growth of unemployment, the decision-makers must take into account not only the economic, but also the socio-political criteria. The latest electoral campaign shows that even the most liberal-rightist parties had to include in their programme a promise to fight unemployment in order to get the support of the voters.

Summing up: economic reforms are inseparably linked with political and social criteria. Programmes which ignore the social goals of sustainable growth and unemployment within a socially acceptable limit have no chance of winning social support.

In order to reach consensus on important policy issues the government of Hanna Suchocka proposed a new mechanism called "The pact on enterprises". This is an agreement between the government and the main social groups: the trade unions and the entrepreneurs. New procedures for reaching compromises on the choice of privatisation paths were agreed. The pact envisages several concessions to the workers such as:

- the distribution of a proportion of shares free of charge to the workers employed in the enterprise to be privatised,
- the right of the workers to select the privatisation path,
- the right of representatives of the workers to participate in the Board of the privatised enterprises,
- more chances of a reduction or liquidation of the bad debts inherited from the past,
- removal of the highly progressive tax on wages and of the tax on fixed assets.

This new form of negotiation in political and social conflicts between all the interested parties makes it possible to speed up formal procedures and creates a better climate for finding workable compromises. The pact awaits confirmation by the new parliament elected in September 1993.

Political stabilisation

The first and the most important condition for the implementation of economic reforms is political stabilisation in the democratically ruled country. There is no doubt that the past four years of transition can be assessed as a period of unquestionable rule of democracy. However, the frequent changes of governments have little in common with political stability.

The overall political support for the market-oriented reforms inaugurated by Tadeusz Mazowiecki's government was eroded with the emerging conflicts among the many split parties, which were divided over the distribution of transition costs, the speed of the transition processes and the general goals of the reform. The unfortunate electoral procedure (proportional representation) favoured small parties, and offered no chance of a majority government enjoying strong and lasting support in the parliament and capable of implementing structural reforms.

The modified electoral procedure for the September 1993 elections created a better chance of political stability.[1] The fate of further economic reform depends upon the chances of the government maintaining its political base in parliament.

Hence progress in the general direction of economic reform (with possible changes in the pace and substance of transition processes) will depend upon the willingness and ability of reliable parties to reach compromise solutions that could allow the smooth functioning of a coalition government.

Impact of changes in external environment

The actual geo-political environment of Poland has improved markedly. Instead of facing two mighty and unfriendly neighbours we now have:

- in the West: a democratic Federal Republic of Germany, a member of the European Union,
- in the East: the successors of the disintegrating Soviet Union: the republics of Belarus, Ukraine and Russia,
- in the North: Lithuania,
- in the South: the Czech Republic and Slovakia.

Poland, unlike other post-communist countries, has no minority problems. Hence, never in contemporary history Poland had such a favourable geo-political situation.

There are also positive developments in our relations with the West:

- The European Union concluded with Poland (also with Hungary and the former Czechoslovak Republic) an Association Agreement, with the prospect of becoming a full member within the decade.
- We have obtained a $ 1 bn Stabilisation Fund, enabling us to regain the internal convertibility of the zloty.
- We are financially supported by the IMF, the World Bank and the EBRD.

---

1) The new voting regulation excluded small parties which were not able to reach a threshold of 5 per cent of overall votes (or 8 per cent threshold for political coalitions). The results of the September 1993 elections show that the new regulation favoured the large coalition of the left, stabilised the centre (Democratic Union), but eliminated totally the many smaller rightist parties, which – if united – would reach 20 to 30 per cent of the seats in the parliament.

- We have obtained an agreement with the Paris Club on a 50 per cent reduction of our convertible currency debt.
- Poland – among others – obtained assistance from the G-24 within the PHARE programme, as well as within bilateral agreements.

In spite of these very positive short-term developments, there is a fundamental weakness in relations between the West and the post-communist countries: the lack of a long-term active strategy of assistance to transition.

The collapse of the Soviet system threatens to become a defeat for the Western world, as long as the West fails to integrate the post-communist countries into the free world. Instead of being integrated, it is disintegrating. Indeed, it is highly probable that what used to be the Soviet Union may become a bottomless black hole presenting a real danger for Western civilisation.

The very existence of Europe as an open society is now endangered both by the need to close the borders to the outside and by what is happening inside. The reunification of Germany and the breakdown in the Exchange Rate Mechanism have upset the delicate balance that keeps every nation a minority within the European Union and has raised the spectre of German domination.

In the Soviet Union, the key fact is economic disintegration. The Caucasus and some of the Asian republics are comparable with Yugoslavia. In the heartland of the former Soviet Union – Russia and Ukraine – the elements of conflicts are in place: 25 million Russians living outside the borders of Russia, many unsettled economic issues between the two countries, conflicts with the Baltic republics, etc.

Instability in the region will have dangerous repercussions far beyond the region. Events in Bosnia have aroused Islamic passions in Indonesia, and armaments are flowing freely from the former Soviet Union.[2)]

In these circumstances one cannot exclude the possibility of general unrest in the vicinity of the former Soviet Union, i.e. in central Europe. This explains why post-communist countries want to be integrated with Western Europe: the main reason is national security.

---

2) Soros, G. (1992), "Nationalist Dictatorship Versus Open Society", lecture at Harvard Club of New York, 18 November.

18.3 Western aid and Western interests

Total assistance from Western countries and multilateral financial institutions on a per capita basis committed in 1990-1991 represents \$ 795 for Hungary, \$ 545 for Poland including debt restructuring (excluding debt restructuring \$ 305) and \$ 310 for Czechoslovakia. Assuming an optimistic disbursement rate of 20 per cent, the per capita figures given above represent some \$ 160 for Hungary, \$ 110 for Poland (and excluding debt restructuring \$ 60) and \$ 60 for CSFR. The total share of grants assistance in overall assistance is around 14 per cent.

In 1990-1993 the PHARE programme (grants) committed to Poland amounted to ECU 805 mn. In the middle of 1993 only the funds committed for 1990 were fully absorbed (disbursed); of funds committed for 1991 only half were absorbed. The remaining funds committed for 1992 and 1993 were distributed at a very small disbursement rate.[3)]

In terms of net transfer of resources, in 1990 there was a net outflow of financial resources from Eastern Europe; the withdrawal of funds by commercial banks and large debt servicing by Poland and Hungary more than offset the inflow of new funds. In 1991 there was a net inflow of \$ 4.1 bn, with only Poland continuing to have a net outflow.[4)]

The fundamental question is not only how much will be spent on assistance, but also what are the basic goals of assistance, as seen by donors and by recipients. These goals must, first of all, serve the long-term interests of the donor countries (political and economic interests). At the same time the goals must be accepted and supported by the recipient countries.

Here are the basic goals as listed in the literature[5)], which seem to fulfil the condition of being accepted by both parties:

---

3) Based on: *Moving Beyond Assistance* (1992), Institute for East-West Studies, New York, and "PHARE podzielony" (1993), *Gazeta wyborcza,* no. 169, 22 July.

4) Western official financial aid for the countries of Eastern Europe is, so far, considerably smaller than the sums implied either in the Marshall Plan equivalent (\$ 17.7 bn a year) or in the suggestion of the President of the Commission of the European Communities to provide a level of support equivalent to that given by the Community to its own depressed regions (\$ 23 bn a year) (United Nations Economic and Social Council (1992), E/1992/45, 6 May).

5) *Moving Beyond Assistance,* op. cit.

- the future prosperity and security of East and West must be interdependent; hence the creation of a politically stable and economically unified Europe is a basic goal for donors and recipients,
- effective economic reform will underpin pluralist democracy and human rights, and will also act as a form of security expenditure in curbing massive migration and in helping to achieve stability,
- the West should also seek to ensure that the cold war division in Europe between East and West is not replaced by a new destabilising division between rich and poor,
- the main long-term aim of Western assistance is to enable the recipients to help themselves to build viable civil societies and self-sustaining market economies,
- the primary goal is to secure the continuity of transition,
- as domestic and foreign private investment for the long term will be the engine for reconstruction, Western assistance should pave the way for private investment.

Western assistance to Eastern Europe includes stabilisation funds, balance of payments support, debt management, the provision of market access, private source funding on a non-commercial basis and technical and non-economic assistance.

Having in mind this list of main goals, let us confront the theory with the reality of assistance in the light of Western interests.

Short-term Western interests

In the period 1988-1990 the dominant interests of the West centred on the weakening of the communist threat. Hence strong support was granted to the political fight for the respect of human rights, the democratic rights of independent trade unions and the weakening of the economic monopoly of the communist party and government. The support for the Solidarity movement illustrates the point.

However, with the beginning of the fall of the Soviet empire, the situation has changed: the revolutionary activities were accepted very warmly by the West, as with the disappearance of confrontation huge military expenditures could be eliminated; in spite of these savings the readiness of the West to share the burdens of adjustment in the East weakened. The EC made it clear, that only sufficiently developed and fully-fledged market economies have a chance of admission to the EC as members.

Greece, Portugal and Spain, admitted in the times of bloc confrontation, were granted financial subsidies. The Association Agreements of the Visegrád countries with the EC do not contain such privileges.

After the Maastricht agreements, arguments were raised that "deepening" of EC integration must be given priority over its "enlargement". Such an approach means that discrepancies between the wealthy West and the poor East will never disappear.

Politically, the post-communist region is characterised by national conflicts, minority problems and social tension; hence the reluctance of the West to become involved in the maintenance of stability in the whole area.

Besides these political reasons for minimal commitment, there are also economic considerations. Post-communist countries are still a negligible partner for the EC. Trade with the EC of the former CMEA 7 members amounted in 1990 to less than 4 per cent of total EC trade. The region is also a potential threat to the agricultural policies of Western Europe. The endangered agricultural and industrial producers of the EC protested against the elimination of administrative restrictions on Western imports in the "sensitive" commodities.

Finally, there are also budgetary considerations. The annual cost of German reunification varies between \$ 100 bn and 160 bn a year, whereas the total budget of the EC is less than ECU 60 bn. In these circumstances there are not sufficient financial means for the "enlargement" of the Community.

Summing up, the logic of the reasoning is based on the following arguments:

- the Eastern threat is gone with the collapse of the Soviet empire,
- in the light of Western internal problems with budgetary deficits, recession and unemployment one can understand the requirements:
  - that short-term assistance be based on commercial criteria and that the grant element in assistance be minimised,
  - that administrative restrictions of free access to western markets be preserved in order to protect the Western producers,
  - that any long-term commitments for financial assistance should be avoided.

In these circumstances there is no need to envisage a new grand design of aid of the type of the Marshall programme with its 88 per cent grant element and with its partner-relationship between the donor and recipients. On the contrary, the IMF suspended disbursement of its three-year $ 1.67 bn Extended Financing Facility because of the Polish government's failure to comply with the financial target by allowing its budget deficit to exceed 3 per cent of GDP. Poland faced the formidable task of stabilisation and restructuring with no net inward transfer of real resources. A policy of conditionality that focuses attention solely on austerity measures, without considering the crucial role of investment for economic development, petrifies recessionary tendencies.

One may wonder whether the reasoning based on these short-term criteria is compatible with the basic goals discussed above, and whether it coincides with the long-term interests of the West.

Longer-term Western interests

First, there is the problem of political stability in Europe.

- The Yugoslav example illustrates the weakness of the non-commitment policy. In the long run Europe cannot be divided into the rich and the poor parts. In such a divided Europe massive economic migration would be inevitable; these migrations would have obvious destabilising effects on Western democracies.
- Equally, Europe cannot tolerate autocratic governments preaching local wars, concentration camps and mass murders resulting in new waves of political migrations.
- Moreover, Europe cannot be happy with the functioning of Chernobyl-type atomic technologies in the centre of the European continent, since environment is indivisible.

Second, in spite of the actually low share of EC trade with Eastern European countries, trade has turned from East to West. Recently published estimates[6] show that – with successful economic reforms – imports of East European economies could have a more than five-fold increase between 1991 and 2010, the share of EC being around $ 100 bn in 2010 at 1991 prices. That is the equivalent in size of the US market. The whole post-communist market with 380 million population can be looked upon as a potential challenge for

---

6) Rollo, Jim, and Stern, John (1992), "Growth and Trade Prospects for Central and Eastern Europe", *The World Economy,* October.

Western business in the long term. However, as long as Western markets are partly inaccessible to Eastern exporters ("sensitive" commodities), such an expansion of trade is impossible.

The crux of the problem is, how can the East European countries obtain foreign exchange sufficient to modernise their economies and service their debts? Since there is very limited readiness to increase aid flows from the West, there remain two possible solutions: (a) expansion of private investment, and (b) export-led growth. Both require stable and free access to Western markets.

However, the Association Agreements, that should liberalise trade and stabilise the conditions of free access, do not fulfil these demands. Such EC actions restrict trade: some crucial products preserve significant protection through non-tariff barriers; safeguard clauses, anti-dumping provisions and rules of origin in the Agreements are deterrents to both future trade and investment. These restrictive measures can be applied to each large exporter. Such behaviour discourages also potential foreign investors. Without real trade liberalisation, without abolition of commodity clauses and local content requirements, the chances for a successful transition and future integration are small.

Third, it is essential that the IMF policies of conditionality be based on long-term development criteria which are as important as short-term stabilisation criteria connected with the fight against inflation. A policy of boosting investment and exports might be the right solution for promoting long-term economic development, but would require a revision of the IMF rules of conditionality.

Fourth, no one can doubt the seriousness of the efforts of the Visegrád countries to transform their political and economic systems. However, these countries are facing much bigger difficulties than initially expected. The fate of the reforms is endangered by social tensions caused by the drastic recession, rising unemployment and inadequate social safety nets. They are on the border between success and failure. They need assistance with a longer time horizon. The increasing social costs of economic transformation threaten the democratisation process; there is an urgent need to find new ways to support economic revitalisation of these countries; otherwise extreme forces on the right or on the left will gain power.

What could be done?

(a) Maybe within the general available funds for long-term assistance, Western donors could provide a higher share of non-reimbursable grants, as opposed to loans on purely commercial terms. Commercial loans are exacerbating the indebtedness problems of the recipient countries, whereas a larger proportion of grants would result in increasing the absorption of foreign capital. The functioning of such grants could be based on the model of the EC Regional Development Funds, co-financing private investment in regions heavily affected by high unemployment. This would ease the social tensions of transition and minimise security risks throughout Europe.
(b) The effectiveness of assistance is not simply a question of the magnitude of resources poured into the country, but of their deployment as well. A long-term commitment to the support of transition is decisive. Experience gained during the early 1990s proves that transition cannot be measured in months, or years, but in decades. Hence the crucial importance of working out a long-term strategy of assistance for both the donors and the recipients.
(c) Next, there is the problem of effective coordination of assistance.There are more than thirty countries and international institutions involved in support of transition. Each has its own preferences and priorities. As a result there is the danger of duplication of efforts or inefficient use of funds.
(d) The success of assistance depends also upon an active participation of the recipients, who should be engaged in planning and coordination of assistance as partners sharing responsibility.

It would be a fatal mistake to revive the ghost of Yalta by re-building the Russian domination of the whole region of the former Soviet empire. Following Machiavelli's warning: "It would be worse than a crime – it would be a mistake."

The integration of post-communist countries into the free world requires a long-term strategy of Western cooperation with countries in transition. This strategy is still lacking. As long as this is the case, smaller countries of Eastern Europe feel highly insecure. Let me conclude with a quotation from Jim Rollo[7]: "The more we help Eastern Europe improve its economic performance – the more we help ourselves."

---

7) Jim Rollo, Director of The Royal Institute of International Affairs, in *International Herald Tribune,* 23 June 1993.

Selected Bibliography

Balcerowicz, L. (1992), *800 dni, szok kontrolowany,* BGW Warszawa.

– (1993), "Demokracja nie zastąpi kapitalizmu", *Rzeczpospolita,* 9 October.

– (1993), "Pożar w zarodku", *Wprost,* no. 21.

Beksiak, J., Gruszecki, T., Jędraszczyk, and Winiecki, J. (1990), *The Polish Transformation, Program and Progress,* London.

Beksiak, J., Grzelońska, U., Rybczyński, M., and Winiecki, J. (991), "List otwarty w sprawie gospodarki", *Rzeczpospolita,* 15 October.

Bruno, M. (1992), "Stabilization and Reform in Eastern Europe", IMF Working Paper 92/30.

Bugaj, R., and Kowalik, T. (1993), "Ryzykowny eksperyment", *Życie gospodarcze,* 10 March.

Central Planning Office (1993), *Ocena sytuacji społeczno-gospodarczej w 1992 roku,* Warsaw.

Central Planning Office (1993), "Sytuacja Gospodarcza w I kwartale 1993 roku", *Przeglad rzadowy,* no. 95.

Central Statistical Office (1993), "Informacja o sytuacji społeczno-gospodarczej w I kwartale", *Rzeczpospolita,* no. 4, 8 May.

Dornbush, R. (1991), "Policies to Move from Stabilization to Growth", *CEPR Discussion Paper,* no. 456, London.

Grosser, I., et al. (1993), "Shared Aspirations, Diverging Results. The Economic Situation in Central and East European Countries and in Slovenia, Croatia, Russia and Ukraine at the Turn of 1992/1993", *WIIW Research Reports,* no. 192, Vienna.

Gabrisch, H. (1993), "Under the Impact of Western Recession. The economic situation of the post-socialist countries in the first quarter of 1993 and outlook for 1993/94", *WIIW Research Reports,* no. 197b, Vienna.

Gelb, A. (1992), *Socialist Transformation: an Overview of CEE ...,* World Bank, CECSE.

Glikman, P. (1993), *Przekształcenia strukturalne potencjału produkcyjnego...,* ZBSE GUS/PAN, Warsaw.

Gomółka, S. (1992), "Polish Economic Reform 1990-1991: Principles, Policies and Outcomes", *Cambridge Journal of Economics,* September.

– (1993), "Poland: Glass Half Full", *Economic Transformation in CEE. A Progress Report,* CEPR, London.

Institute for East-West Studies (1992), *Moving Beyond Assistance,* New York.

Institute of Finance (1993), *Raport o sytuacji finansowej państwa w marcu 1993,* Warsaw, April.

Kabaj, M. (1993), "Aktywna walka z bezrobociem", *Przeglad spoleczny,* no. 9, Warsaw.

Kołodko, G. W. (1992), *Transformacja polskiej gospodarki: sukces czy porażka?*, Polska Oficyna Wydawnicza, BGW, Warsaw.

– (1993), *Kwadratura Pięciokąta,* Poltext, Warsaw.

Kurowski, S. (1993), "Na krótkiej smyczy", *Nowy swiat,* 12 January, Warsaw.

Landesmann, M. (1993), "Industrial Policy and the Transition in East-Central Europe", *WIIW Research Reports,* no. 196, Vienna.

Laski, K. (1992), "Transition from Command to Market Economies in Central and Eastern Europe: First Experiences and Questions", *WIIW Research Reports,* no. 181, Vienna.

–, et al. (1993), *Transition from the Command to the Market System: what went wrong and what to do?, WIIW Working Papers,* no. 1, Vienna.

– (1993), "Fiscal Policy and Effective Demand during Transformation", *WIIW Research Reports,* no. 189, Vienna.

Levcik, F. (1991), "The Place of Convertibility in the Transformation Process", *WIIWReprint Series,* no. 137, Vienna.

Lipiński, J. (1991), "Polityka makroekonomiczna a recesja i inflacja", Ekspertyza dla Rady Ekonomicznej przy Prezesie Rady Ministrów, Warsaw.

– (1991), "Warunki wyjścia z recesji", *Gospodarka narodowa,* no. 11/12.

Lipowski, A., and Kulig, J. (1992), *Państwo czy rynek?,* Poltext, Warsaw.

Mujżel, J. (1991), "Problems of Post-communist Transformation – Recession and Privatization", *Opera minora,* no. 1, Polish Academy of Sciences, Warsaw.

– (1992), "Zwrot antyrecesyjny", *Ine pan,* mimeo, Warsaw.

– (^993), "The Reform of Ownership Relations in Poland", *Opera minora,* Poltext, Warsaw.

National Bank of Poland, Balance of Payments Statistics, Warsaw.

Nuti, D. M. (1992), "Lessons from the Stabilization Programmes of CEE 1998-91", *Economic Papers,* European Economic Community, Brussels.

PHARE Memorandum: Indicative Programme for EC's Assistance to the Republic of Poland (1992), mimeo.

"PHARE podzielony" (1993), *Gazeta Wyborcza,* no. 169, 22 July.

Pinto, B., Belka, M., and Krajewski, S. (1993), *Transforming State Enterprises in Poland,* Łódź University, mimeo.

Portes, R. (ed.) (1993), *Economic Transformation in CEE. A Progress Report,* CEPR, London.

Rollo, J., and Stern, J. (1992), "Growth and Trade Prospects for CEE", *The World Economy,* October.

– (1993), *International Herald Tribune,* 23 June.

Rosati, D. K. (1993), "Poland: Glass Half Empty?", *Economic Transformation in CEE. A Progress Report,* CEPR, London.

Sołdaczuk, J., et al. (1993), *Strategia i Polityka Międzynarodowej Współpracy Gospodarczej w Okresie Transformacji,* IKiC, Warsaw.

Soros, G. (1992), "Nationalist Dictatorship Versus Open Society", lecture at Harvard Club of New York, 18 November.

United Nations Economic and Social Council (1992), Doc. E/1992/45, 6 May.

United Nations Economic Commission for Europe (1992), *Economic Survey of Europe in 1991-1992,* United Nations, New York.

Wilczyński, W. (1992), *Drogi wyjścia z kryzysu polskiej gospodarki,* PWN, Warsaw.

Winiecki, J. (1993), "Co dalej z prywatyzacją?", *Rzeczpospolita,* no. 70, 24 March.

ANNEX TO CHAPTER 18

Objectives and problems of the Polish Government as seen at the end of 1993

The government elected in September 1993 has the difficult task of preserving the successful elements of the economic programme and of correcting the weaknesses of the social programme.

The intentions of the new government were initially declared to be:

- to continue the policy of growth of industrial production (assessed in 1993 at 7 per cent) and of GDP (in 1993 at 4 per cent),
- to maintain the deficit of the 1994 budget below the 5 per cent limit in the 1993 budget (the initial proposal is 83 trillion zloty, i.e. around 4.2 per cent of GDP),
- to maintain the general equilibrium in the consumer's market,
- to decrease the planned inflation rate to 22-26 per cent a year,
- to implement the programme of mass privatisation (however, with modifications),
- to cooperate closely with IMF, the World Bank, the EBRD, and GATT, as well as to encourage foreign private investments in Poland,
- to negotiate further the reduction of the debts with the Paris Club and with the London Club.

The new government intends also to introduce the following changes:

- to intensify action against unemployment; in heavily hit regions this may take priority over the fight against inflation,
- to expand exports in order to counteract the rise of the trade deficit,
- to support efficient state-owned enterprises,
- to strengthen the active role of the state in industrial policy, agricultural policy and trade policy,
- to build up a social safety net in order to protect the poor,
- to correct the income distribution by modifying the tax structure and the wage incentives (by liquidating the "dividend tax" and the so-called "popiwek").

It remains to be seen whether these initial intentions will be kept and how they will be implemented. The main question is how strong and stable will be the consensus within the coalition and within the parties.

The government is facing the following dangers:

- The Peasant Party, headed by Prime Minister W. Pawlak, represents the interests of farmers, whereas the Social Democratic Party (SLD) represents the interests of industrial workers. The first are agricultural producers, the second are consumers. These are often competing interests;
- Within each party there are also differing interests:

(a) The prime minister is responsible for defending the interests of the whole society; however, being the president of the Peasant Party he acts under strong pressure of the agricultural lobby (for protection of domestic producers from competition of foreign producers);

(b) Within the Social Democratic Party three groups of interests can be distinguished:
   - the neo-liberals, who support the continuity of the reforms initiated by the former governments (with some modifications),
   - the trade unions (OPZZ), who are defending the interests of industrial workers,
   - the various lobbies representing different particular interests, often the interests of the former "nomenklatura", of large banks, or large private enterprises.

It is not easy to maintain consensus among such differing groups.

Finally, there is the discrepancy between the often unrealistic expectations of society and the possibilities of realising them.

Electoral promises cannot – at least immediately – be kept, and the expectations must be adjusted to possibilities. This points to the necessity of a wise information policy, presenting to the society in a convincing way the need for such adjustments. A government that does not know how to convince the society will sooner or later face social eruptions and will be ousted, or be tempted to resort to undemocratic measures.

Chapter 19

SYSTEMIC CHANGES IN THE CZECH ECONOMY

Karel Kouba*)

In this short review of systemic changes in the Czech economy in 1990-1993, I restrict myself to the main results, and the social costs, of the liberalisation and stabilisation stages of economic transformation. Further, I am interested in discussing selected open issues in the current stage of institutional change, especially the rather weak microeconomic foundation for maintaining macrostability and overcoming the decline of economic activity.

19.1 Macroeconomic stabilisation in the period of liberalisation

The starting conditions in 1989-1990 for choosing the type of transformation programme for the Czech economy were contradictory. The long-term rate of open and hidden inflation was not in excess of 5 per cent and the monetary overhang was relatively small. But the selection of liberalisation steps came into conflict with extreme distortions of the price structure. With the private sector not yet in existence, prices were completely under administrative control by state and local price authorities and some prices were heavily subsidised.

The external sector was fully controlled by the state monopoly. The exchange rate was heavily overvalued and artificial, and its role was superseded by extensive redistribution processes using different coefficients and administrative tools of foreign trade.

In the preparation for price liberalisation and opening of the economy in 1990, subsidies were abolished and an administrative increase of retail prices by 10 per cent was partly compensated from the state budget. In January 1991, 85 per cent of prices were liberalised and soon 95 per cent. The current account of the balance of payments was liberalised at the same time.

Devaluation in the range of 16 to 35-40 korunas (CSK) per US$ was proposed. Devaluation expectations and a steep decline of foreign currency

---

*) Professor of Economics, Faculty of Social Sciences, Charles University, Prague.

reserves were strongly influenced by nearly one year of discussions. There were three devaluations in 1990: by 16.6 per cent on 8 January, by 55.3 per cent on 15 October, and by 15.98 per cent on 28 December. In January 1991, the so-called "internal convertibility of the crown" regime (the current account liberalisation) was introduced with the exchange rate at 28 CSK per US$ plus 20 per cent import charges. Import charges were abolished within two years after their introduction. The exchange rate was not changed again in 1991-1993.

An exclusive priority of the restrictive fiscal and monetary policies has been control of inflation and of the value of the currency. Price control rules, temporary wages regulation and interest rate limits have served as supporting measures. Fiscal policy aimed at a balanced state budget. In 1990, the government budget of the former Czechoslovakia (CSFR) ended up with a small surplus; in 1991 its deficit was no more than 1.1 per cent of GDP, and in 1992 0.8 per cent; in 1993 the state budget of the Czech Republic (CR) aimed at balance. The central bank was forbidden by law to cover budget deficits by direct credits to the Government. Gross indebtedness – domestic and foreign – of the Czech Government can be estimated at about 22 per cent of GDP at the end of 1992.

Money supply increased in 1990 and 1991 by less than half the yearly inflation rate. Tight monetary policy was continued in 1992 and especially in the beginning of 1993 when VAT was introduced. In 1991-1993 money supply was flexible and the severity of restrictive monetary policy declined from highly restrictive to neutral and finally to slightly expansionary. The influence of restrictive monetary policy has been weakened by a steep increase of involuntary inter-firm indebtedness and very weak financial discipline.

Tripartite agreements between government, employers and trade unions contributed to the modest wage increase in the liberalisation stage of transformation. An important aspect of the price liberalisation was a steep decline of the average real wage by 26.3 per cent in 1991 (see *Table 19.1*). Average real wages then rose by 8.8 per cent in 1992, with a 20.9 per cent increase in nominal wages. Average real wages in the first half of 1993 further increased by 4.9 per cent with a 27.8 per cent increase in nominal wages. This acceleration of wage increases with stagnating level of labour productivity led the government to restoring the wage regulations in spite of the continuing opposition of trade unions and employers. The wage regulation remained in force for the second half of 1993, and, after further wage increases in the third quarter of the year, continues for 1994. Wage regulation applies to state and private enterprises and the banking sector.

Table 19.1

Czech Republic: Selected indicators

(annual per cent change)

	1990	1991	1992
Real GDP	-1.2	-14.2	-7.1
Industrial production	-3.3	-22.3	-10.6
Employment	-0.2	-7.0	-3.0
Unemployment (% labour force)	0.7	4.1	2.6
Inflation: consumer price index	9.9	56.6	11.1
Money wage rate	3.7	15.4	20.9
Real wage rate	-5.6	-26.3	8.8
Productivity of labour	-1.0	-7.7	-4.2
Labour unit costs[a)]	4.5	26.1	27.6

a) Index of money wage rate divided by index of productivity of labour.

Source: Statistical Yearbook of CSFR, and Czech Statistical Office.

Financial, monetary and income policies imposed an effective control on inflation (see *Table 19.2).* After the price jump of 27 per cent in January 1991, inflation fell off for a few months; and from July 1991 the monthly inflation rate was mostly below 1 per cent despite further price deregulation. In January 1993, due to the imposition of taxes on certain kinds of food and the shift to VAT at rates of 5 and 23 per cent, there was a price increase of 8.5 per cent followed by low rates.

One-stroke price liberalisation and massive devaluation have had some unfavourable side effects, which are still subject to critical discussion. In 1990, a possible alternative to the chosen liberalisation programme was a gradual freeing of the rigid price structure and partial devaluation by stages in the course of a few years. An alternative gradual liberalisation would not have been managed without certain costs. It would have required a wide control of regulated prices, subsidies and redistribution processes both in domestic and external sectors. Heavy inflation and devaluation expectations together with the increased risks to the credibility of the reform process would have been the obvious results.

Liberalisation measures are among the irreversible parts of the transformation process.

Table 19.2

Czech Republic: Consumer price index

(% change from previous month)

	1991	1992	1993
January	26.3	0.9	8.5
February	6.2	0.7	1.3
March	4.3	0.6	0.6
April	2.4	0.6	0.6
May	1.9	0.5	0.4
June	1.7	0.4	0.4
July	-0.2	1.1	0.7
August	-0.1	0.6	0.7
September	0.3	1.9	1.4
October	0.2	1.9	1.1
November	1.4	2.2	0.5
December	0.9	0.6	0.8

Source: Czech Statistical Office.

Results of liberalisation

The results of the actual liberalisation programme are, above all, a favourable macroeconomic stability, a low inflation rate held under control, a balanced state budget, a steady exchange rate with a sufficient level of foreign currencies reserves and balance of payments equilibrium. The overall results of macroeconomic stabilisation are mixed. The good results – stability of prices and stable exchange rate – contrast with the very steep decline of GDP and industrial production (see *Table 19.1)* and fairly slow recovery of economic activity in general (see *Table 19.3).*

I consider that the main problem of the current state of systemic transformation is the weak microeconomic foundations for maintaining macroeconomic stability in the process of transforming the still dominant sector of state enterprises.

Table 19.3

Czech Republic: Gross domestic product

(% change from corresponding quarter of previous year)

Quarter	1991	1992	1993
I	2.7	-21.1	-2.2
II	-15.6	-9.1	1.1
III	-17.9	0.8	-1.5
IV	-24.6	4.2	n.a.

Source: Czech Statistical Office.

The relevant issue for the choice of economic policies, and for necessary changes of priorities, is to overcome the decline and stagnation of economic activity in the Czech economy.

The difficulty of choosing macroeconomic policies in the liberalisation stage was characterised by Michael Landesmann as follows:

> The basic policy dilemma of stabilisation in the context of Eastern Europe seems to arise from its two rather contradictory objectives, i.e. how to reconcile the restrictive policies of conventional stabilisation which are believed to be needed to improve the trade balance and to lower the inflation rate, with stimulative or expansionary policies which will help the private sector to grow at a sufficiently rapid pace to take over the task of growth ... Intellectual honesty demands that we recognize that the basic policy dilemma cannot be easily resolved. (Landesmann 1993)

19.2 Steep decline of economic activity and some fallacies in the Czech economic community

A number of Czech economists (e.g. Komárek 1993, Vintrová 1993, Pick 1993) connect the steep decline of the Czech economy in 1990-1992 directly with the so-called shock therapy. Discussions about "shock therapy versus gradualist strategy", even in the international community, were re-opened after the elections in Poland in 1993.

However, medium-term empirical data do not confirm a direct connection between the speed of freeing prices and reaching a realistic exchange rate on one hand and the loss of output on the other hand. If we tentatively define the shock therapy as full price liberalisation and massive devaluation, then the strategy chosen in Czechoslovakia significantly differs from the gradual approach in Hungary. Yet despite different liberalisation strategies, the loss in industrial production in the medium-term period is approximately the same in the two countries (see *Table 19.4*). Other medium-term statistical data do not confirm a seemingly direct connection between the "shock therapy" and loss of output (Kouba 1992). Obviously, such simplified comparisons do not lead to understanding the causes of the unprecedented decline of economic activity in the liberalisation stage of systemic transformation. Even normative conclusions on the speed of transformation and the nature of desired stabilisation policies are then questionable.

Table 19.4

Industrial production index

1985 = 100

	CSFR	Hungary
1990	104.7	89.0
1991	78.8	72.3
1992	67.8	65.0

Source: Bulletin 1992, Federálni statistický úřad; Kozponti statisztikai hivatal; Glówny urzad statystyczny, Prague 1993, p. 5.

The speed and radical nature of liberalisation depend on the starting conditions and political will in the given country. This is subordinate to the main concern in the starting stage of systemic transformation; namely how fast, and by what institutional changes, the way can be opened to the evolutionary development of the market order.

By these comments I do not mean to underestimate the influence of a sudden change of economic variables on social consensus. In the Czech society, and in the development of the Czech political scene, the liberalisation steps made in 1991 did not lead to the loss of social consensus; indeed they rather increased the credibility of the general programme of systemic transformation.

Loss of output has been often connected with the unexpected collapse of Comecon markets. In the Czech economy, the total loss of output in 1991-1992 is estimated by Rodrik to fall within the range of 30 to 50 per cent. The official estimate of the Czechoslovak statistical office is in practice nearly the same. A later analysis by Rodrik (1993) with the use of the multiplier, shows that nearly the whole loss of output in Czechoslovakia can be attributed to this external factor.

In my opinion, these estimates have limited relevance because of their static analyses. Stagnation of output continues even after a considerable part of the loss of output has been compensated by a relatively fast re-orientation to Western markets.

To a certain extent, the attempt to explain the depth of decline by obvious "overshooting" of stabilisation policies through excessive reduction of domestic demand also seems somewhat questionable. In the Czech economy in the first six months of 1993, against the same period of 1992, aggregate demand grew in all sectors except for exports to Slovakia. Private demand grew by 12 per cent, public sector demand by 16 per cent, investment demand by 5 per cent and foreign demand by 10 per cent. The increase of aggregate demand continued in the second half of 1993. However, a significant effect of further growth of aggregate demand on higher use of capacity and overcoming stagnation is doubtful, particularly because of low income elasticity.

Some take the view that the present somewhat expansive monetary policy could be complemented by a small deficit in the state budget, which ambitiously strove for a small surplus in 1993. However, these proposals do not take into account the negative impact of expansionary fiscal policy on restriction of credit resources for development of the private sector. This sector is the main support for the recovery of the economy and suffers from lack of adequate credit. Hence, in this stage of systemic change, expansionary demand policies have very limited free play and only a small influence on recovery of the real economy.

In discussing the decline in output we encounter some extreme views. Some economists and politicians hold that the decline is a result of wrong economic policy. Those who defend the chosen stabilisation programme have a tendency to view the whole decline as a healthy rectification of previous unhealthy growth. In my opinion, except for a few voices (especially Winiecki 1993), the negative effects of unhealthy inventory accumulation have never been carefully analysed. The centrally planned economy was highly wasteful in this respect (see Goldmann and Kouba 1969).

Table 19.5

Czech Republic: GDP and inventories

	GDP	increase in stocks and reserves		total inventories as of 31 December		of which: production inventories[a)]		of which: sales inventories[b)]		of which: investment work in progress	
	bn CSK	bn CSK	% of GDP	bn CSK	% of GDP	bn CSK	% of GDP	bn CSK	% of GDP	bn CSK	% of GDP
Current prices											
1980	415.3	26.26	6.3	382.4	92.1	113.1	27.2	150.2	36.2	82.7	19.9
1985	473.7	9.6	2.0	451.6	95.3	140.2	29.6	177.6	37.5	96.4	20.4
1986	483.0	12.7	2.6	459.8	95.2	199.1	41.2	122.6	25.4	99.7	20.6
1987	495.1	19.9	4.0	475.1	96.0	216.1	43.6	121.1	24.5	98.6	19.9
1988	513.4	4.7	0.9	479.2	93.3	233.8	45.5	120.8	23.5	84.3	16.4
1989	524.5	4.1	0.8	493.8	94.1	227.5	43.4	131.1	25.0	81.5	15.5
1990	567.3	13.2	2.3	526.4	92.8	249.8	44.0	139.4	24.6	89.1	15.7
1991	716.6	47.9	6.7	539.9	75.3	301.7	42.1	186.9	26.1	51.2	7.1
1992[c)]	771.3	-14.6	-1.9	457.6	59.3	271.1	35.1	158.4	20.5	28.2	3.7
1984 constant prices											
1987	478.0	20.1	4.2	.	.	.	.	.	.	.	.
1988	487.8	4.6	0.9	.	.	.	.	.	.	.	.
1989	509.9	3.8	0.7	.	.	.	.	.	.	.	.
1990	503.7	12.1	2.4	.	.	.	.	.	.	.	.
1991	432.1	16.6	3.8	.	.	.	.	.	.	.	.
1992	401.5	-8.0	-2.0	.	.	.	.	.	.	.	.

a) Material in stock + material in transit + fuel + subdeliveries + work in progress + own semifinished products + building site equipment. - b) Product + goods + import and export goods + animals. - c) Total inventories in 1992 do not include inventories of financial and insurance institutions and of some private nonfinancial organisations (not included part is estimated at CSK 30 bn).

Source: Statistical Yearbooks of CSFR and of CR; data estimated by Vladimír Nachtigal, Institute of Economics, Czech National Bank.

Leakages and waste in the formation and distribution of the GDP again reached enormous proportions in the rigidly centralised Czechoslovak economy in the 1970s and 1980s. The analysis is supported by the data on GDP, inventories and their structure during the 1980s and early 1990s. Total inventories in 1980-1990 were always more than 90 per cent of GDP (see *Table 19.5;* for which I am indebted to Vladimír Nachtigal from The Institute of Economics of the Czech National Bank who carefully reconstructed the data). According to international comparison the average stock of inputs per stock of outputs, in manufacturing in 1981-1985 in Czechoslovakia, was three times greater than in developed market economies (Kornai 1992, p. 250).

The deep fall in output can be viewed as a tax paid for the highly centralised, rigid and wasteful economic system which survived during the last two decades with no attempt at reform.

19.3 Supply-side factors as a desired aim of pro-growth policies

I share *János Kornai's* multi-causal attitude to analysis of this "transformational recession" (Kornai 1993), which does not have its foundations in cyclical development. In my opinion, for solving the "puzzle" of this non-standard phenomenon, the usual quantitative analysis at macroeconomic level is not sufficient. The causes are deeply rooted in the microeconomic sphere, in heterogeneous, contradictory and divergent behaviour patterns of the performers in the transformation.

Divergent forces in the transformed economy

Differing behaviour patterns result in quite divergent forces governing the dynamics of output, especially in industry, where the highly concentrated state sector plays a completely dominant role.

Statistical data for 1992 record already in this second year of transition different development tendencies that have up to now escaped deeper analysis. Industrial production in CSFR in 1992 is estimated to have reached 88.5 per cent of the 1991 level. In industrial enterprises with 25 and more employees, it was down by 13.9 per cent in 1992, by 13.7 per cent in the Czech Republic and 14.7 per cent in Slovakia. By contrast, production increased in small industrial enterprises where the share of private firms is rising. In 1992 against 1991, production rose by 36.7 per cent in firms with 25-49 employees and 24.7 per cent in those with 50-74 employees. When measured in size groups, the biggest share of industrial production was attributable to enterprises with 5000 and more employees (29.7 per cent of total production of enterprises with 25 and more employees). The three largest size groups (with 1000 and more employees) account for 68.1 per cent of total production. The smallest enterprises (with 25-49 and 50-74 employees) are the only categories with substantial increases of industrial production; but their share in 1992 industrial production was only 1.1 per cent. Looked at in terms of ownership form, the distribution was as follows:

Per cent shares in industrial production 1992

	CSFR	Czech Rep.	Slovakia
State enterprises	86.5	84.8	91.0
Private enterprises	7.6	8.7	4.7
International firms	3.7	4.5	2.0
Cooperatives	1.6	1.5	1.7

In the first six months of 1993, industrial production reached 95.3 per cent of the year before. In the group of enterprises with the biggest share of private firms (less than 25 employees) production increased by 21.6 per cent. By contrast there was a fall of 6.8 per cent in enterprises with more than 25 employees (*Hospodářské noviny,* 15 September 1993).

In 1993, official statistics reported a large increase of the private sector, which for the first time included the production of enterprises handed over to new owners, including share-holders from privatisation by voucher. The private sector so recorded in statistics has reached 18 per cent of industrial production in the first six months of 1993, their output being 4.9 per cent higher (in constant prices) than in the same period 1992. This tendency is even more conspicuous in the construction industry where the share of the private sector reached 60 per cent in 1993. Its production increased by 30.9 per cent, whereas total production of the construction industry fell by 6.1 per cent.

Corporate governance – the Achilles' heel of privatisation

Of the enterprises so far privatised, 37 per cent were partly or completely privatised by the voucher scheme. Combination of this non-standard method with standard privatisation methods made possible quick changes of ownership structure. After finishing the first wave of voucher privatisation, the share of the private sector in GDP is estimated to have risen from 4 per cent in 1990 to 20 per cent in 1992, and to 44 per cent in the first six months of 1993. At the same time, a second and last privatisation wave has been started with similar non-standard methods.

In my opinion, the prime feature of the legally privatised corporations in the first wave of voucher privatisation, and also of those commercialised in the second wave, is the lack of an effective system of corporate governance.

Most of the vouchers (72 per cent) were entrusted by their owners to newly founded privatisation investment funds (mutual funds). Out of an original 264 investment funds there remained 218 after mergers. The fears of a highly unequal share dispersion did not come true. On the contrary, there occurred a wide concentration of shares in the hands of the strongest investment funds. The approximately 14 largest investment funds own 70-80 per cent of all shares allocated to all investment funds in the first wave. This represents 26.42 per cent of total assets of all shareholding companies privatised in the first wave. In the portfolio of the largest investment funds there are usually a few hundred enterprises (maximum 20 per cent of each allowed to a single investment fund). For example, the biggest investment funds, governed by parent companies of the biggest banks, hold the shares of between 262 and 514 enterprises in their portfolios. The difficulty of effective control of such a large number of enterprises is intensified by the underdeveloped market in potential managers. Investment funds based on banks are not interested in initiating a radical financial restructuring of enterprises with low liquidity. The restructuring which should be effected under the governance of new owners is the weakest point of the privatisation process up to date. Low unemployment – 3.17 per cent in November 1993 – with simultaneous overemployment (note the smaller decline in employment than in output in *Table 19.1)* indicates the slow process of restructuring.

The National Property Fund is a formal holder of shares of approximately nine hundred corporations, i.e. shares not sold in the first wave, and shares of banking houses, metallurgy and enterprises from the second wave. The National Property Fund and ministries have substantially given up the function of performing effective corporate control, and they mostly rely on a fast transfer of property rights in the privatised corporations to new owners.

Corporate governance and restructuring should be considered as the most relevant open issues in the current stage of systemic change. An effective system of corporate governance can be developed only by an evolutionary process. This provides the final test of successful implementation of the voucher scheme.

Modified paternalism in commercialised state enterprises

Czechoslovakia entered the systemic transformation with a highly centralised control of state enterprises. So it has not faced the problems of excessive decentralisation and self-management seen in Poland and Hungary. However, a quiet, troublefree and immediate abolition of the nonfunctioning central planning system (Mlčoch 1993) has not been replaced by effective control machinery in state enterprises, or by monitoring and motivation of their managers, especially in restricting their rent-seeking behaviour. In reality, the managers themselves propose the conditions of their managerial contracts in the same way as they had done under the old regime when they arranged on their own the so-called breakdown of obligatory planning directives.

Because of the absence of effective corporate control, the room for different forms of "moral hazard" has opened wide. Restrictions are mostly unenforceable by law. The rigid supply responses of state enterprises, perverse behaviour forms and general weakening of financial discipline have been reaffirmed.

Instead of restructuring and a painful recovery process, a modified form of paternalism has spread. The state stopped subsidising the state enterprises and declared the end of paternalism. Nevertheless, paternalism survives in the informal bargaining of managers of the state enterprises which suffer from the supply of liquidity from commercial banks. Commercial banks, encumbered by their past but sometimes also by their own recent mistakes and by the burden of bad debts, are keeping alive even obvious bankruptcy candidates. Validation of the law on bankruptcy has been postponed twice since 1991 although a number of economists consider this delay unreasonable or useless. For example, the present writer, during discussions on delaying the law, expressed the fear that we are faced with "bankruptcy of bankruptcies" (Kouba 1992, 1993). Even after April 1993, when the law came into effect, bankruptcy procedures up to November 1993 were initiated for only 30 firms out of one thousand proposals.

The financial sector has been affected by the cancer of inability to pay, by the growth of involuntary interfirm credits which endangers liquidity even of good firms and of private entrepreneurs. Recurrent emissions of bad loans, in spite of high interest rates, do not constitute an adequate incentive for desirable restructuring of state enterprises. Even worse, the credit resources for the private sector are thus restricted and the cost of credit is rising.[1)]

19.4 Concluding remarks

The development of the Czech economy since 1989 brings out a number of critical issues of policy.

In my opinion, there is a rather sham discussion in the Czech economic community on the so-called shock versus gradualist strategy and on the need for alternative strategic steps in an irreversible situation. This misleading discussion does not contribute to the desirable critical analysis of systemic transformation, which has slowed down considerably in the last two years for a number of reasons.

A widening and harmonising of the priorities in combining antiinflation policy with an active anti-recessional policy is possible and desirable. For me, the issues of pro-growth policy are not dominant in macroeconomic approaches to stimulating higher potential product. The focus of crucial systemic changes lies rather in the microsphere, in the design of incentives, in the institutional framework of property rights, in clearly defined entitlements and in effective corporate governance.

Frequent discussions about the need for an industrial policy do not take into account the fact that in the Czech Republic financial institutions have been established for support of small and medium-size entrepreneurship as well as an agency for supporting exports; some regional projects also exist. However, the problem lies in the low effectiveness and the fairly weak financial background of these institutions.

The Czech economy would benefit from an active pro-growth policy, especially from a more extensive financial support of development of small and medium-size entrepreneurship, of aid for exports and a bolder credit policy of commercial banks. It would be advisable to push through implementation of regional programmes, especially the "sunset programmes" despite the strong resistance of lobbies.

A frequent subject of critical discussions is the active role of the state in cultivating the market. Obviously, contemporary markets are non-competitive,

---

1) I consider *Calvo* and *Coricelli's* analysis of output and underdeveloped credit market quite relevant (Calvo and Coricelli 1992).

with rigid monopolistic and oligopolistic structures (see e.g. Mertlík 1993). The markets lack a deeper cultural background with elementary ethics. One big difficulty is that the weaknesses and failures of the "visible" hand in the first transformation stage are frequently more damaging in depth and scope than the failures of the "invisible" hand. This applies especially to the professional incompetence of state administrations that condemn many rational recommendations as mere academic propositions.

From my personal experience in professional and expert participation in the programmed reform experiments in the 1960s, and in the working in practice of current systemic transformation schemes, I have the impression that a number of recommendations, however well founded they may be theoretically, do not take into account the very different nature of the current systemic changes.

Their real course and side-effects are frequently decided by hidden informal processes, clashes of interest and spontaneous activity more than by well-designed economic policies to set them in motion.

It is my impression that in considering the conditions of systemic transformation, Dani Rodrik's message in his essay *The Positive Economics of Policy Reform* (Rodrik 1993) is increasingly relevant: "Economists have always been better at telling policy makers what to do than at explaining why policy makers do what they do ... This experience has made it clear that devising successful policies requires an understanding of the forces that govern policy-making."

References

Bulíř, A., and Kysilka, P. (1993), "Jednociferná inflace je reálná", *Ekonom,* no. 41, Prague.

Calvo, A., and Coricelli, F. (1992), *Output Collapse in Eastern Europe: The Role Of Credit,* The World Bank.

Goldmann, J., and Kouba, K. (1969), *Economic Growth in Czechoslovakia,* Academy of Sciences, Prague.

Komárek, V. (1993), "Czech and Slovak Federal Republic: A New Approach", in *Economic Transformation in Central Europe: A Progress Report,* R. Portes (ed.), Centre for Economic Policy Research, London.

Kornai, J. (1992), *The Socialist System. The Political Economy of Communism,* Princeton, New Jersey, Princeton University Press.

– (1993), "Transformational Recession", Institute for Advanced Study, *Discussion Papers,* no. 1, Budapest.

Kouba, K. (1992), "Šok stejný jako postupné změny", *Prostor,* 5 June, Prague.

– (1992), "Odklad bankrotù není dobrým řešením", *Ekonom,* no. 46.

– (1993), "Nastal bankrot bankrotú?", *Profit,* no. 3, Prague.

Landesmann, M. (1993), "Industrial Policy and the Transition in East-Central Europe", *WIIW Research Reports,* no. 196, Vienna.

Mertlík, P. (1993), *Product Slump in Czecho-Slovakia: A Critical Overview,* Institute of Economic Sciences, Faculty of Social Sciences, Charles University, Prague.

Mlčoch, L. (1993), *The Dynamics of Changes in Behaviour within the Czech Enterprise Sphere,* Institute of Sociology, Prague.

Pick, M. (1993), "Standardní strategie ekonomické transformace v nestandardních podmínkách ČSFR", *Finance a úvěr,* no. 8, Prague.

Rodrik, D. (1993), "The Positive Economics of Policy Reform", *American Economic Review,* May.

– (1993), "Making sense of the Soviet trade shock in Eastern Europe: a framework and some estimates", in *Eastern Europe in Transition: From Recession to Growth?,* Blejer, M., Calvo, G. A., Coricelli, F., and Gelb, A. (eds.), World Bank Discussion Papers.

Vintrová, R. (1993), "Macroeconomic Analysis of Transformation in the CSFR", *WIIW Research Reports,* no. 188, Vienna.

Winiecki, J. (1993), *Heterodox' stabilization in eastern Europe,* European Bank for Reconstruction and Development, London.

Chapter 20

THE TRANSFORMATION PROCESS IN THE NEW SLOVAK REPUBLIC

Igor Kosír[*)]

The Slovak Republic assumed fully independent and sovereign status on 1 January 1993. This major event gave rise to an urgent need to formulate a strategic plan for the transformation and development of the new state consistent with the political principles emerging from the democratic process now adopted.

In spite of the changes made since the collapse of the chronic shortage economy in the former Czecho-Slovakia, the legacy of the past reveals many features still important for strategic development; this legacy predetermines the problems of transformation as well as some of the solutions. For the purpose of strategic design the most important aspects are:

(a) *the extensive model of development,* dictated in the past by a cold war mentality, provided a range of products and production structures incompatible with current and future needs;

(b) *the political orientation of the past* imposed on an autarkic, supply-side pattern of development, within the CMEA system;

(c) *a highly centralised process of allocation* with little, if any, corrective feedback, leading to distortions not only of economic processes but also of the very structure and nature of the production base;

(d) the redistribution of wealth imposed by the former socialist system created a feeling of equality among people and so relieved many social stresses, but at the same time it had a strong demotivating effect on the work force and ultimately led to a serious decline in the productivity of labour throughout the whole economy.

---

*) Director, Centre for Strategic Studies of the Slovak Republic, Bratislava.

From the macroeconomic point of view, three main kinds of disequilibrium were present:

(1) internal: excess of demand over the supply of goods and services – as much as 46-61 per cent;

(2) external: the need for foreign currency was greatly in excess of the export of goods and services;

(3) since the need for efficiency was not recognised, full employment was achieved through hidden unemployment (over-staffing) which further exacerbated the inefficiency and lack of employee motivation.

Slovakia is among the richer countries in Eastern Europe. This relatively high income level is due to massive investments in infrastructure and industry undertaken since the end of World War II; these have transformed its mainly agrarian into an industrial economy. The specialised structure of the Slovak industry, oriented to heavy industry, engineering, armaments production and chemicals, was frequently connected with final production in the Czech lands, giving a new slant to our transformation process.

The first phase of economic reform in Slovakia was realised, in 1991-1992, within the Czecho-Slovak economy, and came into effect in January 1991. The main elements were:

(a) rapid price liberalisation with a coinciding slashing of subsidies to state-owned enterprises;
(b) immediate current account convertibility, made possible by a large exchange rate devaluation;
(c) wage controls to increase international competitiveness and to contain inflation;
(d) restrictive monetary and fiscal policies to maintain macroeconomic stability;
(e) liberalisation and modernisation of economic institutions through a new legal system (e.g. a new commercial code and laws on banking, foreign investment, competition, taxation, social security and environmental protection) with corresponding changes in the administration;
(f) privatisation of many large state-owned enterprises, without prior restructuring, by using an unorthodox method of privatisation by voucher.

The strategy of the former Czecho-Slovakia was aimed at:

(1) internal equilibrium through price liberalisation;

(2) external equilibrium through currency devaluation;

(3) privatisation of national property to create a competitive economic environment and to motivate employees and managers to increase overall efficiency.

Price liberalisation was one of the most important elements of the economic reform. Only the prices of transport, heating and rent are still regulated in Slovakia. The introduction of internal convertibility and the elimination of most restrictions in foreign trade, connected with the abolition of the former state monopoly of foreign economic activities, created an opening for the subsequent rationalisation of our domestic economy. Slovakia maintains internal convertibility of the Slovak crown. The important pillar of our economic reform is the *privatisation process*. However, large-scale privatisation proved more time-consuming than expected and was delayed.

The first year of economic transformation saw a more or less successful implementation of components of the reform programme, and a swift privatisation of many small units such as shops, hotels, restaurants. But after declining by some 15 per cent in 1991, GDP fell further by around 7 per cent in 1992. Especially in Slovakia, economic activity has been declining since 1990 as a result of:

(a) loss of markets in the former CMEA area;

(b) restrictive monetary and fiscal policies;

(c) the restructuring of the economy.

The Slovak economy was developed as complementary to the more developed Czech economy. The old centrally planned system created for the Czech part of our former federation the additional advantages of being the main decision-making centre. That is why the impact of the first phase of the economic reform was stronger in Slovakia. In particular, unemployment became an important political and social problem in 1991-1992, generated by the decline of output. The unemployment rate in Slovakia at over 10 per cent has remained substantially higher than in the Czech lands (at end-1992 only 2.6 per cent). There are a number of reasons (historical, structural and demographic) for this difference.

These features of Slovakian society, by comparison with the Czech Republic, include a larger number of women on maternity leave, a higher proportion of the Romany ethnic group with its much higher average unemployment rate, more school-leavers entering the labour market, a higher share of defence industry, and fewer possibilities for Slovaks than for Czechs to commute to work in the Western European countries. Slovakia, with its above-average share of defence industries, was affected particularly hard by the 91 per cent decline of defence production since 1988 without rapid conversion and restructuring.

The second phase of economic reform was influenced by the main political event of 1992. After the June elections, negotiations started between the Movement for Democratic Slovakia (HZDS) under the leadership of Vladimír Mečiar and the strongest Czech political party, the Civic Democratic Party (ODS), led by Václav Klaus. They agreed on formation of a coalition federal government and on an orderly dissolution of the Czecho-Slovak federation. On 17 July 1992, the Slovak parliament proclaimed its sovereignty and in September it passed its own Slovak constitution.

The basic principles for the process have been set by the Declaration of the Government of the Slovak Republic (July 1992) which assumed the continuation of the direction of reforms, transforming the national economy into a functioning market economy with responsible concern for an ecological and socially progressive development.

What were the basic goals of the new state?

(1) Parliamentary democracy
(2) Market economy
(3) Integration with the European Union.

To continue the transformation process, a federal government was formed and a series of agreements on post-division arrangements concluded. The most important provided for *the establishment of a customs union and of a monetary union* between the new Slovak and Czech states. The federal parliament finally voted on 25 November 1992 to end the joint Czecho-Slovak state on the terms negotiated by the two Prime Ministers Mečiar and Klaus. On 1 January 1993, the independent Slovak and Czech republics came into existence, with the former governments and parliaments becoming institutions of the new states.

This began the second phase of the economic reform in Slovakia. The government and the parliament of the Slovak republic had to create qualitatively new conditions. The youngest European republic needed its own central bank, ministry of defence, ministry of foreign affairs, centre for macroeconomic, regional and European strategies, national agency for development of market economy and other political and economic institutions such as the Presidential Office, embassies and permanent missions abroad. It was a relatively hard beginning. The year 1993 was an extraordinary one for Slovakia, influenced by two basic goals:

(1) creation and a relatively swift development of a new state structure in Slovakia and of Slovak institutions abroad;
(2) continuation of the economic reform in absolutely new conditions, with own responsibility.

The Government of Slovakia has identified *three key priorities for the industrial development of a new state:*

(i) infrastructure development in transport, post and telecommunications, energy, banks and services, as a precondition for the creation of efficient conditions for the development of the other economic branches;
(ii) the development of small and medium-sized businesses and tourism;
(iii) the development of new industrial sectors and products.

The second phase of the economic reform started with the *introduction of a value added tax* (1 January 1993).

The economic policy of Slovakia is concentrated on the following goals:

- to maintain the internal convertibility of the Slovak crown (after an abrupt termination of the currency union 8 February 1993);
- to keep the rise of domestic prices at a minimum.

The main features in the economic development are:

- the termination of the currency union with the Czech lands and high expectations of devaluation;
- a very low level of the foreign currency reserves of the National Bank of Slovakia (in April 1993 $ 122 mn excluding monetary gold);
- devaluation of the Slovak crown (Sk) by 10 per cent in mid-1993;
- the state budget development (at present the deficit is stabilised at Sk 16 bn but a relatively high deficit was forecast for the year 1993);
- negotiations with the IMF;
- the pre-privatisation climate in industry and agriculture;
- the relatively successful development, and the reorientation, of foreign trade (but 20 per cent decline of trade with the Czech Republic).

The year 1993 has been remarkable for the economic transformation process in Slovakia. And the Slovak reform continues. The realisation of the second wave of privatisation, a very important pillar of our transition, is expected in the year 1994, which will be a period of stabilisation.

Chapter 21

SLOVENIA: A NEW STATE AND ITS PROSPECTS

Jože Mencinger*)

Slovenia proclaimed independence on 26 June 1991, after a decade of tense and uncertain political and economic developments. Three months later, on 8 October 1991, the tiny but relatively affluent nation of two million people became fully "independent". In the beginning of 1992, Slovenia was recognised as an independent state by the EC member states and, in May 1992, became a member of the UN.

Political achievements can be considered a "success story", particularly if they are compared with developments in other republics of the former Yugoslavia. This is only partially true for economic attainments. The expectations of an easy double transition – from socialism to capitalism, and from dependence to independence have not materialised. A rather successful stabilisation accomplished predominantly by monetary policy has been accompanied by an enormous drop in economic activity, a rise in unemployment, and shrinking foreign trade. The policies for the "takeoff" from the current state of "zero sum economy" have not yet been found. Fiscal and income policies and even more so, the badly needed systemic changes have been overshadowed by political considerations.

Stabilisation with contraction

Economic activity started to plunge in 1990, after a decade of stagnation and three years of mild contraction. It picked up in the second quarter of 1991, but the "ten days war" in June and the secession in October 1991, pushed production down rapidly. After a decline by 9.3 per cent in 1991 and 6.0 per cent in 1992, economic activity stagnated in 1993. (See *Table 21.1*).

---

*) Professor of Economics, EIPF (Institute of Economics, Faculty of Law), University of Ljubljana, Slovenia.

Dramatic reduction of trade with the former Yugoslav republics is the principal reason for persistent economic decline. The economy was badly hit by the secession itself and, even more so, by the subsequent political and economic developments in the rest of the former federation. The adverse effects were: the diminished supply of raw materials and competitive finished products, the termination of foreign trade links which Slovenia established through Yugoslav companies and vice versa, the property losses, the lessened interests of foreign investors for a tiny market, and, most importantly, the squeeze of the market. A major fall in trade at the end of 1991 continued because of the war in Bosnia and Herzegovina, the UN embargo in Serbia and Montenegro, and worsening economic performance in Croatia.

Table 21.1

Slovenia: Economic indicators, 1989-1993

	(1)	(2)	(3)	(4)	(5)	(6)
	% change from previous period			000	US$ million	
1989	-.81	73.8	-0.31	28.2	852	804
1990	-2.85	50.4	-1.02	44.6	1029	1182
1991/I	-4.70	18.8	-2.76	63.2	990	1202
/II	-3.32	30.2	-2.66	70.1	900	1034
/III	-2.95	34.5	-3.00	78.5	855	760
/IV	-4.09	66.4	-2.42	88.6	1113	1144
1992/I	-7.80	42.6	-2.21	95.1	1245	1413
/II	-3.87	18.5	-1.69	96.3	1272	1242
/III	-0.86	6.2	-1.12	104.4	1360	1239
/IV	0.50	7.5	-1.48	114.7	1295	1413
1993/I	0.02	6.8	-1.35	119.9	1251	1391
/II	-3.34	3.9	-0.68	126.0	1255	1470
/III	-0.39	4.3	-0.76	133.2	1202	1305
/10	1.43	2.9	-0.58	137.4	449	507
/11	1.84	1.5	..	..	414	479
/12	..	1.6	..	..	..	..

(1) industrial production, (2) retail prices, (3) employment, (4) unemployment, (5) exports and (6) imports (both excluding trade with former Yugoslavia).

Employment fell along with the decrease of economic activity; the elasticity of employment to changes in production since 1990 has been high and growing. Thus, total employment fell by 5.6 per cent in 1992, it is estimated to fall by

3.5 per cent in 1993, and 1 per cent in 1994. The reduction was concentrated in the business sector; there has been no significant drop of employment in the public sector. The so-called restructuring of the economy has so far consisted mainly of "firing and retiring". The number of unemployed nearly quadrupled in three years; total unemployment reached 137 thousand in September and the official unemployment rate exceeded 15 per cent.[1)] This was accompanied by the increase of the number of pensioners which doubled in the same period to 408 thousand to which a policy of early retirement added significantly. The ratio of those retired to those employed diminished to a horrifying 1:5. Inflation is currently running at 1.5-2 per cent monthly with no significant acceleration or deceleration. In October 1991, when the tolar was introduced, monthly inflation was 21.5 per cent.

Figure 21.1

Slovenia: Index of industrial production

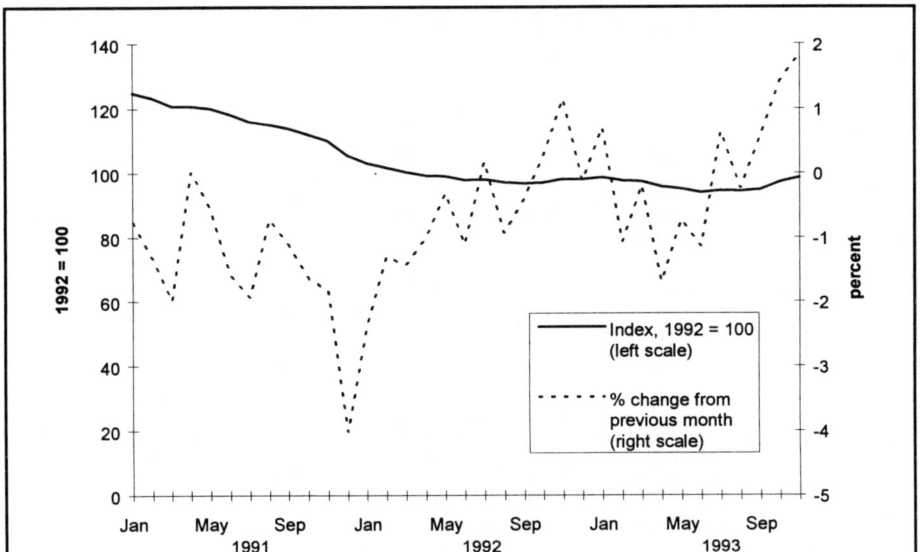

---

1) The unemployment figures are not so bad by ILO standards; according to the latest survey (by the *School of Social Sciences)* the unemployment rate is put at slightly under 9 per cent.

Figure 21.2

Slovenia: Inflation

(% change from previous month)

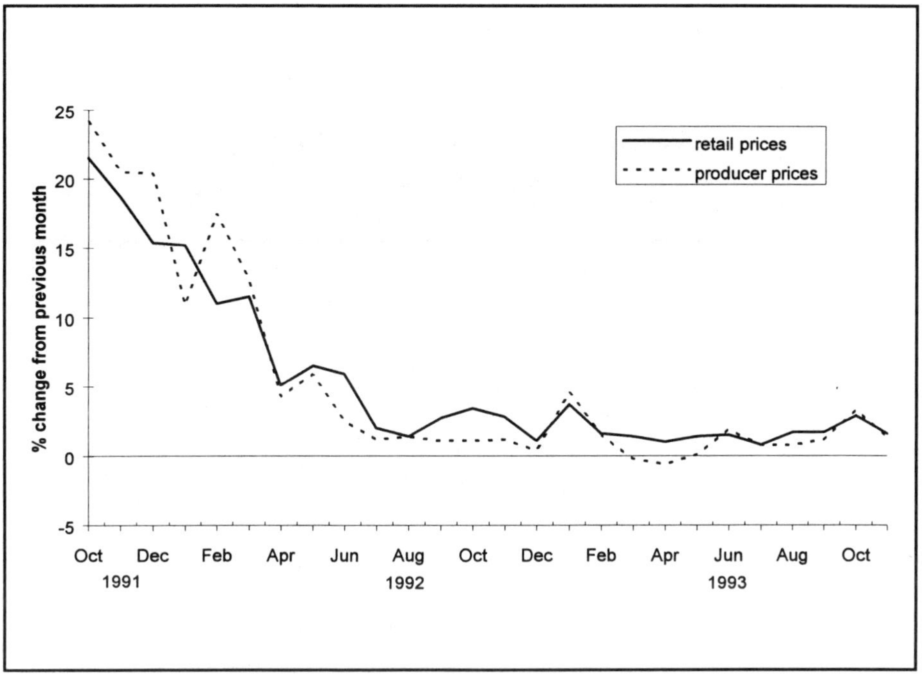

Inflation was steadily suppressed and reached a minimum of 0.7 per cent in July 1993. The general drop comprised major changes in relative prices. Prices of non-tradeables have been growing, prices of tradeables have, except for agricultural goods enjoying different measures of protection, been lagging, and prices of public utilities have remained pegged to tradeables. Inflation at this level has accompanied futile attempts to introduce sound income policies.[2] In four months (in the summer of 1993), the wage bill increased by over 13 per cent in nominal and 5.6 per cent in real terms. This can be explained by traditional structural explanations of inflationary mechanism enhanced by the long-lasting "pre-privatisation environment" (Bole 1993) in which enterprises are able and willing to push wages up so that employees get as much as possible before privatisation is completed.

Figure 21.3

Slovenia: Exports and imports by month

(million of US$)

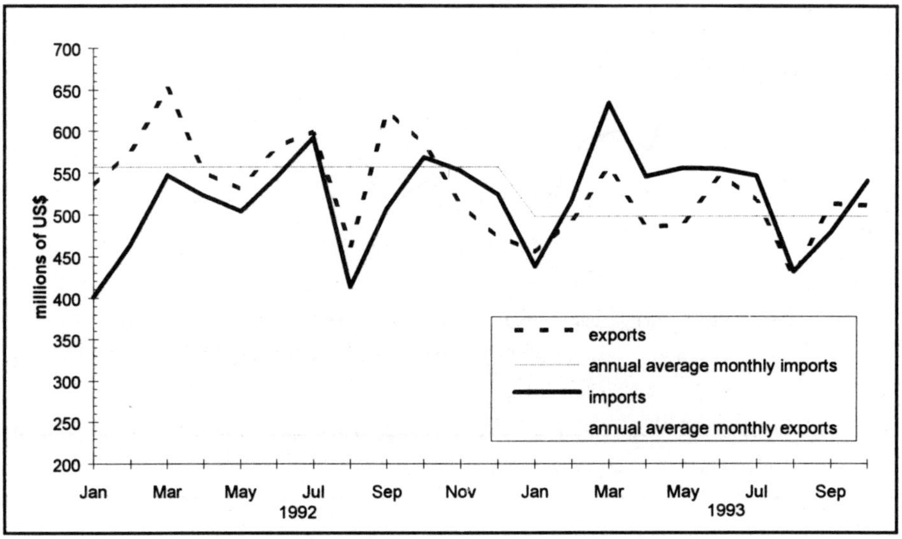

---

2) In the third quarter of 1993, a Wage Contract replaced the Law on Wage Bill Freeze from the beginning of 1993. An increase of inflation by less than 3 per cent a month is not compensated. If prices increase by more than 3 per cent and less than 5 per cent per month or cumulatively in two months, 60 per cent of the increase is compensated by wage increase. If monthly increase or cumulative increase in two months exceeds 5 per cent, 80 per cent of the increase is compensated. Expectations that this Wage Contract would be a far less efficient anchor for wages and social transfers (which are pegged to average wages) turned out correct.

The relative stability of the floating tolar can be considered a success. Two sharp rises of the nominal rates, in October 1991 and in January 1992, were followed by a nearly constant nominal rate until the middle of 1992. Since then, the exchange rate changes have roughly accompanied inflation. Consequently, the real exchange rate fell by a third in the first period, recovered a little, and has since then remained rather stable. The "overvalued" tolar was in 1992 accompanied by a surplus in foreign trade and constant growth of foreign exchange reserves, which at the end of August 1993 reached $ 1,381 mn – a high figure given the size of the economy and the corresponding M1. The success in 1992 can be explained by the lags of foreign trade flows in responding to the real exchange rate changes, by the monetary policy, and by the shifts of supply and demand which resulted in a lower equilibrium real exchange rate. The results in 1993 have been far less impressive; exports dropped by 4.8 per cent and imports grew by 10.6 per cent.[3)]

The boundaries of economic policy in a small open economy

While the relative importance of the elements of depression in Slovenia differ from those in other East European countries, a kind of "transformational recession" has prevailed. The well-known dilemma of "shock versus gradual approach" appeared in Slovenia during the preparations for independence and immediately afterwards. After two years, the reality is more gradual than even the most enthusiastic "gradualists" had suggested, as regards changes both in the economic system and in economic policy. (For indicators of the main features of economic policy see *Figure 21.4* and *Table 21.2.)*

---

3) The drop in total exports was caused by the collapse of trade with former Yugoslavia which plunged by 33 per cent while exports to other countries increased by 3.1 per cent. Total imports were affected in the opposite direction; modest growth of 10.6 per cent reflected a 36 per cent drop in imports from former Yugoslav republics, while imports from other countries increased by 22 per cent.

Table 21.2

Slovenia: Indicators of economic policy since independence
(monthly ratios to 1991/9)

	nominal				real[a)]		
	retail prices	**money supply**	**wage bill**	**tax revenue**	**money supply**	**wage bill**	**tax revenue**
1991/9	1.00	1.00	1.00	1.00	1.00	1.00	1.00
/10	1.21	1.08	1.19	1.60	0.89	0.98	1.32
/11	1.44	1.13	1.27	1.38	0.78	0.88	0.96
/12	1.66	1.18	1.52	1.94	0.71	0.91	1.16
1992/1	1.91	1.41	1.49	1.80	0.73	0.77	0.94
/2	2.12	1.35	1.74	1.84	0.63	0.81	0.86
/3	2.37	1.51	1.94	2.22	0.63	0.82	0.93
/4	2.49	1.62	2.24	2.77	0.64	0.90	1.11
/5	2.65	1.60	2.39	2.85	0.60	0.89	1.07
/6	2.81	1.72	2.68	3.35	0.61	0.95	1.19
/7	2.86	1.84	2.84	3.68	0.64	0.99	1.28
/8	2.90	2.04	2.94	3.48	0.70	1.01	1.19
/9	2.98	2.16	3.02	3.54	0.72	1.01	1.18
/10	3.08	2.27	3.26	3.80	0.73	1.05	1.23
/11	3.17	2.34	3.33	3.84	0.73	1.05	1.21
/12	3.21	2.73	3.93	4.73	0.85	1.22	1.47
1993/1	3.32	2.66	3.42	4.12	0.79	1.02	1.23
/2	3.38	2.69	4.02	4.13	0.79	1.19	1.22
/3	3.43	2.78	3.93	4.79	0.81	1.14	1.39
/4	3.46	2.84	3.88	4.56	0.82	1.12	1.31
/5	3.51	2.92	3.73	4.43	0.83	1.06	1.26
/6	3.56	3.21	3.73	4.63	0.90	1.04	1.30
/7	3.59	3.31	3.87	4.90	0.92	1.07	1.36
/8	3.65	3.33	3.92	4.70	0.91	1.07	1.28
/9	3.71	3.43	4.04	4.71	0.92	1.08	1.27
/10	3.82	3.56	4.23	4.85	0.93	1.11	1.27

a) Nominal values deflated by retail prices.

Figure 21.4

Slovenia: Macroeconomic policies

(1991-1993/10)

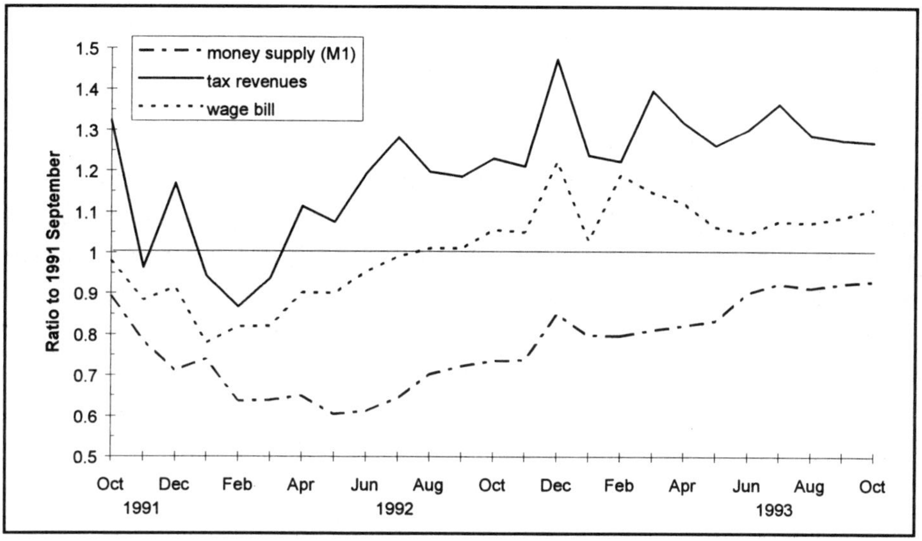

Monetary policy was crucial for preserving the relatively strong tolar alongside the surplus on the current account. It reacted cautiously in removing initial administrative restrictions and intervened sensibly to prevent the substantial nominal appreciations of the tolar that would have resulted from supply and demand in 1992. The exchange rate manipulations were circumscribed by the fight against inflation and by structural changes following the secession from Yugoslavia. Due to the small size of the Slovene market and the divergence between the structure of domestic demand and the structure of supply which was adapted to the Yugoslav market, sales to Yugoslavia could only be replaced by exports but unfortunately at prices much lower than on the protected Yugoslav market, which implied lower real wages, both in the tradeable and non-tradeables sectors. The effects of the temporary shifts in supply and demand for foreign exchange, that preserved the mixture of the strong tolar and growth of foreign exchange reserves with the mixture of plummeting production and rising unemployment, could not be permanent. The foreign trade responses to depreciations that prevailed in 1991, have been followed in 1993 by responses to real appreciations prevailing in 1992. Monetary policy, conceived to keep inflation under control, and to preserve a real exchange rate at competitive levels, became trapped in conflicting goals (Mencinger 1994, forthcoming). In short, monetary policy has to be helped by fiscal and income policies. So far, these have remained weak; the expenditures of the public sector, both of the general government and of social services, have far exceeded the potentials of the economy and the existing real wages have been too high to compete with much lower real wages in the countries of Eastern Europe. A lasting stabilisation with growth requires reduction of costs per unit of output, modest public expenditures, wage restraints, and administrative price controls of non-tradeables. With an import/export ratio over 1:2 and a supply structure adapted to the former Yugoslav market, the tiny economy cannot rely on domestic absorbtion and on standard Keynesian cures. The increase of domestic demand would only marginally affect economic activity, and would, instead, trigger new inflation. The "take-off" is bound to be generated by export demand which however implies lower real costs of production, thus lower real wages and social transfers. The country thus depends crucially on the revival of the world economy and/or severe supply side measures of economic policy. So far, there have been no clear signs for any of them. Thus, the prolongation of the strengthening of economic activity remains uncertain.

Disappointing privatisation

Privatisation in Slovenia also proved to be the most intriguing issue in transition. Two opposite concepts divided political parties and became the root of political instability. The first proposed a gradual, decentralised and commercial privatisation; the second insisted on a mass, centralised and distributive privatisation.

The concept of gradual, decentralised, and commercial privatisation tried to observe major economic and social legacies and seemed suited to the relatively efficient Slovene economy (Bajt 1992). The notion *"decentralised"* implied that enterprises themselves initiate the process of transformation into private companies. The government's role was, consequently, limited to determining the rules and to monitoring the process but not (except in special cases) to implementing it. *"Gradualism"* marked the possibility that initial privatisation by the sale of the existing equity capital or by raising of additional equity capital might be full or partial. The notion *"commercial"* implied that there would be no free distribution of shares at the beginning of the process. Instead, the citizens of Slovenia would be entitled to a discount on the purchase of shares up to a certain value and the employees would enjoy additional discounts.

This concept was in 1991 replaced by the concept of mass, centralised, distributive privatisation. According to this view, the social and economic legacies of the previous system, based on self-management, should be abolished overnight. The notion *"centralised"* related to the role of the government in the privatisation process, implying that the government would carry out the privatisation procedures. By *"mass"* privatisation, it was meant that enterprises were to be immediately converted into joint stock companies by *"free distribution"* of shares to the population. The indirect, two stage approach of free distribution was chosen. In the first stage, shares are transferred to financial intermediaries. In the second stage, the shares of these institutional owners are distributed free of charge to all citizens of Slovenia. Institutional owners should monitor and restructure the companies, and assure that they are efficient and profitable.

The controversy, which was political rather than economic, proved fatal; because of it, Slovenia remained without a privatisation bill for two years during which spontaneous privatisation has abounded in number and forms (Korže 1992). *The Law on the Transformation of Social Ownership* was finally passed on 8 November 1992. Under it, transformation is attained: by restitution to former owners; by debt-equity swaps; by transfer of shares to the Restitution Fund, the Pension Fund, and the Development Fund; by distribution of shares to employees; by managers' and workers' buy-outs; by sales of shares or of the company; and by raising additional equity capital. After restitution to former owners ten per cent of the existing capital goes to the Pension Fund, ten per cent to the Restitution Fund, and twenty per cent to the Privatisation (Development) Fund which is to transfer the shares to the newly established investment companies. Up to twenty per cent of the capital of a company is to be allocated to employees in exchange for their ownership certificates. The rest (40 per cent) is to be sold in 18 months through management and employee buy-outs, public tenders, public auctions, and public offerings of shares, or transferred to the Privatisation Fund. Ownership certificates to facilitate free distribution of shares among employees and citizens at large were distributed in October 1993. The employees can use their certificates (and the certificates of the members of their families) to acquire shares in "their" company, or, together with other citizens, to acquire shares of other companies in public auctions, to acquire shares of state-owned enterprises, or to acquire shares in the investment companies. In short, the privatisation swelled up to an enormous administrative operation.

The outcomes of privatisation will differ; but the efficiency gains will be minor or even negative depending on whether active or passive owners will prevail which depends on the value (administrative evaluation) of the enterprise, the value of ownership certificates in the hands of the employees, and their readiness to use them to acquire shares in "their" company. In small successful firms the insiders will assure the majority directly, in some large firms they will assure the prevalence indirectly by dispersion of shares to general public. In both cases, efficiency might increase slightly; the management will remain unaltered. Loss-making firms will end in the hands of different institutional owners (funds and investment companies) who will be passive owners interested in the sale of such companies and the immediate distribution of proceeds or profits instead of their reinvestment. The general efficiency might even drop.

Short-term prospects

According to estimates in *The Budget Memorandum* (November 1993), a document on economic policy and a provisional budget for 1994 with projections for 1995-1997[4)], one per cent growth is expected in 1994.

The following policies are expected to provide for a modest "take off". *Fiscal policy* is to support expected economic growth by lowering the tax burden and decreasing the role of government, which should provide resources for development. The envisaged real decline in social spending, and a shift from direct to indirect taxes to diminish labour costs and increase competitiveness of the economy, are the two most remarkable features. The changes in the income tax rates are to shift the tax burden from the poorer to the richer strata of the population, while tax allowances for investments are to provide the environment for lowering the interest rate. A budget deficit of 1.2 per cent of

---

4) The document was approved after long deliberations concentrated on the "guns or butter" dilemma. An agreement signed by the parties in the ruling coalition, according to which the law on defence expenditures should be passed before the Budget for 1994, broke the stalemate which threatened the ruling coalition. By this agreement some accounting principles were broken. The opposition boycotted the voting by walking out.

GDP should create additional impulses for growth. *Income policy* is considered crucial for lowering the costs of production and increasing competitiveness. It is to be ensured by a Wage Contract which should provide for a reduction in real wages. It is hoped that increased competitiveness will also change the structure of imports in favour of intermediate and investment goods, and that reduction of wages would also increase savings. Institutional provisions for regulating competition are to enable proper functioning on the domestic market. The *price control* in the infrastructural sector should account for development costs while the price changes of prices (gasoline, electricity, transport) that are controlled by the government should be gradual. The policy of *market promotion* should help to penetrate new markets while retaining cooperation with European countries. *Tariff protection* would remain unchanged on the existing level, but should be enriched by some *non-tariff measures* similar to those in developed countries. The *privatisation,* concentrated in 1994, is supposed to increase the efficiency of the economy and to provide incentives for restructuring.

The Budget Memorandum appears more and more an inconsistent document and its main goals – the reduction of inflation and the squeeze of public expenditures from 48.8 per cent of GDP to 46.6 per cent – unlikely. Recent (simultaneous) changes in the regulation of old age pensions and expenditures for defence, health, and education endanger the proclaimed reduction of public expenditures, while recent increases of wages cast doubts on the reduction of inflation to 13 per cent by the end of 1994 and on the increased competitiveness that should step up exports and provide a modest surplus in the current balance. Instead, it will inevitably result in higher inflation, lower competitiveness, further de-capitalisation of enterprises, and shrinking of employment. The resulting increase of labour costs might stop the recovery of the economy very soon. The administrative operation of privatisation also does not promise to bring about the needed restructuring. The negative impacts of the reductions of trade with the rest of the former Yugoslavia have also not yet been exhausted.

References

Bajt, A. (1992), *A Property Rights Analysis of the Transition Problems in the East,* EIPF (Ekonomski Inštitut Pravne Fakultete), Ljubljana, p. 26.

Bole, V. (1993), "Restrukturiranje gospodarstva", *Gospodarska Gibanja,* EIPF, Ljubljana, pp. 239, 21-34.

Korže, U. (1992), "Decentralized Privatization Strategy: Pitfalls and Benefits – Slovenia", in *Privatization in Central and Eastern Europe 1991*, Simoneti, M., and Bohm, A. (eds.), Central and Eastern European Privatization Network, Ljubljana, pp. 140-153.

Mencinger, J., "The Birth and the Childhood of a Currency – The Experience of Slovenia", in *International Trade and Restructuring in Eastern Europe*, Gács, J. (ed.), (forthcoming).

STATISTICAL APPENDIX
(Chapter 21)

Table A.1

Slovenia: Foreign trade, 1992-1993
(US$ million)

	exports			imports			surplus/deficit		
	total	YU[a)]	other[b)]	total	YU[a)]	other[b)]	total	YU[a)]	other[b)]
1992	6681	1508	5173	6141	1218	4923	540	290	250
1992/1	536	160	376	401	109	292	135	51	84
/2	575	167	408	465	124	341	110	43	67
/3	654	193	461	547	150	397	107	43	64
/4	550	152	398	523	122	401	27	30	-3
/5	531	125	406	504	106	398	27	19	8
/6	581	113	468	545	102	443	36	11	25
/7	599	107	492	592	111	481	7	-4	11
/8	461	106	355	413	77	336	48	29	19
/9	624	111	513	508	86	422	116	25	91
/10	586	110	476	568	104	464	18	6	12
/11	511	90	421	552	64	488	-41	26	-67
/12	474	76	398	524	63	461	-50	13	-63
1993/1	456	72	384	438	60	378	18	12	6
/2	492	80	412	517	65	452	-25	15	-40
/3	558	88	470	634	69	565	-76	19	-95
/4	485	83	403	545	67	479	-60	16	-76
/5	488	73	415	555	57	498	-67	16	-83
/6	547	85	462	554	58	496	-7	27	-34
/7	518	75	442	546	54	492	-28	21	-48
/8	425	100	325	432	47	385	-7	53	-60
/9	513	78	435	479	51	428	34	27	7
/10	512	70	442	540	52	488	-28	18	-46
1992/1-10	5696	1342	4355	5065	1091	3975	633	251	380
1993/1-10	4992	803	4189	5242	581	4661	-250	222	-472

a) Former Yugoslavia. – b) Rest of world.

Source: Statistical Office of Slovenia.

Table A.2

Slovenia: Regional structure of trade, 1-9/1993
(US$ million)

	exports	imports	total	balance	export/ import	share %
Developed countries	3159	3452	6611	-293	.915	72.0
– Germany	1336	1149	2485	187	1.16	27.1
– Italy	564	762	1326	-198	.740	14.4
– France	387	389	776	-2	.995	8.5
– United Kingdom	98	71	169	27	1.38	1.8
– Netherlands	67	87	154	-20	.770	1.7
EC countries	2572	2590	5162	-18	.993	56.2
– Austria	229	397	626	-168	.577	6.8
EFTA countries	317	566	883	-249	.560	9.6
– Japan	18	94	112	-76	.191	1.2
– USA	162	124	286	38	1.31	3.1
OECD non-Europe	234	250	484	-16	.936	5.3
Other developed countries	37	46	83	-9	.804	0.9
Developing countries	1321	1249	2570	72	1.06	28.0
– Croatia	567	451	1018	116	1.26	11.1
– Macedonia	145	68	213	77	2.13	2.3
former Yugoslavia	733	529	1262	204	1.39	13.7
– former USSR	192	149	341	43	1.29	3.7
developing countries Europe	250	282	532	-32	.887	5.8
other developing countries	146	290	436	-144	.503	4.8
Total	4480	4702	9182	-222	.953	100.0

Source: Statistical Office of Slovenia.

Table A.3

Slovenia: Balance of payments, 1-8/1993
(US$ million)

	Inflow	Outflow	Balance
A. Current transactions	4997.8	5056.1	-58.3
1. goods	3957.4	4199.4	-242.0
2. nonfactor services	892.6	735.4	157.1
– transport	291.6	257.1	34.5
– travel	478.2	224.0	254.2
– other	122.8	254.3	-131.5
3. factor services	76.7	121.3	-44.6
4. transfers	71.1	0	71.1
B. Capital transactions			84.2
1. direct investments			83.1
2. other investments			-0.1
3. other			1.2
C. Short-term capital			15.4
D. Errors and omissions			9.1
Changes in the assets of Central Bank			-50.4

Source: ARC and *Bilten,* Bank of Slovenia.

Table A.4

Slovenia: Debts, credit commitments and foreign exchange reserves

(US$ million)

	end-1991	end-1992	31.8.1993
Total debt	1866	1741	1772
Long-term debt	1765	1659	1681
– public	1357	1203	1180
– private	408	456	501
Short-term debt	101	82	75
Loans extended	418	281	247
Net debt	1448	1460	1525
Foreign exchange reserves	365	1163	1381
– Bank of Slovenia	112	716	744
– banks	253	447	637
Net debt – reserves	1083	297	144

Source: Bilten, Bank of Slovenia.

Table A.5

Slovenia: The state budget

(tolar billion)

	1993 (est.)	1994 (proj.)	1994/1993 nominal	1994/1993 real[a)]
Revenues	310.3	382.1	1.23	1.02
direct taxes				
– incomes	54.9	58.5	1.07	0.88
– profits	5.8	7.4	1.27	1.05
indirect taxes				
– sales tax	158.3	207.5	1.31	1.08
– custom duties	50.2	62.6	1.25	1.03
Expenditures	324.7	395.7	1.22	1.01
Current expenditures	291.3	356.1	1.22	1.01
– wages and salaries	74.0	85.2	1.15	0.95
– material costs	13.1	15.9	1.21	1.00
– defense	19.9	34.1	1.70	1.42
– social transfers	65.9	83.8	1.27	1.05
– services to govt.	40.1	45.5	1.13	0.94
– interest, guarantees	28.2	40.2	1.42	1.18
– subsidies to economy	30.7	27.1	0.88	0.73
– transfers to local govts.	14.0	19.8	1.41	1.17
Investments	33.4	39.6	1.19	0.98
– highways	11.0	18.8	1.71	1.41
Surplus/(Deficit)	(16.8)	(16.5)	0.98	0.81

a) Current prices assuming average year to year inflation of 21 per cent.

Table A.6

Slovenia: Public sector revenues and expenditures

(tolar billion, share in GDP)

	1993 (est.)		1994 (proj.)		real percentage change
GDP	1323	100	1617	100	+1.0
Revenues	646	48.8	754	46.6	-3.6
Tax revenues	605	45.7	703	43.5	-10.0
– taxes	308	23.3	376	23.3	+1.0
– contributions for soc. sec.	297	22.5	327	20.2	-9.1
Non-tax revenues	41	3.1	51	3.1	+2.8
Expenditures	658	49.7	773	47.8	-2.9
Pensions	182	13.7	211	13.0	-4.1
Health care	105	7.9	120	7.4	-5.4
Government	301	22.8	360	22.3	-1.2
Local governments	69	5.2	80	5.0	-3.2

Chapter 22

THE CROATIAN ECONOMY IN TRANSITION

Dragomir Vojnić*)

22.1 Some characteristics of transitional crisis

I will first discuss some major issues of the transitional crisis. The Croatian economy, like all the other countries in transition, is passing through a very difficult transitional crisis. That transitional crisis has been manifested in drastic declines of gross domestic product, employment, productivity, all categories of consumption, salaries and wages, and overall standards of living. The drastic falls in production and consumption occurred simultaneously with high rates of escalating inflation. The facts are summarised in *Table 22.1.*

Such a drastic decline of gross domestic product was suffered by no other country in transition, certainly by none with which Croatia can reasonably be compared.[1)]

A fall in gross domestic product in 1993 to one half of that in the prewar year 1990, has little precedent in recent history. It displays a far more difficult situation than the world was enduring in the Great Depression of the 1930s. Industrial production in Croatia fell somewhat less, but by more than two fifths of the prewar level. Economic policy was thus confronted with hardly solvable tasks and problems. Employment decreased to about three quarters of prewar, while unemployment increased by almost three fifths. Labour productivity fell below three quarters of prewar, and average wages of employees to below two fifths. Consumption of goods and services by the population fell by over a half from 1990, and investment by nearly one fifth. During the first nine months of 1993, the unemployment rate was 17.6 per cent and monthly inflation 27.5 per

---

*) Professor of Economics, Institute of Economics, University of Zagreb, Croatia.

1) For comparative economic statistics see, e.g., Gabrisch, H. (1993), "Under the Impact of Western Recession. The economic situation of the post-socialist countries in the first quarter of 1993 and outlook for 1993/94", *WIIW Research Reports,* no. 197b, June.

cent. Although the other countries in transition confront difficult crises, their severity is markedly less than in Croatia.

Table 22.1

Some economic indicators for Croatia

	1991/1990	1992/1991	1993/1992 Jan.-Sept.	1993/1990 Jan.-Sept.
		per cent of previous period		
Gross domestic product (est.)	71.3	76.4	90.4	49.2
Industrial production	71.5	85.4	93.6	56.2
Employment (total)	88.4	88.8	96.4	75.7
Unemployment	157.9	105.1	94.8	157.3
Productivity	83.5	88.7	97.3	72.1
Average wage per worker	83.4	54.1	83.7	37.8
Personal expenditures on goods and services	76.8	70.5	82.6	44.7
Investment	60.0	40.9	71.7	17.6
	1990	**1991**	**1992**	**1993 Jan.-Sept.**
		averages for period		
Unemployment rate (per cent)	9.3	15.5	17.8	17.6
Inflation rate (per cent monthly)	7.4	11.0	21.5	27.5

Source: National Statistics. Centre for Economic Informatics and Statistics, Institute of Economics Zagreb, 1993.

Why was the transitional crisis in Croatia so much more intense than elsewhere? Some particular factors relating to Croatia should be underlined as basic reasons. The first is the extent of war damage (which amounted to nearly $ 20 billion already by mid-1992; *Table 22.2),* war devastation and war expenditures. Over one quarter of the whole state territory was occupied. Huge numbers of refugees and displaced persons – between 300 and 600,000 – have been continuously living in Croatia. These are displaced persons from the occupied territories of Croatia or refugees from the various parts of Bosnia and Herzegovina and Serbia. According to the Croatian Office for Refugees and Displaced Persons (25 August 1993), there were 239,785 refugees and 249,199 displaced persons registered in Croatia, which along with an estimed

37,050 unregistered displaced persons amounts to 526,034 persons. Besides, 77,500 refugees from Croatia are accommodated in other European countries.[2] Average costs for one displaced person or refugee come to about $ 3 daily. However, in spite of all the humanitarian help from abroad, the budget of the Republic of Croatia suffers a huge burden of support expenses for this host of refugees and displaced persons.

Table 22.2

An estimation of war damages in Croatia

at mid-1992, in US$ million

	Direct	Indirect	Total	% of economy	% of costs
Industry	1600	900	2500	18.0	12.6
Agriculture and food industry	780	520	1300	9.3	6.5
Forestry and wood industry	787	396	1183	8.5	6.0
Water utilities	150	140	290	2.1	1.5
Transport and communications	1426	798	2224	16.0	11.2
road communication	90	90	180	-	0.9
road infrastructure	261	215	476	-	1.4
railway	353	249	602	-	3.0
river transport and ports	90	10	100	-	0.5
maritime transport and maritime ports	38	67	105	-	0.5
air transport	94	30	124	-	0.6
post communication and radio and television	500	137	637	-	3.2
Trade	20	900	920	6.6	4.6
Tourism and catering	230	1480	1710	12.3	8.6
Communal utilities and housing	3800	...	3800	27.2	19.2
Economy	8793	5134	13927	100.0	70.1
Social welfare	100	1000	1100		5.6
Education, culture and sport	2500	...	2500		12.6
Public health	2300	...	2300		11.6
Social activities	4900	1000	5900		29.8
Total	13693	6134	19827		100.0

Source: Report on Estimation of the War Damages in Croatia, Drzavni zavod za makroekonomske analize i prognoze Republike Hrvatske (State Bureau for Macroeconomic Analysis and Prognoses of the Republic of Croatia), Zagreb, September 1992.

2) *Economic Development in Croatia* (1993), vol. III, no. 5-7 (May-July), State Bureau for Macroeconomic Analyses and Forecasting of the Republic of Croatia, Zagreb, p. 15.

The second peculiarity is the fact that the Republic of Croatia became an independent, sovereign and internationally recognised state no earlier than in 1992. A group from the Institute of Economics, Zagreb, using a simulation model, have come to the approximate conclusion that one half of the drastic decline in all relevant macroeconomic aggregates is due to the war and its consequences. The other half is due to the loss of markets, both in the former Yugoslavia and in the other ex-socialist countries (Marendić 1992).[3] Recession in the developed economies of the West surely influenced, directly or indirectly, economic development in Croatia. However, that influence, compared with the factors mentioned above (and others not mentioned) had only marginal significance.

To sum up, the transition in Croatia has suffered not only from general causes affecting all countries in transition, but also from special factors: the consequences of the war, and of the emergence of the Republic of Croatia as an independent state.

22.2 Property and market transition

The second issue that I will discuss is the transition of property rights which has begun, as in most ex-socialist countries, with many dilemmas and hesitations. These similarities and hesitations referred to the choice of method for property pluralisation in the movement towards privatisation. A basic question is whether to set off privatisation by a sale (with bigger or smaller benefits), or by some other method such as a public distribution of capital. The difference in Croatia derives from the fact that unlike other countries in transition, it was not state property but *social* property that was dominant. Property rights based on social property are closer to property rights based on private, than on state property. That happens because the macroeconomic environment based on social property assumes a market for goods and services, the independence of economic subjects and the decentralisation of economic decisions.

When the Law for Privatisation of Social Firms was in preparation, a group at our Institute prepared a study of "Privatisation in the Policy of Economic

---

3) Marendić, Božo, and Škegro, Borislav (eds.) et al. (1992), "Conception and Strategy of Economic Development of the Republic of Croatia", in *Economic Movements and Economic Policy of Croatia,* no. 10, National Bank of Croatia and Institute of Economics, Zagreb, p. 147.

Development" (Zdunić 1991).[4)] The starting point was the principle that in Croatia social property should be converted into private property. That means that the transition should be realised not through a return to state property but by direct transformation into private property. This study suggested an "open strategy" providing for different models of privatisation. The following basic methods are suggested:

- participation of various subjects by free distribution of primary share issues;
- participation by internal and external shares;
- coexistence (competition) of social and private property.

All possible combinations of these three basic methods should be permitted, depending on the concrete situation and on all characteristics (sectoral, regional, market, etc.) towards which the enterprise should adjust during the transition. Although the Law for Privatisation of Social Firms also started with the model of open strategy providing for various methods of privatisation, it included some essential differences from the study referred to. All firms which have not been privatised in a given period become the property of the Croatian Fund for Privatisation which has to take forward the process of transformation, or privatisation. Other differences from the cited study relate to the distribution method for one part of social capital.

The basic methods applied are (a) sell; (b) debt to equity conversion; (c) privatisation through additional investment; (d) transfer of shares to the Fund for Development and other funds. The sale includes sale of shares to the employees of the firm, within a limit of DM 20,000, with a 20 per cent discount plus 1 per cent for each year of service. Employees may also pay for their shares over five years (paying only five per cent in the first year). Not more than 50 per cent of the total share capital can be bought by the firm's employees. The Law foresees the participation in the purchase of social capital of the Health, Pension and Disability Insurance Fund to the extent of 30 per cent (in equal amounts of 15 per cent). Although the Denationalisation Law has not yet been introduced, part of the assets will be set aside for compensation of former owners.

30 June 1992 was determined as the deadline for transfer of property rights (into private or state property). Up to that date the Agency for Restructuring and Development and the Croatian Development Fund received requests for so-called

---

4) Zdunić, Stjepan, et al. (1991), *Privatisation in the Policy of Economic Development,* Institute of Economics, Zagreb, March, pp. 91-96.

"autonomous transformation" from 2,422 firms, which equals about two thirds of the total number of 3,600 social firms to which the Law for Privatisation of Social Firms applies.[5)]

The process of transformation of social firms has continued, so that by the end of September 1993 in total 2818 presented their programmes to the Croatian Fund for Privatisation. Distribution of those firms is shown by sectors in *Table 22.3.* 2,082 firms had by then concluded agreements for transformation, and most of the others will have received decisions from the Fund by the end of 1993. Transformation has been completed in 1,759 firms. Of these 845 (48 per cent) have been completely privatised, in 263 (15 per cent) the Funds have become the dominant owners, while in 651 (37 per cent) Funds have minority share holdings. About 350,000 agreements have been made with the buyers of shares. The biggest number of buyers (80 per cent) negotiated progress payments for a period of five years, most of them paying only 5 per cent in the first year. Therefore, the figure of 845 wholly privatised firms must be treated with caution. The final payment was achieved in only 13,620 agreements, only 4 per cent of the total number of agreements signed. The total assets realised from the sale of firms came to about DM 476 million by the end of September 1993, of which DM 176 mn (37 per cent) was in cash and about DM 300 mn (63 per cent) was "old foreign exchange savings", which have been transformed into public debt.[6)] That means that only DM 176 mn are additional financial assets, while DM 300 mn represent a decrease of public debt. Since the total social capital of Croatia has been estimated at about DM 40 billion, the assets concerned represent less than 1.5 per cent. All these assets are credited to the budget of the Republic of Croatia.[7)]

The question then arises why the effects of the transformation are so moderate. There are two big reasons. The first is the very restricted purchasing

---

5) In view of war and other special circumstances, as well as the occupation of parts of Croatia, this number of firms is approximate.

6) "Old foreign exchange savings" represent foreign exchange holdings of the population on the bank accounts of ex-Yugoslavia, which were converted by the Republic of Croatia into public debt which has been regularly serviced with interest of 5 per cent.

7) All data related to the ownership transition and privatisation have been cited from: *Croatian Fund for Privatisation: September Report to the Croatian Parliament* (1993), Zagreb, pp. 11-16.

power of domestic buyers. The second is the very strong reluctance of potential foreign buyers, regarding Croatia as a country of high risk.

A particularly important and difficult problem is the fact that at present it is *state* and no longer *social* property which is dominant in Croatia. From the aspect of the macroeconomic environment which should characterise a market economy, that does not represent progress, but the opposite. Whether such a pattern of property rights will represent a bigger or a smaller problem for the complete transformation of the Croatian economy will depend upon the speed of transformation of (not social any more but) state into private property. The Croatian Fund for Privatisation is obliged, as a rule, to put all the shares acquired by transformations at disposal for sale through the Zagreb stock exchange. Up to now, 188 firms have offered their shares for sale through the stock exchange. The value of shares sold amounts to DM 22.8 mn, which is less than modest.

Table 22.3

Croatia: Enterprises in tranformation, by sector

Sector	**number of requests for transformation**	**%**
Industry	782	27.8
Agriculture and fisheries	231	8.2
Construction	273	9.7
Transport and communications	88	3.1
Trade	406	14.4
Catering industry and tourism	216	7.7
Small business and services	186	6.6
Housing	34	1.2
Financial, technical and business services	360	12.8
Education, science, information and culture	92	3.3
Health and social security	15	0.5
Miscellaneous	135	4.8
Total	2818	100.0

Source: Croatian Fund for Privatisation, September Report to the Croatian Parliament, Zagreb, 1993, pp. 11-16.

In an effort to sell more shares, the Fund, along with the stock exchange, will sell its shares through public issues. Some firms in infrastructure and power supply would, however, remain in public and state ownership.

Because of the high level of interdependence between the transformation of property rights towards the predominant role of private property, and the transformation of market institutions, especially of capital and labour, the present structure of property in Croatia is very inappropriate. Hence, the transition to the market is very slow. During four decades of reforms in Croatia, the market institutions for goods and services were developed. But the institutions, mechanisms and instruments for labour and capital markets are only beginning to appear.

Privatisation in Croatia has largely taken the form of a great number of new small firms. The total number of firms increased from 17,350 in December 1990 to 66,091 in April 1993. The major increases were in trade, industry, building, hotels and catering and financial facilities. These small firms are very significant for development of entrepreneurship and employment, but their role is still marginal in the structure of capital.[8)]

At this rate the transformation of property rights would last not just for many years but for several decades. For these reasons, discussion of the need to speed up the process by privatisation has been intensified in professional and political circles. There are some signs that economic policy will by early 1994 begin a distribution of part of the social, or state capital (by means of shares and vouchers) to the workers and citizens. During September of 1993, distribution of shares to disabled persons of the civil war and to the families of dead soldiers came to about DM 9.6 mn.

It is therefore unnecessary to stress that faster privatisation (including distribution of vouchers) is the essential condition for a more efficient transition of the Croatian economy as a whole. This is at the same time the essential condition for effecting a macroeconomic policy of stabilisation, for more efficient reconstruction and development, and for easing the existing serious tensions.[9)]

---

8) *Economic Development in Croatia* (1993), vol. III, no. 3-4 (March-April), State Bureau for Macroeconomic Analyses and Forecasting of the Republic of Croatia, Zagreb, p. 76.

9) To the social tensions already mentioned – an unemployment rate of 17.6 per cent, monthly inflation rate of 27 per cent, average salary per employee 37 per cent of the prewar level, over one half million of refugees and displaced persons – must be added the increased number of insolvencies: 400 legal persons employing about 65 thousand workers in September 1993. For more detailed information see *Economic Development in Croatia* (1993), vol. III, no. 5-7 (May-July), State Bureau for Macroeconomic Analyses and Forecasting of the Republic of Croatia, p. 58.

22.3 Transformation of the macroeconomic environment

The third issue that I would like to discuss refers to the transformation of the macroeconomic environment. One of the main tasks is the creation of a macroeconomic framework within which the transition will be achieved (to cite *János Kornai)* from "soft budget constraints" to "hard budget constraints".[10] In Croatia (which has a long tradition of reform), the radical reforms in that direction began at the end of 1989 and at the beginning of 1990. These radical changes were intensified in early 1992 when the Republic of Croatia became an independent and internationally recognised state, and when the Croatian dinar was introduced as the national currency. The new legal bases for the monetary and fiscal sphere, for the functions of the central bank and commercial banks, for the function of firms and for labour and property relations and also for foreign direct investments and joint ventures, and for the foreign trade and foreign exchange system, created institutional frameworks which are very similar to those in market economies.

Some other relevant laws will be adopted soon: a Corporation Law (the basis of economic legislation in market economies), a Securities Law, and others, all strengthening the similarity of the macroeconomic environment to that of the developed market economies. Appropriate changes will follow in the tax system and fiscal policy. The intention is to make the tax system more transparent, convenient and attractive to the citizens as well as to foreign investors. It is probable that preparations for the introduction of VAT, when circumstances permit, will continue.

Apart from the special circumstances of this period in Croatia – the war, war damages and war expenditures – the major obstacles to be overcome in the transformation to the "hard budget constraints" relate to property rights and market transition. I think especially here of accelerated privatisation, which, as was said above, is an essential condition for development as well as for the functions of the institutions of labour and the capital market and, in general, for the market allocation of investment. This also refers to the whole financial complex, especially to the privatisation of commercial banks (which still represent an extended arm of the state). It should be mentioned in this connection that the role of the state in this phase of transition of the Croatian economy is very

---

10) Kornai, János (1986), "The Soft Budget Constraints", *Kyklos,* pp. 3-30.

evident. This can be explained partly by the war and partly by the domination of state property. Direct intervention of the state in the monetary sphere, attempting solutions which should be solved by fiscal action (such as selective loans for agriculture, export of ships and equipment etc.) continued during the recent slowing down of the transition to the "hard budget constraints" (Hunke 1991).[11)] The stabilisation programme recently adopted by the Government of the Republic of Croatia should represent a good basis for the further transformation of the macroeconomic environment and for a more stable economic development.

22.4 The macroeconomic stabilisation programme[12)]

The fourth issue to be discussed refers to the macroeconomic stabilisation programme. During 1993, negative tendencies of economic development continued. This is illustrated by almost all the basic current economic indicators (presented in *Table 22.4* for the first nine months of 1993).

The negative tendencies in the development of production, employment and consumption, with further escalation of inflation, are clear. In September, the monthly inflation rate escalated over the psychological barrier of 30 per cent. These developments occurred in conditions of general indexation. It is well known (e.g. from experience in Israel as shown by Michael Bruno) that general indexation can neither slow down inflation nor protect the standard of living (Bruno 1993).[13)] On the contrary, the experience of Croatia shows that indexation, because of the impact of inflationary taxation, decreased real demand and restricted production and consumption. Besides, hyperinflation, causing redistribution at the expense of the poor, worsened the already difficult social situation in Croatia. In this connection, one should remember that the gross

---

11) For more information on relevant issues see Hunke, Steve H., and Schuler, Kurt (1991), "Currency Boards for Eastern Europe", *Heritage Lectures,* 355, The Heritage Foundation, p. 38.

12) This section is written in collaboration with Željko Rohatinski, a senior research fellow of the Institute of Economics, Zagreb.

13) For more consideration of some relevant issues see Bruno, Michael (1993), "Stabilisation and the Macroeconomics of Transition – How Different is Eastern Europe?", *Economics of Transition,* vol. I, no. 1, pp. 5-19.

domestic product of 1993 is only about half that of the prewar 1990 and that the average salary per employee is 37 per cent of 1990. The growing number of retirements in conditions of declining employment means a more and more unfavourable proportion between the active and the dependent population. Every employee in the Croatian economy must support 0.75 retired persons. If we add the half million of refugees and displaced persons, then to every employee there are 1.3 persons to support, on a very low level of average wage and even lower minimum wage. The minimum wage in July 1993, the basis for social help, comes to 124,318 dinars (about DM 60) (see Laski 1992)[14)] in July. The total number of recipients of social assistance amounted at the end of August 1993 to 84,238 persons, including 188,326 household members.[15)] As a whole, the social picture reveals deep impoverishment and disintegration along with deeper social differences. Many discontents arising from disturbance to property rights and from privatisation, and from profiteering, have contributed substantially to the rapid disintegration of the population and to the intensifying of social differences in Croatia. In such a situation, the task of simultaneous renewal, reconstruction, restructuring and development was imposed upon economic policy as crucial necessity, in the sense of a *conditio sine qua non* (Zdunić 1993).[16)] However, in order to begin reconstruction and development, the escalating inflation had to be checked. Recognising the urgent need to confront inflation, at the beginning of October 1993 the government, in coordination with the National Bank of Croatia decided to "carry out the final part of the stabilisation programme". This formulation shows that the government intends to intensify achievement of the stabilisation programme which was in principle already accepted as the basis of economic policy. Analysing the causes and character of escalating inflation, economists in many publications during late

---

14) It goes without saying that in Croatia as in some other countries in transition, the difference between the exchange rate and the rate of internal purchasing power has widened. For more information see Laski, Kazimierz (1992), "Transition from Command to Market Economies in Central and Eastern Europe: First Experiences and Questions", *WIIW Research Reports,* no. 181, pp. 14-24.

15) *Economic Development in Croatia* (1993), vol. III, no. 5-7 (May-July), State Bureau for Macroeconomic Analyses and Forecasting of the Republic of Croatia, Zagreb, p. 15.

16) For more consideration of some relevant issues see Zdunić, Stjepan (1993), "Critical Factors in the Policy of Renewal, Reconstruction, Restructuring and Development of Croatian Economy", *Ekonomski pregled,* no. 1-2, Zagreb, pp. 3-36.

Table 22.4

Croatia: Main economic indicators

per cent of previous period

	I-VIII 93/ I-VIII 92	IX 93/ IX 92	I-IX 93/ I-IX 92
Industrial production*	96.9	91.5	93.6
Equipment and machinery	90.2	91.7	90.4
Raw materials	98.5	92.5	97.7
Consumer goods	97.6	90.9	96.7
Stocks of final goods*	103.6	99.0	103.0
Employment (numbers) (public sector)	93.4	94.4	93.5
Goods and services	91.6	93.0	91.8
Education, health and government	100.4	99.7	100.3
Exports (goods)*	86.3	63.4	83.7
Imports (goods)*	105.9	127.1	108.8
Retail trade*	67.4	65.9	67.6
Net wages and salaries (total)*	74.0	82.9	75.0
Personal revenues (total)*	73.5	80.8	74.3
Government revenues*	86.7	92.7	87.4
Personal consumption*	80.8	79.7	80.6
Investment*	70.4	82.9	71.6
Government consumption*	80.0	93.6	81.4
Producer prices (industry)	1646.9	1941.6	1712.9
Retail prices	1649.0	1963.0	1687.1

* constant prices.

Source: as *Table 22.1.*

1992 and 1993 emphasised that the policy of stabilisation should be executed in two phases. In the first, the "psychology of expected inflation" must be dispelled; in the second phase, the real, structural or chronic inflation must be attacked. Simulations showed that about two thirds of the inflation rate can be attributed to the influence of expected inflation, and about one third to the influence of "real" factors (Rohatinski 1993).[17] The "real" factors comprise the

17) Rohatinski, Željko, and Santini, Guste (1993), *Economic Policy for 1993,* RIFIN, Zagreb, pp. 1-49.

contraction of demand, reflected in declining usage of capacity and labour productivity, growth of expenditures, deficits in public sectors for noneconomic reasons, monopolistic behaviour of producers along with hard tax pressures, and transport- and energy problems, all under the shadow of war and the special conditions of the Croatian economy.

With a view to dispelling, in the first phase, the expectation of inflation, what could be described as the classical approach, which relies on four anchors, was adopted. The first anchor refers to the intervention rate of exchange (fixed at a 20 per cent devaluation); the second to primary money; the third to the discount rate; and the fourth to salaries. These four anchors have been introduced in combination with a reduction of tax rates, an attack on tax evasion and the introduction of internal convertibility of national currency.

In the general economic, political, social and defensive circumstances in Croatia, a crucial condition for realising such a programme is political consensus – which, it seems, the government has successfully realised. The political consensus is especially important in the context of the budget deficit (in the broad sense). The cumulated monetarised internal budget deficit (measured by the growth of money supply) reached in the period January-August 1993, a figure of DM 777 mn, which is over 13 per cent of the estimated gross domestic product (Anušić 1993).[18)]

This level of deficit (accompanied by a 59 per cent share of of gross tax revenues in the gross domestic product), itself generated a price increase of about 16 per cent, in the same period. It can be estimated that about one half of that rate is a result of an increase in primary money supply intended for buying foreign currency, or for foreign exchange transactions in a broader sense. The other half of this inflation rate lies in the consequences (with a formally balanced national budget amounting to 32 per cent of gross domestic product) of soft-budget constraints in firms and the funds of public sectors. This especially refers to infrastructure and energy sectors such as electric power, postal, telegraph and telephone services, railways, and to the health, retirement and disability insurance funds. Currency reserves represent the crucial point of the accepted stabilisation programme. The achieved level of currency reserves ($ 1,222 mn) allows at the same time the essential reduction of its growth on the basis of

---

18) Anušić, Zoran (1993), "Budget Deficit and Inflation: Croatia in the Years 1991 and 1992", *Ekonomski pregled,* no. 7-8, Zagreb.

issue financing, and its usage as a source of assets for potential financing of non-economic state expenditure. Besides, the programme includes stabilisation of the material expenditure of the state budget and funds. The programme also strictly determines the tasks of financial discipline in public firms and in firms mainly the property of the state.

However, as noted above, the central task in achieving the Programme relate to the foreign currency reserves. It should be pointed out that these are not as in the classical sense the result of trends in the balance of trade and payments, but result from specific internal and external foreign currency transfers, especially by the population. Thus commodity exports in January-August 1993, in relation to the same period of 1992, were lower by 13.7 per cent. Consequently, the coverage of imports by exports declined from 108.4 to 88.4 per cent. The 1992 surplus of $ 240 mn was transformed in the same period of 1993 to a deficit of $ 352 mn.

However, thanks to the peculiarities mentioned, foreign exchange reserves increased during the first nine months of 1993 by $ 555 mn along with a simultaneous decrease in external debt. Out of the total reserves of $ 1,222 mn, the central bank controls $ 473 mn. That would be probably enough for realisation of the first phase of the stabilisation programme even without support of the appropriate international financial organisations. The second phase probably does require the support of these international organisations, especially of the IMF. It should be mentioned that foreign exchange reserves could cover three months commodity imports or two months total foreign transactions. It is more important that foreign exchange reserves become an essential component in the structure of total cash assets. Their dinar counterpart at the end of September 1993 was 3.6 times more than the total quantity of domestic currency (M1).

At the same date, the dinar counterpart of foreign exchange reserves of the central bank was 4.8 times as much as the cash circulation. The net foreign currency assets of the central bank came to 62 per cent of its total assets. Such a structure of total cash assets allows foreign exchange reserves to have the function of an informal parallel currency. This parallel currency could soften the negative effects of monetary restrictions without strengthening inflationary pressures. This "substitute domestic currency" may help, especially, the financing of production for export. Such approach to the programme of economic stabilisation starts from the assumption that some expenditures, especially government expenditure, whose financing should rely upon existing foreign currency reserves, will not greatly increase (Rohatinski 1993).[19]

From all this it can be seen that the Croatian government has adopted the stabilisation programme in very difficult circumstances, economic as well as social. However, the urgency of creating conditions for beginning reconstruction and development cannot suffer any delay.

Although the stabilisation programme has only just been adopted (autumn 1993), some positive results can be observed, especially the political consensus and the creation of a social realisation that stabilisation would be to the common advantage. The first concrete market and financial reactions are as expected. The Croatian dinar overnight became not only internally convertible (with restrictions), but also the most demanded commodity. On the basis of supply and demand, a lower rate of exchange against the DM has been forming in the market than that established by the stabilisation programme after the devaluation of 20 per cent (intervention level of 4,440 dinars to the DM). The first threats of dinar insolvency have so far been removed. But more serious problems are going to appear, especially (along with the problems of dinar insolvency) in the spheres of production and personal incomes. Big social problems, which are partly covered by the existing social programme, will become even bigger; not only social and economic policies but government policy as a whole, must pay special attention to them. Although we are able to forecast with great certainty only great uncertainties, it remains clear as already said that the stabilisation programme should not have been any further delayed. We may surely ask why it was not adopted earlier, but the answer is outside the scope of the present paper.

22.5 The problems and prospects of transition

The fifth concern that I would like to discuss refers to the problems and prospects of the transition. The short experience of executing transition policies in ex-socialist countries show that the problems are far greater, and more complicated, conflicting, and controversial, than excpected by any of those who

---

19) More detailed information about these questions can be obtained from Rohatinski, Željko (1993), "The August bases of the October measures", in *Current Economic Development and Economic Policy,* no. 23, National Bank of Croatia and Institute of Economics, Zagreb, pp. 5-80.

have been working on preparing and carrying out the transition. Confronted with such unexpected problems, the experts and politicians began to hesitate on some strategic questions. One of the most important of the strategic questions is probably the time dimension – the speed of transition. Many experts on problems of transition gave numerous arguments in favour of "shock" methods. Others presented arguments for the benefit of realising transition gradually, "step by step". However, if we analyse the various basic tasks of transition, then the conclusion emerges that this is really a quasi-dilemma; everybody agrees that the basic task of transition in the economic sphere is the development of the institutions and legal bases and mechanisms, especially in property relations, and of markets, firms, entrepreneurship and macroeconomic environment, which will promote the improvement of the quality of management and decision-making, and thus more efficient development (Somogyi 1993).[20)]

Everybody also agrees that the basic task of transition in the political sphere is the development of multiparty parliamentary democracy, of the legal state, of the protection of human rights and freedoms, and finally the development of a contemporary civil society. The conclusion follows that transition is a social process which penetrates all economic and political aspects of life. By their nature, these processes are burdened by numerous deviations and dangers. Two groups of deviations have got a common denominator. The first appears under the common denominator "neobolshevism", in the sense of over-accentuation of the role of the state in the transition. The second appears under the common denominator "Latin American syndrome" in the sense of discarding every function not only of the legal, but also of the social state. In some transition countries, both kinds of deviation appear simultaneously. To begin with, those deviations have been manifest in sudden social disintegration and economically unjustified accentuated social differences based on different forms of maffia activity, organised crime, black-marketing, war profiteering etc.

In connection with these very trivial side effects of the transition in some countries, we should remember the wellknown political-economic inter-dependence between pluralism of property rights (in the sense of the dominant

---

20) These questions were the subject of several international meetings. I mention especially the book by Somogyi, Lászlo et al. (1993), *The Political Economy in the Transition Process in Eastern Europe,* Proceedings of the 13th Arne Ryde Symposium, Rungsted Kyst, 11-12 June 1992, Edward Elgar Publishing Company, Vermont, USA, p. 375.

role of private property), market pluralism (in the sense of comprehensive markets, especially labour and capital markets) and pluralism of the political structure (in the sense of the legal functions of the state and protection of human rights and freedom).

The crucial issue for such a series of political-economic interdependencies is property pluralisation which means the dominance of privatisation. Abolition of all monopolies in the market, as well as in political authority, cannot even be theoretically imagined without property privatisation. Privatisation is consequently the condition for economic efficiency and political democracy. However, in all the countries in transition, state property is still dominant. Even Croatia, where up to mid-1992 social property was predominant, is now in the phase of its transformation in which state property dominates.

Although Croatia (in view of the war), may not be the best example for generalisation, it must be said that both sorts of deviation are very noticeable: uncontrolled disintegration of population, big social differences, economically unjustified enrichment, war profiteering, weakening of the social function of the state etc. On the other hand, in the transformation of social into state property, even those mechanisms of control which existed in the self-management system disappeared. Such a conjunction of events increases as a rule the role and influence of the state in all spheres of social life. In Croatia, that tendency is felt not only in the economy, but in all other social activities. A series of laws recently adopted by the Croatian Parliament, relating to science, universities, government administration etc., overaccentuate the role of the state. After so short a time it is impossible to generalise with certainty but we can remind ourselves of a very popular slogan which says that "the best can be the enemy of the good".

The best method of privatisation is without doubt a sale. In this way, the problems of additional investment for development and management quality along with the increase of economic efficiency and profitability, can be solved simultaneously.

However, experience so far in the most of the countries in transition has already shown that domestic purchasing power is very limited. If privatisation were to continue at the current rate, the process would last not several years but several decades. That also applies to Croatia. If the distortions were not inherent in the social process, then the question of the time dimension for property privatisation should not have too great a significance. However, in view of the problems of real life, the conclusion must be that in the process of property transition everything that could be sold under normal circumstances should be sold as soon as possible. For the remaining state capital, methods which would accelerate privatisation should be applied, especially by the distribution of shares and vouchers to the workers and citizens. There are some signs that the Croatian government will to some extent take such action very soon. There should be no illusion that accelerated privatisation will solve all the distortions and problems mentioned. On the contrary, some of them can become even sharper. However, in checking those distortions we will know at least whether we are on the right track, and that despite all the social spasms, troubles and contradictions we can see the light at the end of the tunnel – the exit from deep crisis. At present, we must unfortunately point out that to reach the macroeconomic environment which allows more efficient functing of an integral market, especially for labour and capital, and which promotes the market allocation of investment and more efficient development, a far bigger price must be paid than any of us who have been dealing with reform and transition could have expected. The role of the state in this phase of transition must be substantial, recognised and of high quality, but it must as far as possible be restricted to the creation of the indispensable macroeconomic environment. The legal and social functions of the state must be strongly emphasised.

All the countries in transition are still confronting with huge questions of strategic character. We must understand that the pace and priorities in realisating transition can differ because the countries are differently prepared for it. Croatia and Slovenia in view of their long tradition of reform are qualified for transition better than average. That can be illustrated by the fact that in spite of the war and war damages a "war economy" has not been introduced in Croatia. I might mention that in my book *Economics and Politics of Transition* (Vojnić 1993)[21], recently published in Zagreb, I figuratively put some strategic questions under the title of the old legend Quo Vadis Domine? The answer to this question must be sought by determining the function of the social state in developing a Croatian form of welfare state and economy. That question also relates to the role, having regard to the tradition in Croatia, of self-management, in the sense of participation of workers in management and profits, in the context of the overall

---

21) Vojnić, Dragomir (1993), *Ekonomija i politika tranzicije* (Economics and Politics of Transition), *Informator,* Zagreb and Institute of Economics, Zagreb, pp. 107-112.

transformation of the whole social-economic system. Equally important is the role and place of self-government in the development of government administration and the whole political structure.

Finally, again of equal importance, in question is the whole complex of protection of the human environment and all the problems of pollution. For Croatia this complex relates especially to the protection of sea, rivers, lakes and forests. Great damage has been done already; more damage must be prevented.

These are only some of the questions to which the strategists of economic policy in transition must give answers (Puhovski 1993).[22)]

22.6 In place of conclusions

Finally I would like to summarise a few issues:

(1) The difficulties of realising the transition are far greater and more complex and controversial than was earlier assumed.

(2) The fundamental questions (especially in Croatia) in emerging from the hard transitional crisis relate to renewal, restructuring, reconstruction and development.

(3) Stable development requires a macroeconomic environment where all economic and other actors must behave according to criteria of the "hard budget constraint".

(4) The foundation for such a macroeconomic environment is progress towards privatisation of property rights, including privatisation of banks, along with the functioning of an integrated market of labour and capital markets.

(5) The dilemma of "shock therapy" or gradual movement is in the end only a quasi dilemma. The transition, especially privatisation, must be realised in reasonable terms. It is a social process accompanied by various deviations. Those state assets which cannot soon be sold should be privatised by various promotional methods, including the distribution (through shares and vouchers) of parts of state capital.

(6) Privatisation and the development of institutions and instruments of the labour and capital markets, as well as allocation of investment through the

---

22) For a somewhat broader analysis of these and related questions see Puhovski, Žarko, et al. (1993), *Politics and Economics of Transition,* Centre for the Study of Transformation of Central and Eastern Europe, *Informator,* Zagreb, p. 203.

market, cannot be realised without big social disturbances and tensions. For these reaons it is important that the social processes of the transition should be carried out in ways leading to a gradual exit from the severe crisis.

(7) The strategy of transition, especially in Croatia, must increasingly recognise the role of the legal and social state. It must also define clearly attitudes about the character of the "State and Economics of Welfare" including here all the questions of self-management, self-government and protection of human environment.

(8) The achievement of transition in all the countries concerned, including Croatia and Slovenia, must always take into consideration the known political-economic interdependence between transition of property rights, transition to the market and transition of the political structure. Interdependence between economic efficiency and political democracy must be increased. And this is the only possible way of escape from the hard transitional crisis.

(9) It goes without saying that a decisive factor in the efficient achievement of transition in the post-socialist countries will be the willingness of the developed market economies to support the transition financially and in other ways through the international financial institutions; a special role must fall to the International Monetary Fund, the World Bank and the European Bank. This refers especially to those countries which, like Croatia, have found themselves in extraordinarily difficult situations due to the war and war damages, and to the thousands and thousands of refugees and displaced persons imposed upon them.

(10) In view of the globalisation of all relationships (economic, political, military, defensive, ecological and others) in the contemporary world, the successful achievement of the economics and politics of transition in the countries concerned is a common interest for all nations, especially for the most developed.

(11) In the years to come, the complex problems of the economy, and the policies of transition, will continue to be a very important area of research within the social (and not only the social) sciences. It is essential that the interested international institutions systematically assure financial assets for the realisation of suitable projects; that refers especially to the World Bank and the European Bank, the International Monetary Fund and the funds of the European Community. It applies, too, to the world-known foundations. If we think of institutional performers, then priority in financing should benefit those institutes which especially distinguished themselves in such researches, such as the

Vienna Institute for Comparative Economic Studies; the Institute for International Economic and Political Research; Academy of Sciences of the Russian Federation, Moscow; Institute for Comparative Policy Studies, Florida State University, Tallahassee; as well as many others.

(12) In view of the importance and complexity of the problems confronting the countries in transition, it would be very useful to establish an international institution to deal with financing of reconstruction, restructuring and general development of these countries or to support an existing institution. Such a specialised institution might, for example, be organised most easily within the framework of the existing European Bank.

LIST OF PARTICIPANTS

in the 15th international
Workshop on European Economic Interaction and Integration
Vienna, 21 to 25 November 1993

Karl Aiginger	Professor of Economics, University of Linz, and Austrian Institute of Economic Research (WIFO), Vienna, Austria
Vít Bárta	Economic Transition and Integration Project, International Institute for Applied Systems Analysis (IIASA), Laxenburg, Austria
Amit Bhaduri*)	Professor, Jawaharlal Nehru University, New Delhi, and The Vienna Institute for Comparative Economic Studies (WIIW), Vienna, Austria
Carlo Boffito	Professor, University of Turin, Italy
Oleg T. Bogomolov	Academician, Director, Institute of International Economic and Political Studies, Russian Academy of Sciences, Moscow, Russia
Helen Boss	The Vienna Institute for Comparative Economic Studies (WIIW), Vienna, Austria
Christina Bruck	Associate, The Mitsubishi Bank, Ltd., Vienna Representative Office, Vienna, Austria
Wlodzimierz Brus	Emeritus Professor, University of Oxford, UK
Guillermo A. Calvo*)	Senior Advisor, Research Department, International Monetary Fund, Washington DC, USA
Bernard Cazes	Former Head, Division of Long-Term Studies, Commissariat Général du Plan, Paris, France

*) author, but unable to attend the workshop

Simon Commander	The World Bank, International Bank for Reconstruction and Development, International Development Association, Washington DC, USA
Fabrizio Coricelli	Department of Political Economy, University of Siena, Italy
Robert S. Dohner	Principal Administrator, Central and Eastern Europe Division, Economics Department, Organisation for Economic Co-operation and Development, Paris, France
Georg Fischer	Federal Ministry of Finance, Cabinet of the Federal Minister, Vienna, Austria
Erich Fröschl	Director, Dr. Karl Renner Institute, Vienna, Austria
Ingrid Gazzari	Administrative Director, The Vienna Institute for Comparative Economic Studies (WIIW), Vienna, Austria
Peter Goldscheider	EPIC, Goldscheider und Wurmböck Unternehmensberatungsges. m.b.H., Vienna, Austria
Ilse Grosser	The Vienna Institute for Comparative Economic Studies (WIIW), Vienna, Austria
Peter Haiss	Secretariat of the Managing Board, Bank Austria, Vienna, and Lecturer at the Karl Franzens University, Graz, and at the Institute of European Studies, Vienna, Austria
Peter Havlik	Deputy Director, The Vienna Institute for Comparative Economic Studies, (WIIW), Vienna, Austria
Eduard Hochreiter	Senior Adviser and Head, Foreign Research Division, Austrian National Bank, Vienna, Austria

Gábor Hunya	The Vienna Institute for Comparative Economic Studies (WIIW), Vienna, Austria
John A. Kennerley	Deputy Director, Industry and Technology Division, United Nations Economic Commission for Europe, Geneva, Switzerland
Haruhito Kitamura	Chief Representative, The Mitsubishi Bank, Ltd., Vienna Representative Office, Vienna, Austria
Jan Klacek	Director, Institute of Economics, Czech National Bank, Prague, Czech Republic
Norbert Kloten	Former President of Landeszentralbank in Baden-Württemberg, Stuttgart, and Professor of Economics at Humboldt University, Berlin, Germany
Elena Kohútiková	Chief Executive Director, Economics Department, National Bank of Slovakia, Bratislava, Slovak Republic
Vladimir M. Kollontai	Professor, Institute of World Economics and International Affairs (IMEMO), Russian Academy of Sciences, Moscow, Russia
János Kornai	Professor of Economics, Harvard University, and Collegium Budapest, Institute for Advanced Study, Budapest, Hungary
Igor Kosír*)	Director, Centre for Strategic Studies of the Slovak Republic, Bratislava, Slovakia
Karel Kouba	Professor, Faculty of Social Sciences, Charles University, Prague, Czech Republic
Manmohan S. Kumar*)	Research Department, International Monetary Fund, Washington DC, USA
Ferdinand Lacina	Austrian Federal Minister of Finance, Vienna, Austria

*) author, but unable to attend the workshop

Michael Landesmann	Professor, Johannes Kepler University, Linz, Austria
Jochem Langkau	Deputy Head of the Research Institute, Head of the Department for Economic and Social Research, Friedrich-Ebert-Stiftung, Bonn, Germany
Kazimierz Laski	Professor, Research Director of The Vienna Institute for Comparative Economic Studies (WIIW), Vienna, Austria
Friedrich Levcik	Professor, Consultant, The Vienna Institute for Comparative Economic Studies (WIIW), Vienna, Austria
Zdenek Lukas	The Vienna Institute for Comparative Economic Studies (WIIW), Vienna, Austria
Egon Matzner	Professor of Public Economics and Head of Research Unit for Socioeconomics, Austrian Academy of Sciences, Vienna, Austria
Jože Mencinger	Professor of Economics, EIPF (Institute of Economics, Faculty of Law), University of Ljubljana, Slovenia
Patrick A. Messerlin	Professor of Economics, Institut d'Etudes Politiques de Paris, Paris, France
Costea Munteanu	Associate Professor, Academy for Economic Studies, Bucharest, Romania
Alexander Nekipelov	Deputy Director, Institute of International Economic and Political Studies, Russian Academy of Sciences, Moscow, Russia
Jerzy Osiatynski	Professor, Member of Parliament, Warsaw, Poland
Leon Podkaminer	The Vienna Institute for Comparative Economic Studies (WIIW), Vienna, Austria

Josef Pöschl	The Vienna Institute for Comparative Economic Studies (WIIW), Vienna, Austria
Sándor Richter	The Vienna Institute for Comparative Economic Studies (WIIW), Vienna, Austria
Philipp Rieger	The Vienna Institute for Comparative Economic Studies (WIIW), Vienna, Austria
Dariusz K. Rosati	Professor, United Nations Economic Commission for Europe, Division for Economic Analysis and Projections, Geneva, Switzerland
Christopher T. Saunders	Visiting Fellow, Science Policy Research Unit, University of Sussex, UK
Monika Schopf	The Mitsubishi Bank, Ltd., Vienna Representative Office, Vienna, Austria
Hans Seidel	Professor, Austrian Institute of Economic Research (WIFO), Vienna, Austria
Joseph Smolik	United Nations Economic Commission for Europe, Division for Economic Analysis and Projections, Geneva, Switzerland
Judita Štouračová	Managing Director, Centre for Foreign Economic Relations, Prague, Czech Republic
Erich W. Streissler	Professor, Institute of Economics, University of Vienna, Austria
Jolanta Supińska	Professor, Institute of Social Policy, University of Warsaw, Poland
Miklós Szanyi	Institute for World Economics, Hungarian Academy of Sciences, Budapest, Hungary
Ádám Török	Director, Research Institute of Industrial Economics, Hungarian Academy of Sciences, Budapest, and LICOS Institute, Catholic University of Leuven, Belgium

Witold Trzeciakowski	Professor, Institute of Economics, Polish Academy of Sciences, Warsaw, Poland
Aleksandar M. Vacić †	Professor, Director, United Nations Economic Commission for Europe, Division for Economic Analysis and Projections, Geneva, Switzerland
Hermine Vidovic	The Vienna Institute for Comparative Economic Studies (WIIW), Vienna, Austria
Dragomir Vojnić	Professor of Economics, Institute of Economics, University of Zagreb, Croatia
G.D.N. Worswick	Oxford, UK

INDEX

INDEX